April 22–26, 2014
Lugano, Switzerland

Association for
Computing Machinery

Advancing Computing as a Science & Profession

MODULARITY'14

Proceedings of the 13th International Conference on Modularity (formerly AOSD)

Sponsored by:

AOSA

In cooperation with:

ACM SIGPLAN and ACM SIGSOFT

Association for
Computing Machinery

Advancing Computing as a Science & Profession

The Association for Computing Machinery
2 Penn Plaza, Suite 701
New York, New York 10121-0701

ISBN: 978-1-4503-2772-5 (Digital)

ISBN: 978-1-4503-3077-0 (Print)

Additional copies may be ordered prepaid from:

ACM Order Department
PO Box 30777
New York, NY 10087-0777, USA

Phone: 1-800-342-6626 (USA and Canada)
+1-212-626-0500 (Global)
Fax: +1-212-944-1318
E-mail: acmhelp@acm.org
Hours of Operation: 8:30 am – 4:30 pm ET

Printed in the USA

MODULARITY 2014 – Chairs' Welcome

These are the proceedings of the *13th International Conference on Modularity (Modularity'14,* formerly *AOSD)* in Lugano, Switzerland. This year's conference continues the tradition of being the premier international conference on modularity in software systems.

Modularity'14 addresses all aspects of modularity, abstraction, and separation of concerns as they pertain to software, including new forms, uses, and analysis of modularity, along with the costs and benefits, and tradeoffs involved in their application. The broadening in scope of the conference is also reflected in the change of its name: the International Conference on Aspect-Oriented Software Development (AOSD) has evolved to become the International Conference on Modularity.

Modularity provides the international computer science research community and its many sub-disciplines (including software engineering, languages, and computer systems) with unique opportunities to come together to share and discuss perspectives, results, and visions with others interested in modularity as well as in the languages, development methods, architectures, algorithms, and other technologies organized around this fundamental concept.

Modularity'14 comprises two main parts: Research Results and Modularity Visions. Both parts invited full, scholarly papers of the highest quality on results and new ideas in areas that include but are not limited to complex systems, software design and engineering, programming languages, cyber-physical systems, and other areas across the whole system life cycle.

Research Results invited papers on new ideas and results, stressing the contribution of significant new research with rigorous and substantial validation of its technical claims, based on scientifically sound reflections on experience, analysis, experimentation, or formal models, and emphasizing compelling new ideas. The review process consisted of two rounds, as a further development of the multi-round model that has been used for four years at this conference. The outcome in the first round could be 'accept' and 'reject' as usual, but also 'reject, with a recommendation to resubmit'. The intention behind the third outcome is to push for improvements to papers that are promising, but not quite ready; and letting the same reviewers judge the improved paper. The multi-phase model is being used by multiple conferences in its own right, but it could also be considered to be a highly extended version of the well-known concept of an author response period. It is definitely our experience that this mechanism produces significant improvements in several papers, and we are very happy about the high quality of the selected papers. The Program Committee (PC) meetings were online meetings, heavily supported by online discussions in smaller groups. Submissions where one or more of the authors were members of the PC were reviewed and decided by the External Review Committee (ERC) before the PC meetings, such that the PC was totally isolated from the processing of PC papers. All papers had at least three reviews, and PC papers had at least four reviews. The papers live up to the changed name and broadened scope, including such topics as language mechanisms, semantics, program correctness proofs, user studies (where the user is a programmer), software evolution, concurrency, and more.

Modularity influences system diversity, dependability, performance, evolution, the structure and the dynamics of the organizations that produce systems, human understanding and management of systems, and ultimately system value. Yet the nature of and possibilities for modularity, limits to modularity, the mechanisms needed to achieve it in given forms, and its costs and benefits remain poorly understood. Significant advances in modularity thus are possible and promise to yield breakthroughs in our ability to conceive, design, develop, validate, integrate, deploy, operate, and evolve modern information systems and their underlying software artifacts. Modularity Visions invited submissions presenting compelling insights into modularity in information systems, including its nature, forms, mechanisms, consequences, limits, costs, and benefits, and proposals for future work. Modularity Visions followed a two-phase review process. The first reviewing phase assessed the papers and resulted in the selection of a subset of submissions that were either accepted as-is or deemed potentially acceptable, with all other papers being rejected in this phase. Authors of potentially accepted papers were requested to improve specific aspects of the papers in keeping with the assessment criteria and the nature of Modularity Visions. Authors were given about two months to perform the revisions, after which a second submission occurred. The second submission should have reflected the revision requests sent to the authors. The second and final reviewing phase assessed how the revision requests have been acted upon by the authors, and whether the final paper improved the original submission.

Research Results attracted 53 submissions and accepted 20 papers; of these submissions, five were resubmissions, but they were, of course, extensively rewritten. Modularity Visions received seven submissions and accepted one. Altogether, 21 papers out of 60 submissions were accepted, yielding an acceptance rate of 35%.

The Modularity'14 program includes three keynotes: Julia Lawall from Inria on *Coccinelle: Reducing the Barriers to Modularization in a Large C Code Base*, Eelco Visser from TU Delft on *Separation of Concerns in Language Definition*, and Thomas Würthinger from Oracle Labs on *Graal and Truffle: Modularity and Separation of Concerns as Cornerstones for Building a Multipurpose Runtime*.

Putting together Modularity'14 was a team effort. First of all, we would like to thank the authors and the keynote speakers for providing the contents of the program. We would like to express our gratitude to the program committees, to the external review committee, and to all reviewers, who worked very hard on reviewing papers and providing detailed suggestions for their improvement. We would also like to thank Danilo Ansaloni, this year's Publicity Chair. Special thanks go to Elisa Larghi for helping with the local organization of Modularity'14 and to Giacomo Toffetti Carughi for the design and maintenance of the conference web pages. We thank Hidehiko Masuhara, the General Chair of MODULARITY:aosd.13, for his support. We would like to thank our supporters, the University of Lugano, Oracle Labs, and the city of Lugano. We also thank ACM SIGPLAN and ACM SIGSOFT for their continued support of the Modularity conference.

We hope that you will find this program inspiring and compelling, and that the conference will provide you with a valuable opportunity to share ideas with other researchers and practitioners from institutions around the world.

Walter Binder
General Chair
University of Lugano, Switzerland

Achille Peternier
Organizing Chair
University of Lugano, Switzerland

Erik Ernst
Program Chair Research Results
Aarhus University, Denmark

Robert Hirschfeld
Program Chair Modularity Visions
Hasso-Plattner-Institut Potsdam, Germany

Table of Contents

MODULARITY 2014 – Organization vii

MODULARITY 2014 – Sponsor & Supporters x

Session: Language Mechanisms I
Session Chair: Julia Lawall *(Inria/LIP6)*

- **Delegation Proxies: The Power of Propagation** 1
  Erwann Wernli, Oscar Nierstrasz *(University of Bern)*,
  Camille Teruel, Stéphane Ducasse *(RMOD, INRIA Lille Nord Europe)*
- **Composable User-Defined Operators That Can Express User-Defined Literals** 13
  Kazuhiro Ichikawa, Shigeru Chiba *(The University of Tokyo)*
- **REScala: Bridging Between Object-oriented and Functional Style in Reactive Applications** 25
  Guido Salvaneschi, Gerold Hintz, Mira Mezini *(Technische Universität Darmstadt)*
- **FlowR: Aspect Oriented Programming for Information Flow Control in Ruby** 37
  Thomas F. J.-M. Pasquier, Jean Bacon *(University of Cambridge)*, Brian Shand *(Public Health England)*

Session: Software Evolution
Session Chair: Christoph Bockisch *(University of Twente)*

- **Assessing Modularity using Co-Change Clusters** 49
  Luciana Lourdes Silva, Marco Tulio Valente, Marcelo de A. Maia *(Federal University of Uberlândia)*
- **Blending and Reusing Rules for Architectural Degradation Prevention** 61
  Alessandro Gurgel, Isela Macia, Alessandro Garcia *(Pontifical Catholic University of Rio de Janeiro)*,
  Arndt von Staa *(Pontifical Catholic University of Rio de Janeiro)*,
  Mira Mezini, Michael Eichberg, Ralf Mitschke *(Technische Universität Darmstadt)*
- **Automated Software Remodularization Based on Move Refactoring: A Complex Systems Approach** 73
  Marcelo Serrano Zanetti, Claudio Juan Tessone, Ingo Scholtes, Frank Schweitzer *(ETH Zurich)*

Session: Modularity Visions
Session Chair: Christoph Bockisch *(University of Twente)*

- **Context-Oriented Software Engineering: A Modularity Vision** 85
  Tetsuo Kamina *(University of Tokyo)*, Tomoyuki Aotani, Hidehiko Masuhara *(Tokyo Institute of Technology)*,
  Tetsuo Tamai *(Hosei University)*

Session: Understanding Programmers
Session Chair: Guido Salvaneschi *(Technische Universität Darmstadt)*

- **Type Names without Static Type Checking Already Improve the Usability of APIs (As Long as the Type Names are Correct): An Empirical Study** 99
  Samuel Spiza, Stefan Hanenberg *(University of Duisburg-Essen)*
- **How Do Programmers Use Optional Typing? An Empirical Study** 109
  Carlos Souza, Eduardo Figueiredo *(Federal University of Minas Gerais)*
- **An Empirical Study on How Developers Reason about Module Cohesion** 121
  Bruno C. da Silva, Claudio N. Sant'Anna, Christina von F. G. Chavez *(Federal University of Bahia)*

Session: The Meaning of Programs
Session Chair: Eric Bodden *(EC SPRIDE - Fraunhofer SIT & Technische Universität Darmstadt)*

- **Compositional Reasoning About Aspect Interference** 133
  Ismael Figueroa *(University of Chile & INRIA)*, Tom Schrijvers *(Ghent University)*, Nicolas Tabareau *(INRIA)*,
  Éric Tanter *(University of Chile)*

- **Reusable Components of Semantic Specifications** 145
  Martin Churchill, Peter D. Mosses, Paolo Torrini *(Swansea University)*
- **AspectJML: Modular Specification and Runtime Checking for Crosscutting Contracts** .. 157
  Henrique Rebêlo *(Universidade Federal de Pernambuco)*, Gary T. Leavens *(University of Central Florida)*,
  Mehdi Bagherzadeh, Hridesh Rajan *(Iowa State University)*,
  Ricardo Lima *(Universidade Federal de Pernambuco)*, Daniel M. Zimmerman *(Harvey Mudd College)*,
  Márcio Cornélio *(Universidade Federal de Pernambuco)*, Thomas Thüm *(University of Magdeburg)*

Session: Software Product Lines

Session Chair: Stefan Hanenberg *(Universität Duisburg-Essen)*

- **Probabilistic Model Checking for Energy Analysis in Software Product Lines** 169
  Clemens Dubslaff, Sascha Klüppelholz, Christel Baier *(Technische Universität Dresden)*
- **Systematic Derivation of Static Analyses for Software Product Lines** 181
  Jan Midtgaard *(Aarhus University)*, Claus Brabrand, Andrzej Wąsowski *(IT University of Copenhagen)*

Session: Concurrency

Session Chair: Gary T. Leavens *(University of Central Florida)*

- **Aspectual Session Types** 193
  Nicolas Tabareau, Mario Südholt *(Mines Nantes, Inria & LINA)*, Éric Tanter *(University of Chile)*
- **JEScala: Modular Coordination with Declarative Events and Joins** 205
  Jurgen M. Van Ham *(Technische Universität Darmstadt, Mines Nantes, Inria & LINA)*,
  Guido Salvaneschi, Mira Mezini *(Technische Universität Darmstadt)*,
  Jacques Noyé *(Mines Nantes, Inria & LINA)*

Session: Language Mechanisms II

Session Chair: Walter Cazzola *(Università degli Studi di Milano)*

- **Designing Information Hiding Modularity for Model Transformation Languages** 217
  Andreas Rentschler, Dominik Werle, Qais Noorshams, Lucia Happe, Ralf Reussner
  (Karlsruhe Institute of Technology)
- **JavaScript Module System: Exploring the Design Space** 229
  Junhee Cho, Sukyoung Ryu *(KAIST)*
- **Modular Specification and Dynamic Enforcement of Syntactic Language Constraints when Generating Code** 241
  Sebastian Erdweg *(TU Darmstadt)*, Vlad Vergu *(TU Delft)*, Mira Mezini *(TU Darmstadt)*, Eelco Visser *(TU Delft)*

Author Index 253

MODULARITY 2014 – Organization

General Chair: Walter Binder *(University of Lugano, Switzerland)*

Organizing Chair: Achille Peternier *(University of Lugano, Switzerland)*

Research Results Program Chair: Erik Ernst *(Aarhus University, Denmark)*

Modularity Visions Program Chair: Robert Hirschfeld *(Hasso-Plattner-Institut Potsdam, Germany)*

Workshops Chair: Michael Haupt *(Oracle Labs, Germany)*

Demonstrations Chair: Walter Cazzola *(Università degli Studi di Milano, Italy)*

Student Events Chair: Christoph Bockisch *(University of Twente, The Netherlands)*

Publicity Chair: Danilo Ansaloni *(University of Lugano, Switzerland)*

Administrative Coordinator: Elisa Larghi *(University of Lugano, Switzerland)*

Web Chair: Giacomo Toffetti Carughi *(University of Lugano, Switzerland)*

Steering Committee:
Walter Binder *(University of Lugano, Switzerland)*
Paulo Borba *(Federal University of Pernambuco, Brazil)*
Shigeru Chiba *(The University of Tokyo, Japan)*
Thomas Cottenier *(UniqueSoft LLC, USA)*
Erik Ernst *(Aarhus University, Denmark)*
Richard P. Gabriel *(IBM Research, USA)*
Jeremy Gibbons, SIGPLAN Observer *(University of Oxford, UK)*
William Griswold, SIGSOFT Observer *(UCSD, USA)*
Robert Hirschfeld *(Hasso-Plattner-Institut Potsdam, Germany)*
Jörg Kienzle *(McGill University, Canada)*
David H. Lorenz, Chair *(The Open University of Israel, Israel)*
Hidehiko Masuhara *(The University of Tokyo, Japan)*
Mira Mezini *(Technische Universität Darmstadt, Germany)*
Oscar Nierstrasz *(University of Bern, Switzerland)*
Harold Ossher *(IBM Research, USA)*
Mario Südholt *(École des Mines de Nantes, France)*
Kevin Sullivan *(University of Virginia, USA)*
Éric Tanter *(Universidad de Chile, Chile)*
Steffen Zschaler, Secretary/Treasurer *(King's College London, UK)*

Research Results Program Committee:	Sven Apel *(University of Passau, Germany)* Christoph Bockisch *(University of Twente, The Netherlands)* Eric Bodden *(EC SPRIDE, Germany)* Yvonne Coady *(University of Victoria, Canada)* Cynthia Disenfeld *(Technion, Israel)* Pascal Fradet *(Inria, France)* Lidia Fuentes *(University of Málaga, Spain)* Alessandro Garcia *(Pontifical Catholic University of Rio de Janeiro, Brazil)* Stefan Hanenberg *(Universität Duisburg-Essen, Germany)* Klaus Havelund *(Jet Propulsion Laboratory, USA)* Andy Kellens *(Vrije Universiteit Brussels, Belgium)* Ralf Lämmel *(Universität Koblenz-Landau, Germany)* Julia Lawall *(Inria, France)* Ana Moreira *(Universidade Nova de Lisboa, Portugal)* Jacques Noyé *(École des Mines de Nantes, France)* Bruno C.d.S. Oliveira *(National University of Singapore, Singapore)* Ismael Figueroa Palet *(University of Chile, Chile)* Hridesh Rajan *(Iowa State University, USA)* Awais Rashid *(Lancaster University, UK)* Guido Salvaneschi *(Technische Universität Darmstadt, Germany)* Ina Schaefer *(Technische Universität Braunschweig, Germany)* Alex Villazón *(Universidad Privada Boliviana, Bolivia)*
Research Results External Review Committee:	Mehmet Aksit *(University of Twente, The Netherlands)* Walter Cazzola *(Università degli Studi di Milano, Italy)* Krzysztof Czarnecki *(University of Waterloo, Canada)* Atsushi Igarashi *(Kyoto University, Japan)* Viviane Jonckers *(Vrije Universiteit Brussels, Belgium)* Shmuel Katz *(Technion, Israel)* Gary T. Leavens *(University of Central Florida, USA)* Luigi Liquori *(Inria, France)* Christian Prehofer *(fortiss GmbH, Germany)* Yannis Smaragdakis *(University of Athens, Greece)* Clemens Szyperski *(Microsoft Research, USA)* Eric Wohlstadter *(University of British Columbia, Canada)*

Modularity Visions Program Committee:	Carl Friedrich Bolz *(King's College London, UK)* Shigeru Chiba *(The University of Tokyo, Japan)* Richard P. Gabriel *(IBM Research, USA)* Matthias Hauswirth *(University of Lugano, Switzerland)* Christian Kästner *(Carnegie Mellon University, USA)* David H. Lorenz *(The Open University of Israel, Israel)* Hidehiko Masuhara *(Tokyo Institute of Technology, Japan)* Sean McDirmid *(Microsoft Research Asia, China)* Ina Schaefer *(Technische Universität Braunschweig, Germany)* Kevin Sullivan *(University of Virginia, USA)*

Additional Reviewers	Jorge Barreiros	Eduardo Piveta
	Tom Van Cutsem	Alexander von Rhein
	Michael Dukaczewski	Konstantin Schorp
	Matthias Kowal	Janet Siegmund
	Miguel Monteiro	Tetsuo Tamai
	Carlos Noguera	Edoardo Vacchi

MODULARITY 2014 – Sponsor & Supporters

Sponsor:

aosa
Aspect-Oriented Software Association

In cooperation with:

ACM SIGPLAN

SIGSOFT
Special Interest Group on Software Engineering

Supporters:

Università della Svizzera italiana
Faculty of Informatics

ORACLE LABS

Città di Lugano

Delegation Proxies: The Power of Propagation

Erwann Wernli Oscar Nierstrasz
Software Composition Group, University of Bern,
Switzerland

Camille Teruel Stéphane Ducasse
RMOD, INRIA Lille Nord Europe,
France

Abstract

Scoping behavioral variations to dynamic extents is useful to support non-functional requirements that otherwise result in cross-cutting code. Unfortunately, such variations are difficult to achieve with traditional reflection or aspects. We show that with a modification of dynamic proxies, called *delegation proxies*, it becomes possible to reflectively implement variations that *propagate* to all objects accessed in the dynamic extent of a message send. We demonstrate our approach with examples of variations scoped to dynamic extents that help simplify code related to safety, reliability, and monitoring.

Categories and Subject Descriptors D.3.3 [*Software*]: Programming Languages — Constructs and Features

Keywords Reflection, proxy, dynamic extent

1. Introduction

Non-functional concerns like monitoring or reliability typically result in code duplication in the code base. The use of aspects is the de-facto solution to factor such boilerplate code in a single place. Aspects enable scoping variations in space (with a rich variety of static pointcuts), in time (with dynamic aspects), and in the control flow (with the corresponding pointcuts). Scoping a variation to the *dynamic extent* [39] of an expression is however challenging, since scoping between threads is not easily realized with aspects. Traditional reflection and meta-object protocols suffer from similar limitations.

This is unfortunate since scoping variations to dynamic extents increases the expressiveness of the language in useful ways [38, 39]. With such variations, it is for instance possible to execute code in a read-only manner [4] (thus improving safety), or to track all state mutations to ease recovery in case of errors (thus improving reliability), or to trace and profile methods at a fine-grained level (thus improving monitoring).

We show in this paper that with minor changes to the way dynamic proxies operate, it becomes possible to reflectively implement variations that are scoped to dynamic extents. A dynamic proxy [18, 28, 42] is a special object that mediates interactions between a client object and another target object. When the client sends a message to the proxy, the message is intercepted, reified, and passed to the proxy's *handler* for further processing. To scope variations to dynamic extents using proxies, we must first slightly adapt the proxy mechanism, then implement specific handlers.

Our adaptation of dynamic proxies has the following characteristics: 1) it supports delegation [27] by rebinding self-reference, 2) it intercepts state accesses, both for regular fields and variables captured in closures, 3) it intercepts object creations. We refer to our extension of dynamic proxies as *delegation proxies*.

With delegation proxies, it becomes possible to implement handlers that will wrap all objects the target object accesses. Such a handler wraps the result of state reads and object instantiations, and unwraps the arguments of state writes. A proxy can consequently encode a variation that will be consistently *propagated* to all objects accessed during the evaluation of a message send (*i.e.*, its dynamic extent), without impacting objects in the heap.

Delegation proxies have several positive properties. First, delegation proxies do not lead to *meta-regressions* — infinite recursion that arises in reflective architectures when reflecting on code that is used to implement the reflective behavior itself. In aspect-oriented programming, this arises when an advice triggers the associated pointcut. The solutions to this problem generally add an explicit model of the different levels of execution [15, 40]. With delegation proxies, this problem doesn't appear since the proxy and its target are distinct objects and the propagation is enabled only for the proxy. No variation is active when executing the code of the handler. Second, variations expressed with delegation proxies *compose*, similarly to aspects. For instance, tracing and profiling variations can be implemented with delegation proxies and then composed to apply both variations. Third, delegation proxies naturally support *partial reflection* [41]. Only the objects effectively accessed in the dynamic extent of an execution involving a proxy pay a performance overhead; all other objects in the system remain unaffected, including the target.

In this paper, we explore and demonstrate the flexibility of delegation proxies in Smalltalk with the following contributions:

- A model of proxies based on delegation that intercepts object instantiations and state accesses (including variables in closures) (Section 2);
- A technique to use delegation proxies to scope variations to dynamic extents (Section 2);
- Several examples of useful applications of variations scoped to dynamic extents (Section 3);
- A formalization of delegation proxies and the propagation technique (Section 4);
- An implementation of delegation proxies in Smalltalk based on code generation (Section 5).

MODULARITY '14, April 22–26, 2014, Lugano, Switzerland.

ACM 978-1-4503-2772-5/14/04... $15.00.
http://dx.doi.org/10.1145/2577080.2577081

2. Delegation Proxies

We now describe how delegation proxies work and exemplify them with an implementation of tracing. Let us consider the Smalltalk method `Integer>>fib` [1] which computes the Fibonacci value of an integer using recursion:

```
Integer>>fib
    self < 2 ifTrue: [ ↑ self ].
    ↑ (self - 1) fib + (self - 2) fib
```

Listing 1. Fibonacci computation

The computation of the Fibonacci value of 2 corresponds to the following sequence of message sends (first the receiver of the message, then the message with its arguments):

```
2 fib
2 < 2
false ifTrue: [ ↑ self ]
2 - 1
1 fib
1 < 2
true ifTrue: [ ↑ self ]
[ ↑ self ] value
2 - 2
0 fib
0 < 2
true ifTrue: [ ↑ self ]
[ ↑ self ] value
1 + 0
```

Listing 2. Trace of `2 fib`

To automatically trace message sends, we can use delegation proxies to intercept message sends and print them. Like a dynamic proxy, a delegation proxy is a special object that acts as a surrogate for another object, called its *target*. The behavior of a proxy is defined by a separate object called its *handler*, whose methods are referred to as *traps* [42]. When an operation (message send, state access, etc.) is applied to a proxy, the proxy reifies the operation and instead invokes the corresponding trap in the handler. When an operation is intercepted, the handler can take some action and can reflectively perform the original operation on the target. Figure 1 shows the relationships between a proxy, a handler and a target.

The distinction between proxies and handlers is called *stratification* [9, 28, 42]. Stratification avoids name conflicts between application methods and traps, *i.e.*, between the base-level and the meta-level.

The target and the handler can be regular objects or proxies as well. By using proxies as the targets of other proxies, we obtain a chain of delegation. Each of the variations implemented by the handlers of the proxies in the chain will be triggered in order. This is a natural way to compose different variations together.

A tracing proxy can be obtained by instantiating a proxy with a tracing handler. For convenience, we add method `Object>> tracing` that returns a tracing proxy for any object. For instance, `2 tracing` returns a tracing proxy for the number 2.

```
Object>> tracing
  ↑ Proxy handler: TracingHandler new target: self.
```

Listing 3. Creation of a tracing proxy

To trace messages, the tracing handler must define a *message* trap that prints the name of the reified message. Listing 4 shows the code of such a *message* trap:

[1] In Smalltalk, closures are expressed with square brackets (`[ ... ]`) and booleans are objects. The method `ifTrue:` takes a closure as argument: if the receiver is `true`, the closure is evaluated by sending the message `value`. The up-arrow (`↑ ...`) denotes a return statement.

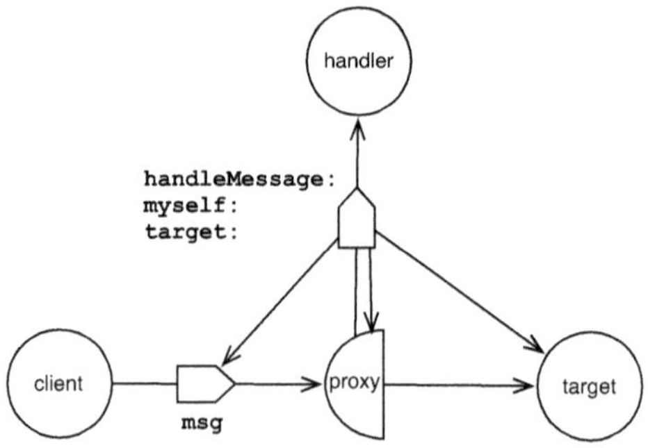

Figure 1. Example of message interception. First, the client sends the message `msg` to a proxy. Then, the proxy intercepts the message and invokes the handler trap associated with message reception (`handleMessage:myself:target:`) with three arguments: the reified message, the proxy itself and the target.

```
TracingHandler>>handleMessage: m myself: p target: t
    Transcript
          print: t asString;
          space;
          print: m asString;
          cr.
    ↑ t perform: m myself: p.
```

Listing 4. A simple tracing handler

The reflective invocation with `perform:` takes one additional parameter `myself`, which specifies how `self` is rebound in the reflective invocation. The handler can thus either rebind `self` to the proxy (delegation) or rebind `self` to the target (forwarding). Delegation proxies thus trivially subsume traditional forwarding proxies. In the case of a reflective invocation with delegation, the method is executed with `self` rebound to the proxy, which allows the proxy to further intercept operations happening during this method execution.

If the target of a proxy is another proxy, proxies form chains of delegation. The identity of the proxy that received the original message send is consistently passed to the handlers.

2.1 Propagation

The tracing handler in the previous section defines a *message* trap. Doing so ensures that messages received by the proxy are traced, including self-sends in the method executed with delegation. However, it would fail to trace messages sent to other objects. The evaluation of `2 tracing fib` would print `2 fib`, `2 < 2`, `2 - 1`, `2 - 2`, but all the messages sent to `1`, `0`, `true`, `false` and `[ ↑ self ]` would not be traced.

To consistently apply a variation during the evaluation of a message send, all objects accessed during the evaluation must be represented with proxies. To achieve this, we can implement a handler that replaces all object references accessed by proxies. This way, the variation will *propagate* during the execution.

In a given method activation, a reference to an object can be obtained from:

- an argument,
- a field read,
- the return value of message sends,
- the instantiation of new objects or the resolution of literals.

The following rules suffice to make sure that all objects are represented with proxies. To distinguish between the initial proxy and the proxies created during the propagation, we call the former the *root* proxy. We need three rules to control how objects must be wrapped:

- *Wrap the initial arguments.* When the root proxy receives a message, the arguments must be wrapped with proxies. We don't need to wrap the arguments of other message sends: the following rules ensure that the arguments were already wrapped in the context of the caller.
- *Wrap field reads.* This way, references to fields are represented with a proxy.
- *Wrap object instantiation.* The return value of primitive message sends that "create" new objects must be wrapped. Such primitive messages include explicit instantiations with `new` and arithmetic computations with `+`, `-`, `/`. Similarly, the resolution of literal must be wrapped.

  We don't need to wrap the return value of other message sends. Indeed, if the receiver and the arguments of a message send are already wrapped, and if the results of state reads and object instantiations are also wrapped in the execution of the method triggered by this message send, this message send will necessarily return a proxy.

Additionally, we need two rules to control how objects must be unwrapped:

- *Unwrap field writes.* When a field is written, we unwrap the value of the assignment before performing it. This way, the proxies created during the propagation are only referred to from within the call stack and don't pollute the heap via the fields of target objects. They can be garbage collected once the propagation is over.
- *Unwrap the initial return value.* The root proxy unwraps the objects returned to the clients.

Applying this technique to the code in Listing 1, the subtractions `self-2` and `self-1` return proxies as well. Figure 2 depicts the situation. This way, tracing is consistently applied during the computation of Fibonacci numbers.

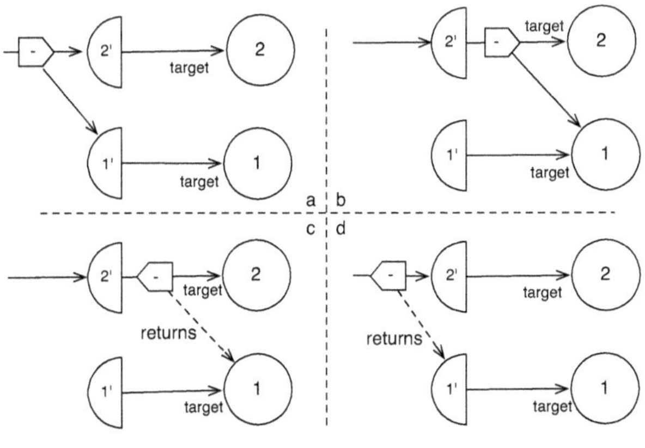

Figure 2. Illustration of propagation during the subtraction 2 - 1. A proxy to 2 receives the subtraction message "-" with a proxy to 1 as argument (a). The message is forwarded to 2 to perform the actual subtraction (b) that returns 1 (c). Finally the result is wrapped (d).

2.2 Traps

In Smalltalk, an object is instantiated by sending the message `new` to a class, which is an object as well. The interception of object instantiations does thus not require a specific trap and is realized indirectly. The following set of traps is thus sufficient to intercept all method invocations, state accesses, and object instantiations:

- `handleMessage:myself:target:`
  The trap for message sends takes as parameters the reified message, the original proxy[2] and the target.
- `handleReadField:myself:target:`
  The trap for field reads takes as parameters the field name, the original proxy and the target.
- `handleWriteField:value:myself:target:`
  The trap for field writes takes as parameters the field name, the value to write, the original proxy and the target.
- `handleLiteral:myself:target:`
  The trap for the resolution of literals (symbols, string, numbers, class names, and closures) takes as parameters the resolved literal, the original proxy and the target.

Instantiations of objects using literals, *e.g.*, the instantiation of a string, are intercepted with the *literal* trap. In Java, an additional trap would be needed to intercept constructor invocations. Similar considerations hold for access to static fields and invocation of static methods.

Similarly to `perform:`, reflective methods to read fields, to write fields and to resolve literals are extended with an additional parameter `myself`. They become `instVarNamed:myself:`, `instVarNamed:put:myself` and `literal:myself:`. The parameter `myself` is needed, because proxies may form chains of delegation. When invoked on a proxy, the reflective operations will trigger the corresponding trap. The parameter `myself` is passed to the traps along the chain to preserve the identity of the proxy that originally intercepted the operation.

With the support of delegation and the ability to intercept state accesses and object instantiations, it becomes possible to implement a handler that realizes the propagation technique. The code of such a propagating handler is shown in Listing 5. We assume the existence of a class `Reflect` to unwrap proxies.

```
PropHandler>>initialize
  isRoot := true

PropHandler>>handleMessage: m myself: p target: t
  ↑ m selector isPrimitive
    ifTrue: [ self wrap: (t perform: m myself: p) ]
    ifFalse: [
      self isRoot
        ifTrue: [
          m arguments: (self wrapAll: m arguments).
          self unwrap: (t perform: m myself: p) ]
        ifFalse: [ t perform: m myself: p ] ]

PropHandler>>handleReadField: f myself: p target: t
  ↑ self wrap: (t instVarNamed: f myself: p).

PropHandler>>handleWriteField: f value: v proxy: p
              target: t
  t instVarNamed: f put: (self unwrap: v) myself: p.
  ↑ v

PropHandler>>handleLiteral: l myself: p target: t
  ↑ self wrap: l

PropHandler>>wrap: anObject
  | handler |
  handler := self class new.
```

[2] In case of chain proxies, the original proxy is not necessarily the one that intercepted the operation but the root of the chain

```
    handler isRoot: false.
    ↑ Proxy handler: handler target: anObject

PropHandler>>wrapAll: aCollection
    ↑ aCollection collect: [ :each | self wrap: each ]

PropHandler>>unwrap: aProxy
    ↑ Reflect targetOf: aProxy

PropHandler>>isRoot: aBoolean
    isRoot := aBoolean
```

Listing 5. Tracing handler implementing the propagation technique.

2.3 Closures

A closure should be evaluated with the variations that are active in the current dynamic extent, and not the variations that were active when the closure was created. For instance, if the closure `[ self printString ]` is created when tracing is enabled, its evaluation during a regular execution should not trace the message `printString`. Conversely, if the closure `[ self printString ]` is created during a regular execution, its evaluation when tracing is enabled should trace the message `printString`. For this to work correctly, closures are always created in an *unproxied* form, and proxying is only applied on demand.

Variables captured in a closure are stored in indexed fields. Let us describe first how creation works and illustrate it with the closure `[ self printString ]` and tracing:

1. The closure is created by the runtime and captures variables as-is. *Tracing example:* the closure captures `self`, which refers to a proxy.
2. The closure creation is intercepted by the *literal* trap of the creator. *Tracing example:* the closure is treated like other literals and thus proxied.
3. If the closure was proxied, the runtime invokes the *write* trap of the closure's proxy for all captured variables. *Tracing example:* the runtime invokes the *write* trap of the closure's proxy passing `0` as field index and the `self` proxy as value. The trap unproxies the value and reflectively invokes `instVarNamed:put:myself:` for field `0`. This overwrites the previous value in the closure with a reference to the base object.

Evaluation of closures follows the inverse scheme:

1. If the closure is evaluated via a proxy, the runtime invokes the *read* trap each time a captured variable is accessed. *Tracing example:* the runtime invokes the *read* trap of the closure's proxy passing `0` as field index. The trap reflectively invokes `instVarNamed:` for field `0` and wraps the result with a proxy. The message `printString` is sent to the proxy.

Note that this scheme is quite natural if we consider that closures could be encoded with regular objects, similarly to anonymous classes in Java. In that case, captured variables are effectively stored in synthetic fields initialized in the constructor. The instantiation of the anonymous class would trigger *write* traps, and evaluation would trigger *read* traps.

Adding method `valueWithHandler:` in `BlockClosure`, tracing `2 fib` can also be achieved with `[ 2 fib ] valueWithHandler: TracingHandler new` instead of `2 tracing fib`. When we evaluate the closure via the proxy, the *literal* trap will wrap `2` before it is used. Closures provide a convenient way to activate a behavioral variation in the dynamic extent of expression.

```
BlockClosure>> valueWithHandler: aHandler
    ↑ (Proxy handler: aHandler target: self) value.
```

Listing 6. Convenience method to wrap and evaluate a closure

2.4 Transparency

Traps are implemented in a separate handler and not in the proxy itself. If an application defines an application-level method whose name collides with the name of a trap, the explicit invocation of this method will be trapped by the handler. It avoids conflicts between the base-level and the meta-level. The proxy can expose the exact same interface as its target.

It is impossible to deconstruct a proxy to obtain its handler or its target without using reflective capabilities. Since security is not a concern, we assume for simplicity the existence of a class `Reflect` that exposes the following methods globally:

- **`Reflect class>>isProxy: aProxy`**
  Returns whether the argument is a proxy or not.
- **`Reflect class>>handlerOf: aProxy`**
  If the argument is a proxy, returns its handler. Fails otherwise.
- **`Reflect class>>targetOf: aProxy`**
  If the argument is a proxy, returns its target. Fails otherwise.

For increased security, these methods could to be stratified with mirrors [9], in which case handlers would need to have access to a mirror when instantiated.

3. Examples

Since delegation proxies subsume dynamic proxies, they can be used to implement all classic examples of dynamic proxies like lazy values, membranes, remote stubs, etc. We omit such examples that can be found elsewhere in the literature [13, 18, 28].

We focus in this section on new examples enabled by delegation proxies. They all rely on the propagation technique presented earlier. We assume that the handlers inherit from the class `PropHandler` that implements the propagation technique for reuse (see Listing 5).

3.1 Object Versioning

To tolerate errors, developers implement recovery blocks that undo mutations and leave the objects in a consistent state [33]. Typically, this requires cloning objects to obtain snapshots. Delegation proxies enable the implementation of object versioning elegantly. Before any field is mutated, the handler shown below records the old value into a log using a reflective field read. The log can be used in recovery block, for instance to implement rollback. Similarly to the other examples that follow, we assume that the handler inherits from a base handler that implements the propagation technique.

```
RecordingHandler>>handleWriteField: f value: v
                    myself: p target: t
    | oldValue |
    oldValue := t instVarNamed: f.
    log add: { t. f. oldValue }.
    ↑ super handleWriteField: f value: v myself: p target: t
```

Listing 7. Recording handler

A convenience method can be added to enable recording with `[...] recordInLog: aLog`.

```
BlockClosure>>recordInLog: aLog
    ↑ self valueWithHandler: (RecordingHandler log: aLog)
```

Listing 8. Enabling recording

The log can then be used to reflectively undo changes if needed.

```
aLog reverseDo: [ :m |
  m first instVarNamed: m second put: m third
]
```

Listing 9. Undoing changes (m stands for mutation)

3.2 Read-only Execution

Read-only execution [4] prevents mutation of state during evaluation. Read-only execution can dynamically guarantee that the evaluation of a given piece of code is either side-effect free or raises an error.

Classical proxies could restrict the interface of a given object to the subset of read-only methods. However, they would fail to enable read-only execution of arbitrary functions, or to guarantee that methods are deeply read-only. Read-only execution can be implemented trivially using propagation and a handler that fails upon state writes.

```
ReadOnlyHandler>>handleWriteField: f value: v myself: p
                target: t
   ReadOnlyError signal: 'Illegal write'.
```

Listing 10. Read-only handler

3.3 Dynamic Scoping

In most modern programming languages, variables are lexically scoped and can't be dynamically scoped. Dynamic scoping is sometimes desirable, for instance in web frameworks to access easily the ongoing request. Developers must in this case use alternatives like thread locals. It is for instance the strategy taken by Java Server Faces in the static method `getCurrentInstance()` of class `FacesContext`[3]).

Dynamic scoping can be realized in Smalltalk using stack manipulation [16] or by accessing the active process. Delegation proxies offer an additional approach to implement dynamic bindings by simply sharing a common (key,value) pair between handlers. If multiple dynamic bindings are defined, objects will be proxied multiple times, once per binding. When a binding value must be retrieved, a utility method locates the handler corresponding to the request key, and returns the corresponding value:

```
ScopeUtils>>valueOf: aKey for: aProxy
   | h p |
   p := aProxy.
   [ Reflect isProxy: p ] whileTrue: [
      h := Reflect handlerOf: p.
      ( h bindingKey == aKey ) ifTrue: [
         ↑ h bindingValue.
      ].
      p := Reflect targetOf: p.
   ].
   ↑ nil. "Not found"
```

Listing 11. Inspection of a chain of proxies

During the evaluation of a block, a dynamic variable can be bound with `[...] valueWith: #currentRequest value: aRequest` and accessed pervasively with `ScopeUtils valueOf: #currentRequest for: self`.

3.4 Profiling

Previous sections already illustrated delegation proxies using tracing. The exact same approach could be used to implement other interceptors like profiling or code contracts. The following handler implements profiling. It stores records of the different execution durations in an instance variable `tallies` for later analysis.

[3] http://www.webcitation.org/6F0F4DFab

```
ProfilingHandler>>initialize
    tallies := OrderedCollection new

ProfilingHandler>>handleMessage: m myself: p target: t
  | start |
  start := Time now.
  [ ↑ super handleMessage: m myself: p target: t ]
    ensure: [
        | duration |
        duration := Time now - start.
        tallies add: {t. m. duration} ]
```

Listing 12. A simple profiling handler

4. Semantics

We formalize delegation proxies by extending SMALLTALKLITE [6], a lightweight calculus in the spirit of CLASSICJAVA [19] that omits static types. This paper does not assume any prior knowledge of it. Our formalization simplifies three aspects of the semantics presented in the previous sections: it doesn't model first-class classes, literals or closures. Consequently, a *literal* trap does not make sense. Instead, we introduce a *new* trap that intercepts object instantiations.

The syntax of our extended calculus, SMALLTALKPROXY, is shown in Figure 3. The only addition to the original syntax is the new expression **proxy** e e.

$$
\begin{array}{rcl}
P & = & \mathit{defn}^* e \\
\mathit{defn} & = & \textbf{class}\ c\ \textbf{extends}\ c\ \{\ f^* \mathit{meth}^*\ \} \\
\mathit{meth} & = & m(x^*)\ \{\ e\ \} \\
e & = & \textbf{new}\ c \mid x \mid \textbf{self} \mid \mathsf{nil} \mid f \mid f = e \\
 & | & e.m(e^*) \mid \textbf{super}.m(e^*) \mid \textbf{let}\ x = e\ \textbf{in}\ e \\
 & | & \textbf{proxy}\ e\ e
\end{array}
$$

Figure 3. Syntax of SMALLTALKPROXY

During evaluation, the expressions of the program are annotated with the object and class context of the ongoing evaluation, since this information is missing from the static syntax. An annotated expression is called a *redex*. For instance, the super call $\textbf{super}.m(v^*)$ is decorated with its object and class into $\textbf{super}\langle c\rangle.m\langle o\rangle(v^*)$ before being interpreted; **self** is translated into the value of the corresponding object; message sends $o.m(v^*)$ are decorated with the current object context to keep track of the sender of the message. The rules for the translation of expressions into redexes are shown below.

$$
\begin{array}{rcl}
o[\![\textbf{new}\ c]\!]_c & = & \textbf{new}\langle o\rangle\ c \\
o[\![x]\!]_c & = & x \\
o[\![\textbf{self}]\!]_c & = & o \\
o[\![\mathsf{nil}]\!]_c & = & \mathsf{nil} \\
o[\![f]\!]_c & = & f\langle o\rangle \\
o[\![f = e]\!]_c & = & f\langle o\rangle = o[\![e]\!]_c \\
o[\![e.m(e_i^*)]\!]_c & = & o[\![e]\!]_c.m\langle o\rangle(o[\![e_i]\!]_c^*) \\
o[\![\textbf{super}.m(e_i^*)]\!]_c & = & \textbf{super}\langle c\rangle.m\langle o\rangle(o[\![e_i]\!]_c^*) \\
o[\![\textbf{let}\ x = e\ \textbf{in}\ e']\!]_c & = & \textbf{let}\ x = o[\![e]\!]_c\ \textbf{in}\ o[\![e']\!]_c \\
o[\![\textbf{proxy}\ e\ e']\!]_c & = & \textbf{proxy}\ o[\![e]\!]_c\ o[\![e']\!]_c
\end{array}
$$

Figure 4. Translating expressions to redexes

Redexes and their subredexes reduce to a value, which is either an address a, nil, or a proxy. A proxy has a handler h and a target t. A proxy is itself a value. Both h and t can be proxies as well.

Redexes may be evaluated within an expression context E. An expression context corresponds to an redex with a hole that can be filled with another redex. For example, $E[expr]$ denotes an expression that contains the sub-expression $expr$.

$$
\begin{array}{rcl}
\epsilon & = & o \mid \textbf{new}\langle o\rangle\, c \mid x \mid \textbf{self} \mid \mathsf{nil} \\
& \mid & f\langle o\rangle \mid f\langle o\rangle = \epsilon \mid \epsilon.m\langle o\rangle(\epsilon^*) \\
& \mid & \textbf{super}\langle c\rangle.m\langle o\rangle(\epsilon^*) \mid \textbf{let}\, x = \epsilon\, \textbf{in}\, \epsilon \\
E & = & [\,] \mid f\langle o\rangle = E \mid E.m\langle o\rangle(\epsilon^*) \\
& \mid & o.m\langle o\rangle(o^*\; E\; \epsilon^*) \mid \textbf{super}\langle c\rangle.m\langle o\rangle(o^*\; E\; \epsilon^*) \\
& \mid & \textbf{let}\, x = E\, \textbf{in}\, \epsilon \mid \textbf{proxy}\, E\, \epsilon \mid \textbf{proxy}\, o\, E \\
o, h, t & = & \mathsf{nil} \mid a \mid \textbf{proxy}\, h\, t
\end{array}
$$

Figure 5. Redex syntax

Translation from the main expression to an initial redex is carried out by the $o[\![e]\!]_c$ function (see Figure 4). This binds fields to their enclosing object context and binds **self** to the value o of the receiver. The initial object context for a program is nil. (*i.e.*, there are no global fields accessible to the main expression). So if e is the main expression associated to a program P, then $\mathsf{nil}[\![e]\!]_{\mathsf{Object}}$ is the initial redex.

$P \vdash \langle \epsilon, \mathcal{S}\rangle \hookrightarrow \langle \epsilon', \mathcal{S}'\rangle$ means that we reduce an expression (redex) ϵ in the context of a (static) program P and a (dynamic) store of objects $\mathcal{S}$ to a new expression ϵ' and (possibly) updated store $\mathcal{S}'$. The store consists of a set of mappings from addresses $a \in \text{dom}(\mathcal{S})$ to tuples $\langle c, \{f \mapsto v\}\rangle$ representing the class c of an object and the set of its field values. The initial value of the store is $\mathcal{S} = \{\}$.

The reductions are summarized in Figure 6. Predicate $\in^*_P$ is used for field lookup in a class ($f \in^*_P c$) and method lookup ($\langle c, m, x^*, e\rangle \in^*_P c'$, where c' is the class where the method was found in the hierarchy). Predicates $\leq_P$ and $\prec_P$ are used respectively for subclass and direct subclass relationships.

If the object context $\langle o\rangle$ of an instantiation with $\textbf{new}\langle o\rangle\, c$ is an object (*i.e.*, not a proxy), the expression reduces to a fresh address a, bound in the store to an object whose class is c and whose fields are all nil(reduction [new]). If the object context of the instantiation is a proxy, the **newTrap** is invoked on the handler instead (reduction [new-proxy]). The trap takes the result of the instantiation $\textbf{new}\langle t\rangle\, c$ as parameter; it can take further action or return it as-is.

The object context $\langle o\rangle$ of field reads and field writes can be an object or a proxy. A local field read in the context of an object address reduces to the value of the field (reduction [get]). A local field read in the context of a proxy invokes the trap **readTrap** on the handler h (reduction [get-proxy]). A local field write in the context of an object simply updates the corresponding binding of the field in the store (reduction [set]). A local field read in the context of a proxy invokes the trap **writeTrap** on the handler h (reduction [set-proxy]).

Messages can be sent to an object or to a proxy. When we send a message to an object, the corresponding method body e is looked-up, starting from the class c of the receiver a. The method body is then evaluated in the context of the receiver, binding **self** to the address a. Formal parameters to the method are substituted by the actual arguments. We also pass in the actual class in which the method is found, so that **super** sends have the right context to start their method lookup (reduction [message]). When a message is sent to a proxy, the trap **messageTrap** is invoked on the handler. The object context $\langle s\rangle$ that decorates the message corresponds to the sender of the message. The trap takes as parameters the message and its arguments, and the initial receiver of the message **proxy** $h\ t$.

Super-sends are similar to regular message sends, except that the method lookup must start in the superclass of the class of the method in which the **super** send was declared. In the case of super-send, the object context $\langle s\rangle$ corresponds to the sender of the message as well as the receiver. The object context is used to rebind **self** (reduction [super]). When we reduce the super-send, we must take care to pass on the class c'' of the method in which the super reference was found, since that method may make further super-sends.

Finally, **let in** expressions simply represent local variable bindings (reduction [let]). Errors occur if an expression gets stuck and does not reduce to an a or to nil. This may occur if a non-existent variable, field or method is referenced (for example, when sending any message to nil, or applying traps on a handler h that isn't suitable). For the purpose of this paper we are not concerned with errors, so we do not introduce any special rules to generate an error value in these cases.

4.1 Identity Proxy

As was discussed in subsection 2.4, the system requires the ability to reflectively apply operations on base objects and proxies to be useful. For simplicity, we extend the language with three additional non-stratified reflective primitives: **send**, **read**, and **write**. The semantics of these primitives is given in Figure 7.

All three primitives take a last argument *my* (shortcut for "myself") representing the object context that will be rebound. When applied to a proxy, the operations invoke the corresponding trap in a straightforward manner, passing *my* as-is. When **read** or **write** is applied to an object address, the argument *my* is ignored. When **send** is applied to an object address, *my* defines how **self** will be rebound during the reflective invocation.

With these primitives, we can trivially define the identity handler, idHandler. idHandler is an instance of a handler class that defines the following methods:

$$
\begin{array}{lcl}
\textbf{newTrap}(t, my) & = & t \\
\textbf{readTrap}(t, f, my) & = & t.\textbf{read}(f, my) \\
\textbf{writeTrap}(t, f, o, my) & = & t.\textbf{write}(f, o, my) \\
\textbf{messageTrap}(t, m, o^*, my) & = & t.\textbf{send}(m, o^*, my)
\end{array}
$$

We can show that sending a message to an identity proxy will delegate the message to the target, and rebind **self** to the proxy.

Let us consider an object s that sends the message $m(o)$ to a proxy $p = \textbf{proxy}\ \mathsf{idHandler}\ t$. Object t is an instance of class c which defines method $m(x)$ with body $e = \textbf{self}\ n(x)$.

$$
\begin{array}{ll}
p.m\langle s\rangle(o) & \\
\mathsf{idHandler}.\textbf{messageTrap}(t, m, o, p) & [\textit{send-proxy}] \\
t.\textbf{send}(m, o, p) & [\textit{send}] \\
p[\![e[o/x]]\!]_c & [\textit{reflect-message}] \\
p[\![\textbf{self}]\!]_c.n\langle p\rangle(o) & [\textit{translation}] \\
p.n\langle p\rangle(o) & [\textit{translation}]
\end{array}
$$

4.2 Propagating Identity Proxy

Following the technique of propagation presented in subsection 2.1, we propose a propagating identity handler, propHandler. This handler defines the behavior of the root proxy and uses another handler $\mathsf{propHandler}^*$ to create the other proxies during propagation. This technique requires the ability to unwrap a proxy. The expression **unproxy** is added to the language as defined in Figure 7. We also assume the existence of the traditional sequencing (;) operation.

The handler propHandler is defined as follows:

$$
\begin{array}{lcl}
\textbf{newTrap}(t, my) & = & \textbf{proxy}\ \mathsf{propHandler}^*\ t \\
\textbf{readTrap}(t, f, my) & = & \textbf{proxy}\ \mathsf{propHandler}^*\ (t.\textbf{read}(f, my)) \\
\textbf{writeTrap}(t, f, o, my) & = & t.\textbf{write}(f, \textbf{unproxy}\ o, my); o \\
\textbf{messageTrap}(t, m, o^*, my) & = & \textbf{unproxy}(t.\textbf{send}(m, \\
& & \quad (\textbf{proxy}\ \mathsf{propHandler}^* o^1, \ldots, \\
& & \quad \textbf{proxy}\ \mathsf{propHandler}^* o^n), my))
\end{array}
$$

$$P \vdash \langle E[\mathbf{new}\langle r\rangle\ c], \mathcal{S}\rangle \hookrightarrow \langle E[a], \mathcal{S}[a \mapsto \langle c, \{f \mapsto \mathsf{nil} \mid \forall f, f \in_P^* c\}\rangle]\rangle \quad \text{where } a \notin \mathrm{dom}(\mathcal{S}) \qquad [\textit{new}]$$

$$P \vdash \langle E[\mathbf{new}\langle \mathbf{proxy}\ h\ t\rangle\ c], \mathcal{S}\rangle \hookrightarrow \langle E[h.\mathbf{newTrap}(\mathbf{new}\langle t\rangle c, \mathbf{proxy}\ h\ t)], \mathcal{S}\rangle \qquad [\textit{new-proxy}]$$

$$P \vdash \langle E[f\langle a\rangle], \mathcal{S}\rangle \hookrightarrow \langle E[o], \mathcal{S}\rangle \quad \text{where } \mathcal{S}(a) = \langle c, \mathcal{F}\rangle \text{ and } \mathcal{F}(f) = o \qquad [\textit{get}]$$

$$P \vdash \langle E[f\langle \mathbf{proxy}\ h\ t\rangle], \mathcal{S}\rangle \hookrightarrow \langle E[h.\mathbf{readTrap}(t, f, \mathbf{proxy}\ h\ t)], \mathcal{S}\rangle \qquad [\textit{get-proxy}]$$

$$P \vdash \langle E[f\langle a\rangle = o], \mathcal{S}\rangle \hookrightarrow \langle E[o], \mathcal{S}[a \mapsto \langle c, \mathcal{F}[f \mapsto o]\rangle]\rangle \quad \text{where } \mathcal{S}(a) = \langle c, \mathcal{F}\rangle \qquad [\textit{set}]$$

$$P \vdash \langle E[f\langle \mathbf{proxy}\ h\ t\rangle = o], \mathcal{S}\rangle \hookrightarrow \langle E[h.\mathbf{writeTrap}(t, f, o, \mathbf{proxy}\ h\ t)], \mathcal{S}\rangle \qquad [\textit{set-proxy}]$$

$$P \vdash \langle E[a.m\langle s\rangle(o^*)], \mathcal{S}\rangle \hookrightarrow \langle E[a[\![e[o^*/x^*]]\!]_{c'}], \mathcal{S}\rangle \quad \text{where } \mathcal{S}[a] = \langle c, \mathcal{F}\rangle \text{ and } \langle c, m, x^*, e\rangle \in_P^* c' \qquad [\textit{message}]$$

$$P \vdash \langle E[(\mathbf{proxy}\ h\ t).m\langle s\rangle(o^*)], \mathcal{S}\rangle \hookrightarrow \langle E[h.\mathbf{messageTrap}(t, m, o^*, \mathbf{proxy}\ h\ t)], \mathcal{S}\rangle \qquad [\textit{message-proxy}]$$

$$P \vdash \langle E[\mathbf{super}\langle c\rangle.m\langle s\rangle(o^*)], \mathcal{S}\rangle \hookrightarrow \langle E[s[\![e[o^*/x^*]]\!]_{c''}], \mathcal{S}\rangle \quad \text{where } c \prec_P c' \text{ and } \langle c', m, x^*, e\rangle \in_P^* c'' \text{ and } c' \leq_P c'' \qquad [\textit{super}]$$

$$P \vdash \langle E[\mathbf{let}\ x = o\ \mathbf{in}\ \epsilon], \mathcal{S}\rangle \hookrightarrow \langle E[\epsilon[o/x]], \mathcal{S}\rangle \qquad [\textit{let}]$$

Figure 6. Reductions for SMALLTALKPROXY

$$P \vdash \langle E[a.\mathbf{send}(m, o^*, \mathit{my})], \mathcal{S}\rangle \hookrightarrow \langle E[\mathit{my}[\![e[o^*/x^*]]\!]_{c'}], \mathcal{S}\rangle \quad \text{where } \mathcal{S}[a] = \langle c, \mathcal{F}\rangle \text{ and } \langle c, m, x^*, e\rangle \in_P^* c' \qquad [\textit{reflect-message}]$$

$$P \vdash \langle E[(\mathbf{proxy}\ h\ t).\mathbf{send}(m, o^*, \mathit{my})], \mathcal{S}\rangle \hookrightarrow \langle E[h.\mathbf{messageTrap}(t, m, o^*, \mathit{my})], \mathcal{S}\rangle \qquad [\textit{reflect-message-proxy}]$$

$$P \vdash \langle E[a.\mathbf{read}(f, \mathit{my})], \mathcal{S}\rangle \hookrightarrow \langle E[o], \mathcal{S}\rangle \quad \text{where } \mathcal{S}(a) = \langle c, \mathcal{F}\rangle \text{ and } \mathcal{F}(f) = o \qquad [\textit{reflect-get}]$$

$$P \vdash \langle E[(\mathbf{proxy}\ h\ t).\mathbf{read}(f, \mathit{my})], \mathcal{S}\rangle \hookrightarrow \langle E[h.\mathbf{readTrap}(t, f, \mathit{my})], \mathcal{S}\rangle \qquad [\textit{reflect-get-proxy}]$$

$$P \vdash \langle E[a.\mathbf{write}(f, o, \mathit{my})], \mathcal{S}\rangle \hookrightarrow \langle E[o], \mathcal{S}[a \mapsto \langle c, \mathcal{F}[f \mapsto o]\rangle]\rangle \quad \text{where } \mathcal{S}(a) = \langle c, \mathcal{F}\rangle \qquad [\textit{reflect-set}]$$

$$P \vdash \langle E[(\mathbf{proxy}\ h\ t).\mathbf{write}(f, o, \mathit{my})], \mathcal{S}\rangle \hookrightarrow \langle E[h.\mathbf{writeTrap}(t, f, o, \mathit{my})], \mathcal{S}\rangle \qquad [\textit{reflect-set-proxy}]$$

$$P \vdash \langle E[\mathbf{unproxy}(\mathbf{proxy}\ h\ t)], \mathcal{S}\rangle \hookrightarrow \langle E[t], \mathcal{S}\rangle \qquad [\textit{unproxy}]$$

Figure 7. Reflective facilities added to SMALLTALKPROXY

The handler propHandler* is defined as follows:

$$\begin{aligned}
\mathbf{newTrap}(t, \mathit{my}) &= \mathbf{proxy}\ \mathsf{propHandler}^*\ t \\
\mathbf{readTrap}(t, f, \mathit{my}) &= \mathbf{proxy}\ \mathsf{propHandler}^*\ (t.\mathbf{read}(f, \mathit{my})) \\
\mathbf{writeTrap}(t, f, o, \mathit{my}) &= t.\mathbf{write}(f, \mathbf{unproxy}\ o, \mathit{my});\ o \\
\mathbf{messageTrap}(t, m, o^*, \mathit{my}) &= t.\mathbf{send}(m, o^*, \mathit{my})
\end{aligned}$$

We can formally express the intuitive explanation of subsection 2.1 about soundness of the propagation.

Let us assume that all values in the expression $E[e]$ are proxies (using the propHandler*). The reduction rules that can match are [new-proxy], [get-proxy], [set-proxy], [super], [let], and [message-proxy]. According to the definition of the propHandler* traps, rule [new-proxy] will preserve the invariant that all values are proxies. Rule [get-proxy] does so as well. Rule [set-proxy] preserves the assumption since it returns the value written, which we know is a proxy. Rules [super] and [let] do as well since they only bind variables with existing values, which we know are proxies. Similarly, rule [message-proxy] will bind **self** with the expected proxy (see previous section). It also binds the variables with the passed arguments, which are known to be proxies. Since all values remain proxies, the evaluation is consistent.

The initial redex is evaluated with nil as object context: $\mathsf{nil}[\![e]\!]_{\mathsf{Object}}$. If the proxy $p = $ **proxy** propHandler nil is used instead of nil, the assumption is initially true, and will not be broken during evaluation.

5. Implementation

We have implemented a prototype of delegation proxies in Smalltalk that relies on code generation. For each existing method in a base class, a hidden method with an additional parameter `myself` and a transformed body is generated. Instead of `self`, `myself` is used in the generated method body (this is similar to Python's explicit `self` argument). Following the same approach as Uniform Proxies for Java [18], proxy classes are auto-generated. Let us consider the class `Suitcase`:

```
Object>>subclass: #Suitcase
  instanceVariableNames: 'content'

Suitcase>>printString
  ↑ 'Content: ' concat: content.
```

Listing 13. Original code of class `Suitcase`

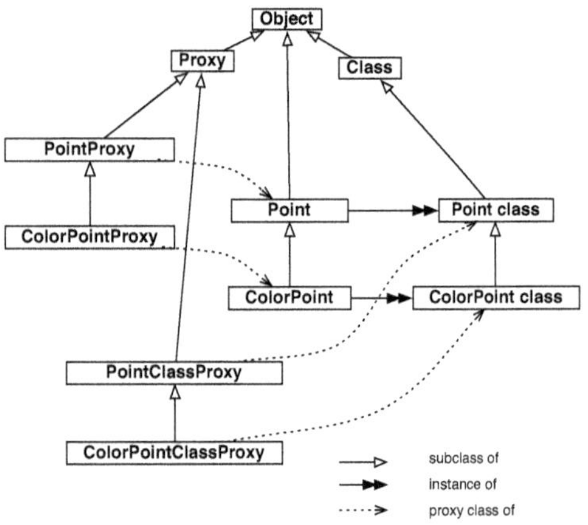

Figure 8. Inheritance of classes, meta-classes, and auto-generated proxy classes.

Applying our transformation, the class `Suitcase` is augmented with synthetic methods to read and write the field `content` and to resolve literals.

```
Suitcase>> literal: aLiteral myself: slf
  ↑ aLiteral

Suitcase>> readContentMyself: slf
  ↑ content

 Suitcase>> writeContent: value myself: slf
  ↑ content := value
```

Listing 14. Synthetic methods to read and write instance variable `content` and literal resolution

In Smalltalk, fields are encapsulated and can be accessed only by their respective object. The sender of a state access is always `myself`, and can thus be omitted from the traps. For each existing method in class `Suitcase`, a hidden method with a transformed body and one additional parameter `myself` is generated.

```
Suitcase>>printStringMyself: slf
  ↑ ( slf literal: 'Content: ' myself: slf )
     concat: (self readContentMyself: slf).
```

Listing 15. A transformed version of method `printString`

A proxy class for `Suitcase` is then generated. It inherits from a class `Proxy`, which defines the `handler` field common to all proxies. The generated class implements the same methods as the `Suitcase` class, *i.e.*, `printString`, `printStringMyself:`, `readContentMyself:`, and `writeContent:myself:`. The methods invoke respectively *message*, *read* and *write* traps on the handler.

```
SuitcaseProxy>> printString
  ↑ self printStringMyself: self

SuitcaseProxy>> printStringMyself: slf
  | msg |
  msg := Message selector: #printString arguments: {} .
  ↑ handler message: msg myself: slf target: target.
```

Listing 16. Sample generated method in proxy class of `Suitcase`

5.1 Classes

Smalltalk has first-class classes whose behaviors are defined in meta-classes. The class and meta-class hierarchies are parallel. Classes can be proxied like any object. Consequently, meta-classes are rewritten and extended with synthetic methods similarly to classes. However, the generated proxy classes do not inherit from `Class`, but `Proxy`, as is shown in Figure 8.

5.2 Closures

Closures are regular objects that are adapted upon creation and evaluation according to subsection 2.3. When a closure defined in an original uninstrumented method is proxied, the code of the closure is transformed lazily.

5.3 Weaving

Sending a message to a proxy entails reification of the message, invocation of the handler's trap, and then reflective invocation of the message on the target. In addition, the handler might take additional actions that entail costs. The handler and the proxy can be woven into specialized classes for less levels of indirection. For instance, a `SuitcaseProxy` with a `Tracing` handler can be woven into a `SuitcaseTracingProxy`:

```
SuitcaseTracingProxy>> printStringMyself: slf
  | msg |
  msg := Message selector: #printString arguments: {} .
  Transcript
          print: target asString;
          space;
          print: msg asString;
          cr.
  ↑ target printStringMyself: slf.
```

Listing 17. Sample woven method

We have implemented a simple weaver that works for basic cases. We plan to mature it in the future and leverage techniques for partial evaluation [20] developed for aspect compilers [29].

5.4 Performance

Delegation proxies have no impact on performance if not used: the transformation adds new code but does not alter the existing one. When used, we need to distinguish between the performance of delegation proxies themselves and the overhead of the propagation technique.

Used sparingly, delegation proxies do not entail performance issues. The situation is similar to traditional forwarding proxies. Used extensively with our propagation technique, the cost of delegation proxies is prohibitive unless weaving is used. With weaving, benchmarks of Fibonacci[4] reveal a performance degradation of below one order of magnitude (8x slower). We believe it is an encouraging result given that delegation proxies enable unanticipated behavioral reflection, which is known to be costly.

With our propagation technique, a given object might be wrapped multiple times, producing multiple equivalent proxies. In the Fibonacci examples, `1`, `2` and `[^ self]` are literals that are intercepted and wrapped thousands of times. This increases the number of objects created and puts pressure on the garbage collector. Future work could address this issue, possibly with caching.

6. Discussion

Scoping Scoping variations to dynamic extents was the motivation for delegation proxies. However, the propagation technique that we have presented covers only one particular form of scoping that can be realized with delegation proxies. Since the propagation is implemented reflectively, it can be customized in many ways.

[4] CogVM 6.0, Mac OS X, 2.3 GHz Intel Core

If a variation is active in all threads, the propagation can for instance be adapted to proxy only instances of application classes and skip kernel classes (string, dictionaries, arrays, etc.). The application and the kernel form two layers. Any application object referenced by a kernel object has necessarily been provided by the application. If application objects are wrapped, this guarantees that kernel objects hold only references to proxies of application objects. Therefore, if a kernel object sends a message to an application object, the propagation will start again. Kernel objects will not unwrap proxies of application objects upon state writes, and the heap might contain references to proxies (the variation must thus be active in all threads). Omitting kernel objects from the propagation could be desirable to improve performance.

It is also be possible to adapt the propagation so that the root proxies doesn't unwrap the objects they returns. Variations that apply security concerns such as access control usually have this requirement [4].

Closure wrapping rules can also be customized in different ways. It is possible to control which closures should "escape" the dynamic extent as proxy or not. If a method parallelizes work internally using multiple threads, the propagation could for instance be customized to propagate to those threads as well. Or if the system uses callbacks, the callbacks could restore the variation that was active when they were created.

Delegation proxies provide flexible building blocks to implement various forms of scopes, possibly blurring the line between static and dynamic scoping, similarly to Tanter's *scoping strategies* [39].

Static Typing There is no major obstacle to port our implementation to a statically-typed language. Delegation proxies preserve the interface of their target, like traditional forwarding proxies. For type compatibility, the generated proxy must inherit from the original class. Reflective operations can fail with run-time type errors. Forwarding and delegation proxies suffer from the same lack of type safety from this perspective.

If closures cannot be adapted at run time with the same flexibility as in Smalltalk, the implementation might require a global rewrite of the sources to adapt the code of the closures at compile-time.

Delegation proxies require that reflective operations have an additional parameter that specifies how to rebind `self`. Naturally, this parameter must be of a valid type: in practice it will be either the target of the invocation or a proxy of the target. Both implement the same interface.

7. Related Work

Method Dispatch MOPs, AOP and proxies are various approaches that enable the interception and customization of method dispatch. MOPs reify the execution into meta-objects that can be customized [23]. AOP adopts another perspective on the problem and enables the definition of join points where additional logic is woven [24]. MOP and AOP share similarities with method combination of CLOS [14].

Many languages provide support for dynamic proxies. When a message is sent to a dynamic proxy, the message is intercepted and reified. Dynamic proxies have found many usefully applications that can be categorized as "interceptors" or "virtual objects" [42]. An important question for proxies is whether to support them natively at the language level or via lower-level abstractions.

Most dynamic languages support proxies via traps that are invoked when a message cannot be delivered [28]. However, modern proxy mechanisms stratify the base and meta levels with a handler [18, 28, 42], including Java that uses code generation to enable proxies for interfaces. The mechanism was extended to enable proxies of classes as well [18].

AOP and MOP inherently suffer from meta-regression issues, unless the meta-levels are explicitly modeled [11, 15, 40]. In contrast to AOP and MOPs, delegation proxies do not suffer from meta-regression issues since the adapted object and the base object are distinct. For instance, the tracing handler in Listing 4 does not lead to a meta-regression since it sends the message `asString` to the target, which is distinct from the proxy (in parameter `myself`). System code can in this way be adapted. Also, delegation proxies naturally enable partial reflection [41] since objects are selectively proxied.

Recent works on proxies in dynamic languages have studied orthogonal issues related to stratification [12, 42], preservation of abstractions and invariants [13, 37], and traps for values [5]. Only Javascript direct proxies support delegation [13]. However, Javascript proxies do not enable the interception of object instantiations; the variables captured in a closure will not be unproxied upon capture and proxied upon evaluation.

In addition to full-fledged MOPs and AOP, reflective language like Smalltalk provide various ways to intercept message sends [17]. Java and .NET support custom method dispatch via JSR 292 [31] and the Dynamic Language Runtime [30].

Composing Behavior Inheritance leads to an explosion in the number of classes when multiple variations (decorations) of a given set of classes must be designed. Static traits [35] or mixins enable the definition of units of reuse that can be composed into classes, but they do not solve the issue of class explosion.

One solution to this problem is the use of decorators that refine a specific set of known methods, *e.g.*, the method `paint` of a window. Static and dynamic approaches have been proposed to decoration. Unlike decorators, proxies find their use when the refinement applies to unknown methods, *e.g.*, to trace all invocations. Büchi and Weck proposed a mechanism [10] to statically parameterize classes with a decorator (called wrapper in their terminology). Bettini *et al.* [8] proposed a similar construct but composition happens at creation time. Ressia *et al.* proposed *talents* [34] which enable adaptations of the behavior of individual objects by composing trait-like units of behavior dynamically. Other works enable dynamic replacement of behavior in a trait-like fashion [7].

The code snippet below illustrates how to achieve the decoration of a `Window` with a `Border` and shows the conceptual differences between these approaches. The two first approaches can work with forwarding or delegation (but no implementations with delegation are available). The third approach replaces the behavior or the object so the distinction does not apply.

```
Window w = new Window<Border>(); // Buchi and Weck
Window w = new BorderWrap( new Window() ); // Bettini
Window w = new WindowEmptyPaint(); // Ressia
w.acquire( new BorderedPaint() );
```

Listing 18. Differences between approaches to decoration

Several languages that combine class-based inheritance and object inheritance (*i.e.*, delegation) have been proposed [25, 43]. Delegation enables the behavior of an object to be composed dynamically from other objects with partial behaviors. Essentially, delegation achieves trait-like dynamic composition of behavior.

Ostermann proposed delegation layers [32], which extend the notion of delegation from objects to collaborations of nested objects, *e.g.*, a graph with edges and nodes. An outer object wrapped with a delegation layer will affects its nested objects as well. Similary to decorators, the mechanism refines specific sets of methods of the objects in the collaboration.

Dynamic Scoping The dynamic extent of an expression corresponds to all operations that happen during the evaluation of the expression by a given thread of execution. Control-flow pointcuts are thus not sufficient to scope to dynamic extents, since they lack control over the thread scope. Control-flow pointcuts are popular and supported by mainstream AOP implementations, *e.g.*, AspectJ's `flow` and `cfbelow`. Aware of the limitations of control-flow pointcuts, some AOP implementations provide specific constructs to scope to dynamic extents, *e.g.*, CaesarJ's `deploy` [2]. Implemented naively, control-flow pointcuts are expensive since they entail a traversal of the stack at run time, but they can be implemented efficiently using partial evaluation [29].

In context-oriented programming (COP) [22, 44], variations can be encapsulated into layers that are dynamically activated in the dynamic extent of an expression. Unlike delegation proxies that support *homogenous* variations, COP supports best *heterogenous* variations [1]. COP can be seen as a form of multi-dimensional dispatch, where the context is an additional dimension.

Other mechanisms to vary the behavior of objects in a contextual manner are roles [26], perspectives [36], and subjects [21]. Delegation proxies can realize dynamic scoping via reference flow, by proxying and unproxying objects accesses during the execution. Delegation proxies can provide a foundation to design contextual variations.

Similarly to our approach, the handle model proposed by Arnaud *et al.* [3, 4] enables the adaptation of references with behavioral variations that propagate. The propagation belongs to the semantics of the handles, whereas in our approach, the propagation is encoded reflectively. Propagation unfolds from a principled use of delegation. Our approach is more flexible since it decouples the notion of propagation from the notion of proxy.

8. Conclusions

We can draw the following conclusions about the applicability of delegation proxies:

- *Expressiveness.* Delegation proxies subsume forwarding proxies and enable variations to be propagated to dynamic extents. This suits well non-functional concerns like monitoring (tracing, profiling), safety (read-only references), or reliability (rollback with object versioning). Since the propagation is written reflectively, it can be customized to achieve other forms of scopes.
- *Metaness.* Delegation proxies naturally compose, support partial behavioral reflection, and avoid meta-regressions. We can for instance trace and profile an execution by using tracing proxies and profiling proxies that form chains of delegation (composition). Objects are wrapped selectively. Adapting objects during an execution will not affect other objects in the system (partial reflection). Proxies and targets represent the same object at two different levels but have distinct identities (no meta-regression).
- *Encoding.* Delegation proxies can be implemented with code generation. In our Smalltalk implementation, only new code needs to be added; existing code remains unchanged. Delegation proxies have thus no overhead if not used. Delegation proxies do not entail performance issues when used sporadically (same situation as with forwarding proxies). The overhead of our propagation technique is of factor 8 when handlers are woven into dedicated proxies. Excluding system classes, if viable, can improve performance further. For optimal performance, the language should provide native support of delegation proxies.

In the future, we plan to further mature our implementation, notably the weaver, and explore native support at the VM level.

Acknowledgments

We thank Jorge Ressia, Mircea Lungu, Niko Schwarz and Jan Kurš for support and feedback about ideas in the paper. We gratefully acknowledge the financial support of the Swiss National Science Foundation for the project "Agile Software Assessment" (SNSF project Np. 200020-144126/1, Jan 1, 2013 - Dec. 30, 2015) and of the French General Directorate for Armament (DGA).

References

[1] S. Apel, T. Leich, and G. Saake. Aspectual feature modules. *IEEE Trans. Softw. Eng.*, 34(2):162–180, Mar. 2008.

[2] I. Aracic, V. Gasiunas, M. Mezini, and K. Ostermann. An overview of CaesarJ. *Transactions on Aspect-Oriented Software Development*, 3880:135 - 173, 2006.

[3] J.-B. Arnaud. *Towards First Class References as a Security Infrastructure in Dynamically-Typed Languages*. PhD thesis, Université des Sciences et Technologies de Lille, 2013.

[4] J.-B. Arnaud, M. Denker, S. Ducasse, D. Pollet, A. Bergel, and M. Suen. Read-only execution for dynamic languages. In *Proceedings of the 48th International Conference on Objects, Models, Components, Patterns (TOOLS EUROPE'10)*. LNCS Springer Verlag, July 2010.

[5] T. H. Austin, T. Disney, and C. Flanagan. Virtual values for language extension. In *Proceedings of the 2011 ACM international conference on Object oriented programming systems languages and applications*, volume 46 of *OOPSLA '11*, pages 921–938, New York, NY, USA, Oct. 2011. ACM.

[6] A. Bergel, S. Ducasse, O. Nierstrasz, and R. Wuyts. Stateful traits and their formalization. *Journal of Computer Languages, Systems and Structures*, 34(2-3):83–108, 2008.

[7] L. Bettini, S. Capecchi, and F. Damiani. On flexible dynamic trait replacement for java-like languages. *Science of Computer Programming*, 2011.

[8] L. Bettini, S. Capecchi, and E. Giachino. Featherweight wrap java. In *Proc. of SAC (The 22nd Annual ACM Symposium on Applied Computing), Special Track on Object-Oriented Programming Languages and Systems (OOPS)*, pages 1094–1100. ACM Press, 2007.

[9] G. Bracha and D. Ungar. Mirrors: design principles for meta-level facilities of object-oriented programming languages. In *Proceedings of the International Conference on Object-Oriented Programming, Systems, Languages, and Applications (OOPSLA'04), ACM SIGPLAN Notices*, pages 331–344, New York, NY, USA, 2004. ACM Press.

[10] M. Büchi and W. Weck. Generic wrappers. In E. Bertino, editor, *ECOOP 2000 - Object-Oriented Programming, 14th European Conference, Sophia Antipolis and Cannes, France, June 12-16, 2000, Proceedings*, volume 1850 of *Lecture Notes in Computer Science*, pages 201–225. Springer, 2000.

[11] S. Chiba, G. Kiczales, and J. Lamping. Avoiding confusion in metacircularity: The meta-helix. In K. Futatsugi and S. Matsuoka, editors, *Proceedings of ISOTAS '96*, volume 1049 of *Lecture Notes in Computer Science*, pages 157–172. Springer, 1996.

[12] T. V. Cutsem and M. S. Miller. On the design of the ECMAScript reflection api. Technical report, Vrije Universiteit Brussel, 2012.

[13] T. V. Cutsem and M. S. Miller. Trustworthy proxies: Virtualizing objects with invariants. In *ECOOP 2013*, 2013.

[14] L. G. DeMichiel and R. P. Gabriel. The Common Lisp object system: An overview. In J. Bézivin, J.-M. Hullot, P. Cointe, and H. Lieberman, editors, *Proceedings ECOOP '87*, volume 276 of *LNCS*, pages 151–170, Paris, France, June 1987. Springer-Verlag.

[15] M. Denker, M. Suen, and S. Ducasse. The meta in meta-object architectures. In *Proceedings of TOOLS EUROPE 2008*, volume 11 of *LNBIP*, pages 218–237. Springer-Verlag, 2008.

[16] P. Deutsch. Building control structures in smalltalk-80. *Byte*, 6(8):322–346, aug 1981.

[17] S. Ducasse. Evaluating message passing control techniques in Smalltalk. *Journal of Object-Oriented Programming (JOOP)*, 12(6):39–44, June 1999.

[18] P. Eugster. Uniform proxies for java. In *Proceedings of the 21st annual ACM SIGPLAN conference on Object-oriented programming systems, languages, and applications*, OOPSLA '06, pages 139–152, New York, NY, USA, 2006. ACM.

[19] M. Flatt, S. Krishnamurthi, and M. Felleisen. Classes and mixins. In *Proceedings of the 25th ACM SIGPLAN-SIGACT Symposium on Principles of Programming Languages*, pages 171–183, New York, NY, USA, 1998. ACM Press.

[20] Y. Futamura. Partial evaluation of computation process: An approach to a compiler-compiler. *Higher Order Symbol. Comput.*, 12(4):381–391, 1999.

[21] W. Harrison and H. Ossher. Subject-oriented programming (a critique of pure objects). In *Proceedings OOPSLA '93, ACM SIGPLAN Notices*, volume 28, pages 411–428, Oct. 1993.

[22] R. Hirschfeld, P. Costanza, and O. Nierstrasz. Context-oriented programming. *Journal of Object Technology*, 7(3), Mar. 2008.

[23] G. Kiczales, J. des Rivières, and D. G. Bobrow. *The Art of the Metaobject Protocol*. MIT Press, 1991.

[24] G. Kiczales, J. Lamping, A. Mendhekar, C. Maeda, C. Lopes, J.-M. Loingtier, and J. Irwin. Aspect-oriented programming. In M. Aksit and S. Matsuoka, editors, *ECOOP'97: Proceedings of the 11th European Conference on Object-Oriented Programming*, volume 1241 of *LNCS*, pages 220–242, Jyvaskyla, Finland, June 1997. Springer-Verlag.

[25] G. Kniesel. Type-safe delegation for run-time component adaptation. In R. Guerraoui, editor, *Proceedings ECOOP '99*, volume 1628 of *LNCS*, pages 351–366, Lisbon, Portugal, June 1999. Springer-Verlag.

[26] B. B. Kristensen. Object-oriented modeling with roles. In J. Murphy and B. Stone, editors, *Proceedings of the 2nd International Conference on Object-Oriented Information Systems*, pages 57–71, London , UK, 1995. Springer-Verlag.

[27] H. Lieberman. Using prototypical objects to implement shared behavior in object oriented systems. In *Proceedings OOPSLA '86, ACM SIGPLAN Notices*, volume 21, pages 214–223, Nov. 1986.

[28] M. Martinez Peck, N. Bouraqadi, M. Denker, S. Ducasse, and L. Fabresse. Efficient proxies in smalltalk. In *Proceedings of the International Workshop on Smalltalk Technologies*, IWST '11, pages 8:1–8:16, New York, NY, USA, 2011. ACM.

[29] H. Masuhara, G. Kiczales, and C. Dutchyn. A compilation and optimization model for aspect-oriented programs. In *Proceedings of the 12th international conference on Compiler construction*, CC'03, pages 46–60, Berlin, Heidelberg, 2003. Springer-Verlag.

[30] Microsoft. Microsoft .net dynamic language runtime.

[31] Oracle. Jsr 292: Supporting dynamically typed languages on the java platform.

[32] K. Ostermann. Dynamically composable collaborations with delegation layers. In *Proceedings of the 16th European Conference on Object-Oriented Programming*, ECOOP '02, pages 89–110, London, UK, 2002. Springer-Verlag.

[33] F. Pluquet, S. Langerman, and R. Wuyts. Executing code in the past: efficient in-memory object graph versioning. In *Proceedings of the 24th ACM SIGPLAN conference on Object oriented programming systems languages and applications*, OOPSLA '09, pages 391–408, New York, NY, USA, 2009. ACM.

[34] J. Ressia, T. Gîrba, O. Nierstrasz, F. Perin, and L. Renggli. Talents: an environment for dynamically composing units of reuse. *Software: Practice and Experience*, 2012.

[35] N. Schärli, S. Ducasse, O. Nierstrasz, and A. P. Black. Traits: Composable units of behavior. In *Proceedings of European Conference on Object-Oriented Programming (ECOOP'03)*, volume 2743 of *LNCS*, pages 248–274, Berlin Heidelberg, July 2003. Springer Verlag.

[36] R. B. Smith and D. Ungar. A simple and unifying approach to subjective objects. *TAPOS special issue on Subjectivity in Object-Oriented Systems*, 2(3):161–178, Dec. 1996.

[37] T. S. Strickland, S. Tobin-Hochstadt, R. B. Findler, and M. Flatt. Chaperones and impersonators: Run-time support for reasonable interposition. In *OOPSLA '12: Proceedings of the ACM International Conference on Object Oriented Programming Systems Languages and Applications*, Oct. 2012. To appear.

[38] É. Tanter. Expressive scoping of dynamically-deployed aspects. In *Proceedings of the 7th ACM International Conference on Aspect-Oriented Software Development (AOSD 2008)*, pages 168–179, Brussels, Belgium, Apr. 2008. ACM Press.

[39] É. Tanter. Beyond static and dynamic scope. In *Proceedings of the 5th symposium on Dynamic languages*, DLS '09, pages 3–14, New York, NY, USA, 2009. ACM.

[40] É. Tanter. Execution levels for aspect-oriented programming. In *Proceedings of AOSD'10)*, pages 37–48, Rennes and Saint Malo, France, Mar. 2010. ACM Press. Best Paper Award.

[41] É. Tanter, J. Noyé, D. Caromel, and P. Cointe. Partial behavioral reflection: Spatial and temporal selection of reification. In *Proceedings of OOPSLA '03, ACM SIGPLAN Notices*, pages 27–46, nov 2003.

[42] T. Van Cutsem and M. S. Miller. Proxies: design principles for robust object-oriented intercession apis. In *Proceedings of the 6th symposium on Dynamic languages*, DLS '10, pages 59–72, New York, NY, USA, 2010. ACM.

[43] J. Viega, B. Tutt, and R. Behrends. Automated delegation is a viable alternative to multiple inheritance in class based languages. Technical report, University of Virginia, Charlottesville, VA, USA, 1998.

[44] M. von Löwis, M. Denker, and O. Nierstrasz. Context-oriented programming: Beyond layers. In *Proceedings of the 2007 International Conference on Dynamic Languages (ICDL 2007)*, pages 143–156. ACM Digital Library, 2007.

Composable User-Defined Operators
That Can Express User-Defined Literals

Kazuhiro Ichikawa

The University of Tokyo
ichikawa@csg.ci.i.u-tokyo.ac.jp

Shigeru Chiba

The University of Tokyo
chiba@acm.org

Abstract

This paper proposes new composable user-defined operators, named *protean operators*. They can express various language extensions including user-defined literals such as regular expression literals as well as user-defined expressions. Their expressiveness is equivalent to Parsing Expression Grammar (PEG). The operators have two important features to be parsed in pragmatic time: overloading by return type and a precedence rule for operators. They can be parsed efficiently even if they express user-defined literals since ambiguities in the grammar are removed by these two features. The overloading by return type enables us to consider static types as non-terminal symbols in the grammar. The compiler can use static type information for parsing. It can resolve ambiguities of the rules with the same syntax but a different type. Protean operators with the same return type require programmers to declare the precedence among them. These precedence rules enable completely removing ambiguities from the grammar since all the rules applicable to the same place are ordered. Thus, the expressions including protean operators can be parsed in pragmatic time. We have implemented a language that is a subset of Java but supports protean operators. We present an experiment to show that the programs including user-defined literals cannot be parsed in pragmatic time in existing approaches but can be efficiently parsed in our approach.

Categories and Subject Descriptors D.3.3 [*Programming Languages*]: Language Constructs and Features

General Terms Languages, Algorithms, Experimentation

Keywords user-defined operators; parsing; syntax extensions

1. Introduction

A Domain Specific Language (DSL) is a simple programming language specially designed for only a limited purpose. Since a DSL is specialized for its application domain, its source code is more concise and intuitive than the equivalent code written in a general purpose language. An internal DSL [11] (or Embedded DSL) is a DSL that is implemented as a library in a general purpose language. It can be used together with the general purpose language

Modularity '14, April 22–26, 2014, Lugano, Switzerland.
Copyright is held by the owner/author(s). Publication rights licensed to ACM.
ACM 978-1-4503-2772-5/14/04. . . $15.00.
http://dx.doi.org/10.1145/2577080.2577092

(called the host language) since a program written in the DSL is still a valid program in the host language. It can be also used together with another DSL implemented on the same host language since both DSL programs are host language programs. An advantage of internal DSLs is this feature, *composability*. On the other hand, internal DSLs have drawbacks in the syntax – the syntax of internal DSLs is restricted by their host language. This paper aims to relax the restriction of the DSL syntax.

Composable user-defined operators are a useful tool for implementing internal DSLs since we can consider that they define their own syntax and semantics. The overloaded operators in C++ are simple user-defined operators but there have been user-defined operators that enable syntax extension. Mixfix operators [7] are one of the most powerful implementation of composable user-defined operators. However, the expressiveness of the mixfix operators is still limited and they cannot express certain kinds of syntax for internal DSLs. A typical problem is that they cannot express user-defined literals. A number of DSLs have their own literals that are not included in general purpose languages for describing programs concisely and safely. For example, flex [15], which is a DSL for generating a scanner, has literals for expressing regular expressions. Without user-defined literals, they must be expressed by character strings; it weakens maintainability and safety since the compiler does not check that the string character fits the literal syntax. User-defined literals introduce a large number of ambiguities and user-defined literals are included at a number of places in the source program. Thus, the parser cannot parse a program in pragmatic time.

In this paper, we propose new composable user-defined operators, named *protean operators*. They can express user-defined literals such as regular expressions and they are designed to be parsed in pragmatic time. There are two important features for efficient parsing: operator overloading and a precedence rule of operators. The first one is that a protean operator is overloaded on its return type and its parameter types. It enables us to consider static types as non-terminal symbols in the grammar. The compiler can use static type information for parsing. It resolves ambiguities of the rules with the same syntax but a different type. Furthermore, it also guarantees their composability. The second feature is that protean operators with the same return type require that the precedence among them is explicitly specified. These precedence rules completely remove ambiguities from the grammar since all the rules applicable to the same place are ordered. The parser can efficiently parse expressions including protean operators since the grammar has no ambiguities. We have developed *ProteaJ*, which is a subset language of Java supporting protean operators. We have conducted an experiment for demonstrating that ProteaJ can parse expressions including user-defined literals efficiently even though a naive parsing method cannot parse them in pragmatic time.

In the rest of this paper, we first show the limitation of existing composable user-defined operators. Then we propose new compos-

```
for (int i = 0; i < 10; i = i + 1) {
  print("Loop " + i + "\n");
}
```

Figure 1. An example of composable operators

```
val v1 = calc1()
val v2 = calc2()
v1 should be (0)
v2 should not be (0)
```

Figure 2. Composable user-defined operators with new syntax

able user-defined operators, named *protean operators*, and we show the parsing method for them in Section 3. In Section 4, we present a programming language supporting protean operators, named *ProteaJ*. Section 5 mentions an experiment for demonstrating the efficiency of our parsing method for protean operators. Section 6 is on related work. We conclude in Section 7.

2. Motivation

Composable user-defined operators are useful for implementing internal DSLs [11]. "Composable" means that operators with similar syntax can be used together at the same time safely. For example, composable operators are distinguished by static types. Figure 1 shows an example of composable operators. In this figure, there are three + operators. The first + operator expresses addition of integer values. The second + operator expresses concatenation of a string and an integer. The third + operator expresses concatenation of two strings. Although these three operators share the same syntax, they are distinguished by their parameter types. In some languages, progammers can define new operators that are not only predefined operators such as +. Figure 2 shows a unit test program using user-defined operators that introduce their own syntax. Line 3 in the figure consists of a binary infix operator `should` and a function call `be(0)`. Line 4 in the figure also includes two binary infix operators `should` and `be`. We can write a unit test program by using these operators as if it is written in a domain-specific or "natural" language. We can consider that composable user-defined operators make a new language on the host language since they have their own syntax and they are separated from the host language syntax, for example, by static types. Programmers can compose a library of composable user-defined operators as an internal DSL.

Mixfix operators [7] are a powerful implementation of composable user-defined operators. Mixfix indicates prefix, postfix, infix, or outfix. Mixfix operators can take operands and each two operands are separated by an operator-name. For example, the following syntax can be expressed by mixfix operators:

```
if _ then _ else _ // prefix
_ [ _ ] // postfix
_ < _ < _ // infix
| _ | // outfix
```

here, an underscore _ indicates an operand. Mixfix operators adopted in several languages such as Isabelle [16], Agda [1], and Pure [12].

However, mixfix operators do not have sufficient syntactic expressiveness for implementing a certain kind of internal DSLs. Mixfix operators cannot express complicated literals since they do not support literal-level syntax extension. The following code is an example of a regular expression literal:

```
Regex r = hel+o ;
```

the right-hand side of = is a regular expression literal that denotes `helo`, `hello`, `helllo`, and so on. Expressing user-defined literals by mixfix operators is difficult since the definition of tokens read by the scanner cannot be changed. For example, the literal `hel+o` should be tokenized into `[h, e, l, +, o]`, but it is tokenized into three tokens `[hel, +, o]` in typical general purpose languages such as C and Java.

Scannerless parsing is one of the implementation techniques of parsers that handle every character as a token and it enables us to handle literals as non-terminal symbols constructed by tokens. Since each character is a token, the syntax rules of user-defined literals can be handled by a parser. For instance, the literal `hel+o` is tokenized into `[h, e, l, +, o]` in a language implementing by a scannerless parser, and we can express the literal `hel+o` by six operators: four operandless operators (`h`, `e`, `l`, and `o`) for recognizing a single character as a sub-expression, an nameless operator (_ _) for concatenating sub-expressions, and a postfix operator (_ +). Mixfix operators can express user-defined literals when the host language is implemented by using a scannerless parser and they support nameless operators.

A typical parser for user-defined operators generates all possible parse trees to parse an expression. Then the compiler selects the most suitable parse tree from all possible trees by using the language semantics since the syntax of a user-defined operator should be allowed to conflict with another operator or the host language syntax. This is for flexible DSL definitions. The type checker is usually used for selecting the suitable parse tree since the type information holds the semantics of programs – what the programmer intends. For example, the expression `hel+o` has some possible parse trees and the interpretation of the expression should be changed by the context. It should be interpreted as an addition of integers if it is used as follows:

```
int i = hel+o;
```

but it should be interpreted as a regular expression literal if it is used as follows:

```
Regex r = hel+o;
```

Therefore, the syntax including regular expression literals should be an ambiguous grammar such as in Figure 3 and the ambiguities must be resolved by the type checker.

A typical scannerless parser is inefficient when parsing a program including user-defined literals. It must generate all possible parse trees but the number of these trees tends to be extremely large due to the ambiguity introduced by user-defined literals. Scannerless Generalized LR (SGLR) [25][23] parser is a well-known implementation of a scannerless parser. The parsing time of SGLR parsers is proportional to the degree of ambiguities (nondeterministics) in the grammar, and the worst-case time complexity is $O(n^3)$ (n is the input length). Note that n in this complexity is the number of tokens and it is equal to the number of characters in the program when an SGLR parser is used. n is sometimes larger than 10000. For example, the definition of the `ArrayList` class in OpenJDK 7 includes more than 12000 characters excluding comments and white-spaces.

3. Proposal: Protean Operators

We propose new composable user-defined operators, named *protean operators*. They can express user-defined literals such as regular expressions and parse them in pragmatic time. There are two important features of protean operators for efficient parsing : (1) overloading based on return type, and (2) parsing precedence. The overloading by return type enables the parser to resolve grammar ambiguities by using type information at parse time. The parsing

```
Stmt → Type Id "=" Expr ";"
Expr → Regex | Sum
Regex → Star+
Star → Letter "+" | Letter
Sum → Sum "+" Id | Id
Id → Letter+
```

Figure 3. An example of grammar including regular expression literals

precedence resolves the remaining ambiguities after the type checking by (1). Since these features resolve all the grammar ambiguities at parse time, protean operators that express user-defined literals can be parsed even in pragmatic time.

3.1 Protean Operators

Protean operators are composable user-defined operators that can have any number of operator-names and operands. Unlike mixfix operators, a protean operator is not only infix, prefix, postfix, and outfix; for example, a "nameless" operator, which is an operator without an operator-name, is a protean operator. Nameless operators are useful for implementing a concise internal DSL since they are invisible. Protean operators support operator precedence and associativity for ease of use. Protean operators are totally ordered by operator precedence. Figure 4 shows examples of protean operators that express regular expression literals. To express a protean operator, we introduce the following notation: `[S]:T` represents that an operator has syntax `S` and a return-type `T`. A double-quoted string denotes an operator-name and `_:T` denotes an operand of type `T`. The optional part enclosed by curly braces indicates an operator associativity. *left-assoc* is left-associative and *non-assoc* is non-associative. The operator precedence is shown in the last two lines in the figure. The literal `hel+o` is parsed as a regular expression literal as shown in Figure 5. The literal `hel+o` consists of four literals `h`, `e`, `l+`, and `o` and they are connected with a nameless operator. The nameless operator takes literals as operands and it returns a new literal expressing a regular expression constructed by the concatenation of the given regular expressions.

The details of the parsing of `hel+o` are the following. We assume that any single character is recognized as a token. First, each alphabetic token is interpreted as a simple `Letter` literal by the corresponding operator taking the token as an operator name such as `[ "h" ]:Letter` and `[ "e" ]:Letter`. These operators can be considered as a simple user-defined literal, which consists of one token. Each `Letter` literal is converted into a `Regex` literal by the nameless operator `[ _:Letter ]:Regex` at (D) in Figure 4. This nameless operator takes a `Letter` object as an operand and it returns an object expressing a regular expression that accepts the given letter. It is used as implicit type coercion. The two `Regex` literals, `h` and `e`, are tied by the nameless operator `[ _:Regex _:Regex ]:Regex` at (A) in Figure 4. The nameless operator takes two operands of type `Regex`, and it expresses a sequence of regular expressions. In this part, it takes the two `Regex` literals, `h` and `e`, as operands and it returns an object expressing a regular expression that accepts `he`. `l+` forms a literal of a regular expression constructed by a postfix unary operator `[ _:Regex "+" ]:Regex` shown at (C) in Figure 4. It represents a regular expression that accepts one or more sequences of `l`. Then `he` and `l+` tied by `[ _:Regex _:Regex ]:Regex`, and they make a literal expressing `hel`, `hell`, `helll`, and so on. Finally, `hel+` and `o` make a literal that expresses the complete regular expression by `[ _:Regex _:Regex ]:Regex`.

Protean operators are overloaded by their return types and their parameter types. Overloading by return type allows defining operators that have the same syntax but a different return type. The interpretation of the expression is changed by the expected type there. This fact is useful for developing internal DSLs since an operator is used only where it is required. For example, an expression `hel+o` can be interpreted as either of the following two patterns:

```
int hel = 2;
int o = 3;
int x1 = hel+o; // 5
Regex x2 = hel+o; // helo, hello, helllo, ...
```

The expression `hel+o` in the third line is interpreted as an addition expression of integers since the right hand of the assignment expects an integer value. Only the expression `hel+o` in the fourth line is interpreted as a regular expression literal since a Regex object is expected. It can be considered that the expected type of an expression determines the parsing of the expression.

If two protean operators share the same return type, the user must specify the *parsing precedence* among them. This precedence determines which operator should be selected when multiple interpretations are possible during parsing. In this paper, the earlier declared operator has the higher parsing precedence. For example, the possessive quantifier `[ _:Regex "++" ]:Regex` has higher precedence than the greedy quantifier `[ _:Regex "+" ]:Regex` since `[ _:Regex "++" ]:Regex` is a special case of `[ _:Regex "+" ]:Regex`. An operator with higher precedence is applied for parsing before operators with lower precedence. If the operator with higher precedence is successfully applied, then the other operators with lower precedence are not applied. The literal `hel++o` is interpreted as `he(l++)o` by applying `[ _:Regex "++" ]:Regex` rather than `he((l+)+)o` by `[ _:Regex "+" ]:Regex` since the former has higher precedence. The literal `hel+o` is interpreted as

```
(A) [ _:Regex _:Regex ]:Regex { left-assoc }
(B) [ _:Regex "++" ]:Regex { non-assoc }
(C) [ _:Regex "+" ]:Regex { non-assoc }
(D) [ _:Letter ]:Regex { non-assoc }
(E-a) [ "a" ]:Letter
(E-b) [ "b" ]:Letter
 ...
(E-z) [ "z" ]:Letter

operator precedence:
  (A) < (B) = (C) < (D) < (E-a) = (E-b) = ... = (E-z)
```

Figure 4. The protean operators expressing regular expression literals

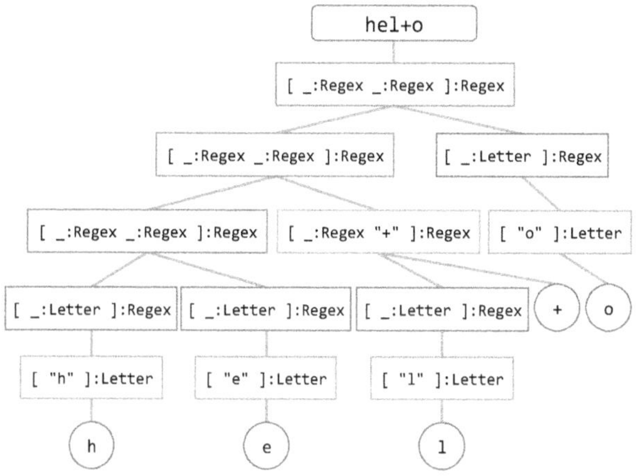

Figure 5. The parse tree for the literal `hel+o`

he(l+)o since [_:Regex "++"]:Regex is applied first and fails and then [_:Regex "+"]:Regex is successfully applied.

A drawback of protean operators is a limited kind of places where the operators are available. Protean operators are available only in the expressions whose expected type are statically determined before parsing the expression. The places where protean operators are available depend on a host language. For example, in typical general purpose languages such as Java, protean operators can be used in the right-hand side of an assignment but they cannot be used in the left hand of an assignment. The expected type of the right hand of an assignment is determined since it is the same type of the left-hand side. However, the expected type of the left-hand side of an assignment is not known before parsing the assignment expression. If we use a protean operator on the left-hand side of an assignment, the compiler emits a parse error. It is a drawback that the compiler cannot distinguish between a syntax error and a type error. Table 1 lists the expected types of every kind of expressions in Java. It reveals that protean operators are available in any kind of expression in Java except the left-hand side of an assignment, the target of a member access, and the operand of a cast. Since the left-hand side of an assignment is usually a simple expression, protean operators would not be desirable there. The target of a member access could be a complicated expression like:

```
boolean b = (hel+o).matches("hello");
```

In such case, the programmers must rewrite the code as follows:

```
Regex r = hel+o;
boolean b = r.matches("hello");
```

Or, they must rewrite by using another protean operator as follows:

```
boolean b = hel+o matches "hello";
```

Here, matches is a binary infix operator. In Java, protean operators are not available in the operand of a cast operator. A cast operator that expresses a type conversion from S (source) to T (target) takes the target type T but it does not take the source type S. Thus, the compiler cannot know the expected type of the operand of a cast since it is the source type S. For example, assuming that ["sin" _:double]:double is an operator that returns the sine value of the given angle, in the following code, the expected type of (sin 0.0) is unknown:

```
int a = (int)(sin 0.0);
```

If the cast operator explicitly specified the source type as follows:

```
int a = (double -> int)(sin 0.0);
```

Then the expected type of (sin 0.0) would be known as double.

In the argument of throw statement in Java, it is difficult to determine available protean operators properly. According to Table 1, the expected type of the argument of throw statement is Throwable; however, it is not proper because, it must throw either an Error, a RuntimeException, an exception declared in the throws clause, or an exception caught in surrounding catch clauses. Our current compiler does not consider this.

This drawback, protean operators are available only in the expressions whose expected type are statically determined, also makes an obstacle to use generics. Assuming that the generic type List[T] is available, we would like to define the following operator:

```
[ "length" "of" _:List[T] ]:int
```

In this operator, the type parameter T cannot be inferred from the return type. Hence, the expected type List[T] of the argument cannot be determined. We cannot use protean operators at the operand of this operator. Since we currently do not have a good solution of this problem, our compiler introduced in section 4 does not support generics.

Place	Expected type
left hand of an assignment	*unknown*
right hand of an assignment	the left-hand side type
target of a method call	*unknown*
target of a field access	*unknown*
operand of a cast	*unknown*
argument of a method call	corresponding parameter type
argument of a constructor	corresponding parameter type
argument of an operator	corresponding parameter type
condition of if, for, while	boolean
argument of switch, case	char or int
argument of throw	Throwable
return expression	the return type of the method
statement expression	void
initial value of a field	the field type

Table 1. The expected types of Java expressions

3.2 Parsing

To efficiently parse an expression including protean operators, we developed a parsing method based on packrat parsing [9] supporting left recursion [26]. This parsing method is a recursive descent parsing with backtracking and it consides type information. In this section, we do not regard operator precedence since a grammar having operator precedence can be translated to a grammar that does not have it. (see 3.3)

Before parsing statements, the definition of protean operators available in the program is parsed. The compiler parses the definitions excluding the body parts of the definitions. It collects the meta-information of the protean operators such as the syntax and type signature of the operator. The collected information is sorted by the return types and the parsing precedences for later use.

The parser first attempts to parse a given piece of code as a statement such as if until it encounters a non-terminal symbol representing an expression. The protean operators cannot be used for statement-level syntax since a protean operator and its operands constitute only an expression. The statements are parsed by using only the syntax rules of the host language. Once the parse encounters an expression, it first determines the expected type of the expression by analyzing the code that the parse has already read. For example, an assignment statement is parsed by this rule:

```
Assignment → Id "=" Expr
```

The right-hand side of the statement Expr is parsed under the expected type obtained from the L-value, in this case, the variable named Id.

The parser first chooses the protean operator that returns the expected type and has the highest parsing precedence. Then it attempts to parse the expression by assuming that the expression is of the chosen operator. If this attempt succeeds, the parser returns the resulting parse tree of the expression. If it fails, the parser backtracks and tries the protean operator with the next highest parsing precedence. If there is no other operator, the parser parses the expression by using the syntax rules of the expressions in the host language. When the parser parses an expression as a protean operator, it performs the following action for each element in the syntax definition of the operator:

- An operator name "n" : read tokens by assuming that they match n
- An operand _:T : parse the successive tokens as an expression of the expected type T

Figure 6 shows the pseude code of the parsing algorithm for statements. We assume that the language supports several control flow statements such as while and it also supports local variables.

The procedure parseStmt is an entry point of the parser. The procedure parseWhileStmt parses a while statement. Since the condition expression in the while statement must return a boolean value, the expected type of the condition expression is boolean. Thus the call parseExpr(*Boolean*, ops, env) parses it. The procedure scan performs token analysis and returns Success if the next token matches the given string, otherwise Failure. The procedure parseVarDecl parses a local variable declaration. The initialization expression of the declaration is parsed by using the expected type specified by the type of the declared variable. The name and the type of the variable is stored into the environment env. The procedure parseExpr parses an expression. It takes an expected type as a parameter and attempts to parse an expression returning a value of that type. If all the attempts fail, it calls another procedure parseExprByPredefinedRule to parse an expression in the host language. The procedure parseExprByOperator parses according to the syntax of each protean operator. If it encounters an operand, it recursively calls parseExpr. It passes the operand type to parseExpr as the expected type.

In this figure, memoization is not shown for simplicity; however, it can be easily applied to the algorithm. To apply memoization, the algorithm must be modified so that the result will be memoised before it is returned and parseExpr will first look up the memoization table to avoid redundant parsing attempts.

3.3 Parsing Speed and Expressiveness

Our parsing method is sufficiently fast to parse protean operators even if they express user-defined literals since the operators can be regarded as Parsing Expression Grammar (PEG) [10] with left recursion as shown later. Our parsing method can be regarded as a variant of recursive descent parsing with memoization for the PEG generated from the operators. The memoization is used for eliminating the cost of backtracking. Our method can be used for scannerless parsing since its parsing-time complexity is $O(n)$. The original packrat pasing does not support left recursion, however, we added the left-recursion support by a small extension. Unfortunately, the worst-case time complexity of the packrat parsing supporting left recursion is not $O(n)$ but such a case seldom occurs in practical programming languages [26]. Most user-defined literals defined by protean operators are also parsed in linear time. Most practical language grammar can be parsed in linear time.

The expressiveness of protean operators is equivalent to PEG. Any protean operator can be expressed by PEG syntax and any PEG syntax can be expressed by protean operators. Each rule of PEG has the form $A \leftarrow e$, where A is a non-terminal symbol and e is a parsed expression. A parsed expression consists of terminal symbols, non-terminal symbols, the empty string, sequence operators $e_1 e_2$, and ordered-choice operators e_1/e_2. Here, e_1 and e_2 are a parsed expression. The other operators such as optional operators can be expressed by the above operators.

We can translate any protean operator to PEGs by replacing the types of the protean operator with non-terminal symbols. For example, the following protean operator:

```
[ _:Regex "+" ]:Regex
```

can be translated into the following PEG syntax:

```
Expr<Regex> → Expr<Regex> "+"
```

Here, *Expr<Regex>* denotes a non-terminal symbol representing an expression of the expected type Regex. A protean operator returning a value of different type is translated into a different non-terminal symbol. If an operator returns Letter, it is translated into a non-terminal symbol *Expr<Letter>*. The parsing precedence is translated into the ordered-choice rule in PEG. For example, see the following protean operators:

```
// entry point
// ops is the definitions of the operators collected before parsing
// env is variable environment
def parseStmt(ops, env) {
  r = parseWhileStmt(ops, env)
  if (r is Success) return r
  else backtrack
  [ parse by the other control flow rules similarly ]
  r = parseVarDecl(ops, env)
  if (r is Success) return r
  else backtrack
  [ parse by the other statement rules similarly ]
  r = parseExprStmt(ops, env)
  if (r is Success) return r
  return Failure
}

// WhileStmt → "while" "(" Expr<Boolean> ")" Stmt
def parseWhileStmt(ops, env) {
  w = scan("while")
  l = scan("(")
  c = parseExpr(Boolean, ops, env)
  r = scan(")")
  s = parseStmt(ops, env)
  if (w is Success && l is Success && c is Success &&
   r is Success && s is Success) return WhileStmt(c, s)
  else return Failure
}

// VarDecl → TypeName<T> Identifier "=" Expr<T>
def parseVarDecl(ops, env) {
  t = parse by the identifier rule
  n = parse by the identifier rule
  e = scan("=")
  v = parseExpr(get a type whose name is t, ops, env)
  if (t is Success && n is Success &&
   e is Success && v is Success) {
    add a variable n whose type is t to env
    return VarDecl(t, n, v)
  }
  else return Failure
}

// ExprStmt → Expr<Void> ";"
def parseExprStmt(ops, env) {
  e = parseExpr(Void, ops, env)
  s = scan(";")
  if (e is Success && s is Success) return ExprStmt(e)
  else return Failure
}

// typ is expected type
def parseExpr(typ, ops, env) {
  // operators have been sorted by parsing precedence
  operators = get operators returning typ from ops
  for (op in operators) {
    r = parseExprByOperator(op, ops, env)
    if (r is Success) return r
    else backtrack
  }
  return parseExprByPredefinedRule(typ, ops, env)
}

// op is an operator
def parseExprByOperator(op, ops, env) {
  for (e in the syntax of op) {
    if (e is an operator-name) {
      if (scan(e to string) is Failure) return Failure
    }
    else if (e is an operand) {
      r = parseExpr(e's type, ops, env)
      if(r is Failure) return Failure
      else append r to the parse tree
    }
  }
  return the parse tree
}

// variable access rule is a predefined
def parseExprByPredefinedRule(typ, ops, env) {
  r = parse by the identifier rule
  v = get a variable by the name of r from env
  if (r is Success && v's type is typ) return VarAccess(v)
  else backtrack
  [ parse by any other predefined rules ]
  return Failure
}
```

Figure 6. the parsing algorithm for statements

PEG			protean operators
parsing rule	$A \leftarrow e$	$\rightarrow$	an operator *op* that returns A and the syntax of *op* is e
terminal	a	$\rightarrow$	an operator-name "a"
non-terminal	T	$\rightarrow$	an operand _ : T
empty string	ε	$\rightarrow$	an operator-name ""
sequence	$e_1 e_2$	$\rightarrow$	a sequence $e_1 e_2$
ordered-choice	e_1 / e_2	$\rightarrow$	an operand _ : X and operators $op_1 > op_2$ op_1 and op_2 return X and the syntax of op_i is e_i

Table 2. The translation from PEGs to protean operators

```
[ _:Regex "++" ]:Regex
[ _:Regex "+" ]:Regex
```

Here, the two different protean operators return the same type. The first operator has higher parsing precedence than the second operator. We traslate these operators into the following PEG syntax:

```
Expr<Regex> → Expr<Regex> "++"
            | Expr<Regex> "+"
```

Note that the ordered choice | chooses the left operand first and then the right operand. So the operator with a higher precedence is the left operand.

On the other hand, any PEG rule can be translated into protean operators. Table 2 presents the translation from PEG to protean operators. In this table, $op_1 > op_2$ denotes that op_1 has a higher parsing precedence than op_2. Terminal symbols in PEG are translated into an operator-name of protean operator. Non-terminal symbols at the left-hand side of $\rightarrow$ are translated into the return types while non-terminal symbols at the right-hand side are translated into the operand types. The left and right operands of an ordered choice are translated into distinct two protean operators. The operator for the left has a higher parsing precedence than the operator for the right.

Operator precedence and associativity

We show below how to translate the protean operators with operator precedence and associativity into the protean operators without them. Assume that operator precedence is represented by a non-negative integer number and the larger number indicates the higher precedence. We show the translation from the protean operator `[S]:T` having operator precedence P and associativity A. The operator syntax S involves n operands and each operand has the type $\mathtt{T}^i$. First, the return type T is translated into the type $\mathtt{T}_\mathtt{P}$. Here, the subscript P is a non-negative integer number that is equivalent to the operator precedence. Second, each operand $\_:\mathtt{T}^i$ in the operator syntax S is translated into the operand $\_:\mathtt{T}^i_{\mathtt{P}+1}$ if the operand is not the left-or-right-most element in the syntax. The left-most operand $\_:\mathtt{T}^1$ is translated into $\_:\mathtt{T}^1_\mathtt{P}$ if the operator associativity A is *left-assoc*. Otherwise, it is translated into $\_:\mathtt{T}^1_{\mathtt{P}+1}$ like the other operand. The right-most operand $\_:\mathtt{T}^n$ is also translated into $\_:\mathtt{T}^n_\mathtt{P}$ if the operator associativity A is *right-assoc*. Otherwise, it is translated into $\_:\mathtt{T}^n_{\mathtt{P}+1}$. For example, the following operator:

```
[ _:Regex _:Regex ]:Regex { left-assoc }
```

with the operator precedence 0, is translated into:

```
[ _:Regex0 _:Regex1 ]:Regex0
```

Then we add an additional operator $[\_:\mathtt{T}_\mathtt{P}]:\mathtt{T}_{\mathtt{P}-1}$ for each return type $\mathtt{T}_\mathtt{P}$ if P is not 0. This operator converts a given argument to the operand to a value of type $\mathtt{T}_{\mathtt{P}-1}$ and returns it. Note that the parsing precedence of the added operator $[\_:\mathtt{T}_\mathtt{P}]:\mathtt{T}_{\mathtt{P}-1}$ is set to the lowest among the operators with the return type $\mathtt{T}_{\mathtt{P}-1}$. Finally, we add the operator $[\_:\mathtt{T}_0]:\mathtt{T}$ for each return type $\mathtt{T}_0$. It converts an operand from $\mathtt{T}_0$ to T. For example, the protean operators in Figure 4 are translated into the operators in Figure 7.

```
[ _:Regex0 ]:Regex
[ _:Regex0 _:Regex1 ]:Regex0
[ _:Regex1 ]: Regex0
[ _:Regex2 "++" ]:Regex1
[ _:Regex2 "+" ]:Regex1
[ _:Regex2 ]: Regex1
[ _:Letter3 ]:Regex2
[ _:Letter0 ]:Letter
[ _:Letter1 ]:Letter0
[ _:Letter2 ]:Letter1
[ _:Letter3 ]:Letter2
[ "a" ]:Letter3
 ...
[ "z" ]:Letter3
```

Figure 7. The definition of the regular expression literals without operator precedence or associativity (the translation from Figure 4)

4. Implementation: ProteaJ

We have developed *ProteaJ*, which is a subset language of Java and supports protean operators. ProteaJ recognizes a single character as a token. It enables protean operators to express user-defined literals. For convenience, a white space is recognized as a token separator by default, however, it can be recognized as a token by using a special keyword `readas`.[1] ProteaJ provides a module system called `operator modules` to implement and export user-defined operators. Programmers can use these operators by importing the modules. We give some examples of DSLs that are implemented in ProteaJ to show the expressiveness of the protean operators. We also give examples in which multiple DSLs are used. We implemented the compiler of ProteaJ in Java. ProteaJ does not support generics since there is a problem when protean operators and generics use together (see section 3.1). ProteaJ also does not support inner classes because they make the compiler complicated. For the same reason, ProteaJ does not support annotations and the other facilities introduced in Java 1.5 or above.

4.1 Definitions of Protean Operators

The definitions of protean operators in ProteaJ are similar to the class and method definitions in Java. Figure 8 shows the definition of protean operators that express regular expressions. This code defines an operator module named `RegexOperators`. This module defines four protean operators. For example, the third one of them defines the greedy quantifier operator `[ _:Regex "+" ]:Regex`. The keyword `readas` indicates that this operator expresses a user-defined literal. It specifies that a white space is recognized as a normal token rather than a token separator. The details on `readas` are mentioned later (see 4.2). `Regex` next to `readas` represents the return type of the operator. The following part `r "+"` represents the syntax of the operator. The identifier `r` represents the operand of the operator and the double-quoted string `"+"` represents the operator-name of the operator. The parameter type of the operand `r` is described in the following part enclosed in parentheses `(Regex r)`. It denotes that the type of the operand named `r` is `Regex`. The following `: priority = 250` represents the operator precedence. The remaining part enclosed in curly braces is the operator body. It is equivalent to the method body of a method declaration.

[1] The keyword `readas` means that the parser *reads* the next input *as* an instance of a specified type.

```
operators RegexOperators {
  readas Regex rs+ (Regex... rs): priority = 200 {
    return new RegexList(rs);
  }
  readas Regex r "++" (Regex r): priority = 250 {
    return new RegexPossessivePlus(r);
  }
  readas Regex r "+" (Regex r): priority = 250 {
    return new RegexPlus(r);
  }
  readas Regex l (Letter l): priority = 300 {
    return new Regex(l);
  }
}
```

Figure 8. The definition of protean operators expressing regular expressions

Figure 9 is the syntax of the declarations of protean operators in ProteaJ. In ProteaJ, an operator is defined in an operator module. An operator declaration consists of two parts, a header and a body. The body part is described as a method body. The header of a declaration consists of modifiers, a return type, syntax, throwable exceptions, and an operator priority. Protean operators can have modifiers `rassoc`, `nonassoc`, and `readas`. The modifiers `rassoc` and `nonassoc` specify operator associativity: `rassoc` specifies right-associative and `nonassoc` specifies non-associative. The default operator associativity is left-associative. ProteaJ provides several notations like PEG notations for describing the syntax of the operator more concisely. ?, *, and + are an annotation for the operand of the operator and they are annotated after the operand. ? indicates an optional operand of the operator. It is used with a default argument as follows:

```
readas Regex r "+" a? (Regex r, Anno a = Anno.greedy)
: priority = 250 {
  return new RegexPlus(r, a);
}
readas Anno "+" () : priority = 300 {
 return Anno.possessive;
}
```

* indicates zero or more repetitions, and + indicates one or more repetitions. They are used with variable arguments. The lines from 2 to 4 in Figure 8 is an example using +. The operator `[ _+:Regex ]:Regex`, which concatenates one or more regular expressions, are defined there. `&` and `!` are a predicate that can be used in the operator syntax. They represent look-ahead; they check the next inputs and might fail parsing by the condition of checking but they do not conume the inputs. They take a type name after the symbol. `& T` is a predicate that tries to parse the next inputs assuming that an expected type is a given type `T` and fails when the look-ahead fails. `! T` is similar to `& T` but it fails when the look-ahead succeeds.

To use protean operators, the 'using' declaration is needed to import the operator module. For example, regular expression literals defined in Figure 8 can be used as follows:

```
using RegexOperators;
...
Regex r = hel+o;
```

the protean operators defined in `RegexOperators` are used for the code `hel+o`. The using-declaration is written at the beginning of programs.Multiple operator modules can be imported in one source file by writing multiple using-declarations. For example, `GrepOperators`, `RegexOperators`, and `FilePathOperators` are used together in the following code:

```
OpModule → "operators" Id "{" OpDef* "}"
OpDef → Header Body
Header → Mod* Type Syntax Params Throws Prty
Mod → "rassoc" | "nonassoc" | "readas"
Syntax → ( OpName | Operand | Opt | Rep | Pred )+
OpName → StringLiteral
Operand → Id
Opt → Id "?"
Rep → Id ( "*" | "+" )
Pred → ( "&" | "!" ) Type
Params → "(" Param ( "," Param )* ")"
Param → Type VarArgs? Id DfltArg?
VarArgs → "..."
DfltArg → "=" Expr
Prty → ":" "priority" "=" IntConst
```

Figure 9. The syntax of the protean operator declarations in ProteaJ

```
using RegexOperators;
using FilePathOperators;
using GrepOperators;

GrepResult r = grep -i hel+o ~/src/Main.java;
```

4.2 Readas Operators, Operator Precedence, Parsing Precedence

In ProteaJ, protean operators can be devided into two categories: expression operators and readas operators, which begins with `readas`. When parsing an expression operator, a white space is reccognized as a separator of tokens. On the other hand, when parsing a readas operator, a white space is a token. The operands of readas operators must be expressions of readas operators. Readas operators are mainly used for defining literals. Readas operators are inconvenient for user-defined expressions since token separators must be explicitly inserted into the definition of the syntax. For convenience, if `readas` is not specified, a white space is automatically recognized as a separator. The operators defined without readas are called expression operators.

The operator precedence of protean operators are specified by integer values.In ProteaJ, the value of a precedence is larger, the binding of an operator is tighter. For example, the third operator in Figure 8 `[ _:Regex "+" ]:Regex` is bound tighter than the first operator in the figure `[ _+:Regex ]:Regex`.

Parsing precedence of protean operators are specified by the order of definitions in ProteaJ. The precedence of an operator defined earlier is higher. For example, the second operator in Figure 8 `[ _:Regex "++" ]:Regex` has higher parsing precedence than the third operator `[ _:Regex "+" ]:Regex`.

Operator precedence and parsing precedence are closed in each operator module. The entire operator precedence and parsing precedence are finally determined by the order of using-declarations. Operators in a module that is imported earlier have lower parsing precedence. Operators imported earlier binds tighter than operators imported later.

4.3 Case Study

The rest of this section, we show several internal DSLs implemented in ProteaJ.

Ruby-like print statement

In ProteaJ, programmers can define a new statement since ProteaJ allows programmers to define an operator returning `void`. Programmers can use such an operator as if an expression of the operator is a user-defined statement since a statement expression is

```
operators RegexOperators {
 readas Regex l "|" r (Regex l, Regex r): priority = 100
 readas Regex rs+ (Regex... rs): priority = 200
 readas Regex r "?+" (Regex r): priority = 250
 readas Regex r "*+" (Regex r): priority = 250
 readas Regex r "++" (Regex r): priority = 250
 readas Regex r "??" (Regex r): priority = 250
 readas Regex r "*?" (Regex r): priority = 250
 readas Regex r "+?" (Regex r): priority = 250
 readas Regex r "?" (Regex r): priority = 250
 readas Regex r "*" (Regex r): priority = 250
 readas Regex r "+" (Regex r): priority = 250
 readas Regex r "{" n "}" (Regex r, Nat n): priority = 250
 readas Regex "[" es+ "]" (ClsElm... es): priority = 270
 readas ClsElm f "-" t (Letter f, Letter t): priority = 280
 readas ClsElm l (Letter l): priority = 300
 readas Regex "." (): priority = 300
 readas Regex l (Letter l): priority = 300
}
```

Figure 10. regular expression literals as an internal DSL

considered as an expression that expects `void` type. The following code is a definition of an operator returning `void`:

```
operators OutputOperators {
  void "p" msg (String msg): priority = 0 {
    System.out.println(msg);
  }
}
```

and we can use this as follows:

```
using OutputOperators;
...
p "Hello world!";
```

In the above code, the last line is a statement expression. We can use p statement, which takes a string argument and prints the string since `OutputOperators` provides the operator `[ p _:String ]: void`.

Regular Expression

Programmers can define complex literals by using readas operators. For example, regular expression literals can be defined as in Figure 10. This operator module `RegexOperators` provides `Regex` literals, which express regular expressions. The following code is an example using `RegexOperators`:

```
using OutputOperators;
using RegexOperators;
...
Regex stnumber = [0-9]{2}(B|M|D)[0-9]{5};
Matcher m = stnumber.matcher(text);
if(m.find()) {
  p "match : " + m.group();
}
```

`Regex` literals are used in the statement of line 4 in the above code. This regular expression literal consists of many operators: `[ _+:Regex ]: Regex`, `[ _:Regex | _:Regex ]: Regex`, `[ _:Regex { _:Nat }]: Regex`, `[ [ _+:ClsElm ] ]: Regex`, and so on. Parentheses `( _ )` are an operator provided by ProteaJ. They reset the parsing precedence and the operator precedence of the expression within them.

Simple Optimization

Another usage of protean operators is performance optimization. For example, the binary operator `[ _:String + _:String]: String`, which is used for string concatenation, is not efficient

```
operators ExStringOperators {
  String buf (StringBuilder buf): priority = 200 {
    return buf.toString();
  }
  StringBuilder l "+" r
  (StringBuilder l, String r): priority = 250 {
    return l.append(r);
  }
  String l "+" r (String l, String r): priority = 300 {
    return l.concat(r);
  }
  StringBuilder s1 "+" s2 "+" s3
  (String s1, String s2, String s3): priority = 350 {
    StringBuilder buf = new StringBuilder();
    return buf.append(s1).append(s2).append(s3);
  }
}
```

Figure 11. Optimized string concatenation operators

when it is successively used more than once. To be more efficient, we should instead use the `StringBuilder` class. Protean operators in ProteaJ can be used in this case.

The definition in Figure 11 is the operators module that defines the optimized string concatenation. When the operators module is used, the single string concatenation such as `"foo" + "bar"` is interpreted as `"foo".concat("bar")`, but the successive string concatenation such as `"foo" + "bar" + "baz"` is interpreted as the following:

```
new StringBuilder().append("foo")
 .append("bar").append("baz").toString()
```

Like this, protean operators enables us to optimize the expressions that conform to the typical patterns. An important fact is that the optimizations are defined by the library, not the compiler.

SQL

In ProteaJ, programmers can implement more complex internal DSLs. For example, they can implement a subset of SQL. We implemented two operator modules, `FilePathOperators` and `SQLOperators`. `FilePathOperators` module enables us to write a file path like `~/Documents/file.txt`. The definition of `FilePathOperators` is shown in Figure 12. `SQLOperators` module defines some SQL operators, for example, select, create table, and insert into. The definitions of these operator modules are available from our web site.[2]With these modules, programmers can write a program shown in Figure 13, for example.

5. Experiment

We have conducted an experiment for demonstrating that ProteaJ can efficiently parse expressions including user-defined literals even though a naive parsing method such as SGLR cannot parse them in pragmatic time. We used JSGLR parser [2], that is a well-known implementation of a SGLR parser in Java, as a parser of a naive parsing method for mixfix operators supporting user-defined literals. Since the parser of ProteaJ cannot be detached from the compiler, we compared a compile time (parse time + code generation time) by ProteaJ and a parse time by JSGLR. The machine used for the experimentation had 2.67GHz Core i5 processor and 8 GB memory. The installed operating system on the machine was OpenSUSE 12.1. We used openJDK 1.7.0.

[2] The source code of ProteaJ and DSLs introduced in this section is available from: `http://www.csg.ci.i.u-tokyo.ac.jp/~ichikawa/ProteaJ.tar.gz`

```
// PrimitiveOperators are predefined operators module
// and they are imported implicitly like java.lang
operators PrimitiveOperators {
  ...
  int a + b (int a, int b): priority = 900 { ... }
  int a - b (int a, int b): priority = 900 { ... }
  int a * b (int a, int b): priority = 1000 { ... }
  int a / b (int a, int b): priority = 1000 { ... }
  ...
}
operators FilePathOperators {
  readas FilePath dir? name
   (DirPath dir = CurDir.v, Identifier name)
   : priority = 100 { ... }
  readas DirPath parent? name "/"
   (DirPath parent = CurDir.v, Identifier name)
   : priority = 200 { ... }
  readas DirPath dir? "./" (DirPath dir = CurDir.v)
   : priority = 200 { ... }
  readas DirPath dir? "../" (DirPath dir = CurDir.v)
   : priority = 200 { ... }
  readas DirPath "/" (): priority = 200 { ... }
  readas DirPath "~/" () : priority = 200 { ... }
}
```

Figure 12. File path operators module

The problem setting of the experiment is as follows:

- Grammar: basic arithmetic operators and file path literals.
  The grammar for the experiment of JSGLR is shown in Figure 14. ProteaJ uses the two operator modules in Figure 12 as the grammar.
- Input: `a/a/a/.../a` (a sequence of `a` separated by `/`)
  The input size is the number of `a` in the input. For example, the input size of `a/a/a` is 3.
  In the experiment of ProteaJ, the input source is more complex since it should be a valid ProteaJ source code. Figure 15 shows the input source for ProteaJ.
- Measurement: an average parse or compile time of ten executions.

The grammar shown in Figure 14 is a simple grammar only including basic arithmetic operators and file path literals. It has ambiguities, for example, `a` can be parsed as both of a variable and a file name. `a/a` might be a division expression of two numbers, a division expression of a number and a file name, a division expression of two file names, and a file path literal. The possible parsing results of the input `a/a/.../a` explode exponentially. The two operator modules shown in Figure 12 express the same grammar as in Figure 14. When the two modules are imported by using-declarations, ProteaJ can parse any expressions that can be expressed by the grammar in Figure 14. Note that the grammar in Figure 12 is more powerful than Figure 14 since identifiers are not only `a`. We have measured the parse or compile time by changing the input size.

Figure 16 shows the result of the experiment. It is a semilog graph. The vertical axis is the parsing time, and the horizontal axis is the input size. The diamond is an average parse time by JSGLR, and the rectangle is an average compilation time (parse time + code generation time) by ProteaJ. This graph is plotted for the input size from 0 to 20. According to the figure, JSGLR parser is getting slow as the input size is getting large. The parsing time increases exponentially. The worst-case time complexity of a GLR parser is $O(n^3)$ if it is implemented carefully. This fact shows that implementing an efficient scannerless GLR parser is difficult. Moreover, JSGLR could not parse when the input size is more than 20, due to a lack of memory.

```
import java.sql.*;

using FilePathOperators;
using SQLOperators;
using OutputOperators;
using ExStringOperators;

public class Main {
  private static boolean existTable
   (String tbl) throws Exception
  {
    ResultSet tables = select tablename from sys.systables
                       where tablename = tbl.toUpperCase();
    return tables.next();
  }

  private static void insertMember
   (int id, String name) throws Exception
  {
    insert into members ( user_id, name ) values ( id, name );
  }

  public static void main(String[] args) throws Exception {
    connect to ./database.db;
    if(existTable("members")) drop table members;
    create table members (
      user_id int not null primary key,
      name varchar(64) not null
    );

    if(existTable("posts")) drop table posts;
    create table posts (
      id int not null generated always as identity,
      date timestamp default current timestamp,
      user_id int,
      comment long varchar
    );

    insertMember(123, "ichikawa");
    insertMember(345, "ohtani");
    insertMember(567, "hiramatsu");
    insert into posts ( user_id, comment )
           values ( 123, "Ohayo!" );

    ResultSet rs = select * from members;
    while(rs.next()) {
      p rs.getInt(1) + " " + rs.getString(2);
    }
    commit;
    disconnect;
  }
}
```

Figure 13. A program using `SQLOperators`

S → *Expr*
Expr → *AddE*
AddE → *AddE* "+" *MulE* | *AddE* "-" *MulE* | *MulE*
MulE → *MulE* "*" *Primary* | *MulE* "/" *Primary* | *Primary*
Primary → "a" | *FilePath*
FilePath → *DirPath* *FileName* | *FileName*
DirPath → *DirPath* *FileName* "/" | *FileName* "/"
  | *DirPath* "./" | "./"
  | *DirPath* "../" | "../"
  | "/" | "~/"
FileName → "a"

Figure 14. The grammar of the language only supporting file-path names and arithmetic calculations

The compilation time by ProteaJ increases linearly with the input size. Figure 17 presents the compilation time by ProteaJ and the input size. The vertical axis is the compilation time and the horizontal axis is the input size. This figure presents the same data as Figure 16 but on a different scale. The graph is plotted with the input size from 0 to 1000. The vertical axis of Figure 16 is on a logarithmic scale, but one of Figure 17 is on a linear scale.

```
using FilePathOperators;

public class Test {
  public static void main(String[] args) {
    FilePath path = a/a/.../a;
    System.out.println(path.getAbsolutePath());
  }
}
```

Figure 15. The input source for the experiment of ProteaJ

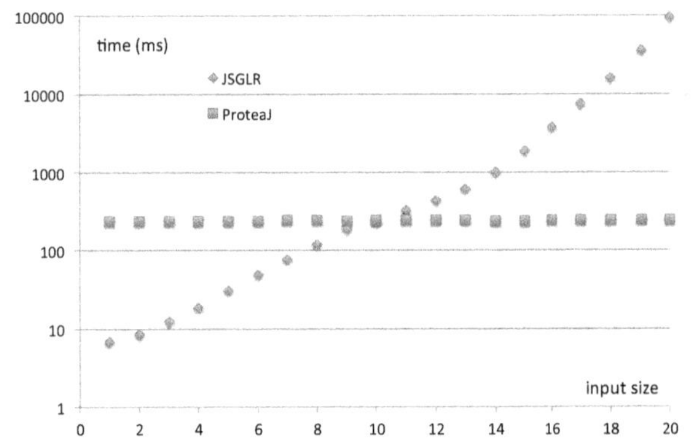

Figure 16. Comparison between ProteaJ compiler and JSGLR parser

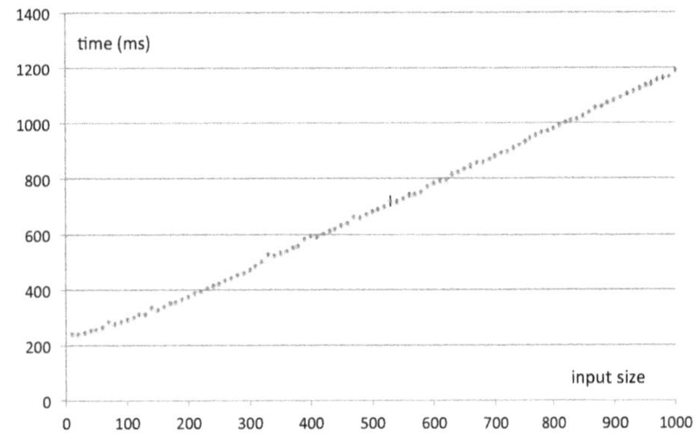

Figure 17. The compilation time by ProteaJ

6. Related Work

The idea of this paper is initially published as ACM Student Research Competition [13]. The detailed discussion and the experiments are new materials of this paper.

Macros

Syntactic macros are a common language facility to extend language semantics. They are based on Abstract Syntax Tree (AST) transformation. We can use them for implementing a new language construct. Lisp is the most famous language that supports syntactic macros. Syntactic macros are powerful especially in Lisp since Lisp programs are represented by simple syntax, S-expressions. We can define any kinds of special form if the syntax is an expression surrounded with parentheses. A drawback of syntactic macros is that they cannot lexically extend the syntax of the host language since they are applied after parsing a program. There are many languages supporting syntactic macros, besides Lisp. For instance, Dylan [4], MetaML [17], Template Haskell, Nemerle [20], and Scala [3] support syntactic macros. They have the same drawback as Lisp macros.

Common Lisp has syntactic macros and it also has a syntax extension system that is known as reader macros. Reader macros switch the scanner and the parser to user-defined ones when a special token is read. We can define a new syntax by using reader macros and we can define the semantics of it by using syntactic macros. Reader macros are very powerful, however, they are not composable. Multiple syntax definitions in different read macros cannot be used at the same time. User-defined scanners and parsers used in reader macros may be implemented by different programmers. Since it is difficult to merge them, the syntax defined in them would be difficult to be used together. Template Haskell [18] and Converge [22] have the same facilities.

Nemerle also provides another macro system like C/C++ lexical macros. It allows programmers to define new syntax, and the semantics of the syntax can be defined by a compile-time metaprogram. The restriction on the syntax is that the first token of the syntax must be unique. User-defined literals are difficult to implement in Nemerle since the syntax must begin with an identifier in the host language.

Mixfix Operators with Empty Syntax

Isabelle [16] and Maude [6] are programming languages supporting mixfix operators with empty syntax. The empty syntax support a nameless operator syntax like the protean operator `[_:Regex _:Regex]:Regex`. Arbitrary Context Free Grammar can be expressed by mixfix operators with empty syntax. Although the mixfix operators with empty syntax have good expressiveness, they cannot express user-defined literals. A naive extension to them by using a scannerless parser is not practical due to the efficiency of the parsing as we mentioned.

External Tools

JastAdd [8] and Silver [24] are language construction systems based on attribute grammar [14]. These systems allow us to describe a language definition in declarative and modular fashion. We can extend an existing language by defining a new lanǵuage extension module. Since they are systems for language developers to implement a new or extended language, they are not suitable in our case; as far as we know, there is no system where programmers can reflectively extend the underlying parser.

Metaborg [5] is a meta-programming toolkit that enables us to create syntax extensions. Since Metaborg uses SGLR parser, programmers can define both of user-defined expressions and user-defined literals on the same way. Metaborg is designed to be used for creating an extended language that has new language features. It is not designed to combine a number of language extensions that are selected by users (not language developpers). It is not suitable in our case.

Type-Oriented Island Parsing

Type-oriented island parsing [19] is a parsing algorithm based on island parsing [21], which is a parsing algorithm for CFG, but uses type information for efficient parsing. It can efficiently parse expressions including composable user-defined operators even if the operators introduce a number of ambiguities into the grammar. It uses static type information to prune parsing paths that will make ill-typed parse trees. However, it is unclear whether or not the type-oriented island parsing can be applied to scannerless parsers since the type-oriented island parsing uses heuristics for parsing tokens.

7. Conclusion

In this paper, we proposed new composable user-defined operators, named *protean operators*. They can express various language extensions including user-defined literals as well as user-defined expressions. They can have any number of operator-names and operands, and their order is arbitrary. Protean operators have two important features for the efficient parsing: *overloading by return type* and *parsing precedence*. The overloading by return type enables the parser to resolve grammar ambiguities by using type information at parse time. The parsing precedence resolves the remaining ambiguities after the type checking by the overloading by return type. Since these features resolve all the grammar ambiguities at parse time, protean operators can be parsed in pragmatic time. We showed an efficient parsing method for protean operators based on packrat parsing supporting left recursion. This parsing method is a recursive descent parsing with backtracking and considering type information. A drawback of protean operators is a limited kind of places where the operators are available. Protean operators are available only in the expressions whose expected type are statically determined before parsing the expression.

We have developed *ProteaJ*, which is a subset language of Java and supports protean operators. ProteaJ provides a module system called operator module to implement and modularize user-defined operators. We implemented the compiler of ProteaJ in Java. It is available from our web site mentioned in section 4.3. We have conducted an experiment for demonstrating that ProteaJ can efficiently parse expressions including user-defined literals even though a naive parsing method such as SGLR cannot parse them in pragmatic time. Currently, the entire operator precedence and parsing precedence are determined by the order of using-declarations; however, it is not clear that this means resolve conflicting operators in any case. To find better composable precedence rules is future work.

References

[1] Agda Wiki. http://wiki.portal.chalmers.se/agda/pmwiki.php.

[2] JSGLR: An SGLR Parse Table Evaluator for Java. http://strategoxt.org/Stratego/JSGLR.

[3] Scala Macros. http://scalamacros.org/.

[4] J. Bachrach and K. Playford. D-Expressions: Lisp Power, Dylan Style. Technical report, 1999.

[5] M. Bravenboer and E. Visser. Concrete syntax for objects: domain-specific language embedding and assimilation without restrictions. In *Proceedings of the 19th annual ACM SIGPLAN conference on Object-oriented programming, systems, languages, and applications*, OOPSLA '04, pages 365–383, New York, NY, USA, 2004. ACM. ISBN 1-58113-831-8. . URL http://doi.acm.org/10.1145/1028976.1029007.

[6] M. Clavel, F. Durán, S. Eker, P. Lincoln, N. Martí-Oliet, J. Meseguer, and J. F. Quesada. Maude: Specification and Programming in Rewriting Logic. *Theor. Comput. Sci.*, 285(2):187–243, Aug. 2002. ISSN 0304-3975. . URL http://dx.doi.org/10.1016/S0304-3975(01)00359-0.

[7] N. A. Danielsson and U. Norell. Parsing mixfix operators. In *Proceedings of the 20th international conference on Implementation and application of functional languages*, IFL'08, pages 80–99, Berlin, Heidelberg, 2011. Springer-Verlag. ISBN 978-3-642-24451-3. URL http://dl.acm.org/citation.cfm?id=2044476.2044481.

[8] T. Ekman and G. Hedin. The Jastadd System — Modular Extensible Compiler Construction. *Sci. Comput. Program.*, 69(1-3):14–26, Dec. 2007. ISSN 0167-6423. . URL http://dx.doi.org/10.1016/j.scico.2007.02.003.

[9] B. Ford. Packrat parsing:: simple, powerful, lazy, linear time, functional pearl. In *Proceedings of the seventh ACM SIGPLAN international conference on Functional programming*, ICFP '02, pages 36–47, New York, NY, USA, 2002. ACM. ISBN 1-58113-487-8. . URL http://doi.acm.org/10.1145/581478.581483.

[10] B. Ford. Parsing expression grammars: a recognition-based syntactic foundation. In *Proceedings of the 31st ACM SIGPLAN-SIGACT symposium on Principles of programming languages*, POPL '04, pages 111–122, New York, NY, USA, 2004. ACM. ISBN 1-58113-729-X. . URL http://doi.acm.org/10.1145/964001.964011.

[11] M. Fowler. Language Workbenches: The Killer-App for Domain Specific Languages? http://martinfowler.com/articles/languageWorkbench.html, 2005.

[12] A. Gräf. The Pure Programming Language. http://code.google.com/p/pure-lang/.

[13] K. Ichikawa. Powerful and Seamless Syntax Extensions on a Statically Typed Language. In *Proceedings of the 12th Annual International Conference Companion on Aspect-oriented Software Development*, AOSD '13 Companion, pages 41–42, New York, NY, USA, 2013. ACM. ISBN 978-1-4503-1873-0. . URL http://doi.acm.org/10.1145/2457392.2457411.

[14] D. Knuth. Semantics of context-free languages. *Mathematical systems theory*, 2(2):127–145, 1968. ISSN 0025-5661. . URL http://dx.doi.org/10.1007/BF01692511.

[15] J. Levine. *Flex & Bison: Text Processing Tools*. O'Reilly Media, 1 edition, 8 2009. ISBN 9780596155971.

[16] L. C. Paulson. *Isabelle: a Generic Theorem Prover*. Number 828 in Lecture Notes in Computer Science. Springer – Berlin, 1994.

[17] T. Sheard. Using MetaML: a Staged Programming Language. In *IN ADVANCED FUNCTIONAL PROGRAMMING*, pages 207–239. Springer-Verlag, 1999.

[18] T. Sheard and S. P. Jones. Template meta-programming for Haskell. *SIGPLAN Not.*, 37(12):60–75, Dec. 2002. ISSN 0362-1340. . URL http://doi.acm.org/10.1145/636517.636528.

[19] E. Silkensen and J. Siek. Well-Typed Islands Parse Faster. In H.-W. Loidl and R. PeÃśa, editors, *Trends in Functional Programming*, volume 7829 of *Lecture Notes in Computer Science*, pages 69–84. Springer Berlin Heidelberg, 2013. ISBN 978-3-642-40446-7. . URL http://dx.doi.org/10.1007/978-3-642-40447-4_5.

[20] K. Skalski, M. Moskal, and P. Olszta. Meta-programming in Nemerle, 2004.

[21] O. Stock, R. Falcone, and P. Insinnamo. Island parsing and bidirectional charts. In *Proceedings of the 12th conference on Computational linguistics - Volume 2*, COLING '88, pages 636–641, Stroudsburg, PA, USA, 1988. Association for Computational Linguistics. ISBN 963 8431 56 3. . URL http://dx.doi.org/10.3115/991719.991768.

[22] L. Tratt. Domain specific language implementation via compile-time meta-programming. *ACM Trans. Program. Lang. Syst.*, 30(6):31:1–31:40, Oct. 2008. ISSN 0164-0925. . URL http://doi.acm.org/10.1145/1391956.1391958.

[23] M. G. J. van den Brand, J. Scheerder, J. J. Vinju, and E. Visser. Disambiguation Filters for Scannerless Generalized LR Parsers. In *Proceedings of the 11th International Conference on Compiler Construction*, CC '02, pages 143–158, London, UK, UK, 2002. Springer-Verlag. ISBN 3-540-43369-4. URL http://dl.acm.org/citation.cfm?id=647478.727925.

[24] E. Van Wyk, D. Bodin, J. Gao, and L. Krishnan. Silver: An Extensible Attribute Grammar System. *Electron. Notes Theor. Comput. Sci.*, 203(2):103–116, Apr. 2008. ISSN 1571-0661. . URL http://dx.doi.org/10.1016/j.entcs.2008.03.047.

[25] E. Visser. Scannerless generalized-LR parsing. Technical report, 1997.

[26] A. Warth, J. R. Douglass, and T. Millstein. Packrat parsers can support left recursion. In *Proceedings of the 2008 ACM SIGPLAN symposium on Partial evaluation and semantics-based program manipulation*, PEPM '08, pages 103–110, New York, NY, USA, 2008. ACM. ISBN 978-1-59593-977-7. . URL http://doi.acm.org/10.1145/1328408.1328424.

RESCALA: Bridging Between Object-oriented and Functional Style in Reactive Applications

Guido Salvaneschi
Software Technology Group
Technische Universität Darmstadt
salvaneschi@informatik.tu-darmstadt.de

Gerold Hintz
Technische Universität Darmstadt
gerold.hintz@stud.tu-darmstadt.de

Mira Mezini
Software Technology Group
Technische Universität Darmstadt
mezini@informatik.tu-darmstadt.de

Abstract

Traditionally, object-oriented software adopts the Observer pattern to implement reactive behavior. Its drawbacks are well-documented and two families of alternative approaches have been proposed, extending object-oriented languages with concepts from functional reactive and dataflow programming, respectively event-driven programming. The former hardly escape the functional setting; the latter do not achieve the declarativeness of more functional approaches.

In this paper, we present RESCALA, a reactive language which integrates concepts from event-based and functional-reactive programming into the object-oriented world. RESCALA supports the development of reactive applications by fostering a functional declarative style which complements the advantages of object-oriented design.

Categories and Subject Descriptors D.1.5 [*Software*]: Programming Techniques—Object-oriented Programming; D.3.3 [*Programming Languages*]: Language Constructs and Features

General Terms Languages, Design

Keywords Functional-reactive Programming; Scala; Event-driven Programming

1. Introduction

Reactive applications are an important class of software systems. In these applications, *events or state changes*, e.g., user interaction, data changes in a Model-View-Controller design, network messages, value acquisition from sensors, etc., trigger computations, which may in turn update the state of the system, eventually triggering new events and/or computations. Even if reactive systems have been studied for a long time, they are still difficult to design and maintain. At the code organization level, proper modularization is hard to achieve because reactions involve cross-module entities and must be triggered in several places in code. At runtime, the normal control flow is interleaved with reactions to events, leading to interactions that are hard to foresee.

MODULARITY '14, April 22–26, 2014, Lugano, Switzerland.

http://dx.doi.org/10.1145/10.1145/2577080.2577083

Object-oriented (OO) reactive applications traditionally adopt the Observer pattern [13], which relies on the concept of *inversion of control* [14] to decouple the observers from observables. Other than that, the pattern does not contribute much to managing the complexity of reactive systems and has been criticized for cluttering code and hindering composability of reactions [19].

Two classes of alternative approaches have emerged to address the complexity of reactive applications. The first class includes languages that support event-driven programming at the language level. Examples are C# [8], Ptolemy [29], EventJava [11], EScala [15], DominoJ [35]. These languages provide first-class representation for events; some of them support expressive event models with advanced features like quantification, implicit events and event correlation. We refer to this class as event-based languages. The second class includes languages with direct representation of reactive values and means to compose computations based on them through dedicated abstractions. The ideas around reactive values were originally explored by synchronous dataflow languages [3, 28] and functional-reactive programming (FRP) [10]. More recently, these concepts have been proposed in a more modern flavor in reactive languages like Scala.React [19], FrTime [6], and Flapjax [25]. We refer to this class as reactive languages.

Both classes have their tradeoffs, which calls for an integration of their concepts. Event-based languages nicely integrate with OO design, support OO modularity, encapsulation, late binding and fine grained updates of object state, but do not achieve the declarative style and the level of expressiveness of reactive languages. With reactive languages, dependencies are defined in a more declarative way and updates are automatically performed by the runtime. But these languages do not fit well into the OO setting. Reactive abstractions do not support fine-grained changes to objects: Objects must be recomputed from scratch, a constraint that enforces immutability and does not integrate with OO modifiable state. In addition, events are still desirable, since they model certain phenomena in a direct and intuitive way.

In this paper, we present a language design that seamlessly integrated reactive values with an advanced event system. Thanks to this solution, it is possible to exploit the benefits of reactive abstractions without losing the advantages of OO design. In our design, both events and reactive values are object attributes in addition to fields and methods and exposed as part of the object interface. Crucially, the design comes with a rich library of operations (API) for bridging the gap between the worlds of events and reactive values making them composable to support a mixed OO and functional style.

We implemented these ideas in RESCALA, a reactive language based on Scala. Building upon existing approaches for event-driven and reactive programming, the key new contribution of RESCALA, its added value, is the unification of imperative, modular events and

reactive values making them composable to support a mixed OO and functional style in designing reactive systems. To the best of our knowledge such a unification has not been proposed before.
To summarize, in this paper, we make the following contributions:

- We provide an analysis of language-level support for reactive applications focusing on event systems and reactive values. We investigate their tradeoffs and how these abstractions relate to the OO and to the functional paradigms.
- We present the design of RESCALA, a language which combines signals and events and supports a mixed functional and imperative style. Thanks to the fluid integration of events and signals, RESCALA raises the level of abstraction in reactive applications, and promotes a gradual migration to a more declarative style.
- We provide a usable implementation of the language and apply RESCALA in several case studies. We demonstrate the crucial role of RESCALA's conversion functions by refactoring four OO reactive applications. We introduce more than 90 signals and show the improvement of the resulting design.

The paper is organized as follows. Section 2 motivates the work analyzing the limitations of signals and events taken singularly. Section 3 presents the design of RESCALA. Section 4 describes our implementation. Section 5 validates our contribution with case studies. Section 6 presents related work. Section 7 concludes and outlines areas of future research.

2. Problem Statement

Traditionally, OO applications implement reactivity by using the Observer pattern. The limitations of this approach have been analyzed elsewhere [19, 25]. For convenience, we briefly summarize them. First, dependencies are not directly specified but rather established by inversion of control – this reverses the intuitive flow of the applications and makes code harder to understand and analyze. Additionally, a lot of boilerplate code is required to implement even elementary functionalities, which further complicates program comprehension. More importantly, separation of concerns is hard to achieve because reactive functionalities are mixed with the application logic. Since callbacks do not return a value, they are not composable, limiting extensibility and reuse and program comprehension cannot be guided by types. Finally, callbacks enforce exclusively an imperative programming style, since reaction is performed via side effects.

Event-based languages have emerged to address these limitations providing abstractions for event-based programming [11, 15, 29]. In this section, we review these approaches with their limitations and motivate the need for complementing event-based languages with abstractions for reactive values, in the spirit of FRP and dataflow programming [6, 7, 10, 19, 22, 25].

2.1 Event-based Languages

Languages in this class, like C#, EventJava [11], Ptolemy [29] and EScala [15] provide dedicated abstractions for events and event-driven interactions. Since RESCALA extends EScala, we take the latter as representatives of event-based langauges to investigate their limitations.

Event abstractions and their advantages. EScala [15] combines concepts from OO and AOP. Beside imperative events, EScala supports implicit events. In the style of AOP, implicit events allow one to capture points in the execution of the program by the `after(`*method*`)` and `before(`*method*`)` pointcuts without having to explicitly trigger events at the boundaries of method executions, which is tedious and error-prone.

```
1  abstract class Figure { ...
2    protected evt moved[Unit] = after(moveBy)
3    evt resized[Unit]
4    evt changed[Unit] = resized || moved || after(setColor)
5    evt invalidated[Rectangle] = changed.map(() => getBounds())
6    ...
7    def moveBy(dx: Int, dy: Int) { position.move(dx, dy) }
8    def setColor(col: Color) { color = col }
9    def getBounds(): Rectangle   ...
10 }
11 class Connector(val start: Figure, val end: Figure) {
12   start.changed += updateStart
13   end.changed += updateEnd
14   ...
15   val updateStart = { _ => ... }
16   val updateEnd = { _ => ... }  ...
17 }
18 class RectangleFigure extends Figure {
19   evt resized[Unit] = after(resize) || after(setBounds)
20   override evt moved[Unit] = super.moved || after(setBounds)
21   ...
22   def resize(size: Size) { this.size = size }
23   def setBounds(x1: Int, y1: Int, x2: Int, y2: Int) {
24     position.set(x1, y1); size.set(x2 - x1, y2 - y1)
25   } ...
26 }
```

Figure 1: EScala Events.

EScala also supports declarative events, which are defined as a combination of other events. For this purpose it offers operators like $e_1||e_2$ (occurrence of one among e_1 or e_2), $e_1\&\&p$ (e_1 occurs and the predicate p is satisfied), $e_1.map(f)$ (the event obtained by applying f to e_1). Event composition allows one to express the application logic in a clear and declarative way. Also, the update logic is better localized because a single expression models all the sources and the transformations that define an event occurrence. Compared to EventJava and Ptolemy, EScala takes a more object-centric view. Events are part of the interface of a class, so event-driven behavior nicely integrates with OO data abstraction, inheritance, and subtype polymorphism.

In Figure 1, we show a slice of a drawing application in EScala. The `Figure` class defines an implicit event `after(moveBy)`, automatically triggered at the end of the execution of the `moveBy` method. The declarative event `changed` is triggered when one of the events `resized`, `moved`, or `after(setColor)` is triggered. The declarative event `invalidated` is defined as a transformation of the event `changed`. Handlers are registered and unregistered to events with the `+=` and `-=` notation (cf. Line 12 in Figure 1). Events are explicitly triggered by the `event()` notation. EScala events integrate with objects in several ways. Events support visibility modifiers (Line 2), abstract events can be refined in subclasses (Line 19). Events can be overridden in subclasses (Line 20) and the inherited definitions can be accessed by `super`. Finally events are late-bound: For example in Line 12 if `start` refers to a `RectangleFigure`, the definition of `changed` in `RectangleFigure` is chosen.

Limitations of event abstractions. While event-based languages address several issues of reactive software, several drawbacks are still in place. The application control flow is still inverted, since updates are performed only indirectly by event handlers that return void and do not support composition. The definition of the events and of the reactions to them (the update logic) are separated, making dependencies hard to grasp in code. More generally, event handlers update the object state in an imperative way. Thus, side effects are inherent to those event models, which limits the migration to a more functional style.

Triggering an event in every point in the code where a variable on which other variables depend on is updated leads to code scatter-

```
1  imperative evt tick[Unit]
2  var hour: Int = 0
3  var day: Int = 0
4  var week: Int = 0
5
6  tick += nextHour _
7  def nextHour() {
8    hour = (hour + 1) % 24
9  }
10 evt newDay [Unit] = tick && (() => hour == 0)
11 newDay += nextDay _
12 def nextDay () {
13   day = (day + 1) % 7
14 }
15 evt newWeek [Unit] = ...
16 newWeek += nextWeek _
17 def nextWeek() {
18   ...
19 }
```

(a)

```
1 val tick = new Var(0)
2 val hour = Signal{ tick() % 24 }
3 val day = Signal{ (tick()/24)%7 + 1 }
4 val week = Signal{ ... }
5
6
```

(b)

Figure 2: Simulation of Elapsed Time (a) with Events and (b) with Signals.

ing and tangling [32]. In addition, new events cannot be introduced transparently by clients: the original codebase must be modified by converting fields into observables and by adding event triggering. Therefore, event definitions are hardly extensible and require careful preplanning.

2.2 Reactive Languages

Some of the issues with event-based languages are addressed by abstractions for reactive values provided by reactive languages. In the following, we briefly present the concept as it is supported by some contemporary languages and discuss its advantages. Subsequently, we focus on the limitations of this concept compared to events, which motivates the need for improving event-based languages with reactive abstractions instead of abandoning events.

A reactive value, a.k.a. *behavior* in FrTime [6] and Flapjax [25], or *signal* in Scala.React [19], is a language concept for expressing functional dependencies among values in a declarative way. Intuitively, a reactive value can depend on variables – sources of change without further dependencies – or on other reactive values. When any of the dependency sources changes, the expression defining the reactive value is automatically recomputed by the language runtime to keep the reactive value up-to-date. In this paper, we focus on signals, an abstraction for reactive values introduced by Scala.React [19], a library implementing reactive abstractions for Scala.

To give an intuition of signals and their advantages over events, we use code extracts from a program that simulates a 2D environment, called the Universe application, which we used as a case study for EScala [15]. The environment is populated by animals and plants; the simulation involves growing of animals and plants, movements of animals, and planning for food search. A tick represents a simulation step equivalent to an hour in the simulation time; elapsed hours, days, and weeks must be updated accordingly.

In Figure 2, we show side-by-side two code fragments that use EScala events (a) and Scala.React signals (b) to model the elapsed time.

Signals (Figure 2b) enable the programmer to specify only the entities that are really part of the application logic: The `tick`, the `hour`, the `day`, and the `week` values. Each of them is declared together with its definition in terms of the other entities (for example, `hour` is defined in terms of `ticks`, Figure 2b, Line 2). The Scala.React library transparently performs all the necessary updates along the dependency chain of values declared as signals, e.g., to update the value of `hour`, when the value of `tick` changes. No additional programming logic is needed for these updates.

On the contrary, modeling dependent time-changing values by using events (Figure 2a) requires to introduce *artificial* entities (like the `newDay` event, the `newWeek` event, and the `nextDay` and the `nextWeek` callbacks). As a result, the code is much more complex. In addition, boilerplate code is introduced to register events (Lines 11 and 16), the definition of each entity is separated from declaration, and the application logic is spread among event definitions and callbacks. For example, the logic of `day`, declared at Line 3, is spread between Line 10, and Line 13.

Generally, by using signals, functional dependencies are expressed in a direct and declarative way. In contrast to the event-based reactivity, dependencies are not inverted. Since each reactive element is defined on the basis of its depending values, signals capture the design intention of the programmer; dependencies among reactive entities are automatically tracked and the runtime is in charge of keeping depending values updated. Another advantage, compared to inversion of control, is that the definition of the reactive behavior is not separated from the source of the change. As a result, reactive code is clearer and easier to read. Furthermore, since signals are reactive values themselves, new signals can be defined as dependents on existing ones. Signals composition fosters rapid implementation of new reactive functionalities and code reuse. Finally, signals identify dependencies which can be used to transparently cache the computed values.

2.3 Need for Complementing Events with Signals

While reactive values can model a computation in a simple and elegant way, they are not enough alone.

First, events are a well established programming model in the OO community, they properly integrate with OO [15] and OO programmers are unlikely to refrain form using them.

Second, most of existing OO reactive applications are event-based – graphic libraries being probably the most widespread example. Rewriting all the existing event-based software to use signals is probably unfeasible.

Third, events are *conceptually* the correct way of modeling phenomena that happen at a point in time. For example, the reception of a network packet could be modeled by a signal that has an `Option` type. The signal evaluates to `None` when no packet is available and to `Some[Packet]` when a packet arrives (Figure 3, Line 1). It is clear, however, that a programmer would be only interested in the *change* of such a signal, making the use of an event much more suitable for this case (Figure 3, Line 3).

```
1 val packet: Signal[Option[Packet]] = Signal{ ... }
2
3 evt packetReceived[Packet] = ...
```

Figure 3: Packet reception with Events and Signals.

Finally, reactive values have been designed in functional languages where they are applied to immutable (typically primitive) values. As such, they conflict with mutable state and incremental computation. For example, a signal of a complex value such as `Signal{aList.filter(_>10)}: Signal[List[T]]` recomputes the `filter` function for all the elements of the list `aList`, every time an element is added to `aList` – with a clear loss of performance. While there are attempts to incrementalize such computations they only work for certain operations and are limited the specific domain of data structures [20]. Instead, events are applicable in general and can be generated by partial modifications of objects (like the insertion of an element into a list). On the receiver part, objects can

```
1 val age = 0
2 val size = 1
3  ...
4 def canLive: Boolean = {
5   (age <= maxAge ) && (size <= 3000) && (size >= 1)
6 }
7 def disease() = { age *= 2 }
8
9 evt shouldDie[Unit] =
10    (after(getOlder) || after(grow) || after(disease)) &&
11    (_ => !canLive()) || killed )
```

(a)

```
1 val age = new Var(0)
2 val size = new Var(1)
3  ...
4 val canLive: Signal[Boolean] = Signal {
5   (age() <= maxAge ) && (size() <= 3000) && (size() >= 1)
6 }
7 def disease() = { age *= 2 }
8
9 evt shouldDie =
10     canLive.changed && !canLive() || killed
11
```

(b)

Figure 4: Dependencies with Implicit Method Events (a). Dependencies as Signals (b).

be updated imperatively minimizing the update by performing fine grained changes.

The discussion so far shows that events and signals have their advantages and disadvantages and event-based applications cannot be refactored to use only signals without loss of desired properties. We derive that there is a need for a language design that supports a fluid transition between the two worlds and seamlessly integrates them into the OO setting. This was the goal driving the design of RESCALA, which we present next.

3. REScala

In this section, we present RESCALA, a reactive language that provides a powerful event system – recapitulated in Section 2 – with seamlessly integrated support for reactive values. Some details on the implementation of RESCALA are in Section 4. Reactive values are called signals in Scala.React [19]; we adopt the same terminology in RESCALA.

As argued in the previous section, to properly support reactive applications, language designs are needed that offer both imperative and functional styles of programming reactivity. But, just having them side-by-side is only half-way to a coherent language design; in addition, imperative and functional abstractions to reactivity should be made composable. To achieve this goal, the key innovation of RESCALA, consists in mechanisms to seamlessly bridge between the imperative and functional styles of reactive behaviors to make them composable.

3.1 Signals

In RESCALA, the general form of a signal *s* is *Signal*{*expr*}, where *expr* is a standard Scala expression. When *expr* is evaluated, all `Signal` and `Var` values it refers to are registered as dependents of *s*; any subsequent change of them triggers a reevaluation of *s*. RESCALA signals integrate seamlessly with OO design. They are class attributes like fields and methods. They too can have different visibilities. Public signals are part of the class interface: Clients can refer to them to build composite reactive values. Conversely, private signals are only for object-internal use.

RESCALA signals cannot be re-assigned new expressions once they are initialized. At first sight, it may seem intuitive to treat signals like object fields, which can be reassigned as needed. However, this makes applications harder to understand; signal values would depend not only on the control flow inside their expression, but also on the control flow of the application, which can assign a different signal expression. Hence, the definition of the dependencies is separated from the declaration of the signal; making signals reassignable comes at the risk of vanishing the motivations that lead to their introduction. Fortunately, our experience suggests that this need does not arise in practice. This design decision enforces uniformity across signals and methods: Method bodies cannot be assigned dynamically, signals expressions cannot be assigned after creation. In RESCALA, this design is technically achieved by declaring them with Scala's `val` modifier.

As expected, RESCALA signals will replace the use of (implicit) events in EScala for encoding functional dependencies between values. For example, consider the snippet from the Universe application in Figure 4a that uses events to express the functional dependency between the `canLive` attribute of an animal on its `age` and `size`. The logic of the simulation is the following: An animal may become ready to die whenever it gets older (as time elapses), whenever it grows (as it eats food), or whenever it has a disease (a disease is implemented by simply doubling the age); the `canLive` method determines at any of these points whether the animal can still be alive. Finally, the animal can die because it is killed by other animals.

The dependency between the `canLive` attribute of an animal on its `age` and `size` can be expressed more declaratively by refactoring the `canLive` method to a signal and turning `age` and `size` into Scala `vars`, as shown in Figure 4b, Lines 1-2. This design comes with a reduced number of events, simplifying the application. In particular, *technical events*, which are not part of the application logic disappear because changes of `age` and `size` are captured directly in the definition of `canLive`. The `change` operator in Line 10 converts a signal into an event and will be explained in details in Section 3.2.2.

3.2 From Events to Signals and Back

RESCALA provides a rich API of functions for converting events to signals and the other way around. The goal is to ensure that the same abstraction/composition mechanisms uniformly apply over them. Conversion functions also facilitate refactoring of code fragments from one style to the other. The complete list of functions supported by RESCALA is shown in the Appendix A. Due to lack of space, in the following, we discuss only a subset of them that is representative enough to give an intuition about the role and expressiveness of the API. As we discuss at the end of this section, RESCALA also supports functions lifting to improve compatibility of existing code with signals.

3.2.1 Integrating Events into Signals

Since RESCALA promotes a mixed OO and functional style, it is important to manage state at the boundary between imperative and functional fragments of applications. For this purpose, RESCALA provides a set of functions for converting events into signals, so that event-based imperative sub-computations can be wrapped up and abstracted over in functional computations.

The *basic function for converting events to signals* is `hold`: given an event `e`, the call `e.hold()` returns a signal representing the value exposed by the most recent occurrence of `e`. For illustration, consider the code snippet in Figure 5, where a signal `click.hold` is built to represent the last position in which the mouse was clicked. Once defined, this signal encapsulates the imperative event and can be composed with other signals and mutable values into more complex signals. In Line 5, the mouse position is combined with a circle that changes its position on the screen – modeled as a `var` (Line 3) – to detect if the last click was on the circle[1].

```
1 evt click: Event[(Int, Int)] = mouse.click
2 // circle = ((centerX, centerY), radius)
3 val circle: Var[(Int, Int),Int] = Var((1,1),10)
4 val lastClickOnCircle: Signal[Boolean] =
5                        Signal{ over(click.hold(), circle()) }
6 val lastClick: Signal[(Int, Int)] = mouse.lastClick
```

Figure 5: `hold` at Work.

The conversion of events to signals by `hold` is stateless in the sense that at any point in time the value of the resulting signal is independent of that signal's previous history. For example the signal `click.hold` in Figure 5 (Line 5), does not remember previous positions of the mouse. To model situations when the value of a signal needs to depend on its previous values, RESCALA's provides *functions for stateful conversion of events to signals* – in the following, we discuss three such functions: `fold`, `list`, and `last(Int)`.

For illustration, suppose that we want to create a reactive value to keep track of the number of mouse clicks. A possible encoding based on events and reactions to events is shown in Figure 6a. The variable `nClick` records the number of observed mouse clicks; it is imperatively updated on any occurrence of the event `click` by the reaction attached to that event (line 4). A signal can then rely on `nClick` to react to the cumulative value. This solution has a number of drawbacks. First, the design is unnecessarily complex because it requires to register an imperative callback when a functional definition is possible. Second, it exposes the state in the `nClick` variable, so the programmer can accidentally modify its value.

```
1 evt click: Event[(Int, Int)] = mouse.click
2 val nClick = Var(0)
3
4 click += { _ => nClick() += 1 }
```

(a)

```
1 evt click: Event[(Int, Int)] = mouse.click
2 val nClick: Signal[Int] = click.fold(0)( (x,_) => x+1 )
3
```

(b)

Figure 6: Tracking State with Events (a) and Stateful Signals with `fold` (b).

What is actually needed is a way to bridge between events and signals in a stateful way, i.e., an operation that turns events into signals whose actual values depend on their past values. This is what the `fold` function in RESCALA's conversion API offers. With the `fold` function the programmer directly specifies how the value of a signal, that captures occurrences of an event, functionally depends on its past values. An initial value can be assigned, otherwise at the beginning the `fold` function evaluates to null. For illustration, Figure 6b shows a code snippet that uses `fold` to encode the logic in Figure 6a in a more concise declarative way. `nClick` is now encoded by accumulatively converting the event `click` to a signal. The initial value for the accumulation is 0, while the accumulation is encoded in the lambda passed as the second parameter to `fold`.

Unlike `fold` that composes the values in a signal's history, functions `list` and `last` just collect them into lists. Given an event `e`, the call `e.list()` returns a signal modeling the whole list of values produced by occurrences of `e`, while the `e.last(n)` returns a signal modeling a sliding window over the last `n` values exposed by occurrences of `e`. In Figure 7, `list` and `last` are used to reify into signals the complete history of the positions of mouse clicks (Line 2), respectively a sliding window over the last `5` values (Line 3). The definition of the `mean` signal (Line 5) illustrates how signals defined by `list` and `last` over the `click` event can be used in the definition of more complex signals; `mean` computes the average position over the last 5 clicks[2].

```
1 evt click: Event[(Int, Int)] = mouse.click
2 val history: Signal[Seq[(Int,Int)]] = click.list()
3 val history5: Signal[Seq[(Int,Int)]] = click.last(5)
4
5 val mean = Signal {
6   val (x,y) = history5().unzip
7   val n = history5().length + 1
8   (x.sum/n, y.sum/n)
9 }
```

Figure 7: Abstracting over State with `list/last(Int)`.

Figure 8 shows the same functionality implemented without the support of conversion functions. The programmer needs to introduce a var (Line 2) and a callback (Line 3). The callback updates the var when the event occurs, so the depending signals (Lines 6-9) are updated. The callback and the var are not part of the application logic and serve the sole purpose of bridging events and signals. The logic of the application is now spread among the callback (adding the element to the list) and the definition of each signal (slicing the last 5 elements). Even worse, the relation between the `click` event and the `history/history5` signal is not explicit any more from the definition of those signals and must be harvested from the control flow.

```
1 evt click: Event[(Int, Int)] = mouse.click
2 val historyV: Var[List[(Int,Int)]] = Var(List())
3 click += { clickPosition =>
4   historyV()= clickPosition :: historyV()
5 }
6 val history: Signal[List[(Int,Int)]] = Signal{ historyV() }
7 val history5: Signal[List[(Int,Int)]] =
8                              Signal{ history.slice(0,5) }
9 val mean = Signal{
10   val (x,y) = history5().unzip
11   val n = history5().length + 1
12   (x.sum/n, y.sum/n)
13 }
```

Figure 8: Abstracting over State without Interface Functions Support.

3.2.2 Integrating Signals into Event-Driven Computations

RESCALA also provides a set of operations that enable to seamlessly integrate signals into event-driven computations.

The most *basic operation for converting signals to events* is `changed()`: Given a signal `s`, `s.changed()` triggers an event every

[1] In real programming practice, one would probably encapsulate this feature in a signal tracking the position of the last click, directly available in the `mouse` interface (Line 6).

[2] The `unzip` function takes a list of pairs and returns a pair of lists. Given the input list $[(l_i, r_i), i \in (0..n)]$, `unzip` returns the lists $[l_i, i \in (0..n)]$ and $[r_i, i \in (0..n)]$.

time the value of the signal is updated, enabling `s` to engage in composite event expressions. For illustration, consider the code snippet in Figure 4b. The refactored definition of `canLive` as a signal must be integrated with the rest of the application, which is in an event-driven style. Specifically, the `canLive` signal and the `killed` event need to be composed in the definition of the complex event `shouldDie`. This is achieved by using `canLive.changed()` to bridge the worlds of signals and of the events (Line 10).

In addition to `changed()`, RESCALA provides *functions for more sophisticated integration of signals into event-driven computations.* In the following, we discuss two such operations: `snapshot` and `toggle`. The `snapshot` function takes the instant value of a signal whenever an event occurs. The `toggle` function switches back and forth between two expressions of a signal when an event is raised. In the following, we motivate and illustrate these functions by examples.

To show the use of the `snapshot` function we further decompose the interface of the `mouse` object. Like in the previous examples, the signal `mouse.position` models a cursor's current position, but now the event `mouse.clicked` carries no value and only models clicks form the user (Figure 9a). The `snapshot` function is applied to the signal `mouse.position` (Line 3) to sample the position of the mouse whenever the user clicks the button[3]. For comparison, Figure 9b, shows the same functionality implemented without the `snapshot` function.

```
1 evt clicked: Event[Unit] = mouse.clicked
2 val position: Signal[(Int,Int)] = mouse.position
3 val lastClick: Signal[(Int,Int)] = position snapshot clicked
4
```

(a)

```
1 evt clicked: Event[Unit] = mouse.clicked
2 val position: Signal[(Int,Int)] = mouse.position
3 val lastClickPos = Var(0,0)
4 val lastClick: Signal[(Int,Int)] = Signal{ lastClickPos() }
5 clicked += { _ =>
6   lastClickPos()= position()
7 }
```

(b)

Figure 9: `snapshot` at Work (a). Tracking the Position of Last Click without `snapshot` (b).

The situation becomes worse when more reactive values are involved. For illustration, consider an application that in reaction to an event occurrence does not simply take a static snapshot of a reactive value, but needs to switch between two reactive values `a` and `b` returning alternatively one of them. This is the case e.g., with a graphical application that models a bouncing ball. When the ball reaches a border, the `xBounce` or the `yBounce` event occur and the moving direction of the ball needs to be inverted. Compared to the simple snapshotting discussed above, without proper support (Figure 10a), the developer would have even more complex callback logic (Lines 14-16). The information about the currently active reactive value (e.g. `posSpeedX` or `negSpeedX`) needs to be explicitly tracked (Lines 11-12); an update of this information would also be needed every time the event fires. Finally, the programmer has to implement the switching logic (Lines 8-9). In summary, interfacing events and signals by such a low-level programming activity basically would annihilate the advantages of reactive values.

This accidental complexity can be avoided by using RESCALA's `toggle` function. For illustration, consider the code snippet in Figure 10b, where `toggle` is used in the context of the graphical application that models a bouncing ball. The inversion of the moving direction is encoded by switching the expression of the `speedX` and `speedY` signals (Lines 3-4), from `speed.x` to `-speed.x`, respectively from `speed.y` to `-speed.y`, whenever the events `xBounce`, respectively `yBounce` are raised.

[3] `snapshot` is a method of `Signal`. Since Scala supports infix notation for methods, in Figure 9a, `snapshot` is invoked on the `position` signal passing `clicked` as a parameter.

3.2.3 Lifting Functions on Ordinary Values to Functions on Signals

To support gradual refactoring of applications to a more declarative style, it is fundamental that existing code can be reused with the abstractions introduced by RESCALA. To enforce compatibility of reactive abstractions with existing components, RESCALA provides conversions that lift a value to the reactive counterpart. The `Signal.lift(f)` function converts a function `f: A=>B` to a function operating on a reactive value `Reactive[A]` (either a signal or a var) and returning a `Signal[B]`. As a result, computations expressed by traditional functions that operate on traditional values can be turned into reactive computations operating on reactive values. In Figure 11, we show how the mean over the last mouse click positions – presented in Figure 7 – can be encoded by leveraging a regular `mean` function working on non-reactive values. The function is lifted (Line 6) and then applied on the reactive values (Line 9).

While we expect that most of the conversions required by programmers are meant to use existing non reactive functions with reactive values, RESCALA also supports the conversion in the opposite direction. When a function expecting a reactive value is applied to a traditional value, the value is automatically promoted – by using Scala's implicit conversions – to guarantee type compatibility.

4. Implementation

RESCALA is implemented as a completely new Scala library. The user API of RESCALA provides both signals and events and subsumes the event-based EScala interface. To explain why a complete reimplementation is needed we briefly summarize the mechanism behind EScala events.

The EScala event system is based on an event graph connecting dependent events. Imperative events and implicit events are the nodes without a predecessor, declarative events form the rest of the graph. For example, if the `e3` declarative event is defined by `evt e3 = e1 || e2`, `e1` and `e2` are connected to `e3` in the graph. Each node maintains a list of the callbacks to execute in case the event associated to the node fires. When a leaf event fires, the graph is traversed in depth-first order starting from the firing event following the connections among events. The callbacks attached to each traversed event are collected. Finally, all handlers are executed in non-deterministic order [15]. Unfortunately, this mechanism is not suitable for signals. If signals are added, intermediate nodes represent signal expressions that depend on each other and must be executed during the traversal – not only at the end, like event handlers. In such a system, glitch freedom requires to control the order of update propagation – as we explain shortly. For this reason, we reimplemented the propagation system from scratch and used the same interface of EScala for events. As a result, EScala programs, that correctly do not rely on the order of handlers executions originated by the same change, are also RESCALA valid programs.

The RESCALA signal system is conceptually similar to existing implementations of other reactive languages [6, 19]. It is based on a directed graph to track dependencies between values and to keep them up-to-date. Dependencies are established in conjunction with the evaluation of signal expressions. To enforce the correct update order, the graph is topologically sorted and change propagation proceeds in order from changed values to the values depending on them. Topological sorting ensures *glitch freedom* [6], the property of avoiding temporary violations of the constraints expressed by

```
val speed = new Point(10,8)
evt xBounce,yBounce = ... // Events

val posSpeedX = Signal{ speed.x }
val posSpeedY = Signal{ speed.y }
val negSpeedX = Signal{ -speed.x }
val negSpeedY = Signal{ -speed.y }
val speedX = Signal{ if switchedX() posSpeedX() else negSpeedX() }
val speedY = Signal{ if switchedY() posSpeedY() else negSpeedY() }

val switchedX = Var(false)
val switchedY = Var(false)
xBounce += {_ =>
  switchedX() = !switchedX()}
yBounce += {_ =>
  switchedY() = !switchedY()}
```

(a)

```
val speed = new Point(10,8)
evt xBounce, yBounce = ... // Events
val speedX = Signal{speed.x}.toggle(xBounce){ -speed.x }
val speedY = Signal{speed.y}.toggle(yBounce){ -speed.y }
```

(b)

Figure 10: Bouncing Ball without `toggle` (a). `Toggle` Function at Work (b).

```
def mean(list: Seq[(Int,Int)]): (Double,Double) = {
  val (x, y) = list.unzip
  val n = list.length + 1.0
  (x.sum / n, y.sum / n)
}
val meanR = Signal.lift(mean)
evt click = new ImperativeEvent[(Int, Int)]
val history = click.last(5)
val meanS = meanR(history)
```

Figure 11: Lifting of Traditional Functions.

signal expressions. For example, consider the dependencies established by the following configuration of reactive values and signal expressions:

```
val x = Var(1)
val y = Signal{ x() * 2 }
val z = Signal{ x() * 3 }
val t = Signal{ y() + z() }
```

Suppose that the value of x is updated to 2. Then y must be updated to 4. If at this point t is updated, it evaluates to 5, which is clearly wrong, since after updating z, the correct – and stable – value of t is 10. To prevent such temporary values (i.e. *glitches*), nodes must be updated in the correct order, in this case x-y-z-t. Compared to EScala, a breadth-first traversal is needed *(i)*. Signal expressions must be evaluated inside signal nodes and the propagation must be stopped in case a signal expression does not change its value *(ii)*. As node dependencies are discovered at runtime, topological sorting cannot be guaranteed in advance and the graph must be restructured when the topological order is violated *(iii)*. Further details on this technique can be found in the technical report [19] and references therein.

RESCALA preserves glitch freedom inside signal-based dependent computations and conversions between signals and events. When the computation escapes the reactive system and involves imperative events and callbacks, side effects can be performed. In that case, like with other event-based languages, side effects can establish data dependencies that are not under the control of the reactive system and the user is responsible of performing the updates in the correct order.

5. Validation

The main hypothesis that motivated RESCALA's design is that the fluid integration of events and signals by conversion functions contributes to improved design quality of reactive object-oriented applications. To validate this hypothesis we performed a side-by-side comparison of alternative designs of four reactive object-oriented applications – designs using events only versus designs using the combination of events and signals via conversion functions.

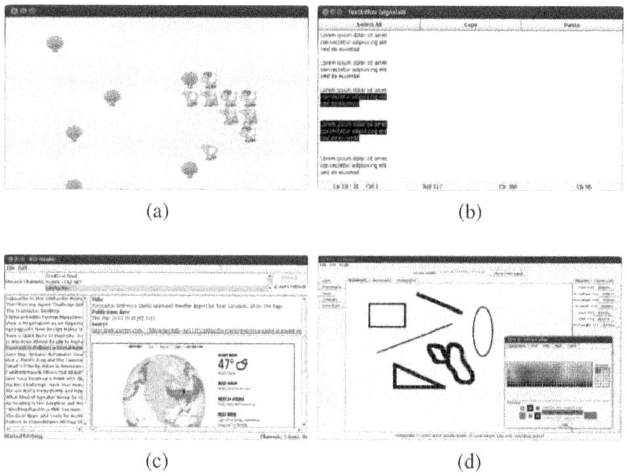

Figure 12: The Case Study Applications: Universe (a), ReactEdit (b), ReactRSS (c), ReactShapes (d).

5.1 Experimental Set Up

Case Studies. Our validation benchmark suite consists of four reactive OO applications (Figure 12), which were initially implemented based on events only and afterwards refactored to introduce signals integrated with events via conversion functions.

The *Universe* simulation [15] has been already presented in the paper. The simulation evolves in rounds and the state of each element at a given step is a function of the other elements and of the state of the simulation in the previous step. This structure allows one to express several aspects of the computation functionally. However, the elements of the simulation are mutable objects that encapsulate state, so the OO and the functional style must be properly combined. A screenshot of this application is shown in Figure 12a.

ReactEdit is a minimal text editor implementing functionalities like text selection, line counting, and cutting-and-pasting of text. In previous work [32], we analyzed a text editor provided as a widget in the SWT graphic library, which is used, among other ap-

Case Study	LOC	Callb.	Events	Signals
Universe				
Events	466	17	8	0
Events+Signals	442	6	12	30
ReactEdit				
Events	644	14	34	0
Events+Signals	632	10	36	22
ReactRSS				
Events	599	16	41	0
Events+Signal	595	14	38	9
ReactShapes				
Events	1161	17	30	0
Events+Signals	1160	5	56	30

Figure 13: Main Metrics for the Case Studies.

plications, in the Eclipse IDE. The analysis showed that a lot of complexity in the code is due to a design of reactivity that favors efficiency, requiring caching of intermediate values and incremental computations. ReactEdit is a minimal version of the SWT widget, which is malleable to investigating various design alternatives based on reactive abstractions[4]. A screenshot of this application is shown in Figure 12b.

ReactRSS is a RSS feed reader displaying a list of channels, which are periodically checked for updates. Fetched items are immediately displayed to the user in a side bar. When the user selects one of them, the HTML content is rendered in the main view. A screenshot of this application is shown in Figure 12c.

ReactShapes is a small drawing program. The user can drag and drop different shapes on a canvas, connect them with lines and change the stroke width and the color of each shape. The application supports an history and an undo function. Finally, the drawing canvas can be shared with other clients that participate in the same task from remote. A screenshot of this application is shown in Figure 12d.

We selected the case studies to cover different kinds of reactive behavior in common OO applications. In most cases, in desktop software, reactivity originates from user interaction, e.g., mouse movements or hitting a button on the keyboard. ReactEdit, ReactRSS and ReactShapes cover this class of applications. Another source of reactivity are asynchronous external events, like messages from the network. The ReactShapes and the ReactRSS applications implement this kind of functionality. Another common example of reactive applications are synchronous simulations, where at each round a change is propagated to all the entities in the application. The Universe case study covers this case.

Research Questions and Methodology. The main question for the validation was: Are designs based on the combinations of events and signals better? We look at improved composability, i.e., increased number of composable abstractions in code as an indication for better design. The secondary question is: If the designs are improved, in what extent are the conversion functions involved in this improvement. In the following, we demonstrate that the studied refactorings do indeed improve composability and that conversion functions play a key role in this respect. To answer this questions, we followed a three-step process.

First, each case study was implemented with events and callbacks. Second, the case studies were refactored to introduce signals and compositions thereof with events via the conversion functions. Typically a refactoring concerned the reactivity for a certain concern of the application, e.g., time management in the Universe synchronous simulation or the palette to select the shape to draw in the GUI of the ReactShapes application. The decision about which concerns to refactor was made by looking at concerns involving functionally dependent values. Those values are good candidates for being expressed by signals. An example is time management in the Universe application, as shown in Figure 2. On the contrary, a criterion for rejecting a refactoring candidate was when a change is *conceptually* modeled in a proper way by events. For example, Figure 19 shows the *select-all, copy and paste* functionalities in the ReactEdit application which are activated by pressing a button in the UI (i.e. an *event*) and do not require composition. However, computations that *depend* on events can still be good candidates for refactoring. For example, building on top of events, we refactored to a signal the *fetching* state of the React RSS application, as shown in Figure 15 and discussed shortly. Finally, in a separate step, various metrics related to answering our research questions were calculated for both versions. The first two steps were performed by students not involved in the third step, which was performed by the first author.

The calculated metrics are presented in Figures 13 and 14. Figure 13 reports, for each version of each application, the non-comment-non-space lines of code (LOCs) measured with CLOC[5], the number of callbacks, the number of observers/events, and the number of signals. For each refactoring, we report more detailed data in Figure 14 (there is a row in the table for each identified refactoring; the concerns are listed in the last column of Figure 14). Column *Conv Funs* shows the number of conversion functions used in each refactoring, further discriminated in the number of conversions from signals to events (column *S*→*E*) and conversions from events to signals (column *S*→*E*). Data in the other columns characterize the effect of each refactoring. Column *Callb.* shows the number of callbacks that where removed after refactoring. When counting signals and events we consider also the signals/event created in intermediate computations (e.g., by a conversion function) if not already counted elsewhere. Column *Signals* shows the number of signals that are introduced in each refactoring; column *Events* shows the number of removed/added events.

5.2 Improved Design

We measure the improvement of composability by calculating two metrics. First, we observe that the number of non-composable abstractions (callbacks) is reduced. Second, we observe that the number of composable reactive abstractions (signals and events) is increased by the refactorings.

Removed Callbacks. Figure 14, *Callbacks* column, shows the number of callbacks that where removed due to the introduction of signals and the associated conversion functions. We observe a systematic reduction of callbacks in the events+signals version of each application by 44% on average.

Since callbacks do not return a value, they are not composable, limiting extensibility and reuse. Conversion functions help reducing the amount of callbacks that are required in each application. With events, a handler is necessary to perform the action associated to the event, which typically imperatively updates some values. Instead, by turning events into signals, we turn their exposed values into reactive values that can freely be composed with other

[4] Since the SWT widget amounts to ~10K LOCs of Java it was not feasible for us to work on the original version.

[5] httpc://cloc.sourceforge.net

Case Study (Signals+Events)	Conv Funs	S → E	E → S	Signals	Callb.	Events	Comp.	Refactored Concern
Universe	2	1	1	+11	-2	-1	+10	Activity of the creatures
	10	5	5	+11	0	0	+11	Statistics
	2	0	2	+3	-2	0	+3	Evolution and reproduction
	9	8	1	+5	-7	+5	+10	Time management
ReactEdit	0	0	0	+7	-3	-3	+4	Statistics tracker
	9	7	2	+15	-1	+5	+20	Caret position and selection
ReactRSS	5	4	1	+1	-2	0	+1	Network fetcher
	2	0	2	+2	0	-2	0	RSS feeds store
	6	5	1	+6	0	-1	+5	UI for items channels and status
ReactShapes	0	0	0	+6	-6	0	+6	State of the canvas
	8	6	2	+7	0	+8	+15	Display information
	2	1	1	+8	-1	+6	+14	UI for menus
	1	1	0	+4	-2	+1	+5	History of executed commands
	1	1	0	+4	-2	+2	+6	Panel for drawing shapes
	1	0	1	+1	-1	+9	+10	Palette for shape selection
Total	+58	+39	+19	+91	-29	+29	+120	

Figure 14: Conversion Functions and their Effect in the Case Studies.

signal expressions. This enables dependencies of computations on the occurrence of events and their exposed values to be expressed declaratively and new event values to be automatically propagated to those dependent computations.

Increased Number of Composable Abstractions. The results of the analysis of the refactorings shown in Figure 14 demonstrate that the refactorings enabled by interface functions increase the number of composable abstractions (Figure 14, *Comp.* column). Not surprisingly, signals largely contribute to increased composability (Figure 14, *Signals* column).

Overall, events increase in the refactorings (Figure 14, *Events* column). This is due to two causes. First, in some cases signals are not directly defined on top of existing events, but over a combination thereof. For example, in Figure 15 the `before(fetch)` and the `after(fetch)` are combined and it is the composed event that is converted to a signal. Second, in some refactorings, the signals added by the refactorings need to interface with the existing event-based part of the application, hence, events must be generated from signals – as in the case discussed for Figure 16. However, we also experienced cases in which events can be simply removed and replaced with signals.

5.3 Use of Conversion Functions

In this sub-section, we elaborate on the role of the conversion functions in the improved design composability. Indeed, in all refactorings, conversion functions are used in almost all the cases (Figure 14, second column). Exceptions are discussed at the end of this section. To give an intuition of how conversion functions are used, we graphically depict event-based applications as a graph (Figure 18a), in which the nodes without a predecessor denote directly triggered events on which other events (indirectly) depend (inner nodes of the graph).

From events to signals. Functions converting from events to signals are used to refactor some reactive functionality to signals, in cases when reactivity originates from events, graphically depicted in Figure 18c. For example, ReactRSS needs to fetch possible updates from the monitored websites. Since the operation is time-consuming, the application displays a message to the user. Figure 15 shows how a signal is used to express the "fetching state". The source of reactivity are the implicit events `before(fetch)` and the `after(fetch)` that express the begin and the end of the fetching phase. After composing these events, the `hold` conversion function is used to capture the state of the RSS fetcher.

```
lazy val fetcherState: Signal[String] =
  ((before(fetch) map { _ => "Started fetching" }) ||
    (after(fetch) map { _ => "Finished fetching" })) hold ""
```

Figure 15: Converting Events to Signals in a Refactoring.

From signals to events. Functions converting from a signal to an event are used when some piece of reactive functionality that is refactored to use signals still needs to interface to events, graphically depicted in Figure 18b. For illustration, we briefly discuss a refactoring in the universe case study. The example refactoring is about the time management concern, which was refactored to use signals (Figure 2) with the advantages already discussed in Section 2. However, the board on which the creatures move in the simulation is mutable and updated imperatively – a design typical of OO style.

This solution allows each creature in the simulation to access the board and change its state without carrying the board as a parameter in each computation. Due to the imperative design of the board, the signal-based time management must be converted to events before interfacing with the board. In Figure 16, an event is obtained from

```
1 time.hour.changed += {x =>
2   board.elements.foreach { _ match {
3       case (pos, be) =>
4         if(be.isDead.getVal)
5           board.clear(pos)
6       else be.doStep(pos)
7 } }   }
```

Figure 16: Converting Signals to Events in a Refactoring.

```
1 val charCountLabel =
2   ReLabel(Signal { "Ch " + textArea.charCount() })
```

Figure 17: Use of Signals in the Graphic Interface.

the signal holding the current week through the `changed` function (Line 1) that fires every new week. A handler attached to the event imperatively removes the dead creatures form the board (Line 5) and makes those evolve that are still alive (Line 6).

Exceptions. There are two refactorings in Figure 15 – namely *"Statistics tracker"* and *"State of the canvas"* – that introduce signals without using conversion functions. We explain the reason for this for the *"Statistics tracker"* refactoring of ReactEdit. The other case in the ReactShapes case study is analogous, thus not further discussed. The *"Statistics tracker"* refactoring focuses on the part of the application concerned with displaying information on the text currently edited, e.g., the number of characters and the number of lines in the text. These values, however, are already available as signals, since the other refactoring of ReactEdit already introduced signals in the model of the application (e.g., text storage and caret position). For this reason, conversion functions are not needed. Note however, that conversion functions are still required in the second refactoring for the events that come from user interaction, so they are indirectly required to enable the *"Statistics tracker"* refactoring. In terms of Figure 18, the scenario discussed in this paragraph corresponds to performing a (b) refactoring *followed by* a (c) refactoring.

Still to answer is the question why, in the refactorings under consideration (*"Statistics tracker"* and *"State of the canvas"*), the conversions S→E are not needed either. Since the overall design of the case studies is OO, the result of a signal-based computation typically produces a side effect at some point. This is usually achieved by converting a signal to an event and binding a callback to the latter – hence the expected use of S→E conversions. When the information is displayed in the GUI, we also need to convert from signals to events, since the Swing library [33] we use (and OO graphic libraries in general) is based on events. Nevertheless, S→E are not needed because we wrapped the classes of the Swing library to directly support signals. For illustration, Figure 17 shows an example of a `Label`, a widget that displays text. The widget is directly attached to a signal when it is created and automatically updates the text according to the changes of the signal. Internally, this requires a conversion from signals to events, but this is encapsulated into the `ReLabel` class (Line 2) and does not appear in the counting of conversion functions in Figure 15.

Discussion. The classification of refactorings discussed above – *signal to events* vs. *events to signals* (i.e. Figure 18c vs. Figure 18b) – is useful to capture the role of interface functions in the refactorings. However, in practice, those cases are often mixed, and a single refactoring comprises both. This circumstance can be inferred from Figure 14 where in several refactorings both E→S and S→E conversions appear. The reason is that, in many cases, the refactoring

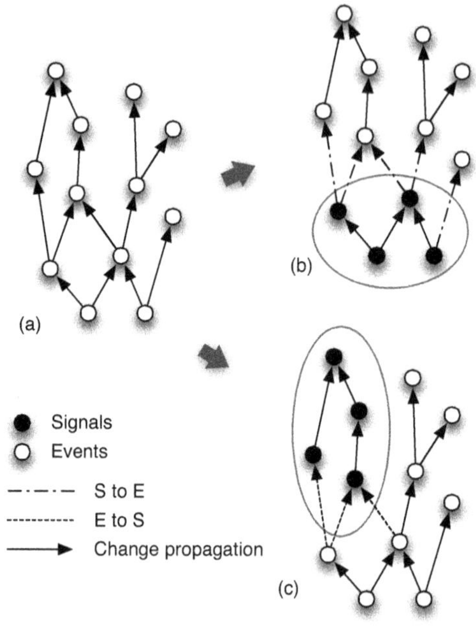

Figure 18: Reafactoring Event-based Applications to use Signals.

```
selectAllButton.clicked +=
  {_=> textArea.selectAll; textArea.requestFocus}
copyButton.clicked +={_=> textArea.copy; textArea.requestFocus }
pasteButton.clicked +={_=> textArea.paste; textArea.requestFocus }
```

Figure 19: User Interaction in the ReactEdit Case Study.

to signals is *surrounded* by the event based systems. As a result the signal based computation introduced by the refactoring needs to interface to events at some point – hence conversion functions are needed in both directions.

One may wonder if the effect of conversion functions is simply to turn each event into a signal and then back to an event, artificially increasing the number of composable abstractions in Figure 14. This is, however, not the case. In the events+signals implementations, there is significantly higher number of signals than conversion functions (Figure 14, cf. column *E→S* and column *Signals*). This means that conversion functions not only introduce signals by turning events into signals, but enable more advanced refactorings towards more declarative style, where signals can be further defined as a composition of the existing ones.

6. Related work

Approaches closely related to RESCALA [6, 15, 17, 19, 25] were already discussed in Section 2. In this section, we focus on the approaches that are related to our research in a broader scope.

Functional-reactive programming was originally designed by Elliott in Haskell [10]. FRP focuses on the abstract representation of continuous time in functional programs. More generally, the term refers to language abstractions to support time-changing values, like signals or event streams. Frappe [7] ports to Java the ideas originally implemented in FRP and Haskell.

Constraint programming supports declarative relations among program entities and automatically enforces their consistency. For example the Kaleidoscope [12] and the graphical toolkits Garnet [26] and Amulet [27] allow the user to introduce constraints that are automatically satisfied by the framework. Compared to the work in this paper, these languages only focus on updating dependencies and do not include an advanced event system like the one of RESCALA. SuperGlue [22] is a statically typed language that allows one to specify constraints among Java components. To reduce coupling, Superglue supports quantification over component types. The runtime is in charge of keeping constraints satisfied in a way that resembles reactive programming. Unlike RESCALA and other reactive programming approaches, Superglue focuses on constraints over components and not on composition of time-changing computations.

Data-flow languages provide abstractions to manipulate streams of values. Conceptually, these languages define nets of operators connected with wires. Examples include Esterel [2] and Lucid [28]. They have a synchronous notion of time which resembles the design of our synchronous timers with contemporary events. Unlike RESCALA, these languages focus on real-time requirements, providing boundaries to memory consumption and propagation time at the cost of sacrificing language expressiveness.

Event-based languages support events as language abstractions. EventJava [11] is a Java extension which borrows ideas from complex event processing and composite event detection. It supports event matching, predicate guarding, reaction to event combination and event correlation. As a consequence, complex reactive behavior can be expressed in a declarative way. Another event-based language is Ptolemy [29]. Whereas the Observer pattern decouples observables from observers, the latter still need to explicitly reference observables. Ptolemy specifically addresses this issue: an object can register to events by referring to the event type instead of referencing the subject that announces the event. Due to the quantification over the event types, observers are decoupled from observables. Finally, Rx [23] is a library originally developed for .NET and ported to other platforms. Rx has received great attention because it provides uniform abstractions, based on LINQ [24], for event composition over heterogeneous sources.

Complex event processing is about performing queries to detect patters on event streams. For example, TelegraphCQ [5], and Cayuga [9] provide SQL-like queries over time-changing event streams. These systems share with reactive programming the concept of reacting to time-changing values and the declarative style of functional relations [21]. However, they are based on SQL-like query languages rather than integrating dedicated abstractions into a general-purpose language.

Self-adjusting computation (e.g. [1]) is a programming technique that automatically derives an incremental version of a given program. In self-adjusting computation, the program is initially executed to compute the result, then a *mutator* performs the updates when the input changes. The focus of self-adjusting computation is on efficient derivation of incremental algorithms, and not on raising the level of abstraction via proper linguistic constructs. For example, in self-adjusting computation, the programmer explicitly interacts with the runtime to initiate the change propagation across the dependencies.

Incremental and automatic update has been successfully applied to data structures and queries. Due to this restricted domain, these approaches can take advantage of techniques developed by research in databases to keep views synchronized with the underlying tables [4]. Willis *et al.* [34] studied queries incrementalization over mutable objects. Object fields are manually annotated and made observable by using AspectJ. Finally, the framework is in charge of tracking the updates and propagating the change to the query result. Rothamel and Liu [30] propose a similar approach based on code generation. While the general problem of incrementalizing and automatically updating generic computations is still a research challenge, incremental update and synchronization of data structures is currently implemented in libraries like Livelinq [18] and GlazedList [16].

7. Summary and Future Work

In this work, we presented RESCALA, a language that seamlessly integrates concepts from event-based programming and reactive languages into object-oriented design. We analyzed the limitations of both approaches and argued that their integration is fundamental to support a mixed functional and OO paradigm. We showed that RESCALA can effectively ameliorate the implementation of reactive applications by fostering a declarative and functional style without relinquishing the advantages of OO design. Finally we provided an evaluation of the language.

In the future, we plan to continue the development of RESCALA. We envisage several research directions. First, we plan to investigate a more direct support of reactive behavior over mutable data by integrating reactive data structures. Second, we want to introduce abstractions from complex event processing like joins and elaborate on matching over event patterns. Finally, we want to apply concepts from reactive programming to the distributed setting. This direction is promising since a huge amount of callbacks, commonly used to react to events in publish-subscribe systems, can be potentially replaced by signals. A more detailed discussion – including the challenge of enforcing glitch-freedom in a distributed setting – can be found in [31].

Acknowledgments

This work has been supported by the German Federal Ministry of Education and Research (BMBF) under grant No. 01IC12S01V SINNODIUM and by the European Research Council, grant No. 321217.

References

[1] U. A. Acar, A. Ahmed, and M. Blume. Imperative self-adjusting computation. In *Proceedings of the 35th annual ACM SIGPLAN-SIGACT symposium on Principles of programming languages*, POPL '08, pages 309–322, New York, NY, USA, 2008. ACM.

[2] G. Berry and G. Gonthier. The Esterel synchronous programming language: design, semantics, implementation. *Science of Computer Programming*, 19(2):87 – 152, 1992.

[3] P. Caspi, D. Pilaud, N. Halbwachs, and J. A. Plaice. LUSTRE: a declarative language for real-time programming. In *Proceedings of the 14th ACM SIGACT-SIGPLAN symposium on Principles of programming languages*, POPL '87, pages 178–188, New York, NY, USA, 1987. ACM.

[4] S. Ceri and J. Widom. Deriving production rules for incremental view maintenance. In *Proceedings of the 17th International Conference on Very Large Data Bases*, VLDB '91, pages 577–589, San Francisco, CA, USA, 1991. Morgan Kaufmann Publishers Inc.

[5] S. Chandrasekaran, O. Cooper, A. Deshpande, M. J. Franklin, J. M. Hellerstein, W. Hong, S. Krishnamurthy, S. R. Madden, F. Reiss, and M. A. Shah. TelegraphCQ: continuous dataflow processing. In *Proceedings of the 2003 ACM SIGMOD international conference on Management of data*, SIGMOD '03, pages 668–668. ACM, 2003.

[6] G. H. Cooper and S. Krishnamurthi. Embedding dynamic dataflow in a call-by-value language. In *ESOP, 15th European conference on Programming*, pages 294–308, 2006.

[7] A. Courtney. Frappe: Functional reactive programming in Java. In *Proceedings of the Third International Symposium on Practical Aspects of Declarative Languages*, PADL '01, pages 29–44, London, UK, 2001. Springer-Verlag.

[8] Microsoft corporation. C# language specification. v.3.0. http://msdn.microsoft.com/en-us/vcsharp/aa336809.aspx.

[9] A. Demers, J. Gehrke, M. Hong, M. Riedewald, and W. White. Towards expressive publish/subscribe systems. In *Proceedings of the*

10th international conference on Advances in Database Technology, EDBT'06, pages 627–644, Berlin, Heidelberg, 2006. Springer-Verlag.

[10] C. Elliott and P. Hudak. Functional reactive animation. In *Proceedings of the second ACM SIGPLAN international conference on Functional programming*, ICFP '97, pages 263–273. ACM, 1997.

[11] P. Eugster and K. R. Jayaram. EventJava: An extension of Java for event correlation. In *Proceedings of the 23rd European Conference on Object-Oriented Programming, ECOOP 2009*, Genoa, pages 570–594, Berlin, Heidelberg, 2009. Springer-Verlag.

[12] B. N. Freeman-Benson. Kaleidoscope: mixing objects, constraints, and imperative programming. In *Proceedings of the European conference on object-oriented programming systems, languages, and applications*, OOPSLA/ECOOP '90, pages 77–88, New York, NY, USA, 1990. ACM.

[13] Gamma, Helm, Johnson, and Vlissides. *Design Patterns Elements of Reusable Object-Oriented Software*. Addison-Wesley, 2000.

[14] D. Garlan and D. Notkin. Formalizing design spaces: Implicit invocation mechanisms. In *Proceedings of the 4th International Symposium of VDM Europe on Formal Software Development: Conference Contributions - Volume I*, VDM '91, pages 31–44, London, UK, 1991. Springer-Verlag.

[15] V. Gasiunas, L. Satabin, M. Mezini, A. Núñez, and J. Noyé. EScala: modular event-driven object interactions in Scala. In *Proceedings of the tenth international conference on Aspect-oriented software development*, AOSD '11, pages 227–240. ACM, 2011.

[16] GlazedLists site. http://www.glazedlists.com/.

[17] D. Ignatoff, G. H. Cooper, and S. Krishnamurthi. Crossing state lines: Adapting object-oriented frameworks to functional reactive languages. In *FLOPS*, pages 259–276, 2006.

[18] LiveLINQ Site. http://www.componentone.com/SuperProducts/LiveLinq/.

[19] I. Maier and M. Odersky. Deprecating the Observer Pattern with Scala.react. Technical report, 2012.

[20] I. Maier and M. Odersky. Higher-order reactive programming with incremental lists. In G. Castagna, editor, *ECOOP 2013 Object-Oriented Programming*, volume 7920 of *Lecture Notes in Computer Science*, pages 707–731. Springer Berlin Heidelberg, 2013.

[21] A. Margara and G. Salvaneschi. Ways to react: Comparing reactive languages and complex event processing. In *REM*, 2013.

[22] S. McDirmid and W. C. Hsieh. SuperGlue: Component programming with object-oriented signals. In D. Thomas, editor, *Object-Oriented Programming, 20th European Conference, Nantes, France*, volume 4067 of *LNCS*, pages 206–229. Springer, 2006.

[23] E. Meijer. Your mouse is a database. *Commun. ACM*, 55(5):66–73, 2012.

[24] E. Meijer, B. Beckman, and G. Bierman. LINQ: Reconciling Object, Relations and XML in the .NET Framework. In *Proceedings of ACM SIGMOD International Conference on Management of Data*, SIGMOD '06, pages 706–706. ACM, 2006.

[25] L. A. Meyerovich, A. Guha, J. Baskin, G. H. Cooper, M. Greenberg, A. Bromfield, and S. Krishnamurthi. Flapjax: a programming language for Ajax applications. Proceeding of the 24th ACM SIGPLAN conference on Object oriented programming systems languages and applications, OOPSLA '09, pages 1–20. ACM, 2009.

[26] B. A. Myers, D. A. Giuse, R. B. Dannenberg, D. S. Kosbie, E. Pervin, A. Mickish, B. V. Zanden, and P. Marchal. Garnet: Comprehensive support for graphical, highly interactive user interfaces. *Computer*, 23(11):71–85, Nov. 1990.

[27] B. A. Myers, R. G. McDaniel, R. C. Miller, A. S. Ferrency, A. Faulring, B. D. Kyle, A. Mickish, A. Klimovitski, and P. Doane. The Amulet Environment: New models for effective user interface software development. *IEEE Trans. Softw. Eng.*, 23(6):347–365, June 1997.

[28] M. Pouzet. *Lucid Synchrone, version 3. Tutorial and reference manual.* Université Paris-Sud, LRI, April 2006.

[29] H. Rajan and G. T. Leavens. Ptolemy: A language with quantified, typed events. In J. Vitek, editor, *ECOOP 2008*, volume 5142 of *LNCS*, pages 155–179, Berlin, July 2008. Springer-Verlag.

[30] T. Rothamel and Y. A. Liu. Generating incremental implementations of object-set queries. In *Proceedings of the 7th international conference on Generative programming and component engineering*, GPCE '08, pages 55–66. ACM, 2008.

[31] G. Salvaneschi, J. Drechsler, and M. Mezini. Towards distributed reactive programming. In R. Nicola and C. Julien, editors, *Coordination Models and Languages*, volume 7890 of *Lecture Notes in Computer Science*, pages 226–235. Springer Berlin Heidelberg, 2013.

[32] G. Salvaneschi and M. Mezini. Reactive behavior in object-oriented applications: An analysis and a research roadmap. In *Proceedings of the 12th annual international conference on Aspect-oriented software development, AOSD'13*, 2013.

[33] Scala Swing library. http://www.scala-lang.org/api/current/index.html#scala.swing.package.

[34] D. Willis, D. J. Pearce, and J. Noble. Caching and incrementalisation in the Java query language. *SIGPLAN Not.*, 43(10):1–18, Oct. 2008.

[35] Y. Zhuang and S. Chiba. Method slots: Supporting methods, events, and advices by a single language construct. In *Proceedings of the 12th Annual International Conference on Aspect-oriented Software Development*, AOSD '13, pages 197–208, New York, NY, USA, 2013. ACM.

A. Signals-events API

In this appendix, we show the RESCALA interface between signals and events. When a signal and an event can be the receiver and an argument, interchangeably, we show the function with the signal as a receiver, i.e, exposed by the `Signal` trait.

- Creates a signal by folding events with a given function.
  `fold[T,A](e: Event[T], init: A)(f :(A,T)=>A): Signal[A]`
- Returns a value computed by `f` on the occurrence of an event.
  `iterate[A](e: Event[_], init: A)(f: A=>A) :Signal[A]`
- Returns a signal holding the latest value of the event e.
  `hold[T](e: Event[T], init: T): Signal[T]`
- Holds the latest value of an event as `Some(val)` or `None`.
  `holdOption[T](e: Event[T]): Signal[Option[T]]`
- Returns a signal which holds the last n events.
  `last[T](e: Event[T], n: Int): Signal[Seq[T]]`
- Collects the event values in a reactive list.
  `list[T](e: Event[T]): Signal[Seq[T]]`
- Delays a signal by n change occurrences.
  `delay[T](n: Int): Signal[T]`
- Counts the occurrences of an event.
  `count(e: Event[_]): Signal[Int]`
- On the event, sets the signal to one generated by the factory.
  `reset[T,A](e: Event[T], init: T)(f: (T)=>Signal[A]): Signal[A]`
- Switches the value of the signal on the occurrence of e.
  `switchTo[U](e: Event[U]): Signal[U]`
- Switches to a new signal once, on the occurrence of e.
  `switchOnce[T](e: Event[_], newSignal: Signal[T]): Signal[T]`
- Switches between signals on the event e.
  `toggle[T](e: Event[_], other: Signal[T]): Signal[T]`
- Returns a signal updated only when e fires.
  `snapshot[T](e: Event[_]): Signal[T]`

FlowR: Aspect Oriented Programming for Information Flow Control in Ruby

Thomas F. J.-M. Pasquier Jean Bacon
University of Cambridge
{thomas.pasquier, jean.bacon}@cl.cam.ac.uk

Brian Shand
Public Health England
brian.shand@phe.gov.uk

Abstract

This paper reports on our experience with providing Information Flow Control (IFC) as a library. Our aim was to support the use of an *unmodified* Platform as a Service (PaaS) cloud infrastructure by IFC-aware web applications. We discuss how Aspect Oriented Programming (AOP) overcomes the limitations of RubyTrack, our first approach. Although use of AOP has been mentioned as a possibility in past IFC literature we believe this paper to be the first illustration of how such an implementation can be attempted.

We discuss how we built FlowR (Information **Flow** Control for **R**uby), a library extending Ruby to provide IFC primitives using AOP via the Aquarium open source library. Previous attempts at providing IFC as a language extension required either modification of an interpreter or significant code rewriting. FlowR provides a strong separation between functional implementation and security constraints which supports easier development and maintenance; we illustrate with practical examples. In addition, we provide new primitives to describe IFC constraints on objects, classes and methods that, to our knowledge, are not present in related work and take full advantage of an object oriented language (OO language).

The experience reported here makes us confident that the techniques we use for Ruby can be applied to provide IFC for any Object Oriented Program (OOP) whose implementation language has an AOP library.

Categories and Subject Descriptors D.2.2 [*Software Engineering*]: Design Tools and Techniques; D.2.4 [*Software Engineering*]: Software/Program Verification

Keywords Information Flow Control, Aspect Oriented Programming, Security

1. Introduction

In 2012 we developed a web portal, in collaboration with Public Health England, to grant access by brain cancer patients to their records [35]. As well as standard authentication and access control we used Information Flow Control (IFC) to track the flow of data end-to-end through the system. For this purpose, we used RubyTrack, a taint-tracking system for Ruby, developed by the SafeWeb project [17].

However, we came to realise certain limitations of the mechanisms we had deployed. For example, to enforce the required IFC policy, we manually inserted IFC checks at selected application component boundaries. In practice, objects and classes are the natural representation of application components within an object oriented language and it seems natural to relate security concerns with those objects. We should therefore associate the primitives and mechanisms to enforce IFC with selected objects. Furthermore, we wish to be able to assign boundary checks on any class or object without further development overhead. We also wish to be able to exploit the inheritance property to define rules that apply to categories of objects (for example defining a boundary check for all possible children of *I/O*). We therefore decided to investigate the use of Aspect Oriented Programming (AOP), and selected the Aquarium library [54], instead of RubyTrack, to use with our Ruby implementation to provide IFC-aware web applications.

We believe the techniques we have used to provide IFC mechanisms for Ruby can be extended to any Object Oriented Language (OO Language) with an AOP library, such as Java [23], C++ [44] or JavaScript [55]. AOP has advantages over our earlier approach: IFC label tracking and enforcement can be applied to any object and/or method invocation; programmers need have minimal concern about the underlying implementation; maintenance overheads are low, for example, when there are changes in the library code. These factors contribute to the overall reliability of software developed using AOP [50].

It has already been pointed out [11] that AOP can be used to implement security functions such as authentication and access control. Our main objective is to separate IFC concerns from the development of the application; we believe that functional issues and security issues should be kept well separated whenever possible. The AOP paradigm allows us to separate the core functionality developed by a programmer from the policy specified by a security expert [50]. Furthermore, the literature on providing IFC through a library [29, 31, 34, 56] has already hinted that AOP techniques could be used to implement IFC.

However, we make some assumptions on the environment and the problems we are addressing. First, we assume that the developer is not adversarial; the aim is to protect against inadvertent disclosure of information through bugs within the application. Second, we focus on the design of web applications using a framework such as Sinatra or Rails to be, for example, deployed on a PaaS (Platform as a Service) cloud, using readily available languages/interpreters. Third, in this context, we assume the application's host ensures that no data can be disclosed outside of the application. Finally, we assume that the organisation running the application is willing to accept a performance overhead in exchange for increased security assurance. Other solutions can be envisioned for other circumstances,

Modularity'14, April 22–26, 2014, Lugano, Switzerland.

ACM 978-1-4503-2772-5/14/04.
http://dx.doi.org/10.1145/2577080.2577090

such as using a particular IFC-aware interpreter or running on an IFC-aware operating system. However, these would require control over the infrastructure that is not available in a standard hosting solution or PaaS, this would require the use of self-managed infrastructure or the use of IaaS (Infrastructure as a Service).

The Ruby standard implementation provides no real multi-threading support (more recent versions are starting to address this). Therefore, Ruby web servers tend to be multi-process rather than multi-threaded, which allows us to handle IFC rule violation effectively; we fail completely any process violating an IFC constraint. This is preferable to (per thread) exception handling which may generate implicit information flows [40]; this is discussed further in section 2.2.

Section 2 gives background on Aspect Oriented Programming and Information Flow Control. Section 3 then gives an overview of our work; we specify the basic principles governing flows and the primitives we added to the language to manipulate IFC labels. Section 4 describes our implementation. Section 5 presents a simple use case to demonstrate the simplicity of the approach then describes the web portal for brain cancer patients mentioned above. In section 6 we show that performance is similar to an equivalent solution and we argue that our approach provides better usability. Section 7 presents related work and section 8 summarises and concludes.

2. Background

Our paper targets readers interested in both AOP usages and IFC implementations. Some may not be familiar with both topics so we give a brief introduction to each, indicating the relevant literature. The last subsection discusses problems that are not addressed in this paper and which are generally not addressed by library-level implementations of IFC. We believe readers should be aware of these issues and options, and suggest further reading in section 7.2.

2.1 Aspect Oriented Programming and Security

Aspect Oriented Programming was introduced in 1997 by Kiczales et al. [22]. It is a programming paradigm extending Object Oriented Programming (OOP) by allowing cross-cutting aspects to be expressed. An aspect is a piece of code named an *advice* together with a *pointcut* determining when it should execute. The pointcut is used to determine the join-points (object methods) where the *advice* code will be executed. Fig. 1 provides an illustration of this concept. In the original specification an *advice* could be executed either *before* or *after* the join-point code is executed. The paradigm was later extended with an *around advice* [23] which has control over whether or not the join-point code should be executed.

An *advice* is composed of a primitive to express when the *advice* should be executed (i.e. *before, after, around*), a pointcut describing where the *advice* should be executed and a block of instructions to specify the behaviour of the *advice*. This is illustrated in Fig. 2 where we define an *advice* to be executed around a call to the method *write* of instances of *File*. The example is in Ruby and using the Aquarium library [54]. The parameters passed to the *advice* are the *join-point* to be executed, the *object* the method belongs to and the *arguments* passed to the method.

A pointcut can be made more expressive by using a regular expression (some implementations may not provide this, however this is provided by the library we are using) to define the methods and classes to which the *advice* should be applied. We can also specify a list of methods to be ignored, or implement different behaviour either after a normal execution or if the method throws an exception.

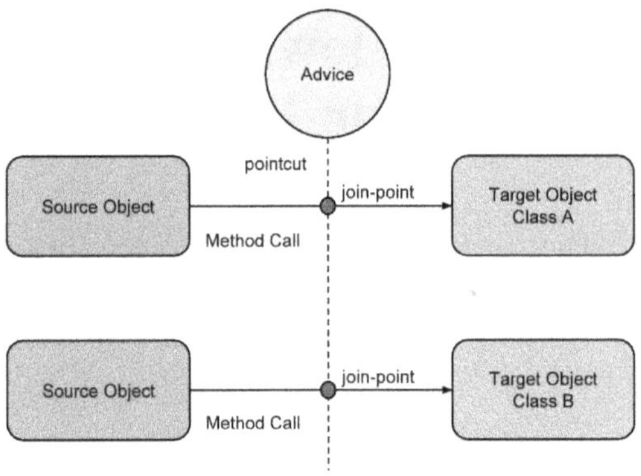

Figure 1. Visual representation of an aspect

2.2 Information Flow Control

It has long been argued that standard security techniques, such as firewalls and access control mechanisms, are not enough to prevent information leakage [9]. Indeed, it is beyond the scope of such mechanisms to determine whether, after the controls they impose, the information is used correctly. For example it is difficult to determine if the confidentiality of decrypted data is respected [40]. We therefore need to protect information flow, that is, how information is transmitted within and between applications.

In 1975, Denning [8] proposed a model to track and enforce rules on information flow within a procedural language. In this model, variables are associated with security classes. The flow of information from a variable a to a variable b is allowed only if the security class of b noted $\underline{b}$ is higher than $\underline{a}$. The security class of an n-function on a classified variable is noted $\underline{a_1} \oplus ... \oplus \underline{a_n}$. This allows the *no-read up, no-write down* principle [4] to be implemented to enforce secrecy. By this means a traditional military classification (public, secret, top secret) can be implemented. A second security class can be associated with each variable to track integrity (quality of data) [6] during *reading down* and *writing up*. Using this model we are able to control and monitor information flow to ensure data secrecy and integrity.

In 1999 Myers [33] proposed *security labels* to replace the security classes of Denning's model [9]. Clearance levels are considered too coarse-grained, permitting unnecessary access and were replaced by the "need-to-know" principle, also known as "Principle of Least Privilege (PoLP)" [42]. Labels are composed of tags representing categories of information or the nature of the information. The *secrecy* label is propagated with data between objects and the *integrity* label is used to define which data are allowed to flow into and within an object. Here, *integrity* relates to the trustworthiness of the source of any data rather than accidental corruption, for example, by hardware. A central authority is not needed in such a model since data flow policy is user-specified (discretionary) rather

```
around method: :write, type: File
             do |join_point, object, *args|
    puts 'hello'
    returned_value = join_point.proceed
    puts 'goodbye'
    return returned_value
end
```

Figure 2. Example: An advice in Ruby using Aquarium

```
y := x mod 2
```

Figure 3. Explicit information flow

```
x := x mod 2
y := 0
if x = 1 then y:= 1
```

Figure 4. Implicit information flow[40]

than centrally mandated. However, system support is needed at runtime for the continuous monitoring of data flows.

IFC implementations must ensure that labels can be allocated to principals but not be forged by them; can be allocated to data and "stick" to them; and that label checking enforces security policy regarding all aspects of information flow.

Practical IFC systems cannot work with policies that only allow data to become more restrictively labelled, for example secret data passed to a principal with top secret clearance becomes top secret when incorporated at that level. There are situations where constraints should be relaxed, for example, to enable the public release of previously classified data. The privilege to override secrecy IFC restrictions is known as the *declassification privilege*. In order to declassify an information item, the owner or owners must agree to remove their policy restrictions. This method of declassification again appears to remove the need for a central authority, as every owner is responsible for its own policy. But since the processes running on behalf of a principal o_i, or the precise hierarchy of principals, is only known at runtime, declassification also requires runtime support.

In this style of language a variable declaration can be augmented with an annotation to describe the policy associated with the data item. Examples can be seen in the solutions proposed by Denning [9] or Myers [33]. It is in these cases the programmers' responsibility to not only understand the algorithm being implemented but also the desired security policy [58]. But the security constraints may not all be clear during the functional design phase and inconsistencies can arise at runtime. It is generally better to separate security concerns from functional ones, limiting the impact they have on each other in the engineered system. We decided in this work to explore the use of AOP to enforce IFC constraints specifically in order to provide this separation.

2.3 Implicit Flow and Covert Channels

In this paper, as in most similar projects on IFC enforced at the library level, we do not address the problem of covert channels and *implicit* flow [2, 10, 15]. *Explicit* flows from x to y, noted $x \Rightarrow y$ are caused by passing data between variables, as illustrated in Fig. 3, or performing operations or method calls on such variables.

An *implicit* flow of information arises from the control structure of the program. Fig, 4 illustrates an *implicit* flow $x \Rightarrow y$ equivalent to the *explicit* flow illustrated in Fig. 3. It is possible to track such an assignment by introducing a process sensitivity level, as defined in the US DoD "orange book"[1], in which case the assignment of y can be detected at runtime. We could consider that any variable modified within the if statement (or any function called from it) must be assumed to create an information flow. However, in the case $x = 0$, no value is assigned to y and therefore no flow is detected even if it exists.

It is possible to prevent such flows remaining unnoticed by applying the label from the if to any assignment happening after

```
x := x mod 2
z := z mod 2
y := 0
w := 0
if x = 1 then y:= 1
if z = 1 then y:= 1
w:= x mod 2
```

Figure 5. Example of label creep

the if statement. However, this means that the number of labels assigned to variables will increase [15], often unnecessarily. This leads to data with higher sensitivity than intended, known as *label creep* [38]. This phenomenon is illustrated in Fig. 5. From the Denning model, briefly described in section 2.2, we expect that $\underline{w} = \underline{x}$; that is, x and w are of the same security level. However, if we enforce process sensitivity levels, we have $\underline{w} = \underline{x} \oplus \underline{z}$ even if we know there is no $z \Rightarrow w$.

To address the concerns brought by the benevolent developer assumption, it has been suggested that an implicit flow can be prevented by the preemptive halting of program execution [2, 41]. However, this could prevent legitimate applications from terminating [2]. Therefore, to deal with potentially malicious code, variable-level runtime taint tracking can be combined with static analysis techniques [52].

At present in our project we do not consider implicit flow nor other covert channels [20] such as timing channels, storage channels [26, 27] or termination channels [53]. We briefly discuss in section 7 how some of these problems could be solved in an AOP context.

3. The FlowR IFC Model

IFC models are used to represent and constrain the flow of information within an application. In this paper, we focus on the aspects of the model relating to a single application rather than a distributed, multi-application environment.

In the DEFCon project [31], AOP was used with Java to enforce IFC by inserting IFC policy around selected methods. In FlowR, we extend those ideas by providing IFC at the level of objects, classes and methods, and provide basic primitives to enforce IFC. Our approach is not specific to Ruby but can be used with any OO Language that supports AOP. Furthermore, our techniques can work with an arbitrary library, without programmers having to know about its inner workings, so requiring little effort from them.

We provide tracking and flow control on what we define as *basic* variables (strings, integers, floats, etc.) and on arbitrary objects, classes or methods (as required).

In this section we first define the labels associated with objects. We then explain how the labels indicate flows that are and are not allowed and how labels are propagated for allowed flows. Finally, we outline how declassification is achieved.

3.1 Security labels

In order to monitor Information Flow we use labels. Our label model is inspired by that proposed by Efstathopoulos et al. [13].

Every tracked object is associated with two labels: a *Receive* label and a *Send* label. The *Receive* label is used to represent the type of information that is allowed to flow into an object, while *Send* labels are used to represent the nature of the information and its sensitivity. *Send* (S) labels are *sticky*, that is, they will propagate and taint any object they interact with, which ensures that no information can flow untracked. *Receive* (R) labels however do not propagate and concern only a single object or class.

[1] http://www.dtic.mil/whs/directives/corres/pdf/850001p.pdf

A label is composed of a set of tags, each representing an individual concern about the information, for example, the origin of the information, its privacy level or its owner. Tags are composed of two elements: a unique identifier t and a marker $+$ or $-$ representing the privileges an object has over the information labelled with this tag. To guarantee that each tag identifier is unique we represent tags using the Ruby concept of *symbol* which associates with a string an integer guaranteed to be unique in the current execution context. t^+ and t^- indicate the tag with identifier t and privileges $+$ or $-$ respectively.

In a *Receive* label. An object with a tag t^- in its *Receive* label is not allowed to receive information labelled with the tag t. An object with a tag t^+ in its *Receive* label is allowed to receive such information. *Receive* labels are not changed by the flow of information.

In a *Send* label. An object with a tag t^+ in its *Send* label is allowed to flow to an appropriately labelled destination object and the tag will propagate. An object with a tag t^- in its *Send* label is allowed to flow to an appropriately labelled destination object, but the tag does not propagate. For details on tag propagation see sections 3.2 and 3.4.

We need to add an additional constraint, that only one tag can be associated with some identifier t. This means that in any label L, either t^- or t^+ can exist, but not both. In order to simplify the notation for the rest of the paper, when we write $t \in L$, we mean $(t^+ \veebar t^-) \in L$.

We also have a special tag, named $default$. Strictly speaking, when unlabeled data are manipulated the empty labels are interpreted as *Send* label $S = \{default^+\}$ and a *Receive* label $R = \{default^+\}$, that is, such data can be freely transmitted. A label therefore implicitly has $default^+$ added to its tags, i.e. it is assumed to contain the default privilege $default^+$. In order to simplify the notation we can omit the default tag in a label. However, it is also possible to explicitly specify the default label. It is forbidden to set the tag $default^-$ in the *Send* label but it may be appropriate to set the tag $default^-$ in the *Receive* label, as we see in an example below.

3.2 Allowed flows and label propagation

We denote the flow of information between two entities A and B as $A \rightarrow B$. We need to define two rules, the first to describe an allowed flow and the second how tags in labels propagate between entities. We define $h(t, L)$ as the function returning the privilege associated with the identifier t in the label L (either R or S). The flow $A \rightarrow B$ is allowed to occur if $\forall t \in S_A, h(t, R_B) = +$ holds true. We define $S'_A = \{t | t \in S_A \wedge h(t, S_A) = +\}$, as the set of tags that should propagate. After the flow, S_B is modified to become $S'_B = S_B \cup S'_A$.

We define the function $ALLOW(A, B)$ which, given two entities A and B returns true if the flow is allowed and false otherwise. We also define the function $PROPAGATE(A, B)$ which propagates the send label from A to B according to the definition we have just given.

Jajodia et al. [19] specify that information flow occurs only if an object changes its state, i.e. changes the value of one or more of its attributes. However, this assumes that methods cannot be altered at run time [18], which is not the case in Ruby. Therefore we need to consider more possible flows.

Flow of information occurs on method call. A method call is the interaction of several entities: the caller C, the callee O, the method parameters $p_1, ..., p_n$ and the returned value r. We distinguish two phases: the calling of the method and the returning phase.

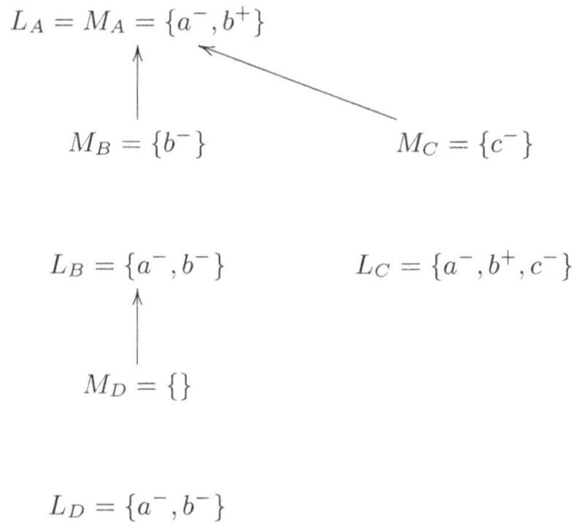

Figure 6. Illustration of label inheritance

During the first phase the flow of information is as follows: $C \rightarrow O$, $p_1 \rightarrow O$, ... $p_n \rightarrow O$. In the second phase the flows first $O \rightarrow r$ and then $r \rightarrow C$. It is important to note that at the end of the second phase we may have $S_r \neq S_O$. This is due to the fact that class/object attributes may have different labels than the class/object they belong to and that there may be label operations within the execution of the method (a method performing an operation on the returned value of another method call, for example). Having different attribute labels may be useful when doing event processing such as in DEFCon [31].

3.3 Methods, instances, class labels

As mentioned earlier, our model has the notion of method label, object label and class label. Object labels are associated with a particular instance of a class, while class labels are associated with all instances of the class or inherited class. Finally, method labels are associated with a particular method of an object or class.

In OO languages classes inherit from their parents. To maintain this logic, the labels defined in a parent class are inherited by its children. Similarly, an object inherits the label of its class and a method inherits the label of its object or class (in the case that this is a static method). It is important to note here that we only support multilevel hierarchical inheritance, but the model could quite easily be extended to support multiple inheritance if implemented in a language supporting this feature.

We now define how labels are inherited. We consider the inheritance from class A to class B. Note that the process would have to be repeated as often as necessary and also that the process is similar when inheriting from class to object or from class or object to method. The inheritance process is identical for *Send* and *Receive* labels.

We note L_A the apparent label for class A (taking into account inheritance) and M_A the label defined at the level of class A. For a class B inheriting from A, $L_B = \{t | t \in L_A \wedge t \notin M_B\} \cup M_B$. Fig. 6 illustrates this principle. For simplicity in the rest of this paper, label will always refer to the apparent label of an object, class or method.

Table 1 illustrates how such a feature can be used to express security concerns throughout an application (we take well known Ruby classes as an example). We first declare that we do not want sensitive information to be written to a file. We also define a tag named $internal$ to protect data that we do not want to leave our

class	receive	send
IO	$\{internal^-\}$	$\{\}$
File	$\{sensitive^-\}$	$\{\}$
NurseReport	$\{\}$	$\{medical^+\}$
Patient	$\{medical^+, default^-\}$	$\{\}$
PublicData	$\{medical^-\}$	$\{\}$

Table 1. Expressing application level security concerns

application (for example a private key used for encryption). We therefore forbid such information to go through any I/O.

We define a class NurseReport which inherits from File to allow the nurse to perform some operation on the report she writes about a patient. We want all data associated with NurseReports to be considered medical. We therefore associate the $\{medical\}$ tag with the *Send* label of NurseReports. An instance of a NurseReport would have the following labels
$R : \{sensitive^-, internal^-\}, S : \{medical^+\}$;
that is, it does not accept sensitive or internal information and contains medical information which it can send to allowed recipients.

We define two other classes inheriting from File that we call Patient and PublicData. Patient labels are as follows:
$R : \{medical^+, internal^-, sensitive^-, default^-\}, S : \{\}$.
As we want our patient well informed, he is only able to read information issued by medical sources (in our case coming from a nurse). He cannot read unlabelled data. PublicData labels are as follows:
$R : \{medical^-, internal^-, sensitive^-\}, S : \{\}$.
This class includes data made public for research. Obviously we do not want confidential medical data to be available to the general public so it is not allowed to flow into PublicData.

However, we want to provide the option for patients to release anonymised data for research purposes. Therefore, we define in the class Patient a method generate_anonymised_record and associate with this method the label $R : \{\}, S : \{medical^-\}$. The medical tag of the data input to the method does not propagate so the data returned by this method would not include the medical tag in its label. It could therefore be used with the PublicData class. Algorithm 1 illustrates how such a method would be used. Section 3.4 contains a general discussion of declassification of data.

Algorithm 1 Example of method label usage

```
p = new Patient
d = new PublicData
d.add(p.generate_anonymised_record)        ▷ succeeds
d.add(p.get_record)                        ▷ fails
```

In order to express real security concerns, we should define a label per patient in order to isolate their respective data. We give an example of this, for records of customers' orders, in section 4.

3.4 Ensuring secrecy and integrity

Information flow control generally enforces two properties throughout the execution of a program. In this section we first describe how we can guarantee the integrity of an entity, then how we can guarantee secrecy of information.

3.4.1 Integrity

Guaranteeing integrity of an entity means accepting data only from trusted sources. The first step to achieve integrity is to set the *Receive* label to $R = \{default^-\}$, that is, no unlabelled data can be read. So far, with this *Receive* label, our entity is unable to receive any information.

Now, we need to set a list of trusted sources. This is done by associating a tag with identifier $source$ with the trusted information and setting the *Receive* label as follows $R = \{source^+, default^-\}$. Here we state that this entity will only accept information associated with the tag with identifier $source$.

Setting $R = \{source\_1^+, source\_2^+, default^-\}$ means that we accept information labelled with one of $source\_1^+$ or $source\_2^+$ or both. Here we are effectively building a white list.

We may also want to prevent onward, indirect propagation of information from a trusted source, i.e. trustworthiness need not be transitive. To achieve this we set the *Send* label of the source to $S = \{source^-\}$. As defined in section 3.2, the tag $source^-$ does not propagate to the *Send* label of the receiver of the information. So an entity that built a white list including the tag $source^+$ would be able to read information directly from the source entity, but would not be able to read it through an intermediate entity. This is important in order to avoid privilege creep.

3.4.2 Secrecy

Secrecy means preventing secret data from being transmitted to an untrustworthy entity. In our context this would generally mean leaving an application or well-known channel. For example, medical data should only be stored in an appropriate database and never be logged or transmitted to a third party server through the network.

In this context the first thing to do is to associate the secret data or the source of the secret data (such as a database) with a tag that will propagate through all the application. That is, we set its *Send* label to $S = \{secret^+\}$. At this point our IFC library will track the data through our application.

The final step to ensure secrecy is to set the receive label of any entity representing a connection outside our application to refuse information with a tag containing this label. This is done simply by setting the entity's *Receive* label to $R = \{secret^-\}$. Here we are effectively building a black list of information which cannot be transmitted to this entity.

3.4.3 Declassification

We have defined how to ensure the secrecy and integrity of information through the manipulation of its associated labels and tags. As mentioned in section 2.2 it is also necessary to be able to declassify information. Declassifying is equivalent to removing a tag from the information in order to allow it to flow to an entity where this would otherwise not be allowed.

Suppose the classified information is stored in data with associated label $S : \{secret^+\}$, $R : \{\}$. To declassify the information we pass the data through a method with the following label $S : \{secret^-\}$, $R : \{\}$. This would mean that the returned value would not carry the $secret^+$ tag and could be used freely. An example of declassification was given above in section 3.3, where a method was defined to input a medical record and output a corresponding declassified, anonymised medical record. Another example is given in section 4.

4. FlowR implementation

We saw in section 3.2, that flows are enforced in two phases: on method call and on method return. This corresponds exactly to the AOP standard *around advice* [23] (discussed in section 2.1). We describe the process in algorithm 2. O is the callee, C is the caller, M the method called, A_s is the set of attributes and $join\_point$ is the *join point* to be executed. We now describe the step described in algorithm 2; *1)* we verify that information is allowed to flow from the caller to the method and we also verify that the information contained in the parameters is allowed to flow in the method; *2)* we propagate the labels from the caller and the parameters to the

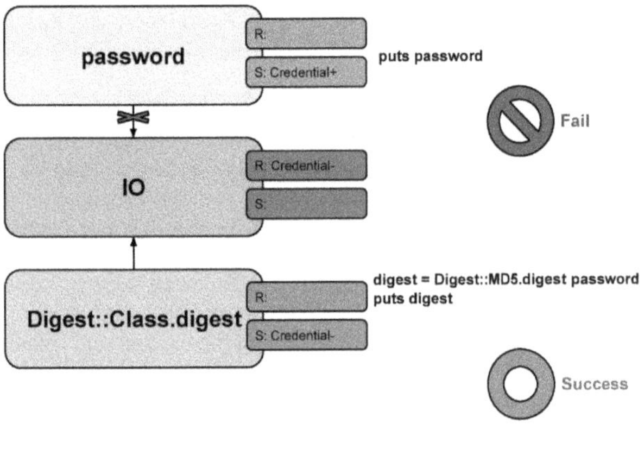

Figure 8. Example 1: Protecting passwords

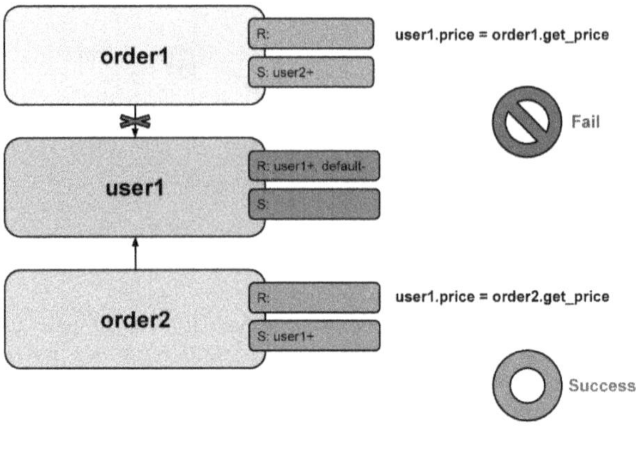

Figure 10. Example 2: Isolating a user's data

callee; *3)* we execute the *join point*; *4)* we propagate the method label to the returned value; *5)* we verify that the information contained in the returned value is allowed to flow to the caller; *6)* we propagate the returned value's labels to the caller. If the flows are found not to be allowed the program is aborted.

We used the AOP library Aquarium [54] to implement this in Ruby. We place an *advice* around any public method of a tracked object (an object is considered to be tracked when there are tags associated with this object). Regardless of the actual object implementation we are therefore able to protect information flow.

Algorithm 2 IFC Around Advice

```
function AROUND(O, C, As, join_point)
    if ALLOW(C, M) then                          ▷ step 1 start
        for all A in As do
            if ¬ALLOW(A, M) then
                FAIL
            end if
        end for                                  ▷ step 1 end
        PROPAGATE(C, O)                          ▷ step 2 start
        for all A in As do
            PROPAGATE(A, O)
        end for                                  ▷ step 2 end
        RV = join_point.execute                  ▷ step 3
        PROPAGATE(M, RV)                         ▷ step 4
        if ¬ALLOW(RV, C) then                    ▷ step 5
            Fail
        end if
        PROPAGATE(RV, C)                         ▷ step 6
        return RV
    else
        FAIL
    end if
end function
```

In order to implement the concepts described in our model (section 3) we provided the API described in table 2. We have instructions to start and stop the tracking of basic variables. Indeed, in some cases, it may be required to activate tracking only on some portion of the code. For example, the loading of a large configuration file could be done before the tracking is activated in order to improve performance. Similarly, *execute_procedure_untracked* allows a single procedure to be executed with tracking deactivated (an illustration of why this may be useful can be found in section 6). Although untracked procedures are executed in Ruby safe mode, the programmer is relied upon to understand the IFC implication of executing a portion of code untracked. The manipulation of this API is illustrated in Fig. 9.

In addition to this API we also support object methods manipulating their labels directly as this may be useful in some circumstances. In Fig. 7 we illustrate how such direct manipulation can be used to prevent information leak on standard output. In this example, we declare that credentials are not allowed to be displayed on the standard output and try to print a password that we previously associated with the credential tag, which causes the program to fail.

A developer should be able to design an application without initially being concerned about IFC, and with the ability to use a legacy library that was built without IFC in mind. Once the application is developed, the original developer, or another expert, can add IFC rules to ensure that the application behaves correctly with respect to information flow.

In this simple example we consider how to protect the user password from being disclosed unintentionally within our application by printing it out "in clear" in the log, displaying it on a page or saving it "in clear" in a database.

Fig. 9 illustrates a simple way to achieve this without any modification to the code of the original application. We first add a method which is executed before the routing of any request received from a client. In this method we associate with the parameter *password* sent by the client, the send tag *credential*, thus ensuring that any data derived from this information will be tracked in our application.

The second step is to activate tracking for our application which is done by calling *FlowR.start_variable_tracking*. Then we need to specify that we do not want *credential* information to leave our application. This is done simply by invoking the method *FlowR.protect_class IO, nil, credential: false*. Here, we say that any information associated with the send tag *credential* is forbidden to flow towards any *I/O* (files, logs, etc.).

We were able to express policy to protect the user password in six lines of code, with minimal knowledge of the application implementation and without modifying the functional implementation. In addition, we also successfully separated security concerns from the implementation itself.

We have confined our password information to our application. However, in order to provide a useful application we should

FlowR API call	Description
start_variable_tracking	start basic variable tracking.
stop_variable_tracking	stop basic variable tracking.
protect_class / protect_classes	protect all public method of a class(es).
protect_object / protect_objects	protect all public method of an instanc(es).
protect_methods_in_class	protect a defined set of methods in a class.
protect_methods_in_object	protect a defined set of methods in a single instance.
execute_procedure_untracked	allow a procedure to execute without variable tracking for performance reasons detailed in section 6.

Object methods	Description
add_receive_tag / add_receive_tags	add a single or a set of tags to the receive label associated with an object instance or class depending on the context of the call.
add_send_tag / add_send_tags	add a single or a set of tags to the send label associated with an object instance or class depending on the context of the call.
declassify	remove specified tag from the send label.
get_send_label / get_receive_label	get the receive or send label associated with the object/class

Table 2. FlowR API

be able to save the password into the database during the registration and verify the password is correct during authentication. The proper thing to do to store a password is to hash it with the salt. Therefore, we determine that once hashed, the data associated with the send tag *credential* loses its secrecy and becomes safe. We can express this with the following method invocation *FlowR.protect_methods_in_class ([:digest], Digest::Class, credential: false, nil)*. This states that the invocation of the method *Digest::Class.digest* declassifies with respect to the *credential* tag. We illustrate these points in Fig. 8.

We now look at another example. In this case a user class is trying to access an order made on a website and stored in the database. In addition to the usual information associated with the order, we maintain in our database the label associated with each entry. When writing to or reading from the database, we ensure that the label associated with instances of orders are propagated to the database by modifying the *ActiveRecord::Base* implementation. An idea of how this is implemented is illustrated in Fig. 11. Again, here we do not need to modify any implementation code, it would work for any children of *ActiveRecord::Base* and this can easily be added after application development.

In the simple example illustrated in Fig. 10, the instances of the order are associated with a *Receive* label containing the tag representing the user to whom the order belongs. Furthermore, the user1 instance of the user class can only read information associated with its own tag *user*1. Therefore, if the user tries to read information belonging to another user the program will simply fail. During the development and testing phases this allows the programmer to detect bugs in the application, and during the release phase to prevent the user accessing data they do not own.

As attributes are also objects it is also possible to assign labels to each attribute. This would represent the different security and confidentiality requirements of the different fields of this structured document. For example, medical records might be shared between medical professionals and social services. Some sensitive information such as HIV status may be restricted to medical professionals

```
FlowR.start_variable_tracking
FlowR.protect_object $stdout, nil, {credential: false}
puts 'nothing happens here' # no problem here
s = 'I can say that!'
s.add_send_tag :label_s
puts s # no problem here
password = '123456789'
password.add_send_tag :credential
puts password # here the program fails
```

Figure 7. Example: Applying flow constraints on standard output

```
before do
  params[:password].add_send_tag :credential unless params[:password].nil?
  params[:verify_password].add_send_tag :credential unless params[:verify_password].nil?
end

FlowR.start_variable_tracking
FlowR.protect_class IO, nil, {credential: false}
FlowR.protect_methods_in_class ([:digest], Digest::Class, {credential: false}, nil)
```

Figure 9. Example: Preventing password leak with FlowR

```
module ActiveIFC
        def before_save
                receive_label = self.get_receive_label
                send_label = self.get_send_label
                # save labels to database
        end

        def after_initialize
                # read label from database
                FlowR.protect_object self, send_label, receive_label
        end

        def after_create
                receive_label = self.get_receive_label
                send_label = self.get_send_label
                # save labels to database
        end
end

class ActiveRecord::Base
        include ActiveIFC
end
```

Figure 11. Example: Integrating IFC in ActiveRecord

only, while more general information may be accessible to social services, for example to detect signs of child abuse. Another use of attribute labelling could be to build an event processing system as described in the DEFcon work [31].

5. Use case: Building a medical web portal

In 2012 we developed a web portal, in collaboration with the Eastern Cancer Registry and Information Centre (ECRIC) – now part of Public Health England – to grant access by brain cancer patients to their records [35]. We used IFC to track the flow of data end-to-end through the system. For this purpose, we used RubyTrack, developed by the SafeWeb project [17]. In the work presented here, we have replaced RubyTrack in the web portal by FlowR.

All cancer patients within an administrative region have their data stored in a data centre managed by the cancer registries. Patients within the Eastern Region who have a brain tumour can opt to have their data made accessible to them on an external website managed by the BrainTrust charity.

The data of those patients are encrypted with a unique key per patient. The keys are stored in a dedicated key server, while the individual patients' anonymised medical data, in transit to them, are stored in a separate server. Any patient-provided data is also held separately, thus maintaining a clear separation between patient data associated with the web portal application and the local image of the data held by the cancer registries. Furthermore, patients are invited periodically to respond to a quality of life survey, in order to track the evolution of their condition over time. Those data are regularly retrieved and added to the Cancer Registry's database to improve statistical data about the patient.

We ensure through the use of IFC, that even in the case of unexpected program behaviour, the integrity of patient data is assured, and patients can access only their own data. That is, we ensure isolation of data per purpose and per user. A single request of the data store can manipulate only data for one patient; moreover, the medical data is anonymous and the associated personal data is held separately in isolation.

The requirement for isolating data per patient is an obvious necessity as we want to ensure that patients can only access or amend their own data. The separation and isolation of medical and personal data for a single patient is there to decrease the risk of re-identification. Indeed, very little information is required to uniquely identify an individual [5]. Through encrypting data with a unique key per patient and per usage, and through ensuring isolation of information per patient and per usage, we can reduce the risk that an attacker who gains access to our data store is able to gain medical information on an identified patient.

Fig. 12 illustrates the architecture of our data store. At reception of data we ensure that the user is authenticated. From this authentication, we are able to build what we call the user context. We identify the purpose of the request and associate the appropriate tags (medical, private, etc.) to the parameters transmitted in the HTTP request. In addition, our database models and our controllers have their own set of IFC constraints.

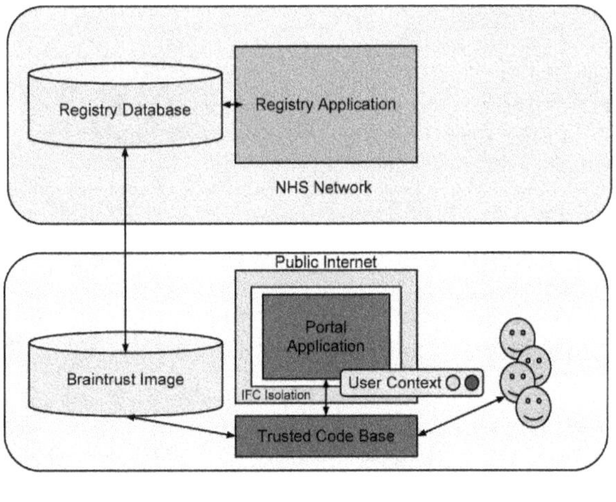

Figure 12. Data store architecture

	RubyTrack	FlowR
Label	a single label	integrity and secrecy
Tag	simple string	symbol + capability
Enforcement	manual by developer at strategic points	at public method call on tracked objects
Engineering	requires overwriting of classes that need to be tracked	minimum

Table 3. Feature comparison of FlowR and RubyTrack

We create an isolation bubble by limiting application access to *IO* classes according to the user context labels and controller labels (in a similar fashion as shown in section 4). In order to propagate labels into and out of the database we store the labels along with the record, i.e. in a row in the database. (We do not support an individual label per column (record field), only per database entry.) We intercept database read and write method calls using the *ActiveRecord* library feature and add the necessary IFC labelling.

Supporting IFC was again done separately from building the actual application, allowing a clear distinction and separation between functional and security concerns.

6. Evaluation

Our tests measure the performance of our solution, FlowR, compared with an equivalent solution, that extends native Ruby with RubyTrack, developed for the SafeWeb project [17]. It is important to note the feature differences that explain the performance difference of FlowR when compared with RubyTrack, as illustrated in table 3.

Our first series of tests concern computing intensive tasks. We demonstrate that FlowR does not perform significantly worse than its equivalent using RubyTrack. In addition, no performance optimisation has been attempted for FlowR, which is beyond the scope of this paper.

Our second series of tests is made on a web application, built to provide patient medical records and similar to the one we built in a previous project [35]. We demonstrate that the performance loss compared with native Ruby is of the same order as the earlier implementation, and acceptable from an end user point of view.

All tests have been performed on an i7 2.2GHz 6GB RAM Fedora 17 GNU/Linux Machine.

6.1 Compute-intensive tasks

We designed two simple tests. The first consists of counting the number of words in text stored in a file on disk ("Les Contemplations" by Victor Hugo). The second test consists of calculating the first n prime numbers. The execution time of the native Ruby code is our time unit. We compare RubyTrack, FlowR and FlowR using untracked procedure calls (section 4).

The results, shown in table 4, show the same order of magnitude for RubyTrack and FlowR. We did not attempt to optimise performance, and the Aquarium library is known to suffer from performance issues [57]. This is because, at present, Aquarium applies advices at runtime whereas AspectJ and AspectC++ apply them at compile time. Furthermore, it is commonly accepted that performing IFC is generally not a good idea while performing computing intensive tasks. Using untracked procedure calls provides much better performance. This figure includes the switching of tracking on, off and on again which induces some overhead. However, this overhead becomes negligible as the execution time becomes large. Therefore, untracked procedure calls can provide performance identical to native Ruby in the case of long computing intensive tasks.

We also measured the execution time for some key primitives which were: starting tracking 325 ms; stopping tracking 108 ms; protecting an additional class 180 ms; adding protection to a single method 5 ms. As mentioned above, adding AOP *advices* at runtime, as in Ruby/Aquarium, incurs performance overhead, and care should be taken in deciding when this is necessary. IFC advices should be added during initialization as much as possible.

On the other hand, the cost of adding a label to an existing object is insignificant (it is simply adding an entry to a hash table). Therefore, adding or removing labels during the lifetime of an application does not amount to a significant performance loss.

6.2 Brain portal: a web portal application

In order to evaluate our library under realistic conditions we used the data store described in section 5. In order to evaluate the performance of our implementation we queried our data store 1000 times, asking for 50 different, randomly chosen data items. We compare the averaged values obtained with native Ruby, RubyTrack and FlowR, as shown in table 5.

We used the "thin" Ruby web server as it provides quite good performance. We first display an unlabelled static page to measure the influence of tracking without flow enforcement. RubyTrack and FlowR add an overhead of 7% and 12% respectively compared to native Ruby. The performance penalties for retrieving a medical record from our database are of the same order (10% and 15% respectively).

We add the IFC advice at initialization; the web server executes the initialization script only once. This removes the very significant overhead generated when creating the advices. Furthermore, as discussed previously, our tracking algorithm is slightly more complicated than RubyTrack and flows are controlled for every protected object (including basic variables), while RubyTrack only enforces flow at strategic points. This explains our performance decrease compared to RubyTrack.

Obtaining more precise results on exactly where compute-time was being spent in our library proved to be impractical, or at least to require too much engineering in the time available. As discussed above in section 6.1, switching on and off advices takes time, i.e. activating IFC slows down the library usually used to trace Ruby application performance. Secondly, activating undiscriminated *I/O*

test	native	RubyTrack	FlowR	untracked
word count	1	6.3	9.8	7.7
prime	1	27	70	1.8

Table 4. Performance comparison of compute-intensive tasks

test	native	RubyTrack	FlowR
hello world	4.1 ms	4.4 ms (+7%)	4.6 ms(+12%)
medical record	62 ms	68 ms (+10%)	71 ms (+15%)

Table 5. Performance comparison for a web portal

protection made the required tracing impossible. This is because the tracer manipulates protected data, which IFC currently prevents it from obtaining via output from the application. We are already working on integrating an IFC-aware, message-passing middleware capable of controlling which connections out of an application are allowed. This will be used to implement debugging and performance monitoring, as well as inter-component communication. At this stage, we can only observe and measure performance "from the outside".

7. Related Work

7.1 Aspect Oriented Programming

Critics of aspect oriented programming [45] argue that AOP reduces the understandability of a program. In our case we are quite confident that expressing constraints in a well-defined and compact fashion in a single file is a better approach than merging them with functional code. Indeed, in standard IFC library, one would need to explore the code in order to understand where IFC constraints are applied.

Others argue [14, 21, 48] that AOP leads to software that is harder than usual to evolve. In our opinion and from experience, the solution we propose is easier to maintain. Indeed, changes to an underlying library implementation do not affect the policy rules defined. The only changes that the security expert needs to keep track of are changes of interface in the case of constraints expressed on methods.

Ramachandran et al. [37] proposed to implement access control using AspectJ [23] around object method calls. In their work each thread is associated with a certain level of clearance, and each object as well. If the current thread level of clearance matches the object on which the program is trying to perform a method call, then the program executes, otherwise it fails. Although our algorithms bear some similarity, [37] does not address information flow control. AspectJ has also been used to implement some of the IFC features of DEFCon [31].

Masuhara et al. [30] discuss the difficulty of implementing crosscutting security features through AOP based on data origin. They propose a new point-cut that they named *dflow*. This point cut allows some procedures to execute on data which flow from object a to b. Although we considered implementing the execution of some programmer-determined procedure on some data with a specific label when it reached a certain object b (effectively providing the same end result), we decided that it was going beyond IFC and therefore beyond the scope of our library.

AOP has been used to implement security features: access control [37, 47], error detection and handling [28], automatic login [51], hardening the security of existing libraries [32] or preventing buffer overflow [43] are some examples where AOP has been used successfully. AOP proves itself a useful and powerful tool as it allows the expression of security concerns that should apply to the whole application while completely decoupling their specification from the application functionality.

7.2 Information Flow Control

Dynamic Library IFC generally presents poor support for implicit flow, as discussed in section 2.3. There are obvious exceptions such as implementation for a purely functional language [39]. In other types of language, solutions include going through static techniques [33] or code rewriting to transform implicit flows into explicit ones [49]. However, AOP techniques present potential alternatives to address implicit flow. Indeed the new "join-point on loop" proposed by Harbulot et al. [16] or "join-point on region" by Akai et al. [1] may be interesting directions to investigate for dynamic implicit flow tracking. We have not yet addressed implicit flow in our work.

Information Flow Control was first enforced statically [9], then Myers introduced some dynamic elements [33] to provide more flexibility at runtime and a decentralised model. More recent work such as SafeWeb [17] or GIFT [25] provides dynamic taint tracking.

We have investigated the provision of IFC at the language level, with its associated tradeoffs. IFC can be provided at other system levels, with different tradeoffs. For example Suh et al. [46] propose a specific hardware architecture to support information flow. Asbestos [13] is an operating system design to provide IFC mechanisms. Finally, there are solutions running on top of a Linux OS [24] or providing a platform for distributed systems [7, 59]. These different levels of implementation, which we discuss in detail in [3], do not necessarily address the same issues. Indeed, while OS level implementation of IFC allows better and easier protection of I/O than the language level, it would require more engineering to create isolation within the application. IFC concerns could have an influence on the application architecture that might be considered too strong.

8. Conclusions and future work

Regardless of the precise implementation properties, we believe that the primitives we propose here are a natural way to express flow constraints within an application in an OO Language. We also believe that the AOP approach discussed in this paper is a good solution to providing IFC when control over the system running an application is not available. That is, our IFC runs above unmodified platforms as well as potentially extending unmodified applications.

We assume a benevolent developer, which is standard for all library-level IFC implementations; and we do not support implicit flow tracking, again, the case for most library-level IFC. We will continue to evaluate the tradeoffs involved in taking the AOP approach compared with using more disruptive and less maintainable mechanisms that might provide higher security and performance. The Brain-Portal implementations using RubyTrack and FlowR have provided a first case study.

Our current implementation does not support multi-threading but this is not inherent to our proposed model. Rather, it is constrained by the AOP library implementation we used and the general poor support of real multithreading in the standard Ruby implementation.

Another issue that may arise when using AOP to enforce IFC is when several AOP advice are implemented over the same object; for example enforcing IFC, logging and authentication. In such a scenario it may be necessary to determine whether composition issues arise, as discussed in [12, 36].

It is important to note that our library does not require the rewriting of any code and therefore *does not modify program behaviour*, except when IFC constraint violation forces the process to abort. So when performance is a critical issue, the library can be used during development, to track unexpected data flows, and ignored in deployment. Again, a tradeoff is involved between performance and security.

In this paper we presented an IFC library implementation using AOP, with primitives to provide IFC concepts, and mechanisms to enforce IFC. We separated application functionality from security concerns. Programmers need not be aware of IFC during application development, and a security specialist can add IFC as a separate phase. This is good engineering practice and achieves better maintainability. However, we described our model informally and a more formal model would be required before substantial future work was carried out.

We believe that using AOP to provide IFC has many advantages which we intend to evaluate further in future work, especially in the context of cloud deployment.

Acknowledgments

This work was supported by the UK Engineering and Physical Sciences Research Council under grant EP/K011510, CloudSafetyNet. We thank Dr Olivier Hermant from MINES ParisTech for his invaluable feedback.

References

[1] S. Akai, S. Chiba, and M. Nishizawa. Region pointcut for AspectJ. In *Proceedings, 8th workshop on Aspects, components, and patterns for infrastructure software*, ACP4IS '09, pages 43–48. ACM, 2009.

[2] T. Austin and C. Flanagan. Efficient purely-dynamic information flow analysis. In *Programming Languages and Analysis for Security (PLAS)*, Dublin, Ireland, 2009. ACM.

[3] J. Bacon, D. Eyers, T. F. Pasquier, J. Singh, I. Papagiannis, and P. Pietzuch. Information Flow Control for secure cloud computing. *submitted to: IEEE Transactions on Network and Service Management,Special Issue on Management of Cloud Services*, 2014.

[4] D. Bell. The Bell-LaPadula model. *Journal of computer security*, 4 (2):3, 1996.

[5] K. Benitez and B. Malin. Evaluating re-identification risks with respect to the HIPAA privacy rule. *Journal of the American Medical Informatics Association*, 17(2):169–177, 2010.

[6] K. J. Biba. Integrity considerations for secure computer systems. Technical report, DTIC Document, 1977.

[7] W. Cheng, D. R. Ports, D. Schultz, V. Popic, A. Blankstein, J. Cowling, D. Curtis, L. Shrira, and B. Liskov. Abstractions for usable information flow control in Aeolus. In *Proceedings, USENIX Annual Technical Conference (Usenix ATC '12)*, 2012.

[8] D. Denning. Secure Information Flow in Computer Systems, 1975. Dissertations Publishing 1975.

[9] D. E. Denning. A lattice model of secure information flow. *Commun. ACM*, 19(5):236–243, May 1976.

[10] D. E. Denning and P. J. Denning. Certification of programs for secure information flow. *Commun. ACM*, 20(7):504–513, July 1977.

[11] B. DeWin, B. DeVanhaute, and B. DeDecker. Security Through Aspect-Oriented Programming. In *Advances in Network and Distributed Systems Security*, volume 78 of *IFIP*, pages 125–138. Springer US, 2002.

[12] C. Disenfeld and S. Katz. A closer look at aspect interference and cooperation. In *Proceedings of the 11th annual international conference on Aspect-oriented Software Development*, AOSD '12, pages 107–118, New York, NY, USA, 2012. ACM.

[13] P. Efstathopoulos, M. Krohn, S. VanDeBogart, C. Frey, D. Ziegler, E. Kohler, D. Mazières, F. Kaashoek, and R. Morris. Labels and event processes in the Asbestos operating system. In *Proceedings, 20th ACM Symposium on Operating Systems Principles*, SOSP '05, pages 17–30. ACM, 2005.

[14] E. Figueiredo, N. Cacho, C. Sant'Anna, M. Monteiro, U. Kulesza, A. Garcia, S. Soares, F. Ferrari, S. Khan, F. Filho, and F. Dantas. Evolving software product lines with Aspects. In *Software Engineering, 2008. ICSE '08. ACM/IEEE 30th International Conference on*, pages 261–270, 2008.

[15] M. Gyung, S. McCamant, P. Poosankam, and D. Song. DTA++: Dynamic Taint Analysis with Targeted Control-Flow Propagation. In *Network and Distributed System Security Symposium (NDSS)*, San Diego, CA, 2011. Internet Society.

[16] B. Harbulot and J. R. Gurd. A join point for loops in AspectJ. In *Proceedings, 5th international conference on Aspect-oriented software development*, AOSD '06, pages 63–74. ACM, 2006.

[17] P. Hosek, M. Migliavacca, I. Papagiannis, D. Eyers, D. Evans, B. Shand, J. Bacon, and P. Pietzuch. SafeWeb: A middleware for securing Ruby-based web applications. In *Middleware*, pages 491–512, 2011.

[18] S. Jajodia and B. Kogan. Integrating an object-oriented data model with multilevel security. In *Proceedings, IEEE Symposium on Security and Privacy*, pages 76–85, 1990.

[19] S. Jajodia, B. Kogan, and R. Sandhu. A multilevel-secure object-oriented data model. *Abrams et al.[AJP95]*, 1995.

[20] V. Kashyap, B. Wiedermann, and B. Hardekopf. Timing- and termination-sensitive secure information flow: exploring a new aproach. In *Symposium on Security and Privacy*, Berkeley, CA, 2011. IEEE.

[21] C. Kastner, S. Apel, and D. Batory. A case study implementing features using AspectJ. In *Software Product Line Conference, 2007. SPLC 2007. 11th International*, pages 223–232, 2007.

[22] G. Kiczales, J. Lamping, A. Mendhekar, C. Maeda, C. Lopes, J.-M. Loingtier, and J. Irwin. *Aspect-Oriented Programming*. Springer, 1997.

[23] G. Kiczales, E. Hilsdale, J. Hugunin, M. Kersten, J. Palm, and W. G. Griswold. An overview of AspectJ. In J. L. Knudsen, editor, *ECOOP 2001 âĂŤ Object-Oriented Programming*, volume 2072 of *Lecture Notes in Computer Science*, pages 327–354. Springer, 2001.

[24] M. Krohn, A. Yip, M. Brodsky, N. Cliffer, M. F. Kaashoek, E. Kohler, and R. Morris. Information Flow Control for standard OS abstractions. *SIGOPS Oper. Syst. Rev.*, 41(6):321–334, Oct 2007.

[25] L. C. Lam and T. cker Chiueh. A general dynamic information flow tracking framework for security applications. In *Computer Security Applications Conference, 2006. ACSAC '06. 22nd Annual*, pages 463–472, 2006.

[26] B. W. Lampson. A note on the confinement problem. *Commun. ACM*, 16(10):613–615, Oct. 1973.

[27] S. B. Lipner. A comment on the confinement problem. *SIGOPS Oper. Syst. Rev.*, 9(5):192–196, Nov. 1975.

[28] M. Lippert and C. Lopes. A study on exception detection and handling using Aspect-Oriented Programming. In *Software Engineering, 2000. Proceedings of the 2000 International Conference on*, pages 418–427, 2000.

[29] F. Marchand de Kerchove, J. Noyé, and M. Südholt. Aspectizing javascript security. In *Proceedings of the 3rd Workshop on Modularity in Systems Software*, MISS '13, pages 7–12, New York, NY, USA, 2013. ACM.

[30] H. Masuhara and K. Kawauchi. Dataflow pointcut in Aspect-Oriented Programming. In *Proceedings, First Asian Symposium on Programming Languages and Systems*, APLAS, pages 105–121. Springer, 2003.

[31] M. Migliavacca, I. Papagiannis, D. M. Eyers, B. Shand, J. Bacon, and P. Pietzuch. DEFCon: High-performance event processing with information security. *USENIX Annual Technical Conference*, June 2010.

[32] A. Mourad, M.-A. Laverdière, and M. Debbabi. An aspect-oriented approach for the systematic security hardening of code. *Computers & Security*, 27(3):101–114, 2008.

[33] A. C. Myers. JFlow: practical mostly-static information flow control. In *Proceedings, 26th ACM SIGPLAN-SIGACT Symposium on Principles of Programming Languages*, POPL '99, pages 228–241. ACM, 1999.

[34] K. Padayachee, J. Eloff, and J. Bishop. Aspect-oriented information flow control, unpublished.

[35] T. Pasquier, B. Shand, and J. Bacon. Information Flow Control for a Medical Web Portal. In *e-Society 2013*. IADIS, March 2013.

[36] R. Pawlak, L. Duchien, and L. Seinturier. Compar: Ensuring safe around advice composition. In *Formal Methods for Open Object-Based Distributed Systems*, pages 163–178. Springer, 2005.

[37] R. Ramachandran, D. J. Pearce, and I. Welch. AspectJ for multilevel security. *ACP4IS '06*, 20:13–17, March 2006.

[38] D. E. Robling Denning. *Cryptography and data security*. Addison-Wesley Longman Publishing Co., Inc., Boston, MA, USA, 1982.

[39] A. Russo, K. Claessen, and J. Hughes. A library for lightweight information-flow security in Haskell. *SIGPLAN Notices*, 44(2):13–24, Sept. 2008.

[40] A. Sabelfeld and A. Myers. Language-based information-flow security. *IEEE Journal on Selected Areas in Communications (JSAC)*, 21 (1):5–19, 2003.

[41] A. Sabelfeld and A. Russo. From dynamic to static and back: Riding the roller coaster of information-flow control research. In *Andrei Ershov International Conference on Perspectives of System Informatics*, Akademgorodok, Novosibirsk, Russia, 2009.

[42] J. Saltzer and M. D. Schroeder. The protection of information in computer systems. *Proc. IEEE*, 63(9):1278–1308, 1975.

[43] V. Shah and F. Hill. An aspect-oriented security framework. In *DARPA Information Survivability Conference and Exposition, 2003. Proceedings*, volume 2, pages 143–145 vol.2, 2003.

[44] O. Spinczyk, A. Gal, and W. Schröder-Preikschat. AspectC++: an aspect-oriented extension to the C++ programming language. In *Proceedings, 40th International Conference on Technology of Object-Oriented Languages and Systems (TOOLS Pacific 2002)*, volume 10 of *CRPIT '02*, pages 53–60. Australian Computer Society, Inc., 2002.

[45] F. Steimann. The paradoxical success of aspect-oriented programming. *SIGPLAN Not.*, 41(10):481–497, Oct. 2006.

[46] G. E. Suh, J. W. Lee, D. Zhang, and S. Devadas. Secure program execution via dynamic information flow tracking. *SIGOPS Oper. Syst. Rev.*, 38(5):85–96, Oct. 2004.

[47] R. Toledo and E. Tanter. Secure and modular access control with Aspects. In *Proceedings of the 12th annual international conference on Aspect-oriented software development*, AOSD '13, pages 157–170, New York, NY, USA, 2013. ACM.

[48] T. Tourwé, J. Brichau, and K. Gybels. On the existence of the AOSD-evolution paradox. *SPLAT: Software engineering Properties of Languages for Aspect Technologies*, 2003.

[49] N. Vachharajani, M. Bridges, J. Chang, R. Rangan, G. Ottoni, J. Blome, G. Reis, M. Vachharajani, and D. August. Rifle: An architectural framework for user-centric information-flow security. In *Microarchitecture, 2004. MICRO-37 2004. 37th International Symposium on*, pages 243–254, 2004.

[50] J. Viega and J. Vuas. Can Aspect-Oriented Programming lead to more reliable software? *Software, IEEE*, 17(6):19–21, 2000.

[51] J. Viega, J. Bloch, and P. Chandra. Applying Aspect-Oriented Programming to security. *Cutter IT Journal*, 14(2):31–39, 2001.

[52] P. Vogt, F. Nentwich, N. Jovanovic, E. Kirda, C. Kruegel, and G. Vigna. Cross site scripting prevention with dynamic data tainting and static analysis. In *Network and Distributed System Security Symposium (NDSS)*, San Diego, CA, 2007. Internet Society.

[53] D. Volpano and G. Smith. Eliminating covert flows with minimum typings. In *Computer Security Foundations Workshop, 1997. Proceedings., 10th*, pages 156 –168, jun 1997.

[54] D. Wampler. Aquarium: AOP in Ruby. In *Proceedings, Aspect Oriented Software Development (AOSD)*, volume 4, 2008.

[55] H. Washizaki, A. Kubo, T. Mizumachi, K. Eguchi, Y. Fukazawa, N. Yoshioka, H. Kanuka, T. Kodaka, N. Sugimoto, Y. Nagai, and R. Yamamoto. AOJS: An Aspect-Oriented Javascript programming framework for web development. In *Proceedings, 8th workshop on Aspects, Components, and Patterns for Infrastructure Software*, ACP4IS, pages 31–36. ACM, 2009.

[56] A. Yip, X. Wang, N. Zeldovich, and M. F. Kaashoek. Improving application security with data flow assertions. In *Proceedings of the ACM SIGOPS 22nd symposium on Operating systems principles*, SOSP '09, pages 291–304, New York, NY, USA, 2009. ACM.

[57] A. Zambrano, A. Alvarez, J. Fabry, and S. Gordillo. Aspect Coordination for Web Applications in Java/AspectJ and Ruby/Aquarium. *Proceedings, 28th International Conference of Chilean Computer Society*, Nov. 2009.

[58] S. Zdancewic. Challenges for information-flow security. In *Proceedings of the 1st International Workshop on Programming Language Interference and Dependence (PLIDâĂŹ04)*, 2004.

[59] N. Zeldovich, S. Boyd-Wickizer, and D. Mazieres. Securing distributed systems with information flow control. In *Networked Systems Design and Implementation (NSDI)*, pages 293–308. Usenix, April 2008.

Assessing Modularity using Co-Change Clusters

Luciana Lourdes Silva
Marco Tulio Valente
Department of Computer Science,
Federal University of Minas Gerais
{luciana.lourdes,mtov}@dcc.ufmg.br

Marcelo de A. Maia
Faculty of Computing,
Federal University of Uberlândia
marcmaia@facom.ufu.br

Abstract

The traditional modular structure defined by the package hierarchy suffers from the dominant decomposition problem and it is widely accepted that alternative forms of modularization are necessary to increase developer's productivity. In this paper, we propose an alternative form to understand and assess package modularity based on co-change clusters, which are highly inter-related classes considering co-change relations. We evaluate how co-change clusters relate to the package decomposition of three real-world systems. The results show that the projection of co-change clusters to packages follow different patterns in each system. Therefore, we claim that modular views based on co-change clusters can improve developers' understanding on how well-modularized are their systems, considering that modularity is the ability to confine changes and evolve components in parallel.

Categories and Subject Descriptors D.1.5 [*Software*]: Programming Techniques - Object-Oriented Programming; D.2.2 [*Software*]: Software Engineering - Design Tools and Techniques; D.2.7 [*Software*]: Software Engineering - Distribution, Maintenance, and Enhancement; D.2.8 [*Software*]: Software Engineering - Metrics; H.3.3 [*Information Storage and Retrieval*]: Information Search and Retrieval

Keywords Modularity, software change, version control systems, co-change graphs, co-change clusters, Chameleon graph partitioning algorithm

1. INTRODUCTION

Modularity is the key concept to embrace when designing complex software systems [3]. The central idea is that modules should hide important design decisions or decisions that are likely to change [27]. In this way, modularity contributes to improve productivity both during initial development and maintenance phases. Particularly, well-modularized systems are easier to maintain and evolve, because their modules can be understood and changed independently from each other.

For this reason, it is fundamental to consider modularity when assessing the internal quality of software systems [21, 24]. Typically, the standard approach to assess modularity is based on coupling and cohesion, calculated using the structural dependencies established between the modules of a system (coupling) and between the internal elements from each module (cohesion) [7, 35]. However, typical cohesion and coupling metrics measure a single dimension of the software implementation (the static-structural dimension). On the other hand, it is widely accepted that traditional modular structures and metrics suffer from the dominant decomposition problem and tend to hinder different facets that developers may be interested in [20, 30, 31]. Therefore, to improve current modularity views, it is important to investigate the impact of design decisions concerning modularity in other dimensions of a software system, as the evolutionary dimension.

Specifically, we propose a novel approach for assessing modularity, based on co-change graphs [5]. The approach is directly inspired by the common criteria used to decompose systems in modules, i.e., modules should confine implementation decisions that are likely to change together [27]. We first extract co-change graphs from the history of changes in software systems. In such graphs, the nodes are classes and the edges link classes that were modified together in the same commits. After that, co-change graphs are automatically processed to produce a new modular facet: co-change clusters, which abstract out common changes made to a system, as stored in version control platforms. Therefore, co-change clusters represent sets of classes that changed together in the past.

Our approach relies on distribution maps [12]—a well-known visualization technique—to reason about the projection of the extracted clusters in the traditional decomposition of a system in packages. We then rely on a set of metrics defined for distribution maps to characterize the extracted co-change clusters. Particularly, we describe some recurrent distribution patterns of co-change clusters, including patterns denoting well-modularized and crosscutting clusters. Moreover, we also evaluate the meaning of the obtained clusters using information retrieval techniques. The goal in this particular case is to understand how similar are the issues whose commits were clustered together. We used our approach to assess the modularity of three real-world systems (Geronimo, Lucene, and Eclipse JDT Core) and observed different patterns of co-change modularity in such systems.

Our main contributions are threefold. First, we propose a methodology for extracting co-change graphs and co-change clusters, including several pre and post-processing filters to avoid noise in the generated clusters. This methodology relies on a graph clustering algorithm designed for sparse graphs, as is the case of co-change graphs, that was capable to identify high density clusters. Second, we propose a methodology to contrast the co-change modularity with the standard package decomposition. This methodology includes metrics to detect both well-modularized and crosscutting co-change clusters. Third, we found that the generated clusters not only are dense in terms of co-changes, but they also have high

MODULARITY '14, April 22–26, 2014, Lugano, Switzerland.

http://dx.doi.org/10.1145/10.1145/2577080.2577086

similarity from the point of view of the meaning of the maintenance issues that originated the respective commits.

The paper is organized as follows. Section 2 presents the methodology to extract co-change graphs and co-change clusters from version control systems. Section 3 presents the results of co-change clustering, when applied to three systems. Section 4 analyzes the modularity of such systems under the light of co-change clusters. Section 5 analyzes the semantic similarity within the set of issues related to the extracted clusters. Section 6 discusses our results and presents threats to validity. Section 7 describes related work and finally Section 8 concludes the paper.

2. METHODOLOGY

This section presents the methodology we followed for retrieving co-change graphs and then for extracting the co-change clusters.

2.1 Extracting Co-Change Graphs

As proposed by Beyer et al. [5], a co-change graph is an abstraction for a version control system (VCS). Suppose a set of change transactions (commits) in a VCS, defined as $T = \{T_1, T_2, \ldots, T_n\}$, where each transaction T_i changes a set of classes. Conceptually, a co-change graph is an undirected graph $G = \{V, E\}$, where V is a set of classes and E is a set of edges. An edge (C_i, C_j) is defined between classes (vertices) C_i and C_j whenever there is a transaction T_k, such that $C_i, C_j \in T_k$, for $i \neq j$. Finally, each edge has a weight that represents the number of transactions changing the connected classes.

2.1.1 Pre-processing Tasks

When extracting co-change graphs, it is fundamental to preprocess the considered commits to filter out commits that may pollute the graph with noise. More specifically, we propose the following pre-processing tasks:

Removing commits not associated to maintenance issues: In early implementation stages, commits can denote partial implementations of programming tasks, since the system is under construction [25]. When such commits are performed multiple times, they generate noise in the edges' weights. For this reason, we consider just commits associated to maintenance issues. More specifically, we consider as maintenance issues those that are registered in an issue tracking system, such as Bugzilla, Jira, etc. Moreover, we only considered issues labeled as *bug correction*, *new feature*, or *improvement*. We followed the usual procedure to associate commits to maintenance issues: a commit is related to an issue when its textual description includes a substring that represents a valid Issue-ID in the system's bug tracking system [10, 34, 40].

Removing commits not changing classes: The co-changes considered by our approach are defined for classes. However, there are commits that only change artifacts like configuration files, documentation, script files, etc. Therefore, we discard such commits in order to only consider commits that change at least one class. Finally, we eliminate unit testing classes from commits because co-changes between functional classes and their respective testing classes are usually common and therefore may dominate the relations expressed in co-change graphs.

Merging commits related to the same maintenance issue: When there are multiple commits referring to the same Issue-ID, we merge all of them—including the changed classes—in a single commit. For instance, the issue GERONIMO-3003 from Geronimo[1] is handled by four commits producing revisions 918360, 798794, 799023, and 799037. In this case, a single change set is generated for the four commits, including 13 classes. Therefore, in the co-change graph an edge is created for each pair of classes in this merged change set. In this way, we will have edges connecting classes modified in different commits (but referring to the same maintenance issue).

Removing commits associated to multiple maintenance issues: We remove commits that report changes related to more than one maintenance issue, which are usually called tangled code changes [15]. Basically, such commits are discarded because otherwise they would generate edges connecting classes modified to implement semantically unrelated maintenance tasks (which were included in the same commit just by convenience, for example). For instance, the revision 565397 of Geronimo includes changes to attend the following six issues: 3254, and 3394 to 3398.

Removing highly scattered commits: We remove commits representing highly scattered code changes, i.e., commits that modify a massive number of classes. Typically, such commits are associated to refactorings (like rename method) and other software quality improving tasks (like dead code removal), implementation of new features, or minor syntactical fixes (like changes to comment styles) [38]. For instance, the commit associated to revision 1355069 of Lucene changed 251 classes, located in 80 packages. In this revision, redundant throws clauses were refactored.

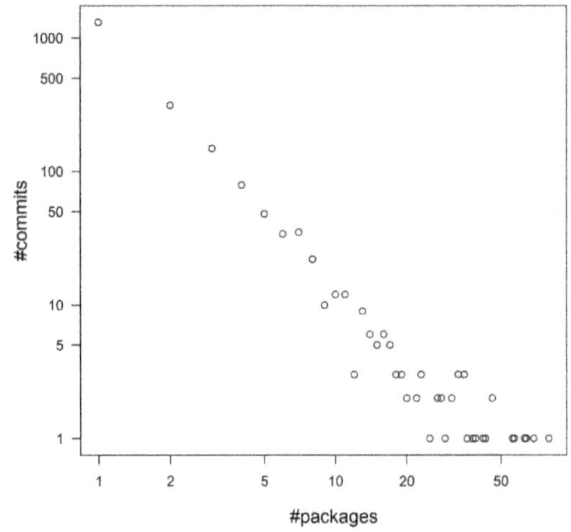

Figure 1. Packages changed by commits in the Lucene system

Recent research showed that scattering in commits tends to follow heavy-tailed distributions [38]. Therefore, the existence of massively scattering commits cannot be neglected. Particularly, such commits may have a major impact when considered in co-change graphs, due to the very large deviation between the number of classes changed by them and by the remaining commits in the system. Figure 1 illustrates this fact by showing a histogram with the number of packages changed by commits made to the Lucene system[2]. As we can observe, 1,310 commits (62%) changed classes in a single package. Despite this fact, the mean value of this distribution is 51.2, due to the existence of commits changing for example, more than 10 packages.

Considering that our goal is to model recurrent maintenance tasks and considering that highly scattered commits typically do not

[1] Geronimo is an application server, http://geronimo.apache.org

[2] An information retrieval library, http://lucene.apache.org.

present this characteristic, we decided to remove them during the co-change graph creation. For this purpose, we define that a package pkg is changed by a commit cmt if at least one of the classes modified by cmt are located in pkg. Using this definition, we ignore commits that change more than *MAX_SCATTERING* packages. In Section 3, we define and explain the values for thresholds in our method.

2.1.2 Post-processing Task

In co-change graphs, the edges' weights represent the number of commits changing the connected classes. However, co-change graphs typically have many edges with small weights, i.e., edges representing co-changes that happened very few times. Such co-changes are not relevant considering that our goal is to model recurrent maintenance tasks. For this reason, there is a post-processing phase after extracting a first co-change graph. In this phase, edges with weights less than a *MIN_WEIGHT* threshold are removed. In fact, this threshold is analogous to the *support* threshold used by co-change mining approaches based on association rules [39].

2.2 Extracting Co-Change Clusters

After extracting the co-change graphs, our goal is to retrieve sets of classes that frequently change together, which we call co-change clusters. We propose to extract co-change clusters automatically, using a graph clustering algorithm designed to handle sparse graphs, as is typically the case of co-change graphs [5]. More specifically, we decided to use the Chameleon clustering algorithm [18], which is an agglomerative and hierarchical clustering algorithm recommended to sparse graphs.

The algorithm operates in two phases:

- *First Phase:* a nearest-neighbor graph is extracted and a min-cut graph partitioning algorithm is used to partition the data items (classes in our case) into a pre-defined number of subclusters M. The number of clusters after this phase is M plus C, where C is the number of connected components in the graph.
- *Second Phase:* Chameleon combines such smaller clusters repeatedly. Clusters are combined to maximize the number of links within a cluster (internal similarity) and to minimize the number of links between clusters (external similarity).

2.2.1 Defining the Number of Clusters

A critical decision when applying Chameleon—and many other clustering algorithms—is to define the number of partitions M that should be created in the first phase of the algorithm. To define the "best value" for M we execute Chameleon multiple times, with different values of M, starting with a *M_INITIAL* value. Furthermore, in the subsequent executions, the previous tested value is decremented by a *M_DECREMENT* constant.

After each execution, we discard small clusters, as defined by a *MIN_CLUSTER_SZ* threshold. Considering that our goal is to extract groups of classes that may be used as alternative modular views, it is not reasonable to have clusters with only two or three classes. If we accept such small clusters, we may eventually generate a decomposition of the system with hundreds of clusters.

For each execution, the algorithm provides two important statistics to evaluate the quality of each cluster:

- $ESim$ - The average similarity of the classes of each cluster and the remaining classes (average *external similarity*). This value must tend to zero because minimizing inter-cluster connections is important to support modular reasoning.
- $ISim$ - The average similarity between the classes of each cluster (average *internal similarity*).

After pruning the small clusters, the following clustering quality function is applied to the remaining clusters:

$$coefficient(M) = \frac{1}{k} * \sum_{i=1}^{k} \frac{ISim_{C_i} - ESim_{C_i}}{max(ISim_{C_i}, ESim_{C_i})}$$

where k is the number of clusters after pruning small clusters.

The measure $coefficient(M)$ combines the concepts of cluster cohesion (tight co-change clusters) and cluster separation (highly separated co-change clusters). The $coefficients$ ranges from [-1; 1], where -1 indicates a very poor round and 1 an excellent round.

The selected M value is the one with the highest $coefficient(M)$. If the highest $coefficient(M)$ is the same for more than one value of M, then the highest $mean(ISim)$ is used as a tiebreaker. Clearly, internal similarity is relevant because maintainers are interested in clusters containing classes that frequently change together.

3. CO-CHANGE CLUSTERING RESULTS

In this section, we report the results we achieved after following the methodology described in Section 2 to extract co-change clusters for three systems.

3.1 Target Systems and Thresholds Selection

Table 1 describes the systems considered in our study, including information on their function, number of lines of code (LOC), number of packages (NOP), and number of classes (NOC), the number of commits extracted for each system, and the time frame used in this extraction. In the study, we considered the following thresholds:

- *MAX_SCATTERING* = 10 packages, i.e., we discard commits changing classes located in more than ten packages. We based on the hypothesis that large transactions typically correspond to noisy data, such as comments formatting and rename method [1, 39]. Excessive pruning is undesirable, so we adopted a conservative approach working at package level.
- *MIN_WEIGHT* = 2 co-changes, i.e., we discard edges connecting classes with fewer than two co-changes because an unitary weight does not reflect how often two classes usually change together [5].
- *M_INITIAL* = $NOC_G * 0.20$, i.e., the first phase of the clustering algorithm creates a number of partitions that is one-fifth of the number of classes in the co-change graph (NOC_G). The higher the M, the higher the final clusters' size because the second phase of the algorithm works by aggregating the partitions. In this case, the ISim tend to be lower because subgraphs that are not well connected are grouped in the same cluster. We made several experiments varying $M's$ value, and observed that whenever M is high, the clustering tend to have clusters of unbalanced size.
- *M_DECREMENT* = 1 class, i.e., after each clustering execution, we decrement the value of M by 1, meaning that no value for *M* is discarded from one iteration to another.
- *MIN_CLUSTER_SZ* = 4 classes, i.e., after each clustering execution, we remove clusters with less than 4 classes.

We defined the thresholds after some preliminary experiments with the target systems. We also based this selection on previous empirical studies reported in the literature. For example, Walker showed that only 5.93% of the patches in the Mozilla system change more than 11 files [38]. Therefore, we claim that commits changing more than 10 packages are in the last quantiles of the heavy-tailed distributions that normally characterize the degree of

Table 1. Target systems (size metrics and initial commits sample)

System	Description	Release	LOC	NOP	NOC	Commits	Period
Geronimo	Web application server	3.0	234,086	424	2,740	9,829	08/20/2003 - 06/04/2013 (9.75 years)
Lucene	Text search library	4.3	572,051	263	4,323	8,991	01/01/2003 - 07/06/2013 (10.5 years)
JDT Core	Eclipse Java infrastructure	3.7	249,471	74	1,829	24,315	08/15/2002 - 08/21/2013 (10 years)

scattering in commits. As another example, in the systems included in the Qualitas Corpus—a well-known dataset of Java programs—the packages on average have 12.24 classes [36, 37]. In our three target systems, the packages have on average 15.87 classes. Therefore, we claim that clusters with less than four classes can be characterized as small clusters.

3.2 Co-Change Graph Extraction

We start by characterizing the extracted co-change graphs. Table 2 shows the percentage of commits in our sample, after applying the preprocessing filters described in Section 2.1.1): removal of commits not associated to maintenance issues (Pre #1), removal of commits not changing classes and also testing classes (Pre #2), merging commits associated to the same maintenance issue (Pre #3), removal of commits denoting tangled code changes (Pre #4), and removal of highly scattering commits (Pre #5).

Table 2. Percentage of commits after each preprocessing filters

System	Pre #1	Pre #2	Pre #3	Pre #4	Pre #5
Geronimo	32.6	25.2	17.3	16.1	14.3
Lucene	39.2	34.6	23.6	23.3	22.4
JDT Core	38.4	32.8	21.7	20.30	20.1

As can be observed in Table 2, our initial sample for the Geronimo, Lucene, and JDT Core systems was reduced to 14.3%, 22.4%, and 20.1% of its original, respectively. The most significant reduction was due to the first preprocessing task. Basically, only 32.6%, 39.2%, and 38.4% of the commits in the Geronimo, Lucene, and JDT Core systems are explicitly associated to maintenance issues (as stored in the systems issue tracking platforms). There were also significant reductions after filtering out commits that do not change classes or that only change testing classes (preprocessing task #2) and after merging multiple commits due to the same maintenance issue (preprocessing task #3). Finally, a reduction affecting 3% of the Geronimo's commits and nearly 1% of the commits of the other systems was achieved by the last two preprocessing tasks.

After applying the preprocessing filters, we extracted a first co-change graph for each system. We then applied the post-processing filter defined in Section 2.1.2, to remove edges with unitary weights. Table 3 shows the number of vertices ($|V|$) and the number of edges ($|E|$) in the co-change graphs, before and after this post-processing task. The table also presents the graph's density (column D).

Table 3. Number of vertices ($|V|$), edges ($|E|$) and co-change graphs' density (D) before and after the post-processing filter

System	Post-Processing					
	Before			After		
	|V|	|E|	D	|V|	|E|	D
Geronimo	2,099	24,815	0.01	695	4,608	0.02
Lucene	2,679	63,075	0.02	1,353	18,784	0.02
JDT Core	1,201	75,006	0.01	823	25,144	0.04

By observing the results in Table 3, two conclusions can be drawn. First, co-change graphs are clearly sparse graphs, having density close to zero in the evaluated systems. This fact reinforces our choice to use Chameleon as the clustering algorithm, since this algorithm is particularly well-suited to handle sparse graphs [18]. Second, most edges in the initial co-change graphs have weight equal to one (more precisely, around 81%, 70%, and 66% of the edges for Geronimo, Lucene, and JTD Core graphs, respectively). Therefore, they connect classes that changed together in just one commit and for this reason were removed by the post-processing task. As result, the number of vertices after post-processing was reduced to 33% (Geronimo), 50% (Lucene), and 68.5% (JDT Core) of their initial value.

3.3 Co-Change Clustering

We executed the Chameleon graph clustering algorithm having as input the co-change graphs created for each system (after applying the pre-processing and post-processing filters).[3] Table 4 shows the value of M that generated the best clusters, according to the clustering selection criteria defined in Section 2.2.1. The table also reports the initial number of co-change clusters generated by Chameleon and the number of clusters after eliminating the small clusters, i.e., clusters with fewer than four classes, as defined by the *MIN_CLUSTER_SZ* threshold. Finally, the table shows the ratio between the final number of clusters and the number of packages in each system (column %NOP).

Table 4. Number of co-change clusters

System	M	# clusters		%NOP
		All	$\|V\| \geq 4$	
Geronimo	108	46	21	0.05
Lucene	68	98	49	0.19
JDT Core	100	35	24	0.32

For example, for the Geronimo system, we achieved the "best clusters" for $M = 108$, i.e., the co-change graph was initially partitioned into 108 clusters, in the first phase of the algorithm. In the second phase (agglomerative clustering), the initial clusters were successively merged, stopping with a configuration of 46 clusters. However, only 21 clusters have four or more classes ($|V| \geq 4$) and the others were discarded, since they represent "small modules", as defined in Section 3.1. We can also observe that the number of clusters is considerably smaller than the number of packages. Basically, this fact is an indication that the maintenance activity in the system is concentrated in few classes.

For the Lucene system, we achieved the best clusters for $M = 68$, since the number of clusters returned in the first phase is M plus the number of connected components.

Table 5 shows standard descriptive statistics measurements regarding the size of the extracted co-change clusters, in terms of number of classes. As we can observe, the extracted clusters have 8.8 ± 4.7 classes, 11.7 ± 7.0 classes, and 14 ± 10.4 classes (average $\pm$ standard deviation) in the Geronimo, Lucene, and JDT Core systems, respectively. Moreover, the biggest cluster has a considerable number of classes: 20 classes (Geronimo), 27 classes (Lucene), and 43 classes (JDT Core).

[3] To execute Chameleon, we relied on the CLUTO clustering package, `http://glaros.dtc.umn.edu/gkhome/cluto/cluto/overview`.

Table 5. Co-change clusters size (in number of classes)

System	Cluster size			
	Min	Max	Avg	Std
Geronimo	4	20	8.8	4.7
Lucene	4	27	11.7	7.0
JDT Core	4	43	14	10.4

Table 6 presents standard descriptive statistics measurements regarding the density of the extracted co-change clusters. The clusters have a density of 0.80 ± 0.24 (Geronimo), 0.68 ± 0.25 (Lucene), and 0.54 ± 0.29 (JDT Core). The median density is 0.90 (Geronimo), 0.71 (Lucene), and 0.49 (JDT Core). Therefore, although co-change graphs are heavily sparse graphs, the results in Table 6 show they have dense subgraphs with a considerable size (at least four classes). Density is a central property in co-change clusters, because it assures that there is a high probability of co-changes between each pair of classes in the cluster. In other words, high-density co-change clusters can be viewed as related program units, at least under evolutionary terms.

Table 6. Co-change clusters density

System	Cluster density				
	Min	Max	Avg	Std	Median
Geronimo	0.31	1.0	0.80	0.24	0.90
Lucene	0.17	1.0	0.68	0.25	0.71
JDT Core	0.18	1.0	0.54	0.29	0.49

Table 7 presents standard descriptive statistics measurements regarding the average weight of the edges in the extracted co-change clusters. For a given co-change cluster, we define this average as the sum of the weights of all edges divided by the number of edges in the cluster. We can observe that the median edges' weight is not high, being slightly greater than two in Geronimo and Lucene, and four in the JDT Core. However, it is important to mention that after applying the preprocessing filters we only considered a small sample of the initial commits to create the co-change graphs (14.3% of the commits in Geronimo, 22.4% of the commits in Lucene, and 20.1% in JDT Core).

Table 7. Average edges' weight

System	Cluster average edges weight				
	Min	Max	Avg	Std	Median
Geronimo	2	5.5	2.4	0.8	2.1
Lucene	2	7.1	2.7	1.0	2.4
JDT Core	2	7.6	4.3	1.5	3.8

4. MODULARITY ANALYSIS

In this section, we investigate the application of co-change clusters to assess the quality of a system's package decomposition. Particularly, we investigate the distribution of the co-change clusters over the package structure. For this purpose, we rely on distribution maps [12], which are typically used to compare two partitions P and Q of the entities from a system S. In our case, the entities are classes, the partition P is the package structure, and Q is composed by the co-change clusters. Moreover, entities (classes) are represented as small squares and the partition P (package structure) groups such squares into large rectangles (packages). In the package structure, we only consider classes that are members of co-change clusters, in order to improve the maps visualization. Finally, partition Q (co-change clusters) is used to color the classes (all classes in a cluster have the same color).

In addition to visualization, distribution maps can be used to quantify the *focus* of a given cluster q in relation to the partition P (package structure), as follows:

$$focus(q, P) = \sum_{p_i \in P} touch(q, p_i) * touch(p_i, q)$$

where

$$touch(p, q) = \frac{|p \cap q|}{|q|}$$

In this definition, $touch(q, p_i)$ is the number of classes of cluster q located in the package p_i divided by the number of classes in p_i that are included in at least a co-change cluster. Similarly, $touch(p_i, q)$ is the number of classes in p_i included in the cluster q divided by the number of classes in q. Focus ranges between 0 and 1, where the value one means that the cluster q dominates the packages that it touches, i.e., it is well-encapsulated in such packages. On the other hand, when co-change clusters crosscut many packages, but touching few classes in each of them, their focus is low. There is also a second metric that measures how *spread* is a cluster q in P, i.e., the number of packages touched by q.

Tables 8 and 9 show the standard descriptive statistics measurements regarding respectively the focus and spread of the co-change clusters. We can observe that the co-change clusters in Geronimo have a higher focus than in Lucene and JDT Core. For example, the median focus in Geronimo is 1.00, against 0.55 and 0.30 in Lucene and JDT Core, respectively. Regarding spread, the values in both systems are similar, on average the spread is 3.50 (Geronimo), 3.35 (Lucene), and 3.83 (JDT Core). Figure 2 shows a scatterplot with the values of focus (horizontal axis) and spread (vertical axis) for each co-change cluster. In Geronimo, we can see that there is a concentration of clusters with high focus. On the other hand, for Lucene, the clusters are much more dispersed along the two axis. Eclipse JDT tends to have lower focus, but also lower spread, even if the maximum spread is the largest of the three systems.

Table 8. Focus

System	Focus				
	Min	Max	Avg	Std	Median
Geronimo	0.50	1.00	0.93	0.12	1.00
Lucene	0.06	1.00	0.57	0.30	0.55
JDT Core	0.07	1.00	0.36	0.26	0.30

Table 9. Spread

System	Spread					
	Min	Max	Avg	Std	Median	Mode
Geronimo	1	8	3.50	2.10	3	1
Lucene	1	8	3.35	1.90	3	3
JDT Core	1	10	3.83	2.60	3	1

In the following sections, we analyze examples of well-encapsulated and crosscutting clusters, using distribution maps,[4] in the Geronimo system (Section 4.1), in the Lucene System (Section 4.2), and the Eclipse JDT (Section 4.3). Section 4.1 emphasizes well-encapsulated clusters, since they are common in Geronimo. On the other hand, Section 4.2 emphasizes crosscutting concerns, which are most common in Lucene. Section 4.3 on Eclipse JDT reports an analysis on both types of clusters.

[4] To extract and visualize distribution maps, we used the Topic Viewer tool [33], available at `https://code.google.com/p/topic-viewer`.

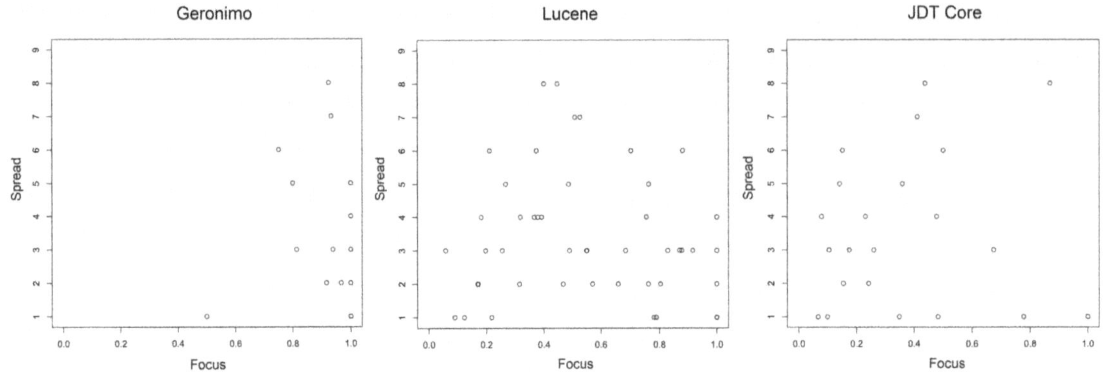

Figure 2. Focus versus Spread

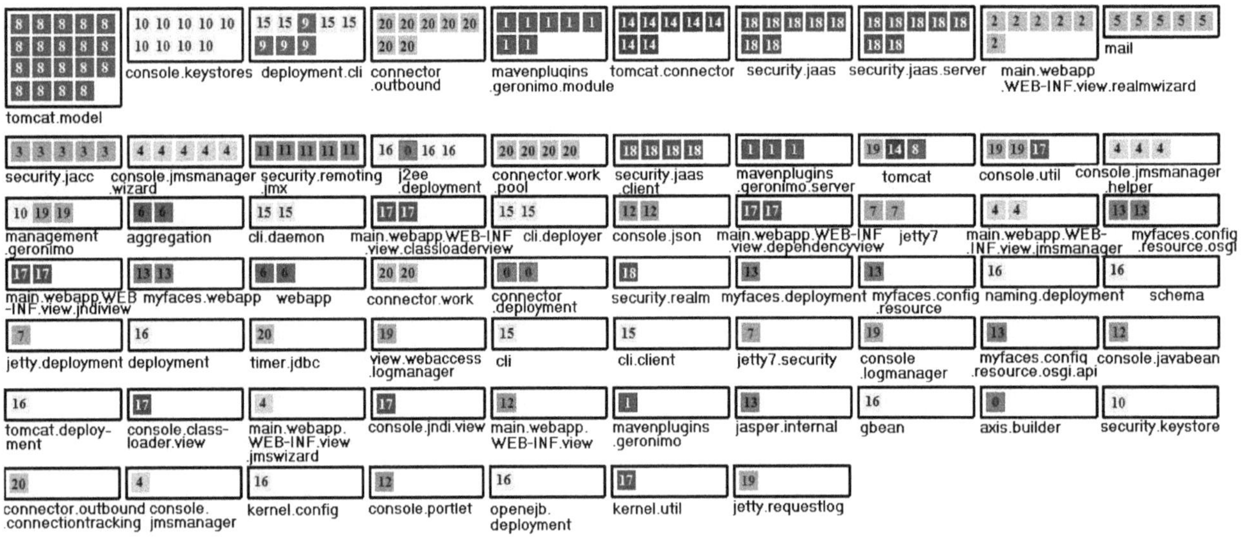

Figure 3. Distribution map for Geronimo

4.1 Distribution Map for Geronimo

Figure 3 shows the distribution map for Geronimo. To improve the visualization, besides background colors, we use a number in each class (small squares) to indicate their respective clusters. The large boxes are the packages and the text below is the package name.

Considering the clusters that are *well-encapsulated* (high focus) in Geronimo, we found three package distribution patterns:

- *Clusters well-encapsulated (focus = 1.0) in a single package (spread = 1).* Four clusters have this behavior. As an example, we have Cluster 2, which dominates the co-change classes in the package `main.webapp.WEBINF.view.realmwizard` (line 1 in the map, column 9). This package implements a wizard to configure or create security domains. Therefore, since it implements a specific functional concern, maintenance is confined in the package. As another example, we have Cluster 5 (package `mail`, line 1 in the map, column 10) and Cluster 11 (package `security.remoting.jmx`, line 1, column 3).
- *Clusters well-encapsulated (focus = 1.0) in more than one package (spread > 1).* We counted eight clusters with this behavior. As an example, we have Cluster 18 (*spread* = *4*), which touches all co-change classes in the following packages: `security.jaas.server`, `security.jaas.client`, `security.jaas`, and `security.realm` (displayed respectively in line 1, columns 7 and 8; line 2, column 6; and line 4, column 6). As suggested by their names, these packages are related to security concerns, implemented using the Java Authentication and Authorization Service (JAAS) framework. Therefore, the packages are conceptually related and their spread should not be regarded as a design problem. In fact, the spread in this case is probably due to a decision to organize the source code in sub-packages.

  As another example, we have Cluster 20 (*spread* = 5), which touches all classes in `connector.outbound`, `connector.work.pool`, `connector.work`, `connector.outbound.connectiontracking`, and `timer.jdbc` (displayed respectively in line 1, column 4; line 2, column 5; line 4, column 4; line 7, column 1; line 5 and column 3). These packages implement EJB connectors for message exchange.
- *Clusters partially encapsulated (focus ≈ 1.0), but touching classes in other packages (spread > 1).*[5] As an example,

[5] These clusters are called octopus, because they have a body centered on a single package and tentacles in other packages [12].

we have Cluster 8 (*focus* = 0.97, *spread* = 2), which dominates the co-change classes in the package `tomcat.model` (line 1 and column 1 in the map), but also touches the class `TomcatServerGBean` from package `tomcat` (line 2, column 8). This class is responsible for configuring the web server used by Geronimo (Tomcat). Therefore, this particular co-change instance suggests an instability in the interface provided by the web server. In theory, Geronimo should only call this interface to configure the web server, but in fact the co-change cluster shows that maintenance in the `model` package sometimes has a ripple effect on this class, or vice-versa.

As another example, we have Cluster 14 (*focus* = 0.92 and *spread* = 2), which dominates the package `tomcat.connector` (line 1 and column 6 in the map) but also touches the class `TomcatServerConfigManager` from package `tomcat` (line 2, column 8). This "tentacle" in a single class from another package suggests again an instability in the configuration interface provided by the underlying web server.

4.2 Distribution Map for Lucene

We selected for analysis clusters that are *crosscutting* (focus $\approx$ 0.0), since they are much more common in Lucene. More specifically, we selected the three clusters in Lucene with the lowest focus and a spread greater than two. Figure 4 shows a fragment of the distribution map for Lucene, containing the following clusters:

- *Cluster 12 (focus = 0.06 and spread = 3)* with co-change classes in the following packages: `index`, `analysis`, and `store`. Since the cluster crosscuts packages that provide very different services (indexing, analysis, and storing), we claim that it reveals a modularization flaw in the package decomposition followed by Lucene. For example, a package like `store` that supports binary `I/O` services should hide its implementation from other packages. However, the existence of recurring maintenance tasks crosscutting `store` shows that the package fails to hide its main design decisions from other packages in the system.
- *Cluster 13 (focus = 0.2 and spread = 3)*, with co-change classes in the following packages: `search`, `search.spans`, and `search.function`. In this case, we claim that crosscutting causes less harm to modularity, because the packages are related to a single service (searching).
- *Cluster 28 (focus = 0.21 and spread = 6)*, with co-change classes in the following packages: `index`, `search`, `search.function`, `index.memory`, `search.highlight`, and `store.instantiated`. These packages are responsible for important services in Lucene, like indexing, searching, and storing. Therefore, as in the case of Cluster 12, the crosscutting behavior of this cluster suggests a modularization flaw in the system.

We also analyzed the maintenance issues associated to the commits responsible for the co-changes in Cluster 28. Particularly, we retrieved 37 maintenance issues related to this cluster. We then manually read and analyzed the short description of each issue, and classified them in three groups: (a) maintenance related to functional concerns in Lucene's domain (like searching, indexing, etc); (b) maintenance related to non-functional concerns (like logging, persistence, exception handling, etc); (c) maintenance related to refactorings. Table 10 shows the number of issues in each category. As can be observed, the crosscutting behavior of Cluster 28 is more due to issues related to functional concerns (59.5%) than to traditional non-functional concerns (8%). Moreover, changes motivated by refactorings (32.5%) are more common than changes in non-functional concerns.

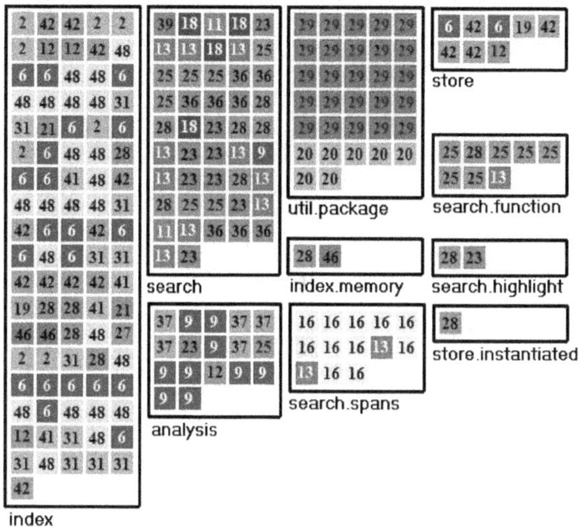

Figure 4. Part of the Distribution map for Lucene

Finally, we detected a distribution pattern in Lucene that represents neither well-encapsulated nor crosscutting clusters, but that might be relevant for analysis:

- *Clusters well-confined in packages (spread = 1).* Although restricted to a single package, these clusters do not dominate the colors in this package. But when considered as a single cluster, they dominate their package. As a concrete example, we have Cluster 20 (*focus = 0.22*) and Cluster 29 (*focus = 0.78*) that are both confined in package `util.packed` (line 1, column 3). Therefore, in this case a refactoring that splits the package in sub-packages can be considered, in order to improve the focus of the respective clusters.

Table 10. Maintenance issues in Cluster 28

Maintenance Type	# issues	% issues
Functional concerns	22	59.50%
Non-functional concerns	3	8.00%
Refactoring	12	32.50%

4.3 Distribution Map for JDT Core

Figure 5 shows the distribution map for JDT Core. We selected three distinct types of clusters for analysis: a *crosscutting* cluster (focus $\approx$ 0.0 and spread >= 3), a clusters confined in a single package with (spread = 1), and a cluster with high spread.

- *Clusters with crosscutting behavior.* We have Cluster 4 (focus = 0.08 and spread = 4) with co-change classes in the following packages: `core.dom`, `internal.core`, `internal.compiler.lookup`, and `internal.core.util`. The `core.util` package provides a set of tools and utilities for manipulating `.class` files and Java model elements. Since the cluster crosscuts packages providing very different services (document structure, files and elements manipulation, population of the model, compiler infrastructure), we claim that it reveals a modularization flaw in the system.
- *Clusters well-confined in packages (spread = 1).* We have Cluster 0 (*focus = 0.48*), Cluster 5 (*focus = 0.35*), and Cluster 6 (*focus = 0.07*) in the `core.dom` package (line 1, column 1).

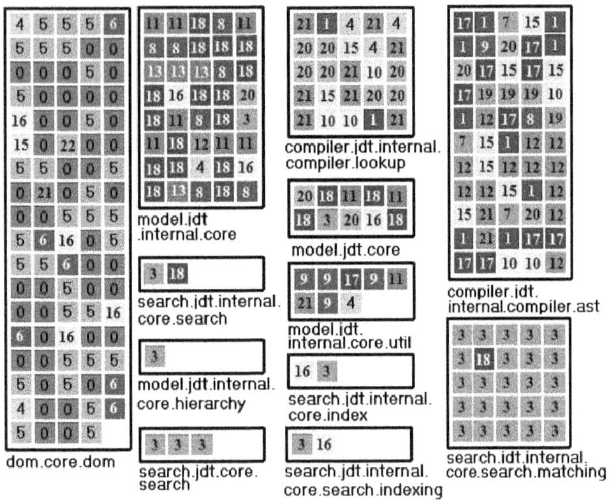

Figure 5. Part of the Distribution map for JDT Core

- *Clusters partially encapsulated (focus $\approx$ 1.0), but touching classes in other packages (spread > 1).* We have Cluster 3 (focus = 0.87 and spread = 8), which dominates the co-change classes in the packages `search.jdt.internal.core.search.matching` and `search.jdt.core.search`. These packages provide support for searching the workspace for Java elements matching a particular description. Their spread should not be regarded as a design problem, because the packages are related to a single service (searching). However, the cluster also touches classes in other packages. For example, the class `core.index.Index` maps document names to their referenced words in various categories.

5. SEMANTIC SIMILARITY ANALYSIS

The previous section has shown that the package modular structure of Geronimo has more adherence to co-change clusters than Lucene's and JDT Core's. We also observed that patterns followed by the relation clusters vs. packages can help to assess the modularity of systems. This section aims at evaluating the semantic similarity of the issues that are related to a specific cluster in order to improve our understanding of the clusters' meaning. We consider that if the issues related to a cluster have high semantic similarity, then the classes within that cluster are also semantically related and the cluster is semantically cohesive. We assume that an issue is related to a cluster if the change set of the issue contains at least a pair of classes from that cluster, not necessarily linked with an edge. In our strategy to evaluate the similarity of the issues related to a cluster, we consider each short description of a issue as a document and the collection of documents is obtained from the collection of issues related to a cluster. We will use Latent Semantic Analysis - LSA [11] to evaluate the similarity among the collection of documents related to a cluster because it is a well-known method used in other studies concerning similarity among issues and other software artifacts [28, 29].

5.1 Pre-processing Issue Description

When analyzing text documents with Information Retrieval techniques, an adequate pre-processing of the text is important to achieve good results. We determined a domain vocabulary of terms based on words found in commits of the target system. The first step is stemming the terms. Next, the stop-words were removed. The final step produces a term-document matrix, where the cells have value 1 if the term occurs in the document and 0 otherwise. This decision was taken after some qualitative experimentation, in which we observed that different weighting mechanisms based on the frequency of terms, such as td-idf [23], did not improved the quality of the similarity matrix.

5.2 Latent Semantic Analysis

The LSA algorithm is applied to the binary term-document matrix and produces another similarity matrix among the documents (issues) with values ranging from -1 (no similarity) to 1 (maximum similarity). The LSA matrix should have high values to denote a collection of issues that are all related among them. However, not all pairs of issues have the same similarity level, so it is necessary to analyze the degree of similarity between the issues to evaluate the overall similarity within a cluster. We used heat maps to visualize the similarity between issues that are related to a cluster. Figures 6 shows examples of similarity within specific clusters. We show for each system the two best clusters in terms of similarity to the left, and the two clusters with several pairs of issues with low similarity to the right. The white cells represent that the issues do not have any word in common, blue cells represent very low similarity, and yellow cells denote the maximum similarity between the issues.

We can observe that even for the cluster with more blue cells, there is still a dominance of higher similarity cells. The white cells in JDT's clusters suggest that there are issues with no similarity between the others in their respective cluster.

5.3 Scoring clusters

We propose the following metric to evaluate the overall similarity of a cluster c:

$$similarity\ score(c) = \frac{\sum\limits_{\substack{0<i,j<n-1 \\ j<i}} similar(i,j)}{(\frac{n^2}{2} - n)}$$

where

$$similar(i,j) = \begin{cases} 0, & \text{if } LSA\_Cosine(i,j) < SIM\_THRS \\ 1, & \text{if } LSA\_Cosine(i,j) \geq SIM\_THRS \end{cases}$$

n = number of issues related to cluster c
$SIM\_THRS = 0.4$

The meaning of the *similarity score* of a cluster is defined upon the percentage of similar pair of issues related to that cluster. So, a cluster with score = 0.5, means that 50% of pairs of issues related to that cluster are similar to each other.

In this work, we had to define a threshold to evaluate if two issues are similar or not. We consider the semantic similarity between two issue reports, i and j, as the cosine between the vectors corresponding to i and j in the semantic space created by LSA. After experimental testing, we observed that pairs of issues (i, j) that had $LSA\_Cosine(i,j) \geq 0.4$ had a meaningful degree of similarity. Nonetheless, we agree that this fixed threshold cannot be free of imprecision. Similar to our study, Poshyvanyk and Marcus [29] used LSA to analyze the coherence of the user comments in bug reports. The system's developers classified as high/very high similar, the comments with average similarity greater than 0.33, so our more conservative approach seems to be quite adequate.

Moreover, because our goal is to have an overall evaluation of the whole collection of co-change clusters, some imprecision in the characterization of similarity between two issues would not affect significantly our analysis of the distribution of clusters' scores. Figures 7 shows the distribution of score values for Geronimo's, Lucene's, and JDT's clusters.

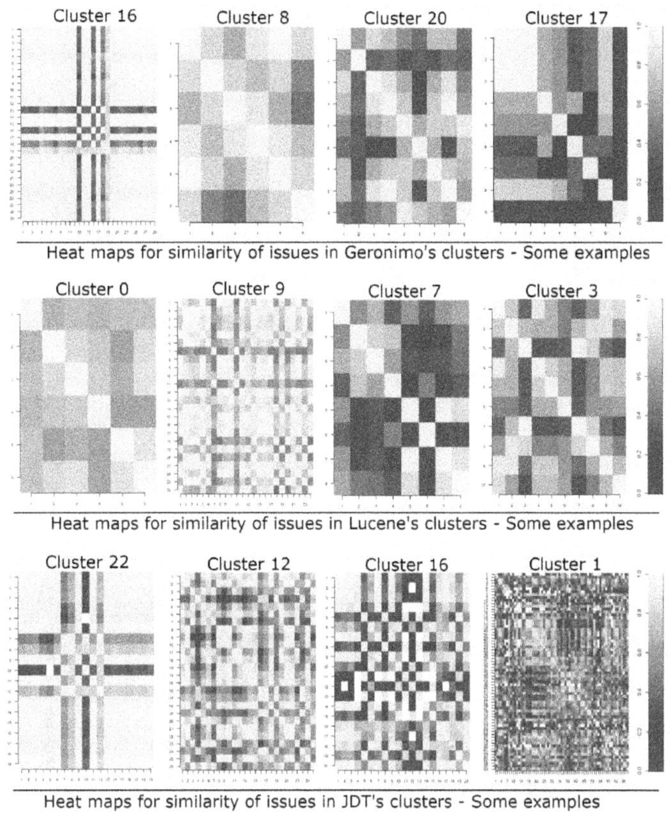

Figure 6. Examples of heat maps for similarity of issues

We can observe that the systems' clusters follow a similar pattern of scoring, with 100% (for Lucene and JDT) and more than 90% (for Geronimo) of clusters having more than half pairs of issues similar to each other.

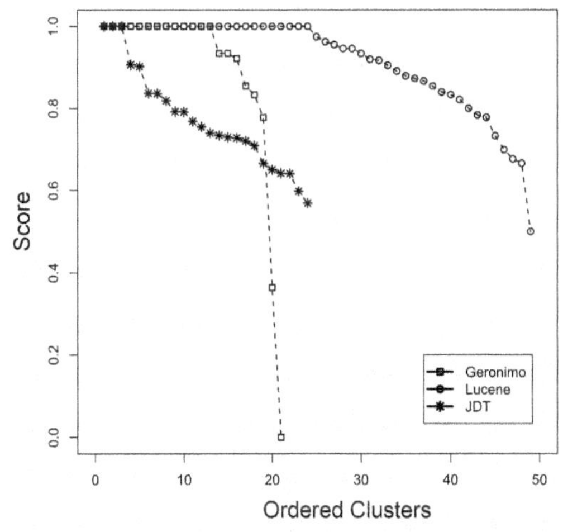

Figure 7. Distribution of the clusters' score

5.4 Correlating Similarity, Focus, and Spread

Another analysis that we carried out with clusters' scores was to evaluate the degree of correlation between the score, focus and spread. Table 11 shows the results obtained by applying the Spearman correlation test. For Geronimo, we observed a strong negative correlation between spread and score. In other words, the higher is the number of similar issues in a cluster, the higher is the capacity of the cluster to encompass a whole package in Geronimo. Interestingly, Lucene does not present the same behavior as Geronimo. We observe a weak correlation between focus and score, but we encounter no significant correlation between spread and score. In the case of Lucene, the higher is the number of similar issues in a cluster, the lower is the number of packages touched by the cluster. In the case of Eclipse JDT Core, there is no significant correlation between focus and score. Although, there is a moderate negative correlation between spread and score, it is only significant at p-value 0.074. Considering that the clusters of the analyzed systems followed a similar pattern of similarity, this result suggests that the reasonable similarity between co-change induces different properties in the clusters, either in spread or in focus.

Table 11. Correlation between score, focus and spread of clusters for Geronimo, Lucene, and JDT Core

Correlation Coefficient *p-value*	**Score Geronimo**	**Score Lucene**	**Score JDT**
Focus	0.264	0.308	−0.015
	0.131	0.016	0.473
Spread	−0.720	−0.178	−0.304
	1.71×10^{-4}	0.111	0.074

6. DISCUSSION

6.1 Practical Implications

Software architects can rely on the approach proposed in this paper to assess modularity under an evolutionary dimension. More specifically, we claim that our approach helps to reveal the following patterns of co-change behavior:

- When the package structure is adherent to the cluster structure, as in Geronimo's clusters (43% well encapsulated), then localized co-changes are likely to occur.
- When there is not a clear adherence between co-change clusters and packages, a restructuring of the package decomposition may be necessary to improve modularity. Particularly, there are two patterns of clusters that may suggest modularity flaws. The first pattern denotes clusters with crosscutting behavior (focus ≈ 0 and high spread). For example, in Lucene and JDT Core we detected 12 and 10 clusters related to this pattern, respectively. The second pattern is the octopus cluster that suggest a possible ripple effect during maintenance tasks. In Geronimo and Lucene, we detected four and five clusters related to this pattern, respectively.

On the other hand, modular designs usually demand well-trained, skilled, and experienced software architects. Nonetheless, we have no evidence that the proposed co-change clusters may fully replace traditional modular decompositions. Indeed, a first obstacle to this proposal is the fact that co-change clusters do not cover the whole population of classes in a system. On the other hand, we believe that they can be used as an alternative modular view during program comprehension tasks. For example, they may provide a better context during maintenance tasks (similar for example to the task context automatically inferred by tools like Mylyn [20]).

6.2 Clustering vs Association Rules Mining

Our approach is centered on the Chameleon hierarchical clustering algorithm, since this algorithm was designed to handle sparse graphs [18]. In our case studies, for example, the co-change graphs have densities ranging from 2% (Geronimo and Lucene) to 4% (Eclipse JDT Core). Particularly, in traditional clustering algorithms, like K-Means [22], the mapping of data items to clusters is a total function, i.e., each data item is allocated to a specific cluster. Likewise K-Means, Chameleon tries to cluster all data items (vertices). However, when some vertices do not share any edge with the rest of the vertices, the number of clustered vertices is fewer than the total number of initial vertices.

An alternative to retrieve co-change relations is to rely on association rules mining [2]. In the context of evolutionary coupling, an association rule $C_{ant} \Rightarrow C_{cons}$ express that commit transactions changing the classes C_{ant} (antecedent term) also change C_{cons} classes (consequent term), with a given probability.

However, hundreds of thousands of association rules can be easily retrieved from version histories. For example, we executed the Apriori algorithm [2] to retrieve association rules for the Lucene system. By defining a minimum support threshold of four transactions, a minimum confidence of 50%, and limiting the size of the rules to 10 classes, we mined 976,572 association rules, with an average size of 8.14 classes. We repeated this experiment with the confidence threshold of 90%. In this case, we mined 831,795 association rules, with an average size of 8.23 classes. This explosion in the number of rules is an important limitation for using association rules to assess modularity, which ultimately is a task that requires careful judgment and analysis by software developers and maintainers.

6.3 Threats to Validity

In this section, we discuss possible threats to validity, following the usual classification in threats to internal, external, and construct validity:

Threats to External Validity: There are some threats that limit our ability to generalize our findings. The use of Geronimo, Lucene, and JDT Core may not be representative to capture co-change patterns present in other systems. However, it is important to note that we do not aim to propose general co-change patterns, but instead we just claim that the patterns founded in the target systems show the feasibility of using co-change clusters to evaluate modularity under a new dimension.

Threats to Construct Validity: A possible design threat to construct validity is that developers might not adequately link commit with issues, as pointed out by Herzing and Zeller [15]. Moreover, we also found a high number of commits not associated to maintenance issues. Thus, our results are subjected to missing and to incorrect links between commits and issues. However, we claim at least that we followed the approach commonly used in other studies that map issues to commits [8–10, 40]. We also filtered out situations like commits associated to multiple maintenance issues and highly scattered commits. Another possible construction threat concerns the time frame used to collect the issues. We considered activity in a period of approximately ten years, which is certainly a large time frame. However, we did not evaluate how the co-change clusters evolved during this time frame or whether the systems' architecture substantially changed.

Finally, our approach only handles co-changes related to source code artifacts (.java files). However, the systems we evaluated have other types of artifacts, like XML configuration files. Geronimo for example has 177 Javascript files, 1004 XML configuration files, 19 configuration files, and 105 image files. Therefore, it is possible that we missed some co-change relations among non-Java based artifacts or between non-Java and Java-based artifacts. On the other hand, considering only source code artifacts makes possible the projection of co-change clusters to distribution maps, using the package structure as the main partition in the maps.

Threats to Internal Validity: Our approach relies on filters to select the commits used by the co-change graphs and clusters. Those filters are based on thresholds that could be defined differently, despite of our careful pre-experimentation. We also calibrated the semantic similarity analysis with parameters that define the dimensionality reduction in the case of LSA, and with a threshold in the case of the LSA_Cosine coefficient that defines when a pair of issues is similar. Although this calibration has some degree of uncertainty, it was not proposed to get better results favoring one system instead of the other. We defined the parameters and constants so that coherent results were achieved in all systems. Moreover, we observed that variations in the parameters' values would affect the results for all systems in a similar way.

7. RELATED WORK

In this section, we discuss work related to our approach. The discussion is organized in three sections: concern mapping, co-change mining, and aspect mining.

7.1 Concern Mapping

Several approaches have been proposed to help developers and maintainers to manage concerns and features. For example, concern graphs model the subset of a software system associated with a specific concern [30, 31]. The main purpose is to provide developers with an abstract view of the program fragments related to a concern. FEAT is a tool that supports the concern graph approach by enabling developers to build concern graphs interactively, as result of program investigation tasks. Aspect Browser [14] and JQuery [16] are other tools that rely on lexical or logic queries to find and document code fragments related to a certain concern. ConcernMapper [32] is an Eclipse Plug-in to organize and view concerns using an hierarchical structure similar to the package structure. However, in such approaches, the concern model is created manually or based on explicit input information provided by developers. Moreover, the relations between concerns are typically only syntactical and structural. On the other hand, in the approach proposed in this paper, the elements and relationships are obtained by mining the version history.

7.2 Co-change Mining

Zimmermann et al. proposed an approach that uses association rule mining on version histories to suggest possible future changes [39]. Their approach differs from ours because they rely on association rules to recommend further changes (e.g., if class `A` usually co-changes with `B`, and a commit only changes `A`, a warning is given suggesting to check whether `B` should not be changed too). On the other hand, we use co-change graphs to retrieve clusters semantically related to a target system's concern. A co-change graph is created from the selection of commits linked to their respective maintenance issues. Furthermore, our goal is not to recommend future changes, but to assess modularity, using distribution maps to compare and contrast co-change clusters with the system's packages.

Beyer and Noack introduced the concept of co-change graphs and proposed a visualization of such graphs to reveal clusters of frequently co-changed artifacts [5]. Their approach clusters all co-change artifacts (code, configuration scripts, documentation, etc), representing files as co-change graphs' vertices. These vertices are displayed as circles and their area is proportional to the frequency that the file was changed. The vertex color represents its respective cluster. However, they do not define pre-processing and post-processing filters. In contrast, we prune many classes during the pre-processing and post-processing phases and after clustering the co-change graphs. Finally, our central goal is not directly related with improving the visualization of co-change clusters, but on using them to assess modularity.

Oliva et al. mined version histories to extract logical dependencies between software artifacts to identify their origins [26]. They conducted a manual investigation of the origins of logical dependencies by reading revision comments and analyzing code diffs. Beck and Diehl combined evolutionary dependencies with syntactic dependencies to retrieve the modular structure of a system [4]. However, they clustered all classes in a system, since their original goal was to compare both approaches to software clustering. On the other hand, since our goal is to assess modularity, we consider only high-density co-change clusters.

Huzefa et al. presented an approach that combines conceptual and evolutionary couplings for impact analysis in source code [17], using information retrieval and version history mining techniques. Gethers et al. proposed an impact analysis that adapts to the specific maintenance scenario using information retrieval, historical data mining, and dynamic analysis techniques [13]. However, they did not use maintenance issues reports to discard noisy commits.

A recent study by Negara et al. revealed that the use of data from version history presents many threats when investigating source code properties [25]. For example, developers usually fix failing tests by changing the test themselves, commit tasks without testing, commit the same code fragment multiple times (in different commits), or take days to commit changes containing several types of tasks. In this work, we proposed five pre-processing tasks and one post-processing task to tackle some of such threats.

7.3 Aspect Mining

Breu and Zimmermann proposed an approach (HAM) based on version history to detect cross-cutting concerns in an object-oriented program to guide its migration to an aspect-oriented program [6]. They defined the notion of transaction, which is the set of methods inserted by the developer to complete a single development task. They also considered that method calls inserted in eight or more locations (method bodies) define aspect candidates. One important difference from their work and ours is that they consider not only methods that were changed together, but also those changes that were the same. Moreover, they rely on a fine-grained notion of change that is interested in finding methods calls to define aspect candidates.

Adams et al. proposed a mining technique (COMMIT) to identify concerns from functions, variables, types, and macros that were changed together [1]. Similarly to HAM, COMMIT is based on the idea that similar calls and references that are added or removed into different parts of the program are candidates to refer to the same concern. This information produces several seed graphs which are concern candidates because nodes in the graph represent program entities to which calls or references have been co-added or co-removed. Their approach differs from ours because they generate independent seed graphs, while we are centered on a unique graph.

8. CONCLUDING REMARKS

In this work, we proposed a method to extract an alternative view to the package decomposition based on co-change clusters. We applied our method to three real software systems, Geronimo, Lucene, and JDT Core, that have approximately ten years of committed changes. Our results show that meaningful co-change clusters can be extracted using the information available in version control systems. Although co-change graphs extracted from repositories are sparse, the co-change clusters were dense and have high internal similarity concerning co-changes and semantic similarity concerning their originating issues. We have shown that co-change clusters and their associated metrics were useful to assess the hierarchical modular decomposition of the target systems. Even if in some cases co-change clusters may be used to restructure the original package decomposition, we suggest that they can also be use as an alternative view during maintenance tasks to improve the developer's understanding of the change impact.

We still need to investigate the reasons that induce co-change clusters and to identify the eventual patterns that produce those clusters, which would contribute in early modularization decisions. We plan to investigate and to compare our approach with other clustering algorithms for sparse graphs, like the approach proposed by Beyer et al. [5]. We also plan to consider co-changes at a finer-granularity level, more specifically among methods, and also including non-source code artifacts, like XML configuration files. Finally, we plan to investigate whether co-change clusters can be used as an alternative to the Package Explorer, supporting a mechanism for the virtual separation of concerns, inspired on the CIDE tool [19]. However, CIDE supports the virtual separation of features whose implementation physically crosscuts many classes. On the other hand, our goal is to support the virtual separation of features with a strong temporal relationship, in terms of co-changes.

Acknowledgments

This work was partially supported by FAPEMIG (grants CEX-APQ-2086-11, PPM-00388-13) and CNPq (grants 475519/2012-4, 304897/2011-6).

References

[1] B. Adams, Z. M. Jiang, and A. E. Hassan. Identifying crosscutting concerns using historical code changes. In *32nd International Conference on Software Engineering*, pages 305–314. ACM, 2010.

[2] R. Agrawal and R. Srikant. Fast algorithms for mining association rules in large databases. In *20th International Conference on Very Large Data Bases (VLDB)*, pages 487–499, 1994.

[3] C. Y. Baldwin and K. B. Clark. *Design Rules: The Power of Modularity*. MIT Press, 2003.

[4] F. Beck and S. Diehl. Evaluating the impact of software evolution on software clustering. In *17th Working Conference on Reverse Engineering (WCRE)*, pages 99–108, 2010.

[5] D. Beyer and A. Noack. Clustering software artifacts based on frequent common changes. In *13th International Workshop on Program Comprehension (IWPC)*, pages 259–268, 2005.

[6] S. Breu and T. Zimmermann. Mining aspects from version history. In *21st Automated Software Engineering Conference (ASE)*, pages 221–230, 2006.

[7] S. Chidamber and C. Kemerer. Towards a metrics suite for object oriented design. In *6th Object-oriented programming systems, languages, and applications Conference (OOPSLA)*, pages 197–211, 1991.

[8] C. Couto, C. Silva, M. T. Valente, R. Bigonha, and N. Anquetil. Uncovering causal relationships between software metrics and bugs. In *16th European Conference on Software Maintenance and Reengineering (CSMR)*, pages 223–232, 2012.

[9] C. Couto, P. Pires, M. T. Valente, R. Bigonha, and N. Anquetil. Predicting software defects with causality tests. *Journal of Systems and Software*, pages 1–38, 2014.

[10] M. D'Ambros, M. Lanza, and R. Robbes. An extensive comparison of bug prediction approaches. In *7th Working Conference on Mining Software Repositories (MSR)*, pages 31–41, 2010.

[11] S. Deerwester, S. T. Dumais, G. W. Furnas, T. K. Landauer, and R. Harshman. Indexing by latent semantic analysis. *Journal of the American Society for Information Science,*, 41:391–407, 1990.

[12] S. Ducasse, T. Gîrba, and A. Kuhn. Distribution map. In *22nd IEEE International Conference on Software Maintenance (ICSM)*, pages 203–212, 2006.

[13] M. Gethers, H. Kagdi, B. Dit, and D. Poshyvanyk. An adaptive approach to impact analysis from change requests to source code. In *26th Automated Software Engineering Conference (ASE)*, pages 540–543, 2011.

[14] W. G. Griswold, J. J. Yuan, and Y. Kato. Exploiting the map metaphor in a tool for software evolution. In *23rd International Conference on Software Engineering (ICSE)*, pages 265–274, 2001.

[15] K. Herzing and A. Zeller. The impact of tangled code changes. In *10th Working Conference on Mining Software Repositories (MSR)*, pages 121–130, 2013.

[16] D. Janzen and K. D. Volder. Navigating and querying code without getting lost. In *2nd International Conference on Aspect-oriented Software Development (AOSD)*, pages 178–187, 2003.

[17] H. Kagdi, M. Gethers, and D. Poshyvanyk. Integrating conceptual and logical couplings for change impact analysis in software. *Empirical Software Engineering (EMSE)*, 2013.

[18] G. Karypis, E.-H. S. Han, and V. Kumar. Chameleon: hierarchical clustering using dynamic modeling. *Computer*, 32(8):68–75, 1999.

[19] C. Kästner, S. Apel, and M. Kuhlemann. Granularity in software product lines. In *30th International Conference on Software Engineering (ICSE)*, pages 311–320, 2008.

[20] M. Kersten and G. C. Murphy. Using task context to improve programmer productivity. In *14th International Symposium on Foundations of Software Engineering (FSE)*, pages 1–11, 2006.

[21] G. Kiczales, J. Lamping, A. Mendhekar, C. Maeda, C. Lopes, J.-M. Loingtier, and J. Irwin. Aspect-oriented programming. In *11th European Conference on Object-Oriented Programming (ECOOP)*, volume 1241 of *LNCS*, pages 220–242. Springer Verlag, 1997.

[22] J. B. MacQueen. Some methods for classification and analysis of multivariate observations. In *5th Berkeley Symposium on Mathematical Statistics and Probability*, pages 281–297, 1967.

[23] C. D. Manning, P. Raghavan, and H. Schtze. *Introduction to Information Retrieval*. Cambridge University Press, 2008.

[24] B. Meyer. *Object-Oriented Software Construction*. Prentice-Hall, 2000.

[25] S. Negara, M. Vakilian, N. Chen, R. E. Johnson, and D. Dig. Is it dangerous to use version control histories to study source code evolution? In *26th European conference on Object-Oriented Programming (ECOOP)*, pages 79–103, 2012.

[26] G. A. Oliva, F. W. Santana, M. A. Gerosa, and C. R. B. de Souza. Towards a classification of logical dependencies origins: a case study. In *12th International Workshop on Principles of Software Evolution and the 7th annual ERCIM Workshop on Software Evolution (EVOL/IWPSE)*, pages 31–40, 2011.

[27] D. L. Parnas. On the criteria to be used in decomposing systems into modules. *Communications of the ACM*, 15(12):1053–1058, 1972.

[28] D. Poshyvanyk and A. Marcus. Using information retrieval to support design of incremental change of software. In *22th IEEE/ACM International Conference on Automated Software Engineering (ASE)*, pages 563–566, 2007.

[29] D. Poshyvanyk and A. Marcus. Measuring the semantic similarity of comments in bug reports. In *1st International ICPC2008 Workshop on Semantic Technologies in System Maintenance (STSM)*, pages 265–280, 2008.

[30] M. P. Robillard and G. C. Murphy. Concern graphs: finding and describing concerns using structural program dependencies. In *24th International Conference on Software Engineering (ICSE)*, pages 406–416, 2002.

[31] M. P. Robillard and G. C. Murphy. Representing concerns in source code. *ACM Transactions on Software Engineering and Methodology*, 16(1):1–38, 2007.

[32] M. P. Robillard and F. Weigand-Warr. Concernmapper: simple view-based separation of scattered concerns. In *OOPSLA workshop on Eclipse technology eXchange*, eclipse '05, pages 65–69, 2005.

[33] G. Santos, M. T. Valente, and N. Anquetil. Remodularization analysis using semantic clustering. In *1st CSMR-WCRE Software Evolution Week*, pages 224–233, 2014.

[34] J. Śliwerski, T. Zimmermann, and A. Zeller. When do changes induce fixes? In *2nd Working Conference on Mining Software Repositories (MSR)*, pages 1–5, 2005.

[35] W. P. Stevens, G. J. Myers, and L. L. Constantine. Structured design. *IBM Systems Journal*, 13(2):115–139, June 1974.

[36] E. Tempero, C. Anslow, J. Dietrich, T. Han, J. Li, M. Lumpe, H. Melton, and J. Noble. Qualitas corpus: A curated collection of Java code for empirical studies. In *Asia Pacific Software Engineering Conference (APSEC)*, pages 336–345, 2010.

[37] R. Terra, L. F. Miranda, M. T. Valente, and R. S. Bigonha. Qualitas.class corpus: A compiled version of the qualitas corpus. *Software Engineering Notes*, pages 1–4, 2013.

[38] R. J. Walker, S. Rawal, and J. Sillito. Do crosscutting concerns cause modularity problems? In *20th International Symposium on the Foundations of Software Engineering (FSE)*, pages 1–11, 2012.

[39] T. Zimmermann, P. Weissgerber, S. Diehl, and A. Zeller. Mining version histories to guide software changes. *IEEE Transactions on Software Engineering*, 31(6):429–445, 2005.

[40] T. Zimmermann, R. Premraj, and A. Zeller. Predicting defects for Eclipse. In *3rd International Workshop on Predictor Models in Software Engineering*, page 9, 2007.

Blending and Reusing Rules for Architectural Degradation Prevention

Alessandro Gurgel, Isela Macia, Alessandro Garcia, Arndt von Staa

OPUS Group, Informatics Department
Pontificial Catholic University of Rio de Janeiro, RJ, Brazil
{agurgel, ibertran, afgarcia, arndt}@inf.puc-rio.br

Mira Mezini, Michael Eichberg, Ralf Mitschke

Technische Universität Darmstadt
Darmstadt, Germany
{mezini,eichberg, mitschke}@ informatik.tu-darmstadt.de

Abstract

As software systems are maintained, their architecture often degrades through the processes of architectural drift and erosion. These processes are often intertwined and the same modules in the code become the locus of both drift and erosion symptoms. Thus, architects should elaborate architecture rules for detecting occurrences of both degradation symptoms. While the specification of such rules is time-consuming, they are similar across software projects adhering to similar architecture decompositions. Unfortunately, existing anti-degradation techniques are limited as they focus only on detecting either drift or erosion symptoms. They also do not support the reuse of recurring anti-degradation rules. In this context, the contribution of this paper is twofold. First, it presents **TamDera**, a domain-specific language for: (i) specifying rule-based strategies to detect both erosion and drift symptoms, and (ii) promoting the hierarchical and compositional reuse of design rules across multiple projects. The language was designed with usual concepts from programming languages in mind such as, inheritance and modularization. Second, we evaluated to what extent developers would benefit from the definition and reuse of hybrid rules. Our study involved 21 versions pertaining to 5 software projects, and more than 600 rules. On average 45% of classes that had drift symptoms in first versions presented inter-related erosion problems in latter versions or vice-versa. Also, up to 72% of all the **TamDera** rules in a project are from a predefined library of reusable rules. They were responsible for detecting on average of 73% of the inter-related degradation symptoms across the projects.

Categories and Subject Descriptors D.2.11 [**Software Architectures**]: languages

Keywords

architectural degradation; design rules, reuse

1. INTRODUCTION

Architectural degradation is a long-standing problem in software engineering. The architecture of software systems is well-known to increasingly degrade through the maintenance and evolution of the source code [7][14][16][28][37]. Hochstein and Lindvall [14] introduced the term architectural degradation to refer to this continuous quality decline. Symptoms of architectural degradation arise through the processes of architectural *erosion* and *drift* [14][28]. Erosion occurs when constraints governing the dependencies between architecture components are violated [28]. Drift symptoms imply the violation of intra-component constraints [28].

In spite of their differences, the erosion and drift processes are often intertwined [14][17]. Violations of component constraints may foster the later introduction of interaction violations or vice-versa, thus, the same or related modules in a program become the locus of both drift and erosion symptoms. The detection of a specific drift symptom may help to reveal erosion symptoms or vice-versa. If any of them remains undetected, it may provoke the emergence of the other one over the system's history [14][18][28]. Hence, the longevity of software projects largely depends on the early detection and repair of architectural degradation problems. Several techniques have been devoted to support architectural degradation detection [1][7][24][27][35][37]. However, there are two main problems with the current state of the art.

First, existing approaches promote the exclusive detection of either erosion or drift symptoms. The detection of either erosion or drift symptoms may not prevent the increasing decay of the software architecture [14][28]. For instance, the removal of the former symptoms may not imply the amelioration of the latter. On the contrary, the strict focus on erosion detection may imply that architects perceive severe drift symptoms too late, when it is hard or costly to address them. The converse is also true. Given the simultaneous occurrence of erosion and drift symptoms [14][18], architects should be able to elaborate hybrid strategies for detecting both forms of degradation using a unified set of abstractions.

Second, to the best of our knowledge, existing approaches only support the specification and checking of rules for particular systems and do not provide any mechanism to reuse them. As a consequence, the specification of such architectural rules becomes a repetitive task, as rules are often similar across multiple projects from the same domain or the same company. In addition, there is recent evidence, gathered from industry [41], presenting convincing results for reusing of anti-drift rules in 7 systems from a same domain. Ideally, architects should be able to reuse anti-drift and anti-erosion rules across projects adhering to similar architecture decompositions. This paper addresses these two problems by proposing **TamDera**[1], a new Domain-Specific Language (DSL), for specifying rules to detect architectural degradation (Section 4).

[1] **TamDera** stands for "Taming Drift and Erosion in Architecture".

MODULARITY'14, April 22–26, 2014, Lugano, Switzerland.

ACM 978-1-4503-2772-5/14/04...$15.00.

The proposed language has two distinguishing features: (i) support for specifying and blending rules for architectural erosion and drift detection in a unified way, and (ii) support for hierarchical and compositional reuse of such rules. It applies usual concepts of programming languages such as inheritance to enable comprehensibility, reusability and maintenance of architectural specifications. For instance, **TamDera** allows architects to define abstract anti-degradation rules that, by means of inheritance, are later specialized in concrete projects. The language was designed to support the detection of architectural degradations symptoms in the source code. **TamDera** allows to define architectural abstractions and mapped them to modules in the source code. The detection relies on static analysis to extract structural dependencies of implementation modules. This facilitates the detection of architectural degradation symptoms during the software build (Section 4.4). A tool implementation to support the language usage and rule enforcement is presented in this paper (Section 4.4).

As a second contribution of this paper, we evaluate the usefulness of supporting blending and reuse of architectural rules with **TamDera**. The study involves 21 releases of 5 projects, and more than 600 anti-degradation rules (Section 5). The findings revealed that developers could benefit from the **TamDera** approach. First, our evaluation provided evidence, observed in multiple projects, on the usefulness of using **TamDera** to detect the co-occurrence of erosion and drift symptoms. The results revealed that the simultaneous occurrence of drift and erosion symptoms – as detected by hybrid **TamDera** rules – in the same code module along the project histories was frequent. On average, 45% of the classes that had drift symptoms in early versions presented erosion problems in later versions and vice-versa. **TamDera** facilitated the early detection of these symptoms by providing a unified set of abstractions for architectural erosion and drift detection. Second, our analysis pointed out several cases where the exclusive detection and removal of a particular symptom was not sufficient to prevent architectural degradation. For instance, we observed that by exclusively detecting erosion symptoms developers would neglect severe drift symptoms in later versions or vice-versa. Finally, we observed that: (i) up to 72% of all the rules defined in a particular project could be reused from a source of reusable **TamDera** rules, and (ii) the reused rules were responsible for detecting 73% of the degradation symptoms on average in each project. A summary of other concluding remarks are presented in Section 7.

2. Background

This section introduces terminology associated with architectural degradation. It also illustrates how symptoms of architectural erosion and drift co-occur through concrete scenarios. These example scenarios will subsequently be used throughout the paper.

2.1 Architectural Degradation Symptoms

Software architecture is concerned with the selection of architecture components and their dependencies as well as with constraints on both of them [28]. *Components* are architectural entities that encapsulate a subset of the system's functionalities [34]. A component of the architecture description is realized by one or more modules in the implementation. The term *module* is used to represent code elements, such as a package, an (implementation-level) interface or a class, which contribute to the implementation of a coherent unit of functionality. In certain cases, inner elements of a module can even contribute to the implementation of different architectural components [34]. *Inner module elements* refer either to methods or fields of a class, or method declarations of an implementation-level interface.

Erosion occurs whenever an implementation decision violates one or more component dependency constraints in the specified architecture. In other words, an erosion symptom is the violation of a constraint at the level of a component dependency. A simple example is an unintended dependency established between two components. *Drift* occurs whenever an implementation decision leads to violations of component constraints in the specified architecture. Typical examples of component constraints are related to modularity principles, such as "narrow component interface" or "single responsibility principle"[28].

The processes of architectural erosion and drift, as well as their relationship, are illustrated below using a motivating example. From hereon, architectural degradation, architectural drift and architectural erosion are also referred to simply as degradation, drift and erosion.

Example of erosion. Figure 1 exemplifies an erosion symptom in the MobileMedia system [8]. This system realizes the architecture pattern Model-View-Controller (MVC)[4]. Each component is realized as a set of modules (classes) in the source code (only a few of them are shown in the figure). The erosion problem concerns an architecture constraint governing the exception handling policy: exceptions are incorrectly propagated through module interfaces across system components. The class `BaseController` defined in the *Controller* component e.g., invokes the *Data* services provided by `AlbumData` and ends up handling exceptions (e.g. `PersistenceException`) thrown by `AlbumData`, which should have been handled within the *Model* component. As a result, dependencies between code modules realizing the *Controller* and *Model* components are accidentally introduced, thereby leading to dependency violations.

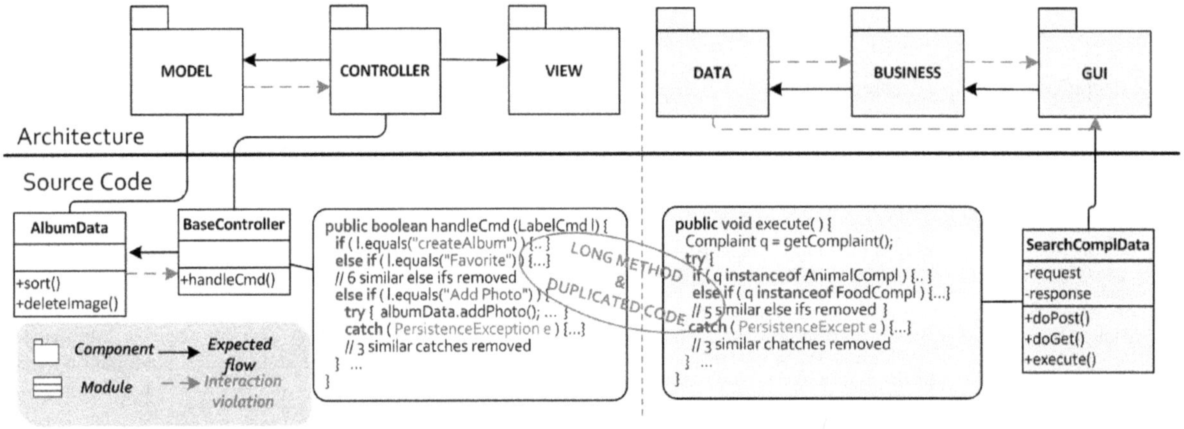

Figure 1. Erosion and drift symptom in MobileMedia (white) and HealthWatcher (gray) architectures

Example of drift. Let us consider again the class `BaseController` in Figure 1. It exhibits the *Large Class* anomaly, as it defines many methods and realizes various non-cohesive functionalities of the system (e.g. video deletion and photo sorting). It also exhibits the *Ambiguous Interface* symptom [11], as it provides an over-generalized component interface - `handleCmd` - for handling all commands. This means that the `BaseController` module (and, therefore, the *Controller* component) is aggregating several responsibilities from different service requests that should be implemented independently. To overcome the drift symptom in a later version, the `BaseController` class was decomposed into smaller classes; each of them being in charge of realizing specific controller responsibilities. Thus, the single interface of the *Controller* component was decomposed in multiple specific interfaces. These examples also illustrate how architecture degradation symptoms could be introduced in anomalous code elements.

Drift symptoms are more difficult to detect than erosion symptoms. The key reason is that code anomalies are not always indicators of drift symptoms [17]. They contribute to drift only when they lead to violations of component constraints in the architecture specification [17][18]. For instance, certain *Large Classes* and *Long Methods*, which are often detected by metrics such as LOC, CAM and CC [15], may occur in modules that are not related to any component constraints.

2.2 Characteristics of Erosion and Drift

Erosion and drift symptoms tend to be intertwined. Drift symptoms often foster the later introduction of erosion symptoms and vice-versa. Drift symptoms impair code comprehension, causing developers to unconsciously introduce dependency violations in their programs [28]. The left-hand side of Figure 1 depicts an example of the close relationship between erosion and drift symptoms in MobileMedia. The class `BaseController` implements different services through its over-generalized interface `handleCmd`. The amount of services exposed by this interface significantly increased throughout the system evolution. This interface bloat in turn forced `BaseController` to handle exceptions propagated from several non-related components. The handling of such exceptions should not be a responsibility of the *Controller* component according to the MVC decomposition, thereby characterizing the occurrence of several dependency violations.

This example illustrates a direct relation between erosion and drift phenomena. Hence, in order to detect the degradation, architects should consider blending the detection of erosion and drift symptoms into the same architecture specification. In this way, developers would be aware of both degradation processes by just considering one architecture document. Therefore, this simultaneous detection would prevent developers from introducing erosion symptoms due to reminiscent drift symptoms and vice-versa. Furthermore, intertwined occurrences of drift and erosion symptoms are also a sign of severe stages of degradation [17][18]. Recent studies revealed that code modules exhibiting both kinds of degradation symptoms tend to be the locus of more severe architecture instabilities in a project history [18][20].

Similar degradation symptoms can infect several projects. It has been noticed that similar degradation symptoms can infect several projects. This occurs, for instance, when multiple projects in the same company share similar constraints either to particular components (e.g. frameworks or libraries) or to dependency among them (i.e. architectural style rules). Projects from different companies can also share similar architecture constraints. This occurs when they follow similar architecture designs. To illustrate this phenomenon, the right part of Figure 1 depicts the architecture of the HealthWatcher system, which follows the Layer style [12]. Certain modules of HealthWatcher suffer from similar erosion and drift symptoms as those occurring in modules of MobileMedia. For instance, `SearchComplData` introduces dependency violations through exception propagation behavior, similar to `BaseController` in MobileMedia (Section 2.1). Also, it reifies drift symptoms related to the implementation of independent responsibilities, such as *GUI* and *Persistence*. It contains large methods with duplicated code. In this way, `SearchComplData` has a similar code structure to `BaseController`. Unlike `BaseController`, it does not suffer from interface bloat. Furthermore, these classes implement components with different responsibilities (i.e. *Controller* and *GUI*).

The re-occurrence of the same degradation symptoms in Figure 1 illustrates the need for *reusing* architectural constraints, instead of defining them from scratch. Architects would benefit from a single reusable abstraction that groups constraints for detecting erosion (anti-erosion) and drift (anti-drift). For instance, an architectural specification can be established to group correlated anti-erosion and drift rules that constrain MobileMedia component elements. This specification encompasses anti-erosion constraints for the exception handling policy and tight coupling between non-related components. Also, the same abstraction groups anti-drift constraints for detecting drift symptoms related to interface bloat, such as large methods in `BaseController`. Therefore, the same abstraction can be reused in HealthWatcher to constrain the dependencies between non-adjacent layers, the exception handling behavior and size boundaries for *GUI* components such as `SearchComplData`. As we can notice, the reuse of hybrid specification of anti-erosion and anti-drift rules can help developers to reduce the effort of specifying such rules in each project. These specifications are also referred to in this paper as hybrid rules.

In addition to the reuse, architects would also benefit from specification mechanisms to specialize previously-defined anti-erosion and anti-drift constraints and associate them with the same reusable abstraction. These mechanisms would allow architects to subtly adjust specific constraints to each system context. As an example, anti-drift rules that are based on size boundaries, such as those applicable to `BaseController`, should be adjusted to other systems (e.g. `SearchComplData` in HealthWatcher).

3. Related Work

This section outlines previous work aimed at supporting the detection of architectural degeneration symptoms. We refer to the motivating example (Section 2.2) to illustrate limitations of anti-erosion and anti-drift techniques.

Anti-erosion techniques. The existing anti-erosion techniques provide mechanisms to: (i) explicitly define the intended architecture of a system, including the description of component dependency rules, and (ii) check if the system's implementation is in conformance to the intended design. Sangal *et al.* [29] and Terra *et al.* [35] proposed DCL, a tool that represents relationships between code elements for a single project and detects violations of such dependencies. Eichberg *et al.* [7] presented a tool that allows the definition and checking of anti-erosion rules. They govern the relationships between the architectural elements of a software system. Marwan and Aldrich [24] developed an embedded language for documenting the system's architecture in the source code and checking its conformance with a prescribed architecture. Morgan *et al.* [27] defined a domain-specific language to specify and check anti-erosion rules in the system implementation. Ubayashi *et al.* [37] presented a programming-level interface to represent the intended architectural design and detect dependency violations in the system's components. ArCon [2] provides instrumental support to validate UML models against anti-erosion rules. It strictly enforces architectural rules in structural models.

However, all these techniques are limited to only support the detection of erosion symptoms. Software projects supported by these tools are susceptible to the progressive introduction of drift symptoms, which can in turn foster the later introduction of more severe degradation symptoms (Section 2.2). Then, when a dependency violation is hopefully detected with these techniques, it is probably too late, for instance, to conduct architecturally relevant refactorings. In the best-case scenario, developers would have to resort to the use of independent techniques for preventing drift.

Furthermore, the techniques presented above rely on anti-erosion rules that are strictly specified for a single system and cannot be reused in other system contexts. For instance, architects cannot maintain a uniform base of anti-erosion rules to constrain the handling of specific exceptions to particular components. This solution would be useful as *GUI* classes cannot handle *Data* exceptions in HealthWatcher and neither *Controller* ones are allowed to handle *Model* exceptions in MobileMedia (Figure 1).

Anti-drift techniques. Other techniques, on the other hand, are limited to only identify symptoms of drift in system implementations. Consequently, developers can introduce unacceptable dependencies between components (Section 2.2). These techniques often refer to the evaluation of structural module properties that may be related to drift symptoms. The problem is that – since they only exploit source code information to detect anomalous code elements [17] – they do not offer means to enable developers to accurately identify which anomalous modules are architecturally relevant. Another limitation is the fact that these properties are strictly specified for a particular system. Therefore, they cannot be reused in other systems even though few adjustments are usually required to detect similar architectural anomalies in different contexts [26] (Section 2.2).

Marinescu *et al.* [22] presented a tool that relies on detection strategies [21] (i.e. combinations of code metrics) to identify anomalous code elements; they may be responsible for introducing drift symptoms. Moha et al. [26] presented a methodology to detect anomalous code structures by combining metric-based evaluations to structural module properties. Mara *et al.* [20] proposed a tool that enables the definition and application of both conventional and history-sensitive detection strategies. However, these techniques are not able to accurately identify which anomalous code elements are related to component dependency problems [17], although the first ones are often the source of latter ones [17][18]. This limitation is due to the fact that they only exploit source code information to detect anomalous code elements [17]; they do not offer means to enable developers to identify which anomalous modules are architecturally relevant.

Taming drift and erosion symptoms. To the best of our knowledge, there is no technique that supports detection of both erosion and drift symptoms. This is harmful to architectural maintenance as it is likely to be often the cause-effect relationships governing these symptoms (Section 2.2). State-of-art work often force developers to learn, at least, two different techniques for dealing with each kind of degradation process. As a consequence, rules for detecting drift and erosion symptoms are specified and analyzed independently, even though they rely on the same architectural abstractions. This creates an additional dependency between the two independent architectural specifications (i.e. anti-erosion and anti-drift) and the enclosed architectural element. As a result, whenever the architectural element changes, both specifications require modifications.

4. The TamDera Language

The proposed language, named **TamDera** (Section 4.1), enables the detection of both symptoms of degradation in the source code. Developers can define and blend anti-erosion and anti-drift rules to produce hybrid, composed rules (Section 4.2). **TamDera** also supports the reuse of these rules in multiple contexts (Section 4.3). **TamDera** is a complementary approach to conventional Architecture Description Languages (ADLs) [37] as it focuses on detecting architecture degradation symptoms in the source via the specification of anti-erosion and anti-drift rules. Therefore, as opposed to ADLs, the rules need to refer to *sets of source code elements* that realize architectural concepts. These concepts could be first described, for instance, in ADL descriptions.

In the following, we introduce a partial description of the *GUI* and *Data* components (Figure 1). It will be used to illustrate the basic abstractions and mechanisms of **TamDera**. We focus on anti-erosion rules (AER) and an anti-drift rule (ADR) obtained from the GUI and Data design descriptions:

"The GUI component's purpose is limited to handle user input and display data information to users. It delegates user requests to the Business component and displays the retrieved data information. In order to avoid this component from addressing other responsibilities, GUI classes are not allowed to directly access services provided by the Data component."

"The Data component provides interfaces for data manipulation and transaction management. It also realizes the handling of exceptional events raised by persistence and transaction management actions. These exceptions are remapped and signalled as general data-related exceptions to the upper layers."

Based on given descriptions we can infer the following architecture rules. First, an anti-erosion rule AER1 establishes that *GUI* classes cannot directly access services from the *Data* component. Second, an anti-drift rule ADR1 should impose upper modularity-related boundaries, for instance on the size and cyclomatic complexity of *GUI* classes; the goal is to avoid the accidental complexity coming from the implementation of several different responsibilities. For illustration purpose, we use size and cyclomatic complexity metrics, but others can also be used such as cohesion. The rules AER1 and ADR1 are combined to prevent the *GUI* component from realizing more responsibilities and introducing more dependencies than expected. The anti-erosion rule AER2 establishes that only Data classes are able to handle persistence and transaction exceptions.

4.1 Concepts and Mappings

Architects usually have a wide range of concerns that are represented by elements in architectural specifications, such as component models or ADL descriptions. Therefore, at the architectural level, each concern is realized by one or more elements of architectural specifications, such as components and interfaces. However, those architecturally-relevant concerns are often realized by multiple module elements in the source code. Therefore, it is not trivial to associate anti-degradation rules with the group of counterpart elements realizing architectural concerns in the source code. In order to support this activity, **TamDera** relies on two main constructs: *architectural concept* and *concept mapping*. They are described below.

Definition 1 (Architectural concept). *An architectural concept is a relevant concern in the mind-set of software architects. It* *identifies the set of module elements that realize this concern and, therefore, share uniform dependency and component constraints.*

Module elements realizing a concept can be classes, interfaces, methods, or fields of a program. An architectural concept consists of anti-degradation rules. These rules should be respected by aggregate sets of module elements comprising the concept. **TamDera** is designed to support the static checking of anti-degradation rules on these elements. **TamDera** is not intended to increase flexibility by supporting description of rules relying on dynamic information (e.g., executions of method X must call method Y). The focus is to support the continuous detection of statically-checked rules to be integrated with the system build (Section 4.4).

The keyword **concept** is used to define an architectural concept with a unique name. Thus, different component constraints, such as size and complexity boundaries, are applied to different modules aggregating various architectural concepts. For instance, architects can specify less-restrictive size boundaries to components that implement core functionalities and which are expected to have a considerable size.

Graphical user interface (GUI), data management and data exceptions (Section 4) are examples of architecturally-relevant concerns captured by elements in the architecture specification. For illustration, Listing 1 shows a **TamDera** specification for these three architectural concepts. These concepts are relevant to the AER1, AER2 and ADR1 rules mentioned in Section 4. `GUIHW` (lines 01-03) and `DataHW` (lines 05-07) concepts refer to elements that respectively realize the *GUI* and *Data* components, whereas the `DataHWException` (lines 09-11) concept denotes specific exception classes pertaining to the *Data* component (Figure 1).

Listing 1

```
01: concept GUIHW {
02:   parent: "Command"
03: }
04:
05: concept DataHW {
06:   name: "healthwatcher.data.*"
07: }
08:
09: concept  DataHWException {
10:   name:  ".*PersistException|.*TransacExpcetion"
11: }
```

Definition 2 (Concept mapping). *A concept mapping is a property of an architectural concept that defines which module elements realize the architectural concept.*

TamDera supports concept mapping through regular expressions that identify properties shared by module elements realizing the concept. Examples of these properties are common names (suffixes, prefixes, and package names), or a common parent (super class or interface) of code elements. The definition of common properties governing element names is made using the keyword **name** (Listing 1). The name-based mapping receives a string (i.e. a regular expression) as input and retrieves all source code elements whose name matches it. Listing 1 illustrates the use of the name-based mapping. The concept `DataHW` is associated with all the code elements included in the package `healthwatcher.data` and in its sub-packages. Parent-based mapping is denoted by the **parent** keyword; it takes the common parent name as a parameter and maps all classes that extend or implement the common parent to the concept. For example, the concept `GUIHW` in Listing 1 is mapped to all classes whose parent class is named `Command`. Parent-based mapping is particularly interesting for programs with well defined interfaces. For instance, design patterns such as Abstract Factory [10] rely on interfaces to structure their solutions.

Table 1: Dependency types considered by **TamDera**

Dependency	Description
*A **invoke** B*	A method of *A* calls a method of *B*
*A **create** B*	Some method of *A* creates an object instance of a class of *B*
*A **declare** B*	The type of a field variable of *A* is a class of *B*
*A **derive** B*	A class of *A* extends or implements a class of *B*
*A **handle** B*	A code element of *A* has a catch block that handles any class exception of *B*
*A **depend** B*	A code element of *A* has some kind of dependency on a code element of *B*

4.2 Blending Anti-Erosion and Anti-Drift Rules

TamDera allows architects to blend anti-erosion and anti-drift rules in the specification of architectural concepts. The mechanisms to describe both forms of rules are described below.

Definition 3 (Anti-erosion rule). *An anti-erosion rule is a construct that establishes a dependency constraint among architectural concepts.*

Anti-erosion rules establish both mandatory and unacceptable dependency constraints among concepts. As a consequence, they prevent the violation of these dependency constrains. Each anti-erosion rule has a source and a target architectural concept. They refer to concepts by their names. The source concept encompasses code elements that are the source of an established dependency. The latter are the concepts whose dependencies with the source concepts are constrained. Table 1 summarizes the dependency types currently supported, which can be extended (Section 4.4). In this table, *A* indicates a set of source concepts and *B* refers to target ones. Some types are not applicable to certain module elements, e.g., ***declare*** is only applicable to classes.

TamDera provides three constructs to establish anti-erosion rules: **cannot**, **only-can** and **must**. The **cannot** construct establishes that source concept elements are prohibited to have a specific dependency type with any target concept element. Listing 2 illustrates the AER1 (line 01) from the HealthWatcher architecture (Figure 1). It uses the construct **cannot** and the relationship ***invoke*** to prohibit the access from `GUHWI` (source concept) code elements to services provided by `DataHW` (target concept) elements. The **only-can** construct (line 03) establishes that only code elements from the source concepts can have a specific dependency type with code elements from the target concepts. For instance, AER2 verifies whether there is a module in the code, which is not realizing the *Data* layer but which is undesirably handling (i.e. catching) an exception comprised by the concept `DataModelHWException`. The last rule (lines 05) uses another construct to state other aspects of the *GUI*'s design description; for conciseness we omit their explanation and refer to [33] for a full description. The three aforementioned constructs are similar to constructs supported by DCL [35].

Definition 4 (Anti-drift rule). *An anti-drift rule defines a component constraint that is relevant to an architectural concept.*

TamDera allows architects to define strategies [21] for preventing drift in the form of anti-drift rules nested in architectural concept bodies. They rely on constraints formulated with metrics and thresholds for capturing deviations from modularity principles in each component. Structural metrics represent the most popular strategy to detect drift symptoms [15][20][26][27]. **TamDera** currently supports several metrics quantifying size, complexity, cohesion and coupling attributes. The language can be extended to support new metrics and strategies (Section 4.4).

Listing 2

```
GUIHW cannot invoke DataModelHW

only DataModelHW can-handle DataModelHWException

GUIHW must-derive AbstractCommand
```

For illustration, Listing 3 shows rules aiming to detect drift symptoms in the HealthWatcher architecture. In particular, the concept `GUIHW` has anti-drift rules to constrain the size (LOC) and the cyclomatic complexity (CC) of its code elements (ADR1). These rules use thresholds (i.e. 100 and 5) to determine limit values. These specific metrics were selected for illustrative purpose and other metrics could be used for detecting similar or different drift symptoms presented in the *GUI* modules of the HealthWatcher system (Section 2.2). The violation of drift rules may imply that developers need to reason about producing and checking anti-erosion rules (Section 2.2).

Listing 3

```
concept GUIHW{
  parent: "Command"
  LOC < 100
  CC < 5
}
```

4.3 Reusing Anti-Degradation Rules

TamDera offers a compositional reuse mechanism for anti-drift rules as well as a hierarchical reuse mechanism of architectural concepts, which in turn enables the hierarchical reuse of anti-drift rules. In addition, it supports the modular specification of rules and concepts in specification files that can be reused across multiple projects. This enables single-project and multi-project reuse of anti-degradation rules.

Compositional reuse enables grouping anti-drift rules into a named set (anti-drift constraint set).

Definition 5 (Anti-drift constraint set). *A constraint set establishes a set of anti-drift rules. The definition of a concept can refer to a constraint set in order to reuse its anti-drift rules.*

Architects use the keyword **constraintset** to specify a set of reusable anti-drift rules in **TamDera**. In general the set of anti-drift rules of an architectural concept includes: (i) the rules explicitly defined within its body (Section 4.2) and (ii) those associated with the referenced constraint sets. Listing 4 illustrates the definition and reuse of a constraint set by the example of the **constraintset** `InheritanceOveruse` (lines 01-03), which constrains the depth of hierarchy class trees via the metric DIT (depth of inheritance tree) [15].The constraint avoids that a piece of coherent functionality gets artificially decomposed into several hierarchy classes. The constraint set is reused in the `GUI` and `Controller` concept definitions (lines 05 and 09 respectively). For conciseness, we omitted the `GUI` and `Controller` anti-drift rules, which are composed with the `InheritanceOveruse` rules.

Listing 4

```
01: constraintset InheritanceOveruse {
02:   DIT < 5
03: }
04:
05: concept GUI{
06:   InheritanceOveruse
07: }
08:
09: concept Controller{
10:   InheritanceOveruse
11: }
```

TamDera supports the reuse of previously defined concepts by means of an inheritance mechanism. The rationale behind hierarchical reuse is that concepts that play similar architectural roles in different projects should be subject to similar anti-degradation rules, i.e., they should belong to the same concept hierarchy tree. This is also the case when, within a single project, architectural concepts share similar structural constraints with subtle differences, such as threshold adjustments.

A concept inheritance establishes a hierarchy relationship between a super-concept and a sub-concept. The concept inheritance mechanism in **TamDera** promotes the reuse of anti-drift rules from the super-concept to the sub-concept. Figure 2 presents the definition of a super concept *GUI* (on the top of the figure). It defines three anti-drift rules (R1, R2, R3). They are in charge of realizing the rule ADR (Section 4). This concept is extended by `ViewMM` (on the left of the figure - lines 02-07), which implicitly inherits all `GUI` rules through the inheritance mechanism. Therefore, all module elements mapped to `ViewMM` must satisfy these rules.

TamDera concepts can be abstract or concrete. Unlike concrete concepts, abstract concepts do not specify a concept mapping (Section 4.1). For instance, the abstract concept `GUI` (Figure 2) has two concrete sub-concepts (`ViewMM` - left and `GUIHW` - right) that define a concept mapping. For evident reasons, only concrete concepts are checked during the anti-degradation rule conformance (Section 4.4).

TamDera allows users to modularize the specification of concepts and anti-degradation rules in several *architectural models.*

Definition 6 (Architectural model). *An architectural model is an abstraction that defines a specification file modularizing the definition of architectural concepts and anti-degradation rules.*

Figure 2 presents three such models: *abstract_rules* (top), HealthWatcher (right) and MobileMedia (left). The *abstract_rules* module defines an abstract concept `GUI` (lines 01-05) and an anti-erosion rule that checks the conformance of AER1. The other models specify rules to constraint the architecture of HealthWatcher and MobileMedia.

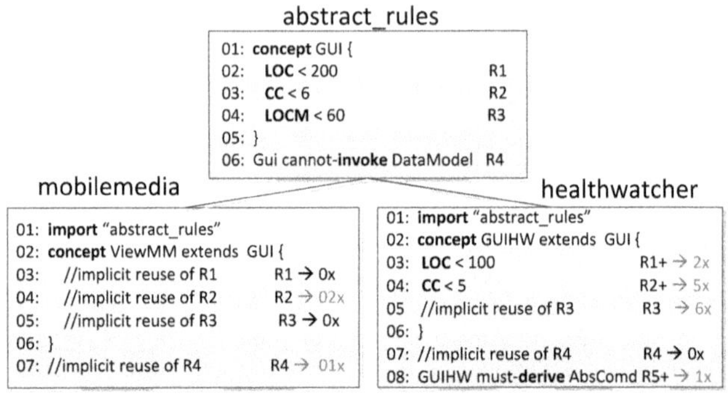

Figure 2: Reuse of anti-degradation rules using **TamDera**

The same architectural model (i.e., specification file) can be used in several projects, thus promoting the reuse of both anti-erosion and drift rules across multiple projects (Section 2.2). For instance, the concept `GUI` from *abstract_rules* and the anti-erosion rule R4 are inherited by both *healthwatcher* and *mobilemedia* models through the **import** construct, which allows the inheritance of concepts and all anti-erosion rules defined in a super architectural model (i.e. imported) to a base one. The base architectural model can define sub-concepts of the inherited concepts from the super architectural model. For example, the concepts `GUIHW` and `ViewMM` reuse `GUI` and its reusable anti-drift rules. This allows architects to specify a library of reusable concepts and promote their reuse in multiple projects.

Extending anti-degradation rules. **TamDera** also enables to override and extend anti-drift rules in sub-concept definitions. Thus, architects can adjust thresholds reused from super concepts according to their needs. This is particularly interesting to enable developers in better coping with particular characteristics of a system. The rationale behind this mechanism is to provide the flexibility to reuse or not (i.e. override) anti-drift rules from parent concepts without necessarily modifying their definitions. Sub-concepts extend a reused anti-drift rule via the declaration of an anti-drift rule using the same metric and the same operator, but specifying different thresholds.

As an example, Figure 2 presents the definition of the concept `GUIHW` (right side), which has the `GUI` as super-concept. `GUIHW` overrides anti-drift rules from `GUI` imposing more restrictive boundaries for the lines of code (line 04 - R1+) and cyclomatic complexity (line 05 - R2+) of its code elements. These rules were overridden to capture existing drift symptoms that occur in `GUI` classes that have less than 200 lines of code.

In addition to overriding inherited rules, a base module can also define new anti-erosion rules that are only applicable to its sub-concepts. For instance, `GUIHW` establishes a new anti-erosion rule (line 9), requiring that `GUIHW` elements extend elements denoted by the concept `AbsComd`.

4.4 Implementation Issues

We have implemented the **TamDera** approach to check the conformance of anti-degradation rules in software systems. In a nutshell, all anti-degradation rules are translated to Prolog queries that use static source code information stored in the knowledge base to check their conformance. In particular, we decided to focus on Java systems to evaluate the feasibility of our approach. This allows us to reuse static analysis platforms for Java programs. The tool was implemented upon the Eclipse platform using XText [38], which is a framework for developing parsers and editors. XText provides features, such as generating editors with syntax coloring and code completion. This facilitates the specification of concepts and their anti-degradation rules.

Design overview. The **TamDera** tool uses Prolog [32] to statically check the conformance of anti-degradation rules. Prolog has been successfully used as a scalable engine to check structural dependencies related to erosion symptoms [7]. There is recent evidence [7] supporting the use of Prolog in the incremental build process of the system. As a consequence, the system can be continuously checked when the source code is modified [7].

Structural properties of module elements, their dependencies and metrics' values are directly represented as Prolog terms (i.e. knowledge base [5]). Thus, a single representation is used for detecting erosion and drift symptoms. This can also foster the tool integration with other programming languages as we can develop translators to represent architectural relevant information as Prolog facts. This characteristic is particularly interesting as recent studies have shown that most software projects nowadays are implemented in four different programming languages [37].

The tool reuses the Bytecode Analysis Toolkit (BAT) [7][39], which receives the system binaries as parameter and retrieves a Prolog-based representation of the system. On the other hand, we use the metric files generated by Together [36] to check the anti-drift rules. It contains metric results based on structural properties (e.g. size and coupling) for each module element in the system under analysis.

Architectural conformance. The tool receives the system specification file whose architecture implementation is being checked as a parameter. It parses the (main) architectural model and also the ones which are referred to through the **import** keyword usage (Section 4.3). In this sense, it evaluates all anti-degradation rules taking into consideration the reuse mechanisms (Section 4.3). Also, it evaluates the concept mappings and stores them in the knowledge base. Our engine uses this information to identify concept code elements that violate any anti-degradation rule. **TamDera** generates an output report which describes each source code element that broke the corresponding anti-degradation rule. **Consistency among rules**. The tool also checks the consistency of anti-degradation rules in architectural models (Section 4.3). In fact, current techniques allow users to unconsciously define an inconsistent set of rules which impair the architectural conformance task [35]. For instance, users can define the rules: A `must-invoke` B and A `cannot-invoke` B. They impose contradictory constraints to the implemented architecture. Similarly to the checking of anti-degradation rules, the tool stores the information about each rule in the knowledge base and checks the consistency among the rules. For instance, we define a function to check if there are two anti-erosion rules that refer to the same concepts (A and B) and dependency types (invoke) but one uses a must relationship while the other uses a cannot one.

5. Evaluation

The usefulness of the **TamDera** language is largely dependent on how frequent the detected symptoms of erosion and drift are inter-related in a program (Section 2.2). The relation of these symptoms can be revealed in two ways (Section 5.4.1). First, their **TamDera** detection rules are logically blended; i.e. associated with the same concept (Section 4.2) in the same architecture model. Second, a drift symptom detected by **TamDera** rules in a program version is perceived to provoke an erosion symptom in a later version. Our evaluation is also intended to assess the adequacy of **TamDera** to promote the reuse of anti-degradation rules. Therefore, we defined two research questions that drive our evaluation: (i) how significant is the number of inter-related erosion and drift symptoms detected with **TamDera** rules, and (ii) to what extent anti-erosion rules and anti-drift rules can be reused in one or more projects.

5.1 Target Systems

We selected software systems for which either the intended architecture specification or the original architects are available. Otherwise, we were not able to investigate the veracity of the rules as well as the degradation symptoms being detected. We also looked for systems adhering to architecture decompositions sharing the same architectural styles and design patterns where opportunities for reusing rules could be explored. At the same time, those systems needed to be from different domains and designed by different developers. The goal was to check whether recurring rules could be actually reused even in extreme cases, where the dominant application domains and developers' backgrounds were different. We also intended to select systems that underwent severe degradation stages, but were continued and redesigned in follow-up projects.

Based on these criteria, we selected three systems: MobileMedia [8], HealthWatcher [12], and MIDAS [19]. However, we took into consideration five projects. The reason is that the original Java projects of the first two systems (Section 2.2) manifested major symptoms of degradation over time. Then, two new follow-up projects [13][30] started. They consisted of significant architecture re-structuring of both MobileMedia and HealthWatcher systems. The systems were partially re-designed with aspectual decompositions and re-implemented with AspectJ [3]. We considered both groups of projects in our evaluation to check if the original design rules from the first project could be reused in the second project. We considered cases where the rules were fully reused (as in the original project) and those that were refined to satisfy the particularities of the second project.

Despite of being projects designed by distinct architects they share -– in many cases (e.g. Section 2.2) – similar design decisions. HealthWatcher [12] is a web system used for registering complaints about health issues in public institutions. Mobile Media is a product line that manages different types of media on mobile devices. MIDAS is a lightweight middleware for distributed sensor applications [19]. These projects were previously used in studies of degradation and refactoring [17][18][19]. This was beneficial to our study as we were also able to access their degradation symptoms from previous independent reports. These documents were helpful to evaluate the adequacy of **TamDera** rules to detect the reported degradation symptoms.

5.2 Study Procedures

The study relied on the use of all **TamDera**'s mechanisms (Section 4) to specify the anti-degradation rules. The process was conducted in two major phases:

Phase 1: Identification of architectural concepts. We accessed the available documentation to support the identification of architecturally-relevant concepts in each project. This activity was driven by the use of high-level component models that were available for all the five projects [33]. There were also specific models for certain versions where the intended architecture decomposition was modified. The subject systems make use of several architectural styles, such as MVC, Layers and Aspectual Design. They also implement several design patterns that are often used to realize architecture decompositions, such as Chain of Responsibility and Façade [10]. We also referred to the documentation of these patterns to guide the specification of architectural concepts. As these pattern elements often rely on abstract classes [10], we naturally mapped the architectural concepts to these classes. Finally, we performed a peer revision with the original architects of each system. The goal was to ensure that the list of concepts and mappings (Section 4.1) specified with **TamDera** were good enough to represent the key decisions of the intended architectures.

Phase 2: Iterative improvement of anti-degradation rule specifications. We also referred to the aforementioned component models in order to specify some of the dependency constraints (i.e. anti-erosion rules). The documentation of styles and patterns were carefully examined to specify the rules for each concept identified in Phase 1. For instance, the responsibilities and characteristics of style and pattern elements were used to specify the anti-drift rules. The system developers also validated and provided us with a list of suggestions to enhance rule definitions based on their architecture knowledge. All the concepts and their corresponding rules are available at the study website [33]. In a final step, we identified opportunities to make the list of concepts and rule specifications more generic. The goal was to possibly enable their reuse across multiple projects. However, this generalization process was performed without acquiring specific knowledge of the 5 projects.

5.3 Assessment Settings

Our study evaluated the occurrence of inter-related erosion and drift symptoms as well as the reuse of their corresponding rules across the 5 projects (Section 5.1). First, we analysed the significance of co-occurring erosion and drift symptoms detected with **TamDera**. This analysis was supported by comparing (Section 5.4.1): (i) the percentage of code elements containing both forms of degradation symptoms, with (ii) the number of code elements containing at least an erosion symptom or a drift symptom. This comparison was important to check to what extent the **TamDera**'s rules were useful to diagnose the simultaneous occurrence of drift and erosion symptoms. Second, the procedures to assess the reuse of **TamDera** rules are described below. Due to space constraints, more details about the study settings are available at [33]. As TamDera has the distinguishing feature of detection both erosion and drift symptoms, we were not able to directly compare the language with other DSLs that describe only anti-erosion rules or only anti-drift rules (Section 3'). Our study does not explicitly evaluate the effort to specify rules. However, the reuse assessment evaluates the degree of rules reused in single and multiple projects, thereby identifying scenarios where specification effort can be reduced.

Reuse assessment. We assessed if the **TamDera** mechanisms promote significant degree of reuse across multiple projects. The reuse assessment relied on quantifying the anti-degradation rules that were reused and contrasts this number with those rules defined from scratch. A rule was considered to be reused if it was used as originally specified. The reuse measure was derived by calculating the percentage of rules that are reused out of the total of them (i.e. both reused and non-reused rules). For a single project, we took into consideration the rules within the project file and the reused rules from the *abstract_rules* file (Section 4.3). As an example, consider the HealthWatcher specification in Figure 2, which reuses 2 rules from the super concept `GUI` (R3 and R4), overrides two rules (R1+ and R2+) and defines a new anti-erosion rule (R5+). Hence, the total number of rules is 5, of which 2 are reused, resulting in a reuse degree of 40% (2 out of 5 rules).

Effective reuse assessment. Then, we identified the reused rules that actually detected architectural design problems. These rules are named effective reused rules. We counted the number of classes containing degradation symptom(s) to evaluate the effective reuse of rules. Then, we distinguished the symptoms that were detected by reused rules from those defined from scratch. Hence, the effective reuse was evaluated as the percentage of degradation symptoms identified by the reused rules out of the total of degradation symptoms (i.e. including those identified by non-reused rules). For illustration, consider the numbers (red values) on the right-hand side of the rules in Figure 2, which correspond to the number of erosion and drift symptoms detected by the corresponding rule. In the case of HealthWatcher, there are 2, 5, 6, 0, 1 degradation symptoms detected by R1, R2, R3, R4, R5 respectively. Hence, the effective reuse is 42.8% (6 out of 14 rules), as 6 degradation symptoms were detected by the reused rule R3. The multi-project effective reuse was evaluated in a similar way, however, by considering only rules that detect degradation symptoms in at least two different projects.

5.4 Study Results

All the results of our study are available at the complementary website [33]. Our evaluation was based on the architectural specification files for 8 versions of HealthWatcher, 7 versions for MobileMedia and 2 versions of MIDAS. Also, we considered the specification files of the first and forth AspectJ versions of MobileMedia and HealthWatcher (Section 5.1). So, we analyzed 21 versions of **TamDera** specifications in total. The evolution history of all the systems underwent architecturally relevant changes. The MobileMedia evolution was guided through the addition of new features [8], whereas the HealthWatcher history mostly encompassed refactorings of specific modules in order to adopt architecturally relevant design patterns [12]. The MIDAS versions are those before and after restructurings to improve the system's modularity and adaptability [19]. Therefore, the anti-degradation rules of the target projects had suffered modifications over their evolutions.

We chose to focus on the data of the versions 1, 4 and 8 of HealthWatcher, the versions 1, 4 and 7 of MobileMedia, the versions 1 and 4 of the aspectual implementation of both systems, and the two versions of MIDAS. We name these versions as HW_1, HW_4, HW_8, MM_1, MM_4, MM_7, HA_1, HA_4, MA_1, MA_2, $MIDAS_{BEF}$ and $MIDAS_{AFT}$, respectively. These versions are those that suffered from the most widely-scoped changes in both implementation and architecture levels along the system's evolution. Therefore, they help us to better illustrate the study results. The analysis encompassed more than 600 anti-degradation rules and more than 300 concept specifications. Table 2 summarizes the amount of concepts, rule types, and the amount of classes in the code that actually manifested degradation symptoms in each analysed version. The number of anti-degradation (ADG) rules is the tally of anti-erosion (AE) and anti-drift (AD) rules.

Table 2. Characteristics of systems' specification files

	MM		MA		HW		HA		MIDAS	
	1	4	1	4	1	4	1	4	B	A
concepts	22	24	28	30	24	45	27	49	28	26
Anti-Erosion rules	22	23	25	33	34	50	36	52	20	20
Anti-Drift rules	25	25	29	35	33	44	37	52	26	22
Anti-Deg. rules	47	48	54	68	67	94	73	104	46	42
classes with Deg.	9	14	8	12	43	49	36	41	45	49

Deg.=degradation; A=After; B=Before

5.4.1 Co-occurring Erosion and Drift Symptoms

Simultaneous occurrences of erosion and drift symptoms. We evaluated the simultaneous occurrence of drift and erosion symptoms detected with **TamDera** in the same modules. Figure 3 shows the results. The percentage of the symptoms was computed based on the total of degradation symptoms for each version described in Table 2 (last row). The histogram presents the percentage of classes containing only erosion symptoms (ES), only drift symptoms (DS) and both of them (DGS). On average 45% of the HealthWatcher and MobileMedia classes, which exhibit degradation symptoms, contain both erosion and drift symptoms. MIDAS was an exception for the reasons discussed below. The high rate of drift and erosion co-occurrences is a first indicator of the usefulness of **TamDera** to support: (i) the retrospective analysis of cause-effect relationships involving drift and erosion symptoms affecting the same modules in the code, and (ii) the early detection and removal of drift (or erosion) symptoms in order to prevent the later occurrence of other erosion (or drift) symptoms caused by the former ones in later versions.

The symbiosis of erosion and drift detection. It could be that an extent of these co-occurring drift and erosion symptoms were just accidentally affecting the same module, but has no conceptual or historical relation. However, we observed that, on average, 85% of co-occurring symptoms were revealed by **TamDera** rules bound to the same architectural concept. These symptoms are referred to as *concept-related.* For instance, the rules AER1 and ADR1 (Section 4) rely on the *GUI* concept and detect both degradation symptoms that occur in `SearchComplData` (Section 2.2). We also observed that, in many cases, a pair of drift and erosion symptoms was concept-related, but they were not necessarily occurring in the same modules. These are typically the case of rules for concepts related to patterns and styles (Section 5.4.2). For instance, each layer from the HealthWatcher architecture is described as an independent concept. These concepts have in common a super-concept, which establishes general anti-drift rules for coupling and size. They also involve anti-erosion rules that constrain the dependencies between non-adjacent layers. Despite these rules being concept-related, they detect erosion and drift rules that occur in different modules (i.e. modules that belong to different layers such as GUI and Data). It would be difficult and time-consuming to detect these concept-related symptoms through the use of individual techniques (Section 3) for drift and erosion.

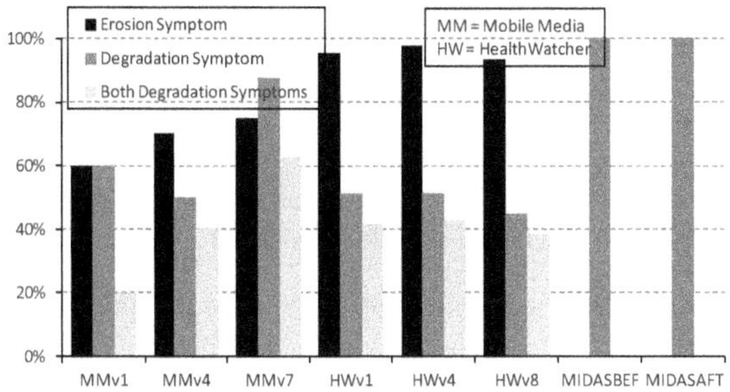

Figure 3: Co-occurring erosion and drift symptoms

Erosion detection alone does not prevent degradation. If we also take MIDAS into consideration, the simultaneous occurrence of erosion and drift symptoms decreases from 45% to 35%, which is still significant (Figure 3). MIDAS was developed using a middleware environment in charge of strictly enforcing the conformance of its implementation to the intended architecture [19]. It means that no dependency violation (i.e. erosion symptom) would remain in the code and, therefore, this system's versions did not exhibit any erosion symptom (Figure 3).

However, the quality of MIDAS architecture had progressively declined until the point where a major restructuring was required [19]. The reason was that several components of MIDAS were progressively exhibiting drift symptoms: they increasingly lost their original conceptual coherence (i.e. purpose) as their implementations had evolved to provide multiple services. In other words, they were increasingly manifesting anomalies related to the "single responsibility" principle [23]. The MIDAS architecture significantly decayed due to the continued incidence of drifts [11]. Even though the developers were concerned with erosion prevention, the MIDAS architecture became susceptible to degradation through an architectural drift process. Hence, this scenario reinforces the importance of the early detection of both degradation symptoms provided by **TamDera** (Section 4). More importantly, we observed in the MIDAS case that the rules would be beneficial to diagnose the following fact: the enforcement of anti-erosion rules might be the actual cause of drift rule violations. This could be easily observed via **TamDera** specifications when both rules are bound to the same architectural concept.

Drift and erosion symptoms throughout systems' evolution. We also observed other interesting cases. Our analysis revealed that erosion symptoms in early versions often result in erosion problems in later versions and vice-versa. For instance, in HealthWatcher, several method declarations were signalling exceptions to other components, but those exceptions were supposed to be internally handled. These were cases of erosion symptoms. Those exception declarations were placed in methods in parent classes and those erosion problems in turn caused drift symptoms in children classes. The latter classes were forced to log the occurrence of these exceptions and throw them as defined in the parent class. This situation increased the internal complexity of children classes as well as their coupling degree with neighbouring components. Also, there were cases where drift symptoms in early versions were the source of later violations in the project history. For instance, the number of responsibilities realized by the *Controller* component increased through successive versions. In later versions, this responsibility overload required the *Controller* to access information from different components, thereby establishing unintended dependencies. The analysis revealed that 66% of drift symptoms in *Controller* classes were sources of later dependency violations.

Identifying and removing co-occurring symptoms is not trivial. When both kinds of symptoms infect the same module, someone could expect that by removing one symptom, the other will be easily detected and fixed as well. For instance, when removing of unacceptable access of `SearchComplData` (erosion symptom) to *Data* services, someone could observe that the class is inadequately addressing other responsibilities, such as handling data-specific objects (drift symptom). This expectation motivated us to investigate how often erosion and drift symptoms that infected the same module were simultaneously fixed. However, this behavior was not observed in more than 61% of all the co-occurrences detected in the target systems. For instance, in the AspectJ project of HealthWatcher all the erosion symptoms in the *GUI* classes were addressed through the modularization of *Persistence* and *Transaction* exceptions. This refactoring reduced the number of responsibilities that *GUI* classes were undesirably dealing with. However, *GUI* classes remained infected by drift symptoms as they introduce a tight coupling degree between *GUI* and *Business* layers. This co-occurring problem could be detected by **TamDera** as the rules for detecting both problems would be defined in the same `GUIHW` concept.

There were also cases where the removal of drift problems did not imply the detection and fix of related erosion symptoms. For instance, around 83% of all the drift problems in the *Controller* classes of MobileMedia were addressed by decomposing them in micro controllers. Thereby, each specific controller was responsible for dealing with a specific functionality. However, after this architecturally-relevant refactoring, the erosion symptoms persisted in the code as *Controllers* continued to deal with exceptions propagated by the *Data* component (Section 2.2). These scenarios provide interesting evidence that: (i) the detection of an erosion problem does not imply that it is easy to identify a concept-related drift problem occurring in the same code module and vice-versa, and (ii) relying on techniques for detecting just one kind of degradation symptom (Section 3) are not enough to enable developers to prevent architectural degradation.

5.4.2 Reuse Analysis

Significant reuse of rules. The second study goal was to analyze the potential reuse of **TamDera** rules in different contexts. We elaborated sources of reusable rules specifying architectural constraints (Section 5.2). These rules were reused in the target projects. Table 3 presents the amount of reused rules for each system. Similarly to Table 2, we distinguish the amount of anti-erosion, anti-drift and anti-degradation rules. An analysis of the last row of Table 3 reveals that 72% of the specified rules were reused on average, taking into consideration the total number of specified rules for the all systems. This finding suggests that architects can significantly save resources on the development and maintenance of architectural rules shared by several projects. Changes applied to shared rules are propagated through the reuse mechanisms of **TamDera** (Section 4.3) to multiple projects.

Reuse of style and pattern constraints. We observed that a large extent of the reused rules, specified in reusable concepts, was related to architectural styles and design patterns (Section 5.2). The definition of each single style or pattern is often formed by a cohesion set of component (anti-drift) and dependency (anti-erosion) constraints. For instance, the *Controller* classes of MobileMedia realize the design pattern Chain of Responsibility (CoR) [10]. This pattern reduces the coupling between the sender of a request to its receiver by delegating the request handling to multiple objects. Listing 5 presents part of a reusable rule associated with the CoR pattern. They define drift and erosion rules for code elements realizing the *Handler* concept. Those elements are architecturally relevant as they handle requests coming from other components. In Listing 5, the client interface as well as other concepts and rules of the CoR were removed from Listing 5 for conciseness. First, it defines an anti-drift rule constraining the coupling strength of each concrete class handling the request (`ConcreteHandler`, lines 01-04) through the metric CBO (coupling between objects) [15]. The coupling threshold is represented by the constant `LOW_COUPLING`. Second, there is also a reusable anti-erosion rule to prohibit direct calls of clients to concrete handlers (line 05). More specifically, those clients are realizing other architectural concepts and should access a specific interface to send their requests. This example shows how drift and erosion rules of a single pattern are mutually-related (Section 2.2): while the former ones enforce structural properties of modules realizing pattern concepts, the latter ones constrain their dependency with other architecturally-relevant concepts of the system.

Table 3: Reuse of architecture rules

	MM		MA		HW		AW		MIDAS	
	1	4	1	4	1	4	1	4	B	A
Anti-Erosion rules	19	19	20	22	16	32	18	50	15	15
Anti-Drift rules	20	21	23	25	27	36	31	54	13	13
Anti-Deg. rules	39	40	43	47	43	68	49	73	28	28
Anti-Deg. rules (%)	82	83	79	70	64	72	67	70	66	60

B=Before; A=After; Deg.=Degradation

Significant detection of degradation symptoms by reused rules. We observed that a significant number of erosion and drift symptoms were detected by reused rules (72% of original rules) in all the 5 projects. They were responsible for detecting on average 73% of the existing symptoms. Table 4 illustrates the effective reuse (Section 5.3) for each system version. These measures represented a balance between the reused rule percentage and the symptoms detected by them. Therefore, the reused rules had similar efficiency to detect architectural deviations in comparison to the non-reused rules unique to each project.

Listing 5

```
01: constraintset ConcreteHandler {
02:   thresholds: LOW_COUPLING
03:   CBO < LOW_COUPLING
04: }
05: Client cannot-invoke ConcreteHandler
```

Overriding anti-drift rules. There was a need to subtly override reused rules in 11% of the cases [33]. For instance, the concept `GUIHW` overrides anti-drift rules from `GUI` to impose more restrictive constraint boundaries (Section 4.3). These boundaries are used to capture symptoms in particular HW *GUI* elements. In such scenarios, we decided not to modify these rules in the `GUI` super-concept. Otherwise, it would potentially generate false positives in the MM analysis. In this context, false positives are related to the use of detection strategies to identify drift symptoms. It represents modules that violate drift rules but do not have the associated drift symptoms. In fact, these restrictive boundaries are not applicable for the `ViewMM` code elements (Figure 2). Rule overriding (Section 4.3) was often useful to avoid false positives and false negatives, in addition to capture particular symptom intricacies of a project. It was also particularly interesting for addressing adjustments required in the aspect-oriented refactorings of the MM and HW architectures (Section 5.1). For instance, concept mappings need to be often overridden to consider: (i) the inclusion of new code elements, and (ii) the renaming or removal of certain classes. Thresholds of drift rules also needed to be replaced in specializations of architectural concepts.

Table 4: Detection of degradation symptoms by reused rules

	MM		MA		HW		HA		MIDAS	
	1	4	1	4	1	4	1	4	B	A
Deg. Symptoms	24	41	20	33	116	140	85	105	50	46
DGRR	21	37	16	27	85	108	58	81	28	25
Reuse of Rules	87	90	80	81	73	77	68	77	56	54

DGRR = degradation symptoms detected by reused rules; B=Before; A=After; Deg.=Degradation

Detection of the same degradation symptom in multiple projects. The reused rules were effective in the detection of the same degradation symptom in multiple projects. We selected a representative set of pairs of system versions, which were sharing reusable rules. Figure 4 presents the results for each of those selected pairs (represented in the x-axis). For instance, the first pair is formed by the first versions of the HW and MM projects. The rules that detect degradation symptoms in both projects are called *common reused rules* in Figure 4. Their percentage (dark grey bar) is computed from the total number of rules defined for the pair of versions. We assessed the percentage of degradation symptoms detected by them, the so-called *similar symptoms*. The analysis reveals that 34% on average of the rules were effectively reused to detect degradation symptoms that occur in both HW and MM projects. Examples of these rules are: (i) anti-erosion rules constraining component dependencies imposed by architectural styles (e.g. R4 - Figure 2), (ii) anti-drift rules to constrain size, complexity and coupling of particular components' elements such as *View* and *Model* (e.g. R3 - Figure 2), and (iii) both anti-erosion and anti-drift rules associated with architecturally-relevant design patterns such as the Command [10].

5.5 Threats to Validity and Study Limitations

Threats to *external validity* are related to the choice of target applications and the generalization of results. We tried to mitigate this threat by selecting applications from different domains and developed by different teams of architects and developers. In fact, they had already been used in previous empirical studies [8][11][17][18][20] with similar purposes. The choice of applications also considered the criteria described in Section 5.1.

We identified two major issues that threaten the *construction validity* of our study: the specification of architectural concepts and their rules, as well as the identification of architectural degradation symptoms. To mitigate this treat, we specified the concepts referring to components explicitly present in high-level diagrams for all projects (Section 5.2). We also performed a detailed revision with the original systems' architects to guarantee that the defined concepts capture the constraints associated with the intended architecture. We only considered those architecture concepts and constraints that were confirmed by systems' architects.

We mitigated the second issue by using reports about architectural degradation and related refactorings in each application as an "oracle" to retrieve the degradation symptoms. These reports were produced in previous empirical studies based on such systems. They provided helpful information regarding: the intended architecture design of target systems and the location of the architec-

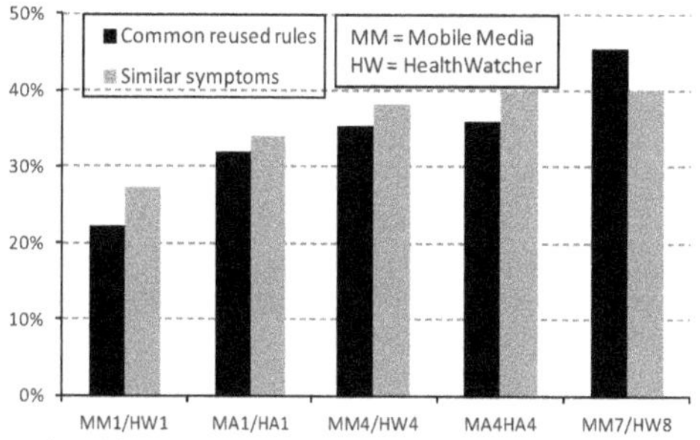

Figure 4: Effective reuse of common degradation symptoms

tural problems in both systems' design and implementation. The information provided by these reports allowed us to carry on a more independent and fair evaluation of the **TamDera** language.

The main issues that threaten the *conclusion validity* of our study are the representativeness of the characteristics and number of used systems. We recognize that we cannot extrapolate much the results of our study to a wide range of projects. Even though those systems share some similar architecture design decisions, they follow different architecture styles and are from different domains. We are aware that the reuse of anti-degradation rules may be affected because of considering systems adhering to similar styles and patterns. However, we followed a pragmatic approach, i.e. we believe that no reuse can be promoted if there is no effort upfront to anticipate general rules applicable to architectures following similar design decompositions.

As far as the number of analyzed programs is concerned, we relied on 21 versions of 5 different systems. Of course, a higher number of systems and versions is always desired. However, the analysis of a bigger sample in this first study would be impracticable for different reasons. First, the relationship between code modules and degradation symptoms need to be confirmed by architects. Second, systems with all the required information and stakeholders available to perform this study are rather scarce. Then, our sample can be seen as appropriate for an exploratory evaluation.

In terms of study limitation, the study assessment does not explicitly evaluate the effort need to specify anti-degradation rules. Effort is an attribute that can only be measured via controlled experiments which deviates from the assessment focus at this point (i.e., evaluates **TamDera's** novel features). However, our study pointed out how the effort to specify rules can be potentially reduced through the reuse mechanism (Section 5.4.2).

A false positive is characterized when an anti-degradation rule is violated by a module that does not have any degradation symptom. On the other hand, a false negative is characterized when rules are not enough to pinpoint a degradation symptom. In respect to anti-drift, it is well known from literature that false positives and negatives largely depends on the ability of architects to select the metrics and define thresholds based on the particular characteristics of the program [18]. Using **TamDera's** reuse mechanisms, architects can combine metrics and reuse or redefine thresholds for system adhering similar architectural decompositions. As far as anti-erosions are concerned, false negatives might occur if the language is not expressive enough to express certain form of constraints governing architectural components. At the moment, **TamDera** does not support the specification of rules related to dynamic information, but the language can be extended to incorporate new constructs to specify object instances and flows of method execution (e.g., similar to AspectJ's cflow construct). In our evaluation, we observed an insignificant set of false positives and negatives. The system original developers reviewed and provided suggestions to iteratively enhance the rule specifications during the first steps of the study (Section 5.2).

6. Concluding Remarks

This paper presents **TamDera**, a language that supports blending of anti-drift and anti-erosion rules to detect both symptoms of architectural degradation. **TamDera** enables the compositional and hierarchical reuse of anti-degradation rules. We evaluated the usefulness of our language by detecting degradation symptoms in 21 versions of 5 different projects.

Our evaluation showed that **TamDera** could help architects and developers to save time and resources. We found that 72% of the anti-degradation rules were reused from existing ones. The analysis also revealed that such reused rules were responsible for identifying on average of 73% of all erosion and drift symptoms in the target projects (Section 5.4.1). More interestingly, there were a broad range of scenarios confirming that individual techniques for drift or erosion would not be sufficient or efficient to support degradation prevention. In cases where both symptoms were affecting the same module in the code, developers detected and removed only one symptom (Section 5.4.1). In addition, many inter-related drift and erosion symptoms do not necessarily affect the same modules in the code (Section 5.4.2), which make them difficult to detect together using existing techniques (Section 3).

Our study pointed out how the effort to specify rules can be potentially reduced thanks to: (i) the degree of reuse achieved once a generic rule is defined, and (ii) the elimination of the need for learning at least two different languages (for anti-degradation rules.. In our agenda, we plan to conduct controlled experiments and case studies with our industry partners to evaluate the effort of using **TamDera** to describe anti-degradation rules.

References

[1] Aldrich, J. ArchJava: Connecting Software Architecture to Implementation. In Proc 24th ICSE, 2002.

[2] ArCon:http://code.google.com/a/eclipselabs.org/p/arcon/.

[3] AspectJ: http://www.eclipse.org/aspectj/.

[4] Buschmann, F. *et al.* Pattern-Oriented Software Architecture: A Pattern Language for Distributed Computing. In Wiley Software Patterns Series, John Wiley & Sons, 2007.

[5] Ceri, S. *et al.* What you always wanted to know about datalog. In IEEE Transactions on Knowledge and Data Engineering, 1989.

[6] Diskin, Z. *et al.* Specifying Overlaps of Heterogeneous Models for Global Consistency Checking. MoDELS companion, 2011.

[7] Eichberg, M. *et al.* Defining and Continuous Checking of Structural Program Dependencies. In Proc. 30th ICSE, 2008.

[8] Figueiredo, E. *et al.* Evolving software product lines with aspects: An empirical study on design stability. In Proc 30th ICSE, 2008.

[9] Fowler, M. Refactoring: Improving the Design of Existing Code. Addison-Wesley, 1999.

[10] Gamma, E. *et. al.* Design Patterns: Elements of Reusable Object-Oriented Software. Addison-Wesley.

[11] Garcia, J. *et al.* Identifying architectural bad smells. In Proc 13th CSMR, 2009.

[12] Greenwood, P. *et al.* On the impact of aspectual decompositions on design stability: An empirical study. In Proc. 21st ECOOP, 2007.

[13] HealthWatcher. http://www.comp.lancs.ac.uk/~greenwop/tao/.

[14] Hochstein, L. and Lindvall, M. Combating architectural degeneration: A survey. Info. & Soft. Technology July, 2005.

[15] Lanza, M. and Marinescu, R. Object-Oriented Metrics in Practice. In Springer, 2006.

[16] Li, Z. Characterizing and Diagnosing Architectural Degeneration of Software Systems from Defect Perspective. In Electronic Thesis and Dissertation Repository. Paper 30. http://ir.lib.uwo.ca/etd/30.

[17] Macia, I. *et al.* Are Automatically-Detected Code Anomalies Relevant to Architectural Modularity? An Exploratory Analysis of Evolving Systems. In Proc. 11st AOSD 2012.

[18] Macia, I. *et al.* On the Relevance of Code Anomalies for Identifying Architecture Degradation Symptoms. In Proc. 16th CSMR, 2012.

[19] Malek, S. *et al.* Reconceptualizing a family of heterogeneous embedded systems via explicit architectural support. In Proc. 29th ICSE. 2007.

[20] Mara, L. *et al.* Hist-Inspect: A Tool for History-Sensitive Detection of Code Smells. In Proc. of the 10th AOSD, 2011.

[21] Marinescu, R. Detection strategies: Metrics-based rules for detecting design flaws. In Proc. 20th ICSM, 2004.

[22] Marinescu, R. *et al.* iPlasma: An integrated platform for quality assessment of object-oriented design. In Proc 21st ICSM, 2005.

[23] Martin, R. Agile Software Development, Principles, Patterns, and Practices. Prentice Hall, 2002.

[24] Marwan A. and Aldrich, J. Static Extraction and Conformance Analysis of Hierarchical Runtime Architectural Structure using Annotations. In Proc. 24th OOPSLA 2009.

[25] McCabe, T.J. A Software Complexity Measure. IEEE Transactions on Software Engineering, 2 (4), 1976.

[26] Moha, N. *et al.* DECOR: A Method for the Specification and Detection of Code and Design Smells. In IEEE TSE, 2010.

[27] Morgan, C. A static aspect language of checking design rules. In Proc. of the 6th AOSD, 2007.

[28] Perry, D.E. and Wolf, A.L. Foundations for the study of software architecture, ACM Software. Eng. Notes 17 (4), 1992.

[29] Sangal, N. *et al.* Using dependency models to manage complex software architecture. In Proc. 20th OOPSLA, 2005.

[30] Soares, S. *et al.* Implementing distribution and persistence aspects with AspectJ. In Proc. 17th OOPSLA, 2002.

[31] Sullivan, K. *et al.* The structure and value of modularity in software design. In Proc. 9th FSE, 2001.

[32] Swi-Prolog. http://www.swi-prolog.org/.

[33] TamDera available at http://www.les.inf.puc-rio.br/opus/tamdera/aosd14/.

[34] Taylor, R. et al. Software Architecture: Foundations, Theory and Practice. Wiley Publishing. 2009.

[35] Terra, R. et al. A Dependency Constraint Language to Manage Software Architectures. In Software: Practice and Experience, 2009.

[36] Together. http://www.borland.com/us/products/together/.

[37] Ubayashi, N. et al. Archfase: A Contract Place Where Architectural Design and Code Meet Together. In Proc. 32sd ICSE, 2010.

[38] XText. http://www.eclipse.org/Xtext/.

[39] http://bitbucket.org/delors/bat.

[40] Oliveira, M. PREViA: An Approach for Visualizing the Evolution of Software Models. Master Thesis. COPPE/UFRJ, 185p. 2011.

[41] Silva, A. et al. Reuse of Domain-Sensitive Strategies for Detecting Code Anomalies: A Multi-Case Study. In SBES'13, 2013.

Automated Software Remodularization Based on Move Refactoring

A Complex Systems Approach

Marcelo Serrano Zanetti, Claudio Juan Tessone, Ingo Scholtes and Frank Schweitzer

Chair of Systems Design – www.sg.ethz.ch – ETH Zurich – Switzerland

{mzanetti, tessonec, ischoltes, fschweitzer}@ethz.ch

Abstract

Modular design is a desirable characteristic of complex software systems that can significantly improve their comprehensibility, maintainability and thus quality. While many software systems are initially created in a modular way, over time modularity typically degrades as components are reused outside the context where they were created. In this paper, we propose an automated strategy to remodularize software based on *move refactoring*, i.e. moving classes between packages without changing any other aspect of the source code. Taking a complex systems perspective, our approach is based on complex networks theory applied to the dynamics of software modular structures and its relation to an n-state spin model known as the *Potts Model*. In our approach, nodes are probabilistically moved between modules with a probability that nonlinearly depends on the number and module membership of their adjacent neighbors, which are defined by the underlying network of software dependencies. To validate our method, we apply it to a dataset of 39 JAVA open source projects in order to optimize their modularity. Comparing the source code generated by the developers with the optimized code resulting from our approach, we find that modularity (i.e. quantified in terms of a standard measure from the study of complex networks) improves on average by 166 ± 77 percent. In order to facilitate the application of our method in practical studies, we provide a freely available ECLIPSE plug-in.

Categories and Subject Descriptors D.2.2 [*Design Tools and Techniques*]: Modules and interfaces, Object-oriented design methods; D2.8 [*Metrics*]: Complexity measures; D.3.3 [*Language Constructs and Features*]: Modules, Packages

Keywords remodularization, refactoring, complex networks

1. Introduction

The modular design of complex software systems is an important factor that contributes to the success of software engineering projects. It is enabled by a set of design principles, among which *information hiding* and *separation of concerns* are the most influential ones [13, 30, 31, 34]. These two principles translate into commissioning different modules to different purposes, such that their internal implementation is transparent to developers making use of their functionalities. This approach has been shown to limit necessary coordination efforts and fosters the simple replacement of obsolete software modules by new ones [9, 39], thus bearing great relevance to the maintenance of sustainable software engineering regimes [37, 42].

In the modular design of software the question about the right level of granularity for a module is quite important. Ideally, to represent a reasonable *module*, a software component should be composed of a *highly cohesive* set of interdependent subcomponents which cannot be easily separated into smaller modules. At the same time, to represent a separate module, such a software component should exhibit a reasonably *low degree of coupling* to other modules. The goal of designing a modular software architecture in which modules exhibit at the same time *high cohesion* and *low coupling* is often achieved in the design phase of a project. However, empirical studies have shown that modularity often deteriorates throughout the subsequent phase of extending and maintaining a software [42–44]. Hence, in order to retain the favorable properties of a modular design, remodularization strategies are needed. They rely on a software restructuring strategy known as *refactoring* [16].

In this paper, we address the question of how automated suggestions for refactoring can be used to improve the modularity of code. In order to minimize the impact on the actual code structures, and thus simplifying the application of our approach in practical settings, we focus on the particular type of *move refactoring*: software constructs are moved between modules without changing other aspects of the source code. If these move refactorings are applied in such a way that the cohesion within modules increases, while the coupling between modules decreases, the modularity of the software improves without affecting the behavior and functionality of the software. While move refactoring is considered as a standard technique to remodularize software, approaches in the literature emphasize difficulties in its practical application that are due to cascades of subsequent move refactorings triggered by the moving of a single software construct [10, 15]. To avoid this caveat, we take a complex systems perspective and frame the remodularization of software based on move refactoring with a scheme similar to simulated annealing [22], in which the system is driven to an equilibrium state [8] by simple local changes. Based on this view, we derive a stochastic optimization algorithm which automates remodularization via move refactoring and validate it in a empirical study on the source code of 39 JAVA open source projects. We show that this approach creates software structures that have higher modularity than the original architectures extracted from the aforementioned empir-

MODULARITY '14, April 22–26, 2014, Lugano, Switzerland.

ACM 978-1-4503-2772-5/14/04... $15.00.
http://dx.doi.org/10.1145/2577080.2577097

ical dataset. We further show that the achievable gain in modularity is related to the level of modularity in the initial architecture, hence indicating the presence of a significant modularization potential in architectures that exhibit low modularity. Although focused in software written in JAVA, we argue that our methodology can be easily extended to other programming languages and paradigms. To foster the reproduction of our results and catalyze their potential impact, we also provide a software prototype of our implementation as an ECLIPSE plug-in.

The rest of this paper is organized as follows: we present our methodology in section 2, discuss our results and their limitations in section 3 and section 4, relate our approach to previous works in section 5 and present our conclusion in section 6.

2. Methods

In this section we describe the steps required to understand and reproduce our results. We start with our empirical datasets, then we move to the interpretation of software constructs and their dependencies in terms of the network structures manipulated during our remodularization strategy, followed by the description of its algorithm. We take inspiration from complex networks theory and apply the Newman's Q modularity measure introduced in [28, 29] and reinterpreted in [43, 44] to score the congruence between coupling and cohesion in a given modular decomposition and finally, we introduce the prototype of an ECLIPSE plug-in implementing a framework that will be expanded to include other approaches, fostering future research on this topic.

2.1 Datasets

We consider two distinct datasets. The first is composed of a curated collection of official releases of 14 JAVA open source software (*OSS*) projects, with a minimum of at least 10 releases each. These releases include the source code as well as the compiled binaries. This dataset is known as QUALITAS CORPUS [35]. The second dataset is composed of 28 JAVA OSS projects, for which fine grained CVS repository logs are available. The logs are aggregated over periods of 30 days such that each aggregation constitutes a full release of the given project. This dataset was previously used in [17, 18, 44], and it was not updated due to the fact that for most of these projects, the development on CVS repositories became obsolete. In Table 1, we present the list of projects, the respective number of snapshots and the date corresponding to the last one.

Table 1. Our datasets of JAVA OSS projects. For the QUALITAS CORPUS dataset, the column "Snapshots" indicate the number of releases of a given project, while in the case of CVS logs it indicates the number of monthly snapshots aggregated over the recorded project history.

	QUALITAS CORPUS	
Project	Snapshots	Last Snapshot Date
ANT	21	2010-12-27
ANTLR	20	2011-07-18
ARGOUML	16	2011-12-15
AZUREUS	57	2011-12-02
ECLIPSE_SDK	40	2011-09-10
FREECOL	28	2011-09-27
FREEMIND	16	2011-02-19
HIBERNATE	100	2012-02-08
JGRAPH	39	2009-09-28
JMETER	20	2011-09-29
JUNG	23	2010-01-25
JUNIT	23	2011-09-29
LUCENE	28	2011-11-20
WEKA	55	2011-10-28

	CVS logs	
Project	Snapshots	Last Snapshot Date
ARCHITECTURWARE	46	2008-02-04
ASPECTJ	62	2008-02-01
AZUREUS	54	2008-01-01
CJOS	87	2008-02-04
COMPOSESTAR	26	2008-07-04
ECLIPSE	83	2008-03-01
ENTERPRISE	64	2008-02-04
FINDBUGS	58	2008-02-04
FUDAA	60	2008-07-01
GPE4GTK	18	2008-07-04
HIBERNATE	50	2008-02-04
JAFFA	59	2008-01-28
JENA	86	2008-02-01
JMLSPECS	71	2008-01-28
JNODE	32	2008-02-03
JPOX	41	2008-01-28
OPENQRM	13	2008-03-01
OPENUSS	44	2008-07-01
OPENXAVA	38	2008-02-04
PERSONALACCESS	39	2008-07-04
PHPECLIPSE	66	2008-07-04
RODINBSHARP	27	2008-07-04
SAPIA	62	2008-07-01
SBLIM	79	2008-07-01
SPRINGFRAMEWORK	59	2008-02-03
SQUIRRELSQL	74	2008-07-04
XMSF	48	2008-07-04
YALE	71	2008-02-01

2.2 Software Dependency Networks

In the following description, we focus on software written in JAVA. However, our approach can be applied right away to software projects developed in other programming languages and paradigms that have suitable abstractions for *modules* and *dependencies*. In particular, we assume that dependencies between JAVA packages represent the *coupling* between modules. Although JAVA was not designed with a specific abstraction for modules [20], it allows *classes* to be grouped into namespaces that are called *packages*. It is considered good practice to organize these packages following modularity principles: high intra-package cohesion and low inter-package coupling [2, 7, 21]. We adopt the same approach and consider a JAVA package as a reasonable approximation for a module. Furthermore, we assume that a package A depends on a package B when a JAVA class (i.e. network node) a in A depends on a class b in B. Here, dependency stands for any kind of relationship between classes such as inheritance, as well as references to attributes or methods. A single link between a and b is created if there is at least one such dependency[1]. By this definition a package is highly cohesive when its classes are tightly connected. Similar approaches were applied in [7, 44]. Figure 1 provides an illustration of our method.

In order to extract such dependency networks (also known as call graphs) from the OSS projects found in the QUALITAS CORPUS dataset, we use a customized version of an OSS parser called DEPENDENCYFINDER [36]. An alternative approach is used to parse the dataset composed of CVS logs. For regular intervals of 30 days, we check out all the corresponding logs and aggregate them, resulting in monthly releases. The dependency network is then extracted by employing the abstract syntax tree parser JDT. For both datasets, the output of this process is a list of links of the form a, b, A, B, meaning class a, which belongs to package A, depends on a class b found in package B.

2.3 A Complex Systems Approach to ReModularization

Our approach to remodularization is based on *move refactoring*, a technique to reorganize source code which does not modify neither the software dependency network, nor the behavior or func-

[1] in this *simplification* links have no weights, but we argue that it can be generalized to weighted links

```
package A;
import B.*;
import C.*;

public class a extends b{
        public static void main (String[] args) {
                        c object_c = new c();
                        object_c.runMethod();
                        ...
        }
        ...
}
```

```
package C;
import D.*;

public class c{
        public static void main (String[] args) {
                        d object_d = new d();
                        object_d.runMethod();
                        ...
        }
        ...
}
```

(a) JAVA source code excerpt

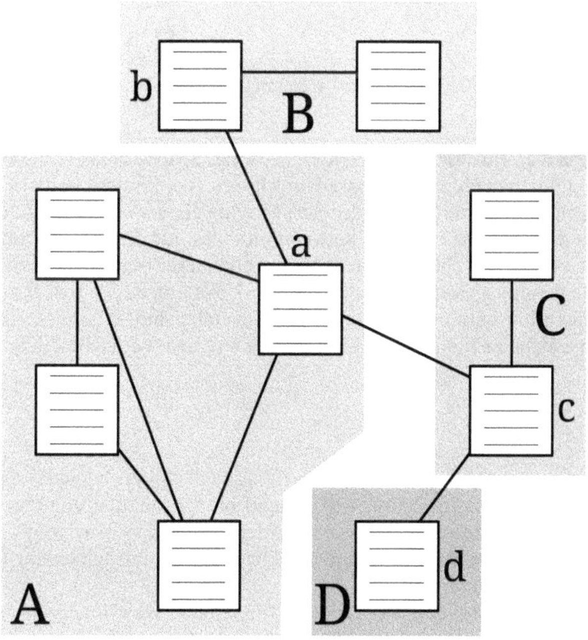

(b) corresponding dependency network

Figure 1. Example of a modular software. (a) Source code excerpt. (b) Corresponding undirected network structure. The shaded areas represent modules (e.g. JAVA packages), which are internally composed of software constructs (e.g. JAVA classes). Links between such elements indicate structural dependencies (e.g. class inheritance, reference to attribute or method, etc).

tionality of the software itself. As an example, consider the modular software system (e.g. written in an object oriented programming language) which is illustrated in Figure 2(a). This system is composed of three coupled modules A, B and C. As described in section 2.2, these dependencies are the result of the interaction between the classes within each module, which can be located internally (intra-module dependencies) or across different modules (inter-module coupling). Too much inter-module coupling hinders modular architectures. For example, in terms of developer cognition, highly coupled modules cannot be easily isolated, forcing the developer to go over all the inter-module dependencies in order to understand the functionalities of a single module. In summary, the more coupling exists between modules, the harder it becomes to maintain and expand the software [12, 24, 38].

Move refactoring offers a simple solution to this problem. It consists of moving software constructs within a module to adjacent modules without changing the dependency structure of the software. In terms of the example discussed above, by carefully moving classes from their original modules into other modules, it is possible to reduce the coupling between modules. Thus, move refactoring applied to a software dependency network translates into relabeling the network nodes (e.g JAVA classes) according to module membership (e.g. JAVA package membership). In Figure 2, we illustrate the result of five move refactorings involving a single class each (the classes are $a1, a2, b1, c1, c2$). The modules in the refactored system, represented by Figure 2(b), are indeed less coupled. It is important to note that when moving content around, while ignoring the semantics of each module, it is likely that the principle of separation of concerns will be violated [13, 30, 34]. We further discuss this issue in section 4.

For small systems, such as the one illustrated in Figure 2, move refactoring is a trivial task and can be performed manually. Due to the structural complexity of software, the larger the system, the harder it is for a developer to grasp which could be suitable move refactoring steps. As described in section 5, most of the literature addresses this issue by means of optimization techniques. In most of these techniques, every possible move needs to be scored by the evaluation of a global optimization criterion (e.g. an *objective function* quantifying coupling and cohesion). In this paper, we propose a stochastic move refactoring strategy that does not require to keep track of such optimization criteria[2]. Besides providing an interesting, new, and simpler, perspective on remodularization based on complex system theory, our approach also addresses concerns in the literature regarding the explicit use of coupling-cohesion metrics when guiding the optimization search.

Our algorithm works as follows: For a modular system composed of n packages and k classes, at each time step, we pick a class c at random and count the number of links $N_j^{(c)}$ connecting it to other classes in each package j, such that $j \in \{module(c')|c' \in \mathcal{N}(c)\}$. Here, $\mathcal{N}(c)$ represents the set of classes adjacent to c (or in other words, the neighborhood of c). The probability $P_j^{(c)}$ that this class will be moved to package j is

$$P_j^{(c)} = \frac{\exp\left(N_j^{(c)}/T\right)}{\sum_{i=1}^{n} \exp\left(N_i^{(c)}/T\right)}. \tag{1}$$

Thus, this randomly picked class has higher probability to be moved into a package where it maintains most of its connections. Indeed, this could be its current package. In such a case this class has higher probability to not undergo move refactoring. The *temperature* parameter T (constant) controls the likelihood of moves that would deteriorate the modularity of this architecture.

[2] see Algorithm 1

This deterioration is characterized by the increase of the number of inter-module links if "bad" moves actually occur. The smaller T, the smaller the chance to select such move refactorings. Although small, this probability is not zero. This nonvanishing probability fosters the exploration of rugged problem landscapes, allowing the search to escape local optima.

From a computational point of view, it is worth remarking that (for projects with large number of classes) the exponential term $\exp\left(N_j^{(c)}/T\right)$ may yield an out-of-bounds error because of numerical precision. In order to avoid this, we can find $N_{max}^{(c)} = \arg\max_{l\in[1,n]} N_l^{(c)}$, i.e. the maximum number of nodes connected to c by inter-module links. Then, we compute

$$P_j^{(c)} = \frac{\exp\left(-\frac{N_{max}^{(c)}-N_j^{(c)}}{T}\right)}{\sum_{i=1}^{n}\exp\left(-\frac{N_{max}^{(c)}-N_i^{(c)}}{T}\right)}, \quad (2)$$

which is equivalent to Eq. 1, and each exponential term is smaller than one.

To summarize, at each step we perform a move refactoring iteration according to the probability distribution P. This procedure is repeated for a finite number of steps. Algorithm 1 presents the pseudocode of our stochastic move refactoring strategy, while in Figure 3 we illustrate one step of this algorithm.

```
initializeParameters(T, n_iterations);
network := loadNetworkFromSourceCode();
for i ← 1 to n_iterations do
    node := pickRandomNode(network);
    normTerm := 0;
    N_max := node.mostLinkedModule.numberOfLinks;
    P := emptyArray();
    for each j in modulesInNeighborhoodOf(node) do
        /*Count the number of links between node and
        module j*/
        N_j := countLinksToModuleJ(node.neighbors, j);
        /*The probability to move node to module j.*/
        /*The temperature parameter T controls the
        likelihood of bad moves.*/
        p := exp - (N_max - N_j)/T;
        normTerm := normTerm + p;
        P.append((p, j));
    end
    /*Normalize the probability distribution P*/
    for j ← 1 to P.length() do
        P[j].p := P[j].p/normTerm;
    end
    /*Decide which module receives node according to
    probability distribution P*/
    node.module := moveRefactoring(node, P);
    network := updateNetwork(node, network);
end
```

Algorithm 1: Stochastic move refactoring algorithm. The temperature parameter T is a constant, therefore a cooling schedule is not required. We emphasize that a node can only be move refactored to adjacent modules in which it maintains software dependencies.

In statistical physics, the model described by Eq. 1 is similar to the n-state *Potts Model* [40]. In a fully connected graph, this system is a paradigmatic model to study the equilibrium phase transition (as a function of temperature) from an ordered state, where all the nodes reside in the same module–to a disordered one–where all the nodes are randomly located in different modules. In the case of complex topologies–like those found in class dependencies–the equilibrium configuration will depend on the modular coherence inside of the software: the more interdependent particular groups of classes are, the more likely they will be assigned–in equilibrium–to the same module.

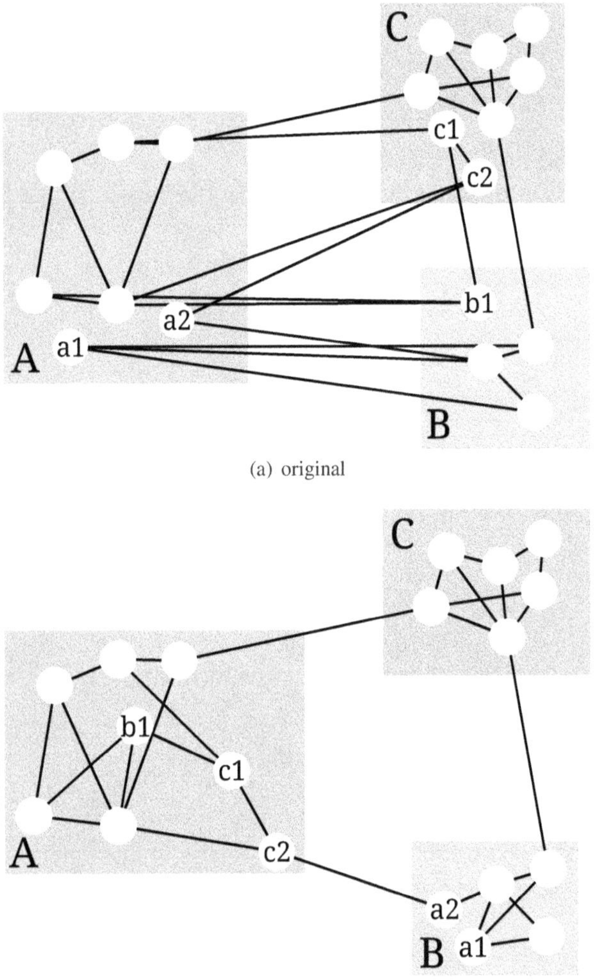

(a) original

(b) refactored

Figure 2. Illustration of move refactoring. Shaded areas represent modules, which are composed of classes (i.e. circles) bound by undirected software dependencies. Moving classes across modules can decrease the coupling between modules. (a) original modular decomposition. (b) modular decomposition after move refactoring. The resulting modules are less coupled. We emphasize that move refactoring only modifies the module membership of a class. The dependencies (i.e. links) on other classes remain untouched.

There are several properties of this system which made it the objective of a large body of literature in the realm of physics. Here, we will simply mention a few properties that are sufficient to understand the relevance of using this model within the context of this paper.

For the n-state *Potts Model*, it is possible to write for each node an individual *objective function*, which dictates the score of the current configuration of package assignment. Let π_c denote the package a class c is assigned to. Then, the objective function for

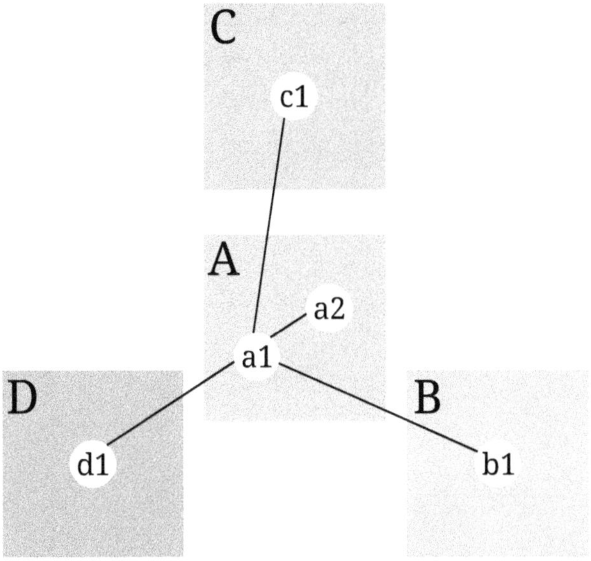

Figure 3. Class $a1$ will be refactored. It can remain in package A, or be moved to package B, C or D. Due to the topology of this simple example (i.e. a single link to each package), each possibility has equal probability to take place. We emphasize that–using Algorithm 1–class $a1$ can only be moved to modules where it maintains software dependencies. Further generalizations are possible and will be investigated in future research.

class c reads

$$u_c = -\sum_{c' \in \mathcal{N}(c)} \delta(\pi_c, \pi_{c'}).$$

The Kronecker delta function δ is equal to one if both arguments are equal (i.e. if classes c and c' belong to the same package), zero, otherwise. The sum runs over all classes c' which have dependency relations with class c, i.e. the neighborhood of c, represented by $\mathcal{N}(c)$. Summing up over all the nodes, we obtain

$$U = \sum_{c=1}^{k} u_c = -\sum_{c=1}^{k} \sum_{c' \in \mathcal{N}(c)} \delta(\pi_c, \pi_{c'}), \tag{3}$$

which measures the total score of the current configuration. Interestingly, when class c is moved from package π_c to another π_c', it is very simple to show that the total change is $\Delta U(\pi_c \rightarrow \pi_c') = 2\Delta u_c$. This implies that the *local* maximization procedure, is equivalent to the *global* maximization. For this particular problem, this is a very important property, as it implies that this simple local rule is equivalent to a global one. This also implies that U in Eq. 3 is the *total energy* of the system.

During the simulations, at every time step there are many possible configurations of module assignment for every node in the source code of the project. Over time, the algorithm *samples* the space of all possible assignments, such that the sampling probability of a given configuration is a function of Equation 3. The process of sampling is thus equivalent to the *Metropolis* algorithm [26], which also allows the convergence time to be determined in a standard way [11, 19, 27]. Because of the results shown in section 3, it is apparent that the energy landscape is not rugged, but smooth. Thereby, the modularization process proposed in this paper always converges to a stationary state, and a simulated annealing approach (meaning the cooling schedule for the temperature) is not needed.

2.4 An Alternative Metric for Coupling and Cohesion

We follow the progress of our automated move refactoring strategy by applying the Newman's Q measure, a quantitative approach widely used in complex networks theory [28, 29]. This was reinterpreted in [42–44] as an alternative method to monitor the evolution of software modularity. In those empirical studies, we focus on JAVA open source projects and show that Q successfully expresses the congruence of the clusters of software dependencies between classes and the decomposition of source code in terms of JAVA packages. It is defined as

$$Q = \frac{\sum_i^n e_{ii} - \sum_i^n a_i b_i}{1 - \sum_i^n a_i b_i} \tag{4}$$

where e_{ij} is the fraction of links that connect nodes in module i to nodes in module j, $a_i = \sum_j^n e_{ij}$ and $b_i = \sum_j^n e_{ji}$ are the column and row sum respectively, while n corresponds to the number of modules. If the network is undirected, the matrix defined by **e** is symmetric and $a_i = b_i$ [28]. We use Q to measure the fraction of links that connect nodes within the same module ($\sum_i^n e_{ii}$) minus the value of the same quantity expected from a randomized network ($\sum_i^n a_i b_i$). If the former is not better than random $Q = 0$ [29]. However, Q would not be defined if all links are concentrated within a single module. For such trivial case, the scaling factor equals zero ($1 - \sum_i^n a_i b_i = 1 - 1 = 0$). To avoid such a division by zero, we define $Q = 0$. In general, $Q \in [-1, 1]$. That is, the less coupled the modules and the higher their cohesion, the closer Q is to 1. As an illustration of its application, $Q = 0.37$ for the network in Figure 2(a), while $Q = 0.84$ for the one in Figure 2(b).

2.5 SOMOMOTO: An Eclipse Plugin for ReModularization

SOMOMOTO is an ECLIPSE plug-in and its name stands for "software modularization and monitoring tool". Its initial goal is providing a framework for remodularization of software written in JAVA. It is a tool that developers can use to monitor the evolution of a modular software architecture, both quantitatively and visually. For the quantitative part, we implement Q as described in section 2.4, and we are planning to include other approaches available in the literature. For the visualization of modular software architectures, we make use of GEPHI's library for graph and network layout [5]. Besides monitoring software modularity, we are also able to act against its deterioration. This is achieved by implementing our automated strategy discussed in section 2.3. Furthermore, we plan to include competing approaches to foster direct comparison with our methodology. We also plan to allow developers to interfere with the algorithm's behavior, for example, by enabling manual move refactoring aided by an interactive network visualization interface. Moreover, we plan to allow the developers to define binding constraints to forbid or prioritize specific move refactoring options, to which any automated approach must comply. The source code, freely distribute with a GPL V3 license, is available at `http://sourceforge.net/projects/somomoto/`.

3. Results

In the following, we apply our strategy to the JAVA OSS datasets described in section 2.1. For each project listed in Table 1, we follow the procedure outlined in section 2.2 to extract the software dependency network of its last snapshot. This network is used as the input of our strategy (see Algorithm 1) and we run it for 20 different values for the temperature parameter T. We choose $T \in [0.01, 1000]$ such that these values are uniformly distributed on a logarithmic scale. We repeat this process 20 times in order to average the dynamics with respect to T.

3.1 The Temperature and the Equilibrium Configuration

In Figure 4 and 5, we depict the Q value and the number of modules with respect to the iterations executed by our strategy. We show three projects belonging to the QUALITAS CORPUS dataset: the IDE ECLIPSE_SDK, the graphical library JUNG and the database interface HIBERNATE, because the results obtained for these three projects are representative for the projects listed in Table 1. In accordance with the theoretical discussion presented in section 2.3, low temperature values (i.e. $T < 0.1$) lead to equilibrium configurations with low inter-module coupling and high intra-module cohesion. This range of temperature makes deteriorating move refactoring steps very unlikely. Thus software modularity improves substantially, as expressed in terms of the high Q values seen in figures 4(a), 4(b) and 4(c).

Interestingly, the highest Q values and the lowest number of modules are obtained within an intermediate temperature range (i.e. $0.1 < T < 10$). For this range, we show in Table 2 that a small improvement in Q (i.e. $\approx 4.0\%$)–with respect to the range $T < 0.1$–is associated with a comparably larger drop in the number of modules (i.e. $\approx 17\%$). Furthermore, as depicted in Figures 5(a), 5(b) and 5(c), the execution of our strategy always leads to a significant drop in the number of modules. For the lowest temperature (i.e. $T = 0.01$) this drop is lowest and corresponds to losing $68.4 \pm 13.2\%$ of the original modules. For higher temperatures, the drop is even larger. Thus, as a side effect of our strategy, a substantial fraction of the original structure of the source code is lost. Although associated with an improvement in modularity, it is not understood how this drop in the number of modules can affect development performance. More research is needed to study if for example, this extra improvement of $\approx 4\%$ in Q values (e.g. from 166% to 170%) justify a further drop of 17% in the number of modules (e.g. from 68% to 85%). As a rule of thumb–if remodularization is expected to preserve the most possible of the original modular structure–only values of $T \ll 0.1$ should be considered.

Table 2. Average values for the change in Q and in the number of modules for different temperature ranges. For the lowest temperature (i.e. $T = 0.01$) our strategy improves Q in $166.6 \pm 77.3\%$, while decreasing the number of modules in $68.4 \pm 13.2\%$.

Temperature Range	ΔQ (%)	Δ Modules (%)
$T = 0.01$ (lowest)	166.6 ± 77.3	-68.4 ± 13.2
$T < 0.1$	166.5 ± 77.6	-68.4 ± 13.2
$0.1 < T < 10$	170.5 ± 105.2	-85.4 ± 9.7
$10 < T$	-50.1 ± 18.6	-82.9 ± 9.7
$T = 1000$ (highest)	-52.1 ± 16.7	-82.4 ± 9.9

Figure 6(a) depicts the relation between Q and the number of modules on the temperature parameter T. In this figure, we only consider the equilibrium values of the former two quantities. We bin the data points with respect to T and calculate the median value. We also show the 90% and 10% quantiles. The first insight is that the variability in Q is almost constant with respect to T, decreasing slightly during the abrupt change between high and low Q values. For small T, the variability in the number of modules is comparably higher, but decreases significantly as T increases. Another insight is the abrupt change in Q about $T = 10$. For $T < 10$ we observe values of Q which are significantly higher than for $T > 10$. This is further illustrated in Figure 6(b), which depicts the potential energy difference between these two states: high potential energy (i.e. high modularity and high Q) and low potential energy (i.e. low modularity and low Q). As a final remark, these two contrasting potential energy levels are the reason why we only observe few equilibrium states in figures 4(a), 4(b) and 4(c): high Q (i.e. high

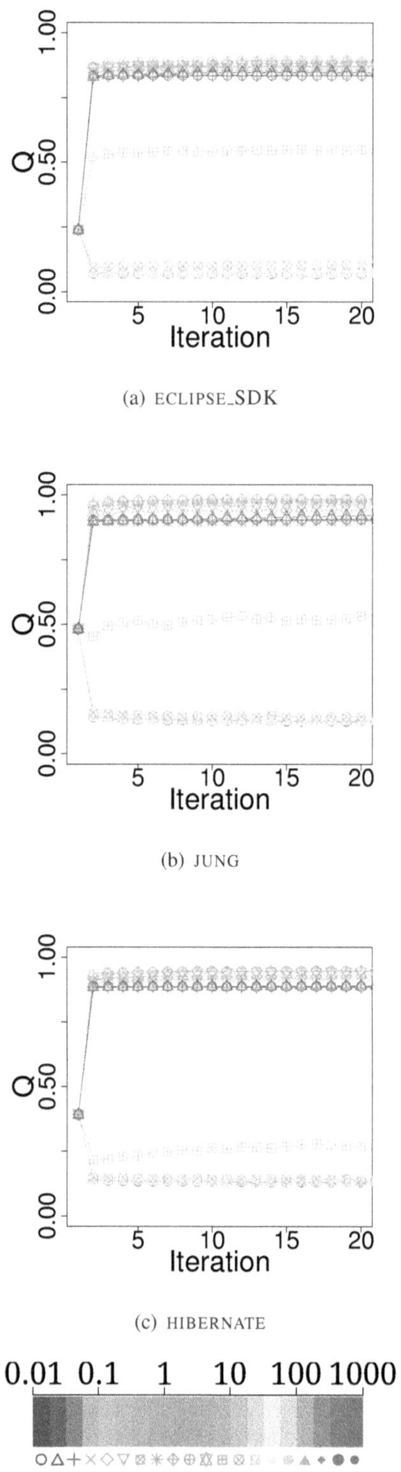

(a) ECLIPSE_SDK

(b) JUNG

(c) HIBERNATE

(d) T

Figure 4. Evolution of Q during move refactoring steps. The iteration number k displayed in the horizontal axis of each figure corresponds to $100 \times m \times k$ move refactoring steps (i.e. m being the number of JAVA classes). Each curve represents the average of 20 runs of our strategy with different values of the temperature parameter T.

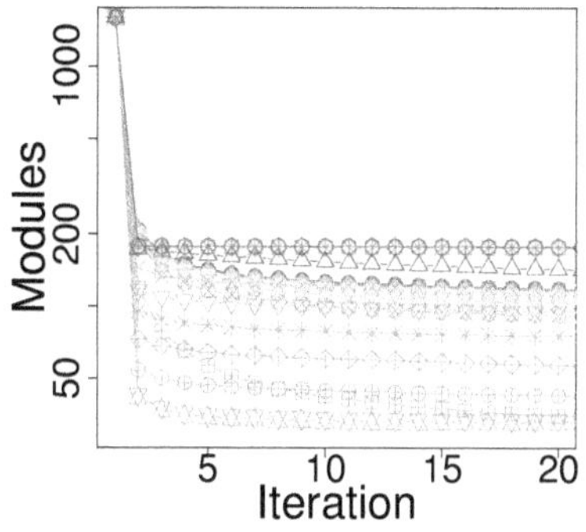

(a) ECLIPSE_SDK

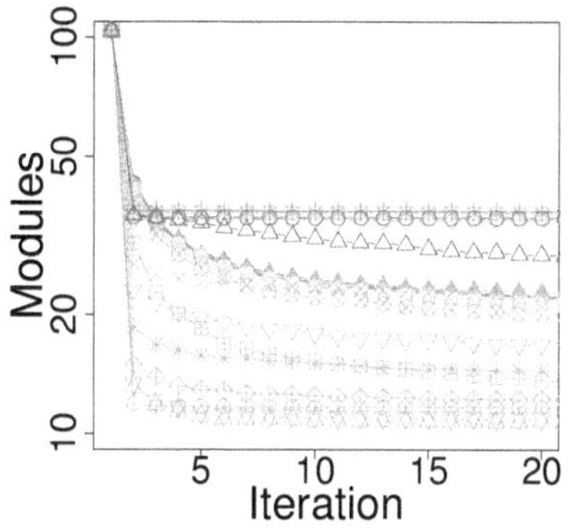

(b) JUNG

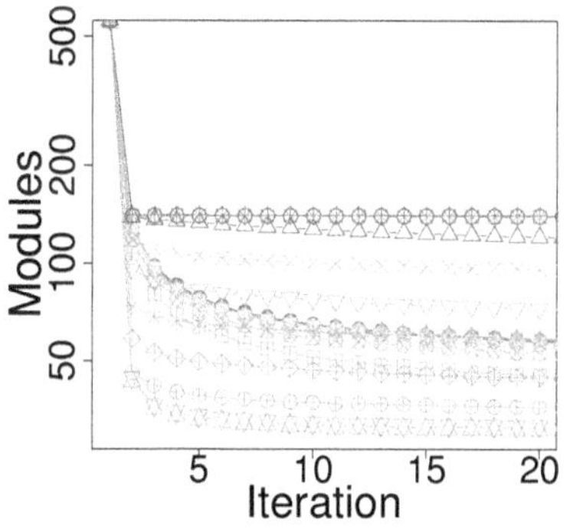

(c) HIBERNATE

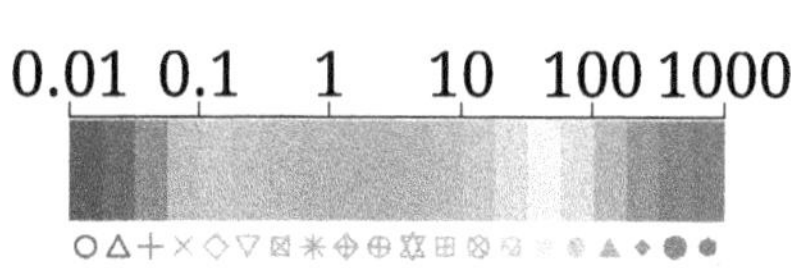

(d) T

Figure 5. Evolution of the number of required modules (i.e. non-empty modules) during move refactoring steps. For intermediary values (i.e. $0.1 < T < 10$) we obtain the highest Q values on the expense of losing a significant fraction of the original modules. Thus, the use of $T < 0.1$ is recommended (see Figure 4).

potential energy), intermediary Q (i.e. transitional state) and low Q (i.e. low potential energy).

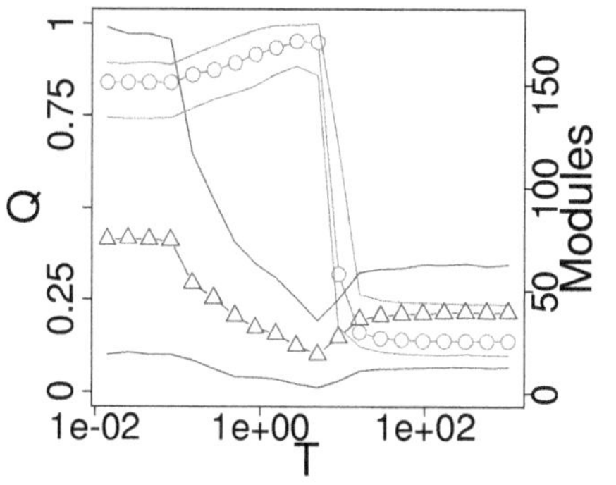

(a) modularity and T

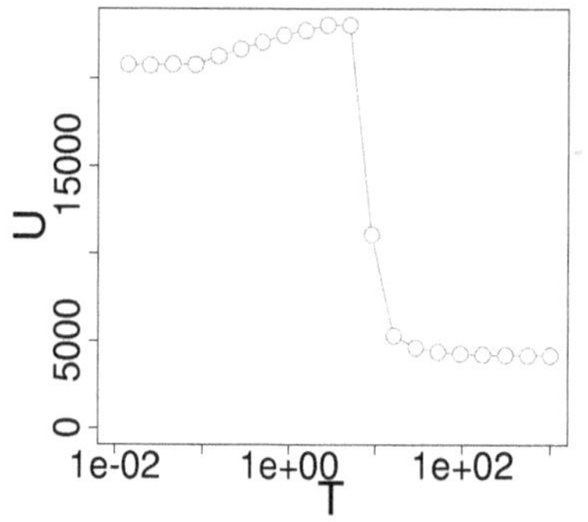

(b) potential energy and T

Figure 6. The role of the temperature T as a control parameter. (a) Dependency of Q (i.e. dashed red circles) and the number of required modules (i.e. dashed blue triangles) with the temperature T. Each curve is obtained by measuring the median value of the corresponding measures, when considering the simulation results aggregated over T. The solid curves above and below the corresponding measure represent the 90.0% and 10.0% quantiles respectively. There is an abrupt change in the value of Q as a function of the control parameter T. (b) Median value of the corresponding potential energy U. Structured or well modularized software falls into the T range mapping to a higher potential energy level (i.e. $T < 10$), while poorly structured software falls into the deep valley with low potential energy level (i.e. $T > 10$).

3.2 Remodularization Performance of our Strategy

In Figure 7(a), we show that the performance of our strategy does not depend on the number of modules (i.e. no correlation between Q and the number of modules). Furthermore, our strategy improved the modularity of all projects considered in this paper, resulting in remodularized software with an average value of $Q = 0.8 \pm 0.1$ for $T = 0.01$. Finally, the worse the modularity of a given architecture, the higher the relative improvement as a result of the application of our strategy. We depict this in Figure 7(b). Further research will investigate if these results hold for different datasets.

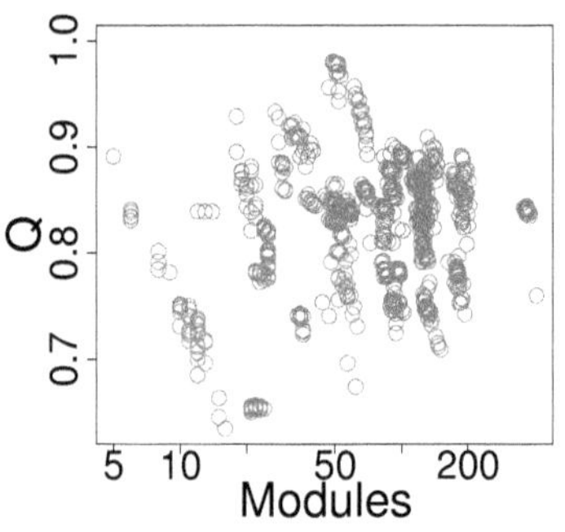

(a) Q does not depend on Modules

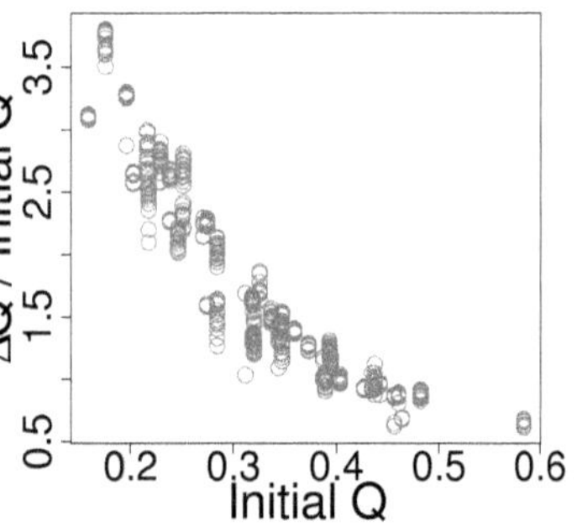

(b) improvement relative to initial Q

Figure 7. The performance of our strategy at equilibrium with $T = 0.01$. (a) In the studied dataset, the number of modules does not correlate with Q, thus we can discard any dependency of this kind. (b) The worse the initial value of Q (i.e. the worse the initial modular design), the larger the improvement achieved.

3.3 Move Refactoring in Empirical Data

In this section, we verify if the move refactoring suggestions discovered by our strategy were actually executed in empirical data. We focus on the CVS logs dataset, which reflects the iterative development process with greater regularity, following closely the coding decisions undertaken by the software developers.

In order to perform this comparison, we first need to be able to detect move refactoring taking place within our datasets. We solve this problem in the following way. We define a time stamped CVS log snapshot s_t, which corresponds to the set of class dependencies and respective package (module) membership observed at time t. Each class in s_t is named with respect to the pattern $package\_name_t.class\_name_t$. To detect move refactoring, we take the simple approach of looking for unique class names ($class\_name_t$) in s_t, verifying if these names are found in s_{t+1}. If the answer is positive, we check for modifications in the respective package names ($package\_name_t$). Thus, move refactoring is detected when $class\_name_t = class\_name_{t+1}$ and $package\_name_t \neq package\_name_{t+1}$. We emphasize that this approach only detects move refactoring of the kind defined in this paper: a refactoring step that only modifies the package membership of a class, without touching upon any of its contents and the network of software dependencies.

With the move refactoring detection method outlined above, we are able to compare our strategy output with the work of the software developers. For each two consecutive CVS log snapshot s_t and s_{t+1}, we extract the respective empirical software dependency networks net_t^e and net_{t+1}^e (see section 2.2). Let D be the set of move refactoring steps performed by the developers between net_t^e and net_{t+1}^e. Furthermore, we use net_t^e as the input of our algorithm and let it run until convergence (for $T = 0.01$). The network of software dependencies resulting from this procedure is defined as net_{t+1}^s. Finally, let S be the set of move refactoring steps performed by our strategy and detected between net_t^e and net_{t+1}^s. We compare these two sets, thresholding on the ΔQ between t and $t+1$, so that we focus on move refactoring taking place during significant improvements in software modularity. For different values of ΔQ, we calculate $precision$ and $recall$ and present the results in Table 3. The results show that our strategy correctly suggest most of the move refactoring steps performed by the software developers, as indicated by the relatively high values listed in the column $recall$. In fact, our algorithm is much more *aggressive* than the developers when suggesting move refactoring steps. This is further discussed this in section 4. Thus, our resulting set of suggestions is much larger than the set chosen by developers. This is the reason why our $precision$ values are relatively small: the software developers do not use move refactoring consistently as mean to restore software modularity.

Table 3. Comparison between the set of move refactoring steps suggested by our strategy S, against the set of steps performed by the developers D upon the empirical data. Quantitatively: $precision = \frac{|S \cap D|}{|S|}$ and $recall = \frac{|S \cap D|}{|D|}$. We present these measures for different values of the threshold parameter ΔQ (i.e. change in modularity measured in empirical data), thus allowing us to focus on the move refactoring steps that had significant impact on software modularity.

Δ Q (%)	$precision$ (%)	$recall$ (%)
1	4.9 ± 15.7	59.9 ± 35.4
5	7.0 ± 16.9	62.4 ± 35.3
10	8.1 ± 19.2	62.7 ± 39.0
15	5.7 ± 8.9	52.4 ± 40.8

3.4 SOMOMOTO in Action

As a simple test case, we employ SOMOMOTO in the remodularization of a JAVA graphical library called JGRAPHX. Figure 8 depicts the software dependency network and the module membership of classes of JGRAPX, before and after remodularization. The resulting network, depicted in Figure 8(b), clearly shows the congruence between the clusters of software dependencies and the source code decomposition into JAVA packages. Network nodes (i.e. classes) bearing the same color are members of the same modules (i.e. packages).

4. Threats to Validity

Here, we address some of the concerns related to the results of our approach. The first issue is our conscious decision of not considering the semantics of modules during the remodularization via automated move refactorings. We are well aware of the fact that there are modules whose contents should not be move refactored, in despite of their significant impact on inter-module coupling. For example, modules responsible for user interfaces may fall within this category. Related to this issue, there might be modules that are

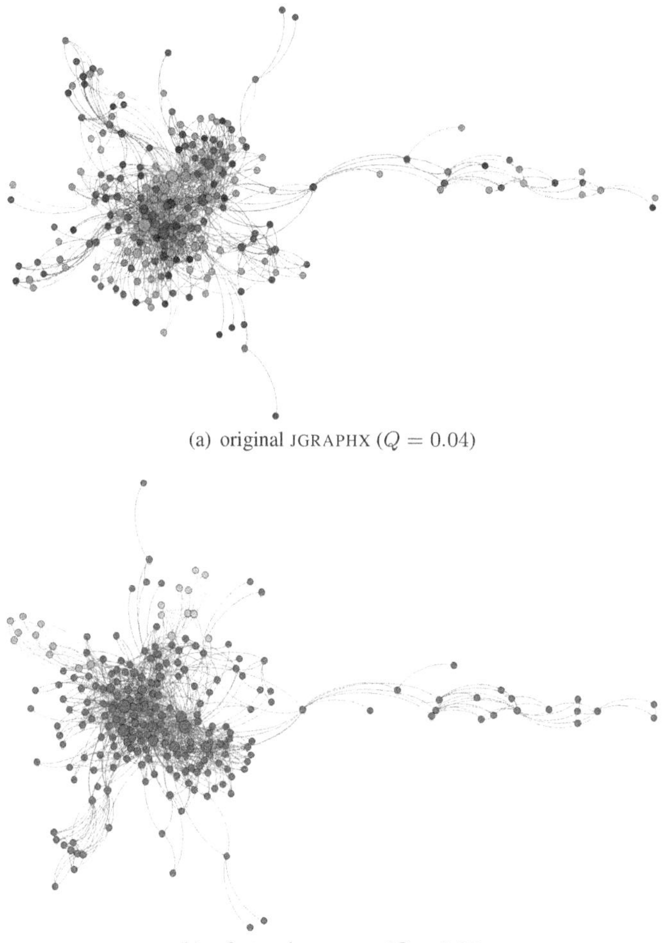

(a) original JGRAPHX ($Q = 0.04$)

(b) refactored JGRAPHX ($Q = 0.85$)

Figure 8. Test case: the remodularization of JGRAPHX (a JAVA graphical library). The JAVA classes are depicted as circles, while their color reflects the corresponding package membership (same color, same package). (a) original. (b) after remodularization by SOMOMOTO.

believed to be already well structured. In such cases, further refactoring them would be detrimental. The simplest solution, which we are planning to include in SOMOMOTO, is to allow developers to mark modules and also classes that should not be remodularized by an automated refactoring strategy. Further ideas related to direct interference in the behavior of the algorithm, allowing it to cope with developer preferences are possible. For example, the contents of obsolete modules might need to be move refactored into other modules. For such cases, our strategy can be applied by focusing on a few modules, redistributing their content.

Another issue that might be circumvented by allowing the direct interference of software developers is the observed significant drop in the number of modules, even for small values of the temperature parameter T. Our results show that at least $\approx 68\%$ become empty. One possible explanation is found in [7], where the authors study a similar dataset of JAVA OSS projects, showing that the minimization of the inter-module coupling and maximization of intra-module cohesion is not a dominating module design principle. Thus, a more realistic perspective on automated remodularization should include complementary quantitative dimensions. These additions, together with the implementation of competing approaches, will be included in our ECLIPSE plug-in, in order to foster direct comparison with our methodology, and also to provide a unified framework for the remodularization of JAVA software. These steps will foster its use in practice. We are further interested in the opinion of software developers on the outcome of our automated move refactoring strategy, also to understand if the seldom use of move refactoring observed in our datasets is a general issue. We expect that move refactoring, based on our automated strategy, will be more frequently applied in practice. As shown in this paper, the underlying problem landscape seems to be smooth, at least with respect to the temperature parameter T. Thus, a convergence to favorable software modularities can be ensured.

5. Related Work

Software evolves in ways that do not necessarily reflect positively in its modularity. In order to cope with the deterioration of the latter, refactoring strategies can be employed. It has been argued in [10, 15], that approaches considering developer expertise–to directly refactor the source code–seldom allow for a significant improvement in software modularity. The difficulties are mainly related to the problem of detecting possible candidates for refactoring. This opens up many opportunities for the development of automated refactoring methodologies. Among the available approaches, the ones that imply a reformulation of software modularity as a combinatorial problem are quite common. Furthermore, most of those are mainly concerned with the minimization of inter-module coupling and maximization of intra-module cohesion [3], as dictated by software engineering wisdom [13, 30, 34], both have potentially high impact on maintenance costs. One of the earliest approaches in this direction offers an optimization search guided by a genetic algorithm [14]. Their search starts with an initial modular decomposition, which at each iteration is replaced by the best decomposition found in a population controlled by the algorithm. A simple variation of this approach is to allow multiple searches to take place in parallel, such that a majority rule is used to determine the best modular decomposition [25]. An alternative way to escape local optima is discussed in [1]. Similar to our own approach, they apply simulated annealing allowing the acceptance of moves that do not always improve the functional being maximized. Moves that improve the respective functional are always accepted. Our approach is different for being completely governed by Eq. 1, such that every move bears a probability of being executed. Their absolute contribution to the energy function influences this probability but do not force an immediate acceptance. The authors also introduce constraints to limit some aspects of the optimization search that are missing here: maximal number of classes that can change their packages, maximal number of classes that a package can contain and the classes that should not change their packages. These are in line with the idea of having software developers interfering with automated approaches more effectively, as discussed in [23, 32]. We plan to include this methodology in future releases of our plug-in. Furthermore, [1] report results on modularity improvement only for highly limited values for these three constraints. These result in small improvement in modularity, which cannot be compared to the results–significantly higher–that we present in our work. Complementary to the discussion above, the work presented in [7] classifies modules by their role within the architecture. They show that modules controlling *io* and *gui* functions are the most congruent regarding cohesion and coupling metrics. Moreover, [6, 33] advocate the use of metrics based on the semantics of modules besides structural dependencies. According to [17, 18], structural dependencies are not uniformly important with respect to the propagation of changes. Thus they emphasize that future research should focus on their semantics rather than the structure. Other approaches in the literature seek to group software constructs into modules according to measures that express their similarity, a technique better known as *clustering*. Examples of works within this context are presented in [4, 23, 32]. In [41], a comparison between different clustering strategies concludes that clustering algorithms do not reproduce the existing modular decomposition of software projects, calling for further research.

6. Conclusion

In conclusion, we have introduced a simple stochastic algorithm that allows to remodularize software architectures based on an automated suggestion of *move refactorings*. This algorithm is based on the assumption that an optimum modular design of software minimizes the *coupling* between modules, while the *cohesion* within modules is maximized. We take a complex networks perspective on modularity in software dependency networks and capture both cohesion and coupling by a network-based, quantitative measure. Furthermore, making use of the n-state *Potts Model* known from statistical physics, our stochastic algorithm provides a complex systems approach to the optimization of software modularity in dependency networks. We validate the remodularization performance of our algorithm by applying it to two datasets which allows us to study the evolution of software dependency networks for 39 JAVA open source software projects. The results of our analysis validate that the modularity of these projects can be increased on average by $166 \pm 77\%$. We further show that the achievable gain in modularity is related to the level of modularity in the initial architecture, hence indicating the presence of a significant modularization potential in architectures that exhibit low modularity. Based on empirical data on the evolution of software modularity in JAVA projects, we further extract *move refactorings* performed by developers to remodularize the software architecture. We then compare the suggestions of our algorithm with the actual actions of developers and compare *precision* and *recall* of the refactoring suggestions. The fact that our approach achieves a comparably high recall while the precision is low highlights that a) our method suggests most of the move refactorings that were identified by developers and b) that our method was able to identify many more move refactoring than were actually implemented by real developers. We argue that this finding opens a number of interesting further research directions: First, it can be seen as a challenge for the assumption that optimal modular designs (from the perspective of developers) coincide with a maximization of cohesion and a minimization of coupling. Reasons for this most likely include the importance of context in the choice of the package decomposition of projects, as well as the existence of dependencies to third-party packages whose modular structure cannot be easily changed. Secondly, it can be interpreted in such a way that our method highlights a significant modularization potential that currently goes unused in actual software projects. Finally, it highlights the necessity of introducing an additional parameter to our algorithm, that influences how *aggressive* it is. In summary, we argue that our work is a promising example for the applicability of models, methods and abstractions from the study of complex systems and complex networks in software engineering.

7. Acknowledgment

We acknowledge ETH ZÜRICH for financial support and also Vahan Hovannisyan for implementing the prototype of our ECLIPSE plug-in.

References

[1] H. Abdeen, S. Ducasse, H. Sahraoui, and I. Alloui. Automatic package coupling and cycle minimization. In *Reverse Engineering, 2009. WCRE'09. 16th Working Conference on*, pages 103–112. IEEE, 2009.

[2] D. Ancona and E. Zucca. True modules for java-like languages. In *ECOOP 2001Object-Oriented Programming*, pages 354–380. Springer, 2001.

[3] N. Anquetil and J. Laval. Legacy software restructuring: Analyzing a concrete case. In *Software Maintenance and Reengineering (CSMR), 2011 15th European Conference on*, pages 279–286. IEEE, 2011.

[4] G. Antoniol, M. Di Penta, and M. Neteler. Moving to smaller libraries via clustering and genetic algorithms. In *Software Maintenance and Reengineering, 2003. Proceedings. Seventh European Conference on*, pages 307–316. IEEE, 2003.

[5] M. Bastian, S. Heymann, and M. Jacomy. Gephi: An open source software for exploring and manipulating networks. In *Proceedings of the ICWSM '09*. AAAI, 2009.

[6] G. Bavota, A. De Lucia, A. Marcus, and R. Oliveto. Software remodularization based on structural and semantic metrics. In *Reverse Engineering (WCRE), 2010 17th Working Conference on*, pages 195–204. IEEE, 2010.

[7] F. Beck and S. Diehl. On the congruence of modularity and code coupling. In *Proceedings of the 19th ACM SIGSOFT symposium and the 13th European conference on Foundations of software engineering*, pages 354–364. ACM, 2011.

[8] E. Bertin. *A concise introduction to the statistical physics of complex systems*. Springer, 2012.

[9] K. Blincoe, G. Valetto, and S. Goggins. Proximity: a measure to quantify the need for developers' coordination. In *Proceedings of the ACM 2012 conference on Computer Supported Cooperative Work*, pages 1351–1360. ACM, 2012.

[10] S. Bryton and F. B. e. Abreu. Modularity-oriented refactoring. In *Software Maintenance and Reengineering, 2008. CSMR 2008. 12th European Conference on*, pages 294–297. IEEE, 2008.

[11] J. Cruz and C. Dorea. Simple conditions for the convergence of simulated annealing type algorithms. *Journal of applied probability*, pages 885–892, 1998.

[12] J. S. Davis. Effect of modularity on maintainability of rule-based systems. *International Journal of Man-Machine Studies*, 32(4):439–447, 1990.

[13] E. W. Dijkstra. On the role of scientific thought. In *Selected Writings on Computing: A Personal Perspective*, pages 60–66. Springer, 1982.

[14] D. Doval, S. Mancoridis, and B. S. Mitchell. Automatic clustering of software systems using a genetic algorithm. In *Software Technology and Engineering Practice, 1999. STEP'99. Proceedings*, pages 73–81. IEEE, 1999.

[15] B. Du Bois, S. Demeyer, and J. Verelst. Refactoring-improving coupling and cohesion of existing code. In *Reverse Engineering, 2004. Proceedings. 11th Working Conference on*, pages 144–151. IEEE, 2004.

[16] M. Fowler. *Refactoring: improving the design of existing code*. Addison-Wesley Professional, 1999.

[17] M. M. Geipel. Modularity, dependence and change. *Advances in Complex Systems*, 15(06), 2012.

[18] M. M. Geipel and F. Schweitzer. The link between dependency and co-change: Empirical evidence. *IEEE Transactions on Software Engineering*, 38(6):1432–1444, 2012.

[19] V. Granville, M. Krivánek, and J.-P. Rasson. Simulated annealing: A proof of convergence. *Pattern Analysis and Machine Intelligence, IEEE Transactions on*, 16(6):652–656, 1994.

[20] R. Hall, K. Pauls, S. McCulloch, and D. Savage. *OSGi in action: Creating modular applications in Java*. Manning Publications Co., 2011.

[21] E. Hautus. Improving java software through package structure analysis. In *The 6th IASTED International Conference Software Engineering and Applications*, 2002.

[22] S. Kirkpatrick, D. G. Jr., and M. P. Vecchi. Optimization by simmulated annealing. *science*, 220(4598):671–680, 1983.

[23] R. Koschke. Atomic architectural component recovery for program understanding and evolution. In *Software Maintenance, 2002. Proceedings. International Conference on*, pages 478–481. IEEE, 2002.

[24] W. Li and S. Henry. Object-oriented metrics that predict maintainability. *Journal of systems and software*, 23(2):111–122, 1993.

[25] K. Mahdavi, M. Harman, and R. M. Hierons. A multiple hill climbing approach to software module clustering. In *Software Maintenance, 2003. ICSM 2003. Proceedings. International Conference on*, pages 315–324. IEEE, 2003.

[26] N. Metropolis, A. W. Rosenbluth, M. N. Rosenbluth, A. H. Teller, and E. Teller. Equation of state calculations by fast computing machines. *The journal of chemical physics*, 21:1087, 1953.

[27] D. Mitra, F. Romeo, and A. Sangiovanni-Vincentelli. Convergence and finite-time behavior of simulated annealing. In *Decision and Control, 1985 24th IEEE Conference on*, volume 24, pages 761–767. IEEE, 1985.

[28] M. E. J. Newman. Mixing patterns in networks. *Phy. Review E*, 67: 026126, 2003.

[29] M. E. J. Newman and M. Girvan. Finding and evaluating community structure in networks. *Physical Review E*, 69:026113, 2004.

[30] D. L. Parnas. On the criteria to be used in decomposing systems into modules. *Communications of the ACM*, 15(12):1053–1058, 1972.

[31] D. L. Parnas, P. C. Clements, and D. M. Weiss. The modular structure of complex systems. *Software Engineering, IEEE Transactions on*, 11 (3):259–266, 1985.

[32] S. Parsa and O. Bushehrian. Genetic clustering with constraints. *Journal of research and practice in information technology*, 39(1):47–60, 2007.

[33] D. Poshyvanyk and A. Marcus. The conceptual coupling metrics for object-oriented systems. In *Software Maintenance, 2006. ICSM'06. 22nd IEEE International Conference on*, pages 469–478. IEEE, 2006.

[34] W. P. Stevens, G. J. Myers, and L. L. Constantine. Structured design. *IBM Systems Journal*, 13(2):115–139, 1974.

[35] E. Tempero, C. Anslow, J. Dietrich, T. Han, J. Li, M. Lumpe, H. Melton, and J. Noble. Qualitas corpus: A curated collection of java code for empirical studies. In *2010 APSEC*, pages 336–345, 2010.

[36] J. Tessier. The dependency finder user manual. . Dependency Finder (2001-2012). Revised BSD License., 2012.

[37] C. J. Tessone, M. M. Geipel, and F. Schweitzer. Sustainable growth in complex networks. *EPL (Europhysics Letters)*, 96:58005, 2011.

[38] Y. Umeda, S. Fukushige, K. Tonoike, and S. Kondoh. Product modularity for life cycle design. *CIRP Annals-Manufacturing Technology*, 57(1):13–16, 2008.

[39] G. Valetto, M. Helander, K. Ehrlich, S. Chulani, M. Wegman, and C. Williams. Using software repositories to investigate socio-technical congruence in development projects. In *MSR '07*, pages 25–25. IEEE, 2007.

[40] F. Y. Wu. The potts model. *Reviews of Modern Physics*, 54:235, 1982.

[41] J. Wu, A. E. Hassan, and R. C. Holt. Comparison of clustering algorithms in the context of software evolution. In *Software Maintenance, 2005. ICSM'05. Proceedings of the 21st IEEE International Conference on*, pages 525–535. IEEE, 2005.

[42] M. S. Zanetti. The co-evolution of socio-technical structures in sustainable software development: Lessons from the open source software communities. In *Proceedings of the 34th ICSE*, pages 1587–1590. IEEE Press, 2012.

[43] M. S. Zanetti. *A complex systems approach to software engineering*. PhD thesis, Diss., Eidgenössische Technische Hochschule ETH Zürich, Nr. 21653, 2013, 2013.

[44] M. S. Zanetti and F. Schweitzer. A network perspective on software modularity. In *Architecture of Computing Systems (ARCS) Workshops 2012*, pages 175–186. GI, IEEE, 2012.

Context-Oriented Software Engineering: A Modularity Vision

Tetsuo Kamina
University of Tokyo
kamina@acm.org

Tomoyuki Aotani
Tokyo Institute of Technology
aotani@is.titech.ac.jp

Hidehiko Masuhara
Tokyo Institute of Technology
masuhara@acm.org

Tetsuo Tamai
Hosei University
tamai@acm.org

Abstract

There are a number of constructs to implement context-dependent behavior, such as conditional branches using `if` statements, method dispatching in object-oriented programming (such as the state design pattern), dynamic deployment of aspects in aspect-oriented programming, and layers in context-oriented programming (COP). Uses of those constructs significantly affect the modularity of the obtained implementation. While there are a number of cases where COP improves modularity, it is not clear when we should use COP in general.

This paper presents a preliminary study on our software development methodology, the context-oriented software engineering (COSE), which is a use-case-driven software development methodology that guides us to a specification of context-dependent requirements and design. We provide a way to map the requirements and design formed by COSE to the implementation in our COP language ServalCJ. We applied COSE to two applications in order to assess its feasibility. We also identify key linguistic constructs that make COSE effective by examining existing COP languages. These feasibility studies and examination raise a number of interesting open issues. We finally show our future research roadmap to address those issues.

Categories and Subject Descriptors D.2.1 [*Software Engineering*]: Requirements/Specifications—Methodologies

General Terms Design, Languages

Keywords Context-oriented programming; Methodology; Use cases

1. Introduction

Context awareness is a major concern in many application areas. It refers to the capability of a system to appropriately behave with respect to its surrounding contexts. A context is identified by observing behavioral changes in the application. An example of a context-aware application is a ubiquitous computing application that differently behaves in relation to situations such as geographical location, indoor or outdoor environment, and weather. In this case, some specific states or situations are contexts. An adaptive user interface is also context aware as it provides different GUI components (behavior) depending on the user's current task (contexts).

There are a number of constructs to implement context-dependent behavior, such as conditional branches using `if` statements, method dispatching in object-oriented programming (such as the state design pattern), and dynamic deployment of aspects in aspect-oriented programming (AOP). Context-oriented programming (COP) [20] also provides another mechanism to implement context-dependent behavior, which is called a *layer*. Uses of those constructs significantly affect the modularity of the obtained implementation, and research in COP shows a number of cases where COP can modularize variations of context-dependent behavior that are difficult to modularize by using other approaches.

However, it is not clear when we should use COP in general because of the lack of a methodology to find context-dependent behavior from the requirements. This problem consists of a stack of subproblems. First, the definition of a context is not clear. A context implies a specific state of a system and/or an environment that affects the system's behavior, but we may find a very large number of such states and environments from the requirements. We need to find the candidate contexts among them and the behavioral variations depending on them that should be implemented by using layers in COP. Second, besides context-dependent behavior, predictable control of change of context-dependent behavior is also important. There are complex relations between contexts (that affect the application's behavior) and variations of behavior, which make the modification of behavioral changes with respect to a change in the specification error prone. Thus, systematic identification of changes in contexts and variations of behavior is required. Third, we need to design modules and dynamic changes of behavior from the identified contexts. For example, selecting modularization mechanisms for context-dependent behavior and context changes is important because these behavior and context changes may be scattered over the whole execution of the application. Finally, we need to map the design to the implementation. A number of COP mechanisms have been proposed thus far [7, 9, 14, 17, 19, 20, 23]; among them, we need to select an appropriate mechanism to implement a design artifact.

This paper presents a preliminary study of our software development methodology, context-oriented software development (COSE) that organizes the specifications of contexts and variations of behavior depending on them. By giving an overview of the devel-

MODULARITY '14, April 22–26, 2014, Lugano, Switzerland.

http://dx.doi.org/10.1145/2577080.2579816

opment process with COP, even if it is not in depth, it would lead us to further research on each stage of the development process. We hypothesize methods to find context-dependent behavior, and they are validated through two case studies. We provide a mechanized modular mapping from a specification developed by COSE to an implementation in our COP language ServalCJ [26][1]. This preliminary study raises a number of interesting open issues. To address these issues, we finally present a future research plan to further explore the effectiveness of COSE that covers a number of research areas including requirements engineering and programming language implementation.

Methodology. On the basis of the use-case-driven approach [21], COSE represents the requirements for a context-aware application using contexts and context-dependent use cases. A context is represented as a Boolean variable that represents whether the system is in that context[2]. A context-dependent use case is a specialization of another use case applicable only under some specific contexts. From these requirements, COSE further derives a design model that is eventually translated into a modular implementation. This design method classifies variations of context-dependent behavior into those implemented by appropriate mechanisms such as layers in COP and other traditional mechanisms such as class hierarchies and `if` statements. This classification drives mechanized mapping from requirements to implementation. We choose ServalCJ as an implementation language because it provides a generalized layer activation mechanism, which supports all existing COP mechanisms as far as we know. This mapping ensures that each specification in the requirements is not scattered over multiple modules in the implementation, and each module is not entangled with multiple requirements.

Case studies. We demonstrate the effectiveness of this method by conducting two case studies of different context-aware applications. The first one is a conference guide system, which serves as a guide for an academic conference including management of an attendee's personal schedule, navigation help inside the venue and around the conference site, and a social networking service (SNS) function such as a Twitter client. The other one is CJEdit, a program editor providing different functionalities relative to cursor position [8]. In these case studies, we successfully organized context-related specifications by applying COSE and directly mapped these specifications to their implementations in ServalCJ.

To examine the existing language features and discuss what features make the methodology effective, we analyze how COSE addresses the aforementioned problems and the key linguistic constructs that make COSE effective through the case studies. We examine several existing implementation techniques to clarify which constructs will be useful for COSE. A notable finding is that, while most existing COP languages directly specify the execution point when the corresponding context becomes active, in the case studies, the implicit layer activation mechanism where context activation is indirectly specified by using conditional expressions is used intensively. Even though the implicit layer activation mechanism may currently suffer from performance problems, it can be a strong tool to separately implement the dynamic changes of behavior specified in the requirements.

[1] This language was previously known as Javanese.

[2] Keays also proposed COP [28], where a context is a named identifier (e.g., location) that identifies the type of *open terms* (holes in the code skeleton) that are filled at runtime with pieces of code corresponding to a specific value of the context (e.g., location="Tokyo"). This paper is based on Hirschfeld's COP [20] where a context is represented as a *layer* that dynamically takes two states, namely active and inactive, and thus can be represented as a Boolean variable.

Research roadmap. Although the case studies indicate that our approach is promising, we also identify a number of interesting open issues, which comprise our future research roadmap. First, to deal with scattered mentions of context-dependent behavior in descriptions of the system-to-be written in inconsistent syntax, we are planning to further develop a systematized method to identify contexts. Second, our approach is based on use cases; however, it is also desirable to explore how similar approaches can be applied when use cases are not appropriate to analyze requirements. Third, we mention issues in the evaluation of our methodology. Fourth, since there is a performance issue in the implicit layer activation, we are planning to study optimization of implicit activation. It is also interesting to analyze when the event-based activation (i.e., the way in which the execution points where context activation occurs are explicitly represented) is useful and desirable. Finally, since both case studies in this paper are standalone and conducted by using just a single language, it is also desirable to study how the same approach can be applied to more sophisticated environments such as distributed, multi-language environments.

Contributions. The main contributions of this paper are as follows:

- Identification of difficulties in the development of context-aware applications and discussion about the existing approaches (Section 2)
- Systematic organization of context-dependent requirements and classification of them into those implemented by appropriate linguistic mechanisms (Section 3)
- Mechanized mapping from the artifacts obtained by COSE to modular implementation in existing COP mechanisms (Section 4)
- Informal evaluation of COSE through case studies, and identification of key linguistic constructs that make it successful (Sections 5 and 6)
- Provision of the future research roadmap (Section 7)

2. Motivation

We explain the motivation to develop a new context-oriented software development methodology by introducing an example of a context-aware application and explaining the difficulties in the development of context-aware applications and the limitations of the existing approaches.

2.1 Example

We introduce a conference guide system, which serves as a guide for an academic conference, as an example of a context-aware application. This system is implemented on an Android smartphone and provides the conference program, management of the attendee's personal schedule, navigation help inside the venue and around the conference site, and a Twitter client to enable the user to submit their comments on the talks during the conference. This system has a couple of context-related behavioral variations listed as follows:

- The conference program is provided online; the user can view the online program using Internet on the smartphone. The downloaded program is cached on the local database in case the online version becomes unavailable. From the program, the user can select sessions that she/he will attend. The selected sessions are listed on the personal schedule. The listing of the selected sessions is available only when some have been selected.

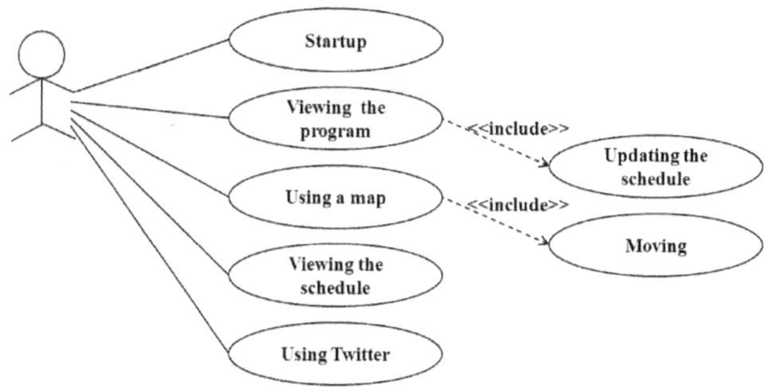

Figure 1. Use case diagram for the conference guide system

- The system provides a map function. When the user is within the conference venue, the map provides a floor plan of that venue. When the user is outside the venue, it provides a city map around the conference site, which is updated when the new position of the user is detected. The positioning is performed on the basis of GPS or the Wi-Fi connection. If the system cannot determine whether it is outdoors or indoors, it provides a static map around the conference site.
- The system provides a Twitter client, which is available only when the Internet is available.

In Figure 1, we summarize the use case diagram for the conference guide system. Besides the "Startup" use case where the user is starting the system, there are four use cases where the user interacts with the system, corresponding to the above itemized listing. Furthermore, the use case "Viewing the program" includes the use case "Updating the schedule" where the user selects sessions to attend, and the use case "Using a map" includes the use case "Moving" where the user is moving and the new position of the user is detected by the positioning system.

2.2 Difficulties

Although this is a simple example, we can observe that there are a number of difficulties in the development of context-aware applications.

Identification of contexts and requirements variability. A context-aware application changes its behavior with respect to current executing context, i.e., there are a number of variations of behavior depending on context. Thus, we need to identify contexts and requirements variability depending on them. For example, in the conference guide system, we may identify contexts such as outdoors, the availability of the list of selected sessions, and the availability of the Internet. However, identification of contexts is not trivial. After the identification of the outdoor context, it is unclear whether we should also identify the indoor context, because it seems that we can represent the indoor context by means of the outdoor context (i.e., indoors=!outdoors).

Different levels of abstraction. Contexts have different abstraction levels, and contexts at the abstract level consist of multiple concrete contexts. For example, the availability of positioning systems depends on the hardware specifications such as the availability of GPS and/or wireless LAN functions. Thus, we need to precisely define contexts in terms of the target machine. This multiple dependency leads to difficulty in precisely defining when the variation of behavior switches at runtime, because there may be a number of state changes in the target machine that trigger a context change, and some states of the executing hardware may barrier or guard the change of abstract contexts.

Multiple dependencies between contexts and behavior. We also need to carefully analyze dependencies between contexts and variations of behavior because some variations depend on multiple contexts. For example, in the conference guide system, if we identify outdoor and indoor situations as different contexts, displaying a static map depends on them, because this behavior is executable only when the system cannot determine whether it is outdoors or indoors. In general, this multiple dependency depends on how we identify contexts, and multiple contexts may barrier or guard the execution of context-dependent behavior. This dependency becomes more complicated when we consider different levels of abstraction of contexts as discussed above.

Requirements volatility in context specification. Technologies for sensing context changes are very complex and evolving continually, indicating that requirements specifications for context sensing are subject to change. For example, at first, it seems appropriate to define the outdoor/indoor contexts on the basis of the status of the GPS receiver. However, this definition may change in the future to use air pressure sensors or other technologies that are not currently implemented in the smartphone (such as an active RFID receiver).

Crosscutting of contexts in multiple use cases. In context-aware applications, a number of contexts are scattered over multiple use cases. For example, in the conference guide system, the conference program is downloaded through the Internet (to let the user access the up-to-date program) only when Internet access is available. Similarly, the availability of the Twitter client depends on the availability of the Internet. Thus, the context "the Internet is available" crosscuts both use cases "Viewing the program" and "Using Twitter." A systematic way to find such a situation and select an appropriate implementation mechanism for this specification is necessary.

Crosscutting of behavior changes. One of the most important properties of context-aware applications is that they change their behavior at runtime. Thus, we need to identify when a variation of behavior switches to another one. However, as discussed above, a variation of behavior may depend on multiple (abstract) contexts, where each context may depend on a number of concrete contexts. Furthermore, changes of such concrete contexts are scattered over the execution of the application. Since their specifications are subject to change, it is desirable to encapsulate them.

Translation to modular implementation. The above difficulties (from the viewpoint of requirements specification) make it difficult to map specifications to modular implementations. We need to carefully trace which requirements are implemented by which modules. It is also desirable that a module in the implementation is not entangled with several requirements but serves only a single requirement. Thus, to support modularity, it is desirable that there is an injective mapping from the specification to the implementation.

2.3 Problems in Existing Approaches

COP languages provide a novel linguistic construct called layers to modularize context-dependent behavior. A number of COP languages have been developed thus far, and some of them share the same abstraction mechanism based on layers and partial methods [7, 9, 14, 19]. On the other hand, little research effort has been devoted for systematizing the design of context-oriented programs. For example, the process of discovering layers from requirements is unclear. Determining when the use of layers is preferable over the use of existing object-oriented mechanisms and `if` statements in order to implement context-dependent behavior also remains unclear. A number of mechanisms have been proposed in COP for dynamic activation of layers. Most of the existing COP languages are based on a dynamically scoped layer activation mechanism using so-called `with`-blocks, which scatters a context activation code over the whole program. Event-based activation of layers with the support of AOP features is proposed to separate the control of layer activation from the base program [9, 23]. A layer activation mechanism that unifies existing COP mechanisms is also proposed [26]. All these mechanisms are useful under the assumption that we have already determined what are contexts and what are behavioral variations depending on them. We require a software development methodology that addresses the aforementioned difficulties.

There have been a number of software development methodologies. Object-oriented methodologies are useful for discovering objects and classes from the requirements and analyzing them. Aspect-oriented software development (AOSD) methodologies [22, 35] are useful for finding crosscutting concerns and modularizing them. Feature-oriented software development (FOSD) [4] is a method that maps feature diagrams [27], which are obtained by analyzing the software to be developed, to implementations. Feature diagrams are useful for analyzing dependencies among features from which software is constructed. Even though these methodologies provide a good starting point to consider how we develop context-aware applications, they do not focus on solutions for the aforementioned difficulties. We need to extend the existing methodologies to systematically identify contexts and behavior depending on them to provide predictable control of change of context-dependent behavior.

Recently, a number of approaches to discover, analyze, and implement contexts and variations of behavior depending on them have been studied. A number of requirements engineering methods [3, 31, 32, 37, 38, 41] mainly focus on discovery and analysis of (abstract) contexts and variations of behavior depending on them. Henrichsen and Indulska propose a software engineering framework for pervasive computing [18]. They do not provide any systematic ways to manage volatile requirements for concrete levels of context, and to modularly implement them. Specifically, they do not identify a set of variations that comprises one single module. Frameworks and libraries for context-aware applications provide context-aware software components and thus enhance reusability, addressing some of the difficulties mentioned above [1, 12, 13, 36]. They are domain specific, and few general solutions for context-aware applications are provided.

The authors previously proposed a metamodel of context-dependent specifications and formalized an injective mapping from specifications to implementations in EventCJ [25]. Although this proposal discusses the entire development process from requirement analysis to the implementation, the mapping from specifications to implementations highly depends on EventCJ [23]. By using this proposal, we can find only context changes that are explicitly triggered by events. Since the metamodel includes detailed specifications of context changes, we need to fix the way of implementation at the earlier stages of development. In contrast, COSE provides a language-independent methodology to elicit contexts and context-dependent behavior[3], enables us to find several types of context changes including implicit ones, and postpones a detailed specification of context changes after designing classes. As a result, the model transformation mentioned in [25] is no longer required but implementations are directly obtained from specifications without transforming the model.

To our knowledge, besides our previous study, this paper is the first attempt to propose a methodology to systematically organize context-dependent requirements and promote modular implementation of them.

[3] Although COSE is language independent, this paper shows mappings from specifications in COSE to implementations in ServalCJ.

2.4 Hypotheses

To address the aforementioned descriptions of context-dependent behavior and problems in existing approaches, we propose the following hypotheses that are assumed in COSE to identify contexts and context-dependent behavior.

HYPOTHESIS 2.1. *The factors dynamically changing the system behavior are candidates for contexts.*

A context is one of the factors that changes the system behavior. Thus, it is a good starting point for identifying contexts to focus on factors that change the system behavior.

HYPOTHESIS 2.2. *A context can be represented as a Boolean variable.*

In many cases, a factor that changes the system behavior takes only two states. For example, the situation whether the user is outdoor takes just two states, yes or no. The availability of the network also takes two states, available or unavailable. The battery level also takes two states, low or not low. Each of these factors can be represented as a Boolean variable.

In some cases, such factors may take more than two states. For example, a location may take a number of values such as "Tokyo," "Lugano," and so on. In such cases, we can consider that each value as a context. For example, we can consider a context like that "whether the user is in Tokyo." This may results in quite a large number of contexts (e.g., we may list thousands of cities), and it is hard to prepare such listing. In general, COP requires pre-listing of variations of behavior, and contexts with a large number are unlikely modularized by using COP but implemented in other techniques such as abstraction over parameters. Thus, in the following sections, we assume that a context can be represented as a Boolean variable.

HYPOTHESIS 2.3. *If multiple variations of context-dependent behavior share the same context, and if such variations are not the specializations of the same behavior, they should be implemented by using a layer.*

This hypothesis explains the situation where "unrelated" variations of behavior are eventually found to be executable in the same situation. This is the situation where the same context is scattered over a number of behavioral variations in the system. A layer in COP can modularize such crosscutting behavior. On the other hand, if the context affects only one single variation of behavior, or if such variations are specialization of the same behavior, we may also consider other implementation mechanisms such as `if` statements and method dispatching in object-oriented programming.

3. Specifying Context-Dependent Requirements and Design

We propose COSE, a use-case-based methodology for context-oriented software engineering. It represents the requirements for a context-aware application using contexts and context-dependent use cases. A context is represented as a Boolean variable that represents whether the system is in that context. A context-dependent use case is a specialization of another use case applicable only in some specific contexts.

On the basis of this requirements model, COSE further derives a design model that is eventually translated into a modular implementation, as shown in Section 4. COSE is based on the use-case-driven approach. It provides a systematic mapping from context-dependent use cases to modules provided by existing COP languages, namely *layers*, just as Jacobson proposed the AOSD method, where each use case is implemented by using an aspect

Table 1. Listing of contexts: the first stage

name	description
hasSchedule	the user has registered at least one session or not
hasNetwork	the Internet is available or not
outdoors	the situation is outdoors or not
hasPositioning	the positioning systems are available or not
batteryLow	the battery level is low or not

Table 2. Refined listing of contexts

name	description
hasSchedule	the user has registered at least one session or not
hasNetwork	the Internet is available or not
outdoors	the situation is outdoors or not
indoors	the situation is indoors or not
batteryLow	the battery level is low or not

Table 3. Use cases for the conference guide system

name	context
Startup	
Startup scheduler	hasSchedule
Startup Twitter	hasNetwork
Viewing the program	
Viewing the online program	hasNetwork
Updating the schedule	
Using a map	
Using a city map	outdoors
Using the floor plan	indoors
Using a static map	!outdoors && !indoors
Moving	
Moving when outdoors	outdoors
Viewing the schedule	hasSchedule
Using Twitter	hasNetwork
Updating timeline frequently	!batteryLow
Updating timeline infrequently	batteryLow

[22]. Our design method classifies variations of context-dependent behavior into those implemented by appropriate implementation mechanisms such as layers in COP and those implemented by other traditional mechanisms such as class hierarchies and `if` statements. The following design constituents are identified:

1. Groups of context-dependent use cases, each of which shares the same contexts. Context-dependent use cases in the same group simultaneously become applicable when the contexts hold. To modularize dynamic behavioral changes, they should be modularized into a layer in COP languages.
2. Classes participating in the use cases by applying the standard use-case-driven approach.
3. Detailed specification of contexts based on the identified classes and frameworks on which the system depends.

In the following sections, we overview each step of COSE using the conference guide system example introduced in Section 2.

3.1 Identifying Contexts and Context-Dependent Use Cases

The first step of COSE is to identify contexts and context-dependent use cases. We extend the original use-case-driven method in [21] with context-dependent use cases that are applicable only in specific contexts. By observing use cases, we can see that there exist a number of variations of behavior with respect to some situations or state of the system. As explained in Hypothesis 2.1, these factors changing the system behavior are candidates for contexts. For example, in the conference guide system, we can identify a use case "Startup" where the user starts the system. We can then identify two specializations of "Startup," namely "Startup scheduler" that prepares the menu for the user's schedule, and "Startup Twitter" that prepares the menu for the Twitter client. All these specializations are applicable only when some situations hold such as the availability of the user's schedule and availability of the Internet. Another example is the use case "Using a map," which is specialized to three use cases "Using a city map," "Using the floor plan," and "Using a static map," which are applicable when the user is outdoors, when the user is indoors, and when the system cannot determine the user's situation, respectively.

More precisely, a context in our model is defined as a Boolean variable that represents whether the system is in that context or not. We list the candidates for contexts in the conference guide system in Table 1. This is the very early stage of listing candidates for contexts that are directly observable from behavior of the system-to-be, and should be refined at later steps.

One important criterion on which we rely to identify contexts is that each context should not depend on other contexts, because such dependencies imply that a context can be represented in terms of others. A context and other contexts should be orthogonal, or if they are not orthogonal, they should be exclusive. In the above listing, we can find such a dependency: the situation where no positioning systems are available is a subcase of the situation where the user is not outdoors, because (assuming that the conference guide system determines the situation using positioning systems) the detection of an outdoor situation relies on the availability of positioning systems. Thus, the context outdoors and hasPositioning are divided into three contexts representing outdoors, indoors, and no positioning is available, and the final one is exactly the case where the system cannot determine whether it is outdoors or indoors. The refined listing of contexts is shown in Table 2.

Note that, as discussed in Section 2, requirements for context changes are often volatile. Thus, at this stage, it is preferable to keep contexts abstract to be prepared for future changes of requirements.

A context-dependent use case is a use case annotated with a proposition where ground terms are contexts that specifies when this use case is applicable. Context-dependent use cases for the conference guide system are summarized in Table 3. The names of use cases are listed in the left column, and conditions in terms of contexts that represent when the use case is applicable are listed in the right column. A name with an indent represents that this use case is a specialization of the use case listed in the above row with the italic font. A use case with an empty condition is context independent.

3.2 Grouping Context-Dependent Use Cases

A situation where multiple use cases are applicable in the same context implies that the context-dependent behavior is scattered over those use cases. To modularize dynamic behavioral changes, these context-dependent use cases should be grouped into one module that is enabled (activated) when the condition holds, and disabled (deactivated) when the condition does not hold. This is the situation where the Hypothesis 2.3 explains, which is rephrased in terms of the use case driven method as follows: *if multiple context-dependent use cases that are not specializations of the same use case share the same context, their behavior should be implemented by using a layer.*

Table 4. Groups of context-dependent use cases

context	use case
hasSchedule	Startup scheduler Viewing the scheduler
hasNetwork	Startup Twitter Viewing the online program Using Twitter
outdoors	Using a city map Moving when outdoors
indoors	Using the floor plan
!outdoors && !indoors	Using a static map
hasNetwork && !batteryLow	Updating timeline frequently
hasNetwork && batteryLow	Updating timeline infrequently

Table 5. Classes for each layer

layer	classes	position
`HasSchedule`	`MainActivity`, `Schedule`	class-in-layer
`HasNetwork`	`MainActivity`, `Program`, `Twitter`	class-in-layer
`Outdoors`	`Map`	layer-in-class
`Indoors`	`Map`	layer-in-class
`StaticMap`	`Map`	layer-in-class

Table 4 lists the groups of context-dependent use cases. We can see that three contexts, hasSchedule, hasNetwork, and outdoors, are assigned to multiple context-dependent use cases. Thus, these use cases are grouped into a layer; from now on, we rename these contexts by capitalizing the first character like `HasSchedule`, `HasNetwork`, and `Outdoors`, respectively, following the tradition of the naming of layers in COP languages.

Now, the question is how to treat the remaining context-dependent use cases. Even though they do not share the condition with other use cases, some of them still have a relationship with other layers in that a subterm of their condition is the condition that activates the layer. For example, the condition for "Using a static map" includes a subterm outdoors, which is the condition that activates the layer `Outdoors`. To uniformly control dynamic changes of behavior, activation of "Using a static map" should be managed in the same way as that of `Outdoors`. Thus, we also identify the context-dependent use case "Using a static map" as a layer, namely `StaticMap`. Similarly, we identify the context-dependent use case "Using the floor plan" as a layer, namely `Indoors`.

Other context-dependent use cases are not implemented by using layers. They are conceptually the same as alternative use cases, and the behavioral variations represented by such use cases should be implemented by traditional OO mechanisms such as inheritance and `if` statements.

3.3 Designing Classes

Each layer in COP consists of (partial) definitions of classes. By straightforwardly extending the original use-case-driven approach, we can identify classes and methods participating in each layer.

First, from use case scenarios, we identify the names of classes. Due to the limited space, we do not describe the details, but briefly illustrate the result. Since the conference guide system is an Android application, each view of the application should be implemented as a subclass of the `android.app.Activity` class from the Android SDK framework[4]. The use case *"Startup"* identifies the `MainActivity` class, which will implement the main view of the application. Similarly, in the use cases *"Viewing the program,"* *"Using a map,"* *"Viewing the schedule,"* and *"Using Twitter,"* we identify an `Activity` class for each of them, namely `Program`, `Map`, `Schedule`, and `Twitter`. There are some other helper classes; however, only the `Activity` classes participate in the context-dependent behavior.

Table 5 summarizes this assignment of classes for each layer. While layers `HasSchedule` and `HasNetwork` consist of multiple classes, other layers consist of just one class `Map`. This table also shows the preferred ways to allocate layers. There are two alternative ways to allocate layers: the class-in-layer style allocates the (partial) classes that implement the context-dependent behavior in the layer, while the layer-in-class style allocates the layer within the class. When a layer is scattered over several classes, the class-in-layer style is preferable, while when a class is scattered over several layers, the layer-in-class style is better. Note that some COP languages support only one style [6]. In this case, we need to conform to the style provided by the implementing language.

3.4 Designing Detailed Specification of Contexts

The contexts identified above are abstract. Since we have identified a number of classes in use case scenarios, we can now provide more concrete definitions for them. In the following, we define when the context becomes active in terms of classes identified above and classes from the framework. As explained later, specifications for some contexts are complex; thus, we need to identify more fine-grained contexts that comprise the specified context.

Section 3.1 defines that the context hasSchedule holds when the user has registered at least one session to attend from the conference program. In terms of the Android SDK framework, this is represented as "a query on the `SQLite` instance returns at least one result." Thus, we define when the layer `HasSchedule` becomes active as follows, which is read as "the `getCount` method on the result of a `query` on an `SQLite` instance (namely `db`) returns an integer value that is greater than 0":

```
HasSchedule(SQLite db) ::
  db.query(..).getCount() > 0
```

Similarly, by inspecting the specification of the Android SDK framework, we define when the layer `HasNetwork` becomes active as "the result of the `getDetailedState` method on the result of `getActiveNetworkInfo` on a `ConnectivityManager` instance (namely `cm`) is equal to `NetworkInfo.DetailedState.CONNECTED`":

```
HasNetwork(ConnectivityManager cm) ::
  cm.getActiveNetworkInfo().getDetailedState() ==
    NetworkInfo.DetailedState.CONNECTED
```

The cases for outdoors and indoors contexts are more complex. They are affected by multiple states of the running machine. First, to determine whether the user is outdoors, the GPS device should be available. Second, the conference guide system determines whether the user is in the conference venue by using the SSID of the connecting wireless LAN, which means that the wireless LAN connection should be available. Thus, the activation of layers `Outdoors` and `Indoors` is determined in terms of more fine-grained contexts:

```
Outdoors :: !WifiAvailable && GPSAvailable
Indoors :: WifiAvailable
```

In other words, `Outdoors` and `Indoors` are composite layers [24].

The context `WifiAvailable` is defined as follows, assuming that `isWifiConnected` is an application method that returns `true` when the wireless LAN is connected and its SSID is some predefined value:

```
WifiAvailable :: Config.isWifiConnected()==true
```

[4] http://developer.android.com/sdk/

The context GPSAvailable is defined as follows using the isProviderEnabled method provided by the framework:

```
GPSAvailable ::
  LocationManager.isProviderEnabled(
    LocationManager.GPS_PROVIDER) == true
```

4. Mapping to Implementation

This section demonstrates how the facts discovered by COSE are systematically translated into a program with existing COP mechanisms. We choose ServalCJ [26], which is a successor of EventCJ [23], as an implementation language because it provides a generalized layer activation mechanism that supports most existing COP mechanisms. A context in ServalCJ is defined as a term of temporal logic with a call stack, which can represent most existing layer activation mechanisms. For example, it can specify two events, of which one activates the corresponding context and the other deactivates that context (as in EventCJ's event-based layer transition). ServalCJ can also specify a control flow under which the corresponding context is active (as in JCop [9]). ServalCJ can select the target where such context specifications are applied, and that target can be a set of objects (*per-instance* activation) or the whole application (*global* activation). Furthermore, ServalCJ supports *implicit activation*, where activation of a context is indirectly specified by using a conditional expression. As shown in the following sections, our methodology clarifies that this mechanism is notably useful for modular implementation.

A ServalCJ program comprises a set of classes, layers, and *context groups* where dynamic layer activation and the target for this activation are specified. Layers and classes identified in Sections 3.2 and 3.3 are directly implemented in layers and classes in ServalCJ. Context specifications in Section 3.4 are directly implemented in context groups in ServalCJ. We explain the details in the following sections.

4.1 Implementing Layers

As in other COP languages, layers and partial methods comprise the mechanism for modularization of context-dependent behavior in ServalCJ.

Figure 2 shows an example of layers and partial methods in ServalCJ for the main view of the conference guide system. The class MainActivity extends the Activity class provided by the Android SDK framework, and overrides the onResume method, which is called from the framework when this view resumes the execution. This method displays the main menu of the conference guide system as buttons for viewing the conference program and using the map. MainActivity also declares two layers HasSchedule and HasNetwork. These layers define the context-dependent behavior of MainActivity[5]. HasSchedule defines the behavior when there is at least one session that the user would like to attend, and HasNetwork defines the behavior when the Internet is available. These layers extend the original behavior of onResume by declaring *after* partial methods, which are executed just after the execution of the original method when the respective layer is active[6]. For example, when HasSchedule is active, onResume also displays the menu button to check the user's schedule.

[5] Although Table 5 shows that it is preferable to implement these layers in the class-in-layer style, in Figure 2, they are implemented in the layer-in-class style because currently ServalCJ only supports the layer-in-class style.

[6] There are also *before* and *around* partial methods that execute before the execution of the original method and instead of the original method, respectively, when the respective layer is active.

```
class MainActivity extends Activity
    implements View.OnClickListener {
  private GridLayout layout;

  @Override
  protected void onResume() {
    super.onResume();
    layout = new GridLayout(this);
    layout.addView(makeMenu("program", "Program"));
    layout.addView(makeMenu("map", "Map"));
  }

  private Button makeMenu(String tag,
                          String label) {
    ..
  }

  layer HasSchedule {
    after protected void onResume() {
      layout.addView(makeMenu("schedule",
                              "Schedule"));
    }
  }
  layer HasNetwork {
    after protected void onResume() {
      layout.addView(makeMenu("twitter",
                              "Twitter"));
    }
  }
}
```

Figure 2. Layers and partial methods in ServalCJ

```
contextgroup Network(ConnectivetyManager cm)
    perthis(this(ConnectivityManager)) {
  context HasNetworkContext if(
    cm.getActiveNetworkInfo().getDetailedState()
      ==NetworkInfo.DetailedState.CONNECTED);
  activate HasNetwork when HasNetworkContext;
}
```

Figure 3. Context group responsible for activation of HasNetwork

4.2 Implementing Layer Activation

In COP languages, we can dynamically activate and deactivate layers, and ServalCJ provides declarative ways to perform such layer activation. These declarations are directly obtained from the design of detailed contexts discussed in Section 3.4.

First, detailed context definitions are further grouped on the basis of the variables and contexts that these definitions refer to. For example, HasNetwork refers to an instance of ConnectivityManager (and this is the only context that refers to that instance); thus, it makes up one group, which we call a *context group*.

Figure 3 shows a context group that is responsible for activation of HasNetwork. The first line specifies the name of the context group, which is Network, followed by a specification of how this context group is instantiated. The perthis clause specifies that the instance of Network is associated with an instance of ConnectivityManager (as specified using the this pointcut), which can be referenced through the variable cm.

```
contextgroup Schedule(MainActivity main)
    perthis(this(MainActivity)) {
  context HasScheduleContext if(
    main.scheduleCounter > 0);
  activate HasSchedule when HasScheduleContext;
}
```

Figure 4. Context group responsible for activation of `HasSchedule`

```
contextgroup Situation {
  context WifiAvailable if(
    Config.isWifiConnected()==true);
  context GPSAvailable if(
    LocationManager.isProviderEnabled(
      LocationManager.GPS_PROVIDER)==true);
  activate Outdoors
    when !WifiAvailable && GPSAvailable;
  activate Indoors when WifiAvaileble;
  activate StaticMap
    when !Outdoors && !Indoors;
```

Figure 5. Context group responsible for activation of `Outdoors`, `Indoors`, and `StaticMap`

Line 3 defines a context `HasNetworkContext`, which is used to specify when `HasNetwork` is active. The syntax of context declaration is as follows:

`context` *ContextName Term* ;

It starts with the keyword `context` followed by the name of the context and the specification of when that context is active. There are several ways to specify context activation, e.g., to specify the join points where that context becomes active and inactive, to specify the control flow under which that context is active, and to specify the condition when that context is active. In Figure 3, we specify the condition, which is declared by using the `if` expression. In the `if` expression, we can use any Boolean-type Java expressions, and in this case, we just copy the expression from the definition in Section 3.4.

Line 6 declares when the layer `HasNetwork` is active using an *activate declaration*. The `when` clause specifies the condition when the layer is active in terms of contexts; i.e., if `HasNetworkContext` is active, `HasNetwork` is active.

We can also declare a context group for `HasSchedule` in a similar way. One subtle issue is that the definition of `HasSchedule` contains an expression that requires local database accesses. If the developer has performance concerns, this definition is not preferred, because in ServalCJ, this condition is tested at every call of the layered method (i.e., a method that consists of a set of partial methods). In our case, the definition of `HasSchedule` is refined to access the counter variable that is introduced to `MainActivity` and updated when the local database is updated:

```
HasSchedule(MainActivity main) ::
  main.scheduleCounter > 0
```

The definition of the context group for `HasSchedule` is shown in Figure 4.

The remaining layers are `Outdoors`, `Indoors`, and `StaticMap`. Since they share the same set of context references, we group them into one context group, which is shown in Figure 5. Since this context group does not refer to any instance variables, it specifies no `perthis` and `pertarget` clauses. This context group is a *singleton*, i.e., it is created at the beginning of execution of the application and remains until it terminates.

Table 6. Listing of contexts for CJEdit

name	description
cursorOnCode	the cursor is on code
RTF	the text renderer renders comments

Context declarations for `WifiAvailable` and `GPSAvailable` are directly obtained from the definitions in Section 3.4. Furthermore, activate declarations for `Outdoors`, `Indoors`, and `StaticMap` are also directly obtained from the definitions in Section 3.4. Note that we can use the logical operators `||`, `&&`, and `!` to compose propositions in the `when` clauses.

Finally, we need to decide the sets of instances where these context groups are applied. ServalCJ supports per-instance activation, where a context group is applied to a specified set of instances, and global activation, where a context group is applied to the whole application. In the conference guide system, we decide that all context groups are global because per-instance activation is not important in this system. All the types of instances that should be under the control of some context groups are subtypes of `Activity`, and their instantiation is totally controlled by the Android SDK framework. There should not be cases where multiple instances of the same `Activity` class coexist simultaneously. A context group is global at the initial setting. Thus, the context groups shown in Figures 3, 4, and 5 are global.

5. CJEdit: Another Case Study

This section demonstrates another case study using COSE. CJEdit [8], which was first implemented by Appeltauer, is a program editor that enhances the readability of programs by providing different text-formatting techniques for code and comments. The code part is rendered in a typewriter format with syntax highlighting, and the comment part is rendered in a rich text format (RTF) that supports multiple fonts, text sizes, decorations, and alignments. Furthermore, CJEdit provides different GUI components depending on whether the programmer writes code or comments. For example, when the user is editing code, CJEdit displays the "execute" menu to quickly test the code currently being edited. This application is implemented using the QtJambi framework[7]. We use this example to investigate how COSE fits the development of existing context-aware applications.

Since the original implementation of CJEdit already exists, we do not perform this case study from scratch. We use the original implementation as a prototype of this case study, and by observing the system's behavior, we first derive the contexts listed in Table 6. The context cursorOnCode holds when the cursor is on code. There is also a context for text-rendering regions: RTF holds when the text renderer renders comment regions.

Table 7 lists context-dependent use cases for CJEdit. In CJEdit, we identify the use case *"Editing a program,"* which includes another use case *"Displaying the source code."* We derive context-dependent use cases from these use cases. *"Editing a program"* is specialized to different use cases with respect to the cursor's position; "Writing code" is applicable only when the context cursorOnCode holds, and "Writing comments" is applicable only when the context cursorOnCode does not hold. "Displaying the source code" is specialized to three different use cases depending on the text region and the cursor's position; "With syntax highlighting" is applicable only when the context cursorOnCode && !RTF holds; "Without syntax highlighting" is applicable only when the context !cur-

[7] `http://qt-jambi.org`

Table 7. Use cases for CJEdit

name	context
Editing a program	
Writing code	cursorOnCode
Writing comments	!cursorOnCode
Displaying the source code	
With syntax highlighting	cursorOnCode && !RTF
Without syntax highlighting	!cursorOnCode && !RTF
RTF format	RTF
Execute	cursorOnCode

Table 8. Layers for CJEdit

layer	use case
`CodeEditing`	Writing code *Execute*
`CommentEditing`	Writing comments
`RenderWithHighlighting`	With syntax highlighting
`RenderWithoutHighlighting`	Without syntax highlighting

Table 9. Classes for each layer of CJEdit

layer	classes
`CodeEditing`	`TextBlock,TextEditor` `FileExecutor`
`CommentEditing`	`TextEditor`
`RenderWithHighlighting`	`SyntaxHighlighter`
`RenderWithoutHighlighting`	`SyntaxHighlighter`

sorOnCode && !RTF holds; "RTF format" is applicable only when the context RTF holds. "*Execute*" is applicable only when the context cursorOnCode holds.

The next step is to group all context-dependent use cases with the same context into one single layer. On the basis of Hypothesis 2.3, we group "*Editing a program*" and "*Execute*" into the layer `CodeEditing`. The remaining context-dependent use cases do not share their context with other use cases; however, we still need to further group each of them as a distinct layer because a subterm of their context is a (subterm of a) context that activates a layer. Thus, we finally obtain the layers listed in Table 8.

Next, we identify the names of classes from the use case scenarios. Table 9 lists important classes for implementing context-dependent behavior. While the `CodeEditing` layer consists of multiple classes, other layers consist of just one class.

Now, we can define the detailed specifications of contexts in terms of classes. As specified in Table 6, the context cursorOnCode holds when the cursor is on code. This condition is represented by using the application method `isCursorOnCode` that returns `true` when the cursor is on code:

```
CursorOnCode :: TextEditor.isCursorOnCode()
```

The context `RTF` is also defined in terms of an application method that returns a text block by inspecting the type of that text block:

```
RTF :: SyntaxHighlighter.getCurrentBlock()
  instanceof RTFBlock
```

We directly implement the above systematized specification using ServalCJ. Layers listed in Table 8 are translated to layer declarations in ServalCJ. Figure 6 illustrates the layers affecting the behavior of `TextEditor`. They change the arrangement of GUI components by introducing partial methods, which are executable only when the corresponding layer is active.

```
class TextEditor {
  void showWidgets() { .. }
  void showToolbars() { .. }
  void showMenu() { .. }

  layer CodeEditing {
    after void showWidgets() { .. }
    after void showToolbars() { .. }
  }
  layer CommentEditing {
    after void showMenu() { .. }
    after void showToolbars() { .. }
  }
}
```

Figure 6. Layers and partial methods for CJEdit

```
contextgroup CJEdit(TextEditor editor)
    perthis(this(TextEditor)) {
  context CursorOnCode if(
    editor.isCursorOnCode());
  context RTF if(
    editor.getHighlighter().getCurrentBlock()
      instanceof RTFBlock);
  activate CodeEditing when CursorOnCode;
  activate CommentEditing
    when !CursorOnCode;
  activate RenderWithHighlighting
    when CursorOnCode && !RTF;
  activate RenderWighoutHighlighting
    when !CursorOnCode && !RTF;
}
```

Figure 7. Context group for CJEdit

The detailed specification of contexts is also directly implemented in the context group shown in Figure 7. Since the methods used in the specification of contexts are instance methods, we bind the instance of `TextEditor` with the local variable `editor` of the context group `CJEdit`, and the condition that specifies which context is active is specified by using the corresponding variable. Activate declarations that specify when the corresponding layers are active are directly obtained from Tables 7 and 8.

6. Discussing Modularity

The case studies demonstrate our hypotheses on when we should use COP. In this section, we summarize the result of case studies and validate our hypotheses. By comparing ServalCJ with other languages and implementation techniques, we also explore what are the key functionalities of the implementing language to make our approach effective. Finally, the case studies lead us to further research on each stage of the development process from the requirement analysis to the implementation.

6.1 Summary of Case Studies

In Section 2.2, we identified several difficulties in development of context-aware applications. Our approach COSE addresses them as follows.

Identification of contexts and requirements variability. As illustrated in Section 3.1, COSE systematizes identification of contexts by observing behavior of the system-to-be, such as use cases and prototypes. Furthermore, we clarify a criterion that should hold for each context, which is that a context should not be a subcase of other contexts. Requirements variability based on contexts is also represented by context-dependent use cases.

Different levels of abstraction. As discussed in Sections 3.1 and 3.4, COSE provides a concretization process for contexts. A context may be composed of other contexts that are less abstract than the composed context. Each level of abstraction of contexts in the specification is also directly represented by the implementation language using composite layers.

Multiple dependencies between contexts and behavior. As discussed above, because of composite layers, a layer can be composed of a number of contexts.

Requirements volatility in context specification. Each context-dependent use case is represented in terms of abstract contexts, and thus it is rigorous for future changes of detailed specifications of concrete contexts. For example, in the conference guide system, the specification of the outdoor context may change according to future evolution of sensor technologies that detect outdoor and indoor situations. Context-dependent use cases depending on the outdoor context will not be affected by such changes because the detailed specification of the outdoor context is abstracted from the context-dependent use cases. We may also separately perform such changes because definitions of contexts are encapsulated in context groups in ServalCJ.

Crosscutting of contexts in multiple use cases. COSE groups a number of variations of behavior that are executable under the same contexts and scattered across multiple use cases into one single layer. As discussed in Section 3.2, it also provides a guideline for when to use COP.

Crosscutting of behavior changes. Dynamic changes of contexts and behavior depending on them, which are scattered across the whole execution of the program, are separated as specifications of contexts and directly implemented by using context groups. Specifically, definitions of such changes are declaratively specified and totally separated from the base program.

Modular translation to the implementation. Layers and classes identified in Sections 3.2 and 3.3 are directly implemented in layers and classes in ServalCJ. Context specifications in Section 3.4 are directly implemented in context groups in ServalCJ. Each requirement in the specification is not scattered across multiple modules in the implementation, and each module is not entangled with multiple requirements.

6.2 Validating the Hypotheses

The results of case studies discussed above confirm the validity of Hypotheses 2.1 and 2.2. The case studies reveal that the factors changing the system behavior are actually "candidates" for contexts, and each context can be represented as a Boolean variable. This representation of contexts further derives a criterion to identify contexts, which is that each context at the abstract level should not depend on other contexts. A context and other contexts should be orthogonal, or if they are not orthogonal, they should be exclusive. This criterion enhances the exhaustiveness of contexts and makes it easy to discuss the equivalence between contexts.

For the Hypothesis 2.3, however, we need to further discuss the validity of our decision to implement the variations of context-dependent behavior using layers, because there are other alternatives to implement such variations, and above case studies do not discuss the cases where we do not use COP even when COSE indicates that we should use that.

We can validate it by using Tables 4 and 5. First, the layers `HasSchedule` and `HasNetwork` crosscut across multiple classes, and thus the same concern may scatter over those classes if we naively implement them using `if` statements. Applying design patterns may also produce this scattering problem. Extracting such scattered code as a common superclass requires an additional class hierarchy, which may be orthogonal to the existing hierarchies. Applying multiple inheritance, mixins [11], and traits [40] makes it difficult to take a look at the all classes that are composed with the same context-dependent behavior. In contrast, layers in COP provide a good solution to separate such concerns. More importantly, using the techniques other than COP makes it hard to separate behavior changes from the base program, which is possible in (some variants of) COP languages.

On the other hand, the layers `Outdoors`, `Indoors` and `StaticMap` in Table 5 exist only one single class `Map` and thus they do not seem to contribute to separation of crosscutting concerns. From Table 4, however, we can observe that `Outdoors` consists of two use cases, which are implemented by different methods, and using `if` statements would results in scattering of the same conditions over those methods. We may also avoid this scattering by, for example, to allow the `Map` object to have a state of the current situation, and to define behavioral variations for each state by using the state design pattern. The problem in applying design patterns is the scattering and tangling of behavioral changes. The state changes of the `Map` object are triggered by external environment changes, which are observed by the framework. We need to embed state changes of the `Map` object by implementing appropriate event handlers of possibly multiple modules (such as Wifi and GPS related classes). Thus, it becomes hard to localize the overall state changes in the `Map` object. By applying COSE with appropriate COP languages, we can separate such context changes into one single module.

Similar discussion holds in the case study of CJEdit. Thus, all decisions in this paper to implement variations of context-dependent behavior using layers are valid.

6.3 Comparison with Other Activation Mechanisms

The implementation in ServalCJ discussed in Section 4 implies that, in our approach, it is not necessary to *transform* the model of the requirements into that of the implementation. Instead, the implementation is *directly obtained* from the requirements. There are injective mappings from layers and contexts discovered in the requirements to those in the implementing language. Thus, this mapping promotes separation of concerns in that requirements are not scattered across several modules in the implementation, and each module is not entangled with a number of requirements.

The implementations in the case studies rely on the specific linguistic constructs provided by ServalCJ. In this section, we identify what are the properties that the implementing languages should have to make COSE effective, and compare ServalCJ with other languages and implementation techniques, such as ContextJ [7], EventCJ [23, 24], and a pseudo AOP language with the dynamic layer activation mechanism, with respect to those properties. Table 10 summarizes the result of the comparison. The leftmost column shows the numbers and titles of the following sections.

We do not argue that programming languages that do not support features listed below are not useful in COSE. In such languages, we may still apply useful workarounds to implement specifications organized by COSE, which would not be a bad choice in some circumstances such as availability of libraries and a development environment, and programmer's preference. Nevertheless, Table 10 indicates that recent progress in COP languages effectively supports COSE, which will be a good input for future language design.

Table 10. Comparison with other activation mechanisms

	ContextJ	AOP+COP	EventCJ	ServalCJ
6.3.1 Separation of context-dependent behavior[8]	a	a	a	a
6.3.2 Separation of context changes	n/a	a	a	a
6.3.3 Expressing relations between layers and contexts	n/a	n/a	a	a
6.3.4 Implicit activation	n/a	n/a	n/a	a

6.3.1 Separation of context-dependent behavior

First, in COSE, the implementing language should separate context-dependent behavior that is dynamically enabled and disabled from the base program. Layers of COP languages provide an effective way to achieve this purpose. Each partial method implements the context-specific behavior of the base method, and a layer packs all partial methods executable under the same context into one single module. Besides COP, other programming paradigms such as AOP and feature-oriented programming (FOP) [34] also provide such a modularization mechanism; however, for these paradigms, we also require an additional mechanism for dynamic composition of modules. For example, dynamic aspect deployment [10] may be applied for this purpose.

6.3.2 Separation of context changes

We can also see that, in COSE, specifications and implementations of dynamic changes of contexts and behavior depending on them are also separated from other specifications and modules, respectively. From the implementation viewpoint, such dynamic changes can easily be scattered over the whole application execution. Such scattering behavior can be avoided by using the pointcut-advice mechanism provided by AspectJ [29] (provided that it is also equipped with some imperial layer activation mechanism), or other COP languages with AOP features such as EventCJ and JCop [9].

In some COP languages, layer activation is controlled in a *per-thread* manner, whereby the generation of the event activating the layer and layer activation occur synchronously. In such languages, it is difficult to separate dynamic changes of behavior. For example, in ContextJ, layer activation is expressed by using the `with`-blocks, which ensures that layers are active only within the explicitly specified dynamic scope:

```
with (activeLayers) { onResume(); }
```

However, context changes are triggered by external events that asynchronously occur with the dynamic change of behavior. For example, in this case, we need to remember the active layer within the body of the event handler that handles the change of contexts to activate context-dependent behavior that does not appear in the scope of the event handler:

```
void someEventHandler(Event e) {
  activeLayers.add(Outdoors);
}
```

In this case, the scattering problem is readily encountered, and the base program is entangled with the concerns about dynamic changes of behavior.

6.3.3 Expressing relations between layers and contexts

From COSE, we can also see that a variation of behavior may depend on multiple contexts. For example, from Table 4, we can see that the use case "Using a static map," which is implemented in the layer `StaticMap`, depends on both contexts outdoors and indoors, one of which, namely outdoors, is further decomposed into two contexts `WifiAvailable` and `GPSAvailable`. To separate context-dependent behavior from the detailed specification of contexts, such an abstraction mechanism is necessary. From the implementation viewpoint, composite layers [24], which are supported by EventCJ and ServalCJ, are useful for this purpose.

[8] ServalCJ (and EventCJ) only supports the layer-in-class style. Thus, the same layer may be scattered across multiple classes. In fact, such layers exist in both case studies. This scattering can be addressed by supporting the class-in-layer style in the syntax.

6.3.4 Implicit activation

In most existing COP languages, we need to explicitly specify the join point where the context change occurs. In COP languages with AOP features, we perform such specification using the pointcut sublanguage. In COP languages with `with`-blocks, we explicitly inject the layer activation block into the base program. However, from the case studies, we have learned that a more declarative way to specify the condition when the corresponding context is active is heavily used in the context specification, which is directly implemented by using the implicit layer activation mechanism provided by ServalCJ (i.e., the `if` condition that specifies the condition when the corresponding context is active). This fact indicates that, even though it currently suffers from performance problems, the implicit layer activation mechanism can be a strong tool to modularly implement dynamic changes of behavior from the specification.

It is also possible to manually translate implicit layer activation into the explicit activation by identifying the join points where the condition is changed. However, when there are such multiple join points, we need to list all of them, which is an error-prone task. Furthermore, explicitly specifying the join points using pointcut often encounters the fragile pointcut problem [30].

6.4 Open Issues

Our preliminary case studies on COSE raise the following open issues that should be further explored.

First, both case studies in this paper are simple. Although these case studies demonstrate the effectiveness of COSE, they do not promise success in more complex cases. In large systems, we may have a large number of dynamic changes in behavior, some of which are context dependent. Eliciting contexts from such systems may be time consuming. Furthermore, in both case studies, the target system is standalone and implemented by using one single programming language. We should not consider that the results of the case studies immediately imply that we can easily apply COSE to distributed systems implemented by using multiple programming languages.

Second, COSE represents variations of context-dependent behavior using use cases. There should be some cases where we may prefer to use methods other than use cases, such as feature diagrams and goal models. The results in this paper do not ensure that we can also apply similar context-oriented extensions to those methods.

Third, the case studies do not convey compelling results regarding costs and benefits of COSE. The results ensure modularity of the products. However, they do not reveal how such modularity affects the real software production process and the quality of its products. We believe that COSE would have a significant impact on software development, in particular on software maintenance, because it provides comprehensive abstractions, clarifies complex relations between contexts and behavior, and provides good modularity in its products. However, this hypothesis should be validated through a lot of control experiments. Furthermore, the hypotheses explained in Section 2.4 should also be validated through a number of demonstration experiments and industrial software development.

Finally, as mentioned above, there are open issues in the performance of implicit activation, which is heavily used in the case studies. The performance problem of implicit activation is not significant in the case studies. However, this assumption will not always hold in applications of larger sizes. In some cases, we may optimize implicit activation, but there may be other cases where such optimization is not feasible. The case studies do not clarify when to use implicit activation and when to use other mechanisms such as event-based activation.

7. Future Research Roadmap

In this paper, we presented COSE and proposed that it can be employed for the effective development of context-aware applications. Specifications systematized by COSE effectively represent different levels of abstraction of contexts, which makes the system rigorous with respect to the change of detailed definitions of contexts. Context-dependent use cases are used to discover a layer, a modularization unit in COP, from the specification. The injective mapping from specifications to implementations ensures that each specification in the requirements is not scattered across multiple modules in the implementation, and each module is not entangled with multiple requirements. The comparison among several implementation techniques shown in Section 6.3 reveals the key linguistic constructs that make COSE effective and indicates important research directions for context-oriented software development.

This paper presents preliminary studies on COSE. Although these studies reveal that our approach is promising, there are also a number of open issues. In this section, we show our future research roadmap.

7.1 Systematizing Context Identification

The applications mentioned in the case studies are simple, and the number of identified contexts is not large. In large systems, the number of "candidates for contexts" will be very large. Furthermore, the system-to-be will be described by using natural languages including diagrams in inconsistent syntax. In some cases, such descriptions will be scattered over various documents, spreadsheets, and emails. This unstructured piling up of descriptions easily results in a situation where conceptually the same contexts are described in different words and notations.

In Section 3, we list the factors changing the system behavior as candidates for contexts. This is the most fundamental property of contexts. To systematize identification of contexts and deal with a large number of candidates for contexts, more precise criteria to find candidates for contexts will be necessary. For example, for a factor changing the system behavior to be identified as a context in COP, it should affect the behavior of a number of objects in the system. Moreover, all the contexts in the case studies are external with respect to the affected entities.

From this perspective, we are planning to develop a systematic context elicitation process that is applicable in the early stages of a requirements elicitation process.

7.2 Requirements based on Other Methods

Using use cases is a fantastic way to figure out functional requirements of the system-to-be. Use cases do not require any special languages to describe them; thus, people from various backgrounds can easily understand them. Nevertheless, they effectively describe the system behavior. Furthermore, they prevent hasty design; design methods based on use cases are well studied.

However, use cases are not all around. They are not suitable for figuring out non-functional requirements or for describing requirements specifications of platforms such as operating systems and frameworks. There are also a number of methods for analyzing requirements that are not based on use cases. It is natural to raise the question whether it is possible to apply methods similar to that described in this paper to other requirements analysis methods.

Goal-oriented methods for requirements engineering [15, 33] are complementary approaches suitable for eliciting requirements variability and constraints. Non-functional requirements are derived from their *soft goals*. Their variability and constraints may depend on executing contexts. Although a goal-based approach for contextualization is proposed in [3], further research should be conducted to explore, for example, approaches to align goal-based approaches and use-case-driven approaches.

Feature modeling presents a compact representation of all products of a software product line (SPL). Feature models are represented by means of feature diagrams [27]. Features provide requirements for architectures (including non-functional ones) and reusable functions. At the programming language level, layers in COP resemble features in FOP [5, 42]. This similarity indicates that we may develop a context-oriented extension of FOSD [4].

Application of context-oriented software development described in this paper to these major requirements engineering methods will be our new challenge.

7.3 Evaluation

To ensure that our methodology is effective, it will be necessary to perform further evaluation. For example, we need to evaluate the costs and benefits of our methodology, and the validity of the decision to use layers to implement context-dependent behavior instead of other mechanisms, through control experiments that compare our methodology with other software development methods. It is difficult to conduct control experiments, and it will take a long time to derive quantitative evaluations. Meanwhile, we think that it is also important to conduct a number of demonstration experiments and collect experiences of the application of our approach. In particular, we believe that application of our methodology to industrial software development is notably important.

Since one purpose of our study is to enhance modularity, the evaluation will be performed from the viewpoint of modularity. For example, an experimental study of how our approach makes it easy to deal with volatile requirements regarding contexts, and analysis of effects of requirement changes should be performed.

7.4 Implicit Activation

In both case studies in this paper, contexts are implemented by means of context conditions. As mentioned above, this fact implies the importance of implicit layer activation. However, there is a performance problem in implicit layer activation. A naive implementation strategy is to evaluate the condition that specifies when the corresponding context is active at every call of the layered methods, and when that condition holds and the corresponding context is not active, then that context is activated. This strategy will not produce a serious problem if the number of layered method calls is not so high. However, in the case where calls of layered methods frequently and repeatedly occur (e.g., in the case where calls of layered methods are included within a loop statement), this strategy may result in a serious performance problem.

Thus, to develop an optimization mechanism for implicit layer activation so that the evaluation of the context condition occurs only when necessary is an important research topic. There are several approaches for this purpose.

One approach is to develop an ad hoc method that optimizes parts of the program where calls of layered methods may frequently occur, such as loop statements. For example, if we can determine that the context condition will never change during the execution of the loop, we may rewrite the loop so that the context condition is evaluated just once at the entrance of that loop.

For a more effective approach, we may research a method to statically analyze when the value of the context condition changes. For example, assuming that c is a condition for the context C, if we can derive a pair of predicates (p, q) for which it can easily be checked that $p \implies c$ and $q \implies \neg c$, we can insert evaluations of c where the values for p or q change. We are currently considering an application of predicate abstraction for model checking for this purpose.

In both cases, the optimization requires whole program analysis because the change of context condition may occur anywhere in the program execution. To make the whole program analysis lightweight and feasible in the case when the whole code is not available for analysis, it is also necessary to study the application of whole program analysis without the whole program [2] to COP programs.

The emphasis on implicit activation does not mean that event-based activation of contexts is not necessary. First, in the case where layered methods are frequently called and optimization of implicit layer activation is difficult for some reason, event-based activation should be used. There are also some cases where the specification of context is defined in terms of events (even though this did not happen in our case studies). For example, there may be a specification of stateless objects whose contexts are changed by clicking buttons. In this case, it is better to implement context activation in an event-based manner than to introduce a state for each object to manage context activation using the implicit activation mechanism. There are also some cases where context changes can be observed from both conditions and events.

The problem is that there are no clear guidelines about when to use implicit activation and when to use the event-based mechanism. To create such guidelines, we need to study this problem both from the programming language perspective and the programming practice one. From the programming language perspective, as mentioned above, it is necessary to figure out the feasibility of efficient implementation of implicit activation. Meanwhile, formalization of implicit activation is also desirable to precisely study the semantics of implicit activation. We think that implicit activation is a special case of functional reactive programming (FRP) [16] in that the change of condition (value) reactively changes the result of activation (computation). Understanding implicit activation in terms of FRP may further clarify the semantics of implicit activation.

From the programming practice perspective, through a number of other case studies, we are planning to discover common *patterns* in context activation, which will serve as guidelines.

7.5 Distributed, Multi-Language Environment

Both case studies in this paper are standalone applications written in one single programming language. In real products, however, systems are implemented by using multiple programming languages and sometimes comprise a number of components and services over networks. To apply our methodology to such systems, there are two problems.

First, to our knowledge, ServalCJ is the only language that has all the desirable properties shown in Section 6.3. We need to explore how to realize the mechanism supported by ServalCJ in a wide range of programming languages including those suitable for high performance computing such as C and C++ and scripting languages such as JavaScript.

Second, little research effort has been devoted in COP for sharing the same context among multiple application processes. Sharing context among processes over the network is possible in programming languages supporting network-transparent communications between processes such as ContextErlang [39]. Further research is necessary to support network-transparent context in other programming models, and develop a mechanism to share contexts among multiple programming languages, which possibly communicate with each other over the network.

On the basis of these technical elements, we will further study the applicability of COSE to more realistic and sophisticated software development situations.

References

[1] Gregory D. Abowd, Christopher G. Atkeson, Jason Hong, Sue Long, Rob Kooper, and Mike Pinkerton. Cyberguide: A mobile context-aware tour guide. *Wireless Networks*, 3(5):421–433, 1997.

[2] Karim Ali and Ondřej Lhoták. Whole-program analysis without the whole program. In *ECOOP'13*, volume 7920 of *LNCS*, pages 378–400, 2013.

[3] Raian Ali, Fabiano Dalpiaz, and Paolo Giorgini. Goal-based self-contextualization. In *CAiSE 2009*, pages 37–43, 2009.

[4] Sven Apel and Christian Kästner. On overview of feature-oriented software development. *Journal of Object Technology*, 8(5):49–84, 2009.

[5] Sven Apel, Thomas Leich, Marko Rosenmüller, and Gunter Saake. FeatureC++: On the symbiosis of feature-oriented and aspect-oriented programming. In *GPCE'05*, pages 125–140, 2005.

[6] Malte Appeltauer, Robert Hirschfeld, Michael Haupt, Jens Lincke, and Michael Perscheid. A comparison of context-oriented programming languages. In *COP'09*, pages 1–6, 2009.

[7] Malte Appeltauer, Robert Hirschfeld, Michael Haupt, and Hidehiko Masuhara. ContextJ: Context-oriented programming with Java. *Computer Software*, 28(1):272–292, 2011.

[8] Malte Appeltauer, Robert Hirschfeld, and Hidehiko Masuhara. Improving the development of context-dependent Java application with ContextJ. In *COP'09*, 2009.

[9] Malte Appeltauer, Robert Hirschfeld, Hidehiko Masuhara, Michael Haupt, and Kazunori Kawauchi. Event-specific software composition in context-oriented programming. In *Proceedings of the International Conference on Software Composition 2010 (SC'10)*, volume 6144 of *LNCS*, pages 50–65, 2010.

[10] Ivia Aracic, Vaidas Gasiunas, Mira Mezini, and Klaus Ostermann. An overview of CaesarJ. In *Transactions on Aspect-Oriented Software Development I*, volume 3880 of *LNCS*, pages 135–173, 2006.

[11] G. Bracha and W. Cook. Mixin-based inheritance. In *OOPSLA 1990*, pages 303–311, 1990.

[12] Cinzia Cappiello, Marco Comuzzi, Enrico Mussi, and Barbara Pernici. Context-management for adaptive information systems. *Electronic Notes in Theoretical Computer Science*, 146:69–84, 2006.

[13] Stefano Ceri, Florian Daniel, Federico M. Facca, and Maristella Matera. Model-driven engineering of active contet-awareness. *World Wide Web*, 10:387–413, 2007.

[14] Pascal Costanza and Robert Hirschfeld. Language constructs for context-oriented programming – an overview of ContextL. In *Dynamic Language Symposium (DLS) '05*, pages 1–10, 2005.

[15] Anne Dardenne, Axel van Lamsweerde, and Stephen Fickas. Goal-directed requirements acquisition. *Science of Computer Programming*, 20:3–50, 1993.

[16] Conal Elliott and Paul Hudak. Functional reactive animation. In *ICFP'97*, pages 263–273, 1997.

[17] Carlo Ghezzi, Matteo Praella, and Guido Salvaneschi. Programming language support to context-aware adaptation–a case-study with Erlang. In *SEAMS'10*, pages 59–68, 2010.

[18] Karen Henrichsen and Jadwiga Indulska. A software engineering framework for context-aware pervasive computing. In *PERCOM'04*, 2004.

[19] Robert Hirschfeld, Pascal Costanza, and Michael Haupt. An introduction to context-oriented programming with ContextS. In *GTTSE 2007*, volume 5235 of *LNCS*, pages 396–407, 2008.

[20] Robert Hirschfeld, Pascal Costanza, and Oscar Nierstrasz. Context-oriented programming. *Journal of Object Technology*, 7(3):125–151, 2008.

[21] Ivar Jacobson, Magnus Christerson, Patrik Jonsson, and Gunnar Övergaard. *Object-Oriented Software Engineering: A Use Case Driven Approach*. Pearson Education, 1992.

[22] Ivar Jacobson and Pan-Wei Ng. *Aspect-Oriented Software Development with Use Cases*. Pearson Education, 2005.

[23] Tetsuo Kamina, Tomoyuki Aotani, and Hidehiko Masuhara. EventCJ: a context-oriented programming language with declarative event-based context transition. In *AOSD '11*, pages 253–264, 2011.

[24] Tetsuo Kamina, Tomoyuki Aotani, and Hidehiko Masuhara. Introducing composite layers in EventCJ. *IPSJ Transactions on Programming*, 6(1):1–8, 2013.

[25] Tetsuo Kamina, Tomoyuki Aotani, and Hidehiko Masuhara. Mapping context-dependent requirements to event-based context-oriented programs for modularity. In *Workshop on Reactivity, Events and Modularity (REM 2013)*, 2013.

[26] Tetsuo Kamina, Tomoyuki Aotani, and Hidehiko Masuhara. A unified context activation mechanism. In *COP'13*, 2013.

[27] Kyo C. Kang, Sholom G. Cohen, James A. Hess, William E. Novak, and A. Spencer Peterson. Feature-oriented domain analysis (FODA) feasibility study. Technical Report CMU/SEI-90-TR-21, Software Engineering Institute, Carnegie Mellon University, 1990.

[28] Roger Keays and Andry Rakotonirainy. Context-oriented programming. In *MobiDE'03*, pages 9–16, 2003.

[29] Gregor Kiczales, Erik Hilsdale, Jim Hugunin, Mik Kersten, Jeffrey Palm, and William G. Grisword. An overview of AspectJ. In *ECOOP'01*, pages 327–353, 2001.

[30] Christian Koppen and Maximilian Störzer. PCDiff: Attacking the fragile pointcut problem. In *European Interactive Workshop on Aspects in Software*, 2004.

[31] Alexiei Lapouchnian and John Mylopoulous. Modeling domain variability in requirements engineering with contexts. In *ER 2009*, volume 5829 of *LNCS*, pages 115–130, 2009.

[32] Sotirious Liaskos, Alexei Lapouchnian, Yijun Yu, Eric Yu, and John Mylopoulos. On goal-based variability acquisition and analysis. In *RE'06*, pages 79–88, 2006.

[33] Lin Liu and Eric Yu. Designing information systems in social context: a goal and scenario modelling approach. *Information Systems*, 29(2):187–203, 2004.

[34] Christian Prehofer. Feature-oriented programming: A fresh look at objects. In *ECOOP'97*, volume 1241 of *LNCS*, pages 419–443, 1997.

[35] Awais Rashid, Peter Sawyer, Ana Moreira, and João Araújo. Early aspects: a model for aspect-oriented requirements engineering. In *RE'02*, pages 199–202, 2002.

[36] Daniel Saliber, Anind K. Dey, and Gregory D. Abowd. The context toolkit: Aiding the development of context-enabled applications. In *CHI'99*, pages 434–441, 1999.

[37] Mohammed Salifu, Bashar Nuseibeh, Lucia Rapanotti, and Thein Than Tun. Using problem descriptions to represent variability for context-aware applications. In *VaMoS 2007*, 2007.

[38] Mohammed Salifu, Yujun Yu, and Bashar Nuseibeh. Specifying monitoring and switching problems in context. In *RE'07*, pages 211–220, 2007.

[39] Guido Salvaneschi, Carlo Ghezzi, and Matteo Pradella. ContextErlang: Introducing context-oriented programming in the actor model. In *AOSD'12*, 2012.

[40] Nathanael Schärli, Stéphane Ducasse, Oscar Nierstrasz, and Andrew P. Black. Traits: Composable units of behaviour. In *ECOOP 2003*, volume 2743 of *LNCS*, pages 248–274, 2003.

[41] Alistair Sutcliffe, Stephen Fickas, and McKay Moore Sohlberg. PC-RE: a method for personal and contextual requirements engineering with some experience. *Requirements Engineering*, 11(3):157–173, 2006.

[42] Fuminobu Takeyama and Shigeru Chiba. Implementing feature interactions with generic feature modules. In *Software Composition 2013*, volume 8088 of *LNCS*, pages 81–96, 2013.

Type Names without Static Type Checking already Improve the Usability of APIs (As Long as the Type Names are Correct): An Empirical Study

Samuel Spiza, Stefan Hanenberg

Department for Computer Science and Business Information Systems,
University of Duisburg-Essen, Essen, Germany

samuel.spiza@stud.uni-due.de
stefan.hanenberg@icb.uni-due.de

Abstract

In the discussion about the usefulness of static or dynamic type systems there is often the statement that static type systems improve the documentation of software. In the meantime there exists even some empirical evidence for this statement. One of the possible explanations for this positive influence is that the static type system of programming languages such as Java require developers to write down the type names, i.e. lexical representations which potentially help developers. Because of that there is a plausible hypothesis that the main benefit comes from the type names and not from the static type checks that are based on these names. In order to argue for or against static type systems it is desirable to check this plausible hypothesis in an experimental way. This paper describes an experiment with 20 participants that has been performed in order to check whether developers using an unknown API already benefit (in terms of development time) from the pure syntactical representation of type names without static type checking. The result of the study is that developers do benefit from the type names in an API's source code. But already a single wrong type name has a measurable significant negative impact on the development time in comparison to APIs without type names.

Categories and Subject Descriptors D.3.3 [*Programming Languages*]: Language Constructs and Features

General Terms Human Factors, Languages

Keywords programming languages, type systems, empirical research

1. Introduction

While there is a long ongoing debate about the possible pros and cons of static or dynamic type systems (see [1, 3, 18, 27]) in programming languages, there is in the meantime some empirical knowledge available which permits one to lead such a discussion based on statements for which some empirical evidence exists. At least some experiments have been performed in this area (see [8, 9, 13–15, 20, 25, 26]) that give such discussions now more substance than the often mentioned and often criticized '*deep but anecdotal analysis by language designers*' [16, p. 13] (see furthermore [10] among others).

While from first glance it appears that the whole discussion about static and dynamic type systems is rather a discussion from the old ages of programming it turns out that the whole discussion is still up-to-date. Even in modern programming languages there is the fight between static and dynamic type systems especially in web-programming languages where it seems that in the last decade dynamic type systems play a stronger role. Programming languages such as PHP, JavaScript or Ruby, which are often used in web-programming, do not have a static type system. Taking results of previous experiments into account it is at least worth to think about whether it is worthwhile to implement a static type system for such languages.

However, for language designers it is always the question whether it is worth to design and implement a static type system for a new or existing language. The design and implementation of such a type system might be complex and time consuming and as long it is unclear whether the resulting language benefits from such a type system there are no hard arguments for the introduction of static types.

One of the often mentioned arguments for static type systems is that static type systems such as the one implemented in Java (i.e. type systems that rely on explicitly declared type names) provide some kind of implicit documentation, i.e. a documentation that actually helps developers to use the code (see [18, p. 5]). In fact, this (possible) characteristic of static type systems has been evaluated in controlled experiments (see [13–15]) and it turned out that static type systems (based on nominal, declarative types) do indeed improve the usability of undocumented APIs (in comparison to dynamic type systems without any type declarations).

However, a direct follow up question from these experiments is whether the same results can be achieved by a very simple extension of a language: instead of implementing a complete type system it is also possible to extend the syntax of the language in a way that developers are allowed to write down parameters types, return types, etc. although these syntax constructs are actually not checked. In such a situation the type declarations are actually only used for documentation purposes and not for any kind of static type checking.

For example, instead of adding a completely new type system to the programming language JavaScript (which was actually done

MODULARITY '14, April 22–26, 2014, Lugano, Switzerland.
Copyright © 2014 ACM 978-1-4503-2772-5/14/04... $15.00.
http://dx.doi.org/10.1145/2577080.2577098

in TypeScript[1]) it is worth to think about whether the existing positive effect of declarative type systems could be achieved just by permitting (or even forcing) developers to declare types in the code (although these types would not be statically checked). If it turns out that the benefit of static type systems can be reduced to the additional type names in the code, a large number of dynamically typed language could already benefit just by performing these small syntactical changes to the language.

Hence the question is whether such a simple extension is able to provide the same benefit that has been experimentally shown for static type systems. A more fine-grained question is, whether the use of correct type names (which would have been guaranteed by the static type checker) improve the usability of code and whether incorrect type names reduce the usability of the code (or simple have the same impact as no information at all).

While the whole discussion of type systems seems to be only a matter of programming language designers, it turns out that there is a more high-level question which is directly related to the question of modularity. A (declared) type name represents a description of a fine-grained module which can be replaced by a different implementation. The static type check then performs some checks that guarantee the absence of certain errors in the way how these modules are used. Hence, the more general question is whether the presence of module interfaces in the code improve the usability of these modules and whether it is necessary to statically check these module interfaces in order to get such a benefit.

This paper describes an experiment that has been performed at the University of Duisburg-Essen with 20 subjects which addresses the question whether the pure syntactical representation of type names (without static type checks) help developers to use an unknown API (in comparison to developers who do have neither a syntactical representation of the type names nor a static type check). The result of the study is that the type names do help developers to a certain extent (although the effect seems to be smaller than the combination of type names and static type checking). But the experiment also shows that incorrect type names reduce the usability of APIs with declared types in comparison to APIs that do not have such type declarations.

Structure of the paper. Section 2 gives an overview of related work. Section 3 describes the experiment by discussing initial considerations, the programming tasks given to the subjects, the general experimental design, and threats to validity. Then, section 4 describes the results by describing the measured data, giving descriptive statistics and performing significance tests on the measurements. Finally, section 5 summarizes and concludes the paper.

2. Related Work

While there are countless works available about different kinds of type systems (see [1, 18] for an overview of different type systems), there are relatively few experiments available about the usability of type systems (apart from the experiments the authors contributed to). We describe the related work in two sections. First, we describe controlled experiments that focus on (static) type systems. Then, we describe works that present studies about the use and usability of type constructs.[2]

2.1 Empirical Studies of Type Systems

To our knowledge most of the experiments that test the usability of type systems were done by at least one of the authors of the present paper. In order to distinguish these works from works by other authors we describe related experiments in two different sections.

2.1.1 Studies by different authors

The first experiment we are aware of about the usability on static type systems was performed by Gannon in the late 1970s. Gannon showed a positive impact of static type systems in comparison to untyped systems in a programming experiment on thirty-eight subjects [8]. The programming language used in the experiment is no longer available or in use. The experimental design followed a two-group within-subject experiment. The result of the study was that the programming reliability was increased for subjects who used the language with static type checking.

Prechelt and Tichy studied the impact of static type checking on procedure arguments by using the programming languages ANSI C (which performed type checking on procedure arguments) and K&R C (which does not) [20]. The experiment divided 34 subjects into four groups where each group had to solve two programming tasks, one using ANSI C and one using K&R C. The result of the study was that for one task subjects were faster in solving the programming task when using the statically type checked ANSI C. For the other programming task, no significant difference was measured.

Daly et al. observed in a pilot-study programmers who used a new static type system for the (originally dynamically typed) language Ruby [5]. Although the authors did not perform direct measurements on the subjects (and taken into account that the number of subjects was very low, because only three subjects participated) they concluded that the benefits of static typing could not be shown. It should be mentioned that the authors speculated that this might had to to do with the programming tasks given to the subjects.

Another study by Prechelt which did not explicitly study the impact of type systems compared seven different programming languages [19]. The author concluded from the work that that humans writing in programming languages with a dynamic type system (the scripting languages) require less development time.

2.1.2 Our own experiment series

The study presented here is part of a larger experiment series that empirically analyzes the impact of static type systems on software development (see [11]) – more specially on the resulting development times. The experiment series was not completely designed upfront. Instead, whenever from one experiment new insights arise, we try to consider them directly in future experiments. The experiment series was motivated by the observation that there is relatively little empirical knowledge about the usability of static type systems (see [10] for a more detailed discussion).

The first study in this series by Hanenberg [9] let subjects use a statically and dynamically typed programming languages in order to solve two programming tasks. Subjects using the dynamically typed programming language were significantly faster for a smaller task while no significant difference was found for a larger task.

In a follow up experiment the influence of type casts was measured [26]. Twenty-one subjects divided into two groups took part in a within-subjects design. The result of the study was that type casts do influence the development time of completely trivial programming tasks in a negative way while tasks with more than eleven lines of code showed no significant difference.

Steinberg and Hanenberg analyzed to what extent static type systems help to identify and fix type errors as well as semantic errors in an application [25]. The study was based on 31 subjects. The result of the experiment was that static type systems have a positive impact on the time required to fix type errors, but did not reveal any differences with respect to fixing semantic errors.

[1] See http://www.typescriptlang.org/

[2] It should be noted that the related work section is very closely related to previous works such as [13–15]. This has to do with the fact that to our knowledge no additional empirical studies on the usability of static or dynamic type systems appeared in the meantime.

Mayer et al. studied in [15] to what extent static types help to use undocumented APIs. It turned out that for 3/5 programming tasks the application of static types were beneficial. While one of these two tasks where static type systems did not turn out to be beneficial was rather critically considered by the authors as problematic task (whose results should not be over-interpreted), still one task showed a positive impact of dynamic types.

Kleinschmager et al. performed an experiment on 33 subjects which combined repetitions of previous experiments [14]. Among others, the key findings from [15] (that static type systems help using undocumented APIs) were confirmed; this time without any exception.

In order to study different kinds (and different aspects) of static type systems Hoppe and Hanenberg ran a study on generic types in Java [13]. Again, it was checked whether generic type declarations helped developers to use an unknown API. Additionally, it was checked whether generic types have potentially the disadvantage when extending software. Finally, it was checked whether the previously measured positive effect on debugging also holds for generic types.

A more recent study by Endrikat et al. tested the influence of type systems in comparison to documentation [7]. The experiment was based on a 4-group random factorial design where each group was assigned to the variables type system (with the treatments static or dynamic type system) and the variable documentation (with the treatments with and without documentation). The programming tasks were (again) to use a given API. It turned out that developers with the static type system were significantly faster solving the task. Documentation had only a close to significant (positive) effect (in comparison to no documentation). Hence, even in the presence of documentation the positive effect of static type systems was measurable.

2.2 Empirical Studies on Language Usage and Usability

While the previously described works have their focus directly on type systems and type system usability there are a number of different works that are closely related, although they to not have controlled studies of type systems in their focus.

Souza and Figueiredo [22] studied the usage of static type annotations in the programming language Groovy by analyzing the source code of more than 6000 projects. The study is based on the characteristic that Groovy gives developers the option to use or not to use static type declarations in the code. The interesting result it that the study seems to confirm the results of the previously described experiments, i.e. that type declarations are a good means to document code. It turned out that type declarations were significantly more often used in method signatures than for example for local variables. This seems to suggest that developers intuitively use the positive documentation effect of static type systems that have been just recently shown in an experimental way.

Parnin et al. studied the usage of Generic Java by analyzing 20 open source projects [17]. Although the experiment in [13] showed that APIs benefit from generic type information in comparison to raw types, it turned out that generic types is a language construct that is not that exhaustively used as one could expect: half of the projects did not use generics at all and in most cases were generic types only used for collections.

A study by Stefik and Siebert [23] analyzed to what extent the syntax of a programming language influences its usability. While the authors tested a large number of different syntax constructs, the use of type declarations was part of the study as well. One of these results with respect to type declarations was that the authors of the study observed difficulties that novices had with (the syntax of) static type annotations.

3. Experiment Description

First, we discuss some initial considerations for the experiment. After that, details about the experimental design are explained. After describing the experiment execution, we finally discuss threats to validity.

3.1 Initial Considerations for Experimental Design

The intention of the experiment is to identify whether the pure syntactical representation of type names is sufficient to achieve the same positive effect that has been shown in previous experiments in the comparison of static and dynamic types (see [13–15]). According to previous experiments and the literature on type systems our expectations were that type names help in situations where an unknown API has to be used under the assumption that the type names represent the expected types. In case the type names are wrong we expect that the type names do not have any influence on the resulting usability (i.e. we assume that wrong type information have the same impact as no type information).

If we want to write this down in form of testable hypotheses we come to the following ones[3]:

- H_0^a: The existence of type names (under the condition that the type names are correct) in the code (in dynamically typed programming languages) does not have a measurable influence on the development time in comparison to code where no type names occur.[4]
- H_0^b: Wrong type names in the code (in dynamically typed programming languages but which permit to declare types) do no influence on development time in comparison to (dynamically typed) code where no type names occur.[5]

The motivation for testing the first hypothesis H_0^a is that it seems clear that if the type names are correct, they directly provide developers knowledge about what parameters are passed to or returned from the API. Hence, developers save time because they do not need to search through the code what classes possibly match the expected objects. The motivation for testing the second hypothesis H_0^b is that from our perspective developers relatively easily identify when a type name is wrong. Hence, we do not assume that it really influences the development time, because the moment when developers are aware of the problem they directly work in exactly the same way as they would if no type information were be available.

As a next step we need to define the environment used in the experiment and the programming tasks that need to be performed. Our goal was to use languages as similar as possible and which do not need exhaustive additional training for the subjects. Since the subject were expected to come from the University of Duisburg–Essen and since the language being used in education is Java our intention was to use a Java-like language. Additionally, the language must allow to use optional type names in the code without performing any type checking because this is the main goal of the experiment. From our perspective the programming language Dart[6] fulfills these requirements. Dart provides an optional type checker that can be switched off. In that case the type declarations are still in the code but they are not statically checked.

[3] Hypotheses are written down in a form that states that no differences between two measurements are found.

[4] Again, the experimenters expect that the type names do have an influence on the development time. The null hypothesis is formulated in that way because of statistical reasons.

[5] Here, the experimenters indeed assume no difference between the measured development times.

[6] http://www.dartlang.org/

3.2 Environment and Measurement

According to previous experiments we used the Emperior programming environment [6, 12, 25]. This environment consists of a simple text editor (with syntax highlighting) with a tree view that shows all necessary source files for the experiment. From within the text editor subjects were allowed to edit and save changes in the code and also to run both the application and test cases.

Subjects worked on each individual task one after another (without knowing the next ones). Every time a programming task was fulfilled and a new programming task was given to the subject a new IDE was opened which contained all necessary files. For each task subjects were provided executable test cases (without the source code of these test cases). We measured the development time until all test cases for the current programming task passed. Hence, a solution is assumed to be correct if all test cases are fulfilled. It might be possible that different solutions differ with respect to their quality. For example, developers might spend more time on finding appropriate names for local variables while others do not use local variables at all but pass directly the results of expressions to method calls. Others might even document their code. However, in correspondence to the previous study only the time until the tests are fulfilled is used as a primary measurement. The test cases were written in a way that the resulting data structures have to match, i.e. the correct objects have to be passed to other methods and the correct objects from other methods have to be used.

In order to reduce the time required by each subject (and in case one programming task is too hard for a subject) we defined an upper time limit for each programming task. For each task we defined an upper limit of 40 minutes following the approach we did in previous experiments (see [13]). I.e. after 40 minutes we interrupted the subjects and let them continue with the next task. The measurement for these subjects is then 40 minutes (although we are aware that it is possible that each subject that ran into the limit potentially would have required much more time).

The whole programming environment (IDE with programming tasks, test cases, etc.) including the operating system (Ubuntu 11.04) was stored on an USB stick which was used to boot the machines used in the experiment. This (again) followed our previous procedures.

3.3 Experimental Design

The experiment in this paper follows a within-subject design that has been applied in previous experiments [6, 15, 26]. Within-subject means that the subjects are measured twice: one time for the first treatment (type names) and one time for the other treatment (no type names). According to the motivation of previous experiments the idea was that a within-subject design requires a relatively low number of subjects.

In this design we split the set of subjects into two groups. The first group receives a set of programming tasks where the type names are in the code. Afterwards, the same subjects receive comparable programming tasks without such type names in the code. The other group starts without type names and continues with type names. Table 1 illustrates the corresponding design.

Table 1. General experimental design

	Technique for all tasks (round 1)	Technique for all tasks (round 2)
Group A	No Type Names	Type Names
Group B	Type Names	No Type Names

The potential problem with this approach is the learning and the carry-over effect. A learning effect appears when subjects solve a similar programming task for a second time (although using the same treatment with respect to type names). A carry-over effect appears when the developers solve the same programming task for the second time with a different treatment (such as using no type names in the first round and using type names in the second round).

The problem becomes serious when these effects are too large. For example, it is possible that the carry-over effect to so large that the subjects are alway faster in the second round than in the first round. In this situation the within-subject measurement (i.e. the comparison of the first and the second round) would not reveal any meaningful results, because the second measurement is always smaller. However if the learning effect is lower than the effect that is to be measured the design is still applicable (see [15, 26] for a more detailed discussion). In order to reduce the carry-over effect the programming tasks for round 1 and round 2 are in different domains. In order to make both domains comparable both structures are similar. In fact the code for each domain was constructed by renaming the classes, methods, fields and packages from the other domain).

In order to test the second hypotheses H_0^b developers had to fix a given piece of code that uses an API that contains a wrong type name in its declaration (respectively no type names in the control group). We did that because we were not interested in the time required to create the code until the subjects are aware that there is a problem in the API description. However, we expect that such kind of programming task would lead to a very high carry-over effect. Because of that the programming task for the second hypothesis is only tested between-subject, i.e. we do not use a second measurement on each subject for this task.

3.4 Base Application and Programming Tasks

Since the main motivation for the experiment came from the results of the two previous experiments (see [14, 15]) and since the experiment by Kleinschmager et al. showed relatively clear results, we decided to use programming tasks from the experiment by Kleinschmager et al. that revealed such clear results. Additionally, we decided to use the same base application (small text-based adventure) for the experiment. We transformed this text-based adventure for the second group.

3.5 Programming Tasks

Three of the five programming tasks from the experiment by Kleinschmager et al. revealed clear results (with a relatively large effect size in favour for static type systems). The characteristics of these programming tasks is to use an unknown API in order to implement some part of the game. We directly used these three programming tasks[7] in the experiment in order to test the first hypothesis. Additionally, we made some modifications to the programming tasks. We did this in order to reduce the problem that one of the subjects would have read a publication about the previous experiment. A direct copy of the programming tasks would lead to the potential problem that subjects at least partially know the solution upfront.

Additionally, we changed the second domain in the experiment. Kleinschmager et al. used originally a small game as the first and an EMail system as the second domain. However, we felt that the EMail system was not that inuitive as it could be (which potentially increase the problem with the carry-over effect). Our intention was to provide a more intuitive domain to developers. We used a car insurance system as the target domain.

All of these tasks have in common that a relative high number of classes need to be identified by the subjects, instances of these classes need to be constructed, and these instances must be used as

[7] These tasks are the programming tasks CIT3–5 from [14] where a detailed description of these tasks can be found.

parameters or target objects in relative simple code that does not contain any loops or conditions.

Figure 1. Possible solution for task 2 (with type names)

```
static Monster task() {
  HillGiant h = new HillGiant();
  Giants g = new Giants();
  h.setGroup(g);
  Behavior b = new Behavior();
  h.setStrategy(b);
  RandomItemBuilder ri = new RandomItemBuilder();
  h.setDropableItemGenerator(ri);
  SubjectAttributes s = new SubjectAttributes();
  Resistances r = new Resistances();
  s.setResiliences(r);
  UnarmedAttackType u = new UnarmedAttackType();
  DefaultDamageType d = new DefaultDamageType();
  u.setDamageStyle(d);
  s.setStyle(u);
  h.setStats(s);
  return h;
}
```

Figure 1 illustrates a potential solution code for the second task (with type names in the code). Here, developers had to identify how a HillGiant object needs to be initialized and how to get the corresponding objects required for the initialization (such as an UnarmedAttackType object, etc.).

For the second hypothesis H_0^b developers where given a piece of code that leads to an error. Figure 2 describes the corresponding code. The problem with the code is that the second parameter of the setInvolved invocation on the report object is wrong. Here, the result of the method getPaymentHandling() is expected. However, the (wrong) type name in the target object explicitely requests a ThirdParty object. I.e. the main problem for subjects is to identify that the expected type in the target method is wrong. The code in Figure 2 shows how the corresponding solutions probably look like.

Again, for the second hypothesis H_0^b no second domain was created because we assumed a very high carry-over effect for this kind of task.

Figure 2. Source code given to subject in Task 4, the comment describes how the code can be fixed

```
static AccidentReport task(
  DateData dayOfAccident, Description info,
  Customer user, ThirdParty person,
    DamagedCar automobile) {
        AccidentReport report = new AccidentReport();
        report.setBrokenVehicle(automobile);

    /* Expected correction:
       report.setInvolved(
         user,
         person.getPaymentHandling()); */

        report.setInvolved(user,person);
        report.setAccidentData( dayOfAccident,info);
        return report;
}
```

3.6 Experiment Execution

The experiment was performed with 20 subjects. However, three subjects were not able to work on task 4 (they skipped the experiment after the first tasks). All subjects were undergraduate students (in their 5th or higher semester) at the University of Duisburg–Essen. All subjects were volunteers and were randomly assigned to the two groups. The experiment was performed at the University of Duisburg-Essen within a time period of one month. The machines used by the subjects where IBM Thinkpads R60, with 1GB of RAM.

3.7 Threats to Validity

The experimental design and also the underlying research question is comparable to the previous experiments. Hence, the threats to validity are comparable, too. While some threats are rather general (students as subjects, small programming tasks, artificial development environment) and are already discussed in detail in other related experiments (see for instance [9, 26]) others such as the learning effect are specific to the experimental within-subject design (which has been also applied previously, see detailed discussion in [15]). Because these threats already have been explained elsewhere we do not repeat them here.

However, some threats are special for this experiment and we need to remind the reader that the main motivation for the experiment is to check whether the results of the previous experiment by Kleinschmager et al. [14] can be replicated without having a static type check.

While some authors (see [28]) argue that a number of different kinds of threats to validity should be reported[8], we reduce ourselves here just to the distinction between internal and external threats.

Internal threat – language: In fact, the previous experiment made use of the programming languages Java and Groovy while the here described experiment makes use of the programming language Dart. We expect that the programming language itself (and most important the error messages by each programming language) plays a major role in experimentation. Hence, there is the internal threat that the switch of the programming language is responsible for any changes in the results. From our perspective this threat is not that large, because of the similarity of the languages Java and Dart. At least the specific properties of Dart (closures, mixins, to-level functions, etc.) have not been used in the experiment so that Dart can be considered in the context of the present experiment as a dynamically typed Java.

Internal threat – programming tasks: The main motivation for the experiment is to check first whether the type names play a role and whether the correctness of the type names plays a role. However, the programming tasks for the correct and incorrect type names are different: while for the correct type names new code has to be written, for wrong type names code has to be fixed. One could argue that both kinds of programming tasks are too different in order to be compared with each other. However, our motivation for the second kind of programming task was that we only wanted to measure the effect of the wrong type name and not (additionally) the time required for writing new code.

Internal threat – between-subject design for incorrect type names: In assition to the two different kinds of programming tasks there is also a difference in the experimental design. The task that is intended to check the hypothesis concerning incorrect type names is measured between-subject and not (as the other tasks) within subjects. As a consequence the statistical power of the resulting tests is less than for the within-subject measurement. Since the authors' assumption is that they do not find a difference in time for wrong type names there is the problem that in case no difference was measured, this is only a problem of the statistical power of the underlying test (and the low number of subjects).

[8] Wohlin et al. argue that the grouping of the threats to validity should follow the grouping by Cook and Campell who distinguish between conclusion validity, internal validity, construct validity, and external validity [4].

Internal threat – only one task for wrong type names: In addition to the previously mentioned threats there is the problem that only one programming task is used for the second hypothesis H_0^b. This has in fact two different kinds of implications. First, a larger number of programming tasks would (again) increase the statistical power of the applied significance tests. In that way a larger number of tasks could reveal a difference which is not revealed by a single task. Second, it is possible that only for the specified task no difference can be shown although such a difference exists. We still used only one programming task because we think that a repetition of a similar task has a too large carry-over effect. Hence, the decision to use only one programming task can be considered as trade-off between the reduced statistical power and the expected large carry-over effect.

4. Experiment Results

We start presenting the results by describing the measured data and by describing the descriptive statistics first in section 4.1. Then, we describe the results of performing corresponding significance tests in section 4.2 and 4.3. With respect to the performed significance tests we follow the same method which has been applied in previous works (see [14, 15]): First, we run a repeated measures ANOVA in order to test the data round by round. Then we run a within-subject analysis where we combine both rounds.

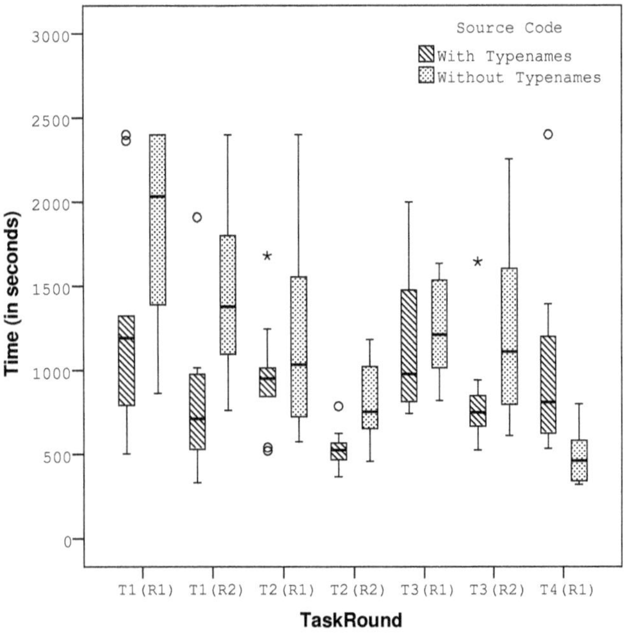

Figure 3. Boxplot for measured data

4.1 Measurements and Descriptive Statistics

Table 2 shows the observed development time for all tasks. In addition to the raw data the table also shows the sums of development times for the programming tasks 1-3 with the correctly used type names in the code. Furthermore, the differences between the sums are listed in one column. Finally, the measured (between-subject) development time for the incorrectly used typed names in the code are shown. Note that there is no second round for task four because of the chosen between-subject measurement of this task.

It is possible to get a first impression of the tendencies of the measurements from the raw data.

- **Tasks with correct type names (tasks 1–3):** For task one it looks like that the existence of the type names has a positive influence on the development times. Only three subjects (subjects 11, 15 and 17) required more development time with the type names in the code in comparison to the code without type names. And all of these subjects come from the group that started with the type names first (which might be an indicator for some carry-over effect). Although task 2 seems to be similar to task 1, 9/10 subjects in the group starting with the type names required more time with the type names compared to the group without the type names. All subjects from the group starting without type names required less development time with type names. Task three's results seem to be some kind of mixture between the first and the second task. Five subjects required more time for the solutions with type names and one of them was in the group starting without the type names. If we build the sums of development times for the tasks one to three, it turns out that four subjects required more time with the solutions with type names, all of them in the group starting with the type names in the code. In addition to the direct time measurement it is interesting to count how often subjects were not able to finish a programming task in time. Eight times subjects did not finish a programming task and only in one case this was the case for the task with type names.
- **Task with incorrect type names (task 4):** For the programming task with the incorrect type names it turns out that only the fastest subject from the group with the type names in the code required less time than the slowest subject from the group without the type names in the code. It is subject 20 who is the fastest subject from TN group and who is slower than all subjects from the No TN group except subject three (who is the slowest subject in the TN group).

Hence, a first impression from the raw measured data is that for one task there seems to be a relatively clear benefit for the code with the type names. For task two it is quite unclear and task three seems to have at least a tendency towards a benefit of type names. With respect to the incorrect type names, it relatively clearly looks as if the group without type names performed better that the group with the incorrect type names.

Taking a look into the descriptive statistics (see Figure 3) reveals also a slightly positive impression for the programming tasks 1-3 with type names and programming task 4 without type names:

- **Tasks with correct type names (tasks 1-3):** The minimum times for the tasks 1-3 are (as well as the sums of times) smaller for the tasks with the type names than the minimum development times for the tasks without type names. The maximum times are never higher for the tasks with type names: Only for task 1 both are equal, just because one subject ran into the time limit. Also, the means and median are always lower for the tasks with the type names. Additionally, the standard deviations for the tasks without type names are higher.
- **Task with incorrect type names (task 4):** For the task with incorrect type names all descriptive numbers are lower for the tasks without type names.

The previous descriptions did not take into account the comparison between subjects in the same round, i.e. they did not compare the measured data of for example task 1 in a way that only the measurements between the subjects that solved the tasks for the first time were taken into account. The boxplot (see Figure 3) describes

Table 2. Measured development times (time in seconds) – Start = Kind of system subjects started with, No TN = No Type Names in the code, TN = Type names in the code, light grey highlighted cells = subjects who ran out of time, dark gray highlighted cells = cells with unexpected results

		Task 1		Task 2		Task 3		Sums		Diff	Wrong Typename
Subject	Start	TN	No TN	TN	No TN	TN	No TN	TN	No TN		
1	No TN	1909	2400	507	1555	1645	1536	4061	5491	-1430	-
2	No TN	1017	2400	468	2400	527	1029	2012	5829	-3817	204
3	No TN	532	1390	539	739	668	1014	1739	3143	-1404	562
4	No TN	978	1848	513	1409	687	1287	2178	4544	-2366	417
5	No TN	735	2400	626	1860	816	1609	2177	5869	-3692	456
6	No TN	518	1414	436	576	802	842	1756	2832	-1076	234
7	No TN	671	2218	569	724	848	1303	2088	4245	-2157	200
8	No TN	810	1199	565	1038	695	1635	2070	3872	-1802	335
9	No TN	690	2400	786	1026	942	1134	2418	4560	-2142	517
10	No TN	332	863	366	611	638	820	1336	2294	-958	351
11	TN	1305	1198	845	785	805	1134	2955	3117	-162	819
12	TN	1203	1801	948	896	813	1236	2964	3933	-969	2400
13	TN	1179	1700	1006	654	1300	797	3485	3151	334	803
14	TN	1323	2400	1680	1181	1934	2255	4937	5836	-899	-
15	TN	2364	1187	886	719	890	1085	4140	2991	1149	1395
16	TN	672	1560	953	679	855	969	2480	3208	-728	1000
17	TN	2400	2400	1243	1105	1999	1604	5642	5109	533	-
18	TN	983	1096	1014	1022	1477	2236	3474	4354	-880	640
19	TN	504	763	542	467	744	613	1790	1843	-53	612
20	TN	794	984	522	458	1066	729	2382	2171	211	536

Table 3. Descriptive statistics of experiment results (time in seconds), TN = Type Names in the code, No TN = No Type Names in the code

	Task 1		Task 2		Task 3		Sums		Diff	Wrong TN	
	TN	No TN	TN	No TN	TN	No TN	TN	No TN		TN	No TN
min	332	763	366	458	527	613	1336	1843	-3817	536	200
max	2400	2400	1680	2400	1999	2255	5642	5869	1149	2400	562
arith. mean	1046	1681	751	995	1008	1243	2804	3920	-1115	1026	364
median	894	1630	598	841	832	1134	2400	3903	-964	811	351
std. dev.	584	592	326	494	431	455	1153	1267	1305	618	134

exactly this. There, for each round the data is being compared. The boxplot seems to suggest the following interpretation[9]:

- **Tasks with correct type names (tasks 1–3):** While it seems relatively clear that for the second round the times for the tasks with type names are smaller than the development times without type names, it seems at least unclear whether this is the case for the first round.

While the examination of the raw measurements and the descriptive statistics gives already a first impression it is necessary to perform inference statistics in order to come to a conclusion about the results of the experiment.

4.2 Repeated Measures ANOVA on Correct Type Names

Running a repeated measures ANOVA means that we analyse each round individually and we compare all tasks (i.e. tasks 1–3) together. Because of the different nature of task 4 we do not include it in this analysis here.

A repeated measures ANOVA on the measurements implies that we use the measured development times as dependent variable. The independent variables are the within-subject variable programming task (with the treatments 1–3) and the between-subject variable type information (with the treatments with and without type names).

For the first round we see that the variable programming task is a significant factor ($p<.01$, $\eta_p^2=.33$) while the factor type information is not ($p=.15$, $\eta_p^2=.11$). An interesting observation is that there is a significant interaction between programming task and type information ($p=.05$, $\eta_p^2=.2$) which means that the task treatment and the type information influence together the resulting measurements in a significant way.

The second round reveals slightly different results (a phenomena that happened also in previous studies, see [14, 15]). Again, the variable programming task turns out to be significant ($p<.01$, $\eta_p^2=.47$). But now, the between-subject variable type information turns out to be significant, too ($p<.01$, $\eta_p^2=.33$). Finally, the interaction between programming task and type information is close to significant ($p<.08$, $\eta_p^2=.13$).

Because of the significant interaction in round 1 and the close to significant interaction in round 2 we think it is worthwhile to take a look closer look into the interaction (see Figures 4 and 5). In both rounds we see that that the differences between the lines differ for different tasks and for different type information. An interesting observation here is that both diagrams differ slightly. While for round 1 it looks like there is hardly any difference between both groups for task three there is a larger difference between the lines for the same task in round 2. In both diagrams we see that the differences between both lines are different between the tasks: this illustrates the interaction.

More interesting is round 2 because the factor type information turned out significant. Here, the interaction diagram shows that the

[9] Note, that the previous descriptions of task 4 were already between subject, i.e. the boxplot does not reveal any new information for task 4.

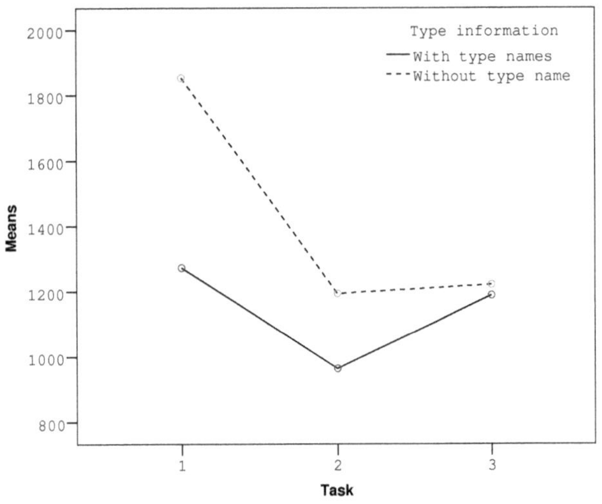

Figure 4. Interaction diagram for round 1

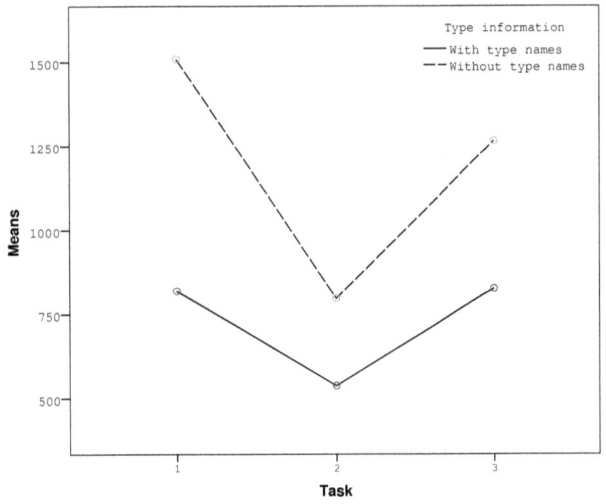

Figure 5. Interaction diagram for round 2

means for solutions with type names are always smaller than the means for the solutions without type names.[10]

4.3 Task-by-Task Comparison

The previous analysis shows for both rounds a significant effect of the programming tasks. Because of that we study the programming tasks in more detail. A first (maybe obvious) possible analysis of the tasks is to study each task in each round in separation. However, the disadvantage of this approach is that the necessary statistical method has a relatively small statistical power: it turns out that in round 1 only task 1 has a significant difference in the means ($p<.05$ computed using the Mann-Whitney-U-Test) while task 2 and task 3 have not ($p=.4$ and $p=.5$). For round 2 the results are different. Here, the means for task 1 and task 2 are significantly different while task 3 is only close to significant (task 1: $p<.01$, task 2: $p<.03$, task 3: $p=.052$).

However, the application of the Mann-Whitney-U-Test does not take into account that we have a within-subject measurement for each subject and for each task. I.e. it is possible to apply a paired test on the measurements. According to previous approaches (see [14, 15]) we perform a (paired) Wilcoxon test on each individual task and for each individual round.

Table 4 shows the results for the Wilcoxon tests for each group. It turns out that the group starting with no type names always has a decreased development time in the second run when the type names are in the code. For the second group, it turns out that for the second task subjects had a benefit in the second run. For tasks 1 and 3 no significant differences were measured.

According to the interpretation which takes into account possible learning effects (see [15] for a more detailed discussion) a positive impact for task 1 and 3 was measured. For task 2 it is not possible to draw any conclusion from the within-subject study.[11]

Table 4. Individual within-subject analysis (Wilcoxon-test) for both groups No TN first and Type Names first

Task	**Task 1**	**Task 2**	**Task 3**
P-values			
NO TN FIRST	.005	.005	.009
Dominating approach	TN	TN	TN
TYPE NAMES FIRST	.14	.001	.72
Dominating approach	–	No TN	–
Result			
Dominating approach	TN	–	TN

Combining the measurements for each group (i.e. assuming a counterbalance effect of the experimental design) and running again a Wilcoxon test reveals the same situation. For task one an task 3 the differences are significant ($p<.05$) while for task two the differences are not significant ($p>.2$).

4.4 Non-Paired Comparison on Wrong Type Names

While the previous analysis took into account that for task 1–3 there was a between-subject measurement, task 4 (which is the task with the wrong type name in the method header) was measured between-subjects. Hence, the Mann-Whitney-U-Test must be applied again and since there are no multiple tasks only a single test can be performed.

Applying the Mann-Whitney-U-Test reveals a significant lower development time using no type names ($p<.001$).

4.5 Summery of the analysis

The results of the analysis can be summarized as follows. First, a significant difference between type names and no type names was measured for those tasks where the type names were correct, i.e. the hypothesis H_0^a was rejected and the type names decreased the development times. However, task 2 did not show this effect. Second, a significant difference between type names and no type names was measured for the task with incorrect type names, i.e. the hypothesis H_0^b was rejected and no type names (i.e. the code without type declarations) decreased the development time.

5. Summary and Conclusion

While the discussion about possible pros and cons about static and dynamic type systems goes on and while there are in the meantime some empirical studies available which can be used for arguing for or against these type systems this study focused on one specific

[10] The same is true for round 1, but the factor type information did not turn out to be significant.

[11] In order to ease the reading of the paper we do not report the ranks here.

issue which can be considered as a special case in the discussion. Instead of focusing on static or dynamic type systems, this study focused only on the possible effect of type names in the code, i.e. only on the piece of syntax.

The motivation for this study was driven by the fact that previous studies on API usage showed a positive effect of static types using a Java-like type system where the type names are in the code. These studies were based on the statement by Pierce that the syntactic representation of types helps documenting the code (see [18]). Hence, it seemed plausible to ask whether a pure synactic representation of static types (without static type checking) is able to achieve the same results.

In order to answer this question an experiment was constructed which used the Java-like programming language Dart which provides different kinds of usage modes and where type names are optional. One of the possible usage modes in Dart is that the type check is omitted which has been applied in the experiment. Four programming tasks were given to the subjects. Three tasks where the type names in the code were correct and one task where a type name in the API was not correct. The three programming tasks were not completely newly designed for the experiment. Instead, they were taken from previous experiments where in each of the tasks a positive impact of the static type system had been shown. As measurements the development times for each tasks were taken. The experiment had been performed with 20 subjects at the University of Duisburg–Essen, Germany.

The results of the experiment were that to a certain extent the type names already helped developers using the API: The analysis of development times per round showed a positive impact of the type names in the second round (but not in the first round) and the within-subject analysis revealed a positive effect of type names for two tasks while for one task the results were inconclusive.

If we compare these results to the experiment where the programming tasks were originally developed for (see [14]) we see that the results of the here presented study do not show the same strength in favor for type names. The second task is an indicator that the effect of only the type names is weaker than the effect of type names in combination with static type checking.

An interesting result is the observation for the task with the incorrect type name. The motivation for this task was that static type systems guarantee the correctness of type names in the code, i.e. a wrong type name will be detected by the type checker. The experimenters expected no difference between the measured times with and without type names. However, the interesting observation is that a wrong type information is not only some kind of information that does not have any influence on the resulting development times. A wrong type name has a measurable, significant negative influence on the development times.

Although we do not know why wrong type names have such a negative influence, we speculate that developers first will assume that a given type name is correct and will use such parameters in a way as expected by the type description. We assume that in case an error occurs developers will first look into those classes that match the corresponding (wrong) type and subjects might wonder what exactly the problem is. We assume that the behavior is different when no information is available at all. We assume that in such cases developers directly read the code from the perspective what types might match into the parameters (instead of wondering why a certain type does not match). We believe that this might be one possible explanation for the measured differences.

Altogether, the results of the study can be summarized in the following way:

- **Correct type names help humans to use a new set of classes:** Two of three tasks (or all tasks in the second round in combination in the between-subject analysis) revealed a positive effect of type names on the development time and correct type names significantly reduced the time required to solve the programming tasks.
- **Incorrect type names hinder humans using an API:** The only task we have in the experiment showed a negative impact of the group working with type names when the type name was incorrect. The group required significantly more time to solve the programming task.

Of course, the results of the study should not be overestimated because to our knowledge this is the only study so far which purely tests the influence of the syntactic construct type name. However, if we assume that multiple replications of this study will reveal a similar effect we think that this should have an influence on language design based on the following discussion.

There seems to be some tendency to equip programming languages with static type names but without enforcing type checks. The programming language Dart is one of these examples, TypeScript is an example of a language which provides a type system that does not aim to be type sound. Based on the results of this study, we consider these tendencies to be rather problematic. Incorrect types (based on a nominal type system which adds type names to the syntax) possibly reduce the usability of APIs and other code. Hence, incorrect types are some kind of risk that systems with type names but without type checks imply.

Of course, it might be possible to argue that in real code such wrong type names would not occur. But unfortunately, we do not have any empirical knowledge about how often type errors actually occur. In order to study such a question, the use of controlled experiment is probably rather not the right way and maybe mining source code repositores (see for example [2, 21]) would be able to answer this question. Another possible argument could be that before delivering any code it is always necessary to run some code reviews. It is at least unclear whether these code reviews would be able to detect and fix possible errors in type names.

Another interesting issue is a comparison between the here described experiment and the experiment performed by Prechelt and Tichy (see [20]) who analyzed the effect of static type checking on procedure arguments and who concluded that the static type checking actually helps. The here described experiment is somehow related; and it is possibly a contrast to the results by Prechelt and Tichy, because our study showed that also only the type names help – as long they are correct.

Hence, an implication of this experiment is that the measured differences between static and dynamic type systems in previous experiments (see [8, 9, 13–15, 20, 25, 26]) is in fact a combination of the effect of static type checking and usability based on type names. Consequently, we think that it is desirable and necessary to perform experiments which check whether the use of languages with static type systems without type declarations (i.e. type systems that are purely based on type inference) are able to show the same effect that has been shown so far.

Altogether, we think that the here described experiment is an argument for static type checking in programming languages. Although the use of pure type names might already achieve a good part of the positive effect resulting from static type systems that rely on declared type names, there is the risk that such type names might be wrong and cause a reduced usability of the code. Consequently, as long as it is unclear whether the type system causes higher costs in API development, there does not seem to be a hard argument to omit static type checking – especially in situations where the type names are already statically declared in the code.

Of course, it is necessary to mention that the here described experiment is just a first experiment in this direction and that further experimentation is needed. In general the whole question to what extent syntactic elements in the code have a possible effect on the development time is relatively open (see for example [24]). Additionally, it is always necessary to mention that each experiment comes with a set of threats to validity that need to be taken into account. For example, the here described experiment was executed using the programming language Dart and it is unclear to what extent the actual programming language influences the results of the study. However, from our perspective this experiment gives the next piece of the puzzle "understanding the influence of type systems on developers" and we hope that the more experiments will be available the more fine-grained we will be able to understand the long-discussed topic about static and dynamic types.

Acknowledgments

We thank the volunteers from the University of Duisburg-Essen for their participation in the experiment.

References

[1] Kim B. Bruce. *Foundations of object-oriented languages: types and semantics*. MIT Press, Cambridge, MA, USA, 2002.

[2] Oscar Callaú, Romain Robbes, Éric Tanter, and David Röthlisberger. How developers use the dynamic features of programming languages: the case of smalltalk. In *Proceedings of the 8th International Working Conference on Mining Software Repositories, MSR 2011 (Co-located with ICSE), Waikiki, Honolulu, HI, USA, May 21-28, 2011, Proceedings*, pages 23–32, 2011.

[3] Luca Cardelli. Type systems. In Allen B. Tucker, editor, *The Computer Science and Engineering Handbook*, chapter 103, pages 2208–2236. CRC Press, 1997.

[4] T.D. Cook and D.T. Campbell. *Quasi-experimentation: design & analysis issues for field settings*. Rand McNally College, 1979.

[5] Mark T. Daly, Vibha Sazawal, and Jeffrey S. Foster. Work in progress: an empirical study of static typing in ruby. *Workshop on Evaluation and Usability of Programming Languages and Tools (PLATEAU),Orlando, October 2009*, 2009.

[6] Stefan Endrikat and Stefan Hanenberg. Is aspect-oriented programming a rewarding investment into future code changes? A socio-technical study on development and maintenance time. In *Proceedings of the 2011 IEEE 19th International Conference on Program Comprehension*, ICPC '11, pages 51–60, Kingston, CA, 2011. IEEE Computer Society.

[7] Stefan Endrikat, Stefan Hanenberg, Romain Robbes, and Andreas Stefik. How do API documentation and static typing affect API usability? In *Proceedings of the ICSE 2014 (accepted for publication)*, ICSE '14, 2014.

[8] J. D. Gannon. An experimental evaluation of data type conventions. *Commun. ACM*, 20(8):584–595, 1977.

[9] Stefan Hanenberg. An experiment about static and dynamic type systems: Doubts about the positive impact of static type systems on development time. In *Proceedings of the ACM international conference on Object oriented programming systems languages and applications*, OOPSLA, pages 22–35, New York, NY, USA, 2010. ACM.

[10] Stefan Hanenberg. Faith, hope, and love: An essay on software science's neglect of human factors. In *Proceedings of the ACM international conference on Object oriented programming systems languages and applications*, OOPSLA '10, pages 933–946, Reno/Tahoe, Nevada, USA, October 2010.

[11] Stefan Hanenberg. A chronological experience report from an initial experiment series on static type systems. In *2nd Workshop on Empirical Evaluation of Software Composition Techniques (ESCOT)*, Lancaster, UK, 2011.

[12] Stefan Hanenberg and Stefan Endrikat. Aspect-orientation is a rewarding investment into future code changes - as long as the aspects hardly change. *Information & Software Technology*, 55(4):722–740, 2013.

[13] Michael Hoppe and Stefan Hanenberg. Do developers benefit from generic types? an empirical comparison of generic and raw types in java. In *Proceedings of the 2013 ACM SIGPLAN International Conference on Object Oriented Programming Systems Languages & Applications, OOPSLA 2013, part of SPLASH 2013, Indianapolis, IN, USA, October 26-31, 2013*, pages 457–474. ACM, 2013.

[14] Sebastian Kleinschmager, Stefan Hanenberg, Romain Robbes, Éric Tanter, and Andreas Stefik. Do static type systems improve the maintainability of software systems? An empirical study. In *IEEE 20th International Conference on Program Comprehension, ICPC 2012, Passau, Germany, June 11-13*, pages 153–162, 2012.

[15] Clemens Mayer, Stefan Hanenberg, Romain Robbes, Éric Tanter, and Andreas Stefik. An empirical study of the influence of static type systems on the usability of undocumented software. In *Proceedings of the 27th Annual ACM SIGPLAN Conference on Object-Oriented Programming, Systems, Languages, and Applications, OOPSLA 2012, part of SPLASH 2012, Tucson, AZ, USA, October 21-25, 2012*, pages 683–702. ACM, 2012.

[16] Leo A. Meyerovich and Ariel S. Rabkin. Empirical analysis of programming language adoption. In *Proceedings of the 2013 ACM SIGPLAN International Conference on Object Oriented Programming Systems Languages & Applications, OOPSLA 2013, part of SPLASH 2013, Indianapolis, IN, USA, October 26-31, 2013*, pages 1–18. ACM, 2013.

[17] Chris Parnin, Christian Bird, and Emerson R. Murphy-Hill. Adoption and use of java generics. *Empirical Software Engineering*, 18(6):1047–1089, 2013.

[18] Benjamin C. Pierce. *Types and programming languages*. MIT Press, Cambridge, MA, USA, 2002.

[19] Lutz Prechelt. An empirical comparison of seven programming languages. *IEEE Computer*, 33:23–29, 2000.

[20] Lutz Prechelt and Walter F. Tichy. A controlled experiment to assess the benefits of procedure argument type checking. *IEEE Trans. Softw. Eng.*, 24(4):302–312, 1998.

[21] Gregor Richards, Christian Hammer, Brian Burg, and Jan Vitek. The eval that men do - a large-scale study of the use of eval in javascript applications. In *ECOOP 2011 - Object-Oriented Programming - 25th European Conference, Lancaster, UK, July 25-29, 2011 Proceedings*, pages 52–78, 2011.

[22] Carlos Souza and Eduardo Figueiredo. How do programmers use optional typing? an empirical study. In *To appear in: Proceedings of Modularity 14 (AOSD'14),2014*. ACM, 2014.

[23] Andreas Stefik and Susanna Siebert. An empirical investigation into programming language syntax. *Trans. Comput. Educ.*, 13(4):19:1–19:40, November 2013.

[24] Andreas Stefik, Susanna Siebert, Melissa Stefik, and Kim Slattery. An empirical comparison of the accuracy rates of novices using the quorum, perl, and randomo programming languages. In *Proceedings of the 3rd ACM SIGPLAN workshop on Evaluation and usability of programming languages and tools, PLATEAU 2011, Portland, OR, USA, October 24, 2011*, pages 3–8, 2011.

[25] Marvin Steinberg and Stefan Hanenberg. What is the impact of static type systems on debugging type errors and semantic errors? - submitted.

[26] Andreas Stuchlik and Stefan Hanenberg. Static vs. dynamic type systems: An empirical study about the relationship between type casts and development time. In *Proceedings of the 7th symposium on Dynamic languages*, DLS '11, pages 97–106, Portland, Oregon, USA, 2011. ACM.

[27] Laurence Tratt. Dynamically typed languages. *Advances in Computers*, 77:149–184, July 2009.

[28] Claes Wohlin, Per Runeson, Martin Höst, Magnus C. Ohlsson, Bjöorn Regnell, and Anders Wesslén. *Experimentation in software engineering: an introduction*. Kluwer Academic Publishers, Norwell, MA, USA, 2000.

How Do Programmers Use Optional Typing? An Empirical Study

Carlos Souza
Software Engineering Lab
Federal University of Minas Gerais (UFMG)
carlosgsouza@gmail.com

Eduardo Figueiredo
Software Engineering Lab
Federal University of Minas Gerais (UFMG)
figueiredo@dcc.ufmg.br

Abstract

The recent popularization of dynamically typed languages, such as Ruby and JavaScript, has brought more attention to the discussion about the impact of typing strategies on development. Types allow the compiler to find type errors earlier and potentially improve the readability and maintainability of code. On the other hand, "untyped" code may be easier to change and require less work from programmers. This paper tries to identify the programmers' point of view about these tradeoffs. An analysis of the source code of 6638 projects written in Groovy, a programming language which features optional typing, shows in which scenarios programmers prefer to type or not to type their declarations. Our results show that types are popular in the definition of module interfaces, but are less used in scripts, test classes and frequently changed code. There is no correlation between the size and age of projects and how their constructs are typed. Finally, we also found evidence that the background of programmers influences how they use types.

Categories and Subject Descriptors D.2.3 [*Software Engineering*]: Cooding Tools and Techniques

General Terms Experimentation, Language

Keywords Type Systems; Static Analysis; Groovy

1. Introduction

Type systems are one of the most important characteristics of a programming language and also a major topic of research in software engineering [13, 29, 32, 34]. A programming language's type system determines when the type of an expression is defined [29]. Statically typed languages, such as Java and C#, require programmers to explicitly define the type of a declaration, which can then be used by the compiler to check for type errors. On the other hand, in dynamically typed languages, such as Ruby and JavaScript, the definition of the type of an expression only happens at run time.

Discussions about what is the best type system for a particular situation have become increasingly important in recent years due to the rapid popularization of dynamically typed languages. According to the TIOBE Programming Community Index [35], a well-known ranking that measures the popularity of programming languages, 27% of the programming languages used in industry are dynamically typed. A decade ago, this number was only 17%. Among the 10 languages on top of the ranking, four are dynamically typed: JavaScript, Perl, Python and PHP. None of these languages were among the top 10 rank before 1998.

Several factors may be considered when choosing between a dynamically or statically typed language. Dynamically typed languages tend to allow programmers to code faster and to adapt their programs to frequently changing requirements more easily. Also, by removing the repetitive work of defining types, these languages allow programmers to focus on the problem to be solved rather than on the rules of the language [36].

Statically typed languages also have their advantages. They allow compilers to find type errors statically [24]. Typed declarations increase the maintainability of systems because they implicitly document the code, telling programmers about the nature of expressions [4, 25]. Systems built with these languages tend to be more efficient since they do not need to perform type checking during execution [2, 5]. Finally, modern development environments, such as Eclipse and IDEA, are able to assist programmers with functionalities such as code completion based on the information provided by statically typed declarations [3].

Some languages try to combine characteristics from both static and dynamic type systems. Groovy [18] is one of these languages. Although Groovy is mostly a dynamically typed language, it gives programmers the option to use type annotations as a means to document their code. It is also possible to turn static type checking on so the compiler can find type errors before execution. This allows developers to choose the most appropriate paradigm for each situation.

Understanding the point of view of programmers about the use of types is an important matter. Programming language developers can consider this information in their design so they can develop the most appropriate features for their target audience. Tools can be created or improved to overcome weaknesses of languages. Finally, programmers can benefit from this knowledge when choosing programming languages or typing paradigms for a given context.

This paper presents a large scale empirical study about how programmers use optional typing in Groovy. Through the analysis of a massive dataset with almost seven thousand Groovy projects, we were able to identify when programmers prefer to type or not their declarations. Our results show the point of view of programmers about the use of types. This analysis complements, with a different point of view, existing studies based on controlled experiments [9, 14, 19, 20, 22, 25, 31].

The remainder of this paper is organized as follows. Section 2 introduces the main concepts of the Groovy programming language and Section 3 presents the study settings. Section 4 describes the

MODULARITY '14, April 22–26, 2014, Lugano, Switzerland.

ACM 978-1-4503-2772-5/14/04... $15.00.
http://dx.doi.org/10.1145/2577080.2582208

results of the study, which are then discussed in Section 5. Threats to the validity and related work are presented in Sections 6 and 7. Finally, Section 8 concludes this study and suggests future work.

2. The Groovy Language

Groovy is a dynamically typed programming language designed to run on the Java Virtual Machine. Its adoption has grown remarkably over the last years. According to the TIOBE Programming Index, Groovy is the 22nd most popular language in the software industry [35], ahead of languages like Haskell and Scala. It builds upon the strengths of Java, but has additional features inspired by dynamic languages such as Python and Ruby, such as metaprogramming, closures and script support. Like Java, Groovy code is compiled to bytecode, allowing it to seamlessly integrate with existing Java classes and libraries. These factors have attracted a large number of Java programmers who want to use Groovy's dynamic functionality without having to learn a completely different language or change the execution platform of their systems.

When Groovy was first launched, in 2007, it was a purely dynamically typed language. However, it allowed programmers to optionally type their declarations. Examples of typed and untyped declarations combined in the same file are shown in Listing 1. This kind of typing should not be confused with static typing since the Groovy compiler does not use these type annotations to look for errors. For example, the snippet of code shown in Listing 2 compiles without any errors. Nevertheless, during runtime, the *string* variable references an instance of the *Integer* class and an exception is thrown when the method *toUpperCase* is invoked since the *Integer* class does not have such method.

Listing 1 Typed and untyped declarations mixed together

```
class DynamicTyping {
  private String typedField
  private untypedField

  DynamicTyping(typedParam){}

  def untypedMethod(untypedParam,int typedParam){
    def untypedVariable = 1.0
    return untypedVariable
  }

  int typedMethod(){
    String typedVariable = ""
    return typedVariable
  }
}
```

Listing 2 Types are not checked by default by the Groovy compiler

```
String string = new Integer(1)
string.toUpperCase()
```

Since version 2.0, Groovy allows programmers to explicitly activate static typing by using the *@TypeChecked* annotation. This makes Groovy a gradually typed language [15–17, 33, 34]. In this mode, the Groovy compiler looks for type errors and fails if it finds any. Listing 3 shows an example of static typing in Groovy. Trying to compile the class *TypeCheckedGroovyClass* produces an error since the method *sum* is supposed to receive two parameters of the type *int*, but it is actually called with two parameters of the type *String*.

Listing 3 Forcing the compiler to check types

```
@TypeChecked
class TypeCheckedGroovyClass {

  static int sum(int a, int b) {
    a + b
  }

  public static void main(String[] args) {
    println sum("1", "2")
  }
}
```

The *@TypeChecked* annotation is reasonably recent and most Groovy programmers still do not use it. Typing annotations on the other hand are very popular. Although they do not provide static type checking, they are capable of documenting the code and aiding in the integration with development tools. In the remainder of this text, we refer to declarations with type annotations as "typed", while the word "untyped" is used for declarations with no type annotations.

3. Study Settings

The study presented in this paper consists in the static analysis of the source code of a corpus of 6638 Groovy projects. Its goal is to find in which contexts Groovy programmers type or do not type their declarations. In this section, we present five research questions that guide our analysis, the data collection and analysis procedures and the characterization of the studied dataset.

We have shared all the artifacts of this study in our project website. [1] This includes the source code of the programs used in the data collection and analysis procedures, the analyzed data (except the source code of the analyzed projects) and detailed results. Our goal is to allow this study to be easily replicated or extended.

3.1 Research Questoins

We aim to answer the following research questions about the usage of types by Groovy programmers:

- **Question Q1: Do programmers use types more often in the interface of their modules?** We believe that the benefits of the use of types are more clear in declarations that define the interface of modules. In such cases, programmers are specifying how the rest of the program should interact with a module, potentially improving readability and maintainability. On the other hand, in declarations that are hidden from external modules, we expect programmers to opt for the simplicity and flexibility offered by untyped declarations more often.
- **Question Q2: Do programmers use types less often in test classes and scripts?** Many studies analyze typing paradigms in the main classes of a program. However, little is known about this question in scripts or test classes. We want to understand if programmers consider different typing strategies in these scenarios.
- **Question Q3: Does the experience of programmers with other languages influence their choice for typing their code?** We believe that programmers familiar with a dynamically typed language are more confortable with the lack of types and end up using types less often in Groovy.

[1] http://github.com/carlosgsouza/groovonomics

- **Question Q4: Does the size, age or level of activity of a project have any influence on the usage of types?** We hypothesize that as these metrics grow, there is an increased concern about keeping code more maintainable. This can lead programmers to use types more often as a means to improve code readability.
- **Question Q5: In frequently changed code, do developers prefer typed or untyped declarations?** It makes sense to assume that developers try to increase the maintainability of frequently changed code. One way to achieve that is improving the readability of such code with the use of types. On the other hand, the flexibility of untyped declarations is capable of increasing the changeability of those files. We want to understand which one of these strategies is actually preferred by Groovy developers.

3.2 Data Collection Procedure

The projects used in this study were obtained from GitHub, a popular source control service based on Git. For each project, it was necessary to retrieve its source code, metadata, commit history, and the metadata of all of its developers. GitHub does not offer a listing of all hosted projects, but it offers two search mechanisms, a REST API and a Web based search page. Unfortunately, the GitHub API is too limited for our requirements. It imposes a limit of one thousand results and does not allow filtering projects by their programming language.

In order to retrieve an extensive dataset, it was necessary to write a bot to simulate human interactions with the GitHub webpage and search for projects. Some special care was necessary to make this work. For instance, because the number of results is limited to one thousand projects, we had to segment the queries. Multiple requests were made, each of them asking for the name of all projects created on a given month. Results were then combined into a single list. Another problem faced was that GitHub denies excessive requests from the same client. By adding artificial delays between requests, it was possible to overcome this limitation.

With the name of all projects in hand, it was then possible to use the GitHub REST API to query their metadata. That metadata also contains the identifiers of the developers and of the commits of that project. Using those identifiers we once again used the GitHub REST API and obtained the background of all developers and the file changes of all projects.

3.3 Dataset

Our dataset consists of 6638 projects with almost 9.8 million lines of code. Table 1 shows descriptive statistics for the size, age and number of commits of these projects. There are more than 1.5 million declarations of all types and visibilities in our dataset. Note that the value of the median of the number of lines is relatively small. Most projects have 529 lines of code or less. This was expected. Since Groovy is a very expressive language, with many traits of functional programming languages, programmers can write more concise code leading to smaller programs. In addition, by manually inspecting our dataset, we found a significant number of projects with a small number of Groovy files among files written in other languages. Also, we found many small projects created with learning purposes only.

	Mean	Median	Sd	Max	Total
Size (LoC)	1,471	529	4,545	149,933	9,770,783
Commits	31	5	175	6,545	203,375
Age (Days)	361	280	333	1,717	2,395,441

Table 1. Characterization of Projects

Table 2 shows the number of declarations by kind and visibility and Table 3 shows the use of visibilities according to kind of declaration. Note that most fields are declared with private visibility while most methods are public. This is explained by the fact that, in Groovy, the default visibilities for fields and methods are private and public respectively.

	Mean	Median	Sd	Max	Total
Field	54	19	163	5,268	366,148
Constructor Parameter	3	0	16	933	18,956
Method Parameter	30	6	110	3,554	202,617
Method Return	53	15	165	4,893	357,997
Local Variable	88	21	361	16,427	602,645
Public	74	20	239	7,942	507,296
Protected	6	0	32	1,394	42,646
Private	58	21	178	5,268	395,776
All Declarations	227	71	744	29,862	1,548,363

Table 2. Number of Declarations per Project

The projects of our dataset were developed by 4481 people. While 96% of the projects were developed by small groups of 3 people or fewer, there were projects with up to 58 people involved. These developers have different backgrounds. Figure 1 shows what are the most popular languages used by the Groovy developers in other GitHub projects. Java is the most popular among them. Almost 2500 out of of the 4481 developers of projects in our dataset also have Java projects hosted on GitHub.

	Private	Protected	Public
Field	346,462	2,996	16,690
Constructor Parameter	680	246	18,030
Method Parameter	27,174	10,897	164,546
Method Return	21,460	28,507	308,030

Table 3. Number of Declarations by Visibility

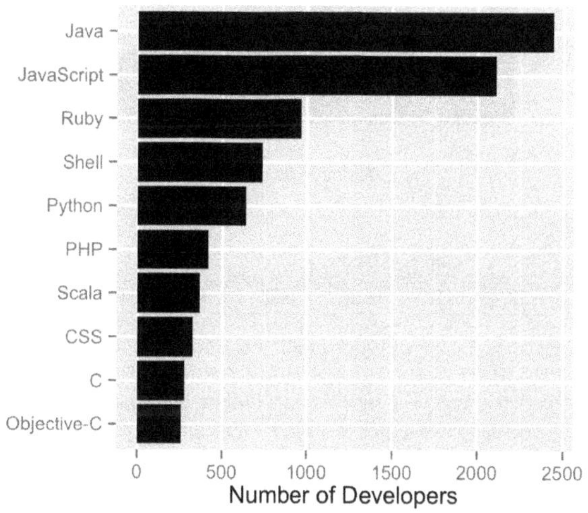

Figure 1. Most popular languages among Groovy developers

3.4 Analysis

In order to understand where programmers use types, we developed a static code analyzer based on the Groovy metaprogramming library. This analyzer is capable of retrieving the declaration information of parameters and returns of methods, parameters of constructors, fields and local variables. In addition, the analyzer can tell if a declaration is part of a test class or a script and what is its visibility.

A relevant decision we made was not to compile projects, which would require all dependencies to be resolved. This is not feasible given the size of our dataset. Instead, we generated the AST for each file using the *CONVERSION* phase of the Groovy compiler. At this phase, the compiler has not tried to resolve any dependencies yet, but it is capable of generating an AST with enough information to determine whether a declaration is typed or not. This makes it possible to analyze each Groovy file separately without having to compile the whole project. The downside of this approach is that we cannot analyze Groovy code in conjunction with its dependencies. For example, it is impossible to determine whether programmers tend to type code that interacts with other typed modules since we have not resolved any dependencies to these modules. However, our choice was fundamental in order to execute a study with such an extensive dataset.

4. Results

This section presents the data obtained from our analysis and its statistical treatment. We show how the usage of types varies according to the kind and visibility of declarations, nature of code, programmers' background, project maturity and frequency of changes. The interpretation of these results is left to Section 5, which answers the proposed research questions (Section 3.1) based on this data and raises new research questions.

4.1 Overall Result

Figure 2 shows a histogram and the descriptive statistics for the relative usage of types in declarations of projects. This value can vary from 0 (a project does not declare any types) to 1 (all declarations of a project are typed). All declarations are considered.

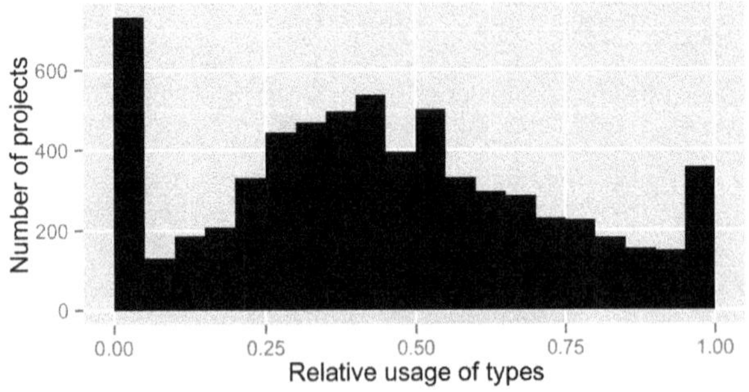

n	mean	std. dev.	Quartiles 1st	2nd	3rd	4th
6638	0.45	0.28	0.25	0.42	0.64	1.00

Figure 2. Usage of types in all declarations of all projects

Note that there is a significant number of projects for which the relative usage of types is either approximately 0 or 1. These are mostly small projects. About 95% of them have less than 1000 lines of code and 22% of them have less than 100 lines of code. In such projects, it is easier to be consistent on the typing strategy since there are just a few declarations. We initially considered not including these projects in the rest of our analysis since they could not represent well the entire population of Groovy projects. However, doing so did not alter the results significantly and we decided to include all projects in our analysis regardless of their size. In the rest of this section, this data will be presented in more detail so we can understand which factors lead programmers to use types or not.

4.2 Kind of Declaration

This section investigates whether programmers use types differently depending on the kind of the declaration. For each project, we measured the relative usage of types in fields, constructor parameters, method returns, method parameters and local variables. These results are displayed in box plots in Figure 3 along with the corresponding descriptive statistics. Note that the size of each sample, *n*, is different since not all projects have all types of declarations. For instance, there are only 1670 out of 6638 projects that declare constructor parameters. On the other hand, 6000 projects have declarations of fields.

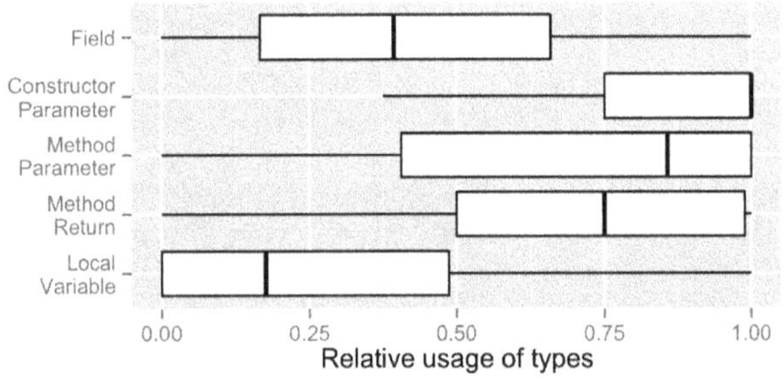

Declaration Type	n	mean	median	std. dev.
Field	6000	0.43	0.39	0.33
Constructor Parameter	1670	0.80	1.00	0.35
Method Parameter	4867	0.67	0.86	0.36
Method Return	5881	0.68	0.75	0.31
Local Variable	5845	0.29	0.18	0.32

Figure 3. Usage of types in all declarations by type of declaration

The results presented in Figure 3 suggest that programmers use types differently depending on the type of a declaration. Local variables, for example, are typed less often. Half of the projects have only 18% or less of their local variables typed. Conversely, methods and constructors are typed in most cases. Note that the median for constructor parameters is equal to 1.00, which means that at least half of the projects with constructor parameters type all declarations of this kind. Since local variables are never part of a module interface, these results suggest a positive answer for Question Q1, i.e, declarations that compose module interfaces are typed more often than other declarations.

The box plot graph and the descriptive statistics are not enough to determine whether the difference in the usage of types in any two kinds of declaration is significant. In order to do that, a significance test should be applied. We start by defining a hypothesis below, which can then be rejected or accepted by this test.

H0 There is no difference in how programmers type different kinds of declarations

H1 Programmers type their declarations differently depending on the kind of the declaration

The appropriate significance test should be chosen carefully. It needs to compare multiple treatments, which represent the 5 distinct kinds of declaration. We first considered applying repeated *t-tests* or *Mann-Whitney U-tests* in order to compare every two kinds of declaration, i.e, fields vs. local variables, fields vs method returns, etc. However, applying repeated tests over the same sample increases the probability of getting Type-I errors (rejecting the null hypothesis when it actually should be accepted).

A valid alternative for our scenario is to use One-Way Between Groups ANOVA, which compares all means simultaneously and maintains the Type-I error probability at the designated level. ANOVA computes a p value which indicates whether at least two treatments are significantly different from each other. The smaller the value of p, the "more significant" is the difference and, consequently, the stronger the rejection of the null hypothesis.

Given the level of significance, α, we can reject the null hypothesis if $p < \alpha$. Typically, $\alpha = 0.05$ or $\alpha = 0.01$ are used, but in this study we decided to use a very small value for this purpose, $\alpha = 0.001$. This value might seem too small at first, which would require the difference between two treatments to be unnecessarily high in order to be considered significant. However, since we are analyzing such a large dataset, this value of α seems reasonable [23]. For the treatments described in Figure 3 the p value reported by ANOVA is 0. This allows us to strongly reject the null hypothesis, even though we are using such an extreme value for α, and state that at least two treatments are different from each other.

The results above show a very clear influence of the kind of variable over the usage of types. However, it is also desirable to know which kinds of variables are different from each other and how different they are. For this purpose, we apply the Tukey Honest Significant Differences (Tukey HSD) test in conjunction with ANOVA. This method calculates, for every two treatments, a p value indicating whether they are significantly different. It also reports a confidence interval for the difference between the means of these two treatments. The results of the Tukey Honest Significant Differences are displayed in Table 4. Confidence intervals were calculated with a confidence of 0.999 $(1 - \alpha)$.

		p	Difference
Local Variable	Contructor Parameter	0	(-0.55, -0.47)
Field	Contructor Parameter	0	(-0.41, -0.34)
Method Parameter	Contructor Parameter	0	(-0.17, -0.10)
Method Return	Contructor Parameter	0	(-0.16, -0.09)
Local Variable	Field	0	(-0.16, -0.11)
Method Return	Field	0	(0.22, 0.26)
Method Parameter	Field	0	(0.22, 0.27)
Method Parameter	Local Variable	0	(0.35, 0.40)
Method Return	Local Variable	0	(0.36, 0.41)
Method Return	Method Parameter	0.95	(-0.02, 0.03)

Table 4. Tukey Honest Significant Differences Test results for the comparison between the usage of types by kind of declaration

The table above shows that there are only two kinds of declaration for which there is no significant difference, parameters and returns of methods. This result is reasonable. Since returns and parameters of methods are declared together as part of a method signature, programmers probably use the same typing strategy in both declarations. All other declaration types can be considered significantly different from each other. In particular, note that these results clearly show that local variables and constructor parameters are the least and most typed declarations respectively. Another interesting insight provided by these results is that parameters of methods and parameters of constructors are typed differently. Although these are essentially the same kind of declaration in Groovy, they seem to be perceived differently by programmers when it comes to typing.

4.3 Declaration Visibility

This section presents an analysis about how programmers use types according to the the visibility of a declaration. We follow the same approach as in the previous section. Figure 4 shows the box plots for the usage of types per declaration visibility along with the descriptive statistics. The ANOVA test reported a p value equal to 0 for these treatments, allowing us to strongly reject the null hypothesis. Finally, the results of the Tukey HSD Test are reported in Table 5. These results show that all treatments are different from each other since all p values are equal to 0.

Protected declarations are those typed most often. Note how skewed is the distribution for these elements in Figure 4. Almost all 2387 projects which use protected visibility in their declarations have all of their protected fields, methods and constructors typed. The confidence intervals reported by the Tukey HSD test show very large differences between these declarations and those with either private or public visibility. Although public declarations are not typed as much, they are also typed very often. At least half of the projects type 75% or more of their declarations. Conversely, private declarations are those with the smallest relative use of types. These results again suggest a positive answer for Question Q1, which hypothesizes that declarations that are part of a module definition are typed more frequently.

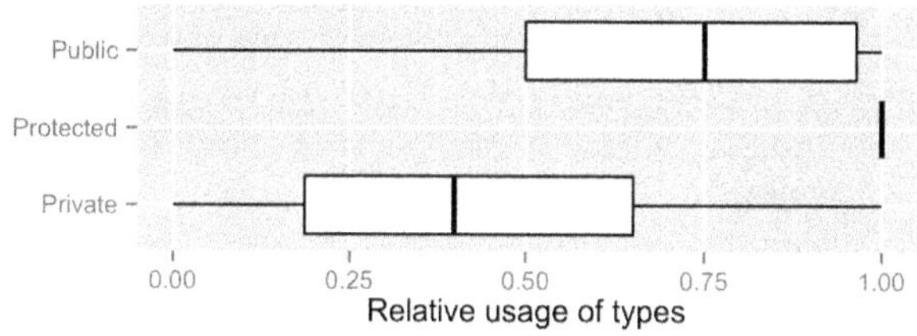

Declaration Visibility	n	mean	median	std. dev.
Public	5852	0.69	0.75	0.29
Protected	2387	0.93	1.00	0.19
Private	6023	0.43	0.40	0.32

Figure 4. Usage of types in all declarations by type of declaration

		p	Difference
Protected	Private	0	(0.47, 0.52)
Public	Private	0	(0.24, 0.28)
Public	Protected	0	(-0.27, -0.22)

Table 5. Tukey Honest Significant Differences Test results for the comparison between the usage of types by visibility of declaration

4.4 Test Classes and Main Classes

We now analyze the use of types in test classes in comparison to main classes. We used a simple heuristic to determine the kind of the class. In Groovy, like in Java, it is common to organize test classes and main classes in different source folders. The convention adopted by build tools popular among Groovy programmers, such as Gradle and Maven, assumes that test classes and main classes are in the *src/test/groovy* and *src/main/groovy* directories respectively. Based on these conventions, we can assume that all classes inside a *test* directory, but not in a *main* directory, are test classes.

For every project, we measured the usage of types in test classes and main classes. Script files are not considered in this analysis. We found test classes in 4350 of the 6638 projects in our dataset. Results are displayed in Figure 5 and show the relative usage of

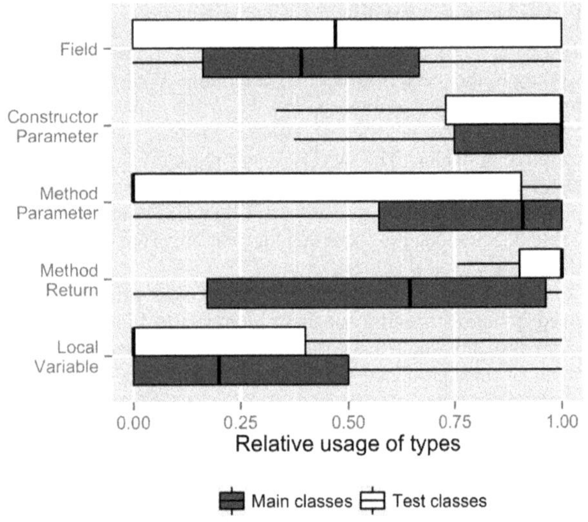

Declaration Type	Class Type	n	mean	median	std. dev.
Field	Test	1769	0.48	0.47	0.43
	Main	5857	0.43	0.39	0.33
Constructor Parameter	Test	124	0.77	1.00	0.41
	Main	1623	0.80	1.00	0.34
Method Parameter	Test	1524	0.34	0.00	0.43
	Main	4593	0.71	0.91	0.35
Method Return	Test	4334	0.85	1.00	0.31
	Main	5299	0.54	0.60	0.39
Local Variable	Test	2842	0.23	0.00	0.35
	Main	5548	0.30	0.19	0.32

Figure 5. Usage of types by declaration type in test classes and main classes

types by declaration type. White and gray box plots correspond to test classes and main classes respectively.

In order to compare the usage of types in test and main classes, we use a slightly different approach. In this analysis, there are two independent variables, the kind of declaration and the kind of class. Thus, we are required to use Factorial ANOVA, which is the generalization of the One Way ANOVA for multiple factors. Multiple values of p are calculated by this test, each one corresponding to the comparison of treatments according to one of the factors. We report the p value corresponding to the factor representing the kind of class. We also apply the Tukey HSD test, for which results are displayed in Table 6. This time we want to show what is the difference of the relative usage of types between the same kinds of declaration, but in different kinds of classes. For example, the third row of Table 6 shows that there is a significant difference in how programmers type local variables in main and test classes. The difference between the relative usage of types in main classes and test classes falls in the $(0.05, 0.11)$ interval.

The ANOVA test reported once again a p value equal to 0, implying that the usage of type is different in test and main classes. Figure 5 and Table 6 show that this difference is significant for all kinds of declarations except constructor parameters. While local variables in main classes are not typed very often, they are typed even less in test classes. At least half of the projects type none of the declarations of this kind in test classes. The difference in declarations of parameters of methods is even more evident since they are often typed in main classes, but almost never typed in test classes. The confidence interval reported by the Tukey HSD Test in this case is $(-0.36, -0.44)$. The large width of the box plots for fields and method parameters is noteworthy. This indicates that many projects type either almost all or none of these declarations.

Curiously, method returns are significantly more typed in test classes. The difference reported by the confidence interval in Table 6 for this case is (-0.31, -0.26). At least half of the projects type all of their method returns in test classes. Although counterintuitive this result can be easily explained. Automated testing frameworks usually enforce a certain method signature for test methods. JUnit for example, which is used in 2525 of the 4350 projects with test classes, requires test methods to be typed as *void*. Other popular test frameworks, such as TestNG, have similar requirements. This implies that, in this case, developers type their methods not because they want to, but because they have to.

Declaration Type	p	Difference
Constructor Parameter	0.98	(-0.08, 0.16)
Field	0	(-0.08, -0.02)
Local Variable	0	(0.05, 0.11)
Method Parameter	0	(0.36, 0.44)
Method Return	0	(-0.31, -0.26)

Table 6. Tukey Honest Significant Differences Test results for the comparison between the usage of types by main and test classes

4.5 Script Files and Class Files

In Groovy, programmers can write code in the form of scripts, not requiring the definition of classes for simple tasks. This section investigates how programmers type their code in such scripts. Similar to what was done in the previous section, we measured the usage of types in script and class files in all projects and compared the obtained data. We do not consider test classes in this analysis. Determining whether a file corresponds to a script or a class is fairly simple since, in Groovy, scripts are compiled into a class extending *groovy.lang.Script*.

Figure 6 shows the distribution of the relative usage of types in class and script files. Note that constructors and fields are not considered since there is no way to declare those elements in scripts. Also, we do not present an analysis of declarations grouped by visibility since, although allowed, defining the visibility of a declaration inside a script does not make much sense.

The execution of the ANOVA test reported a p value equal to 0, revealing that the declarations are typed significantly different in script files. Table 7 displays the results for the Tukey HSD test, which provide detailed results by the kind of declaration. There is no significant difference on the usage of types in local variables. On the other hand, declarations of parameters or returns of methods are typed much less frequently in scripts. Note however that the value for the last quartile of these declarations is very high, superior to 0.8. This indicates that, although most projects prefer not to use types in method returns, there are a few projects that consistently type most of them.

Along with the results of the analysis of test classes, the results presented in this section show that the answer for Question Q2 is positive. There are large differences in how programmers type scripts and classes. Although it is not clear from our analysis what is the reason for such phenomena, we will raise some hypothesis in our discussion, presented in Section 5.

4.6 Programmers' Background

In this section, we analyze how programmers use types in their declarations according to their backgrounds. Projects are distributed in three groups based on the type system of the languages their

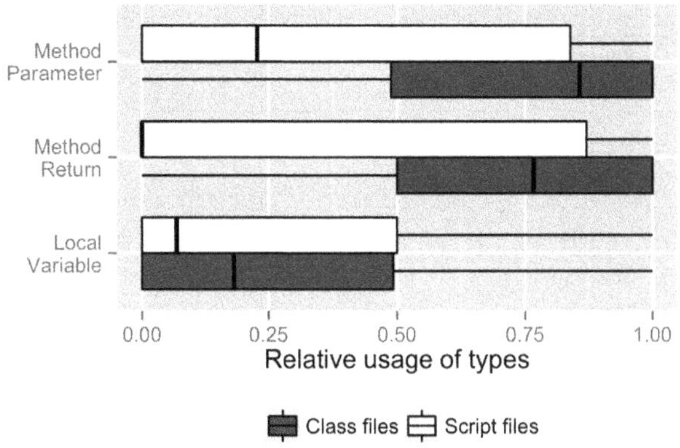

Declaration Type	File Type	n	mean	median	std. dev.
Method Parameter	Script	504	0.40	0.23	0.42
	Class	4647	0.69	0.86	0.35
Method Return	Script	583	0.34	0.00	0.43
	Class	5662	0.70	0.77	0.30
Local Variable	Script	1775	0.28	0.07	0.37
	Class	5246	0.30	0.18	0.32

Figure 6. Usage of types by declaration type in script files and class files

Declaration Type	p	Difference
Local Variable	0.39	(-0.01, 0.04)
Method Parameter	0	(0.24, 0.35)
Method Return	0	(0.30, 0.40)

Table 7. Tukey Honest Significant Differences Test results for the comparison between the usage of types in script files and class files

developers have used on GitHub. The first group comprises those projects of programmers who developed only in statically typed languages, such as Java or C#. The projects of those who developed only in dynamically typed languages, such as Ruby or JavaScript, comprise the second group. Finally, the third group is formed by the projects of those programmers with both dynamically and statically typed languages in their portfolio. We refer to these three groups by the names *Static Only*, *Dynamic Only* and *Static and Dynamic* respectively.

Figures 7 and 8 show results by declaration type and visibility. The p value reported by the ANOVA test is equal to 0, implying that there is a significant difference in how programmers with different backgrounds type their declarations. The results of the Tukey HSD test are reported in Tables 8 and 9. These tables are divided in three parts, each one corresponding to the comparison between the data of two of the three groups.

There are significant differences in the usage of types between all groups. These differences, however, are not as clear as those found in the previous anlayses. Let's start with the comparison between projects in the *Static and Dynamic* and the *Dynamic Only* groups. There are significant differences only in private declarations and declarations of fields. Still, these differences are not very large, $(0.01, 0.08)$ for fields and $(0.02, 0.09)$ for private declarations. All in all, these two groups present very similar behavior when typing their declarations, apart from those two exceptions.

The comparison between the *Static* and the other groups shows more clear differences. Most of the p values reported by the Tukey

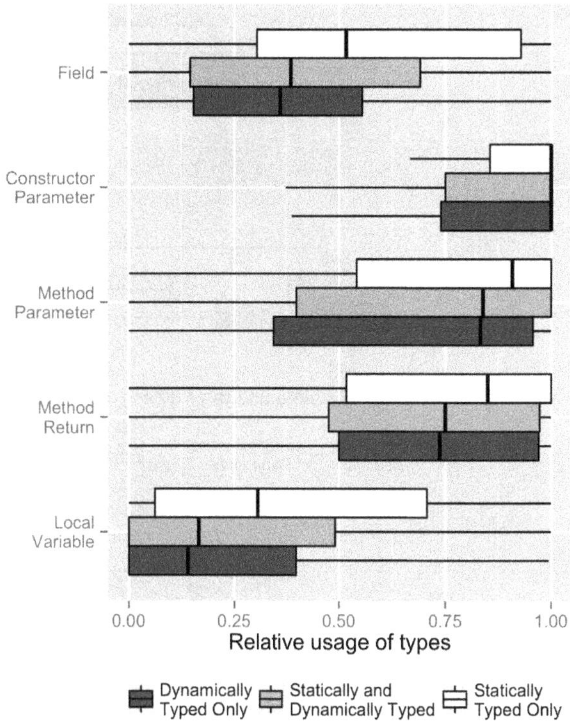

Declaration Type	Background	N	Mean	Median	Std. Dev.
Field	Static	782	0.56	0.52	0.35
	Both	3183	0.43	0.39	0.34
	Dynamic	2035	0.38	0.36	0.29
Constructor Parameter	Static	224	0.83	1.00	0.33
	Both	991	0.80	1.00	0.35
	Dynamic	455	0.80	1.00	0.34
Method Parameter	Static	662	0.73	0.91	0.34
	Both	2694	0.67	0.84	0.36
	Dynamic	1511	0.65	0.83	0.37
Method Return	Static	764	0.73	0.85	0.30
	Both	3205	0.66	0.75	0.32
	Dynamic	1912	0.68	0.74	0.29
Local Variable	Static	798	0.39	0.31	0.36
	Both	3230	0.28	0.17	0.32
	Dynamic	1817	0.25	0.14	0.30

Figure 7. Usage of types by declaration type and programmer background

HSD test are equal to 0. However, constructor parameters and protected declarations never present significant differences. This indicates a strong influence of these types of declarations over the programmers' behavior. There are other two other cases that do not present significant differences, method returns and public declarations, both in the comparisons between programmers of the *Dynamic* and *Static* groups. It is important though to say that the p value reported in these two cases is relatively small, 0.01. These differences are considered not significant only because we are using a very strict confidence level, but would be considered significantly different under a confidence level of 0.05.

The results reported in this section suggest a positive answer for Question Q3, i.e, programmers use types differently depending on their background. This difference is larger when comparing

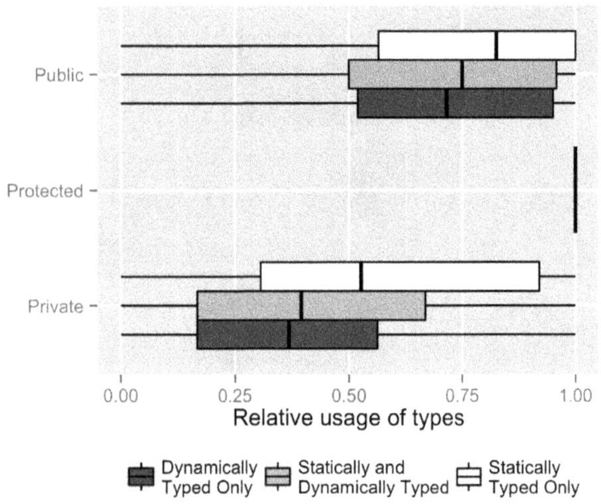

Declaration Type	Background	n	mean	median	std. dev.
Public	Static	757	0.73	0.83	0.29
	Both	3191	0.68	0.75	0.30
	Dynamic	1904	0.69	0.71	0.27
Protected	Static	287	0.92	1.00	0.20
	Both	1275	0.94	1.00	0.18
	Dynamic	825	0.93	1.00	0.20
Private	Static	787	0.56	0.53	0.34
	Both	3196	0.43	0.40	0.33
	Dynamic	2040	0.38	0.37	0.28

Figure 8. Usage of types by declaration visibility and programmer background

	Declaration Type	p	Difference
Static and Dynamic vs. Static	Field	0	(-0.17, -0.07)
	Constructor Parameter	1.0	(-0.12, 0.06)
	Method Parameter	0	(-0.11, 0.00)
	Method Return	0	(-0.11, -0.01)
	Local Variable	0	(-0.15, -0.05)
Dynamic vs. Static	Field	0	(-0.23, -0.12)
	Constructor Parameter	0.99	(-0.12, 0.07)
	Method Parameter	0	(-0.14, -0.02)
	Method Return	0.01	(-0.10, 0.00)
	Local Variable	0	(-0.18, -0.07)
Static and Dynamic vs. Dynamic	Field	0	(0.01, 0.08)
	Constructor Parameter	1.00	(-0.07, 0.06)
	Method Parameter	0.84	(-0.02, 0.06)
	Method Return	0.94	(-0.05, 0.02)
	Local Variable	0.12	(-0.00, 0.06)

Table 8. Tukey Honest Significant Differences Test results for the comparison between the usage of types by declaration type and programmers background

those projects of the *Static* group with projects of the other groups. These results are statistically strong, but should be generalized with care. The detailed results reported by the Tukey HSD test reveal many exceptions, specially in the comparison between the groups comprising the projects of those programmers who have at least one dynamically typed language in their portfolio, *Static and Dynamic*

	Declaration Visibility	p	Difference
Static and Dynamic vs. Static	Public	0.00	(-0.10, 0.00)
	Protected	1.00	(-0.07, 0.09)
	Private	0.00	(-0.18, -0.08)
Dynamic vs. Static	Public	0.01	(-0.10, 0.01)
	Protected	1.00	(-0.08, 0.09)
	Private	0.00	(-0.23, -0.13)
Static and Dynamic vs. Dynamic	Public	0.98	(-0.04, 0.03)
	Protected	1.00	(-0.05, 0.06)
	Private	0.00	(0.02, 0.09)

Table 9. Tukey Honest Significant Differences Test results for the comparison between the usage of types by declaration visibility and programmers background

and *Dynamic Only*. This comparison reveals that, for all kinds and visibilities of declarations, the difference is either not significant or small.

4.7 Project Size, Age and Number of Commits

This section investigates whether programmers use types differently in their code depending on the project characteristics. We analyze three project metrics: age, number of lines of code and number of commits. We start by analyzing the correlation between these metrics and the relative use of types in declarations by type and visibility. The Spearman rank correlation coefficient is used for this purpose. This coefficient, which ranges from -1 to 1, is a measure of the dependence between two variables. A positive value means that two variables are correlated, i.e, as the value of one grows, so does the value of the other. A negative value means an inverse correlation. Values close to 1 or -1 indicate very strong relationships and values above 0.5 or below -0.5 can be considered strong correlations.

Declaration Type/Visibility	Size	Age	Commits
Field	0.221	-0.063	0.153
Constructor Parameter	-0.072	-0.132	-0.053
Method Parameter	-0.123	-0.079	-0.004
Method Return	-0.071	0.168	-0.027
Local Variable	0.057	-0.049	0.112
Public	-0.063	0.119	-0.024
Protected	-0.286	-0.020	-0.165
Private	0.213	-0.068	0.160

Table 10. Spearman Correlation between the usage of types and the size, age and number of commits of projects

Table 10 shows the Spearman correlation coefficient between the usage of types and the age, size and number of commits of a project. Most of values in this table are close to 0. There are a few coefficient values which could indicate a relationship, such as *Size* vs. *Protected* or *Commits* vs. *Private*, but these relationships are still considerably weak. All in all, these values do not seem to suggest any direct relationship between these metrics and the usage of types.

The lack of correlation between the relative usage of types and these metrics does not necessarily imply that they have no influence on the usage of types. A possibility is that this influence appears only in the most mature projects, where the values of all of these three metrics are large enough. In order to determine whether this is true, we conduct now a comparison between mature projects and the rest of the dataset. We define a mature project as a project that is 100 days old or more and has, at least, 2KLoC and 100 commits. These numbers were defined by manually inspecting our dataset and finding that there are popular and mature projects that barely exceed these three metrics. According to our criteria, there are 223 mature projects in our dataset, which are characterized in Table 11.

	Mean	Median	Std. Dev.	Max	Total
Size (LoC)	9947	5627	14594	149933	2218189
Commits	487	213	800	6545	108583
Age (Days)	600	574	350	1469	133697

Table 11. Descriptive statistics for mature projects

Figures 9 and 10 show the box plots for the usage of types in mature projects and others by declaration type and visibility respectively. The ANOVA test reported a p value equal to 0.0518 for this analysis, which implies that there are no treatments that are significantly different from each other. Because of this, we do not report the results for the Tukey HSD test. This result, along with the very low correlation coefficients reported in Table 10, implies that the answer for Question Q4 is negative. There is no significant difference in how programmers type declarations in mature projects compared to declarations in other projects.

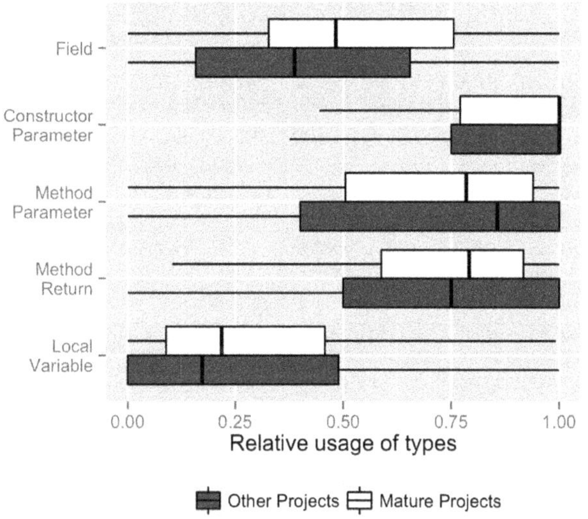

Declaration Type	Project Type	n	mean	median	std. dev.
Field	Mature	221	0.53	0.48	0.27
	Other	5779	0.43	0.39	0.33
Constructor Parameter	Mature	172	0.83	1.00	0.30
	Other	1498	0.80	1.00	0.35
Method Parameter	Mature	222	0.69	0.78	0.29
	Other	4645	0.67	0.86	0.37
Method Return	Mature	222	0.72	0.79	0.24
	Other	5659	0.68	0.75	0.32
Local Variable	Mature	223	0.32	0.22	0.28
	Other	5622	0.29	0.17	0.32

Figure 9. Usage of types in projects by declaration type and project maturity

4.8 Frequency of changes

This section investigates whether programmers prefer to type their declarations in frequently changed code or not. Only the mature

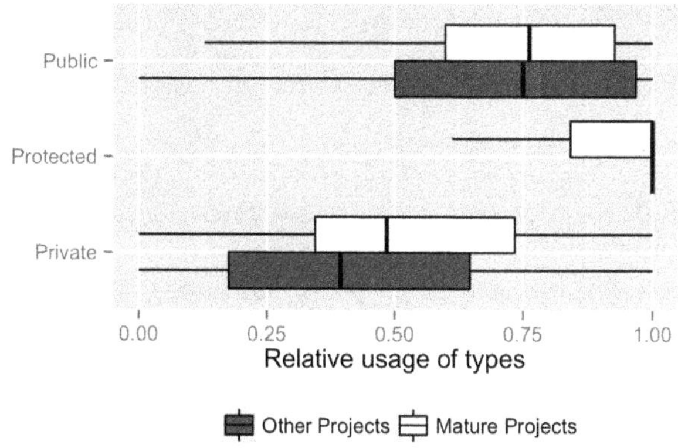

Declaration Type	Project Type	n	mean	median	std. dev.
Public	Mature	223	0.72	0.76	0.24
	Other	5629	0.69	0.75	0.29
Protected	Mature	183	0.88	1.00	0.21
	Other	2204	0.94	1.00	0.19
Private	Mature	221	0.53	0.48	0.26
	Other	5802	0.43	0.40	0.32

Figure 10. Usage of types in projects by declaration visibility and project maturity

projects defined in the previous section are considered since we would not be able to obtain meaningful results from small and young projects.

We found that in most of the mature projects programmers prefer untyped declarations in frequently changed code. We calculated the Spearman correlation coefficient between the frequency of changes of a file and the usage of types in that file for all mature projects. In projects where types are used more often in frequently changed files, this coefficient is positive, and negative when untyped declarations are preferred. Figure 11 displays the cumulative distribution of this coefficient across the mature projects dataset. It shows that 65% of them present a negative Spearman correlation coefficient and that almost half of these present strong correlations, i.e., inferior to -0.5. On the other hand, only 10% of the mature projects present strong positive correlations.

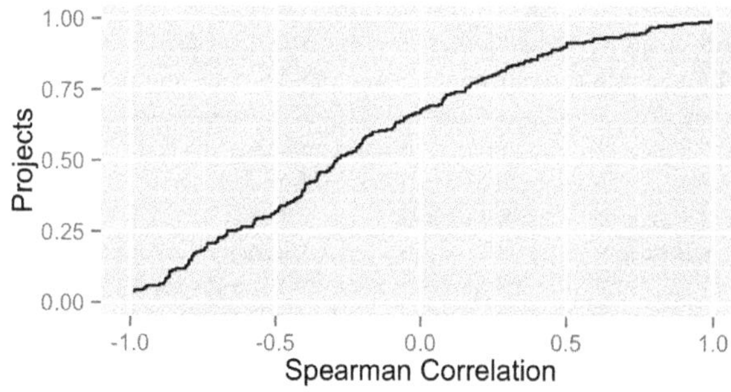

Figure 11. Spearman ranking for the correlation between frequency of changes of files and the usage of types in mature projects

5. Discussion

In this section, we discuss the results of our study in the light of the research questions proposed in Section 3.1. Although we were able to obtain a good understanding of the usage of types in different contexts, the cause for such results is still unclear in many of them. We provide several hypotheses with the goal of identifying future research topics that can provide more detailed insights about such causes.

Q1: Do programmers use types more often in the interface of their modules?

The analysis of the usage of types by kind and visibility of declarations, presented in Sections 4.2 and 4.3, provides clear evidence that the answer for Q1 is affirmative. Private declarations are typed less often than protected and public declarations. Also, fields, methods and constructors are typed more often than local variables. Although fields are significantly less typed than methods and constructors, this can be explained by the fact that most fields are declared privately as shown in Section 3.3. In Groovy, similar to what happens with Java, interactions with fields of other modules usually happen through accessor methods.

While it is clear that module definitions are typed more often, the cause for such phenomena is still open to discussion. We believe that the main motivation for this is the implicit documentation provided by types. In these scenarios, types provide useful hints about the behavior of modules [8] and define pre and post condition of contracts [11, 13, 26, 27, 30, 37]. Users of a well defined module learn how to use it faster and do not need to read its implementation to understand how to use it. Programmers may consider that delicate contracts, such as those defined by protected methods, should be well documented and thus are typed more often.

Constructor parameters and protected declarations are always the elements typed most often. In addition, the analyses of different contexts, i.e, main and test classes, mature and non-mature projects and programmers' backgrounds, show no significant difference in the usage of types. This reveals that the presence of these particular declarations is considered by programmers as a more important factor in their choice whether to type a declaration than these contexts. We hypothesize that programmers consider documentation more important in these elements. Constructors usually define the dependencies of an object, at least for its creation. In addition, they might be the first element that a programmer interacts with when dealing with a new module. Protected declarations are often used as a means to delegate the implementation of a method to subclasses, which requires a well defined contract so the superclass can work properly. Moreover, they give subclasses and other classes in the same package access to internal elements of a class, forming a tightly coupled relationship [6].

We can also speculate that declarations that are not part of a module definition, which are local variables and those with private visibility, require less documentation and thus are typed less often. Programmers can easily find all the references to these elements. Local variables are only used inside the block of code where they are declared, while all the references to elements declared privately are in the same file. This makes it easier for a programmer to infer the type of such a declaration even when it is not explicitly defined.

Documentation may not be the only reason why programmers type declarations in modules interfaces. We can think of at least two other reasons. First, a programmer might type a declaration so that he or she can get code assistance from the development environment. For example, typing the declaration of a method parameter allows the development environment to provide code completion for that parameter inside the method. Another possibility is that, even though Groovy is actually a dynamically typed language, programmers might type their declarations thinking that the compiler will check for type errors, which would lead to safer interactions between modules.

Q2: Do programmers use types less often in test classes and scripts?

There are notable differences between the usage of types in either test classes or scripts and the main classes of a program. Sections 4.4 and 4.5 show that, in these scenarios, programmers use types less often. If we are right about our hypothesis that programmers type their modules as a means to document their code, this could explain this less frequent use of types. Scripts and test classes are usually not designed as reusable modules. Test classes have the sole goal of verifying a program's functionality and not interfering with it while scripts cannot be instantiated or referenced by other modules. In these scenarios, programmers might perceive documentation as less important. It is curious however that test code itself is usually perceived as a form of documentation [1, 28]. Because of this, we were expecting programmers to actually use more types in test classes as a means to improve the documentation they provide. Perhaps, although programmers use test classes as documentation, they might not write them with this goal in mind.

An alternative explanation for the fact that scripts and tests are typed less frequently is that most of them are probably simpler than main classes. As found in the recent work of Hanenberg et al. [20], untyped code potentially has a positive impact on the development time of easier tasks. In such case, programmers might not type their declarations in scripts or test classes since this would allow them to finish their tasks faster.

Q3: Does the experience of programmers with other languages influence their choice for typing their code?

The analysis presented in Section 4.6 indicates that the answer for Question Q3 is affirmative. The choice for using types on a language with optional typing, such a Groovy, is in fact influenced by the programmers' experience with other languages. In general, those programmers who have only statically typed languages in their portfolio type more often than the others. However, the two groups with projects written by programmers who have either statically and dynamically typed languages or only dynamically typed languages are very similar in most cases. Apparently programmers who develop in an "untyped" language get used to the lack of types, leading them to declare types less often. This hypothesis supports the work of Daly et al. which suggests that programmers have ways of reasoning about types that compensate for the lack of static type information [9].

Q4: Does the size, age or level of activity of a project have any influence on the usage of types?

We initially believed that, as these metrics grow, the maintenance of projects becomes more difficult, leading programmers to use more types as a means to make code more readable. However, the analysis presented in Section 4.7 shows no evidence of such behavior. We consider two hypotheses in order to explain these results. First, the considered metrics might not actually correlate to the need for maintenance of projects. Second, even if these metrics are a good indicative of the necessity of better maintainability, once projects start growing and aging, programmers might not have the opportunity or desire to make their code more maintainable.

Q5: In frequently changed code, do developers prefer typed or untyped declarations?

In frequently changed code, there are arguments in favor and against using types. Since types act as documentation, programmers might use them to make code more maintainable and easier to change [24]. On the other hand, untyped code is simpler and can potentially be changed faster [32]. The results presented in Section 4.8 however suggests that the latter is considered more often than the former.

In most projects, the usage of untyped declarations grows as the frequency of changes in a file increases. Apparently, programmers understand that untyped code makes maintenance tasks easier. One can argue that the causal relationship is the opposite, i.e., these files have to be changed more often due to the use of untyped declarations. However, it is very unlikely that programmers would not notice that untyped declarations would be causing such problems and would not add types to those declarations in order to fix them.

6. Threats to Validity

In this section, we discuss potential threats to validity of our study. As usual, we have arranged possible threats in two categories, internal and external validity [38].

Internal Validity

Perhaps the most relevant internal threat to our study is that in a large scale empirical study such as ours, there might be many confounds which are difficult to identify. In Section 4.6 we consider that the GitHub portfolio of a programmer represents well his experience with other languages and type systems, but this might not be true for all programmers. They may have projects in their portfolio that they have not worked on or projects hosted elsewhere written in other languages. There is also the possibility of a programmer having multiple GitHub accounts with different languages in each one, causing such a programmer to be measured twice with different inferred backgrounds. Due to the large number of programmers considered in our study, we expect these special cases not to have a large influence on the results.

There are other factors that might have influenced programmers besides the ones considered in this study. Some frameworks require programmers to use typed or untyped declarations in some cases. For example, we found that the data collected in test classes is biased by the fact that popular testing frameworks, such as JUnit, require test methods to have their returns declared as *void*. There might be other similar cases that we are not aware of.

External Validity

Although we have analyzed a very extensive number of Groovy projects, it cannot be said that we have covered all possible scenarios. By manually inspecting our dataset, we could find only a few projects with characteristics of software developed inside an organization. Most of them were developed by small groups of people or open source communities. Enterprise projects are probably hosted privately on GitHub or in private servers, and hence unavailable to us.

The behavior observed for Groovy projects can be very different in other languages. Most languages are not like Groovy and feature either static or dynamic typing, forcing programmers to choose a single typing strategy for all scenarios in a single project. Even a language with a hybrid typing paradigm might implement different strategies which will be perceived differently by the programmers of that language. Finally, the tools used to code in a given language might influence programmers to chose different type strategies.

7. Related Work

There are multiple studies in the literature that compare different typing strategies. Although we are not aware of any studies that analyze this question using a large scale case study as ours, we know of multiple controlled experiments with significant results. One of the goals of this paper is to complement these results by providing a a different point of view to their analyses.

In a recent experiment, Hanenberg et al. [20] studied the impact of the use of types on the development time of programmers while performing tasks on an undocumented API. The experiment divided 27 people in two groups. They developed in two languages, one statically typed, Java, and the other dynamically typed, Groovy. Results revealed a positive impact of the use of types when these were used to document design decisions or when a high number of classes had to be identified by programmers. On the other hand, for easier tasks, programmers developed faster in the dynamically typed language. Our analysis suggest that programmers are aware of these tradeoffs and consider them when choosing whether or not to type their declarations. In potentially simpler scenarios, such as scripts and tests, we show a lower usage of types. Conversely, programmers type the interface of their modules very often, probably as a means to document their codem which potentially improves the development time in more complex scenarios.

Daly et al. conduct an experiment in order to compare the performance of two groups working on small development tasks [9]. One group used Ruby, a dynamically typed language, while the other used DRuby, a statically typed version of Ruby. Results showed that the DRuby compiler rarely managed to capture any errors that were not already evident for programmers. Most subjects involved in the study had previous experience with Ruby, which suggests that programmers get used to the lack of typing. Our analysis of the programmers' backgrounds supports this argument. It shows that those programmers who have worked with dynamically typed languages in fact use types less often.

8. Conclusions and Future Work

In this paper we conducted a large scale case study in order to investigate how types are used in Groovy. Our goal is to find what are the point of view of programmers about what typing strategies are more suitable to which contexts. Our main findings are:

- Groovy programmers type declarations that define the interface of modules more often than other declarations
- Types are less popular in test classes and script files
- Those programmers who have developed in at least one dynamically typed language use types less frequently than those who have only worked with statically typed languages
- Apparently, there is no influence of the size, age or level of activity of a project on how programmers use types
- In most projects, the files that change more frequently are also those files with a lower usage of types

We believe that these results are valuable to the developers of programming languages and development tools who can base their designs on real user data. Also, programmers can understand the tradeoffs between using or not types in their projects. Our results provide a different point of view and complement previous studies, which analyzed typing strategies through the use of controlled experiments. We hope that the questions raised in our discussion can inspire other researchers to analyze our findings in more detail.

In future work we want to conduct controlled experiments and qualitative studies in order to evaluate some of our results in more details. In particular, we have started a new study with the goal of finding what is the impact of the use of the documentation provided by types and the documentation provided by unit tests on the development time of maintenance tasks. Another work in progress is a framework for the static source code analysis of massive datasets called Elastic Repository Analysis - ERA[2]. This framework is based on the artifacts we built to analyze the Groovy projects in this study. ERA will help researchers retrieve large numbers of projects from GitHub and process these projects quickly on the cloud using Amazon Web Services.

[2] http://github.com/carlosgsouza/ERA

Acknowledgments

Many thank to Stefan Hanenberg for the inspiration and the invaluable contributions.

This work was partially supported by FAPEMIG, grants APQ-02376-11 and APQ-02532-12, and CNPq grant 485907/2013-5.

References

[1] K. Beck. Test-driven development: by example. Addison-Wesley Professional, 2003.

[2] K. Bruce. Foundations of object-oriented languages: types and semantics. The MIT Press, 2002.

[3] M. Bruch, M. Monperrus, and M. Mezini. Learning from examples to improve code completion systems. In Proceedings of the International Symposium on the Foundations of Software Engineering (FSE), 213222, 2009.

[4] L. Cardelli. Type systems. ACM Computing Surveys, 28(1), 263264, 1996.

[5] M. Chang, B. Mathiske, E. Smith, A. Chaudhuri, A. Gal. M. Bebenita, C. Wimmer, and M. Franz. The impact of optional type information on jit compilation of dynamically typed languages. SIGPLAN Notices, 47(2), 1324, 2011.

[6] S. Chidamber and C. Kemerer. A metrics suite for object oriented design. IEEE Transactions on Software Engineering, 20(6), 476-493, 1994.

[7] J. Cohen. Statistical power analysis for the behavioral sciences (2nd ed.). Hillsdale, NJ: Lawrence Erlbaum, 1988.

[8] B. Curtis. Five paradigms in the psychology of programming. MMC, 1987.

[9] M. Daly, V. Sazawal, and J. Foster. An empirical study of static typing in ruby. In Proceedings of the Workshop on Evaluation and Usability of Programming Languages and Tools (PLATEAU), 2009.

[10] N. Fenton and S. Pfleeger. Software metrics: a rigorous and practical approach. PWS Publishing Co., 1998.

[11] C. Flanagan. Hybrid type checking. ACM SIGPLAN Notices. Vol. 41. No. 1, 2006.

[12] M. Fowler, Domain-specific languages. Pearson Education, 2010.

[13] M. Furr et al. Static type inference for Ruby. In Proceedings of the ACM symposium on Applied Computing (ACM SAC), 2009.

[14] J. Gannon. An experimental evaluation of data type conventions. Communications of the ACM, 20, 8, 584595, 1977.

[15] K. Gray. Safe cross-language inheritance. In Proceedings of the European Conference on Object-Oriented Programming (ECOOP), pp. 5275.

[16] K. Gray. Interoperability in a scripted world: Putting inheritance & prototypes together. In Proceedings of Foundations of Object-Oriented Languages (FOOL), 2011.

[17] K. Gray, R. Findler, M. Andflatt. Fine-grained interoperability through contracts and mirrors. In Proceedings of the International Conference on Object-Oriented Programming, Systems, Languages, and Applications (OOPSLA), pp. 231245, 2005.

[18] Groovy programming language. http://groovy.codehaus.org/. Accessed in 10/10/2013.

[19] S. Hanenberg, An experiment about static and dynamic type systems: doubts about the positive impact of static type systems on development time. SIGPLAN Notices, 45(10), 2235, 2010.

[20] S. Hanenberg et al. An empirical study on the impact of static typing on software maintainability. Empirical Software Engineering - An International Journal, 1-48, 2013.

[21] ISO, and IEC FCD. 25000, Software engineering-software product quality requirements and evaluation (SQuaRE) - Guide to SQuaRE. International Organization for Standardization, 2004.

[22] S. Kleinschmager, S. Hanenberg, R. Robbes, and A. Stefik. Do static type systems improve the maintainability of software systems? An empirical study. In Proceedings of the 20th IEEE International Conference on Program Comprehension (ICPC), 153 162, 2012.

[23] S. Labovitz, Criteria for selecting a significance level: A note on the sacredness of. 05. The American Sociologist 3.3, 220-222, 1968.

[24] L. Lamport, and L. Paulson. Should your specification language be typed. ACM Transactions on Programming Languages and Systems, 21(3), 502526, 1999.

[25] C. Mayer, S. Hanenberg, R. Robbes, E. Tanter, and A. Stefik. Static type systems (sometimes) have a positive impact on the usability of undocumented software: An empirical evaluation. Technical Report 20120418-005, 2012.

[26] E. Meijer and D. Peter. Static typing where possible, dynamic typing when needed: The end of the cold war between programming languages. In Proceedings of the International Conference on Object-Oriented Programming, Systems, Languages, and Applications (OOPSLA), 2004.

[27] B. Meyer. Object-oriented software construction, Vol. 2. Prentice hall, 1988.

[28] L. Meyerovich and A. Rabkin. Empirical analysis of programming language adoption. In Proceedings of the International Conference on Object-Oriented Programming, Systems, Languages, and Applications (OOPSLA), 1-18, 2013.

[29] B. Pierce. Types and programming languages. MIT press, 2002.

[30] R. Plosch. Design by contract for Python. Proceedings of the Asia Pacific Software Engineering Conference (APSEC), 1997.

[31] L. Prechelt and W. Tichy. A controlled experiment to assess the benets of procedure argument type checking. IEEE Transactions of Software Engineering, 24(4), 302312, 1998.

[32] J. Siek, and W. Taha. Gradual typing for objects. In Proceedings of the European Conference on Object-Oriented Programming (ECOOP), 2-27, 2007.

[33] J. Siek, W. Andtaha. Gradual typing for objects. In Proceedings of European Conference on Object-Oriented Programming (ECOOP), 227, 2007.

[34] A. Takikawa et al. Gradual typing for first-class classes. ACM SIGPLAN Notices. Vol. 47. No. 10. ACM, 2012.

[35] Tiobe programming community index. http://www.tiobe.com/index.php/content/paperinfo/tpci/index.html. Accessed in 23/09/2013.

[36] L. Tratt. Dynamically typed languages. Advances in Computers, vol. 77, 149-184, 2009.

[37] P. Wadler and R. Findler. Well-typed programs cant be blamed. Proceedings of the 18th European Symposium on Programming Languages and Systems (ESOP), 1-16, 2009.

[38] C. Wohlin et al. Experimentation in software engineering. Springer Publishing Company, 2012.

An Empirical Study on How Developers Reason about Module Cohesion

Bruno C. da Silva, Claudio N. Sant'Anna, Christina von F. G. Chavez
Department of Computer Science
Federal University of Bahia
Salvador, Bahia – Brazil
{brunocs, santanna, flach}@dcc.ufba.br

Abstract

Several cohesion metrics have been proposed to support development and maintenance activities. The most traditional ones are the structural cohesion metrics, which rely on structural information in the source code. For instance, many of these metrics quantify cohesion based how methods and attributes are related to each other within a given module. Recently, conceptual cohesion metrics have been proposed for computing cohesion based on the responsibilities a given module realizes. Besides different flavors of cohesion, there is a lack of empirical evidence about how developers actually perceive cohesion and what kind of cohesion measurement aligns with developers' perception. In this paper we fill this gap by empirically investigating developers opinion through a web-based survey, which involved 80 participants from 9 countries with different levels of programming experience. We found that: most of the developers are familiar with cohesion; and they perceive cohesion based on class responsibilities, thus associating more with conceptual cohesion measurement. These results support the claim that conceptual cohesion seems to be more intuitive and closer to the human-oriented view of software cohesion. Moreover, the results showed that conceptual cohesion measurement captures the developers' notion of cohesion better than traditional structural cohesion measurement.

Categories and Subject Descriptors D.2.8 [*Metrics*]: Product metrics

General Terms Measurement, Experimentation, Human Factors

Keywords Module cohesion; Empirical software engineering

1. Introduction

Cohesion has been recognized across decades as an important quality attribute for software modules [34] [2] [10] [26] [25]. Amongst several definitions, cohesion can be defined as the degree to which a module is focused on a single concern of software [8] [26] [24]. A concern is any concept, feature, requirement or property of the problem or solution domain of software [28]. In particular, highly cohesive modules are focused on a single concern. In consequence, they are easier to maintain because, in general, they are easier to read, their implementation logic is clearer and they are less likely to undergo changes [32] and faults [25] [22].

However, measuring cohesion is not straightforward. Indeed, several researchers have attempted to provide an objective and effective way to measure such quality attribute [5] [17] [2] [21] [16] [3]. Most of them rely on structural information extracted from the source code. For example, several cohesion metrics quantify cohesion by counting pairs of methods of a class that access the same attributes. This notion of cohesion is dependent on the source code structure and does not consider any abstract information regarding the concerns implemented by the classes. In contrast, there is an alternative group of recently proposed cohesion metrics which attempts to measure cohesion in a conceptual way [24] [22] [32]. For example, the C3 metric [24] computes the average similarity of the methods in a given class based on textual mining source code comments and identifiers. If the methods inside a given class have low textual similarity, then the methods most likely participate in the implementation of different concerns. In this case, C3 indicates low cohesion. Similarly, MWE [22] executes a text mining method to identify topics in the source code and then computes cohesion based on how topics are distributed over each software module. LCbC [32] measures cohesion by just counting the number of concerns a module realizes. It takes as input a previous identification of what concerns the module implements. Conceptual cohesion metrics are aligned with the assumption that software engineers would prefer to reason about module cohesion in terms of a set of concerns instead of a set of code segments structurally associated to each other [8].

Despite several attempts throughout decades to measure cohesion, it is still unaddressed to what extent such structural and conceptual cohesion metrics reflect developer's perception of module cohesion. Besides, it is unclear how developers reason when rating module cohesion. Presumably, it is easier for humans, when decomposing a problem into modules, to find distinct concerns implemented by a module than to mentally calculate the degree of structural relatedness amongst methods and attributes. However, there is no empirical evidence to support this argument. Moreover, there is no evidence whether or not developers know the concept of module cohesion as it is in software engineering theory. Therefore, the main goal of this paper is to provide empirical evidence about how developers perceive module cohesion and assess at what extent such perception associates with structural and conceptual cohesion measurement.

To achieve this goal, we performed an empirical study where we investigated: (i) what rationale developers used to rate cohesion of different modules and (ii) to what extent the ratings they gave were

MODULARITY '14, April 22–26, 2014, Lugano, Switzerland.

ACM 978-1-4503-2772-5/14/04...$15.00.
http://dx.doi.org/10.1145/2577080.2577096

related to structural and conceptual cohesion measurements. The study included a web-based closed-access survey involving 80 participants from nine countries and different levels of experience and academic degrees. The survey comprised questions related to: general perception of module cohesion; module cohesion comparison and rating; cohesion reasoning; and participant profile. In summary, we found that most of the participants were familiar with cohesion. Those who showed themselves as not familiar with cohesion were most likely the least experienced ones. In general, developers perceive cohesion in a conceptual manner, i.e., based on class responsibilities. The conceptual cohesion perception was predominant even among participants who declared themselves not familiar with cohesion and among developers with different levels of programming experience. These results support the claim that conceptual cohesion seems to be more intuitive and closer to the human-oriented view of cohesion [8].

The contribution of this paper is threefold. First, our study and its results built up empirical evidence about how developers perceive cohesion and which cohesion measurement associates with their opinion. It represents a stepping stone towards understanding the applicability of structural and conceptual cohesion measurement. Second, we found that, in the context of our study, conceptual cohesion metrics were better representative of developers' perception of cohesion than structural metrics. Finally, the study design, the survey details, the materials, coded topics, and the statistics were all made publicly available in the companion website [31].

The remainder of this paper is organized as follows: Section 2 discusses related work; Section 3 describes in details the study design; Section 4 presents and provides discussion about the study results; Section 5 points out threats to validity; and Section 6 presents the conclusion and future work.

2. Related Work

Etzkorn et al. [8] compared various cohesion metrics with ratings of two separate teams of developers over two software packages. Their goal was to determine which of these metrics best match human-oriented view of cohesion. The developers rated class cohesion on a scale from 0 to 1. The ratings were then statistically correlated with a set of well-known structural cohesion metrics. Etzkorn et al. [8] study differs from ours in many ways. First, one of our goals is to better understand through a qualitative approach how developers perceive module cohesion. Second, we do not aim at comparing developers' ratings with an exhausted list of similar cohesion metrics. Rather, we analyzed two metrics representative of two distinct ways of measuring cohesion (structural and conceptual cohesion). Third, instead of rating cohesion through a numerical scale, we asked participants to rate which class was more cohesive in a given pair of classes. Also we asked them to explain their reasoning by means of open questions.

Similarly, Counsell et al. [6] presented a study involving twenty-four subjects drawn from IT experienced and novice groups of developers. Subjects were asked to rate, in scale from 1 to 10, cohesion of ten classes sampled from two systems on a controlled classroom environment. Three research hypotheses guided their study, which involved quantitative analysis. Two hypotheses addressed whether or not cohesion as perceived by developers associates with class size and comment lines. The third hypothesis evaluated whether there is a noticeable difference between the ratings of experienced developers and novice ones. Besides the research methodology, their study differs from ours as they compared cohesion ratings with two other class features: size and amount of comments. Interestingly, one of their findings stated that cohesion is a subjective concept involving a combination of class factors and raters experience rather than any single, individual class feature per se. In our study we address the investigation of what would be the developers perception of such subjective concept, without having in advance any specific module feature as candidate to be associated with cohesion.

There are other related studies which applied web-based surveys to explore how programmers rate different software quality attributes like readability [4], complexity [18] and coupling [1]. These studies applied mainly quantitative analysis. However, qualitative inquiry provides an interesting way of building knowledge on how human subjects reason about software quality attributes. In our case, besides doing quantitative analysis, we mainly focused on a qualitative investigation of how developers reason about cohesion by coding participants' responses.

3. Study Design

The following research questions guided our study:

RQ1. How do developers perceive module cohesion? How do they reason about it?

RQ2. To what extent do structural cohesion and conceptual cohesion measurements relate with how developers rate cohesion of modules?

In order to address these research questions we collected developers' opinion to understand their perception and analyze how they react when having to reason about module cohesion. At first glance, interviewing would fit well as a research instrument for collecting developers' opinion. However, this would constrain some important requirements for our study. Such kind of study needs to provide classes' source code to participants' analysis and give them reasonable time to express their opinion. Interviewing would intimidate them by the presence of researchers or by the pressure of time. Also, interviewing is not an effective choice for collecting a reasonable amount of data without large cost. Therefore, we decided to conduct a survey as a web-based questionnaire. This technique has become one of the primary instruments in software engineering research [30], and it can be used for both qualitative and quantitative inquiry. Combining both types of research methods are the best way for finding answers and for building a convincing body of evidence to support or reject research hypotheses [29].

The following sections present in details how the survey was structured and applied.

3.1 Survey Overall Structure

The survey was divided in three groups of questions according to three categories of information: (i) information about participant familiarity with the class cohesion concept; (ii) information about how participants rate cohesion by analysing classes; and lastly, (iii) information about participants' profile. Figure 1 illustrates the flow of questions divided into these three groups. For simplicity, questions from the second and third groups were abstracted away in the figure as they are explained in details in the following sections.

We found reasonable to define questions in this order as it is recommended to approach "the most important stuff first" [29]. Thus, we left participants' profile questions at the end, which is probably the less motivating part to answer. We started with approaching the participants' knowledge about cohesion. For this, we applied the "funnel shape" [29]. First we asked broader questions about cohesion definition. Then, we narrowed down to questions that forced participants to concretely apply their perceived concept of cohesion by comparing and rating classes.

It is important to note the decision point between first and third questions in the first group (Figure 1). Obviously, we only ask participants to explain what a highly cohesive class is if he or she declares him/herself familiar with such concept. Otherwise, we skip question 1.2 and jump to the cohesion definition (item 1.3). Item 1.3 is not a question. Instead it is a set of statements defining what cohesion means. In this part of the survey, we were

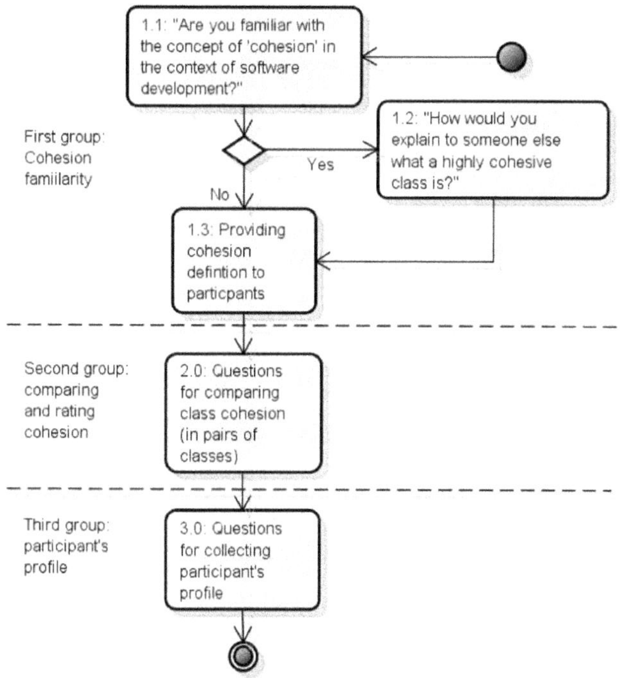

Figure 1. Questions flow overview.

concerned about having a single page summarizing different flavors of cohesion definition extracted from different well-known authors in this field. This would not bias the participant by presenting a partial view of cohesion. Moreover, for the sake of consistency, we decided to show this page to all the participants, that is, even to participants who declared him/herself familiar with the concept of cohesion.

3.2 Comparing and Rating Cohesion between two Classes

The second group of questions (see Figure 1) plays a central role in this survey. With them we aim at inducing participants to compare cohesion between two given classes and extract information about how they rate cohesion and how they explain their decisions. Given a pair of classes to be analyzed by participants we asked them to choose which class in the pair was more cohesive. Then we asked them to explain the rationale behind their choice. All participants were asked to compare three pair of classes during the survey. In the following subsection, we explain why this number of pairs of classes and how we selected the classes. The companion website [31] presents the complete survey as it was applied.

3.2.1 Class selection criteria for cohesion comparison

To address the second research question we carefully selected pairs of classes for being compared by the participants. We aimed to strategically define measurement scenarios that would allow the participants to compare classes with high and low values of conceptual and structural cohesion. Moreover, we were concerned with avoiding confounding factors such as, classes with different sizes, naming conventions and comments density.

We ended up with three measurement scenarios, which guided us to select three pairs of classes.

Measurement scenario 1: *Both classes with similar conceptual cohesion measurement and distinct structural cohesion measurement.* The goal here is to analyse if participants' ratings match the difference of structural cohesion. This requires a pair of classes with the following characteristics: (i) classes equally cohesive in terms of conceptual cohesion, and (ii) one class much more cohesive than the other in terms of structural cohesion.

Measurement scenario 2: *Classes with opposite structural and conceptual cohesion measurements.* For example, if class A is more conceptually cohesive than class B, then B must be more structurally cohesive than A. This scenario exposes situations where the two different ways of measuring cohesion are contradictory. Thus we can analyse whether and at what extent participants' interpretation follow the structural or the conceptual measurement.

Measurement scenario 3: *Both classes with similar structural cohesion measurement and distinct conceptual cohesion measurement.* This scenario is similar to the first one but now what varies between the classes is the degree of conceptual cohesion. The goal here is, therefore, to analyse if participants' ratings match the difference of conceptual cohesion when structural cohesion is the same for both of the classes.

It is worth highlighting that participants did not have access to the classes' measurements in any part of the survey. Besides, we tried to minimize confounding factors that could affect participant's interpretation of class cohesion, as described as follows.

Size. It is a well-known confounding factor when analysing module properties [19]. So, we selected classes with similar LOC (Lines of Code). In addition, we filtered out too large classes that could be tiring and less motivating for participants to read and understand.

Context. We selected classes within a relatively simple context, which could be easily and shortly explained in a single survey page. Simple contexts do not require previous reading about the system the classes are related to.

Naming conventions. Participants might have more difficult to understand classes whose source code is poorly named, without following any convention for naming identifiers. Thus, we selected classes with similar naming conventions. In very few cases, it was necessary to refactor some identifiers' names in order to balance the readability of the selected classes.

Source code comments. Finally, the presence of comments in the source code is another factor that may affect class comprehension. So, we selected pairs of classes with balanced amount of comments.

Finding pairs of classes which matches that set of requirements and measurement scenarios is not a trivial activity. We had to be very cautious as class comparison is a key part of the survey. Additionally, due to the subjectivity of some criteria we had to carry out this activity manually. That was challenging and took a reasonable effort when designing the study.

3.2.2 Cohesion Metrics

In order to measure structural and conceptual cohesion we chose two metrics – LCOM (Lack of Cohesion in Methods) by [16] (also known as LCOM5) and LCbC (Lack of Concern-based Cohesion) [32], representing ways of measuring structural cohesion and conceptual cohesion, respectively. Structural cohesion is the most traditional view of cohesion available in literature and in software metrics tools. We chose LCOM5 as it is available in an open source plugin for Eclipse IDE called Metrics[1].

Regarding LCbC, we have been working and studying this metric as well as other conceptual cohesion metrics in our research group for some years. We are not aware of any other simpler and

[1] The Metrics Eclipse plugin is available at http://metrics.sourceforge.net/

flexible metric for this purpose. No matter how a class is internally structured, LCbC just counts the number of concerns a class realizes. To compute this metric, it is necessary to identify and map concerns to source code elements. This concern mapping process can be done manually or by applying any automated or semi-automated concern mining technique. As we worked with just six classes (three pairs) it did not take to much time to manually identify and map concerns to the classes' source code. Also, LCbC is part of a concern-driven metrics suite which has been used in recent works [14] [11] [12].

For practical reasons, we could not include more than one representative metric for structural and conceptual cohesion. As explained in Section 3.2.1, most of the study design effort was to strictly balance five confounding factors combined with two cohesion metrics and three measurement scenarios in order to select classes for the study. The addition of more cohesion metrics would make it very difficult to manually fulfill all the class selection criteria in reasonable time.

3.2.3 Selected Pairs of Classes

After analysing classes from several open source projects in well-known repositories such as SourceForge and Github, we ended up with three pairs of classes from two software systems written in Java. The first system is for managing hotels[2]. It has features for controlling bookings, billings and guests data. From this system, we selected four classes for the first and second measurement scenarios, as detailed in Figure 2. We obtained the pair of classes for the third measurement scenario from the FamilyTree project[3]. This is an open source academic system used by other empirical studies [23]. The source code of all selected classes is available at the companion website [31] exactly as it was presented to the participants.

Figure 2 also shows the corresponding structural cohesion (LCOM5) and conceptual cohesion (LCbC) measurements for each class. In addition, to facilitate interpretation, Figure 2 indicates the corresponding measurement scenario for each pair of classes. For example, in the first comparison, ">LCOM5" indicates that the class in the left-hand side has a higher LCOM5 value and "=LCbC" indicates that both classes have the same LCbC value, which matches with the first measurement scenario. In the third comparison, both classes have quite similar LCOM5 measurement[4], whereas the left-hand side class has a higher LCbC value, thus the corresponding signals for this comparison are "=LCOM5" and ">LCbC". Participants did not have access to this information.

3.3 Collecting Participant's Profile

Software engineers experience may influence on how they reason about software properties like cohesion. Thus participant's academic and professional background should be considered in this kind of study. However, there is no agreed way to collect programming experience data in empirical software engineering. Researchers have used distinct, sometimes not reported, ways of collecting and quantifying it. Some other researchers do not collect it at all [9].

To build the third (and last) part of the survey questionnaire (see Figure 1 for the overview structure) we followed the results of a recent study on programming experience measurement [9]. It suggests a set of questions to measure participants' experience in

[2] FGMP - Hotel Management, available at http://sourceforge.net/projects/fgmp-hm/

[3] FamilyTree project available at http://www.soberit.tkk.fi/ mmantyla/ISESE2006/

[4] We considered a difference of 0.1 in LCOM5 as not sufficient to say both classes have different cohesion degrees according to this metric

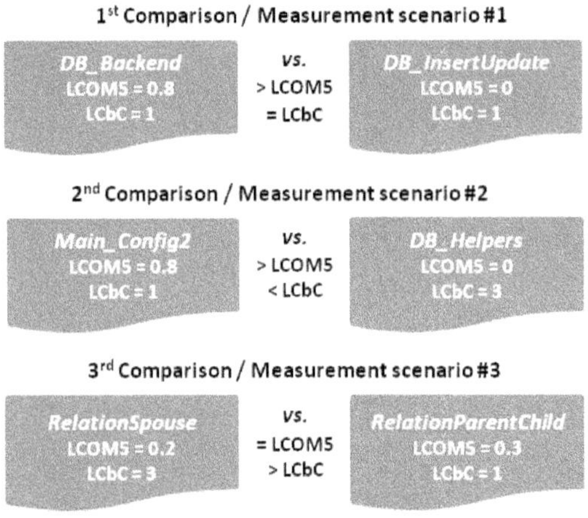

Figure 2. Classes for comparison.

software engineering empirical studies [9]. The companion website [31] shows all the questions we used for collecting participant's profile regarding professional and academic background.

3.4 Survey Sampling

The population for this study refers to software developers around the world with any experience on object-oriented programming and acting on any position in the software engineering field.

Any survey-based empirical study faces the problem of gathering participants, especially when dealing with such a broad population. That is why most of the survey-based software engineering studies use a non-probabilistic sampling [29]. This kind of sampling gathers participants who are easily accessible or the researchers have some justification for believing that they are representative of the population. Within non-probabilistic sampling, we referred to *Convenience* and *Snowball* sampling methods. The former consists of obtaining responses from people who are available and willing to take part. The latter involves asking people who have participated in the survey to nominate other people they believe would be willing to take part. We used snowball sampling only with some participants who showed interest in the study results, as we found they would be more willing to indicate other potential participants to be invited.

Some works have reported a low rate of participation, what have motivated recent investigation on this topic [33]. We report the following factors and procedures we used to invite developers. They helped us to achieve a reasonable number of participants and improve our response rate. We apply here the same terminology used in [29] [27] [33].

Personalized vs. Self-recruited survey. In self-recruited surveys, participants get to known somehow of the survey and decide to participate, while in personalized surveys each member of the sample is known and is personally invited to participate. The former can be easily spread by means of e-mail lists or social networks. However, researchers have no control of who participates in. We opted for a personalized survey to have control of who would be invited to participate. Thus, we were able to assure one response for each person and customize e-mail messages for invitations and reminders.

Reciprocity and Liking. People tend to comply with a request if they feel they owe the requester a favor (reciprocity) or if they have positive affect towards (liking). We addressed reciprocity by inviting people who had invited us to participate in previous studies; and by inviting people who had some previous connection with us either by academic or by professional purposes. To address liking, in every invitation e-mail we tried to make a connection by using the person's name and first asking how they were feeling. We could confirm that people who had prior and stronger connection with the authors respond more than people who had subtle or no connection.

Authority and Credibility. Response rates may rise with the authority and credibility of the survey invitor. We approached this factor by emphasizing our affiliation as researchers/professors. The response rate might have risen as some respondents were former students of the authors or they had previously known our research laboratory.

Brevity. In general, the longer the survey takes to be completed the lower is the response rate. However, to keep empirical soundness, researchers have to carefully evaluate whether important questions can be removed. Thus, every time we prepared a new version of the questionnaire we made inspections to discuss and decide what could be removed or shorten in order to improve brevity. This is the main reason why we used just three pairs of classes to be compared by respondents.

Compensation Value and Likelihood. One of the strongest motivators is when the respondents feel that they get something back for their invested time. The return can come in many forms including monetary incentives, prizes, and gift cards. We provided a fifty dollars Amazon gift card for a drawing to participants who completed the survey. We highlighted this offer in every survey message such as invitations, reminders and welcome message.

Reminders. People easily forget to accomplish tasks they are not required to do. Therefore, we sent reminders to potential participants who had not answered the survey within a week. In addition, instead of programming automatic reminders, we decided to customize reminders messages according to whom we would send.

3.5 Data Collection

The data collection was preceded by a pilot study involving three participants with experience on software engineering industry and academy. We carried out the pilot study including all the expected steps for the survey execution (from invitation messages to data analysis). After analyzing their feedback and responses we made some adjustments on survey questions and presentation of the classes.

Afterwards, we executed the survey data collection. It lasted forty days, from February 23rd, 2013 to April 8th, 2013. We sent invitations in batches almost every day until March 03rd, 2013 by means of personalized e-mail messages. During data collection we monitored survey responses in order to have a crisp notion about how the web-based system were performing and how the respondents were acting in terms of their answers.

4. Results and Analysis

In this section, we firstly describe the participants' profile and general statistics about who responded the survey. Then we present and discuss the results in the light of the two research questions.

4.1 Participants' Profile

From 228 invitations sent to software developers around the world we had 34 incomplete responses (15%) and 80 full responses, representing a 35% of response rate. This number of participants is at least equivalent or superior to some recent studies in software engineering which used closed access survey [1] [33]. All the survey messages and the questionnaire were provided in English and Portuguese. We used the Portuguese version for Brazilian and Portuguese potential participants, although they were able to switch from the Portuguese to the English version. As expected, most of the participants were from Brazil and used the Portuguese version. At the end we had: 47 responses in Portuguese (58%), comprising one from Portugal and the others from Brazil; and 33 responses in English (42%) from 9 different countries (Canada, Germany, Chile, Japan, USA, Iran, Poland, Spain, and Brazil). The reminders played an important role as 33 responses (42%) were completed after we sent customized reminders messages.

Figures 3-6 summarize the participants profile in terms of occupation, academic degree and self-estimation on programming experience. Most of them declared themselves as software developers, system analysts, researchers and students. Some of them were software architects/designers and lecturers/professors. Few of them were testers, business analysts and project managers. Just one answered as unemployed or retired and other two answered as system administrator and software engineer. It is important to note that job position was a multiple choice question, so it was possible to have participants choosing more than one position (e.g., student and software developer). In terms of academic degree, which was approached as a single choice question, two participants checked as undergraduate (2%), whereas nearly 31% checked as graduate (without post-graduate degrees). About 66% of the participants held some post-graduate degree.

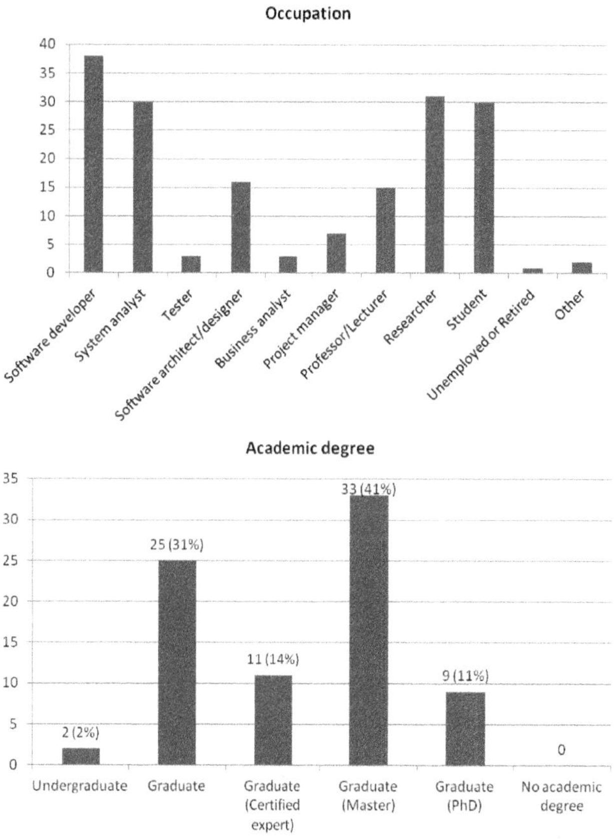

Figure 3. Participants' occupation and academic degree.

We asked them to self-estimate their programming experience in two different ways as depicted in Figure 4. As explained in Section 3.3, we followed a set of questions to measure programming experience suggested by previous work on this topic [9]. First, we asked them to rate their experience on a scale from 1 to 10 (1 - very inexperienced and 10 - very experienced). Nearly 81% marked 7 or higher. Second, we asked them to compare their experience to colleagues' in a scale from 1 to 5. 65% declared themselves more experienced than colleagues by checking 4 or 5.

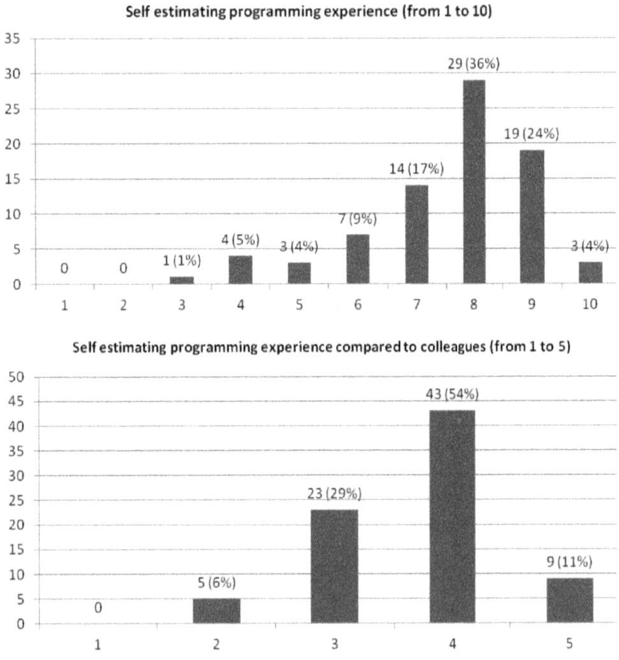

Figure 4. Participants' self estimation on programming experience.

Regarding their experience with Java programming language (Figure 5), 12% checked 1 and 2, which means little experience, whereas 57% declared themselves well experienced (4 and 5 rates). With respect to object-oriented programming (OOP) (second chart of Figure 5), the ratings follow similar trend, with the difference that all participants declared themselves average experienced to very well experienced.

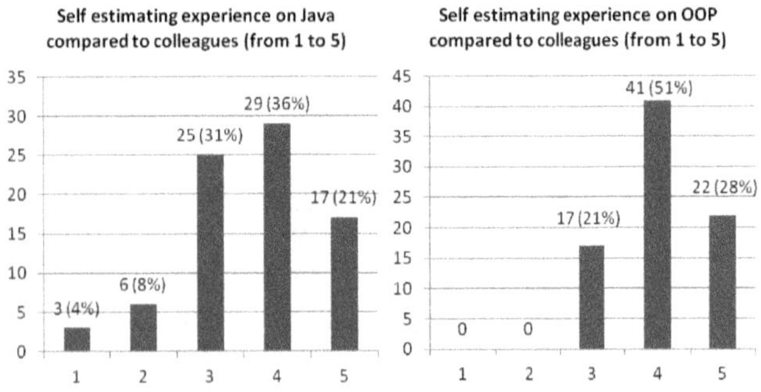

Figure 5. Participants' self estimation on Java and OOP.

The boxplot charts in Figure 6 show, respectively, the overall number of years of programming experience and the number of years of programming experience in large software projects. The plots are very similar, except that in the first one, experience varies from 1 to 29 years, whereas in the second one, experience varies between 0 and 15 years.

In summary, our set of participants includes developers with varied degrees of programming experience. We consider this result as positive for two reasons. First, it allowed us to make cross analysis between degrees of programming experience and the perception of cohesion. Second, the group of participants includes a

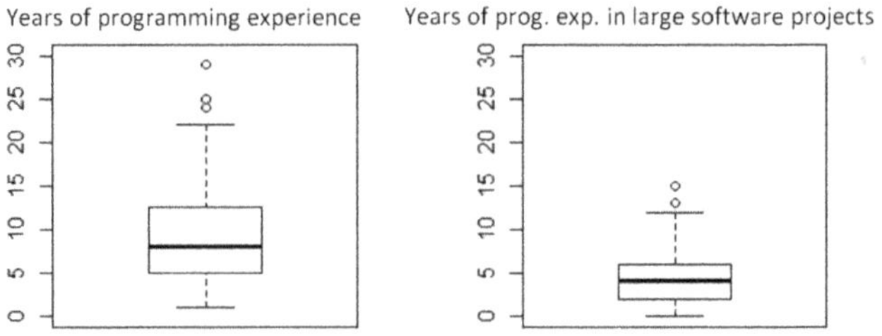

Figure 6. Participants' programming experience in years.

representative set of developers with sufficient experience to answer the survey without difficulty.

4.2 How do developers perceive module cohesion? How do they reason about it?

To answer this research question we need to analyze answers of three parts of the survey, as presented in the following subsections.

4.2.1 "Are you familiar with the concept of cohesion in the context of software development?"

This is the first question of the survey (see Section 3.1 for the overall survey structure). From 80 respondents, 71 (89%) answered YES (familiar with cohesion) and 9 (11%) answered NO (not familiar with cohesion) for this question. Interestingly, most of the participants declared themselves as familiar with cohesion. Note that, at this point of the survey, no definition about cohesion was presented to the participants yet.

Having this result in mind, it is important to investigate whether cohesion familiarity is related with participant experience. To address this point, we cross-checked the survey first question responses with two other questions about participant's profile as follows.

Cohesion Familiarity vs. Years of Programming Experience. As explained in 4.1, participants' programming experience varies from 1 to 29 years. Additionally, we found that 35 participants declared having 10 years or more of programming experience. We consider these ones as the most experienced participants. They represent 44% of our sample. When analysing their first question responses, we found that only two of them checked as not familiar with cohesion. The other seven not familiar with cohesion are spread over the participants with less than 10 years of programming experience.

Cohesion Familiarity vs. Academic Degree. We found that the distribution over academic degree considering only the 71 participants familiar with cohesion is very similar to this distribution considering all participants (see the second chart in Figure 3, which shows the distribution of academic degree for the entire sample). However, from the nine participants not familiar with cohesion, six are undergraduate or graduate programmers without post-graduate degree, whereas just three have Masters or PhD. Of these three, one has more than 10 years of programming experience but no experience in large software projects.

On the developers familiarity with cohesion. We can conclude that most of the participants of our sample are familiar with cohesion. Those who are not familiar with cohesion are most likely the least experienced ones.

4.2.2 "How would you explain to someone else what a highly cohesive class is?"

To analyse answers for this question we coded responses from the 71 participants who declared themselves familiar with cohesion.

Two members of our research group conducted the open coding process separately. One of them is co-author of this paper. Then, they had a meeting to cross-check, discuss and resolve conflicts in order to obtain the resulting coded responses.

As a result, we obtained 11 topics related to how participants explain what a highly cohesive class is. The distribution of these topics is shown in Figure 7. Each response may touch one or more topics as it is plausible to describe high cohesion by using a combination of correlated concepts. The top two topics are *class responsibilities* and *coupling*. Most of the participants (56) explain a highly cohesive class by using the concept of cohesion in terms of class responsibility, for example: *"it is a class with a well defined scope of responsibilities"*; *"(...) It should not take responsibility for functions other than its own"*; *"(...) When it performs a well-defined role"*; *"Singular in purpose. It does one thing, and only one thing"*; *"All the included functionalities are conceptually highly related"*. This represents 78% of the 71 participants. We grouped in this topic similar terms like *features, concerns, functionality, role*, etc. Participants who touched this topic had a rationale and perception aligned with conceptual cohesion.

Thirteen participants mentioned the property of coupling in their explanation. This represents 18% of the 71 participants. Although high coupling does not necessarily mean low cohesion (and vice-versa), this is somewhat acceptable as we know that coupling and cohesion may be related to each other in many situations. Thus, some people prefer to explain cohesion by mentioning other concepts they might know better such as coupling.

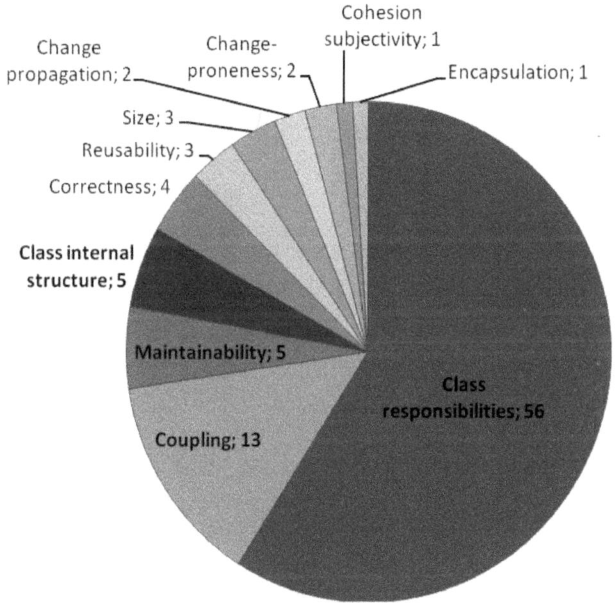

Figure 7. Coded topics from how participants explain highly cohesive classes (survey first question).

The *maintainability* topic, which we grouped with readability and comprehension, was mentioned by five participants (7%). Interestingly, some participants explained cohesion by mentioning external quality attributes such as maintainability, reusability and change-proneness. The presence of such topics is somehow understandable as cohesion may affect these properties.

In five responses (7%), participants explained high cohesion based on *class internal structure*. They mentioned the relationship between methods and attributes within a class. For example: *"Attributes and methods of this class have a strong logical relationship. I would say data-flow should be equally distributed within this class. If you think of a Def-Use-Graph almost all nodes should be connected to achieve high cohesion"*; *"Methods of this class implement features by calling each other"*; *"Its members are concerned mostly with themselves and other members of the same class"*. This kind of responses reveals rationale and perception more aligned with structural cohesion.

Some not expected topics had few occurrences, such as *Correctness*. Curiously, four participants (5%) mentioned that cohesion is related to whether a class correctly fulfills its requirements. For them, cohesion degree depends on whether a class is correct or not with respect to what it is supposed to do. We made available all the coded responses in the companion website [31], including the ones from the other questions.

4.2.3 Rationale for Rating and Comparing Cohesion

Additionally, we analysed how participants reason about cohesion by investigating their rationale when rating and comparing cohesion between classes. As explained in Section 3.2, for each one of the three pairs of classes, we asked the participants to selected the most cohesive class. Then, we asked them to explain the reasoning behind their choice. This was done in the second group of questions of the survey. To analyse their answers, we carried out an open coding process for their responses about this.

Regardless the classes the participants chose as more cohesive, the most coded topic for all the three scenarios was *class responsibilities*. Again, most of the participants used the notion of class responsibilities to justify their choice when comparing cohesion between classes. From the 80 responses, for the first comparison scenario, *class responsibilities* was coded in 60 responses. Class *suitability to split* was the second most coded topic. It appeared in 15 responses. It was followed by *coupling* and *class internal structure* with 8 occurrences each. Turning to the second comparison scenario, conceptual cohesion perception (by means of *class responsibilities* topic) was found in 67 responses, *class suitability to split* in 17, *class internal structure* in 7, and *coupling* in 5 responses. Finally, for the third comparison, *class responsibilities* had 71 occurrences, *coupling* had 4, *class internal structure* had 2, and *class suitability to split* had just 1 occurrence.

Interestingly, we found the topic *Suitability to split* in the second group of questions to explain cohesion ratings but not in the first question – the one about highly cohesive class explanation (see Figure 1 for the questions overall structure). This is probably due to the set of statements defining the concept of cohesion we provided the participants after the first question. One of the statements say that a highly cohesive class should be difficult to split, according to Bieman and Kang [2].

> **On the developers' perception about module cohesion.** By analysing how the participants explained class cohesion and how they reasoned when comparing cohesion between classes, we conclude that developers perceive cohesion in a conceptual manner, i.e., based on class responsibilities. We identified other ways of thinking about cohesion, which were coded during our analysis, such as coupling and structural cohesion. However any of them were intensively used as conceptual cohesion perception was.

4.3 To what extent structural cohesion and conceptual cohesion relate with how developers rate cohesion?

In order to answer this question, we quantitatively analyzed the cohesion ratings for the three comparison scenarios. Also we qualitatively analyze participants' explanation about their respective ratings. In addition, we cross-analyzed these data with cohesion familiarity and participant's experience to verify whether such factors associate with the results.

4.3.1 Cohesion Ratings and Respective Rationale

Figure 8 shows the ratings distribution for the three scenarions of comparison. We applied the Fleiss Kappa statistical test [13] to quantitatively assess the degree of inter-rater agreement for each scenario, by using the R tool. This test is applicable as we had a fixed number of raters assigning nominal-scale ratings to a number of items. The Kappa coefficient κ lies in [0,1] and indicates the level of agreement among raters: 1 indicates total agreement among all raters and 0 no agreement. As a result, for the first and third scenarios we found a slight agreement, with coefficients 0.193 and 0.155, respectively. For the second one we found fair agreement, with coefficient 0.234. This means that in first and third scenarios of comparison, the respondents slightly agreed to each other by means of rating in the same way, whereas in the second question their ratings fairly agreed. These categories (slight and fair agreement) were suggested by [20]. Although it is used by some related works, for instance [18], they are not universally accepted. Literature recommends further analysis of the results to give support for any conclusions [15], as we do in the following.

To better interpret the results of Figure 8 it is important to refer to Figure 2 to recall the measurement set corresponding to each scenario.

First scenario. In the first scenario, the second class (DB_InsertUpdate) is more cohesive than the first one (DB_Backend) in terms of structural cohesion, measured by means of the LCOM5 metric. On the other hand, they are equally cohesive in terms of conceptual cohesion, measured by means of the LCbC metric. Turning to participants' ratings, only 5% (4 participants) rated the second class as more cohesive. On the other hand, 37% (30 participants) rated both classes with quite similar cohesion, which matches with the conceptual cohesion measurement. Finally, 45 participants (57%) rated the first class as more cohesive, which does not match with structural cohesion neither with conceptual cohesion. Therefore, analysing quantitatively the amount of ratings for each category, we observe that most of the ratings do not match with structural cohesion measurement.

These results showed an issue to be further investigated – *Why did 45 participants rate the first class (DB_Backend) as more cohesive?* So, we turned to the responses where they explained their rationale. After analysing the coded explanations, we found that of these 45 participants, 29 justified their ratings by using conceptual cohesion perception. Basically, most of them found the second class (DB_InsertUpdate) less cohesive because they considered that it contains two different concerns: inserting and updating information in database. Although this interpretation does not match with our initial measurement, as we considered inserting and updating as a single concern, called *data base writing*, it can be seen as correct. Other 12 responses mentioned that the class should be split into two, for instance: *"(...) you could say that the Backend is more cohesive than InsertUpdate, as the second can be split into Insert and Update."*. This viewpoint is also associated with conceptual cohesion, as they claim the class should be split because it has multiple responsibilities. *Class coupling* were mentioned in 8 responses, whereas *class internal structure* were mentioned only in 7 out of the 45 responses. In summary, despite 57% (45) of the participants did not rate according to any of the target cohesion measurements, we found that most of them applied the conceptual cohesion perception to explain their reasoning.

We also investigated the reasoning of the four participants (5%) who chose the second class (DB_InsertUpdate) as more cohesive. At first sight, as it match with the structural cohesion measurement, we would expect explanations related with this kind of cohesion perception. However, none of them used the structural cohesion view. Three found more responsibilities in the first class than in the second one. For example, one participant explained: *"the first class handles database connections, which includes opening, closing and returning connections. The second one only updates the database"*. *Readability* and *comprehension*, *complexity*, *suitability to split*, and *encapsulation* are topics with one occurrence each.

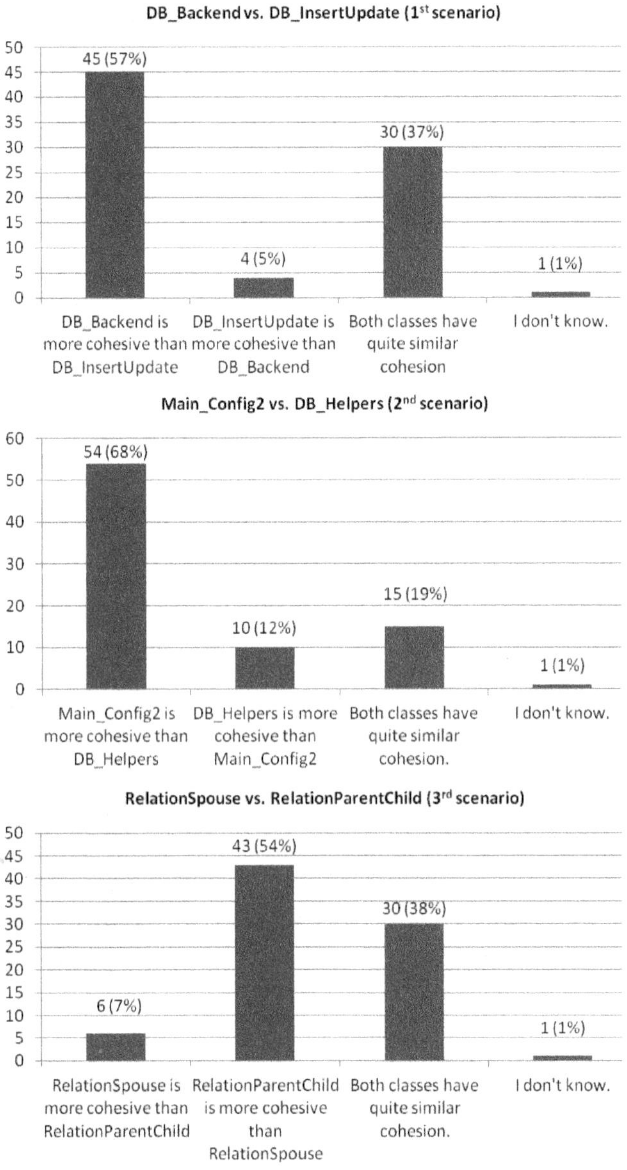

Figure 8. Cohesion ratings for the three scenarios.

Finally, we analysed the explanations from those who rated both classes with similar cohesion. From the 30 participants of this group (37%), 28 mentioned the *class responsibilities* topic and two mentioned the *suitability to split* topic. Other three topics had one occurrence each: *poor method decomposition*, *encapsulation*, and *class internal structure*. These observations indicate the association between the ratings of this group and conceptual cohesion measurement.

In summary, in the first scenario, most of the ratings matched with the conceptual cohesion measurement. Moreover, when analysing the coded explanations, we found that most of them refer to the conceptual cohesion perception, even when the ratings do not match with it.

Second scenario. In this scenario, the first class (Main_Config2) is more cohesive than the second one (DB_Helpers) in terms of conceptual cohesion measurement, whereas the opposite stands for structural cohesion measurement. 54 participants (68%) rated the first class as more cohesive, which matches with the conceptual cohesion measurement. 15 participants (19%) chose both classes with similar cohesion. 10 (12%) rated the second class as more cohesive, which matches with the structural cohesion measurement. Therefore, just analysing quantitatively this result, we can conclude that most ratings associate with the conceptual cohesion measurement.

Analysing the explanations of the participants who chose the second class as more cohesive (those that apparently matched with structural cohesion), we did not find any rationale referring to structural cohesion perception. Interestingly, all of these 10 participants gave explanations related with conceptual cohesion. 8 of them explicitly mentioned the identification of multiple concerns in Main_Config2 class, for instance: *"(...) it contains DB information and billing information and currency information"*. Basically, they found that Maing_Config2 works with distinct and unfocused properties (billing, database, hotel information, etc.). The other 2 seem to have mistakenly checked the wrong answer – they explained the first class as more cohesive but picked the alternative *"second class is more cohesive"*.

The reasons for rating both classes as similarly cohesive were: *class responsibilities* (12 occurrences); *suitability to split* (6 occurrences); *coupling* and *class internal structure* with 1 occurrence each. In fact, 12 out of 15 participants justified their answers by mentioning class responsibilities. This shows that most of the participants who considered both classes similarly cohesive also had a conceptual cohesion perception.

Finally, we analysed the explanations behind the 54 ratings that matched with conceptual cohesion measurement. 45 participants said that the first class (Main_Config2) was more cohesive because it was focused on a single behavior of the software (*class responsibilities* topic). 10 participants argued that this class is less suitable to split than the second one. This justification is somehow related to *class responsibilities*. Six participants justified their ratings by mentioning structural relatedness of class internal members. This shows that these six participants used the structural cohesion perception. Four participants applied the coupling concept as a proxy for cohesion, and one argued in terms of class comprehension. Overall, these results show that most of the participants used the conceptual cohesion perception. This reinforces the association between participants' ratings and the conceptual cohesion measurement.

Third scenario. In this scenario, both classes are similarly cohesive in terms of structural cohesion measurement. However, in terms of conceptual cohesion measurement, the second one (RelationParentChild) is more cohesive than the first one (RelationSpouse). 43 participants, who represent 54% of the sample, rated the second class as more cohesive. These ratings match with the conceptual cohesion measurement. 30 participants (38%) rated both classes as similarly cohesive. These ratings match with the structural cohesion measurement. Six participants (7%) rated the first class as more cohesive. Therefore, it is clear to observe that most of the ratings associate with conceptual cohesion. However, further analysis is necessary to clarify other issues: *Why did 7% of the participants rate the first class as more cohesive? And why did 38% rate both classes similarly cohesive?*

Four of the six participants who rated the first class (RelationSpouse) as more cohesive seem to had done that by mistake. They explained their decisions as if the second class was more cohesive. The other 2 justified their decisions by mentioning the difficult to understand the intention of the classes, and by using odd arguments like *"the first class is more cohesive because it makes several imports"*.

Apparently the 30 ratings for both classes with similar cohesion match with structural cohesion measurement. However, just two explanations behind them were actually related to structural cohesion perception. In addition, we coded 24 responses related to conceptual cohesion perception. However, 23 of them considered that both classes had the same number of concerns, thus assuming both classes similarly cohesive. For instance, one participant wrote: *"Both handles specific functionality"*. Only 2 mentioned structural cohesion in their reasoning, for example: *"I don't see substantial differences in the usage pattern of members"*. Other 6 responses mentioned issues related to *coupling* (3 occurrences), *class similarity* (2 occurrences) and *reusability* (1 occurrence). These results show, therefore, that most of the participants' rationale was based on conceptual cohesion.

Finally, we analysed the responses of the 43 participants who chose the second class as more cohesive, matching with the conceptual cohesion measurement. We found terms related to the *class responsibilities* topic in all of them. This indicates that these participants' rationale is strongly aligned with conceptual cohesion.

On the association between participants' reasoning and cohesion measurement. Most of the ratings in the three scenarios do not associate with structural cohesion measurement. Actually, participants rated cohesion mostly based on class responsibilities, which shows they used the conceptual cohesion point of view. Even the participants who rated differently from the conceptual cohesion measurement applied the conceptual cohesion perception for justifying their decisions. These results indicate that the perception of conceptual cohesion is predominant, which was also observed when addressing the previous research question (see Section 4.2).

4.3.2 Cohesion Ratings vs. Cohesion Familiarity

In this section, we assess whether familiarity with the concept of cohesion associates with the cohesion ratings the participants gave. To do that, we cross-analysed the ratings with answers of the survey first question (see Section 4.2.1), which asks whether or not the participant is familiar with cohesion.

First, we applied the Fisher exact test, which is a statistical test used to examine the significance of the association between two kinds of classification (two categorical variables) – in our case the nominal-scale cohesion ratings and bivariate cohesion familiarity (Yes/No). With this test we aimed at verifying whether the following *null hypothesis* is rejected: *There is no association between participant's previous familiarity with cohesion and participant's cohesion ratings*. After applying the Fisher exact test we got the following p-values respectively for the three scenarios: 0.170, 0.175, and 0.054. Therefore, we could not reject the null hypothesis for any of them. Hence, it is not possible, according to this quantitative assessment, to assume that there is an association between participants' previous familiarity with cohesion and participants' ratings on class cohesion. Then, we turned to the coded responses to try to find any possible association between these two variables.

Just nine participants considered themselves not familiar with cohesion in the beginning of the survey. Thus, we analysed the corresponding ratings and explanations of these nine participants for the three scenarios. Regarding the first scenario, none of them rated the second class as more cohesive, that is, none of their ratings matched with structural cohesion measurement. Of these nine, one participant checked the *"I don't know"* alternative. Four of the ratings matched with the conceptual cohesion measurement, that is, the alternative *"both classes have quite similar cohesion"*. After analysing the corresponding coded explanations, we found that, regardless the ratings, most of them (5 out of 9) justified their answers using the conceptual cohesion perception. Just two applied the structural cohesion perception.

Turning to the second scenario, one participant chose the second class (DB_Helpers) as more cohesive, which apparently corresponds to lower structural cohesion measurement. However, the participant justified his or her choice by applying the conceptual cohesion perception. He or she identified two different concerns in Main_Config2 class but did not identify additional concerns in DB_Helpers. This scenario also had one participant who checked "I don't know". So, there are seven remaining responses. Analysing the coded explanations of them, five used the conceptual cohesion perception, three mentioned class suitability to split, and two used the structural cohesion reasoning. It is worth recalling that we often found two or more coded topics in a single response.

Analysing the third scenario, most of the participants (6 out of 9) considered both classes with similar cohesion, apparently matching with structural cohesion measurement. However, from these six, just two explained their choice based on the structural cohesion perception. The others (4) justified their choice based on similarity of classes' responsibilities, as they did not find additional concerns on the RelationSpouse class. The participant who checked the RelationSpouse class as more cohesive actually did it mistakenly according to his/her explanation. He or she explicitly explained RelationSpouse as less cohesive by using the conceptual cohesion perception and pointing additional concerns on it. Besides, we confirmed that the two who checked RelationParentChild as more cohesive, matching with conceptual cohesion measurement, indeed used the conceptual cohesion perception.

On the association between developer's ratings and previous familiarity with cohesion. Conceptual cohesion perception was predominant even among participants who declared themselves not familiar with cohesion in the beginning of the survey. The overall conclusion for this sample subset follows the conclusion for the entire sample presented in previous subsections. This indicates that no matter whether or not developers have previous familiarity with cohesion, if they are provided with a brief explanation of what cohesion means (in different views – structural and conceptual), they apply the conceptual cohesion perception. These results support the claim that conceptual cohesion seems to be more intuitive and closer to the human-oriented view of cohesion.

4.3.3 Cohesion Ratings vs. Participants' Experience

Another possible factor that could influence the cohesion ratings is the participant's previous experience in programming. As shown in Figure 6, we asked participants the number of years they have in programming (in general) as well as in programming on large software projects.

Following the same strategy for the previous analysis, we applied the Fisher exact test. However, in this case we had to transform the years of programming experience variable, which is continuous, into a categorical variable. Thus, we split the years of programming experience data into the following categories: 5 years or less ($<= 5$), more than 5 years but less than or equals 12 ($> 5 AND <= 12$), and more than 12 years (> 12). The first and third ranges represent the lower quartile and upper quartile, respectively (see Figure 6), whereas the second category comprises the interquartile range. The *null hypothesis* for the Fisher test was: *There is no association between participant's cohesion ratings and participant experience in programming*. As a result, we could not reject this null hypothesis for any of the three scenarios, as we found the respective p-values 0.7, 0.8 and 0.5. Therefore, we turned to the coded explanation trying to find any possible association between these two variables.

Based on participants' programming experience, we split the participants from the sample in two groups: the least experienced and the most experienced developers based on the lower and upper quartiles of programming experience distribution (Figure 6). The least experienced developers were 21 participants with 5 years or less of programming experience. The most experienced ones were 20 developers with more than 12 years of programming experience. Then we counted the occurrences of the coded topics in the three scenarios as summarized in Table 1. The columns represent the three scenarios for both groups of developers (≤ 5 and > 12 years of programming experience), and the rows represent the coded topics from the participants' explanation. Regardless their experience, most of the participants used the conceptual cohesion perception (see "Class responsibilities." row). Other topics were used but with very few occurrences compared with *Class responsibilities*. *Class internal structure*, for example, had one occurrence on each group of participants for each scenario of comparison.

Table 1. Programming experience and coded topics for cohesion ratings explanation

	≤ 5 years			> 12 years		
Topics	**1st**	**2nd**	**3rd**	**1st**	**2nd**	**3rd**
Class responsibilities	17	17	17	14	17	17
Suitability to split	4	6	1	3	1	1
Reusability/modularization	1	1	2	4	0	0
Class internal structure	1	1	1	1	1	1
Readability/Comprehension	1	1	1	0	0	0
Complexity	1	0	0	0	0	0
Coupling	0	0	0	2	3	1

In summary, we could not reject the null hypothesis which states that there is no association between participant's cohesion ratings and participant experience in programming, by using Fisher exact test. However, we could observe that the *class responsibilities* topic was mostly mentioned both by the least experienced and the most experienced developers. We made the same analysis considering participants' experience in large software projects and the results are very similar.

On the association between developer's ratings and experience. We can conclude that conceptual cohesion represents the most common way of reasoning about cohesion regardless the developers' experience on programming. This is another important finding which supports the claim that conceptual cohesion seems to be more intuitive and closer to the human-oriented view of cohesion.

5. Threats to Validity

Construct validity. Threats to construct validity concern the question how we know we are really measuring the attribute we want to measure. There are many ways to measure participants' ratings regarding class cohesion that may influence the results. We opted to treat developers' cohesion ratings as a categorical (nominal scale) variable based on a class cohesion paired comparison, as in [18]. This scale is less powerful for applying statistical tests. Instead, we could have provided a set of classes and asking participants to give a cohesion rate within a range (e.g. from 0 to 1) for each class, as in [8], or we could have used a Likert scale (from 1 - very low cohesion to 5 - very high cohesion). However, with our choice it is cognitively easier for participants to make a decision comparing two concrete examples without needing to give a numerical rate for each analyzed class. Although this is less powerful by means of statistical tests, this helped us to achieve more reliable results by means of qualitative analysis.

Another possible threat is related to the way we provided classes to participants' analysis. Participants could only analyze the classes under study without having access to other project documents. However, we selected classes relatively easy to understand. Also, we shortly described the overall purpose of each class and their corresponding context in the project. This is the choice for simplifying, as much as possible, participants' analysis task, allowing them to focus on what is most important.

To measure cohesion, we used two metrics – LCOM5 and LCbC – which influenced on two parts of our study: (i) in the class selection process for matching the measurement scenarios (Section 3.2.1); and (ii) in the comparison between developers' ratings with cohesion measurement (Section 4.3). We explained the reasons for choosing these two metrics in Section 3.2.2. However, we could have used other metrics, for instance, LCOM3 or LCOM4 [3] for structural cohesion, and C3 [25] or MWE [22] for conceptual cohesion. They would probably lead us to select other classes for the study in order to match the measurement scenarios. Nonetheless, our main focus relied on capturing how developers reason about class cohesion and how their opinions associate with two different ways of measuring cohesion (structural and conceptual), regardless specific metrics applied. Additionally, we claim that LCbC has a higher potential to measure conceptual cohesion than C3 and MWE, as these two metrics compute cohesion based on topics extracted from source code comments and identifiers by executing automated text mining techniques. There is not enough evidence to rely on textually mined topics as proxies for class responsibilities.

Internal validity. Read and interpret class code is a quite subjective task and there are distinct confounding factors that may influence it. Thus, we carefully defined a set of criteria to select classes to be analyzed by developers, as explained in Section 3.2.1. Participants' experience may also affect how the code is interpreted and how cohesion is rated. We discussed the participants' profile in Section 4.1, where we presented the set of participants with varied but sufficient experience to analyze code and rate cohesion. Also, the varied participants' experience was considered positive to enable cross analysis between research questions and experience factors such as years of programming and academic degree.

Conclusion validity. This comprises lack of statistical calculations or misuse of statistical assumptions that leads to incorrect conclusions made by the researcher. This study is predominantly qualitative and most of the analysis relies on discussion over qualitative data (coded responses) and by using basic statistic description illustrated and summarized in charts. Additionally, in Section 4.3.1 we used the Fleiss Kappa test to quantitatively assess the level of agreement among participants when rating cohesion. Then, we used the Fisher exact test in two situations: (i) in Section 4.3.2 to find a possible association between participant's previous familiarity with cohesion and participant's cohesion ratings; and in Section 4.3.3 to test the association between cohesion ratings and categorized participant's programming experience. In none of these two situations we could reject the corresponding null hypotheses, which led us to rely on qualitative analysis.

External validity. The main question related to external validity is whether the results discussed here can be considered to other groups of developers and classes of other systems. As discussed in Section 3.4, we applied convenience sampling instead of probabilistic sampling, as most of state-of-the-art software engineering papers do [18] [1]. However, our sample was not restricted to a group of developers with specific characteristic. As explained in Section 4.1, the analysis of the participants profile revealed an heterogeneous set of participants from nine countries with varied experience in programming and academic degree. Additionally, we limited this study to six Java classes from open source systems, mainly because we had to provide source code of only a limited number of class pairs to be analyzed in a relatively short amount of time. However, we excluded language features special to Java and the overall content of each class could be written in other object-oriented programming language.

6. Conclusion

Although cohesion measures have been addressed in several works during the last decades, little is known about developers reasoning on module cohesion. The understanding of how developers perceive cohesion is important to know how they reason about such important quality attribute during software development and maintenance. This work provides empirical evidence on how developers perceive module cohesion and whether or not such perception associates with conceptual cohesion and structural cohesion – two state-of-the-art ways of measuring cohesion.

The study involved a web-based survey with 80 participants from 9 countries and different levels of experience and academic degree. The survey comprised questions related to: general perception of module cohesion; module cohesion pair-wise comparison and rating; cohesion reasoning; and participant profile. We applied quantitative and mostly qualitative analysis through developer's responses. In summary, the results indicated that most of the developers are familiar with cohesion and those who are not familiar with cohesion are most likely the least experienced ones. Some developers use other popular concepts to explain cohesion such as "coupling" and "size" or more general concepts such as "maintainability" and "reusability". However, most of the developers perceive cohesion in a conceptual manner, i.e., based on class responsibilities, thus associating more with conceptual cohesion measurement. Moreover, this is the most common way of reasoning about cohesion regardless the developers' experience on programming.

These results support the claim that conceptual cohesion seems to be more intuitive and closer to the human-oriented view of cohesion observed on software developers. Although structural cohesion measurement has been the most common way of measuring cohesion both in academic works and in commercial software tools, our findings point out that conceptual cohesion measurement captures better the real notion of cohesion as perceived by developers in contrast with the traditional structural cohesion measurement. This result reinforces the need for improving knowledge and technology on conceptual cohesion measurement. Conceptual cohesion metrics can take advantage of evolving concern mining techniques [7]. So, in future, we suggest the implementation of conceptual cohesion metrics in software measurement tools integrated with automated concern mining techniques. Also, we recommend investigation on how developers maintain high (low) cohesive modules by analyzing how the changes on such modules are carried out.

Acknowledgments

This work was partially supported by CNPq: National Institute of Science and Technology for Software Engineering (grant 573964/2008–4) and Universal Project (grants 486662/2013-6); CAPES: PROCAD-NF (grant 720/2010), and FAPESB (grant DTE 058/2011).

References

[1] G. Bavota, B. Dit, R. Oliveto, M. Di Penta, D. Poshyvanyk, and A. De Lucia. An empirical study on the developers' perception of

software coupling. In *Proceedings of the 2013 International Conference on Software Engineering*, ICSE '13, pages 692–701, Piscataway, NJ, USA, 2013. IEEE Press.

[2] J. M. Bieman and B.-K. Kang. Cohesion and reuse in an object-oriented system. *SIGSOFT Softw. Eng. Notes*, 20(SI):259–262, Aug. 1995.

[3] L. C. Briand, J. W. Daly, and J. Wüst. A unified framework for cohesion measurement in object-orientedsystems. *Empirical Softw. Engg.*, 3(1):65–117, July 1998.

[4] R. P. Buse and W. R. Weimer. Learning a metric for code readability. *IEEE Transactions on Software Engineering*, 36(4):546–558, 2010.

[5] S. R. Chidamber and C. F. Kemerer. A metrics suite for object oriented design. *IEEE Trans. Softw. Eng.*, 20(6):476–493, June 1994.

[6] S. Counsell, S. Swift, A. Tucker, and E. Mendes. Object-oriented cohesion subjectivity amongst experienced and novice developers: an empirical study. *SIGSOFT Softw. Eng. Notes*, 31(5):1–10, Sept. 2006.

[7] R. S. Durelli, D. S. M. Santibáñez, N. Anquetil, M. E. Delamaro, and V. V. de Camargo. A systematic review on mining techniques for crosscutting concerns. In *Proceedings of the 28th Annual ACM Symposium on Applied Computing*, SAC '13, pages 1080–1087, New York, NY, USA, 2013. ACM.

[8] L. Etzkorn and H. Delugach. Towards a semantic metrics suite for object-oriented design. In *Proceedings of the Technology of Object-Oriented Languages and Systems*, TOOLS '00, pages 71–, Washington, DC, USA, 2000. IEEE Computer Society.

[9] J. Feigenspan, C. Kästner, J. Liebig, S. Apel, and S. Hanenberg. Measuring programming experience. In *Proceedings of the 20th International Conference on Program Comprehension (ICPC)*, pages 73–82, Los Alamitos, CA, 2012.

[10] N. E. Fenton and S. L. Pfleeger. *Software Metrics: A Rigorous and Practical Approach.* PWS Publishing Co., Boston, MA, USA, 2nd edition, 1998.

[11] E. Figueiredo, N. Cacho, C. Sant'Anna, M. Monteiro, U. Kulesza, A. Garcia, S. Soares, F. Ferrari, S. Khan, F. Castor Filho, and F. Dantas. Evolving software product lines with aspects: an empirical study on design stability. In *Proceedings of the 30th International Conference on Software engineering*, ICSE '08, pages 261–270, New York, NY, USA, 2008. ACM.

[12] E. Figueiredo, C. Sant'Anna, A. Garcia, and C. Lucena. Applying and evaluating concern-sensitive design heuristics. *Journal of Systems and Software*, 85(2):227 – 243, 2012.

[13] J. L. Fleiss. Measuring Nominal Scale Agreement Among Many Raters. *Psychological Bulletin*, 76(5):378–382, 1971.

[14] A. Garcia, C. Sant'Anna, E. Figueiredo, U. Kulesza, C. Lucena, and A. von Staa. Modularizing design patterns with aspects: a quantitative study. In *Proceedings of the 4th international conference on Aspect-oriented software development*, AOSD '05, pages 3–14, New York, NY, USA, 2005. ACM.

[15] K. Gwet. *Handbook of Inter-Rater Reliability (3rd Edition): The Definitive Guide to Measuring the Extent of Agreement Among Multiple Raters.* Advanced Analytics Press, 3 edition, 2012.

[16] B. Henderson-Sellers. *Software Metrics.* Prentice Hall, UK, 1996.

[17] M. Hitz and B. Montazeri. Measuring coupling and cohesion in object-oriented systems. In *Proc. Intl. Sym. on Applied Corporate Computing*, 1995.

[18] B. Katzmarski and R. Koschke. Program complexity metrics and programmer opinions. In *Proc. 20th IEEE International Conference on Program Comprehension*, pages 17–26. IEEE, 2012.

[19] A. G. Koru and J. J. Tian. Comparing high-change modules and modules with the highest measurement values in two large-scale open-source products. *IEEE Trans. Softw. Eng.*, 31:625–642, 2005.

[20] J. R. Landis and G. G. Koch. The Measurement of Observer Agreement for Categorical Data. *Biometrics*, 33(1):159–174, Mar. 1977.

[21] Y. S. Lee and B. S. Liang. Measuring the coupling and cohesion of an object-oriented program based on information flow. In *Prof. Intl. Conference on Software Quality*, 1995.

[22] Y. Liu, D. Poshyvanyk, R. Ferenc, T. Gyimothy, and N. Chrisochoides. Modeling class cohesion as mixtures of latent topics. In *25th IEEE International Conference on Software Maintenance, September 20-26, 2009, Edmonton, Alberta, Canada*, pages 233–242. IEEE, 2009.

[23] M. V. Mäntylä and C. Lassenius. Drivers for software refactoring decisions. In *Proceedings of the 2006 ACM/IEEE international symposium on Empirical software engineering*, ISESE '06, pages 297–306, New York, NY, USA, 2006. ACM.

[24] A. Marcus and D. Poshyvanyk. The conceptual cohesion of classes. In *Proceedings of the 21st IEEE International Conference on Software Maintenance*, ICSM '05, pages 133–142, Washington, DC, USA, 2005. IEEE Computer Society.

[25] A. Marcus, D. Poshyvanyk, and R. Ferenc. Using the conceptual cohesion of classes for fault prediction in object-oriented systems. *IEEE Transactions on Software Engineering*, 34:287–300, 2008.

[26] R. C. Martin. *Agile Software Development: Principles, Patterns, and Practices.* Prentice Hall PTR, Upper Saddle River, NJ, USA, 2003.

[27] T. Punter, M. Ciolkowski, B. Freimut, and I. John. Conducting on-line surveys in software engineering. In *Proceedings of the 2003 International Symposium on Empirical Software Engineering*, ISESE '03, pages 80–, Washington, DC, USA, 2003. IEEE Computer Society.

[28] M. P. Robillard and G. C. Murphy. Representing concerns in source code. *ACM Trans. Softw. Eng. Methodol.*, 16(1), Feb. 2007.

[29] C. B. Seaman. Qualitative methods in empirical studies of software engineering. *IEEE Trans Softw. Eng.*, 25:557–572, 1999.

[30] F. Shull, J. Singer, and D. I. K. Sjberg. *Guide to Advanced Empirical Software Engineering.* Springer Publishing Company, Incorporated, 1st edition, 2010.

[31] B. Silva. Developers reasoning about module cohesion: companion website, Oct. 2013. URL `http://homes.dcc.ufba.br/~brunocs/CohesionSurveyResults.html`.

[32] B. Silva, C. Sant'Anna, C. Chavez, and A. Garcia. Concern-based cohesion: Unveiling a hidden dimension of cohesion measurement. In *Proc. 20th IEEE International Conference on Program Comprehension*, pages 103–112. IEEE, 2012.

[33] E. Smith, R. Loftin, E. Murphy-Hill, C. Bird, and T. Zimmermann. Improving developer participation rates in surveys. In *Proceedings of the 6th International Workshop on Cooperative and Human Aspects of Software Engineering*, May 2013.

[34] W. P. Stevens, G. J. Myers, and L. L. Constantine. Structured design. *IBM Systems Journal*, 13(2):115 –139, 1974.

Compositional Reasoning About Aspect Interference

Ismael Figueroa[1,3] * Tom Schrijvers[2] Nicolas Tabareau[3] Éric Tanter[1]

[1]PLEIAD Lab, Computer Science Dept (DCC)—University of Chile, Chile
[2]Dept. of Applied Mathematics and Computer Science—Ghent University, Belgium
[3]ASCOLA Team—INRIA, France
ifiguero@dcc.uchile.cl, tom.schrijvers@ugent.be, nicolas.tabareau@inria.fr, etanter@dcc.uchile.cl

Abstract

Oliveira and colleagues recently developed a powerful model to reason about mixin-based composition of effectful components and their interference, exploiting a wide variety of techniques such as equational reasoning, parametricity, and algebraic laws about monadic effects. This work addresses the issue of reasoning about interference with effectful aspects in the presence of unrestricted quantification through pointcuts. While global reasoning is required, we show that it is possible to reason in a compositional manner, which is key for the scalability of the approach in the face of large and evolving systems. We establish a general equivalence theorem that is based on a few conditions that can be established, reused, and adapted separately as the system evolves. Interestingly, one of these conditions, local harmlessness, can be proven by a translation to the mixin setting, making it possible to directly exploit previously established results about certain kinds of harmless extensions.

Categories and Subject Descriptors F.3.3 [*Studies of Program Constructs*]; D.3.2 [*Language Classifications*]: Functional Languages; D.3.3 [*Programming Languages*]: Language Constructs and Features

Keywords aspect-oriented programming, monads, equational reasoning, compositional reasoning, interference

1. Introduction

Aspect-oriented programming promotes separation of concerns at the textual level, but semantic interactions between components of an aspect-oriented program are challenging to predict and control. Consequently, the general issue of interference has received a lot of attention in the AOP literature and related areas, such as feature-oriented programming [23]. A wide range of techniques have been studied, such as program analyses [25], type-and-effect systems [6, 7], model checking [15, 18] and equational reasoning [21, 22].

Oliveira *et al.* developed MRI, which stands for *Modular Reasoning about Interference*, a purely functional model of incremental programming with effects [22]. Effects are made explicit through the use of monads. MRI enables both modular reasoning and reasoning about non-interference of effects using a range of reasoning techniques like equational reasoning and parametricity. MRI has been used to express two theorems about harmless mixins. The central notion is that a mixin is harmless if the advised program is equivalent to the unadvised program, provided we ignore the effects introduced by the mixin. In MRI, harmlessness can be defined with respect to any computational effect, as long as an associated projection function exists to ignore the introduced effects. MRI therefore subsumes Dantas and Walker's notion of harmless advice, which is specific to I/O effects [7].

While originally formulated as "EffectiveAdvice" [21] with a suggested connection to aspect-oriented programming, MRI does not address quantification; advices are mixins which are applied explicitly. The lack of quantification greatly simplifies modular reasoning, because it is enough to study a single module/function and a mixin in isolation. In addition, MRI only focuses on step-wise applications of mixins, in which the composition of a base component with a mixin can then be treated as a new base component for a subsequent mixin application. In contrast, in the pointcut/advice model of AOP, several aspects live in an aspect environment and are all woven at each join point.

This work addresses the challenge of reasoning about aspect interference in the presence of quantification. It has been argued that unrestricted quantification hampers modular reasoning, thereby requiring a form of global reasoning [17]. Recovering modular reasoning can be achieved by restricting quantification, for instance following the Open Modules approach [1]. Yet, as we demonstrate in this paper, while unrestricted quantification hampers *modular* reasoning, it is amenable to *compositional* reasoning: global harmlessness results can be obtained through the composition of smaller proofs. This compositionality makes it possible to evolve an aspect-oriented system and *reuse* previously-established results.

The contribution of this paper is to develop a framework for establishing harmlessness results about aspect-oriented systems in a compositional manner. Like MRI, we develop a purely functional model with monadic effects, using Haskell as a convenient source language for System F_ω and elaborating the model as a Haskell library[1]. We formulate a general behavioral equivalence theorem between a given aspect-oriented system run with respect to two different aspect environments, modulo projection of additional side-effects. This general theorem is proven assuming four sufficient conditions that have to be established separately. When an aspect-oriented system evolves, only some of these conditions may need to be re-established in order to preserve the general theorem.

In Section 2, we illustrate the challenges of reasoning about aspect interference with quantification. Section 3 briefly introduces

* Funded by a CONICYT-Chile Doctoral Scholarship

MODULARITY '14, April 22–26, 2014, Lugano, Switzerland.

ACM 978-1-4503-2772-5/14/04. . . $15.00.
http://dx.doi.org/10.1145/2577080.2577093

[1] http://pleiad.cl/research/cri

the necessary background on monads and reasoning, and describes a general model of monadic AOP. Section 4 exposes the main theorem of compositional reasoning, discussing and illustrating each of the sufficient conditions. Section 5 presents a concrete minimal implementation of monadic AOP, which is used in Section 6 to study the local harmlessness condition in details. This section shows how we can exploit the formal results of MRI [22] in our setting. Section 7 discusses related work and Section 8 concludes. Several proofs are included in the paper; others can be found in an extended version available online as a technical report [13].

2. Reasoning about Aspect Interference

To illustrate the challenges of reasoning about aspect interference, we introduce a simple base program (written in an imaginary ML-like language) defined in terms of some known functions f and g.

$$\begin{array}{l} \mathit{prog}\ x\ y = \\ \quad \mathbf{let}\ r_1 = f\ x\ \mathbf{in} \\ \quad \mathbf{let}\ r_2 = g\ y\ \mathbf{in} \\ \quad r_1 + r_2 \end{array}$$

In the following, we present different changes to a system composed of this program and some aspects, and consider questions related to semantic equivalence. We define aspects as a pointcut/advice pair, and use run to execute programs with certain aspects.

Adding aspects We first add an aspect to the existing system. For instance, to log all calls to f we define a new system:

$$s_1 = run\ [(\mathit{call}\ f, \mathit{log})]\ \mathit{prog}$$

with a typical implementation of the logging advice:

$$\begin{array}{l} \mathit{log}\ \mathit{proceed}\ x = \\ \quad \mathit{print}\ \texttt{"Entering function ..."} \\ \quad \mathit{proceed}\ x \end{array}$$

Is the behavior of s_1 equivalent to the original program? Strictly speaking, they are not equivalent if we consider the output generated by $print$. However, we observe that the return value of the system is left unchanged, and that if we *ignore* the printed output, both systems are equivalent. This corresponds to the notion of *harmlessness* established in MRI [22]. In the general case, establishing that applying the logging aspect is harmless requires to reason globally about the aspect and the composed system.

Some questions arise when we see, intuitively, that the logging advice is harmless for every function on which it may be applied. This property of logging when seen as a mixin is formalized and proven in MRI, but can we use this knowledge when the advice is applied to a system via quantification?

Widening quantification We now widen the quantification of the logging aspect, modifying the pointcut to match additional join points. For instance, if we now want to log calls to g, it suffices to define a combined pointcut:

$$s_2 = run\ [(\mathit{call}\ f \vee \mathit{call}\ g, \mathit{log})]\ \mathit{prog}$$

Intuitively, this change is also harmless. But how to prove it formally? Do we need to reason globally about the system from scratch? or can we reuse some facts from the proof that logging f in the system is harmless?

Evolving the base program We now evolve the base program by replacing the use of f with that of another function h:

$$\begin{array}{l} \mathit{prog}'\ x\ y = \\ \quad \mathbf{let}\ r_1 = h\ x\ \mathbf{in} \\ \quad \mathbf{let}\ r_2 = g\ y\ \mathbf{in} \\ \quad r_1 + r_2 \end{array}$$

$$s_3 = run\ [(\mathit{call}\ f \vee \mathit{call}\ g, \mathit{log})]\ \mathit{prog}'$$

A first observation is that $\mathit{call}\ f$ will never match. We must change references to f also in the aspect environment:

$$s_4 = run\ [(\mathit{call}\ h \vee \mathit{call}\ g, \mathit{log})]\ \mathit{prog}'$$

Changing f for h will most assuredly modify the semantics of the base program, and consequently of the system. This is expected when the base program is evolving. However, we may want to know if the logging aspect is still harmless in this new system. The question is: what amount of reasoning do we need to perform? Do we need to prove again that logging is harmless with respect to the whole system, or can we reason compositionally and only verify that the advice is harmless with respect to h?

Widening quantification, revisited Let us now consider a memoization aspect, with the following advice definition:

$$\begin{array}{l} \mathit{memo}\ \mathit{proceed}\ x = \\ \quad \mathbf{if}\ (\mathit{member}\ x\ \mathit{table})\ \mathbf{then}\ \mathit{table}\ [x] \\ \quad\quad\quad\quad \mathbf{else\ let}\ r = \mathit{proceed}\ x\ \mathbf{in} \\ \quad\quad\quad\quad\quad \mathit{insert}\ (\mathit{table}, x, r) \\ \quad\quad\quad\quad\quad r \end{array}$$

The advice maintains a reference to a lookup $table$ of precomputed values, indexed by argument x. If the result bound to x is already in the table, it is immediately returned. Otherwise the value is computed, stored in the table for future references, and returned.

It is intuitively clear that adding memoization on calls to f is harmless. In fact, if we manually apply $memo$ as a mixin on top of f, then we even know formally that it is harmless [22].

Now, if we follow the quantification widening scenario from above—which was harmless with the logging advice—is the harmlessness of memoization preserved?

$$s_5 = run\ [(\mathit{call}\ f \vee \mathit{call}\ g, \mathit{memo})]\ \mathit{prog}$$

The answer to the question actually depends on the context in which the advice is applied. In a context where f and g actually are the same function, or one of both is never applied, then harmlessness is preserved. But if f and g are different functions that are both applied, the behavior of the composed system is drastically affected because the same lookup table is used to store results from both functions!

Compositional reasoning The examples presented above illustrate that, in presence of quantification, it is generally not enough to establish local properties for aspects, but it is also required to reason about the context in which those aspects are applied. Therefore, the modular reasoning techniques developed in the case of MRI are not directly applicable in a setting with quantification, because some form of global reasoning is generally required.

But global reasoning need not be monolithic. The contribution of this work is to provide a formal framework to establish global equivalence properties in a compositional manner. Compositional reasoning facilitates the task of formally establishing properties about aspect-oriented programs. In practice, while it is possible to apply monolithic global reasoning to tiny systems like the ones considered in this section, this approach hardly scales to larger systems. Furthermore, compositional reasoning accomodates software evolution: it makes it possible to reuse previously-established results that are stable under the considered change scenarios.

3. Monads, Reasoning, and Monadic AOP

The compositional reasoning framework proposed in this work is formulated in a monadic setting. We first briefly review monads and monadic reasoning, and then describe a monadic formulation

$$
\begin{array}{lll}
\textbf{class } \mathit{Monad}\ m \textbf{ where} & \text{-- State} & \text{-- Writer} \\
\quad \mathit{return} :: a \to m\ a & \mathbb{S}_\mathrm{T} \quad :: \mathbb{S}_\mathrm{T}\ s\ m\ a & \mathbb{W}_\mathrm{T} \quad :: \mathbb{W}_\mathrm{T}\ w\ m\ a \\
\quad (\gg\!=) :: m\ a \to (a \to m\ b) \to m\ b & \mathit{run}\mathbb{S}_\mathrm{T} :: \mathbb{S}_\mathrm{T}\ s\ m\ a \to s \to m\ (a, s) & \mathit{run}\mathbb{W}_\mathrm{T} :: \mathbb{W}_\mathrm{T}\ w\ m\ a \to m\ (a, w) \\
\textbf{class } \mathit{MonadTrans}\ t \textbf{ where} & \pi_S \quad :: s \to \mathbb{S}_\mathrm{T}\ s\ m\ a \to m\ a & \pi_W \quad :: \mathbb{W}_\mathrm{T}\ w\ m\ a \to m\ a \\
\quad \mathit{lift} :: \mathit{Monad}\ m \Rightarrow m\ a \to t\ m\ a & \textbf{class } \mathit{Monad}\ m \Rightarrow \mathbb{S}_\mathrm{M}\ m \mid m \to s \textbf{ where} & \textbf{class } (\mathit{Monoid}\ w, \mathit{Monad}\ m) \Rightarrow \\
 & \quad \mathit{get} :: m\ s & \qquad \mathbb{W}_\mathrm{M}\ w\ m \mid m \to w \textbf{ where} \\
 & \quad \mathit{put} :: s \to m\ () & \quad \mathit{tell} :: w \to m\ ()
\end{array}
$$

Figure 1. Monads and monad transformer types used in this paper.

of AOP, which serves as the foundation for the formal development in the following sections.

3.1 Monads and Monadic Reasoning in a Nutshell

Monads are a denotational approach to modeling and reasoning about computational effects in pure functional languages [20, 28], and are widely used in Haskell. A monad is defined by a type constructor m and functions *bind* ($\gg\!=$ in Haskell) and *return*. At the type level a monad is a regular type constructor, although conceptually we distinguish a value of type a from a *computation in monad* m of type $m\ a$. Those computations produce values of the given type and may perform side effects, such as a mutable state and error handling. Additionally, monads provide a uniform interface for computational effects, as specified in the *Monad* type class (Figure 1). The *return* function promotes a value of type a into a computation of type $m\ a$. Computations are composed sequentially using the $\gg\!=$ operator. The concrete definitions of *return* and $\gg\!=$ depend on the computational effect being implemented.

Monad transformers A monad transformer is a type constructor that allows one to construct a *monad stack* that combines several effects [19]. The *MonadTrans* type class (Figure 1) defines an interface for monad transformers. The purpose of the *lift* operation is to promote a computation from an inner layer of the monad stack, of type $m\ a$, into a computation in the monad defined by the complete stack, with type $t\ m\ a$. Each specific transformer t must declare how to make $t\ m$ an instance of the *Monad* class.

Monadic programming in Haskell Monadic programming in Haskell is provided by the standard Monad Transformers Library (known as *mtl*), which defines a set of monad transformers that can be flexibly composed together. Throughout this paper we will use the state ($\mathbb{S}_\mathrm{T}$) and writer ($\mathbb{W}_\mathrm{T}$) monad transformers. In Figure 1 we summarize the types of their constructors ($\mathbb{S}_\mathrm{T}$,$\mathbb{W}_\mathrm{T}$), evaluation functions ($\mathit{run}\mathbb{S}_\mathrm{T}$, $\mathit{run}\mathbb{W}_\mathrm{T}$), and projection functions (π_S, π_W). The projection functions remove the corresponding effect from the monad stack (here, by discarding the threaded state or writer).

Polymorphism in the monad stack In addition to the particular monad transformers, the *mtl* defines a set of type classes associated to particular effects. This allows us to constrain a monad stack such that it presents a particular effect, while being polymorphic in the actual shape of the stack. Figure 1 shows the $\mathbb{S}_\mathrm{M}$ and $\mathbb{W}_\mathrm{M}$ classes that abstract the state and writer effects. The *get* operation retrieves the current value, which can be updated using *put*. Similarly, the *tell* operation appends a value w to its output. Note that the $\mathbb{S}_\mathrm{T}$ and $\mathbb{W}_\mathrm{T}$ transformers are the canonical instances of these type classes, and that the evaluation functions provide the initial values for these computations.

Equational reasoning and observational equivalence Equational reasoning is the process of transforming a program by replacing expressions in a manner similar to high-school algebra. Expression e_1 can be replaced by e_2 only if the two are *equivalent*. Observational equivalence, denoted as $\equiv$ in the paper, is an equivalence relation between expressions that holds whenever two expressions have the same observable behavior. That is, $e_1 \equiv e_2$ iff for every program context C, both $C[e_1]$ and $C[e_2]$ yield the same value, or both diverge. For example, consider the η-reduction rule from the λ-calculus, which states that $\lambda x \to f\ x \equiv f$ (when x is no free in f). Also, Haskell provides the **do** notation as syntactic sugar for $\gg\!=$, hence $\textbf{do}\ \{x \leftarrow f; g\ x\} \equiv f \gg\!= \lambda x \to g\ x$.

Monad laws Monad laws are crucial for equational reasoning in a monadic setting [28]. A proper monad is one that obeys the following three laws:

$$
\begin{array}{lll}
\mathit{return}\ x \gg\!= f & \equiv f\ x & \text{-- left identity} \\
p \gg\!= \mathit{return} & \equiv p & \text{-- right identity} \\
(p \gg\!= f) \gg\!= h & \equiv p \gg\!= \lambda x \to (f\ x \gg\!= h) & \text{-- associativity}
\end{array}
$$

The first two laws, left and right identity, state that *return* neither changes the value nor performs any computational effect. The associativity law states that only the order of computations is relevant in a $\gg\!=$ expression. In the same way, monad transformers need to satisfy the following laws:

$$
\begin{array}{lll}
\mathit{lift} \circ \mathit{return} & \equiv \mathit{return} & \text{-- identity preservation} \\
\mathit{lift}\ (m \gg\!= f) & \equiv \mathit{lift}\ m \gg\!= (\mathit{lift} \circ f) & \text{-- comp. preservation}
\end{array}
$$

Note that Haskell does not enforce that declared instances of the *Monad* or *MonadTrans* classes actually respect these laws. This has to be proven separately for each considered instance.

3.2 Monadic AOP

Our approach to compositional reasoning relies on a monadic formulation of AOP, but is independent from the concrete implementation of an aspectual computation monad transformer. Previous work by Tabareau *et al.* [26] develops a full-fledged polymorphic transformer. In Section 5, we describe a simple monomorphic implementation of the model, which we use to develop local reasoning about interference using the techniques of MRI [22].

In this section, we define an aspectual computation monad transformer denoted $\mathbb{A}_\mathrm{T}$ in an abstract manner, by prescribing its interface and properties. The theorem of compositional reasoning in Section 4 is established based on this abstract specification only.

Join point model We consider a join point model in which join points are function applications. In existing AOP languages, there are many ways by which pointcuts select advised entities: for instance, by name (*e.g.* method names in AspectJ [16], function names in AspectML [8]), by reference equality (*e.g.* AspectScheme [12], AspectScript [27]), by their type (*e.g.* AspectJ, AOHaskell [26]), using a mechanism to explicitly attach tags or types to join points (*e.g.* Ptolemy [24], JPIs [4]), etc.

Here, we abstract over these concrete design choices by introducing an abstract join point type, on which pointcuts predicate:

$$
\begin{array}{l}
\textbf{data } \mathit{Jp}\ m\ a\ b \\
\textbf{type } \mathit{Pc}\ m\ a\ b = \mathit{Jp}\ m\ a\ b \to \mathit{Bool}
\end{array}
$$

The type variables respectively denote the underlying monad stack, and the argument and return types of the applied function. The concrete representation of Jp can hold more information (*e.g.* contextual information, tags) or less, if some information is not meant to be used in pointcuts.

A denotational model cannot assume implicit generation of join points, so we require the presence of an *open application* operator $\#$ that takes a function of type $a \to \mathbb{A}_T\ m\ b$ and returns a function of the same type whose application produces a join point (this effect is encapsulated in the $\mathbb{A}_T$ monad transformer):

$$(\#) :: (a \to \mathbb{A}_T\ m\ b) \to (a \to \mathbb{A}_T\ m\ b)$$

An open application is realized explicitly using $\#$: $f\ \#\ 2$ is the same as $f\ 2$ except that the application generates a join point that is subject to aspect weaving. Note that, in general, there is no reason to assume a single manner to generate join points, so there can indeed be a *family* of operators $\#^i$, which are interpreted by the aspect weaver as needed. Finally, one can view a partial open application $f\ \#^i$ as an open function, whose application produces join points.

An advice is a function that executes in place of a join point matched by a pointcut. The first argument of the advice, typically called $proceed$, is a function which represents the original computation at the matched join point. An aspect simply pairs a pointcut with an advice.

$$\begin{array}{l}\mathbf{type}\ Advice\ m\ a\ b = (a \to m\ b) \to (a \to m\ b)\\ \mathbf{type}\ Aspect\ m\ a\ b = (Pc\ m\ a\ b, Advice\ m\ a\ b)\end{array}$$

Aspect environment The aspects to be deployed in a given aspectual computation are specified in a list of aspects called an *aspect environment*:

$\mathbf{type}\ AEnv\ m = ...$ -- an ADT to be specified

Supporting polymorphic aspects implies that the aspect environment should be an heterogeneous list. Preserving type safety of aspect weaving then requires some care, as discussed elsewhere [26]. In order to avoid accidental complexity, we do not consider this issue in this paper.

Aspectual computation Given a concrete $\mathbb{A}_T$ transformer, we require a function that evaluates an $\mathbb{A}_T$ computation given an aspect environment:

$$run\mathbb{A}_T :: Monad\ m \Rightarrow AEnv\ (\mathbb{A}_T\ m) \to \mathbb{A}_T\ m\ a \to m\ a$$

Abstracting open applications Similarly to the $\mathbb{S}_M$ and $\mathbb{W}_M$ type classes, we introduce a type class to define an abstract interface for performing open applications:

$$\begin{array}{l}\mathbf{class}\ Monad\ m \Rightarrow \mathbb{A}_M\ m\ \mathbf{where}\\ \quad \#^i :: (Int \to m\ Int) \to (Int \to m\ Int)\\ \mathbf{instance}\ Monad\ m \Rightarrow \mathbb{A}_M\ (\mathbb{A}_T\ m)\ \mathbf{where} \ldots\end{array}$$

The only operation of this class is $\#^i$, and we require that any monad $\mathbb{A}_T\ m$ be an instance of this class. Note that $\mathbb{A}_M$ allows a form of type-based reasoning about open applications: any function of type $\forall m.D\ m \Rightarrow a \to m\ b$, where D is a class constraint that does not entail $\mathbb{A}_M$, cannot perform any open applications (and hence cannot emit join points).

3.3 Necessary Properties of $\mathbb{A}_T$

To be a correct model, the $\mathbb{A}_T$ transformer needs to satisfy a number of properties. First, it has to satisfy the monad transformer laws, and when applied to any monad m, the monad laws must be satisfied as well.

Moreover, for all aspect environments $aenv$, the function $run\mathbb{A}_T\ aenv$ must be a *monad morphism*.

Definition 1. *A monad morphism h is a function of type*

$$h :: \forall a.M_1\ a \to M_2\ a$$

that transforms computations in one monad M_1 into computations in another monad M_2. The function satisfies two laws:

$$\begin{array}{rcll}h \circ return & \equiv & return & \\ h\ (m \gg\!= f) & \equiv & h\ m \gg\!= h \circ f & (\forall m, f)\end{array}$$

For $run\mathbb{A}_T$, the first monad is $\mathbb{A}_T\ m$ and the second monad is just m. Moreover, the two monad morphism laws have an intuitive meaning in this setting: the first law expresses that weaving has no impact on pure computations, and the second law expresses that weaving is compositional.[2]

In the same spirit, we also require that a third law holds for $run\mathbb{A}_T\ aenv$:[3]

$$run\mathbb{A}_T\ aenv \circ lift \equiv id$$

This law expresses that $run\mathbb{A}_T\ aenv$ is a left inverse of $lift$. In words, weaving an effectful computation that does not involve open applications has no impact.

These laws have to be established whenever a concrete $\mathbb{A}_T$ transformer is implemented. We will come back to this when presenting a simple $\mathbb{A}_T$ transformer in Section 5.

3.4 Running Example in Monadic Style

Section 2 used pseudo-code to describe a base program and aspects. In Haskell, the base program is defined in monadic style using the **do** notation as follows:

$$\begin{array}{l}prog\ x\ y = \mathbf{do}\ r_1 \leftarrow f\ \#^i\ x\\ \qquad\qquad\quad r_2 \leftarrow g\ \#^j\ y\\ \qquad\qquad\quad return\ (r_1 + r_2)\end{array}$$

The program can be run as an aspectual computation in the $\mathbb{A}_T$ transformer with a logging aspect on open applications of f as follows:

$$run\mathbb{A}_T\ [(fPc, log)]\ (prog\ 5\ 12)$$

The pointcut fPc is left undefined at this stage, since in this abstract model we do not prescribe a specific way to denote functions. The definitions of the log and $memo$ advices in monadic style is given in Figure 2. Their types reflect their side effects.

4. Compositional Reasoning, Formally

This section formalizes our approach to compositional reasoning about aspect interference. This approach revolves around the following general theorem, which provides a framework for the reasoning. The theorem considers an AOP $system$ that is run with respect to a particular aspect environment $aenv$. The theorem states that, under four sufficient conditions, the system preserves its observable behavior under an alternative aspect environment $aenv'$ that may introduce additional effects. With the four conditions it provides a step-by-step guide to proving non-interference.

A key property of the theorem is that it supports *compositional* reasoning. Compositionality is achieved because the theorem splits the system into two parts, an open function $f\ \#^i$ and a *context* c, whose conditions are independent, can be proven separately, and can be reused in different compositions. Moreover, the system

[2] If $\mathbb{A}_T$ supports dynamic deployment of aspects (as in [26]), weaving cannot be compositional. We can nevertheless prove the monad morphism laws for the static fragment, and deal with dynamic deployment on a case-by-case basis.

[3] This law actually subsumes the first monad morphism law, as $return \equiv lift \circ return$.

$$
\begin{array}{l}
\mathit{log} :: \mathbb{W}_{\mathrm{M}}\ \mathit{String}\ m \Rightarrow \mathit{Advice}\ m\ a\ b \\
\mathit{log}\ \mathit{proceed}\ x = \mathbf{do} \\
\quad \mathit{tell}\ \texttt{"Entering function ..."} \\
\quad \mathit{proceed}\ x \\
\mathit{memo} :: (\mathit{Ord}\ a, \mathbb{S}_{\mathrm{M}}\ (\mathit{Map}\ a\ b)\ m) \Rightarrow \mathit{Advice}\ m\ a\ b \\
\mathit{memo}\ \mathit{proceed}\ x = \mathbf{do} \\
\quad \mathit{table} \leftarrow \mathit{get} \\
\quad \mathbf{if}\ \mathit{member}\ x\ \mathit{table}\ \mathbf{then}\ \mathit{return}\ (\mathit{table}\ !\ x) \\
\quad\quad \mathbf{else\ do}\ y \leftarrow \mathit{proceed}\ x \\
\quad\quad\quad\quad\quad \mathit{table}' \leftarrow \mathit{get} \\
\quad\quad\quad\quad\quad \mathit{put}\ (\mathit{insert}\ x\ y\ \mathit{table}') \\
\quad\quad\quad\quad\quad \mathit{return}\ y
\end{array}
$$

Figure 2. Logging and memoization advice in monadic style.

can easily be decomposed into all the individual open functions (rather than just two parts) by repeated application of the theorem. In fact, the third condition below, which relates to the context, is an instance of the theorem and thus explicitly invites this systematic decomposition.

Theorem 1. *Given an expression:*

$$\mathit{system} :: \forall m.C\ m \Rightarrow A \rightarrow \mathbb{A}_T\ m\ B$$

Here A and B are some types, and m is a type variable constrained by some type class constraints C that at least require m to be an instance of Monad.

We assume that system is given in terms of the following decomposition:

$$\mathit{system} \equiv c\ (f\ \#^{i})$$

where c, f and i are arbitrary values of the following types (with C_f entailed by C; again A' and B' are some types):

$$
\begin{array}{l}
c :: \forall m.C\ m \Rightarrow (A' \rightarrow \mathbb{A}_T\ m\ B') \rightarrow A \rightarrow \mathbb{A}_T\ m\ B \\
f :: \forall m.C_f\ m \Rightarrow A' \rightarrow \mathbb{A}_T\ m\ B'
\end{array}
$$

Also, we are given two aspect environments $aenv$ and $aenv'$ of types:

$$
\begin{array}{l}
\mathit{aenv}\ \ :: \forall m.D\ m \Rightarrow \mathit{AEnv}\ (\mathbb{A}_T\ m) \\
\mathit{aenv}' :: \forall m.D\ m \Rightarrow \mathit{AEnv}\ (\mathbb{A}_T\ (T\ m))
\end{array}
$$

where T is some instance of MonadTrans and D is a type class constraint that requires m to be at least an instance of Monad.

The given projection function:

$$\pi :: \forall m\ a.\mathit{Monad}\ m \Rightarrow T\ m\ a \rightarrow m\ a$$

is a left-inverse of lift that removes the additional T effect from the monad stack $T\ m$.

If the four conditions on c and f given below hold, then we have that:

$$\mathit{run}\mathbb{A}_T\ \mathit{aenv}\ \mathit{system} \equiv \pi\ (\mathit{run}\mathbb{A}_T\ \mathit{aenv}'\ \mathit{system})$$

The four conditions on c and f are:

1. *Compositional weaving*

$$\forall \mathit{env}.\mathit{run}\mathbb{A}_T\ \mathit{env}\ (c\ (f\ \#^{i})) \equiv \mathit{run}\mathbb{A}_T\ \mathit{env}\ c\ (\mathit{lift} \circ \mathit{run}\mathbb{A}_T\ \mathit{env} \circ (f\ \#^{i}))$$

2. *Compositional projection*

$$\pi \circ \mathit{run}\mathbb{A}_T\ \mathit{aenv}' \circ c\ (\mathit{lift} \circ \mathit{lift} \circ \pi \circ \mathit{run}\mathbb{A}_T\ \mathit{aenv}' \circ (f\ \#^{i})) \equiv \pi \circ \mathit{run}\mathbb{A}_T\ \mathit{aenv}' \circ c\ (\mathit{lift} \circ \mathit{run}\mathbb{A}_T\ \mathit{aenv}' \circ (f\ \#^{i}))$$

3. *Contextual harmlessness*

$$\mathit{run}\mathbb{A}_T\ \mathit{aenv} \circ c \circ (\lambda g \rightarrow \mathit{lift} \circ g) \equiv \pi \circ \mathit{run}\mathbb{A}_T\ \mathit{aenv}' \circ c \circ (\lambda g \rightarrow \mathit{lift} \circ \mathit{lift} \circ g)$$

4. *Local harmlessness*

$$\mathit{run}\mathbb{A}_T\ \mathit{aenv} \circ (f\ \#^{i}) \equiv \pi \circ \mathit{run}\mathbb{A}_T\ \mathit{aenv}' \circ (f\ \#^{i})$$

Proof. The proof proceeds by straightforward equational reasoning:

$$
\begin{array}{l}
\quad \mathit{run}\mathbb{A}_T\ \mathit{aenv}\ \mathit{system} \\
\equiv\ \{\text{-system decomposition -}\} \\
\quad \mathit{run}\mathbb{A}_T\ \mathit{aenv}\ (c\ (f\ \#^{i})) \\
\equiv\ \{\text{-compositional weaving -}\} \\
\quad \mathit{run}\mathbb{A}_T\ \mathit{aenv} \circ c\ (\mathit{lift} \circ \mathit{run}\mathbb{A}_T\ \mathit{aenv} \circ f\ \#^{i}) \\
\equiv\ \{\text{-local harmlessness -}\} \\
\quad \mathit{run}\mathbb{A}_T\ \mathit{aenv} \circ c\ (\mathit{lift} \circ \pi \circ \mathit{run}\mathbb{A}_T\ \mathit{aenv}' \circ f\ \#^{i}) \\
\equiv\ \{\text{-contextual harmlessness -}\} \\
\quad \pi\ (\mathit{run}\mathbb{A}_T\ \mathit{aenv}' \circ c\ (\mathit{lift} \circ \mathit{lift} \circ \pi \circ \mathit{run}\mathbb{A}_T\ \mathit{aenv}' \circ f\ \#^{i})) \\
\equiv\ \{\text{-compositional projection -}\} \\
\quad \pi\ (\mathit{run}\mathbb{A}_T\ \mathit{aenv}' \circ c\ (\mathit{lift} \circ \mathit{run}\mathbb{A}_T\ \mathit{aenv}' \circ f\ \#^{i}) \\
\equiv\ \{\text{-compositional weaving -}\} \\
\quad \pi\ (\mathit{run}\mathbb{A}_T\ \mathit{aenv}'\ (c\ (f\ \#^{i}))) \\
\equiv\ \{\text{-system decomposition -}\} \\
\quad \pi\ (\mathit{run}\mathbb{A}_T\ \mathit{aenv}'\ \mathit{system})
\end{array}
$$

□

We now explain and illustrate how the theorem can be used.

4.1 System Decomposition

The starting point is to *view* the system as the composition of a particular function f and a context c. For instance, we can write our running example as $c_1\ (f_1\ \#^{i})$ where

$$
\begin{array}{l}
f_1 = f \\
c_1 = \lambda f\ x\ y \rightarrow \mathbf{do}\ r_1 \leftarrow f\ x \\
\qquad\qquad\qquad\quad\ \ r_2 \leftarrow g\ \#^{j}\ y \\
\qquad\qquad\qquad\quad\ \ \mathit{return}\ (r_1 + r_2)
\end{array}
$$

Here the context c_1 is just *system* abstracted over $f\ \#^{i}$. Note that the same *system* can be decomposed in many different ways, in order to focus on different open functions.

4.2 Compositional Weaving

The first condition states that weaving the composite system is equivalent to weaving the context c and the function f separately and then composing them.

While the compositional weaving condition is formulated in terms of the specific c and f, it comes *almost* for free from the three laws that $\mathit{run}\mathbb{A}_T\ \mathit{env}$ satisfies (recall Section 3.3).

To see why, let us consider the essential ways in which c can use f. There are two permitted ways:

1. c does nothing with f, and thus whether f is woven or not is inconsequential.

2. c invokes f (once or more), which means embedding it in its larger computation (once or more) with $\gg\!=$, which is where the second law comes in. Note that the second law can be used repeatedly to tackle a larger computation sequence $m \gg\!= f_1 \gg\!= \ldots \gg\!= f_n$.

However, there is also one way in which the condition can be violated:

3. The context c is itself weaving the open function with a custom aspect environment. One such example is:

$$c = \lambda f \to \mathit{lift} \circ \mathit{run}\mathbb{A}_{\mathrm{T}}\ [\,] \circ f$$

where c weaves the function with an empty aspect environment, irrespective of the aspect environment used to weave c itself.

This illegal use of f can be avoided by introducing a measure of parametricity. Instead of using the fixed monad transformer $\mathbb{A}_{\mathrm{T}}$ and its fixed function $\#^i$ in c and f, we make c and f parametric in the particular type and function definition. This parameterization is conveniently achieved by imposing the $\mathbb{A}_{\mathrm{M}}$ constraint on the monad stack instead of applying the $\mathbb{A}_{\mathrm{T}}$ transformer. It prevents c from invoking the weaving function $\mathit{run}\mathbb{A}_{\mathrm{T}}$ locally on f because $\mathit{run}\mathbb{A}_{\mathrm{T}}$ only works for $\mathbb{A}_{\mathrm{T}}\ m'$ and not for all possible m that instantiate $\mathbb{A}_{\mathrm{M}}$.

We summarize our technique for establishing compositional weaving in the following conjecture.

Conjecture 1. *Provided that f and c have the following polymorphic types:*

$$\begin{aligned} c &:: \forall m.(C\ \ m, \mathbb{A}_M\ m) \Rightarrow (A' \to m\ B') \to A \to m\ B \\ f &:: \forall m.(C_f\ \ m, \mathbb{A}_M\ m) \Rightarrow \ \ A' \to m\ B' \end{aligned}$$

the condition of compositional weaving holds.

We believe that this conjecture can be proven with logical relations, but that is out of the scope of this paper.

4.3 Compositional Projection

The second condition expresses that composing the projected context c and projected function f is equivalent to projecting the composition.

This condition has a similar shape as that for compositional weaving. Hence, in the case that the projection function π is a monad morphism, then the same solution as for compositional weaving applies. For instance, the projection π_W of the writer effect (used in the logging advice) is well-known (and easily verified) to be a monad morphism. This means that, if the system abstracts over the implementation of the writer effect with the type class constraint $\mathbb{W}_{\mathrm{M}}$, then its projection is indeed compositional.

However, it is a very strong requirement for the projection function to be a monad morphism. For instance, the projection π_S of the state effect is *not* a monad morphism:

$$\begin{aligned} \pi_S\ 0\ (\mathit{get} \gg\!= \lambda x \to \mathit{put}\ (x+1) \gg \mathit{get}) \ &\equiv\ \ \mathit{return}\ 1 \\ \pi_S\ 0\ (\mathit{get} \gg\!= \lambda x \to \mathit{put}\ (x+1)) \gg \pi_S\ 0\ \mathit{get} \ &\equiv\ \ \mathit{return}\ 0 \end{aligned}$$

This explains why we must be careful when adding the memo advice of Figure 2, which has a memo table as its state, to our running example. If the pointcut of this advice matches both the function f on the one hand and the function g in the context c on the other hand, then the two uses of the advice may interfere through the shared state. For instance, the result for $f\ 3$ may be stored in the table and later wrongly used as if it were the result for $g\ 3$. This problem is not discovered when we consider the impact of memo on c and f separately. On the contrary, memo is contextually and locally harmless, but globally harmful. We only discover this problem because compositional projection does not hold. This illustrates why compositional projection is a crucial condition.

In some cases, the use of memo in a larger system is nevertheless harmless. As we cannot take the monad morphism route to establishing this, we need to resort to alternative techniques.

- If the woven function $\mathit{run}\mathbb{A}_{\mathrm{T}}\ \mathit{aenv}' \circ (f\ \#^i)$ does not use the projected effect, then projection is indeed compositional. This is for instance the case when memo does not advise f. We can formally capture this as:

  $$\exists h, \mathit{lift} \circ h \equiv \mathit{run}\mathbb{A}_{\mathrm{T}}\ \mathit{aenv}' \circ (f\ \#^i)$$

  Let us now reason about the relevant part of the left-hand side of the condition:

  $$\begin{aligned} & \mathit{lift} \circ \mathit{lift} \circ \pi \circ \mathit{run}\mathbb{A}_{\mathrm{T}}\ \mathit{aenv}' \circ (f\ \#^i) \\ \equiv\ & \{\text{-assumption -}\} \\ & \mathit{lift} \circ \mathit{lift} \circ \pi \circ \mathit{lift} \circ h \\ \equiv\ & \{\text{-}\pi \text{ is left inverse of } \mathit{lift} \text{ -}\} \\ & \mathit{lift} \circ \mathit{lift} \circ h \\ \equiv\ & \{\text{-assumption -}\} \\ & \mathit{lift} \circ \mathit{run}\mathbb{A}_{\mathrm{T}}\ \mathit{aenv}' \circ (f\ \#^i) \end{aligned}$$

  If we plug this conclusion into the left-hand side of the compositional projection condition, we obtain its right-hand side. In other words, the condition follows from the assumption.

- The dual assumption from the above is that the context c does not use the projected effect. This is for instance the case when memo advises f but not c. Unfortunately, this case is not as straightforward. While c does not directly interfere with the effect, it may indirectly create interference by invoking f repeatedly and those invocations may interfere with one another through their shared effect. This requires reasoning about the compatibility of an advised f with itself. For instance, in the case of memo it is perfectly fine for multiple invocations of f to share the memo table; in fact, that is exactly the point of memoization. A counterexample is an advice that monitors whether a function is invoked at most n number of times, where n is the first input its called with, and raises an error when that limit is exceeded. This advice is perfectly fine for a function in isolation that takes n (recursive) calls, but when there are multiple separate invocations, then the error may be triggered inadvertently.

Note that we can safely memoize both f and g in our example, if separate tables are used. This amounts to using two instances of memo that each act on a different $\mathbb{S}_{\mathrm{T}}$ layer in the monad stack. In this setup, the state of the components is isolated from each other. Hence, this scenario involves the two classes of compositional projection discussed above.

4.4 Contextual Harmlessness

The third condition expresses that as far as the context c is concerned, the aspect environments aenv and aenv' are indistinguishable. There are various ways in which aenv and aenv' can be related for this to be true, for example:

- Unused aspects (pc, a), where the pointcut pc does not match any join point in c, can be freely added or removed.
- Two aspects (pc_1, a_1) and (pc_2, a_2) can be reordered if they either do not match on the same applications in c or their advices commute ($a_1 \circ a_2 \equiv a_2 \circ a_1$).
- The pointcut of an aspect can be replaced by one that matches the same join points in c.
- The advice of an aspect can be replaced by one that behaves in the same way with respect to c.

- Multiple aspects can be replaced simultaneously by another set of aspects that together behave in the same way on c, redistributing the work among themselves, *e.g.* splitting a predicate into two disjoint ones.

Note that the contextual harmlessness condition is a variant of the general theorem itself, but on a smaller system that only consists of the context c. Hence, it can be proven by recursively decomposing the context and invoking the general theorem on the two parts. This insight is essential to scale up our approach from a two-function system to arbitrarily complex systems.

For instance, in the running example we can build a simpler system from c_1, namely $c_1\ (\mathit{lift} \circ h)$, where $h :: C\ m \Rightarrow A' \rightarrow m\ B'$ is universally quantified. This form is *smaller* than the original system because it features fewer open applications; h's type is constrained to not feature any. The resulting system has the form:

$$\begin{aligned} \mathit{system}' = \lambda x\ y \rightarrow \textbf{do}\ & r_1 \leftarrow \mathit{lift}\ (h\ x) \\ & r_2 \leftarrow g\ \#^j\ y \\ & \mathit{return}\ (r_1 + r_2) \end{aligned}$$

which can be decomposed as $\mathit{system}' = c_2\ (f_2\ \#^j)$:

$$\begin{aligned} f_2 &= g \\ c_2 &= \lambda g\ x\ y \rightarrow \textbf{do}\ r_1 \leftarrow \mathit{lift}\ (h\ x) \\ &\qquad\qquad\qquad\quad r_2 \leftarrow g\ y \\ &\qquad\qquad\qquad\quad \mathit{return}\ (r_1 + r_2) \end{aligned}$$

Here we can consider the harmlessness of the extended environment aenv' separately for g and c_2. Note that since c_2 does not contain any more open applications, contextual harmlessness is trivally established for it.

4.5 Local Harmlessness

The fourth condition requires the harmlessness of the extended aspect environment aenv' with respect to a single function seen in isolation. In our recursively decomposed example, this means we can study the impact of aenv' on f and g individually.

We do not go into detail here, but devote Section 6 to adapting the techniques of MRI for proving this condition in our setting. These techniques involve both regular proofs based on equational reasoning over the actual implementations of function and advice, as well as the more lightweight parametricity-based techniques that only need to consider the types.

5. A Simple Monadic AOP Model

In order to illustrate concrete applications of compositional reasoning about aspect interference, we now describe a simple monomorphic monadic model of pointcut/advice AOP in Haskell. The model is a simplification of the monadic embedding of aspects of Tabareau *et al.* [26]. The main differences are that this model:

1. does not support polymorphic aspects; only functions of type $\mathit{Int} \rightarrow m\ \mathit{Int}$, for some monad m, are open to advice.
2. only has pure pointcuts, *i.e.* pointcuts that cannot use monadic effects.
3. uses an abstract syntax tree of computations that expose function applications as join points and turn it into a monad transformer.
4. does not support dynamic aspect deployment; $\mathbb{A}_\mathrm{T}$ computations are evaluated under a fixed aspect environment.
5. uses a more general model of *tagged* open weaving to specify quantification.

Section 8 discusses potential extensions to the model.

$$\begin{aligned} &\textbf{instance}\ \mathit{Monad}\ m \Rightarrow \mathit{Monad}\ (\mathbb{A}_\mathrm{T}\ m)\ \textbf{where} \\ &\quad \mathit{return} \;\; = \mathbb{A}_\mathrm{T} \circ \mathit{return} \circ \mathit{Return} \\ &\quad m \gg\!= f = \mathbb{A}_\mathrm{T}\ (\mathit{un}\mathbb{A}_\mathrm{T}\ m \gg\!= \lambda r \rightarrow \textbf{case}\ r\ \textbf{of} \\ &\qquad \mathit{Return}\ x \rightarrow \mathit{un}\mathbb{A}_\mathrm{T}\ (f\ x) \\ &\qquad \mathit{OpenApp}\ t\ g\ x\ k \rightarrow \\ &\qquad\quad \mathit{return}\ (\mathit{OpenApp}\ t\ g\ x\ (\lambda y \rightarrow k\ y \gg\!= f))) \\ &\textbf{instance}\ \mathit{MonadTrans}\ \mathbb{A}_\mathrm{T}\ \textbf{where} \\ &\quad \mathit{lift}\ ma = \mathbb{A}_\mathrm{T}\ (ma \gg\!= \lambda a \rightarrow (\mathit{return} \circ \mathit{Return})\ a) \end{aligned}$$

Figure 3. $\mathbb{A}_\mathrm{T}$ instances for the *Monad* and *MonadTrans* type classes.

5.1 An Embedding of Open Applications

We implement $\mathbb{A}_\mathrm{T}$ as a monad transformer that captures open function applications in a syntactic form.[4] The interpreter function $\mathit{run}\mathbb{A}_\mathrm{T}$ interprets the open applications by weaving them with the aspect environment.

Join point model Join points represent open function application. In order not to deal with function equality or type comparisons as in [26], we rely on *tagged* applications: pointcuts match join points based on tag equality (pcTag). Here, tags are just integers:

$$\begin{aligned} &\textbf{type}\ \mathit{Tag} = \mathit{Int} \\ &\textbf{data}\ \mathit{Jp}\ m\ a\ b = \mathit{Jp}\ \mathit{Tag} \\ &\mathit{pcTag}\ t\ (\mathit{Jp}\ t') = t \equiv t' \end{aligned}$$

Note that in this simple instantiation of monadic AOP, join points only embed the tag of an open application, and neither the applied function nor the argument.

Defining the monad transformer The $\mathbb{A}_\mathrm{T}$ transformer extends a given monad m with the ability to expose some open function applications. A computation $\mathbb{A}_\mathrm{T}\ m\ a$ is denoted by an alternating sequence of computations in the monad m and exposed open function applications starting with the former.

$$\begin{aligned} &\textbf{data}\ \mathbb{A}_\mathrm{T}\ m\ a = \mathbb{A}_\mathrm{T}\ \{\mathit{un}\mathbb{A}_\mathrm{T} :: m\ (\mathit{Result}\mathbb{A}_\mathrm{T}\ m\ a)\} \\ &\textbf{data}\ \mathit{Result}\mathbb{A}_\mathrm{T}\ m\ a \\ &\quad = \mathit{Return}\ a \\ &\quad \mid \mathit{OpenApp}\ \mathit{Tag} && \text{-- tag} \\ &\qquad\qquad (\mathit{Int} \rightarrow \mathbb{A}_\mathrm{T}\ m\ \mathit{Int}) && \text{-- function} \\ &\qquad\qquad \mathit{Int} && \text{-- argument} \\ &\qquad\qquad (\mathit{Int} \rightarrow \mathbb{A}_\mathrm{T}\ m\ a) && \text{-- continuation} \end{aligned}$$

The $\mathit{Result}\mathbb{A}_\mathrm{T}$ value indicates what comes next after an m computation. Either the computation is done, which is denoted by the *Return* constructor, or an open function application comes next, denoted by the *OpenApp* constructor. In particular, $\mathit{OpenApp}\ t\ g\ x\ k$ denotes the open application of g to x with tag t, followed by the continuation k that proceeds the computation with the result of the open application. Figure 3 shows the instances for the *Monad* and *MonadTrans* type classes. Observe that for open applications, $\gg\!=$ extends the corresponding continuation k with operation f.

Open Applications Function *openApp* creates the denotation of tagged open applications:

$$\mathit{openApp}\ t\ f\ x = \mathbb{A}_\mathrm{T}\ (\mathit{return}\ (\mathit{OpenApp}\ t\ f\ x\ \mathit{return}))$$

Because *return* is the left and right identity of $\gg\!=$, we use it as the continuation that proceeds with the result of the open application. Hence, in isolation, open applications provide a semantics-preserving connection point for composition through $\gg\!=$. Using *openApp*, $\mathbb{A}_\mathrm{T}$ can be declared as an instance of the $\mathbb{A}_\mathrm{M}$ type class:

[4] Our $\mathbb{A}_\mathrm{T}$ implementation is a close cousin of a free monad.

$$
\begin{array}{l}
\textbf{instance } \mathit{Monad}\ m \Rightarrow \mathbb{A}_M\ (\mathbb{A}_T\ m) \textbf{ where} \\
\quad f\ \#^t\ x = \mathit{openApp}\ t\ f\ x
\end{array}
$$

5.2 Running $\mathbb{A}_T$ Computations

We define the $run\mathbb{A}_T$ interpreter function which evaluates an $\mathbb{A}_T$ computation:

$$
\begin{array}{l}
run\mathbb{A}_T\ aenv\ m = un\mathbb{A}_T\ m \gg= go \textbf{ where} \\
\quad go\ (Return\ r) = return\ r \\
\quad go\ (OpenApp\ t\ f\ x\ k) = \\
\qquad un\mathbb{A}_T\ (weave\ f\ aenv\ (Jp\ t) \gg= \\
\qquad\quad \lambda woven\_f \rightarrow woven\_f\ x \gg= k) \gg= go
\end{array}
$$

This function is defined in terms of the locally-defined go function. In case of $Return\ r$ values, it simply unwraps and $returns$ value r. When it encounters an open application, it creates a join point $Jp\ t$ and uses the $weaver$ to apply the matching aspects deployed in $aenv$. This yields the $woven\_f$ function which is applied to argument x. The result of the application is given to continuation k, whose resulting computation is evaluated recursively using go.

5.3 Aspect Weaving

The weaver is defined recursively on the aspect environment as follows.

$$
\begin{array}{l}
weave :: Monad\ m \Rightarrow (Int \rightarrow m\ Int) \rightarrow AEnv\ m \rightarrow \\
\qquad\qquad\qquad\qquad Jp\ m\ Int\ Int \rightarrow m\ (Int \rightarrow m\ Int) \\
weave\ f\ [\,]\ \_ \qquad\qquad = return\ f \\
weave\ f\ ((pc, adv) : asps)\ jp = \\
\quad weave\ (\textbf{if}\ pc\ jp\ \textbf{then}\ (adv\ f)\ \textbf{else}\ f)\ asps\ jp
\end{array}
$$

For each aspect it applies the pointcut to the join point. Then it continues weaving on the rest of the aspect environment using either $(adv\ f)$ if the pointcut matches, or f otherwise.

5.4 Properties of $\mathbb{A}_T$

To exploit the general result of the previous section, we need to establish that $\mathbb{A}_T$ is a proper aspectual monad transformer that satisfies the necessary properties described in Section 3.

Lemma 1 (Monad laws for $\mathbb{A}_T$)**.** *$\mathbb{A}_T$ fulfills the monad transformer laws. In addition, for any monad m, $\mathbb{A}_T\ m$ fulfills the monad laws.*

Lemma 2 ($run\mathbb{A}_T$ monad morphism)**.** *For any aspect environment $aenv$, $run\mathbb{A}_T\ aenv$ is a monad morphism. Furthermore, it is also a left inverse of lift.*

The proofs proceed by straightforward co-induction and equational reasoning on the shape of the monadic composition, and are available in the companion technical report [13]. Crucially, the proofs rely on the monad and monad transformer laws for $\mathbb{A}_T$.

Given the importance of the compositionality of weaving (which corresponds to the second law of monad morphisms), we show its proof in Figure 4. This law is fundamental for the formalization of Section 4, as well as for the theorem of the following section. The proof consists of folding and unfolding the definitions of $run\mathbb{A}_T$, its internally-defined function go, and the $\gg=$ operation of $\mathbb{A}_T$; it also uses the monad laws on m, and the identity $un\mathbb{A}_T \circ \mathbb{A}_T \equiv \mathbb{A}_T \circ un\mathbb{A}_T \equiv id$. A crucial step is the application of the co-induction hypothesis, which allows us to start folding the definitions until its final form.

$$
\begin{array}{l}
run\mathbb{A}_T\ aenv\ (m \gg=_{\mathbb{A}_T} f) \\
\equiv \{\text{-unfold } \gg=_{\mathbb{A}_T} \text{-}\} \\
run\mathbb{A}_T\ aenv\ (\mathbb{A}_T\ (un\mathbb{A}_T\ m \gg=_m \lambda r \rightarrow \textbf{case}\ r\ \textbf{of} \\
\quad Return\ x \qquad\quad \rightarrow un\mathbb{A}_T\ (f\ x) \\
\quad OpenApp\ t\ x\ g\ k \rightarrow return_m\ (\\
\qquad OpenApp\ t\ x\ g\ (\lambda y \rightarrow k\ y \gg=_{\mathbb{A}_T} f)))) \\
\equiv \{\text{-unfold } run\mathbb{A}_T \text{ and } un\mathbb{A}_T \circ \mathbb{A}_T \equiv id\ \text{-}\} \\
(un\mathbb{A}_T\ m \gg=_m \lambda r \rightarrow \textbf{case}\ r\ \textbf{of} \\
\quad Return\ x \qquad\quad \rightarrow un\mathbb{A}_T\ (f\ x) \\
\quad OpenApp\ t\ x\ g\ k \rightarrow return_m \\
\qquad (OpenApp\ t\ x\ g\ (\lambda y \rightarrow k\ y \gg=_{\mathbb{A}_T} f))) \gg=_m go \\
\equiv \{\text{-associativity of } \gg=_m + \text{distributing } go \text{ over } \textbf{case}\ \text{-}\} \\
un\mathbb{A}_T\ m \gg=_m \lambda r \rightarrow \textbf{case}\ r\ \textbf{of} \\
\quad Return\ x \qquad\quad \rightarrow un\mathbb{A}_T\ (f\ x) \gg=_m go \\
\quad OpenApp\ t\ x\ g\ k \rightarrow return_m \\
\qquad (OpenApp\ t\ x\ g\ (\lambda y \rightarrow k\ y \gg=_{\mathbb{A}_T} f)) \gg=_m go \\
\equiv \{\text{-folding } run\mathbb{A}_T + un\mathbb{A}_T \circ \mathbb{A}_T \equiv id + \text{left identity} + go\ \text{-}\} \\
un\mathbb{A}_T\ m \gg=_m \lambda r \rightarrow \textbf{case}\ r\ \textbf{of} \\
\quad Return\ x \qquad\quad \rightarrow run\mathbb{A}_T\ aenv\ (f\ x) \\
\quad OpenApp\ t\ x\ g\ k \rightarrow un\mathbb{A}_T\ (\mathbb{A}_T\ (return_m \\
\qquad (OpenApp\ t\ x\ g\ (\lambda y \rightarrow k\ y \gg=_{\mathbb{A}_T} f)))) \gg=_m go \\
\equiv \{\text{-left identity of } m + \text{folding } run\mathbb{A}_T \text{-}\} \\
un\mathbb{A}_T\ m \gg=_m \lambda r \rightarrow \textbf{case}\ r\ \textbf{of} \\
\quad Return\ x \qquad\quad \rightarrow return\ x \gg=_m run\mathbb{A}_T\ aenv \circ f \\
\quad OpenApp\ t\ x\ g\ k \rightarrow run\mathbb{A}_T\ aenv \\
\qquad (\mathbb{A}_T\ (return_m\ (OpenApp\ t\ x\ g\ (\lambda y \rightarrow k\ y \gg=_{\mathbb{A}_T} f)))) \\
\equiv \{\text{-folding } \gg=_{\mathbb{A}_T} \text{-}\} \\
un\mathbb{A}_T\ m \gg=_m \lambda r \rightarrow \textbf{case}\ r\ \textbf{of} \\
\quad Return\ x \qquad\quad \rightarrow return\ x \gg=_m run\mathbb{A}_T\ aenv \circ f \\
\quad OpenApp\ t\ x\ g\ k \rightarrow run\mathbb{A}_T\ aenv \\
\qquad ((\mathbb{A}_T\ (return_m\ (OpenApp\ t\ x\ g\ k) \gg=_{\mathbb{A}_T} f))) \\
\equiv \{\text{-co-induction hypothesis -}\} \\
un\mathbb{A}_T\ m \gg=_m \lambda r \rightarrow \textbf{case}\ r\ \textbf{of} \\
\quad Return\ x \qquad\quad \rightarrow return\ x \gg=_m run\mathbb{A}_T\ aenv \circ f \\
\quad OpenApp\ t\ x\ g\ k \rightarrow run\mathbb{A}_T\ aenv \\
\qquad (\mathbb{A}_T\ (return_m\ (OpenApp\ t\ x\ g\ k))) \\
\quad \gg=_m run\mathbb{A}_T\ aenv \circ f \\
\equiv \{\text{-factoring } run\mathbb{A}_T\ aenv \circ f \text{ from the } \textbf{case} \text{ branches -}\} \\
un\mathbb{A}_T\ m \gg=_m \lambda r \rightarrow (\textbf{case}\ r\ \textbf{of} \\
\quad Return\ x \qquad\quad \rightarrow return\ x \\
\quad OpenApp\ t\ x\ g\ k \rightarrow run\mathbb{A}_T\ aenv \\
\qquad (\mathbb{A}_T\ (return_m\ (OpenApp\ t\ x\ g\ k)))) \\
\quad \gg=_m run\mathbb{A}_T\ aenv \circ f \\
\equiv \{\text{-associativity of } m\ \text{-}\} \\
(un\mathbb{A}_T\ m \gg=_m \lambda r \rightarrow \textbf{case}\ r\ \textbf{of} \\
\quad Return\ x \qquad\quad \rightarrow return\ x \\
\quad OpenApp\ t\ x\ g\ k \rightarrow run\mathbb{A}_T\ aenv \\
\qquad (\mathbb{A}_T\ (return_m\ (OpenApp\ t\ x\ g\ k)))) \\
\quad \gg=_m run\mathbb{A}_T\ aenv \circ f \\
\equiv \{\text{-unfolding of } run\mathbb{A}_T + un\mathbb{A}_T \circ \mathbb{A}_T \equiv id\ \text{-}\} \\
(un\mathbb{A}_T\ m \gg=_m \lambda r \rightarrow \textbf{case}\ r\ \textbf{of} \\
\quad Return\ x \qquad\quad \rightarrow return\ x \\
\quad OpenApp\ t\ x\ g\ k \rightarrow return_m \\
\qquad (OpenApp\ t\ x\ g\ k \gg=_m go)) \gg=_m run\mathbb{A}_T\ aenv \circ f \\
\equiv \{\text{-folding } go\ \text{-}\} \\
(un\mathbb{A}_T\ m \gg=_m go) \gg=_m run\mathbb{A}_T\ aenv \circ f \\
\equiv \{\text{-folding } run\mathbb{A}_T \text{-}\} \\
run\mathbb{A}_T\ aenv\ m \gg=_m run\mathbb{A}_T\ aenv \circ f
\end{array}
$$

Figure 4. Proof of the second monad morphism law for $run\mathbb{A}_T$.

6. Local Harmlessness

In Section 4, we have shown how the first three conditions of Theorem 1 can be met. This section develops local harmlessness results using the monadic AOP model of Section 5. We now discuss how local harmlessness of the updated aspect environment $aenv'$ with respect to the initial environment $aenv$ can be established in this setting. Concretely, we must prove that:

$$runA_T\ aenv \circ (f\ \#^i) \equiv \pi \circ runA_T\ aenv' \circ (f\ \#^i)$$

We observe that the problem of reasoning about aspect interference for an isolated function woven by aspects is directly analogous to the work of MRI in the model of mixins. Therefore, we can benefit from the established results of MRI in at least two ways:

- Translate AOP programs into the setting of MRI; establish the required program equivalence in this setting, and interpret this result back into the AOP model. This approach allows us to reuse directly all the theorems proven in the MRI model.
- Lift the reasoning techniques developed in MRI to the AOP setting, to establish similar harmlessness results. This path is potentially more general and avoids a translation to MRI, but it does entail the need to re-establish all theorems proven in the MRI model in the AOP model.[5]

Here, we adopt the first approach, leaving the second one as a possible line of future work.

AOP-MRI translation We present a commutative correspondence diagram that gives a high-level overview of the chosen technique. In this diagram, the local harmlessness condition of Theorem 1 is represented by path (d). Instead of proving this directly, the goal is to obtain (d) by the composition of paths (a), (b) and (c).

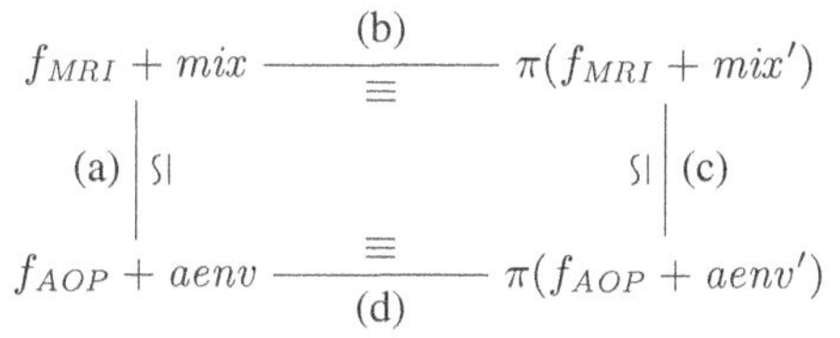

f_MRI + mix
(b)
≡
π(f_MRI + mix')
(a)
(c)
f_AOP + aenv
≡
(d)
π(f_AOP + aenv')

Starting from an AOP system composed by function f_{AOP} and aspect environment $aenv$, step (a) involves finding a function f_{MRI} and a mixin mix, such that their composition is equivalent to this initial system. In the same way, step (c) requires to find a mixin mix' equivalent to aspect environment $aenv'$. Given this, we can reuse the reasoning techniques and established results of MRI to determine the equivalence of step (b) between f_{MRI} composed with mix and the projection of f_{MRI} composed with mix'.

A drawback of this approach is that it is not known how to perform steps (a) and (c) in a general manner, because there are AOP programs that cannot be expressed using mixins, as illustrated later. Still, we can prove that a connection exists for a wide family of functions and aspect environments (Theorem 2 below).

We now briefly summarize the MRI model and prove a theorem connecting MRI to AOP. Then, using the Fibonacci function as a concrete example, we show how to prove that the logging and memoization aspects from Figure 2 are locally harmless.

6.1 Background: the MRI Framework

MRI models inheritance by the composition of mixins through open recursion. This inheritance model is defined as [22]:

```
type Open s = s → s
new :: Open s → s
new a = fix (λf → a f)
(⊕) :: Open s → Open s → Open s
a1 ⊕ a2 = λsuper → a1 (a2 super)
```

[5] Tabareau *et al.* [26] adapt the use of parametricity to enforce non-interference of pointcuts, advice and base programs to the AOP model, but formal results have not been established.

The type $Open\ s$ represents an open component of type s. new is a fixpoint combinator that closes, or instantiates, an open component that is potentially extended. Finally, the $\oplus$ operator defines component composition. The following diagram (taken from [22]) illustrates the inheritance model:

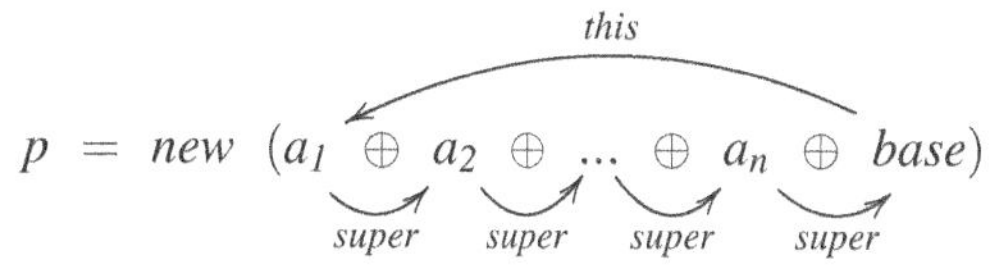

To create a component $\oplus$ instantiates $super$ references for every extended component, and new instantiates the self-reference $this$.

MRI formally captures the notion of *harmlessness* that has been used in this paper. Given a mixin mix and base component bse, then mix is harmless if:

$$\pi\ (new\ (mix \oplus bse)) \equiv run\mathbb{I} \circ new\ bse$$

for some projection π. Here $run\mathbb{I}$ is the projection of the identity monad, which has no computational effect.

MRI provides two harmless mixin theorems [22]. Using these theorems it is formally proven that logging is harmless for any arbitrary function. It is also proven that memoization is harmless when applied to the Fibonacci function. In the examples of next section we detail the specific techniques used in these proofs.

6.2 Connecting MRI to AOP

There is a direct connection between an advice and a mixin, as witnessed by the types of these entities: both type synonyms $Advice\ m\ a\ b$ and $Open\ (a \to m\ b)$ denote the same type $(a \to m\ b) \to (a \to m\ b)$. This reveals that any MRI mixin can be used as an advice. However the converse is not generally true if an advice performs open applications. For instance an aspect could trigger infinite regression by matching join points emitted on its own advice. However, if an advice uses a type class constraint that does not entail $\mathbb{A}_M$ (which means that it cannot perform any open application), this cannot happen.

To connect a base function f_{AOP} with an open recursive equivalent function, we need a stronger constraint. Namely, we ask that f_{AOP} is equivalent to the fixpoint of an open recursion f_{MRI} (that does not make use of open application) in the following way:

$$f_{AOP} \equiv fix\ (\lambda f \to f_{MRI}\ (f\ \#^t))$$

Putting these together, we can state a general theorem that relates MRI to AOP and eases considerably the establishment of steps (a) and (c) of the correspondence diagram.

Definition 2 (AOP agnostic function). *A function*

$$f :: \forall m.C\ m \Rightarrow (A \to m\ B) \to (A \to m\ B)$$

is AOP-agnostic *iff C is a type class constraint that entails $Monad$ but not $\mathbb{A}_M$. This means that the function does not emit join points.*

Theorem 2. *Given AOP-agnostic functions*

$$f_{MRI} :: \forall m.C\ m \Rightarrow (A \to m\ B) \to (A \to m\ B)$$
$$adv_i :: \forall m.D_i\ m \Rightarrow (A \to m\ B) \to (A \to m\ B)$$

and given an aspect environment

$$aenv = [(pcTag\ t_1, adv_1), ..., (pcTag\ t_n, adv_n)]$$

we have that

$$runA_T\ aenv \circ f_{AOP}\ \#^t \equiv new\ (adv'_k \oplus ... \oplus adv'_1 \oplus f_{MRI})$$

where f_{AOP} is such that

$$f_{AOP} \equiv fix\ (\lambda f \to f_{MRI}\ (f\ \#^t))$$

and $[adv'_1, ..., adv'_k] = [adv_i \mid pcTag\ t_i\ (Jp\ t) \equiv True]$ *is the list of all advices in* $aenv$ *whose* $pcTag\ t_i$ *pointcut matches* $\#^t$ *applications.*

Proof. The proof proceeds by equational reasoning and coinduction:

$$
\begin{aligned}
& run\mathbb{A}_T\ aenv \circ f_{AOP}\ \#^t \\
\equiv\ & \{\text{-definition of } f_{AOP}\text{ -}\} \\
& run\mathbb{A}_T\ aenv \circ fix\ (\lambda f \to f_{MRI}\ (f\ \#^t))\ \#^t \\
\equiv\ & \{\text{-unfolding of the fixpoint -}\} \\
& run\mathbb{A}_T\ aenv \circ f_{MRI}\ (f_{AOP}\ \#^t)\ \#^t \\
\equiv\ & \{\text{-compositionality of weaving -}\} \\
& run\mathbb{A}_T\ aenv \circ f_{MRI}\ (run\mathbb{A}_T\ aenv \circ f_{AOP}\ \#^t)\ \#^t \\
\equiv\ & \{\text{-co-induction hypothesis -}\} \\
& run\mathbb{A}_T\ aenv \circ f_{MRI}\ (new\ (adv'_k \oplus ... \oplus adv'_1 \oplus f_{MRI}))\ \#^t \\
\equiv\ & \{\text{-weaving -}\} \\
& adv'_k \circ ... \circ adv'_1 \\
& \qquad \circ f_{MRI}\ (new\ (adv'_k \oplus ... \oplus adv'_1 \oplus f_{MRI})) \\
\equiv\ & \{\text{-definition of } \oplus \text{ -}\} \\
& adv'_k \oplus ... \oplus adv'_1 \\
& \qquad \oplus f_{MRI}\ (new\ (adv'_k \oplus ... \oplus adv'_1 \oplus f_{MRI})) \\
\equiv\ & \{\text{-folding the } new \text{ fixpoint -}\} \\
& new\ (adv'_k \oplus ... \oplus adv'_1 \oplus f_{MRI})
\end{aligned}
$$

□

The same proof can be made for any model of AOP as described in Section 3; one just has to accommodate the proof according to the concrete way (in particular the ordering) in which aspects are woven.

Example that cannot use Theorem 2 We now present an aspect-oriented implementation of the Fibonacci function that cannot be translated into MRI by Theorem 2. In this example, taken from [1], the function is split into a base case that simply returns 1, and an advice that handles the recursive calls. The composed function $plainFib$ combines the base program and advice to provide the regular unoptimized version of Fibonacci.

$$
\begin{aligned}
& plainFib\ n = run\mathbb{A}_T\ [(pcTag\ t, fibAdv)]\ (fibBase\ \#^t\ n) \\
& fibBase\ \_ = return\ 1 \\
& fibAdv\ proceed\ n = \\
& \quad \mathbf{if}\ (n \leqslant 2)\ \mathbf{then}\ proceed\ n \\
& \qquad \mathbf{else\ do}\ f_1 \leftarrow fibBase\ \#^t\ (n-1) \\
& \qquad\qquad\quad f_2 \leftarrow fibBase\ \#^t\ (n-2) \\
& \qquad\qquad\quad return\ (f_1 + f_2)
\end{aligned}
$$

We cannot apply Theorem 2 because of the type of $fibAdv$. Since $fibAdv$ performs open applications of $fibBase$, its type necessarily contains a type class constraint that entails $\mathbb{A}_M$; thus violating the initial condition of Theorem 2. In fact, it does not seem possible to define $fibAdv$ using mixins, because the full aspect environment is woven upon each open application, whereas mixins can only execute the next component using $super$.

Applying the theorem We now present an example, using the Fibonacci function as a concrete value for f, on how to follow the steps of the correspondence diagram to prove the harmlessness of the logging and memoization advices of Figure 2. We consider the starting environment $aenv$ to be empty; and illustrate the case of adding each aspect individually. Figure 5 presents the Fibonacci function in the AOP and MRI models, along with their plain, logged and memoized versions.

6.3 Harmlessness of Logging

The local harmlessness of *log* applied to fib_{AOP} corresponds to the following lemma:

Lemma 3. $plainFib_{AOP} \equiv \pi_W \circ logFib_{AOP}$

Proof. Following the commutative correspondence diagram, by composition of Lemmas 4, 5 and 6. □

Step (a) We must translate $plainFib_{AOP}$ into MRI. We choose $plainFib_{MRI}$ as its translation, hence we must prove the following:

Lemma 4. $plainFib_{AOP} \equiv plainFib_{MRI}$

The proof is direct consequence of Theorem 2, using the equality

$$fib_{AOP} \equiv fix\ (\lambda f \to fib_{MRI}\ (f\ \#^t))$$

that can be proven by equational reasoning and induction on the integer argument.

Step (b) For the second step we need to prove:

Lemma 5. $plainFib_{MRI} \equiv \pi_W \circ logFib_{MRI}$

Here we benefit from the results of MRI. In MRI the local harmlessness of logging is proven for any arbitrary component, like fib_{MRI}; hence it holds for this particular case [22].

In fact the general harmlessness of logging is an application of the *harmless mixin theorem* of MRI [22]. This theorem is proven using: (i) parametricity to ensure that the base component cannot access the effects used by the mixin; (ii) a mixin combinator to guarantee that *super* is called exactly once, and that the arguments and return values are not modified; and (iii) the algebraic laws for monadic effects. Consequently, any mixin that satisfies this theorem is also harmless for functions that are AOP-agnostic (Definition 2).

Step (c) Finally, we prove the equivalence between $logFib_{AOP}$ and $logFib_{MRI}$:

Lemma 6. $\pi_W \circ logFib_{AOP} \equiv \pi_W \circ logFib_{MRI}$

Again, this is a direct consequence of Theorem 2.

6.4 Harmlessness of Memoization

Proving the harmlessness of memoization involves the same steps as that of logging. In this case we greatly benefit from the established results of MRI, because proving step (b) is rather complex.

The issue is that, conversely to logging, memoization is not harmless in general; hence this property must be proven for each particular function. The main difficulty of such a proof is to show that the function maintains an invariant on the memoization table: namely, that the stored values actually correspond to the results of the original function. In [22] this is proven for fib_{MRI}, developing a long equational reasoning proof—the Coq proof assistant is used to manage the complexity of the proof.

It is in complex situations like this that the interest of following the steps of the AOP-MRI correspondence diagram is justified. In addition, we can benefit from new results about harmlessness of specific mixins.

7. Related Work

There is a large body of work on modular reasoning and interference. Here, we only discuss the most directly related work; an extensive and recent review of the area, which also covers reasoning techniques in functional, object-oriented, and feature-oriented programming can be found in [22].

We have extensively related our work to the work on EffectiveAdvice [21] and its successor, MRI [22]. The present work

$$
\begin{array}{l}
\mathit{fib}_{AOP} :: \mathbb{A}_{\mathrm{M}}\ m \Rightarrow Int \rightarrow m\ Int \\
\mathit{fib}_{AOP}\ n = \textbf{case}\ n\ \textbf{of} \\
\quad 0 \rightarrow return\ 1 \\
\quad 1 \rightarrow return\ 1 \\
\quad \_ \rightarrow \textbf{do}\ y \leftarrow \mathit{fib}_{AOP}\ \#^t\ (n-1) \\
\qquad\qquad x \leftarrow \mathit{fib}_{AOP}\ \#^t\ (n-2) \\
\qquad\qquad return\ (x+y) \\
plainFib_{AOP} :: Monad\ m \Rightarrow Int \rightarrow m\ Int \\
plainFib_{AOP} = run\mathbb{A}_{\mathrm{T}}\ [\,] \circ \mathit{fib}_{AOP}\ \#^t \\
logFib_{AOP} :: Monad\ m \Rightarrow Int \rightarrow \mathbb{W}_{\mathrm{T}}\ String\ m\ Int \\
logFib_{AOP} = run\mathbb{A}_{\mathrm{T}}\ [(pcTag\ t, log')] \circ \mathit{fib}_{AOP}\ \#^t \\
memoFib_{AOP} :: Monad\ m \Rightarrow Int \rightarrow \mathbb{S}_{\mathrm{T}}\ (Map\ Int\ Int)\ m\ Int \\
memoFib_{AOP} = run\mathbb{A}_{\mathrm{T}}\ [(pcTag\ t, memo)] \circ \mathit{fib}_{AOP}\ \#^t
\end{array}
$$

$$
\begin{array}{l}
\mathit{fib}_{MRI} :: Monad\ m \Rightarrow Open\ (Int \rightarrow m\ Int) \\
\mathit{fib}_{MRI}\ this\ n = \textbf{case}\ n\ \textbf{of} \\
\quad 0 \rightarrow return\ 1 \\
\quad 1 \rightarrow return\ 1 \\
\quad \_ \rightarrow \textbf{do}\ y \leftarrow this\ (n-1) \\
\qquad\qquad x \leftarrow this\ (n-2) \\
\qquad\qquad return\ (x+y) \\
plainFib_{MRI} :: Monad\ m \Rightarrow Int \rightarrow m\ Int \\
plainFib_{MRI} = new\ \mathit{fib}_{MRI} \\
logFib_{MRI} :: Monad\ m \Rightarrow Int \rightarrow \mathbb{W}_{\mathrm{T}}\ String\ m\ Int \\
logFib_{MRI} = new \circ (log \oplus \mathit{fib}_{MRI}) \\
memoFib_{MRI} :: Monad\ m \Rightarrow Int \rightarrow \mathbb{S}_{\mathrm{T}}\ (Map\ Int\ Int)\ m\ Int \\
memoFib_{MRI} = new\ (memo \oplus \mathit{fib}_{MRI})
\end{array}
$$

Figure 5. Fibonacci function. Left: in the simple pointcut/advice model of Section 5. Right: in the MRI setting (taken from [22])

was motivated by the desire to bring the reasoning power of MRI to aspect-oriented programming with quantification. The monadic embedding of aspects in Haskell developed recently [26] is a practical programming system that extends EffectiveAdvice with quantification, but it does not describe how to do formal reasoning. Compared to the simple monadic AOP system presented in this paper, it supports polymorphic aspects while preserving type soundness thanks to anti-unification, and supports dynamic deployment of aspects. Scaling up this work to that more complete model of AOP is future work.

Kiczales and Mezini argue that strictly modular reasoning about programs written in the presence of quantification is not feasible, and introduce a notion of aspect-aware interfaces that rely on a global reasoning step to infer precise dependencies [17]. Aspect-aware interfaces have not been used to perform formal reasoning.

Aldrich introduced the concept of Open Modules [1] to allow modular reasoning on aspects. Technically, modularity is obtained by using a special module sealing operator that hides internal join points from external advices. While formally establishing modular reasoning results, the approach has strong limitations when it comes to dealing with realistic aspects because the model does not support effects. Also, proving the equivalence of two modules relies on "global" reasoning with unrestricted quantification; our framework could be used to enhance that part of the reasoning.

There is a vast literature on interference analysis in the setting of AOP. Starting from his pioneering work on superposition for distributed systems [14], Katz has later refined it to give a classification of aspects [15]. He distinguishes between spectative superposition (that amounts to harmlessness), regulative superposition (that can modify which actions occur, but cannot change the computation performed by an individual action) and invasive superposition (that can change anything).

Inspired by these categories, Djoko Djoko *et al.* [10] have recently proposed to capture observer, aborter and confiner aspects directly in the language under consideration. Namely for each category, they define a specific aspect language with the property that any aspect written in that language belongs to the category.

Rinard *et al.* [25] present a classification for different kinds of interference, using program analyses for automatic classification. No proofs are given that the analyses are actually correct.

Dantas and Walker define an object calculus extended with harmless advices [7]. In their work, harmless advice is advice that can only change the termination of a program and perform I/O operations. Harmlessness is guaranteed using a type-and-effect system related to information flow type systems that prevent information flow from advice to base component using protection domains. Their notion of harmlessness is a particular instance of the more general notion studied in MRI and in this work.

Douence *et al.* [11] present a formal approach to establish that two stateful aspects commute, and in that sense do not interfere. Their work, specific to stateful effect, is also based on equational reasoning, but the language under consideration is only partially defined and no theorem is stated.

A well-known situation of non-interference has been captured by Clifton and Leavens as *observers* [5]. They have later proposed an extension of AspectJ with annotations to control two forms of interference on control and heap effects [6]. The correctness of annotations is also checked using a type-and-effect system.

Translucid contracts use grey box specifications and structural refinements in verification to enforce control-flow properties [3]. Using the interference combinators of MRI, similar properties can be enforced at the level of types [22].

Krishnamurthi *et al.* present a technique for modular model checking of aspects [18]. Given a set of properties to satisfy and a fixed set of pointcuts, they generate sufficient conditions on the pointcuts themselves to enable modular verification.

Recently, Disenfeld and Katz define a compositional model checking method for events and aspects specification using temporal logic on event detection [9]. The technique is used to detect interference in systems where aspects may be activated during the execution of other aspects.

8. Conclusions and Future Work

In the pointcut/advice model of aspect-oriented programming, unrestricted quantification through pointcuts forces global reasoning. We show that such global reasoning can be compositional. Compositionality is crucial for formal reasoning to scale up to large systems; equivalence proofs are hard to develop, so they should be partially reused as much as possible when a system evolves. We develop a framework for compositional reasoning about interference, using monads to express and reason about effects in a pure functional setting.

We introduce a general equivalence theorem that relies on four sufficient conditions—namely compositional weaving, compositional projection of effects, contextual and local harmlessness—that can be proven and reused independently. We demonstrate how the framework can be used to reason about a variety of scenarios related to the evolution of aspect-oriented programs.

A promising line of future and ongoing research is to study means to strengthen compositional reasoning to achieve modular reasoning under certain scenarios. A first approach is to use parametricity. For instance, Tabareau *et al.* [26] use parametricity to define non-interfering pointcuts and advices, following the techniques of MRI [22]. Additionally, Tabareau *et al.* provide *protected pointcuts* as a mechanism to recover modular reasoning. However, the approach is not yet formalized.

Because, ultimately, unrestricted quantification is incompatible with modular reasoning, it is appealing to combine the coarse-grained modular reasoning provided by Open Modules [1] with our compositional reasoning techniques for reasoning about equivalence of modules.

Finally, the model of AOP presented in this paper is very simplified compared to that of [26]; hence an additional challenge is to scale the expressiveness of the model while preserving the results established in this paper.

Acknowledgments. This work was supported by the INRIA Associated Team REAL and FONDECYT Project 1110051, and by the Fund for Scientific Research - Flanders (FWO-Vlaanderen).

References

[1] J. Aldrich. Open modules: Modular reasoning about advice. In A. P. Black, editor, *Proceedings of the 19th European Conference on Object-Oriented Programming (ECOOP 2005)*, number 3586 in Lecture Notes in Computer Science, pages 144–168, Glasgow, UK, July 2005. Springer-Verlag.

[2] *Proceedings of the 9th ACM International Conference on Aspect-Oriented Software Development (AOSD 2010)*, Rennes and Saint Malo, France, Mar. 2010. ACM Press.

[3] M. Bagherzadeh, H. Rajan, G. T. Leavens, and S. Mooney. Translucid contracts: Expressive specification and modular verification for aspect-oriented interfaces. In *Proceedings of the 10th ACM International Conference on Aspect-Oriented Software Development (AOSD 2011)*, Porto de Galinhas, Brazil, Mar. 2011. ACM Press.

[4] E. Bodden, É. Tanter, and M. Inostroza. Join point interfaces for safe and flexible decoupling of aspects. *ACM Transactions on Software Engineering and Methodology*, 2014. To appear.

[5] C. Clifton and G. T. Leavens. Observers and assistants: A proposal for modular aspect-oriented reasoning. In *In FOAL Workshop*, 2002.

[6] C. Clifton, G. T. Leavens, and J. Noble. MAO: Ownership and effects for more effective reasoning about aspects. In E. Ernst, editor, *Proceedings of the 21st European Conference on Object-oriented Programming (ECOOP 2007)*, number 4609 in Lecture Notes in Computer Science, pages 451–475, Berlin, Germany, july/august 2007. Springer-Verlag.

[7] D. S. Dantas and D. Walker. Harmless advice. In *Proceedings of the 33rd ACM SIGPLAN-SIGACT Symposium on Principles of Programming Languages (POPL 2006)*, pages 383–396, Charleston, South Carolina, USA, Jan. 2006. ACM Press.

[8] D. S. Dantas, D. Walker, G. Washburn, and S. Weirich. AspectML: A polymorphic aspect-oriented functional programming language. *ACM Transactions on Programming Languages and Systems*, 30(3):Article No. 14, May 2008.

[9] C. Disenfeld and S. Katz. Specification and verification of event detectors and responses. In *Proceedings of the 12th annual international conference on Aspect-oriented software development*, AOSD '13, pages 121–132, New York, NY, USA, 2013. ACM.

[10] S. Djoko Djoko, R. Douence, and P. Fradet. Aspects preserving properties. *Science of Computer Programming*, 77(3):393 – 422, 2012.

[11] R. Douence, P. Fradet, and M. Südholt. Composition, reuse and interaction analysis of stateful aspects. In K. Lieberherr, editor, *Proceedings of the 3rd ACM International Conference on Aspect-Oriented Software Development (AOSD 2004)*, pages 141–150, Lancaster, UK, Mar. 2004. ACM Press.

[12] C. Dutchyn, D. B. Tucker, and S. Krishnamurthi. Semantics and scoping of aspects in higher-order languages. *Science of Computer Programming*, 63(3):207–239, Dec. 2006.

[13] I. Figueroa, T. Schrijvers, N. Tabareau, and É. Tanter. Compositional reasoning about aspect interference – extended with supplementary material. Technical Report TR/DCC-2013-8, Computer Science Department, University of Chile, Oct. 2013.

[14] S. Katz. A superimposition control construct for distributed systems. *ACM Trans. Program. Lang. Syst.*, 15(2):337–356, Apr. 1993.

[15] S. Katz. Aspect categories and classes of temporal properties. In A. Rashid and M. Aksit, editors, *Transactions on Aspect-Oriented Software Development I*, volume 3880 of *Lecture Notes in Computer Science*, pages 106–134. Springer Berlin Heidelberg, 2006.

[16] G. Kiczales, E. Hilsdale, J. Hugunin, M. Kersten, J. Palm, and W. Griswold. An overview of AspectJ. In J. L. Knudsen, editor, *Proceedings of the 15th European Conference on Object-Oriented Programming (ECOOP 2001)*, number 2072 in Lecture Notes in Computer Science, pages 327–353, Budapest, Hungary, June 2001. Springer-Verlag.

[17] G. Kiczales and M. Mezini. Aspect-oriented programming and modular reasoning. In *Proceedings of the 27th international conference on Software engineering (ICSE 2005)*, pages 49–58, St. Louis, MO, USA, 2005. ACM Press.

[18] S. Krishnamurthi, K. Fisler, and M. Greenberg. Verifying aspect advice modularly. In *Proceedings of the 12th ACM SIGSOFT International Symposium on Foundations of Software Engineering (FSE-12)*, pages 137–146, 2004.

[19] S. Liang, P. Hudak, and M. Jones. Monad transformers and modular interpreters. In *Proceedings of the 22nd ACM Symposium on Principles of Programming Languages (POPL 95)*, pages 333–343, San Francisco, California, USA, Jan. 1995. ACM Press.

[20] E. Moggi. Notions of computation and monads. *Information and Computation*, 93(1):55–92, July 1991.

[21] B. C. d. S. Oliveira, T. Schrijvers, and W. R. Cook. EffectiveAdvice: discplined advice with explicit effects. In AOSD 2010 [2], pages 109–120.

[22] B. C. D. S. Oliveira, T. Schrijvers, and W. R. Cook. MRI: Modular reasoning about interference in incremental programming. *Journal of Functional Programming*, 22:797–852, Nov. 2012.

[23] C. Prehofer. Semantic reasoning about feature composition via multiple aspect-weavings. In S. Jarzabek, D. C. Schmidt, and T. L. Veldhuizen, editors, *Proceedings of the 5th ACM SIGPLAN/SIGSOFT Conference on Generative Programming and Component Engineering (GPCE 2006)*, pages 237–242, Portland, Oregon, Oct. 2006. ACM Press.

[24] H. Rajan and G. T. Leavens. Ptolemy: A language with quantified, typed events. In J. Vitek, editor, *Proceedings of the 22nd European Conference on Object-oriented Programming (ECOOP 2008)*, number 5142 in Lecture Notes in Computer Science, pages 155–179, Paphos, Cyprus, July 2008. Springer-Verlag.

[25] M. Rinard, A. Salcianu, and S. Bugrara. A classification system and analysis for aspect-oriented programs. In *Proceedings of the 12th ACM Symposium on Foundations of Software Engineering (FSE 12)*, pages 147–158. ACM Press, 2004.

[26] N. Tabareau, I. Figueroa, and É. Tanter. A typed monadic embedding of aspects. In J. Kinzle, editor, *Proceedings of the 12th International Conference on Aspect-Oriented Software Development (AOSD 2013)*, pages 171–184, Fukuoka, Japan, Mar. 2013. ACM Press.

[27] R. Toledo, P. Leger, and É. Tanter. AspectScript: Expressive aspects for the Web. In AOSD 2010 [2], pages 13–24.

[28] P. Wadler. The essence of functional programming. In *Proceedings of the 19th ACM Symposium on Principles of Programming Languages (POPL 92)*, pages 1–14, Albuquerque, New Mexico, USA, Jan. 1992. ACM Press.

Reusable Components of Semantic Specifications

Martin Churchill Peter D. Mosses Paolo Torrini
Swansea University, Swansea, UK
martin.churchill@keble.oxon.org, {p.d.mosses, p.torrini}@swansea.ac.uk

Abstract

Semantic specifications of programming languages typically have poor modularity. This hinders reuse of parts of the semantics of one language when specifying a different language – even when the two languages have many constructs in common – and evolution of a language may require major reformulation of its semantics. Such drawbacks have discouraged language developers from using formal semantics to document their designs.

In the PLANCOMPS project, we have developed a component-based approach to semantics. Here, we explain its modularity aspects, and present an illustrative case study. Our approach provides good modularity, facilitates reuse, and supports co-evolution of languages and their formal semantics. It could be particularly useful in connection with domain-specific languages and language-driven software development.

Categories and Subject Descriptors F.3.2 [*Logics and Meanings of Programs*]: Semantics of Programming Languages; D.3.1 [*Programming Languages*]: Formal Definitions and Theory; D.2.13 [*Software Engineering*]: Reusable Software

Keywords modularity; reusability; co-evolution; component-based semantics; fundamental constructs; funcons; modular SOS.

1. Introduction

Various programming constructs are common to many languages. For instance, assignment statements, sequencing, conditional branching, loops and procedure calls are almost ubiquitous among languages that support imperative programming; expressions usually include references to declared variables and constants, arithmetic and logical operations on values, and function calls; and blocks are provided to restrict the scope of local declarations. The details of such constructs often vary between languages, both regarding their syntax and their intended behaviour, but sometimes they are identical.

Many constructs are also 'independent', in that their contributions to program behaviour are unaffected by the presence of other constructs in the same language. For instance, consider conditional expressions '$E_1 \mathbin{?} E_2 : E_3$'. How they are evaluated is unaffected by whether expressions involve variable references, side effects, function calls, process synchronisation, etc. In contrast, the behaviour of a loop may depend on whether the language includes break and continue statements.

We consider a semantic specification framework to have *good modularity* when independent constructs can be specified separately, once and for all. Such frameworks support verbatim reuse of the specifications of common independent constructs between different language specifications. They also reduce the amount of reformulation needed when languages evolve.

It is well known that various semantic frameworks do not have good modularity. For example, using structural operational semantics (SOS) [39] we might start by specifying the evaluation of conditional expressions as follows.

$$\boxed{E \rightarrow E'}$$

$$\frac{E_1 \rightarrow E_1'}{E_1 \mathbin{?} E_2 : E_3 \rightarrow E_1' \mathbin{?} E_2 : E_3} \quad (1)$$

$$\texttt{true} \mathbin{?} E_2 : E_3 \rightarrow E_2 \quad (2)$$

$$\texttt{false} \mathbin{?} E_2 : E_3 \rightarrow E_3 \quad (3)$$

The transition formula $E \rightarrow E'$ asserts the possibility of a step of the computation of the value of E such that, after making the step, E' remains to be evaluated. The inference rule (1) specifies that computing the value of '$E_1 \mathbin{?} E_2 : E_3$' involves computing the value of E_1; the axioms (2) and (3) specify how the computation proceeds after E_1 has computed the value `true` or `false`. If the computation of the value of E_1 does not terminate, neither does that of '$E_1 \mathbin{?} E_2 : E_3$'; if it terminates with a value other than `true` or `false`, the computation of '$E_1 \mathbin{?} E_2 : E_3$' is stuck: it cannot make any further steps.

If we are specifying the semantics of a simple imperative language, we would specify the evaluation of an assignment expression '$I = E$', assigning the value of E to a simple variable named I, as follows.

$$\boxed{\rho \vdash (E, \sigma) \rightarrow (E', \sigma')}$$

$$\frac{\rho \vdash (E, \sigma) \rightarrow (E', \sigma')}{\rho \vdash (I = E, \sigma) \rightarrow (I = E', \sigma')} \quad (4)$$

$$\rho \vdash (I = V, \sigma) \rightarrow (V, \sigma[\rho(I) \mapsto V]) \quad (5)$$

The environment ρ represents the current bindings of identifiers (e.g., to declared variables) and the store σ represents the values currently assigned to variables. The formula $\rho \vdash (E, \sigma) \rightarrow (E', \sigma')$ asserts that, after making the step, E' remains to be evaluated, and σ' reflects any side-effects. Axiom (5) specifies that when the value V of E has been computed, it is also the value of the enclosing expression; the resulting store σ' reflects the assignment of that value to the variable bound to I in ρ.

However, if conditional expressions are included in the same language as the above assignment expressions, conventional SOS requires their semantics to be specified using the same form of

MODULARITY '14, April 22–26, 2014, Lugano, Switzerland.
Copyright is held by the owner/author(s). Publication rights licensed to ACM.
ACM 978-1-4503-2772-5/14/04...$15.00.
http://dx.doi.org/10.1145/2577080.2577099

transition formulae, $\rho \vdash (E,\sigma) \rightarrow (E',\sigma')$, so we need to reformulate rules (1–3) as follows.

$$\frac{\rho \vdash (E_1,\sigma) \rightarrow (E_1',\sigma')}{\rho \vdash (E_1 \mathbin{?} E_2 : E_3,\sigma) \rightarrow (E_1' \mathbin{?} E_2 : E_3,\sigma')} \qquad (6)$$

$$\rho \vdash (\texttt{true} \mathbin{?} E_2 : E_3,\sigma) \rightarrow (E_2,\sigma) \qquad (7)$$

$$\rho \vdash (\texttt{false} \mathbin{?} E_2 : E_3,\sigma) \rightarrow (E_3,\sigma) \qquad (8)$$

In effect, we have to *weave* the extra arguments of the required transition formulae (here ρ, σ and σ') into the original rules.

Different SOS rules would be needed for specifying conditional expressions in other languages. For example, in a pure functional language, the transition formulae could be simply $\rho \vdash E \rightarrow E'$; in a process language, they would involve labels on transitions, e.g., $E \xrightarrow{a} E'$. The notation used to specify a language construct depends not only on the features of that particular construct, but also on the features of all the *other* constructs in the language. This flagrant disregard for modularity means that in conventional SOS, it is simply not possible to specify the semantics of conditional expressions (or any other programming constructs) once and for all.

A further issue affecting potential reuse of parts of language specifications is the common practice of using notation from the concrete syntax of a language when defining its semantics. For instance, the SOS rules illustrated above are based on the following fragment of a grammar for expressions:

$$E : \mathsf{exp} ::= \mathsf{exp} \mathbin{?} \mathsf{exp} : \mathsf{exp} \qquad (9)$$

Such grammars provide a concise and suggestive specification of the compositional structure of programs, and are generally preferred to the original style of abstract syntax specification developed by McCarthy [22]. They are typically highly ambiguous, but semantics is defined on abstract syntax trees, making it independent of parsing and disambiguation issues. Regarding modularity, however, the use of concrete terminal symbols entails that our SOS rules for '$E \mathbin{?} E : E$' cannot be directly reused for a language using different concrete syntax for conditional expressions, e.g., '$\texttt{if}\ E\ \texttt{then}\ E\ \texttt{else}\ E$'.

Without support for reuse and co-evolution, the development and subsequent revision of a formal semantics for a major programming language is inherently a huge effort, often regarded as disproportionate to the benefits [13].

Our component-based approach to semantics addresses both the above modularity issues. Its crucial novel feature is the introduction of an *open-ended* collection of so-called *fundamental constructs*, or *funcons*. Many of the funcons correspond closely to simplified language constructs. But in contrast to language constructs, each funcon has a fixed interpretation, which we specify, *once and for all,* using a modular variant of SOS called MSOS [28]. For example, the collection includes a funcon written '$\textbf{if-true}(E_1, E_2, E_3)$', whose interpretation corresponds directly to that of the language construct '$E_1 \mathbin{?} E_2 : E_3$' considered above.

To specify the semantics of a language, we translate all its constructs to funcons. Thanks to the closeness of funcons to language constructs, the translation is generally rather simple to specify. For instance, the translation of '$E_1 \mathbin{?} E_2 : E_3$' is trivial, simply using '**if-true**' to combine the translations of E_1, E_2, E_3; translation of conditional expressions that have a different type of condition involves inserting operations to test the value of E_1.

Each funcon has both static and dynamic semantics. Translation of a language to funcons therefore defines both the static and dynamic semantics of the language. Sometimes it is necessary to adjust the induced static semantics by inserting further funcons. For example, our '**if-true**' funcon requires its second and third arguments to have a common supertype, but the intended static semantics of '$E_1 \mathbin{?} E_2 : E_3$' might require checking for inclusion between the minimal types of E_2 and E_3. Funcons for making such static checks have vacuous dynamic semantics.

The funcon specifications are expected to be highly reusable components of language specifications. When the syntax or semantics of a language construct changes, however, the specification of its translation to funcons has to change accordingly (since we never change the semantics of funcons) so the translation specification itself is inherently not so widely reusable. We explain all this further, and provide some simple introductory examples, in Sect. 2.

The main contribution of this paper is in Sect. 3, where we illustrate the modularity and practical applicability of our approach by presenting excerpts from a case study: a component-based semantics of Caml Light [18]. This language is used for teaching functional programming, but also has imperative features. For selected language constructs, we give conceptual explanations of the funcons involved in their translations, and present the MSOS specifications of the semantics of the funcons. We have made the complete case study available online.[1] We have also tested the correspondence between our component-based semantics of Caml Light and the standard implementation of the language, by running programs using a (modular!) interpreter generated from the MSOS specifications of the funcons [1, 2]. Preliminary tool support for our language specifications is based on SDF [11] and Prolog; the PLanCompS project [38] is developing further tool support. We are also carrying out major case studies, to demonstrate the extent to which funcons can be reused in specifications of different languages.

Finally, we discuss related work and alternative approaches in Sect. 4, before concluding and outlining further work in Sect. 5.

2. Component-Based Semantics

In this section, we first explain the general concepts underlying *fundamental constructs* (*funcons*), giving some simple examples. We then consider how to specify translations from programming languages to funcons. Finally, we recall MSOS (a modular variant of SOS) and show how we use it to specify, once and for all, the static and dynamic semantics of funcons.

2.1 Funcon Syntax

As mentioned in the Introduction, many funcons correspond closely to simplified programming language constructs. However, each funcon has fixed syntax and semantics. For example, the funcon written $\textbf{assign}(E_1, E_2)$ always has the effect of evaluating E_1 to a variable, E_2 to a value (in any order), then assigning the value to the variable. In contrast, a language construct written '$E_1 = E_2$' may be interpreted as an assignment or as an equality test, depending on the language.

Signatures The *signature* of a funcon determines its name, how many arguments it takes (if any), the sort of each argument, and the sort of the result. For any sort X of values, let $\mathsf{comp}(X)$ be the sort of computations which, whenever they terminate normally, compute values of sort X. The following computation sorts reflect fundamental conceptual distinctions in programming languages.

- The sort of *commands* $\mathsf{comm} = \mathsf{comp}(\mathsf{skip})$ is for funcons that are executed for their effects: the sort skip has only one value.
- The sort of *expressions* $\mathsf{expr} = \mathsf{comp}(\mathsf{value})$ is for funcons that compute values of the language-dependent sort value (they might also have effects).
- The sort of *declarations* $\mathsf{decl} = \mathsf{comp}(\mathsf{env})$ is for funcons that compute environments, mapping identifiers to values.

[1] `www.plancomps.org/churchill2014`

assign(*var*, *value*)	: *comm*
assigned-value(*var*)	: *expr*
bound-value(*id*)	: *expr*
effect(*value*)	: *comm*
given	: *expr*
if-true(*boolean*, *comp*(X), *comp*(X))	: *comp*(X)
seq(*skip*, *comp*(X))	: *comp*(X)
supply(*value*, *comp*(X))	: *comp*(X)
while-true(*expr*, *comm*)	: *comm*

Table 1. Some funcon signatures

Note that *comp*(X) includes X as a subsort: we regard values as terminated computations.

Table 1 shows the signatures of some funcons. The funcons **if-true** (conditional choice), **seq** (sequencing) and **supply** (value-passing) are polymorphic: the sort variable X in their signatures may be instantiated (uniformly) with any value sort.

The following sorts used in Table 1 are all value sorts: *boolean* (the values **false** and **true**), *id* (identifiers, denoting values given by **bound-value**), *skip* (the value **skip**), *value* (all values) and *var* (imperative variables). Further value sorts include familiar data types such as *int* (the unbounded integers) and instances of generic data types such as *list*(X) and *map*(X, Y). Abstraction values of sort *abs*(X, Y) are formed from computations. New value sorts can be defined using algebraic data types and subsort inclusions.

Lifting We can lift operations from value sorts to computation sorts. For example, consider the negation operation **not**(*boolean*) : *boolean*. By lifting the signature to **not**(*expr*) : *expr* we can use **not** as a funcon. The value of **not**(E) is computed by first computing the value of E, then (provided that this is a *boolean* value) applying the negation operation. The same principle applies to funcons with a value sort argument, such as **assigned-value**. Its lifted signature is **assigned-value**(*expr*) : *expr*, and the computation of the argument value is followed by applying the original funcon to it. When we lift value operations and funcons with two or more value sort arguments, the argument values may be computed in any order; the funcons **given** and **supply** can be used to restrict to sequential evaluation of lifted arguments, when required, as illustrated below.

The lifted signatures determine a set of *well-sorted terms* for each sort. The well-sortedness of a funcon term is independent of its context.

2.2 Language Semantics

We next consider how to specify translations from programming languages to funcons. The translation of complete programs to funcon terms determines the static and dynamic semantics of the programs.

The starting point for specifying a translation to funcons is a context-free grammar for the abstract syntax of the source language. We define functions mapping abstract syntax trees generated by the grammar to terms of the appropriate computation sorts. The functions are compositional: the translation of a composite language construct is a combination of the translations of its components. We specify the translation functions inductively, by equations (much as in denotational semantics).

The following examples illustrate how to specify the translation of some simple language constructs to funcons. Their main purpose is to show the form of the equations used to define the translation functions. Section 3 provides excerpts from a component-based semantics for a complete language, demonstrating how our approach scales up, and how to translate some less straightforward language constructs to funcons.

Expressions Let *exp* be the nonterminal symbol for expressions in some programming language. We specify that the function *expr*⟦_⟧ translates abstract syntax trees generated by *exp* to funcon terms of sort *expr* thus:

expr⟦*exp*⟧ : *expr*

Using the name '*expr*' for both the function and its target sort makes it easy to see that our funcon terms below are well-sorted. Note that language constructs are always inside ⟦· · ·⟧, and funcons outside, so clashes of notation between them are insignificant. Let the meta-variable E, optionally subscripted and/or primed, range over abstract syntax trees generated by *exp*.

Recall the conditional expressions specified in SOS in Sect. 1. When their conditions are boolean-valued, the intended semantics of these expressions correspond exactly to the semantics of the funcon **if-true** (lifted from *boolean* to *expr* in its first argument), so we can specify their translation very simply indeed:

expr⟦E_1 ? E_2 : E_3⟧ =   [*exp* ::= *exp* ? *exp* : *exp*]
if-true(*expr*⟦E_1⟧, *expr*⟦E_2⟧, *expr*⟦E_3⟧) (10)

The variant where E_1 is a numerical expression can be specified by inserting the appropriate value operations to compute **true** when the value of E_1 is non-zero, and **false** otherwise:

expr⟦E_1 ? E_2 : E_3⟧ =
if-true(**not**(**equal**(*expr*⟦E_1⟧, 0)), *expr*⟦E_2⟧, *expr*⟦E_3⟧) (11)

Notice that the well-sortedness of the terms in the above equation comes from lifting the value operations **not** and **equal** to the computation sort *expr*. Lifting also allows the following straightforward translation of equality test expressions.

expr⟦E_1 == E_2⟧ =   [*exp* ::= *exp* == *exp*]
equal(*expr*⟦E_1⟧, *expr*⟦E_2⟧) (12)

To specify left-to-right evaluation of E_1, E_2, we can use the funcons **supply** and **given**, as follows.

expr⟦E_1 == E_2⟧ =
supply(*expr*⟦E_1⟧, **equal**(**given**, *expr*⟦E_2⟧)) (13)

When identifiers can be bound only to (imperative) variables, we translate an identifier I occurring in an expression so that it gives the value currently assigned to the variable:

expr⟦I⟧ =   [*exp* ::= *id*]
assigned-value(**bound-value**(*id*⟦I⟧)) (14)

If identifiers can also be bound to other sorts of values, we use a funcon (not illustrated here) that inspects the assigned value when its argument is a variable, and otherwise returns its argument.

Statements Let *stm* be the nonterminal symbol for statements S in some programming language. The corresponding sort of funcons is *comm* (commands), so we use the following translation function.

comm⟦*stm*⟧ : *comm*

An assignment statement 'I = E ;' corresponds to a straightforward combination of the **assign** and **bound-value** funcons:

comm⟦I = E ;⟧ =   [*stm* ::= *id* = *exp* ;]
assign(**bound-value**(*id*⟦I⟧), *expr*⟦E⟧) (15)

The following translation of assignment *expressions* illustrates repeated use of a previously computed value.

$\mathit{expr}[\![I = E]\!] =$ $\boxed{\mathit{exp} ::= \mathit{id} = \mathit{exp}}$

$$\textbf{supply}(\mathit{expr}[\![E]\!], \textbf{seq}(\textbf{assign}(\textbf{bound-value}(\mathit{id}[\![I]\!]), \textbf{given}), \textbf{given})) \quad (16)$$

The combination of assignment expressions and the following expression-statements (which discard the value of E) makes the separate specification of assignment *statements* in (15) redundant.

$\mathit{comm}[\![E\ ;]\!] =$ $\boxed{\mathit{stm} ::= \mathit{exp}\ ;}$

$$\textbf{effect}(\mathit{expr}[\![E]\!]) \quad (17)$$

Our translation of if-else statements uses the same polymorphic **if-true** funcon as that of conditional expressions above:

$\boxed{\mathit{stm} ::= \texttt{if (}\ \mathit{exp}\ \texttt{)}\ \mathit{stm}\ \texttt{else}\ \mathit{stm}}$

$\mathit{comm}[\![\texttt{if(}\ E\ \texttt{)}\ S_1\ \texttt{else}\ S_2]\!] =$

$$\textbf{if-true}(\mathit{expr}[\![E]\!], \mathit{comm}[\![S_1]\!], \mathit{comm}[\![S_2]\!]) \quad (18)$$

For if-then statements without an else-part, we can exploit the usual 'desugaring', which we specify by the following equation.

$\mathit{comm}[\![\texttt{if(}\ E\ \texttt{)}\ S]\!] =$ $\boxed{\mathit{stm} ::= \texttt{if (}\ \mathit{exp}\ \texttt{)}\ \mathit{stm}}$

$$\mathit{comm}[\![\texttt{if(}\ E\ \texttt{)}\ S\ \texttt{else}\ \{\ \}]\!] \quad (19)$$

Provided that we do not introduce circularity between such equations, they give the effect of translating a language to a kernel sublanguage, followed by translation of the kernel constructs to funcons. When the grammar of the kernel is of particular interest, we could exhibit it, and separate the specification of desugaring from the specification of the translation of the kernel to funcons.

The translation of the empty statement '{ }' used above is as simple as one might expect:

$\mathit{comm}[\![\{\ \}]\!] =$ $\boxed{\mathit{stm} ::= \{\ \}}$

$$\textbf{skip} \quad (20)$$

While-statements correspond exactly to our **while-true** funcon (without any lifting):

$\mathit{comm}[\![\texttt{while(}\ E\ \texttt{)}\ S]\!] =$ $\boxed{\mathit{stm} ::= \texttt{while (}\ \mathit{exp}\ \texttt{)}\ \mathit{stm}}$

$$\textbf{while-true}(\mathit{expr}[\![E]\!], \mathit{comm}[\![S]\!]) \quad (21)$$

Our final illustrative example of specifying translations demonstrates a technique used frequently in our Caml Light case study in Sect. 3. Statement sequences may consist of more than two statements, but our **seq** funcon for sequencing commands takes only two arguments. In the following equation, we use '$\cdots$' *formally* as a meta-variable ranging over *stm** (possibly-empty sequences of statements).

$\mathit{comm}[\![S_1\ S_2\ \cdots]\!] =$ $\boxed{\mathit{stm} ::= \mathit{stm}\ \mathit{stm}^{+}}$

$$\textbf{seq}(\mathit{comm}[\![S_1]\!], \mathit{comm}[\![S_2\ \cdots]\!]) \quad (22)$$

To translate a sequence of just two statements, '$S_1\ S_2\ \cdots$' matches '$\cdots$' with the empty sequence, and we can then regard '$S_2\ \cdots$' as a single statement, whose translation is specified by our other equations. To translate a sequence of three or more statements, '$S_1\ S_2\ \cdots$' matches '$\cdots$' with a non-empty sequence, and we can use the above equation recursively to translate '$S_2\ \cdots$'. For instance, the above equations translate a sequence of the form '$S_1\ S_2\ S_3$' to a funcon term $\textbf{seq}(C_1, \textbf{seq}(C_2, C_3))$, where each C_i is the translation of the single statement S_i.

We give many further examples of specifying translations from language constructs to funcons in Sect. 3.

2.3 Funcon Semantics

The preceding subsections illustrate how we use sorts and signatures to specify the syntax of funcons, and how we specify translation functions that map programs to funcon terms. We now explain how to specify the semantics of each funcon, once and for all.

MSOS Modular SOS [28] is a simple variant of structural operational semantics (SOS). It allows a particularly high degree of reuse without any need for reformulation. The specification of each language construct in MSOS is independent of the features of the other constructs included in the language. This is achieved by incorporating all auxiliary entities used in transition formulae (environments, stores, etc.) in *labels* on transitions. Thus transition formulae for expressions are always of the form $E \xrightarrow{L} E'$ (and similarly for other sorts of constructs).

The MSOS notation for labels ensures automatic propagation of all *unmentioned* auxiliary entities between the premise(s) and conclusion of each rule. For this to work, the labels on adjacent steps of a computation are required to be *composable*, and a set of *unobservable* labels is distinguished.[2]

For example, the following MSOS rules for conditional expressions '$E_1\ ?\ E_2 : E_3$' could be used for both imperative and for purely functional languages:

$\boxed{E \xrightarrow{L} E'}$

$$\frac{E_1 \xrightarrow{L} E_1'}{(E_1\ ?\ E_2 : E_3) \xrightarrow{L} (E_1'\ ?\ E_2 : E_3)} \quad (23)$$

$$(\texttt{true}\ ?\ E_2 : E_3) \xrightarrow{\tau} E_2 \quad (24)$$

$$(\texttt{false}\ ?\ E_2 : E_3) \xrightarrow{\tau} E_3 \quad (25)$$

The variable τ varies over all *unobservable* labels. By not mentioning specific auxiliary entities, the rules assume neither their presence nor their absence, ensuring reusability. This also makes the rules significantly simpler to read.

The MSOS rules for assignment expressions are as follows.

$\boxed{E \xrightarrow{L} E'}$

$$\frac{E \xrightarrow{L} E'}{(I = E) \xrightarrow{L} (I = E')} \quad (26)$$

$$(I = V) \xrightarrow{\rho, \sigma, \sigma' = \sigma[\rho(I) \mapsto V], \tau} V \quad (27)$$

The notation used on the transition arrow in (27) above indicates that when assignment expressions are included in a language, the labels on transitions are to have an environment ρ and a pair of stores σ, σ'. The inclusion of τ in a label specifies that any further components must be unobservable.

If we include the above conditional expressions and assignment expressions in the same language, no changes at all are needed – in marked contrast to the weaving that would be required in SOS, as illustrated in Sect. 1.

I-MSOS Although MSOS successfully addresses the modularity issues of SOS, the requirement to label all transitions is an unwelcome notational burden. The *Implicitly-Modular SOS (I-MSOS)* framework [34] combines the benefits of MSOS regarding reusability with the familiar notational style of ordinary SOS: auxiliary entities not actually mentioned in a rule are implicitly propagated between its premise(s) and conclusion *without* requiring the introduction of explicit labels on transitions.

[2] In fact labels in MSOS are the morphisms of a *category*, and the unobservable labels are identity morphisms.

All that is needed is to declare the notation used for the transition formulae being specified (which is in any case normal practice in SOS descriptions of programming languages, e.g. [37]), distinguishing any required auxiliary arguments from the syntactic source and target of transitions. Here, we do this by insisting on some notational conventions commonly followed in SOS:

- Environments ρ (and any other entities that are *preserved* by successive transitions) are written before a turnstile, e.g., $\mathsf{env}\,\rho \vdash E \rightarrow E'$.
- Stores σ (and any other entities that can be *updated* by transitions) are written after the syntactic source and target, e.g., $(E, \mathsf{store}\,\sigma) \rightarrow (E', \mathsf{store}\,\sigma')$.
- Signals ε (and any other entities *emitted* by transitions) are written as labels on transition symbols, e.g., $E \xrightarrow{\mathsf{exception}\,\varepsilon} E'$.

The markers such as env, store and exception are used in case further entities are needed in the same position.

The I-MSOS rules for conditional expressions are formulated *exactly* as (1–3) in Sect. 1; those for assignment expressions need to be augmented with 'store' markers, but entities propagated between the premise and conclusion of a rule can be left implicit:

$$\boxed{\mathsf{env}\,\rho \vdash (E, \mathsf{store}\,\sigma) \rightarrow (E', \mathsf{store}\,\sigma')}$$

$$\frac{E \rightarrow E'}{(I = E) \rightarrow (I = E')} \tag{28}$$

$$\mathsf{env}\,\rho \vdash (I = V, \mathsf{store}\,\sigma) \rightarrow (V, \mathsf{store}\,\sigma[\rho(I) \mapsto V]) \tag{29}$$

When specifying funcons, the so-called 'patience' rules for evaluation of lifted arguments are left implicit, which significantly improves the conciseness of our specifications. For instance, the second argument V_2 of **assign** below (30) can be lifted from *value* to *expr*, but the rule for its patient evaluation, corresponding to (28), does not need to be given.

It is straightforward to generate MSOS rules directly from I-MSOS rules (and label categories from transition formulae declarations). The foundations of MSOS [28], together with its recently developed modular bisimulation theory and congruence format [7], provide correspondingly modular foundations for I-MSOS specifications.

Typing Rules MSOS and I-MSOS can also be used to specify typing rules, allowing auxiliary entities such as typing contexts to be left implicit in most rules. Typing formulae such as $E : T$ are similar to big-step evaluation formulae, where an expression (statically) computes a type. Following convention, we denote the current typing context by Γ. When specifying typing rules for a funcon with arguments of value sorts, the arguments are lifted to expressions.

I-MSOS Specifications of Funcons The following I-MSOS rules define the semantics of the funcons whose signatures are listed in Table 1. In these rules the meta-variable C ranges over *comm*, D over *decl*, E over *expr*, T over *type*, V over *value*, and X over arbitrary computations (including their computed values).

Assignment commands: $\boxed{(C, \mathsf{store}\,\sigma) \rightarrow (C', \mathsf{store}\,\sigma')}$

$$(\mathbf{assign}(V_1, V_2), \mathsf{store}\,\sigma) \rightarrow (\mathbf{skip}, \mathsf{store}\,\sigma[V_1 \mapsto V_2]) \tag{30}$$

$$\boxed{C : \mathbf{comm}}$$

$$\frac{E_1 : \mathbf{var}(T),\ E_2 : T}{\mathbf{assign}(E_1, E_2) : \mathbf{comm}} \tag{31}$$

A well-typed command has a unique type, written **comm**.

Variable references: $\boxed{(E, \mathsf{store}\,\sigma) \rightarrow (E', \mathsf{store}\,\sigma')}$

$$(\mathbf{assigned\text{-}value}(V), \mathsf{store}\,\sigma) \rightarrow (\sigma(V), \mathsf{store}\,\sigma) \tag{32}$$

$$\boxed{E : T}$$

$$\frac{E : \mathbf{var}(T)}{\mathbf{assigned\text{-}value}(E) : T} \tag{33}$$

Identifier references: $\boxed{\mathsf{env}\,\rho \vdash E \rightarrow E'}$

$$\mathsf{env}\,\rho \vdash \mathbf{bound\text{-}value}(I) \rightarrow \rho(I) \tag{34}$$

$$\boxed{\mathsf{env}\,\Gamma \vdash E : T}$$

$$\mathsf{env}\,\Gamma \vdash \mathbf{bound\text{-}value}(I) : \Gamma(I) \tag{35}$$

Side-effects: $\boxed{C \rightarrow C'}$

$$\mathbf{effect}(V) \rightarrow \mathbf{skip} \tag{36}$$

$$\boxed{C : \mathbf{comm}}$$

$$\frac{E : T}{\mathbf{effect}(E) : \mathbf{comm}} \tag{37}$$

Given value: $\boxed{\mathsf{given}\,V \vdash E \rightarrow E'}$

$$\mathsf{given}\,V \vdash \mathbf{given} \rightarrow V \tag{38}$$

$$\boxed{\mathsf{given}\,T \vdash E : T'}$$

$$\mathsf{given}\,T \vdash \mathbf{given} : T \tag{39}$$

Conditional choice: $\boxed{E \rightarrow E'}$

$$\mathbf{if\text{-}true}(\mathbf{true}, X_1, X_2) \rightarrow X_1 \tag{40}$$

$$\mathbf{if\text{-}true}(\mathbf{false}, X_1, X_2) \rightarrow X_2 \tag{41}$$

$$\boxed{E : T}$$

$$\frac{E : \mathbf{boolean},\ X_1 : T,\ X_2 : T}{\mathbf{if\text{-}true}(E, X_1, X_2) : T} \tag{42}$$

Sequencing: $\boxed{C \rightarrow C'}$

$$\mathbf{seq}(\mathbf{skip}, X) \rightarrow X \tag{43}$$

$$\boxed{C : \mathbf{comm}}$$

$$\frac{C : \mathbf{comm},\ X : T}{\mathbf{seq}(C, X) : T} \tag{44}$$

Supplying a value: $\boxed{\mathsf{given}\,V \vdash X \rightarrow X'}$

$$\frac{\mathsf{given}\,V \vdash X \rightarrow X'}{\mathsf{given}\,\_ \vdash \mathbf{supply}(V, X) \rightarrow \mathbf{supply}(V, X')} \tag{45}$$

$$\mathsf{given}\,\_ \vdash \mathbf{supply}(V_1, V_2) \rightarrow V_2 \tag{46}$$

$$\boxed{\mathsf{given}\,T \vdash X : T'}$$

$$\frac{\mathsf{given}\,T_1 \vdash E : T \qquad \mathsf{given}\,T \vdash X : T'}{\mathsf{given}\,T_1 \vdash \mathbf{supply}(E, X) : T'} \tag{47}$$

While-loops: $\boxed{C \to C'}$

$$\textsf{while-true}(E, C) \to \\ \textsf{if-true}(E, \textsf{seq}(C, \textsf{while-true}(E, C)), \textsf{skip}) \quad (48)$$

$\boxed{C : \textsf{comm}}$

$$\frac{E : \textsf{boolean},\ C : \textsf{comm}}{\textsf{while-true}(E, C) : \textsf{comm}} \quad (49)$$

Soundness Funcons have signatures specifying the maximal sorts in which each argument and the resulting terms are contained, with respect to a natural subtyping relation. Value sorts (as an open-ended set), together with types of the form $\mathit{abs}(T_1, T_2)$ (corresponding to abstractions at the typing level) define syntactic types that can be used to type funcon terms, thus making it possible to specify inductively minimal sorts of computed values. Each funcon is associated to a typing rule which allows us to derive typing judgements for all the related terms, given a typing assignment for the identifiers in the environment (i.e., a typing context). Well-formed terms, constructed by application of funcons to arguments according to their signatures, are meant to be those that can be typed.

We have polymorphism, needed for languages such as Caml Light and Java, and deal with it by simply allowing for identifiers that represent type variables, mapped to types by the environment. The type of a funcon term thus depends on the typing context, as well as on type parameters. For example, the funcon **bound-value** has a typing rule such that when the argument I (an identifier) is assigned type T in the typing context Γ, $\textsf{bound-value}(I)$ also has type T – this holds when T is a value sort such as *bool*, as well as when it is a type expression depending on type variables.

All the dynamic rules for the funcons used in our component-based semantics of Caml Light are type preserving. This guarantees type soundness, in the sense that if the translation of a Caml Light expression to a funcon term has type T and it computes a value V, then V is included in the set of values determined by T.

3. An Illustrative Case Study

Caml Light descends from Caml, a predecessor of the language *OCaml*, and is similar to the core of Standard ML [24]. It has first-class functions, assignable state, exception handling mechanisms, and pattern matching. It is statically typed, and supports algebraic data types and polymorphism.

The syntax and semantics of Caml Light are specified in its reference manual [18]. It contains a formal context-free grammar of 'concrete abstract syntax': this generates Caml Light programs, but disambiguation details are abstracted away. However, the explanation it gives of the intended semantics is completely informal.

In this section, after introducing the syntax of Caml Light, we illustrate our approach by presenting excerpts from a component-based semantics of the language. Section 3.2 gives an overview of the required values and funcons; Sect. 3.3 specifies the translation of Caml Light abstract syntax (trees) into combinations of funcons; and Sect. 3.4 specifies the static and dynamic semantics of the funcons using I-MSOS. The full specifications can be found online.[3]

3.1 Caml Light

Caml Light is a language built around *expressions* which compute values, including numbers, strings, function abstractions, tuples and lists. Commands (or statements) are not a separate syntactic category, but rather expressions that compute a particular null value, written `()`. Expressions are given a type, which includes ground types (e.g. `int`), tuple types (e.g. `int*int`) and function type (e.g. `int->int`). Commands and `()` have type `unit`.

[3] `www.plancomps.org/churchill2014`

```
let rec (fib : int -> int) = fun n ->
  if n < 2 then n else fib(n-1) + fib(n-2);;

let rec append zs ys =
  match zs with
  | [] -> ys
  | x::xs -> x::(append xs ys);;

let insertion_sort a =
  for i = 1 to array_length a - 1 do
    let val_i = a.(i) in
    let j = ref i in
    while !j > 0 & val_i < a.(!j - 1) do
      a.(!j) <- a.(!j - 1);
      j := !j - 1
    done;
    a.(!j) <- val_i
  done;;
```

Table 2. Example Caml Light programs

Some example Caml Light programs can be found in Table 2. First, we see a recursively defined Fibonacci function `fib`, with the explicit type `int->int`. The function is defined using the `fun` constructor, introducing a closed function abstraction. Identifiers may be bound to particular values within an expression using `let` bindings, and recursive functions using the `let rec` construct. Formal arguments can also appear as parameters before the '`=`', as in the definitions of `append` and `insertion_sort`.

As well as expressions, values and types, Caml Light supports matching values against *patterns* which bind identifiers. This is demonstrated in the `append` example, where the first argument `zs` is matched against two patterns: the empty list `[]`, and the list-constructor pattern `x::xs`, which binds `x` to the head and `xs` to the tail of a nonempty list.

Caml Light also supports imperative behaviour, as can be seen in the `insertion_sort` example, acting on an array. Arrays are mutable: their content may be updated. An assignable reference cell is constructed using `ref`, and it may be accessed using explicit dereferencing '`!`' and updated using '`:=`'. In this example we also see two different looping constructs.

An extract of the Caml Light reference grammar is given in Table 3 (using meta-variables as nonterminal symbols, for brevity).

3.2 Values and Funcons

In Sect. 2, we introduced some basic funcons for commands and expressions. We next consider the further funcons used in our Caml Light case study, involving declarations, abstractions, patterns and exception handling. They are listed in Table 4, together with their signatures. We discuss their semantics informally here, focusing on dynamic semantics; see Sect. 3.4 for their formal specifications, including static semantics.

Declarations We bind an identifier to a particular value in a declaration using the **bind-value** funcon. To limit the visibility of a declaration to an arbitrary computation, we use the **scope** funcon, which is lifted to act on declarations in its first argument.

Abstractions Values of sort *func* are function abstractions which compute a value from a given value: $\mathit{func} = \mathit{abs}(\mathit{value}, \mathit{value})$. Such abstractions can be constructed using the binary **abs** constructor, which abstracts an expression over a given pattern. They can be turned into self-contained function closures using the **close** funcon, to ensure static scoping. Abstractions may be applied to argument values using the **apply** funcon. The abstraction $\textsf{prefer-over}(A_1, A_2)$ applies A_1, but then applies A_2 if A_1 fails.

Constants

$$C ::= \texttt{()} \mid \texttt{[]} \mid \textit{literals for numbers, characters, strings}$$

Expressions

$$\begin{aligned} E ::= {} & I \mid C \mid \texttt{(} E \texttt{)} \mid \texttt{begin}\, E \,\texttt{end} \mid \texttt{(} E \texttt{:} T \texttt{)} \\ & \mid E\ (\texttt{,} E)^{+} \mid K\ E \mid E \texttt{::} E \mid \texttt{[} E\ (\texttt{;} E)^{*} \texttt{]} \\ & \mid \texttt{[|} E\ (\texttt{;} E)^{*} \texttt{|]} \mid \texttt{\{} L \texttt{=} E\ (\texttt{;} L \texttt{=} E)^{*} \texttt{\}} \\ & \mid E\ E \mid Op\ E \mid E\ Op\ E \mid E\ \texttt{\&}\ E \mid E\ \texttt{or}\ E \\ & \mid E \texttt{.} L \mid E \texttt{.} L \texttt{<-} E \mid E \texttt{.(} E \texttt{)} \mid E \texttt{.(} E \texttt{)} \texttt{<-} E \\ & \mid \texttt{if}\, E \,\texttt{then}\, E\ (\texttt{else}\, E)^{?} \mid \texttt{while}\, E \,\texttt{do}\, E \,\texttt{done} \\ & \mid \texttt{for}\, I \texttt{=} E\ (\texttt{to} \mid \texttt{downto})\ E \,\texttt{do}\, E \,\texttt{done} \\ & \mid E \texttt{;} E \mid \texttt{match}\, E \,\texttt{with}\, SM \mid \texttt{fun}\, MM \\ & \mid \texttt{function}\, SM \mid \texttt{try}\, E \,\texttt{with}\, SM \\ & \mid \texttt{let}\ (\texttt{rec})^{?}\ LB\ (\texttt{and}\, LB)^{*}\ \texttt{in}\, E \end{aligned}$$

Simple Matchings

$$SM ::= P \texttt{->} E\ (\texttt{|}\ P \texttt{->} E)^{*}$$

Multiple Matchings

$$MM ::= P^{+} \texttt{->} E\ (\texttt{|}\ P^{+} \texttt{->} E)^{*}$$

Let Bindings

$$LB ::= P \texttt{=} E \mid I\ P^{+} \texttt{=} E$$

Patterns

$$\begin{aligned} P ::= {} & I \mid \texttt{\_} \mid P\, \texttt{as}\, I \mid \texttt{(} P \texttt{)} \mid \texttt{(} P \texttt{:} T \texttt{)} \mid P \texttt{|} P \\ & \mid C \mid K\ P \mid P\ (\texttt{,} P)^{+} \mid \texttt{[]} \mid P \texttt{::} P \\ & \mid \texttt{[} P\ (\texttt{;} P)^{*}\ \texttt{]} \mid \texttt{\{} L \texttt{=} P\ (\texttt{;} L \texttt{=} P)^{*} \texttt{\}} \end{aligned}$$

Type Expressions

$$T ::= \texttt{'} I \mid \texttt{(} T \texttt{)} \mid T \texttt{->} T \mid T\ (\texttt{*} T)^{+}$$

Table 3. An extract of the Caml Light reference grammar, with EBNF replaced by $\cdot^{*}$, $\cdot^{+}$, $\cdot^{?}$, and nonterminals by meta-variables (I ranges over identifiers, K over constructors, and L over labels)

Patterns A pattern is another sort of abstraction, computing an environment from a given value: *patt* = *abs*(*value*, *env*). An example pattern is **any**, which matches any value and produces no bindings, accurately modelling the '_' wildcard in Caml Light. The funcon **only** takes a value and matches just that value, again producing no bindings. The pattern **bind**(I) matches any value, and binds I to it. Compound patterns may be constructed out of more primitive patterns. For example, if F is a binary data constructor, the pattern **invert** F (P_1, P_2) will match values of the form $F(X,Y)$ provided X matches P_1 and Y matches P_2, combining the generated bindings.

Exceptions The computation **throw**(V) terminates abruptly, and so can be seen to compute a value of any sort, vacuously. The **catch** funcon handles abrupt termination of its first argument by applying a function to the thrown value. The **catch-else-rethrow** funcon is a variant on this: it rethrows the exception should it fail to be in the domain of the handler.

abs(*expr*)	: *func*
abs(*patt*, *expr*)	: *func*
accum(*env*, *decl*)	: *decl*
any	: *patt*
apply(*func*, *value*)	: *expr*
bind(*id*)	: *patt*
bind-value(*id*, *value*)	: *decl*
catch(*expr*, *func*)	: *expr*
catch-else-rethrow(*expr*, *func*)	: *expr*
close(*func*)	: *expr*
closure(*comp*(X), *env*)	: *comp*(X)
else(*comp*(X), *comp*(X))	: *comp*(X)
generalise-all(*decl*)	: *decl*
instantiate-if-poly(*expr*)	: *expr*
invert F (*patt*, ..., *patt*)	: *patt*
match(*value*, *patt*)	: *decl*
only(*value*)	: *patt*
patt-union(*patt*, *patt*)	: *patt*
prefer-over(*abs*(X, Y), *abs*(X, Y))	: *abs*(X, Y)
restrict-domain(*abs*(X, Y), *type*)	: *abs*(X, Y)
scope(*env*, *comp*(X))	: *comp*(X)
throw(*exception*)	: *comp*(X)
when-true(*boolean*, *comp*(X))	: *comp*(X)

Table 4. Funcon signatures (see also Table 1)

id⟦I⟧	: *id*	Identifiers
value⟦C⟧	: *value*	Constants
expr⟦E⟧	: *expr*	Expressions
abs⟦SM⟧	: *abs*	Simple Matchings
decl⟦LB⟧	: *decl*	Let Bindings
patt⟦P⟧	: *patt*	Patterns
type⟦T⟧	: *type*	Type Expressions

Table 5. Translation function signatures

3.3 Language Semantics

We translate Caml Light (abstract syntax trees) into funcon trees. The signatures of the translation functions are listed in Table 5. For Caml Light, the *value* sort contains ground constants (integers, Booleans, strings, floats, chars) as well as records (maps, wrapped in a data constructor), variants for disjoint unions (a value tagged with a constructor), tuples, and functions (as abstractions).

We next show some of the equations specifying the translation of Caml Light programs to funcon terms. We will first consider dynamic semantics, specifying a translation which captures the intended runtime behaviour. Often, this translation will also capture the static semantics correctly (since each funcon by design has a natural combination of dynamic and static semantics). If it does not, we may need to add funcons to the translation to reflect the intended compile-time behaviour.

3.3.1 Dynamic Semantics

Conditional Caml Light's conditional construct on Booleans is translated straightforwardly into the **if-true** funcon we have already seen:

$$\mathit{expr}[\![\texttt{if}\ E_1\ \texttt{then}\ E_2\ \texttt{else}\ E_3]\!] = \mathbf{if\text{-}true}(\mathit{expr}[\![E_1]\!], \mathit{expr}[\![E_2]\!], \mathit{expr}[\![E_3]\!]) \quad (50)$$

Note that here we are lifting **if-true** to be applied to computations that *might* compute a Boolean in the first argument, from the base signature $\mathbf{if\text{-}true}(\mathit{boolean}, \mathit{comp}(X), \mathit{comp}(X)) : \mathit{comp}(X)$.

Lifting can also be applied to pure data operations, such as $\mathbf{not}(\mathit{boolean}) : \mathit{boolean}$.

$$\mathit{expr}[\![\texttt{not}\ E_1]\!] = \mathbf{not}(\mathit{expr}[\![E_1]\!]) \quad (51)$$

We also use the **if-true** funcon to provide meaning to other productions, e.g., Caml Light's Boolean 'and' operator:

$$\mathit{expr}[\![E_1\ \texttt{\&}\ E_2]\!] = \mathbf{if\text{-}true}(\mathit{expr}[\![E_1]\!], \mathit{expr}[\![E_2]\!], \mathbf{false}) \quad (52)$$

Sequencing The sequencing construct of Caml Light is translated as follows:

$$\mathit{expr}[\![E_1\ ;\ E_2]\!] = \mathbf{seq}(\mathbf{effect}(\mathit{expr}[\![E_1]\!]), \mathit{expr}[\![E_2]\!]) \quad (53)$$

Here, we explicitly discard the computed value of the first expression, using the **effect** funcon.

Pattern matching We translate Caml Light's simple matching construct SM to a function abstraction using $\mathit{abs}[\![\_]\!]$. Our analysis of a match expression is as an application of such an abstraction to the matched expression, inserting **prefer-over** to take into account what happens when the pattern fails to match the given value:

$$\mathit{expr}[\![\texttt{match}\ E\ \texttt{with}\ SM]\!] = \mathbf{apply}(\mathbf{prefer\text{-}over}(\mathit{abs}[\![SM]\!], \mathbf{abs}(\mathbf{any}, \mathbf{throw}(\texttt{'Match\_failure'}))), \mathit{expr}[\![E]\!]) \quad (54)$$

Function application The funcon **apply** corresponds directly to Caml Light's call-by-value function application:

$$\mathit{expr}[\![E_1\ E_2]\!] = \mathbf{apply}(\mathit{expr}[\![E_1]\!], \mathit{expr}[\![E_2]\!]) \quad (55)$$

The signature of **apply** indicates that it should be applied to an abstraction and an argument *value*, which is then lifted to take a computation argument. We would specify call-by-name semantics by forming a (parameterless) abstraction from the argument expression, to prevent its premature evaluation.

Function abstraction Caml Light is a functional language, and we represent functions as abstraction values. We use the **close** funcon to specify static bindings, and also specify what should happen if the simple matching SM fails to match the given argument.

$$\mathit{expr}[\![\texttt{function}\ SM]\!] = \mathbf{close}(\mathbf{prefer\text{-}over}(\mathit{abs}[\![SM]\!], \mathbf{abs}(\mathbf{any}, \mathbf{throw}(\texttt{'Match\_failure'})))) \quad (56)$$

Simple matchings We will next see how $\mathit{abs}[\![\_]\!]$ translates simple matchings SM to abstractions. For a single body, the binary **abs** funcon captures matchings accurately; sequences of simple matchings are combined using **prefer-over**.

$$\mathit{abs}[\![P_1\ \texttt{->}\ E_1]\!] = \mathbf{abs}(\mathit{patt}[\![P_1]\!], \mathit{expr}[\![E_1]\!]) \quad (57)$$

$$\mathit{abs}[\![P_1\ \texttt{->}\ E_1\ \texttt{|}\ P_2\ \texttt{->}\ E_2\ \cdots]\!] = \mathbf{prefer\text{-}over}(\mathit{abs}[\![P_1\ \texttt{->}\ E_1]\!], \mathit{abs}[\![P_2\ \texttt{->}\ E_2\ \cdots]\!]) \quad (58)$$

Declarations Local declarations are provided in Caml Light by the '`let` LB `in` E' construct, corresponding to the **scope** funcon:

$$\mathit{expr}[\![\texttt{let}\ LB\ \texttt{in}\ E]\!] = \mathbf{scope}(\mathit{decl}[\![LB]\!], \mathit{expr}[\![E]\!]) \quad (59)$$

Value-definitions are translated to declarations:

$$\mathit{decl}[\![P\ \texttt{=}\ E]\!] = \mathbf{match}(\mathit{expr}[\![E]\!], \mathbf{prefer\text{-}over}(\mathit{patt}[\![P]\!], \mathbf{abs}(\mathbf{any}, \mathbf{throw}(\texttt{'Match\_failure'})))) \quad (60)$$

An identifier expression refers to its bound value.

$$\mathit{expr}[\![I]\!] = \mathbf{bound\text{-}value}(\mathit{id}[\![I]\!]) \quad (61)$$

The preceding two equations account for dynamic semantics. To accurately model Caml Light's let-polymorphism, further details are required, which we will outline in Sect. 3.3.2 below.

Catching exceptions Caml Light's try construct corresponds directly to the **catch-else-rethrow** funcon:

$$\mathit{expr}[\![\texttt{try}\ E\ \texttt{with}\ SM]\!] = \mathbf{catch\text{-}else\text{-}rethrow}(\mathit{expr}[\![E]\!], \mathit{abs}[\![SM]\!]) \quad (62)$$

Also here, a more refined analysis will be required to accurately capture Caml Light's static semantics.

Basic Patterns We have funcons corresponding directly to Caml Light's basic patterns.

$$\mathit{patt}[\![I]\!] = \mathbf{bind}(\mathit{id}[\![I]\!]) \quad (63)$$

$$\mathit{patt}[\![\_]\!] = \mathbf{any} \quad (64)$$

$$\mathit{patt}[\![C]\!] = \mathbf{only}(\mathit{value}[\![C]\!]) \quad (65)$$

Compound data Caml Light expressions include tupling. We represent tuple values using the **tuple-empty** and binary **tuple-prefix** data constructors. These are lifted to computations in the usual way. We use a small auxiliary translation function $\mathit{expr\text{-}tuple}[\![\_]\!]$:

$$\mathit{expr}[\![E_1\ \texttt{,}\ E_2\ \cdots]\!] = \mathit{expr\text{-}tuple}[\![E_1\ \texttt{,}\ E_2\ \cdots]\!] \quad (66)$$

$$\mathit{expr\text{-}tuple}[\![E_1]\!] = \mathbf{tuple\text{-}prefix}(\mathit{expr}[\![E_1]\!], \mathbf{tuple\text{-}empty}) \quad (67)$$

$$\mathit{expr\text{-}tuple}[\![E_1\ \texttt{,}\ E_2\ \cdots]\!] = \mathbf{tuple\text{-}prefix}(\mathit{expr}[\![E_1]\!], \mathit{expr\text{-}tuple}[\![E_2\ \cdots]\!]) \quad (68)$$

The translation of the corresponding pattern constructors involves **invert** F (where F can be an arbitrary data constructor).

$$\mathit{patt}[\![P_1\ \texttt{,}\ P_2\ \cdots]\!] = \mathit{patt\text{-}tuple}[\![P_1\ \texttt{,}\ P_2\ \cdots]\!] \quad (69)$$

$$\mathit{patt\text{-}tuple}[\![P_1]\!] = \mathbf{invert\ tuple\text{-}prefix}(\mathit{patt}[\![P_1]\!], \mathbf{only}(\mathbf{tuple\text{-}empty})) \quad (70)$$

$$\mathit{patt\text{-}tuple}[\![P_1\ \texttt{,}\ P_2\ \cdots]\!] = \mathbf{invert\ tuple\text{-}prefix}(\mathit{patt}[\![P_1]\!], \mathit{patt\text{-}tuple}[\![P_2\ \cdots]\!]) \quad (71)$$

Compound patterns Patterns may also be combined using sequential choice, reusing the **prefer-over** funcon.

$$\mathit{patt}[\![P_1\ \texttt{|}\ P_2]\!] = \mathbf{prefer\text{-}over}(\mathit{patt}[\![P_1]\!], \mathit{patt}[\![P_2]\!]) \quad (72)$$

One may also bind an identifier to the value matched by a pattern:

$$\mathit{patt}[\![P\ \texttt{as}\ I]\!] = \mathbf{patt\text{-}union}(\mathit{patt}[\![P]\!], \mathbf{bind}(\mathit{id}[\![I]\!])) \quad (73)$$

3.3.2 Accounting for Static Semantics

The translation specified above accurately reflects the dynamic semantics of Caml Light programs. The funcons used in the translation also have static semantics, which provides a 'default' static semantics for the programs. In most cases, this agrees with the intended static semantics of Caml Light – but not always. In such cases, we modify the translation by inserting additional funcons which affect the static semantics, but which leave the dynamic semantics unchanged. We consider some examples.

Catching exceptions The translation of `try` E `with` SM above (62) allows any value to be thrown as an exception and caught by the handler. In Caml Light, however, the values that can be thrown and caught are restricted to those included in the type `exn`, so static semantics needs to check that $\mathit{abs}[\![SM]\!]$ has type `exn->`X for some X. This can be achieved using **restrict-domain**(A, T), which has a type only if the argument type of the abstraction A is T, and which dynamically behaves just like A.

$$\mathit{expr}[\![\texttt{try}\ E\ \texttt{with}\ SM]\!] = \quad (74)$$
$$\textbf{catch-else-rethrow}(\mathit{expr}[\![E]\!],$$
$$\textbf{restrict-domain}(\mathit{abs}[\![SM]\!],$$
$$\textbf{bound-type}(\textbf{typeid}(\texttt{'exn'}))))$$

Using polymorphism Caml Light has polymorphism, where a type may be a type schema including universally quantified variables. The interpretation of variable inspection, using just the **bound-value** funcon, does not account for instantiation of polymorphic variables. We can rectify this as follows.

$$\mathit{expr}[\![I]\!] = \textbf{instantiate-if-poly}(\textbf{bound-value}(\mathit{id}[\![I]\!])) \quad (75)$$

The funcon **instantiate-if-poly** takes all universally quantified type variables in the type of its argument, and allows them to be instantiated arbitrarily; it does not affect the dynamic semantics.

Generating polymorphism Expressions with polymorphic types in Caml Light arise from let definitions, where types are generalised as much as possible, up to a constraint regarding imperative behaviour known as *value-restriction* [42]. The appropriate funcon is **generalise-all**, which finds all generalisable types in its argument environment and explicitly quantifies them, universally. Whether this generalisation should be applied is determined entirely by the outermost production of the right-hand side (E) of the let definition.

$$\mathit{decl}[\![P = E]\!] = \textbf{generalise-all}(\mathit{decl\text{-}mono}[\![P = E]\!]) \quad (76)$$
$$\text{if } E \text{ is generalisable}$$

$$\mathit{decl}[\![P = E]\!] = \mathit{decl\text{-}mono}[\![P = E]\!] \quad (77)$$
$$\text{if } E \text{ is not generalisable}$$

The translation funcon $\mathit{decl\text{-}mono}[\![\_]\!]$ is the same as the version of $\mathit{decl}[\![\_]\!]$ specified in Sect. 3.3.1 for dynamic semantics.

$$\mathit{decl\text{-}mono}[\![P = E]\!] = \quad (78)$$
$$\textbf{match}(\mathit{expr}[\![E]\!], \textbf{prefer-over}(\mathit{patt}[\![P]\!],$$
$$\textbf{abs}(\textbf{any}, \textbf{throw}(\texttt{'Match\_failure'}))))$$

Assignment and dereferencing In Caml Light, many built-in operators (e.g., assignment, dereferencing, allocation, and raising exceptions) are provided in the initial library as identifiers bound to functions (and may be rebound in programs). We reflect this by using the funcon **scope** to provide an initial environment to the translations of entire Caml Light programs.

3.4 Funcon Semantics

In Sect. 2.3, we explained and illustrated how to define the static and dynamic semantics of some simple funcons using *Implicitly-Modular SOS* [34]. We now define some further funcons used in the semantics of Caml Light, involving abstractions, environments, patterns, etc. See Table 4 for the signatures of the funcons.

3.4.1 Scoping

We represent bindings of identifiers to values by environments ρ. The environment $\{I \mapsto V\}$ maps I to V; ρ_1/ρ_2 is the environment where bindings in ρ_1 override bindings for the same identifiers in ρ_2. The current environment is preserved by successive transitions, so in I-MSOS notation it appears before the turnstile.

A declaration computes an environment, and can be made local to a computation X using the **scope** funcon. The following I-MSOS rules define its dynamic semantics.

$$\boxed{\mathsf{env}\ \rho \vdash X \to X'}$$

$$\frac{\mathsf{env}\ (\rho_1/\rho) \vdash X \to X'}{\mathsf{env}\ \rho \vdash \textbf{scope}(\rho_1, X) \to \textbf{scope}(\rho_1, X')} \quad (79)$$

$$\mathsf{env}\ \rho \vdash \textbf{scope}(\rho_1, V) \to V \quad (80)$$

Rule (80) applies only when V is a value, which is always independent of the current bindings. The lifted **scope** funcon, which takes a declaration (computing an environment) as its first argument, is defined by an implicit patience rule determined by the signature.

The following I-MSOS rule defines the static semantics of the lifted **scope** funcon. Notice that the type of a declaration D is a typing context Γ_1.

$$\boxed{\mathsf{env}\ \Gamma \vdash X : T}$$

$$\frac{\mathsf{env}\ \Gamma \vdash D : \Gamma_1 \qquad \mathsf{env}\ (\Gamma_1/\Gamma) \vdash X : T}{\mathsf{env}\ \Gamma \vdash \textbf{scope}(D, X) : T} \quad (81)$$

3.4.2 Abstractions

An abstraction **abs**(X) is a value constructed from a computation X that may depend on a given argument value. Abstractions have types $\mathit{abs}(T_1, T_2)$, where T_1 is the type of the argument and T_2 is the type of the computation when given that type of argument.

$$\boxed{\mathsf{given}\ T \vdash X : T'}$$

$$\frac{\mathsf{given}\ T_1 \vdash X : T_2}{\mathsf{given}\ \_ \vdash \textbf{abs}(X) : \mathit{abs}(T_1, T_2)} \quad (82)$$

The funcon **apply** takes an abstraction **abs**(X) and an argument value V, and supplies V to X.

$$\boxed{X \to X'}$$

$$\textbf{apply}(\textbf{abs}(X), V) \to \textbf{supply}(V, X) \quad (83)$$

(The funcon **supply** was introduced in Sect. 2.) The **apply** funcon is lifted in both arguments. Its typing rule is standard:

$$\boxed{E : T}$$

$$\frac{E_1 : \mathit{abs}(T_2, T) \qquad E_2 : T_2}{\textbf{apply}(E_1, E_2) : T} \quad (84)$$

The unary abstraction constructor **abs**(X) allows X to depend on a single given argument value. The *binary* abstraction funcon **abs**(P, X) takes also a pattern P, which is matched against the given value to compute an environment. This allows nested abstractions to refer to arguments at different levels, using the identifiers bound by the respective patterns.

The following rule defines the dynamic semantics of the binary **abs** funcon.

$$\boxed{E \to E'}$$

$$\textsf{abs}(P, X) \to \textsf{abs}(\textsf{scope}(\textsf{match}(\textsf{given}, P), X)) \tag{85}$$

Here **match** is a pattern-matching funcon, defined in Sect. 3.4.4. Patterns are themselves abstractions, and have types of the form $\textit{abs}(T, \Gamma)$ where Γ is a typing context. The static semantics of binary **abs** is as follows.

$$\boxed{\textsf{env}\,\Gamma \vdash E : T}$$

$$\frac{\textsf{env}\,\Gamma \vdash P : \textit{abs}(T_1, \Gamma_1) \qquad \textsf{env}\,(\Gamma_1/\Gamma) \vdash X : T_2}{\textsf{env}\,\Gamma \vdash \textsf{abs}(P, X) : \textit{abs}(T_1, T_2)} \tag{86}$$

We will omit the typing rules in the rest of this section, for brevity.

3.4.3 Static Scoping

When an abstraction $\textsf{abs}(X)$ is applied, evaluation of $\textsf{bound-value}(I)$ in X gives the value *currently* bound to I, which corresponds to dynamic scopes for non-local bindings. To specify static scoping, we use the **close** funcon, which takes an abstraction and returns a closure formed from it and the current environment.

$$\boxed{\textsf{env}\,\rho \vdash E \to E'}$$

$$\textsf{env}\,\rho \vdash \textsf{close}(\textsf{abs}(X)) \to \textsf{abs}(\textsf{closure}(X, \rho)) \tag{87}$$

The funcon **closure** can be used to set the current environment for any computation X:

$$\boxed{\textsf{env}\,\rho \vdash X \to X'}$$

$$\frac{\textsf{env}\,\rho \vdash X \to X'}{\textsf{env}\,\_ \vdash \textsf{closure}(X, \rho) \to \textsf{closure}(X', \rho)} \tag{88}$$

$$\textsf{env}\,\_ \vdash \textsf{closure}(V, \rho) \to V \tag{89}$$

3.4.4 Basic Patterns

Matching the value of an expression E to a pattern P computes an environment. It corresponds to the application of P to E:

$$\boxed{D \to D'}$$

$$\textsf{match}(E, P) \to \textsf{apply}(P, E) \tag{90}$$

Patterns may be constructed in various ways. For example, the pattern $\textsf{bind}(I)$ matches any value and binds the identifier I to it:

$$\boxed{P \to P'}$$

$$\textsf{bind}(I) \to \textsf{abs}(\textsf{bind}(I, \textsf{given})) \tag{91}$$

The wildcard pattern **any** also matches any value, but computes the empty environment $\emptyset$:

$$\textsf{any} \to \textsf{abs}(\emptyset) \tag{92}$$

Other patterns do not match all values. An extreme example is the pattern $\textsf{only}(V)$, matching just the single value V:

$$\textsf{only}(V) \to \textsf{abs}(\textsf{when-true}(\textsf{equal}(\textsf{given}, V), \emptyset)) \tag{93}$$

3.4.5 Failure and Back-Tracking

The funcon $\textsf{when-true}(E, X)$ guards a computation X with a Boolean-valued condition E. When the value of E is **false**, the funcon emits the signal 'failed **true**' while its computation makes a transition to the funcon **stuck** (which has no further transitions).

The signal 'failed **false**' indicates that the computation is proceeding normally, and is treated as unobservable.

$$\boxed{X \xrightarrow{\textsf{failure}\ B} X'}$$

$$\textsf{when-true}(\textsf{true}, X) \xrightarrow{\textsf{failure false}} X \tag{94}$$

$$\textsf{when-true}(\textsf{false}, X) \xrightarrow{\textsf{failure true}} \textsf{stuck} \tag{95}$$

The funcon **else** allows recovery from failure.

$$\frac{X \xrightarrow{\textsf{failure false}} X'}{\textsf{else}(X, Y) \xrightarrow{\textsf{failure false}} \textsf{else}(X', Y)} \tag{96}$$

$$\frac{X \xrightarrow{\textsf{failure true}} X'}{\textsf{else}(X, Y) \xrightarrow{\textsf{failure false}} Y} \tag{97}$$

$$\textsf{else}(V, Y) \xrightarrow{\textsf{failure false}} V \tag{98}$$

3.4.6 Compound Patterns

The funcon **else** is used in the definition of the operation **prefer-over** on abstractions and (as a special case) on patterns:

$$\boxed{P \to P'}$$

$$\textsf{prefer-over}(\textsf{abs}(X), \textsf{abs}(Y)) \to \textsf{abs}(\textsf{else}(X, Y)) \tag{99}$$

For patterns, **prefer-over** corresponds to ordered *alternatives*, as found in Caml Light.

Another way to combine two patterns, also found in Caml Light, is *conjunctively*, requiring them both to match, and uniting their bindings. This corresponds to the funcon **patt-union**:

$$\textsf{patt-union}(\textsf{abs}(X), \textsf{abs}(Y)) \to \textsf{abs}(\textsf{map-union}(X, Y)) \tag{100}$$

Here, the data operation **map-union** is lifted to computations.

3.4.7 Exceptions

We specify exception throwing and handling in a modular way using the emitted signals 'exception $\textsf{some}(V)$' and 'exception **none**' (the latter is unobservable).

$$\boxed{X \xrightarrow{\textsf{exception}\ V} X'}$$

$$\textsf{throw}(V) \xrightarrow{\textsf{exception some}(V)} \textsf{stuck} \tag{101}$$

If the first argument of the funcon **catch** signals an exception $\textsf{some}(V)$, it applies its second argument (an abstraction) to V.

$$\boxed{E \xrightarrow{\textsf{exception}\ V} E'}$$

$$\frac{X \xrightarrow{\textsf{exception none}} X'}{\textsf{catch}(X, Y) \xrightarrow{\textsf{exception none}} \textsf{catch}(X', Y)} \tag{102}$$

$$\frac{X \xrightarrow{\textsf{exception some}(V)} X'}{\textsf{catch}(X, Y) \xrightarrow{\textsf{exception none}} \textsf{apply}(Y, V)} \tag{103}$$

$$\textsf{catch}(V, Y) \xrightarrow{\textsf{exception none}} V \tag{104}$$

The following funcon corresponds to a useful variant of **catch**: exceptions are propagated when the application of the abstraction to them fails.

$$\boxed{E \to E'}$$

$$\textsf{catch-else-rethrow}(E, A) \to \textsf{catch}(E, \textsf{prefer-over}(A, \textsf{abs}(\textsf{throw}(\textsf{given})))) \tag{105}$$

For funcons whose I-MSOS rules do not mention the exception entity, exceptions are implicitly propagated to the closest enclosing funcon that can handle them. When the translation of a program to funcons involves **throw**, it needs to be enclosed in **catch**, to ensure that (otherwise-)unhandled exceptions cause abrupt termination.

This concludes the presentation of our Caml Light case study.

4. Related Work

Heering and Klint proposed in the early 1980s to structure complete definitions of programming languages as libraries of reusable components [12]. This motivated the development of ASF+SDF [3], which provides strong support for modular structure in algebraic specifications. However, an ASF+SDF definition of a programming language does not, in general, permit the reuse of the individual language constructs in the definitions of other languages. As discussed in [33], the main hindrances to reuse in ASF+SDF are coarse modular structure (e.g., specifying all expression constructs in a single module), explicit propagation of auxiliary entities, and direct specification of language constructs.

At the end of the 1980s, Moggi [25] introduced the use of monads and monad transformers in denotational semantics. (In fact Scott and Strachey had themselves used monadic notation for composition of store transformations in the early 1970s, and an example of a monad transformer can also be found in the VDM definition of PL/I, but the monadic structure was not explicit [32].) Monads avoid explicit propagation of auxiliary entities, and monad transformers are highly reusable components. Various monad transformers have been defined (e.g., see [20]) with operations that in many cases correspond to our funcons; monads also make a clear distinction between values and computations. One drawback of monad transformers is that different orders of composition can lead to different semantics; in contrast, our funcons are independent of the order in which they are added. The concept of monad transformers inspired the development of MSOS, our modular variant of SOS.

An alternative way of defining monads has been developed by Plotkin and Power [40] using Lawvere theories instead of monad transformers. Recently, Delaware et al. [8] presented modular monadic meta-theory, combining modular datatypes with monad transformers, focusing on modularisation of theorems and proofs.

Kutter and Pierantonio [17] proposed the Montages variant of abstract state machines (ASMs) with a separate module for each language construct. Reusability was limited partly by the tight coupling of components to concrete syntax. Börger and others [4, 5] gave modular ASM semantics for JAVA and C#, identifying features shared by the two languages, but did not define components intended for wider reuse.

Doh and Mosses [9] first proposed replacing the conventional modular structure of specifications in action semantics [26, 27] by a component-based structure, defining the abstract syntax and action semantics of each language construct in a separate module. Iversen and Mosses [14] introduced so-called Basic Abstract Syntax (BAS), which is a direct precursor of our current collection of funcons. They specified a translation from the Core of Standard ML to BAS, and gave action semantics for each BAS construct, with tool support using ASF+SDF [6]. The action notation used in action semantics can itself be regarded as a primitive collection of funcons; having to deal with both BAS and action notation was a drawback. Mosses and others [15, 29–31] have reported on subsequent work that led to the present paper.

Levin and Pierce developed the TinkerType system [19] to support reuse of conventional SOS specifications of individual language constructs. The idea was to have a variant of the specification of each construct for each combination of language features. To define a new language with reuse of a collection of previously specified constructs, TinkerType could determine the union of the auxiliary entities needed for their individual specifications, and assemble the language definition from the corresponding variants. This approach alleviated some of the symptoms of poor reusability in SOS.

Another system supporting practical use of conventional SOS is Ott [41], which was used by Owens [36] to specify a sublanguage of OCaml corresponding closely to Caml Light. A type soundness theorem was proved, based on HOL code generated by Ott from the language specification. Ott facilitates use of SOS, but any reuse of previous specifications requires manual copying, pasting and editing, which is not evident in the resulting specification.

Ott supports also reduction semantics based on evaluation contexts. This framework is widely used for proving meta-theoretic results (e.g., type soundness). The PLT-Redex tool [16] runs programs by interpreting their reduction semantics, and has been used to validate language specifications. However, evaluation context grammars appear to be inherently non-modular, which seems to preclude use of reduction semantics to define reusable components.

Competing approaches with a high degree of inherent modularity include Rewriting Logic Semantics [23] and the K Framework [21]. The lifting of funcon arguments from value sorts to computation sorts is closely related to strictness annotations in K. It appears possible to specify individual funcons independently in K, and to use the K Tools to translate programming languages to funcons [35], thereby incorporating our component-based approach directly in that framework.

Haeri and Schupp [10] are developing a novel framework that focuses on reusable components of language implementations. It will be interesting to see how well it scales up to larger languages.

5. Conclusions and Further Work

We regard our Caml Light case study as significant evidence of the applicability and modularity of our component-based approach to semantics. The *key novel feature* is the introduction of an open-ended collection of fundamental constructs (funcons). The abstraction level of the funcons we have used to specify the semantics of Caml Light appears to be optimal: if the funcons were closer to the language constructs, the translation of the language to funcons would have been a bit simpler, but the I-MSOS rules for the funcons would have been considerably more complicated; lower-level funcons (e.g., comparable to the combinators used in action semantics [26, 27]) would have increased the size and decreased the perspicuity of the funcon terms used in the translation.

Caml Light is a real language, and we have successfully tested our semantics for it by generating funcon terms from programs, running them using Prolog code generated from the I-MSOS rules that define the funcons, then comparing the results with those given by running the same programs on the latest release of the Caml Light system (which is the *de facto* definition of the language). The test programs and funcon terms are available online[4] together with the generated Prolog code for each funcon. At the time of writing, we have not yet checked whether our test programs exercise every translation equation, nor whether running them uses every rule of every funcon. Nevertheless, we are reasonably confident in the accuracy of our specifications.

The work reported here is part of the PLANCOMPS project [38]. Apart from developing and refining the component-based approach to language specification, PLANCOMPS is developing a chain of tools specially engineered to support its practical use.

Ongoing and future case studies carried out by the PLANCOMPS project will test the reusability of our funcons. We are already reusing many of those introduced for specifying Caml Light in a component-based semantics for C#. The main test will

[4] `www.plancomps.org/churchill2014`

be to specify the corresponding JAVA constructs using essentially the same collection of funcons as for C#. The project is also aiming to test whether the approach is equally applicable to domain-specific languages, where the benefits of reuse in connection with co-evolution of languages and their specifications could be especially significant.

We are quite happy with the perspicuity of our specifications. Lifting value arguments to computation sorts has eliminated the need to specify tedious 'patience' rules in the small-step I-MSOS of funcons. The funcon names are reasonably suggestive, while not being too verbose, although there is surely room for improvement. When the PLANCOMPS project has completed its case studies, it intends to finalise the definitions of the funcons it has developed, and establish an open-access digital library of funcons and language specifications. Until then, the names and details of the funcons presented here should be regarded as tentative.

In conclusion, we consider our component-based approach to be a good example of modularity in the context of programming language semantics. We do not claim that any of the techniques we employ are directly applicable in software engineering, although component-based specifications might well provide a suitable basis for generating implementations of domain-specific languages.

Acknowledgments

Thanks to the anonymous reviewers and Neil Sculthorpe for their helpful comments on the submitted version of this paper. The reported work was supported by an EPSRC grant (EP/I032495/1) to Swansea University for the PLANCOMPS project.

References

[1] C. Bach Poulsen and P. D. Mosses. Deriving pretty-big-step semantics from small-step semantics. In *ESOP'14*, LNCS. Springer, 2014. To appear.

[2] C. Bach Poulsen and P. D. Mosses. Generating specialized interpreters for modular structural operational semantics. In *LOPSTR'13*, LNCS. Springer, 2014. To appear.

[3] J. A. Bergstra, J. Heering, and P. Klint, editors. *Algebraic Specification*. ACM Press/Addison-Wesley, 1989.

[4] E. Börger and R. F. Stärk. Exploiting abstraction for specification reuse. the Java/C# case study. In *FMCO 2003*, volume 3188 of *LNCS*, pages 42–76. Springer, 2003.

[5] E. Börger, N. G. Fruja, V. Gervasi, and R. F. Stärk. A high-level modular definition of the semantics of C#. *Theor. Comput. Sci.*, 336 (2-3):235–284, 2005.

[6] M. G. J. v. d. Brand, J. Iversen, and P. D. Mosses. An action environment. *Sci. Comput. Program.*, 61(3):245–264, 2006.

[7] M. Churchill and P. D. Mosses. Modular bisimulation theory for computations and values. In *FoSSaCS 2013*, volume 7794 of *LNCS*, pages 97–112. Springer, 2013.

[8] B. Delaware, S. Keuchel, T. Schrijvers, and B. C. Oliveira. Modular monadic meta-theory. In *ICFP'13*, pages 319–330. ACM, 2013.

[9] K.-G. Doh and P. D. Mosses. Composing programming languages by combining action-semantics modules. *Sci. Comput. Program.*, 47(1): 3–36, 2003.

[10] S. H. Haeri and S. Schupp. Reusable components for lightweight mechanisation of programming languages. In *Software Composition 2013*, volume 8088 of *LNCS*, pages 1–16. Springer, 2013.

[11] J. Heering and P. Klint. *The Syntax Definition Formalism SDF*, chapter 6. In Bergstra et al. [3], 1989.

[12] J. Heering and P. Klint. Prehistory of the ASF+SDF system (1980–1984). In *ASF+SDF95*, pages 1–4. Programming Research Group, University of Amsterdam, 1995. Tech. rep. 9504.

[13] P. Hudak, J. Hughes, S. P. Jones, and P. Wadler. A history of Haskell: Being lazy with class. In *HOPL-III*, pages 1–55. ACM, 2007.

[14] J. Iversen and P. D. Mosses. Constructive action semantics for Core ML. *Software, IEE Proceedings*, 152:79–98, 2005.

[15] A. Johnstone, P. D. Mosses, and E. Scott. An agile approach to language modelling and development. *Innov. Syst. Softw. Eng.*, 6(1-2): 145–153, 2010.

[16] C. Klein et al. Run your research: On the effectiveness of lightweight mechanization. In *POPL'12*, pages 285–296. ACM, 2012.

[17] P. W. Kutter and A. Pierantonio. Montages specifications of realistic programming languages. *J. Univ. Comput. Sci.*, 3(5):416–442, 1997.

[18] X. Leroy. Caml light manual, Release 0.74, December 1997. URL `http://caml.inria.fr/pub/docs/manual-caml-light`.

[19] M. Y. Levin and B. C. Pierce. Tinkertype: A language for playing with formal systems. *J. Funct. Program.*, 13(2):295–316, Mar. 2003.

[20] S. Liang, P. Hudak, and M. Jones. Monad transformers and modular interpreters. In *POPL'95*, pages 333–343, 1995.

[21] D. Lucanu, T.-F. Serbanuta, and G. Rosu. K Framework distilled. In *WRLA 2012*, volume 7571 of *LNCS*, pages 31–53. Springer, 2012.

[22] J. McCarthy. Towards a mathematical science of computation. In *Information Processing 1962*, pages 21–28. North-Holland, 1962.

[23] J. Meseguer and G. Rosu. The rewriting logic semantics project: A progress report. In *FCT 2011*, volume 6914 of *LNCS*, pages 1–37. Springer, 2011.

[24] R. Milner, M. Tofte, and D. Macqueen. *The Definition of Standard ML*. MIT Press, Cambridge, MA, USA, 1997.

[25] E. Moggi. An abstract view of programming languages. Technical Report ECS-LFCS-90-113, Edinburgh Univ., 1989.

[26] P. D. Mosses. *Action Semantics*, volume 26 of *Cambridge Tracts in Theoretical Computer Science*. Cambridge University Press, 1992.

[27] P. D. Mosses. Theory and practice of action semantics. In *MFCS'96*, volume 1113 of *LNCS*, pages 37–61. Springer, 1996.

[28] P. D. Mosses. Modular structural operational semantics. *J. Log. Algebr. Program.*, 60-61:195–228, 2004.

[29] P. D. Mosses. A constructive approach to language definition. *J. Univ. Comput. Sci.*, 11(7):1117–1134, 2005.

[30] P. D. Mosses. Component-based description of programming languages. In *Visions of Computer Science*, Electr. Proc., pages 275–286. BCS, 2008.

[31] P. D. Mosses. Component-based semantics. In *SAVCBS'09*, pages 3–10. ACM, 2009.

[32] P. D. Mosses. VDM semantics of programming languages: Combinators and monads. *Formal Aspects Comput.*, 23:221–238, 2011.

[33] P. D. Mosses. Semantics of programming languages: Using ASF+SDF. *Sci. Comput. Program.*, 2013.

[34] P. D. Mosses and M. J. New. Implicit propagation in structural operational semantics. In *SOS 2008*, volume 229(4) of *Electr. Notes Theor. Comput. Sci.*, pages 49–66. Elsevier, 2009.

[35] P. D. Mosses and F. Vesely. Funkons: Component-based semantics in K. In *WRLA 2014*, LNCS. Springer, 2014. To appear.

[36] S. Owens. A sound semantics for OCaml light. In *ESOP 2008*, volume 4960 of *LNCS*, pages 1–15. Springer, 2008.

[37] B. C. Pierce. *Types and Programming Languages*. MIT Press, Cambridge, MA, USA, 2002.

[38] PLanCompS. PLANCOMPS: Programming language components and specifications, 2011. URL `http://www.plancomps.org`.

[39] G. D. Plotkin. A structural approach to operational semantics. *J. Log. Algebr. Program.*, 60-61:17–139, 2004.

[40] G. D. Plotkin and A. J. Power. Computational effects and operations: An overview. In *Proc. Workshop on Domains VI*, volume 73 of *Electr. Notes Theor. Comput. Sci.*, pages 149–163. Elsevier, 2004.

[41] P. Sewell, F. Z. Nardelli, S. Owens, et al. Ott: Effective tool support for the working semanticist. *J. Funct. Program.*, 20:71–122, 2010.

[42] M. Tofte. Type inference for polymorphic references. *Inf. Comput.*, 89(1):1–34, 1990.

AspectJML: Modular Specification and Runtime Checking for Crosscutting Contracts

Henrique Rebêlo[λ], Gary T. Leavens[θ], Mehdi Bagherzadeh[β], Hridesh Rajan[β], Ricardo Lima[λ], Daniel M. Zimmerman[δ], Márcio Cornélio[λ], and Thomas Thüm[γ]

[λ]Universidade Federal de Pernambuco, PE, Brazil
{hemr, rmfl, mlc}@cin.ufpe.br
[θ]University of Central Florida, Orlando, FL, USA
leavens@eecs.ucf.edu
[β]Iowa State University, Ames, IA, USA
{mbagherz, hridesh}@iastate.edu
[δ]Harvey Mudd College, Claremont, CA, USA
dmz@acm.org
[γ]University of Magdeburg, Germany
thomas.thuem@ovgu.de

Abstract

Aspect-oriented programming (AOP) is a popular technique for modularizing crosscutting concerns. In this context, researchers have found that the realization of design by contract (DbC) is crosscutting and fares better when modularized by AOP. However, previous efforts aimed at supporting crosscutting contract modularity might actually compromise the main DbC principles. For example, in AspectJ-style, reasoning about the correctness of a method call may require a whole-program analysis to determine what advice applies and what that advice does relative to DbC implementation and checking. Also, when contracts are separated from classes a programmer may not know about them and may break them inadvertently. In this paper we solve these problems with *AspectJML*, a new specification language that supports crosscutting contracts for Java code. We also show how AspectJML supports the main DbC principles of modular reasoning and contracts as documentation.

Categories and Subject Descriptors D.2.4 [*Software/Program Verification*]: Programming by contract, Assertion Checkers; F.3.1 [*Specifying and Verifying and Reasoning about Programs*]: Assertions, Invariant, Pre- and postconditions, Specification techniques

General Terms Design, Languages, Verification

Keywords Design by contract, aspect-oriented programming, crosscutting contracts, JML, AspectJ, AspectJML

1. Introduction

Design by Contract (DbC), originally conceived by Meyer [32], is a useful technique for developing a program using specifications.

MODULARITY '14, April 22–26, 2014, Lugano, Switzerland.
Copyright © 2014 ACM 978-1-4503-2772-5/14/04... $15.00.
http://dx.doi.org/10.1145/2577080.2577084

The key mechanism in DbC is the use of behavioral specifications called "contracts". Checking these contracts against the actual code at runtime has a long tradition in the research community [7, 11, 14, 25, 27, 44, 51]. This idea of checking contracts at runtime was popularized by Eiffel [33] in the late 80s. In addition to Eiffel, other DbC languages include the Java Modeling Language (JML) [27], Spec# [4], and Code Contracts [14].

It is claimed in the literature [6, 15, 21, 29–31, 40, 41, 45] that the contracts of a system are de-facto a crosscutting concern and fare better when modularized with aspect-oriented programming [22] (AOP) mechanisms such as pointcuts and advice [21]. The idea has also been patented [30]. However, Balzer, Eugster, and Meyer's study [3] contradicts this intuition by concluding that the use of aspects hinders design by contract specification and fails to achieve the main DbC principles such as documentation and modular reasoning. Indeed, they go further to say that *"no module in a system (e.g., class or aspect) can be oblivious of the presence of contracts"* [3, Section 6.3]. According to them, contracts should appear in the modules themselves and separating such contracts as aspects contradicts this view [32].

However, plain DbC languages like Eiffel [33] and JML [27] also have problems when dealing with crosscutting contracts. Although mechanisms such as invariant declarations help avoid scattering of specifications, the basic mechanisms for pre- and postcondition specification do not prevent scattering of crosscutting contracts. For example, there is no way in Eiffel or JML to write a single pre- and postcondition and apply it to several methods of a particular type. Instead, such a pre- or postcondition must be repeated and scattered among several methods.

To cope with these problems this paper proposes *AspectJML*, a simple and practical aspect-oriented extension to JML. It supports the specification of crosscutting contracts for Java code in a modular way while keeping the benefits of a DbC language, like documentation and modular reasoning.

In the rest of this paper we discuss these problems and our AspectJML solution in detail. We also provide a real case study to show the effectiveness of our approach when dealing with crosscutting contracts.

JML Contracts

```
01 class Package {
02  double width, height;
03  //@ invariant this.width > 0 && this.height > 0;
04  double weight;
05  //@ invariant this.weight > 0;
06
07  //@ requires width > 0 && height > 0;
08  //@ requires width * height <= 400; // max dimension
09  //@ ensures this.width == width;
10  //@ ensures this.height == height;
11  //@ signals_only \nothing;
12  void setSize(double width, double height){
13   this.width = width;
14   this.height = height;
15  }
16
17  //@ requires width > 0 && height > 0;
18  //@ requires width * height <= 400; // max dimension
19  //@ requires this.width != width;
20  //@ requires this.height != height;
21  //@ ensures this.width == width;
22  //@ ensures this.height == height;
23  //@ signals_only \nothing;
24  void reSize(double width, double height){
25   this.width = width;
26   this.height = height;
27  }
28
29  //@ requires width > 0 && height > 0;
30  //@ requires width * height <= 400; // max dimension
31  //@ signals_only \nothing;
32  boolean containsSize(double width, double height){
33   if(this.width == width && this.height == height){
34    return true;
35   }
36   else return false;
37  }
38
39  //@ signals_only \nothing;
40  double getSize(){
41   return this.width * this.height;
42  }
43
44  //@ ...
45  //@ signals_only \nothing;
46  void setWeight(double weight) {
47   this.weight = weight;
48  }
49 ... // other methods
50 }
51
52 class GiftPackage extends Package {
53  //@ ...
54  //@ signals_only \nothing;
55  void setWeight(double weight) {
56   ...
57  }
58  ... // other methods
59 }
60
61 class Courier {
62  //@ ...
63  void deliver(Package p, String destination) {
64   ...
65  }
66 }
```

AspectJ Contracts

```
67  privileged aspect PackageContracts {
68   pointcut instMeth():
69    execution(!static * Package+.*(..));
70
71   pointcut sizeMeths(double w, double h):
72    execution(void Package.*Size(double, double))
73     && args(w, h);
74
75   pointcut setOrReSize(double w, double h):
76    execution(void Package.setSize(double, double))
77     || execution(void Package.reSize(double, double))
78     && args(w, h);
79
80   pointcut reSizeMeth(double w, double h):
81    execution(void Package.setSize(double, double))
82    && args(w, h);
83
84   pointcut allMeth(): execution(* Package+.*(..));
85
86   before(Package obj): instMeth() && this(obj) {
87    boolean pred = obj.width > 0 && obj.height > 0
88     && obj.weight > 0;
89    Checker.checkInvariant(pred);
90   }
91
92   before(double w, double h): sizeMeths(w, h){
93    boolean pred = w > 0 && h > 0
94     && w * h <= 400; // max dimension
95    Checker.checkPrecondition(pred);
96   }
97
98   before(Package obj, double w, double h):
99   reSizeMeth(w, h) && this(obj){
100   boolean pred = obj.width != w && obj.height != h;
101   Checker.checkPrecondition(pred);
102  }
103
104  after(Package obj, double w, double h) returning():
105   setOrReSize(w, h) && this(obj){
106    boolean pre = obj.width == w
107     && obj.height == h;
108    Checker.checkNormalPostcondition(pred)
109  }
110
111  after() throwing(Exception ex): allMeth() {
112   boolean pred = false;
113   Checker.checkExceptionalPostcondition(pred);
114  }
115
116  after(Point obj): instInv() && this(obj) {
117   boolean pred = obj.width > 0 && obj.height > 0
118    && obj.weight > 0;
119   Checker.checkInvariant(pred);
120  }
121  // other advice for checking contracts
122  }
123
124  privileged aspect GiftPackageContracts {...}
125
126  privileged aspect CourierContracts {...}
127
128  aspect Tracing {
129   after() returning(): execution(* Package.*(..)) {
130    System.out.println("Exiting"+thisJoinPoint);
131   }
132  }
```

Figure 1. The JML and AspectJ contract implementations of the delivery service system [35].

2. Design by Contract and Modularity

In this section we discuss three existing problems in modularizing crosscutting contracts in practice. The first two problems are related to AOP/AspectJ [21, 22], and the third problem is related to design by contract languages like JML [27].

2.1 A Running Example

Figure 1 illustrates a simple delivery service system [35] that manages package delivery. It uses contracts expressed in JML [27] (lines 1-66) and AspectJ [21] (lines 67-126). In addition, the system includes a crosscutting concern, tracing, modularized with AspectJ (lines 128-132).

In JML specifications, preconditions are defined by the keyword **requires** and postconditions by **ensures**. The specification **signals_only \nothing** is an exceptional postcondition which says that no exception (including runtime exceptions but excluding errors) can be thrown. For example, all methods declared in class `Package` are not allowed to throw exceptions. The invariants defined in class `Package` restricts package's dimension and weight to be always greater than zero.

The AspectJ code that corresponds to the JML+Java code is shown in lines 67-126. The main motivation in applying an AspectJ-like language is that we can explore some modularization opportunities that are otherwise not possible in a DbC language like JML. For instance, in the `PackageContracts` aspect, the second **before** advice (lines 92-96) checks the common preconditions, which are scattered in the JML side, for any method with name ending in `Size` and taking two arguments of type **double**. Similarly, the **after-returning** advice (lines 104-109) checks the common postconditions for both methods `setSize` and `reSize`. This advice only enforces the constraints after normal termination. In JML, postconditions normal postconditions are only required to hold when a method returns normally [27]. A third example is the **after-throwing** advice (lines 111-114), which forbids any method in `Package` or subtypes from throwing any exception. This is illustrated in the JML counterpart with the scattered specification **signals_only \nothing**. This second kind of postcondition in JML is called an exceptional postcondition [27].

2.2 The Modular Reasoning Problem

If we consider plain JML/Java without AspectJ, the example in Figure 1 supports modular reasoning [26, 28, 34, 39]. For example, suppose one wants to write code that manipulates objects of type `Package`. One could reason about `Package` objects using just `Package`'s contract specifications (lines 1-50) in addition to any specification inherited from its supertypes [13, 26, 28].

Consider the Java and AspectJ implementation of the delivery service system (without the JML specifications). This is represented by the right-hand-side of Figure 1. In addition to the classes in the base/Java code, Figure 1 defines three aspects for contract checking and one aspect for tracing. In plain AspectJ, advice declarations are applied by the compiler without explicit reference to aspects from a module or a client module; therefore by definition, modular reasoning about the module `Package` does not consider the advice declared by these four aspects. The aspect behavior is only available via non-modular reasoning. That is, in AspectJ, a programmer must consider every aspect that refers to the `Package` class in order to reason about the `Package` module. So the answer to the question "What advice/contract applies to the method `setSize` in `Package`?" cannot (in general) be answered modularly. Therefore, a programmer cannot study the system one module at a time [2, 3, 20, 36, 39, 49].

2.3 Lack of Documentation Problem

In a design by contract language the pre- and postconditions and invariant declarations are typically placed directly in or next to the code they are specifying. Hence, contracts increase system documentation [3, 34, 37]. In AspectJ, however, the advising code (that checks contracts) is separated from the code it advises and this forces programmers to consider all aspects in order to understand the correctness of a particular method. In addition, the physical separation of contracts can be harmful in the sense that an oblivious programmer can violate a method's pre- or postconditions when these are only recorded in aspects [3, 34, 37].

Consider now the tracing concern (Figure 1), modularized by the aspect `Tracing`. It prints a tracing message after the successful execution of any method in the `Package` class when called. For this concern, different orders of composition with other aspects (that check contracts) lead to different behaviors/outputs. As a consequence, the **after-returning** advice (line 129) could violate `Package`'s invariants and pass undetected if this advice runs after those advice (in the `PackageContracts` aspect) responsible for checking the `Package`'s invariant. Without either documentation or the use of AspectJ's **declare precedence** [21] to enforce a specific order on aspects, it is quite difficult–perhaps impossible–to understand the order in which pre- and postconditions will be executed until they are actually executed.

Another problem caused by the lack of documentation implied by separating contracts as aspects is discussed by Balzer, Eugster, Meyer's work [3]. They argue that programmers become aware of contracts only when using special tools like AJDT [23], they are more likely to forget to account for the contracts when changing the classes.

2.4 Lack of Support for Crosscutting Contract Specification in DbC Languages

Balzer, Eugster, and Meyer's study [3] helped to crystallize our thinking about the goals of a DbC language and about the parts of such languages that provides good documentation, modular reasoning, and contracts in general without obliviousness. One straightforward way to avoid the previous two problems discussed is to use a plain DbC language like JML [27].

We make two observations about the JML specifications in Figure 1. First, a DbC language like JML can be used to modularize some contracts. For example, the invariant clauses (declared in `Package`) can be viewed as a form of built-in modularization. That is, instead of writing the same pre- and postconditions for all methods in a class (and its subclasses), we declare a single invariant that modularizes those pre- and postconditions. Second, specification inheritance is another form of modularization. In JML, an overriding method inherits method contracts and invariants from the methods it overrides.[1]

However, DbC languages (like JML) do not capture all forms of crosscutting contract structure [19, 21] that can arise in specifications. For example, consider the JML specifications illustrated in lines 1-66 of Figure 1. In this example there are three ways in which crosscutting contracts are not properly modularized with plain JML constructs:

(1) We cannot write preconditions constraining the input parameters on the methods `setSize`, `reSize`, and `containsSize` (in `Package`) to be greater than zero and less than or equal to 400 (the package dimension) only once and apply them to these or other methods with the same design constraint;

(2) The two normal postconditions of the methods `setSize` and `reSize` of `Package` are the same. They ensure that both `width` and `height` fields are equal to the corresponding method parameters. However, we cannot write a simple and local quantified form of these postconditions and apply them to the constrained methods; and

(3) The exceptional postcondition **signals_only \nothing** must be explicitly written for all the methods that forbid exceptions. This is the case for all declared methods in `Package` and `GiftPackage` classes. There is no way to modularize such a JML contract in one place and apply it to all constrained methods.

[1] Even though inheritance is not exactly a crosscutting structure [19, 21], most DbC languages avoid repeating contracts for overriding methods.

2.5 The Dilemma

It is clear that we face a dilemma with respect to crosscutting contracts. If we use AspectJ to modularize them, the result is a poor contract documentation and compromised modular reasoning. If we go back to a DbC language such as JML, we face the scattered nature of common contracts shown previously. This dilemma leads us to the following research question: Is it possible to have the best of both worlds? That is, can we achieve good documentation and modular reasoning while also specifying crosscutting contracts in a modular way?

In the following, we discuss how our AspectJML DbC language provides constructs to specify crosscutting contracts in a modular and convenient way and overcomes the problems discussed previously.

3. The AspectJML Language

AspectJML extends JML [27] with support for crosscutting contracts [31]. It allows programmers to define additional constructs (in addition to those of JML) to modularly specify pre- and postconditions and check them at certain well-defined points in the execution of a program. We call this the *crosscutting contract specification* mechanism, or XCS for short.

XCS in AspectJML is based on a subset of AspectJ's constructs [21]. However, since JML is a design by contract language tailored for plain Java, we need special support to use the traditional AspectJ syntax. To simplify the adoption of AspectJML, the included AspectJ constructs are based on the alternative @AspectJ syntax [5].

The @AspectJ (often pronounced as "at AspectJ") syntax was conceived as a part of the merge of standard AspectJ with AspectWerkz [5]. This merge enables crosscutting concern implementation by using constructs based on the metadata annotation facility of Java 5. The main advantage of this syntactic style is that one can compile a program using a plain Java compiler, allowing the modularized code using AspectJ to work better with conventional Java IDEs and other tools that do not understand the traditional AspectJ syntax. In particular, this restriction applies to the JML common tools, including the JML compiler on which `ajmlc`, the AspectJML compiler, is based [8, 42, 43].

Figure 2 illustrates the @AspectJ version of the tracing crosscutting concern previously implemented with the traditional syntax (see Figure 1). Instead of using the **`aspect`** keyword, we use a class annotated with an **`@Aspect`** annotation. This tells the AspectJ/ `ajc` compiler to treat the class as an aspect declaration. Similarly, the **`@Pointcut`** annotation marks the empty method `trace` as a pointcut declaration. The expression specified in this pointcut is the same as the one used in the standard AspectJ syntax. The name of the method serves as the pointcut name. Finally, the **`@AfterReturning`** annotation marks the method `afterReturningAdvice` as an **`after returning`** advice. The body of the method is used to modularize the crosscutting concern (the advising code). This code is executed after the matched join point's execution returns without throwing an exception.

In the rest of this section, we present how AspectJML supports crosscutting contract specification. The presentation is informal and based on our running example.

3.1 XCS with Pointcuts-Specifications

The combination of pointcuts and specifications is AspectJML's way to modularize crosscutting contracts at source code level. Recall that a *pointcut designator* enables one to select well-defined points in a program's execution, which are known as *join points* [21]. Optionally, a pointcut can also include some of the

```
@Aspect
class Tracing {
 @Pointcut("execution(* Package.*(..))")
 public void trace() {}

 @AfterReturning("trace()")
 public void afterReturingAdvice(JoinPoint jp) {
  System.out.println("Exiting"+jp);
 }
}
```

Figure 2. The tracing crosscutting concern implementation of Figure 1 using @AspectJ syntax.

values in the execution context of intercepted join points. In AspectJML, we combine these AspectJ pointcuts with JML specifications.

The major difference, in relation to plain AspectJ, is that a specified pointcut is always processed when using our AspectJML compiler (ajmlc). In standard AspectJ, a single pointcut declaration does not contribute to the execution flow of a program unless we define some AspectJ advice that uses such a pointcut. In AspectJML, we do not need to define an advice to check a specification in a crosscutting fashion. Although it is possible to use advice declarations in AspectJML we do not require them. This makes AspectJML simpler and a programmer only needs to know AspectJ's pointcut language [21] in addition to the main JML features.

Specifying crosscutting preconditions

Recall our first crosscutting contract scenario described in Section 2.4. It consists of two preconditions for any method, in `Package` (Figure 1) with a name ending with `Size` that returns **`void`** and takes two arguments of type **`double`**. For this scenario, consider the JML annotated pointcut with the following preconditions:

```
//@ requires width > 0 && height > 0;
//@ requires width * height <= 400; // max dimension
@Pointcut("execution(* Package.*Size(double, double))"+
 "&& args(width, height)")
void sizes(double width, double height) {}
```

The pointcut `sizes` matches all the executions of methods ending with "`Size`" of class `Package` like `setSize` and `setWeight`. As observed, this pointcut is exposing the intercepted method arguments of type **`double`**. This is done in @AspectJ by listing the formal parameters in the pointcut method. We bind the parameter names in the pointcut's expression (within the annotation **`@Pointcut`**) using the argument-based pointcut **`args`** [21].

The main difference between this pointcut declaration and standard pointcut declarations in @AspectJ is that we are adding two JML specifications (using the **`requires`** clause). In this example the JML says to check the declared preconditions before the executions of intercepted methods.

Specifying crosscutting postconditions

We discuss now how to properly modularize crosscutting postconditions in AspectJML. JML supports two kinds of postconditions: normal and exceptional. Normal postconditions constrain methods that return without throwing an exception. To illustrate AspectJML's design, we discuss scenarios (2) and (3) from Section 2.4. For scenario (2), we use the following specified pointcut:

```
//@ ensures this.width == width;
//@ ensures this.height == height;
@Pointcut("(execution(* Package.setSize(double, double))"+
 "|| execution(* Package.reSize(double, double)))"+
 "&& args(width, height)")
void sizeChange(double width, double height) {}
```

This pointcut constrains the executions of the `setSize` and `reSize` methods in `Package` to ensure that, after their executions, the fields `width` and `height` have values equal to the ones passed as arguments. To modularize the crosscutting postcondition of scenario (3), we use the following JML annotated pointcut declaration:

```
//@ signals_only \nothing;
@Pointcut("execution(* Package+.*(..))")
void packageMeths() {}
```

The above specification forbids the execution of any method in `Package` (or a subtype, such as `GiftPackage`) to throw an exception. If any intercepted method throws an exception (even a runtime exception), a JML exceptional postcondition error is thrown to signal the contract violation. In this pointcut, we do not expose any intercepted method's context.

Multiple specifications per pointcut

All the crosscutting contract specifications discussed above consist of only one kind of JML specification per pointcut declaration. However, AspectJML can include more than one kind of JML specification in a pointcut declaration. For example, assume that the `Package` type in Figure 1 does not include the `containsSize` method or its JML specifications. In this scenario, we can write a single pointcut to modularize the recurrent pre- and postconditions of methods `setSize` and `reSize`. Therefore, instead of having separate JML annotated pointcuts for each crosscutting contract, we specify them in a new version of the pointcut `sizes`:

```
//@ requires width > 0 && height > 0;
//@ requires width * height <= 400; // max dimension
//@ ensures this.width == width;
//@ ensures this.height == height;
@Pointcut("execution(* Package.*Size(double, double))"+
  "&& args(width, height)")
void sizes(double width, double height) {}
```

This pointcut declaration modularly specifies both preconditions and normal postconditions of the same intercepted size methods (`setSize` and `reSize`) of `Package`.

Pointcut expressions without type signature patterns

In AspectJ, a pointcut expression can be defined without using a type signature pattern. A type signature pattern is a name (or part of a name) used to identify what type contains the join point. For example, the following AspectJ pointcut:

```
pointcut sizes(): execution(* *Size(double, double));
```

selects any method ending with "`Size`" and has two arguments of type **`double`**. In AspectJ, this pointcut matches any type in a system. Since we omit the type signature pattern, any type is candidate to expose the join points of interest. In AspectJ, although not required, we can also use a wildcard (`*`) to represent a type signature pattern that intercepts any type in the system (i.e., `execution(* *.*Size(double, double))`.

However AspectJML has a different semantics compared with AspectJ. For example, recall the previous pointcut method `sizes` in AspectJML:

```
//@ requires width > 0 && height > 0;
//@ requires width * height <= 400; // max dimension
@Pointcut("execution(* *Size(double, double))"+
  "&& args(width, height)")
void sizes(double width, double height) {}
```

this pointcut method still selects the same methods ending with "`Size`" and that has two arguments of type **`double`**. The main difference is that even with the absence of the target type, AspectJML restricts the join points to the type (`Package` in this case) enclosing the pointcut declaration (see Figure 3). AspectJML works in this manner to avoid the obliviousness problem (see Section 4 for more details).

Specification of unrelated types

Another issue to consider is whether or not AspectJML can modularize inter-type[2] crosscutting specifications. All the crosscutting contract specifications we discuss are related to one type (intra-type) or its subtypes. However, AspectJ can advise methods of different (unrelated) types in a system. This quantification property of AspectJ is quite useful [16, 52] but can also be problematic from the point of view of modular reasoning, since one needs to consider all the aspect declarations to understand the overall system behavior [2, 20, 39, 47–49]. Instead of ruling this completely out, the design of AspectJML allows the specifier to use specifications that constrain unrelated inter-types, but in an explicit and limited manner (see Section 4 for more details about non-obliviousness in AspectJML).

As an example, recall the running example in Figure 1. We know that all the methods declared in `Package` and its subtype `GiftPackage` are forbidden to throw exceptions (see the **`signals_only`** specification). Suppose now that the `deliver` method in type `Courier` also has this constraint. Note that the type `Courier` is not a subtype of `Package`. They are related in the sense that the method `deliver` depends on the `Package` type due to the declaration of a formal parameter. Consider further that `Courier` contains many methods that are not dependent on `Package` in any way. Consider the following type declaration:

```
interface ExceptionSignalling {
 @InterfaceXCS
 class ExceptionSignallingXCS {
  //@ signals_only \nothing;
  @Pointcut("execution(* ExceptionSignalling+.*(..))")
  void allMeth() {}
 }
}
```

This type declaration illustrates how we specify crosscutting contracts for interfaces. In @AspectJ, pointcuts are not allowed to be declared within interfaces. We overcome this problem by adding an inner class that represents the crosscutting contracts of the outer interface declaration. As a part of our strategy, the pointcut declared in the inner class refers only to the outer interface (see the reference in the pointcut predicate expression). Now any type that wants to forbid its method declarations to throw exceptions need only to implement the interface `ExceptionSignallingConstraint`. Such an interface acts like a marker interface [18]. This is important to avoid obliviousness and maintain modular reasoning.

Note that the inner class is marked with the **`@InterfaceXCS`** annotation. This is to distinguish from any other inner class that could be also declared within our crosscutting contract interface. Without this mechanism, the AspectJML compiler will not be able to find the crosscutting contracts for the interface `ExceptionSignalling`.

Collected XCS examples

Some of the main the crosscutting contract specifications used so far in this section (discussed as scenarios in Section 2.4) with pointcuts-specifications are illustrated in Figure 3 (the shadowed part illustrates the XCS in AspectJML's pointcuts and specifications).

3.2 AspectJML Expressiveness

So far we have used the **`execution`** and **`within`** pointcut designators to select join points. This conforms with the supplier-side

[2] Inter-types here are not the AspectJ feature [21] that allows adding methods or fields with a static crosscutting mechanism. Instead, they are unrelated modules in a system; that is, types that are not related to each other but can present a common crosscutting contract structure.

```
01 class Package {
02  double width, height;
03  //@ invariant this.width > 0 && this.height > 0;
04  double weight;
05  //@ invariant this.weight > 0;
06
07  //@ requires width > 0 && height > 0;
08  //@ requires width * height <= 400; // max dimension
09  @Pointcut("execution(* *Size(double,double))"+
10   "&& args(width, height)")
11  void sizes(double width, double height) {}
12
13  //@ ensures this.width == width;
14  //@ ensures this.height == height;
15  @Pointcut("(execution(* setSize(double,double))"
16   + "|| execution(* reSize(double, double)))"+
17   "&& args(width, height)")
18  void sizeChange(double width, double height) {}
19
20  //@ signals_only \nothing;
21  @Pointcut("execution(* Package+.*(..))")
22  void packageMeths() {}
23
24  void setSize(double width, double height){...}
25
26  //@ requires this.width != width;
27  //@ requires this.height != height;
28  void reSize(double width, double height){...}
29
30  boolean containsSize(double width, double height){...}
31  double getSize(){...}
32
33  //@ ...
34  void setWeight(double weight) {...}
35 ... // other methods
36 }
37 class GiftPackage extends Package {
38  //@ ...
39  void setWeight(double weight) {...}
40  ... // other methods
41 }
```

Figure 3. The crosscutting contract specifications used so far for the delivery service system [35] with AspectJML.

checking adopted by most runtime assertion checkers (RAC) of DbC languages. Such RAC compilers typically operate by injecting code to check each method's precondition at the beginning of its code, and injecting code to check the method's postcondition at the end of its code. This checking code is then run from within the method's body at the supplier side.

AspectJML also includes other primitive pointcut designators that identify join points in different ways [21]. For instance, we can use the **call** pointcut. This would provide runtime checking at the call site. Code Contracts [14] is an example of a DbC language that provides runtime checking at the call site. However, it supports only precondition checking. Since JML also supports client-side checking [38], the **call** pointcut enables client-side checking for AspectJML in relation to specified crosscutting contracts.

```
//@ requires width > 0 && height > 0;
//@ requires width * height <= 400; // max dimension
@Pointcut("(execution(* Package.*Size(double, double))"+
          "|| call(void Package.*Size(double, double)))"
         "&& args(width, height)")
void sizeMeths(double width, double height) {}
```

This is an example of a crosscutting precondition specification, in AspectJML, that takes into account both **execution** and **call** pointcut designators.

AspectJML also supports AspectJ's control-flow based pointcuts (e.g., **cflow**) [21].

4. AspectJML's Benefits

In this section we discuss the main AspectJML benefits when used for crosscutting contract specification.

Enabling modular reasoning

Recall that our notion of modular reasoning means that one can verify a piece of code in a given module, such as a class, using only the module's own specifications, its own implementation, and the interface specifications of modules that it references [13, 26, 28, 34, 39].

With respect to whether or not AspectJML supports modular reasoning like a DbC language such as JML, consider the client code, which we will imagine is written by Cathy, shown in Figure 4.

```
// written by Cathy
public class ClientClass {
 public void clientMeth(Package p)
  { p.setSize(0, 1); }
}
```

Figure 4. `setSize`'s Client code.

To verify the call to `setSize`, Cathy must determine what specifications to use. If she uses the definition of modular reasoning [26, 28, 34, 39], she must use the specifications for `setSize` in `Package`. Let us assume that she uses the JML specifications of Figure 1. Hence, she uses:

(1) The pre- and postconditions located at the method `setSize` (lines 7-11);

(2) The first invariant definition in line 3, which constrains the `Package` dimension (`width` and `height`) fields; and

(3) The second invariant (line 5) related to the `Package`'s weight.

Cathy only needs these three steps, including seven JML pre- and postcondition, and invariant specifications, when using plain JML reasoning. (`Package` has no supertype; otherwise, she would also need to consider specifications inherited from such supertypes.) After obtaining these specifications, she can see that there is a precondition violation regarding the width value of `0` passed to `setSize` (in Figure 4).

Suppose now that Cathy wants to perform again the same modular reasoning task, but using the AspectJML specifications in Figure 3 instead of the JML specifications in Figure 1. In this case she needs to find the following pieces of specified code:

(1) The first invariant definition in line 3, that constrains the `Package` dimension (`width` and `height`) fields;

(2) The second invariant (line 5) related to the `Package`'s weight;

(3) The preconditions of the pointcut (lines 7-8) `sizeMeths`, since it intercepts the execution of method `setSize`;

(4) The normal postconditions (lines 13-14) located at the pointcut `setOrReSize`; and

(5) The exceptional postcondition (line 20) of pointcut `allMeth`.

As before, this task involves only modular reasoning and she can still detect the potential precondition violation related to `Package`'s width. In this case, Cathy needed the same seven specifications, but with two more steps (five in total) to reason about the correctness of the call to `setSize`. So, although AspectJML supports modular reasoning, Cathy must follow a slightly more indirect process to reason about the correctness of a call. This confirms that the obliviousness issue present in AspectJ-like languages [16] does not occur in this example. Cathy is completely aware of the contracts of `Package` class, though it does take her longer to determine them.

Enabling documentation

This example shows that, despite the added indirection, reasoning with AspectJML specifications does not necessarily have a modularity difference compared to reasoning with JML specifications. Only the location where these specifications can appear can be different, due to the use of pointcut declarations in AspectJML.

Our conclusion is that an inherent cost of crosscutting contract modularization and reuse is the cost of some indirection in finding contract specifications, which is necessary to avoid scattering (repeated specifications). However, using AspectJML, users also have several new possibilities for crosscutting contracts.

Taming obliviousness

Since AspectJML allows pointcut declarations in AspectJ-style, one can argue that a programmer can specify several unrelated modules in one single place. This phenomenon brings into focus again whether AspectJML allows the controversial obliviousness property of AOP [2, 20, 39, 47–49].

The answer is no. AspectJML rules out this possibility. If one tries to write such pointcuts, they will have no effect with respect to crosscutting specification and runtime checking. This happens because AspectJML associates the specified pointcut with the type in which it was declared (see the discussion in the next section and the generated code in Figure 5). Hence, only join points within the given type or its subtypes are allowed. The cross-references generated by AspectJML (see Section 5.1) can help visualize the intercepted types.

Even though there is no way in AspectJML to specify unrelated modules anonymously, the declared pointcuts can still be used within aspect types that can crosscut unrelated types. Those pointcuts can be used to modularize other kinds of crosscutting concerns using the standard AspectJ pointcuts-advice mechanisms [21].

5. Implementation

We implemented the AspectJML crosscutting contract specification technique in our JML/ajmlc compiler [42, 43], which is available online at: `http://www.cin.ufpe.br/%7ehemr/JMLAOP/ajmlc.htm`. To the best of our knowledge, the AspectJML compiler is the first compiler for runtime assertion checking that supports crosscutting contract specifications.

Compilation strategy

The ajmlc compiler itself was described in a previous work [43]. Unlike the classical JML compiler, jmlc [8, 10], it generates aspects to check specifications. It also has various code optimizations [42] and better error reporting. The main difference between the previous ajmlc and the new one is support for AspectJML features like specified pointcuts. Instead of saying JML/ajmlc, we now say AspectJML/ajmlc.

Figure 5 shows the **`before`** advice generated by the ajmlc compiler to check the crosscutting preconditions of class `Package` defined in Figure 3.[3] The variable `rac$b` denotes the precondition to be checked. This variable is passed as an argument to `JMLChecker.checkPrecondition` method, which checks such preconditions; if it is not true, then a precondition error is thrown. As discussed in Section 4, the exposed object type is `Package`. Hence, this precondition can only be checked to join points of `Package` or its subtypes like `GiftPackage` (see Figure 1).

[3] The ajmlc compiler provides a compilation option that prints all the checking code as aspects instead of weaving them.

```
/** Generated by AspectJML to check the precondition of
  * method(s) intercepted by sizeMeths pointcut. */
before (Package object$rac, final double width,
  final double height) :
  (execution(* p.Package.*Size(double,double))
  && this(object$rac) && args(width, height)) {
  boolean rac$b = (((width > +0.0D) && (height > +0.0D))
   && ((width * height) <= 400.0D));
  JMLChecker.checkPrecondition(rac$b, "errorMsg");
 }
```

Figure 5. Generated before advice to check the crosscutting preconditions of `Package` in Figure 3.

Ordering of checks

As ajmlc generates AspectJ aspects to check contracts, it also enforces aspect precedence. For instance, if we have advising code for other crosscutting concerns, it can only be allowed to execute after the preconditions are satisfied; otherwise, a precondition violation is thrown.

Analogously, the postconditions are checked after all the advising code's execution. This ordering prevents undetected postcondition violations, which could happen if postconditions were checked before the execution of the advising code.

Contract violation example in AspectJML

As an example of runtime checking using AspectJML/ajmlc, recall the client code illustrated in Figure 4. In this scenario, we got the following precondition error in the AspectJML RAC:

```
Exception in thread "main"
org.jmlspecs.ajmlrac.runtime.JMLEntryPreconditionError:
by method Package.setSize regarding code at
File "Package.java", line 13 (Package.java:13), when
  'width' is 0.0
  'height' is 1.0
  ...
```

As can be seen, in this error output, the shadowed input parameter `width` is displaying `0.0`. But the precondition requires a package's width to be greater than zero. As a result, this precondition violation occurs during runtime checking when calling such client code.

5.1 Tool Support

In aspect-oriented programming, development tools like AJDT [23], allow programmers to easily browse the crosscutting structure of their programs. For AspectJML, we are developing analogous support for browsing crosscutting contract structure. We use the existing functionality of AJDT to this end.

For example, consider the crosscutting contract structure of the `Package` class using AspectJML/AJDT (see Figure 6). Note the arrows indicating where the crosscutting contracts apply. In plain AspectJ/AJDT this example shows no crosscutting structure information, because it has only pointcut declarations without advice. In AspectJ, we need to associate the declared pointcuts to advice in order to be able to browse the crosscutting structure of a system. We have implemented an option (that is enabled by default) in AspectJML that generates the cross-references information for crosscutting contracts, thus allowing one to visualize the crosscutting structure.

To enable the crosscutting contract structure view, AspectJML generates an **`around`** advice in AspectJ, without effect in the base code, to associate with the corresponding pointcut in AspectJML pointcuts. For instance, considering the `Package` type (Figure 6), AspectJML generates an AspectJ aspect called `PackageCrossRef`. Figure 6 illustrates this in practice. Once compiled, we can see that the method `reSize` in Package is intercepted by the pointcut sizes from `PackageCrossRef`. Through

```
class Package {
    double width, height;
    //@ invariant this.width > 0 && this.height > 0;
    double weight;
    //@ invariant this.weight > 0;

    //@ requires width > 0 && height > 0;
    //@ requires width * height <= 400; // max dimension
    @Pointcut("execution(* *Size(double,double))"+
            "&& args(width, height)")
    void sizes(double width, double height) {}

    void setSize(double width, double height){
        this.width = width;
        this.height = height;
    }

    //@ requires this.width != width;
    //@ requires this.height != height;
advised by PackageCrossRef.around(double,double): sizes(BindingTypePatt
        this.width = width;
        this.height = height;
    }

    //... other methods
}
```

Figure 6. The crosscutting contract structure in the `Package` class using AspectJML/AJDT [23].

the cross-references, we go to the **around** advice (in the aspect `PackageCrossRef`) that actually activates the arrow through AJDT. But the cross-reference code we generate for AspectJML allows the programmers from a javadoc-link to point to the right pointcut `sizes` in type `Package`. The generated code looks as follows:

```
/** Generated by AspectJML to enable the crossref for
 * the XCS pointcut {@link Package#sizes(double, double)}*/
 pointcut sizes(double width, double height): ... ;
 Object around(...): sizes(width, height) && ...
```

Figure 7 shows another example where the use of the AspectJ/AJDT helps an AspectJML programmer to write a valid pointcut declaration. As depicted, the AspectJML programmer got an error from AJDT because he/she forgot to bind the formal parameters of the pointcut method declaration with the pointcut expression by using the argument-based pointcut **`args`**. The well-formed pointcut can be seen in Figure 6. All the AJDT IDE validation is inherited by AspectJML.

Note that the AJDT is just a helpful functionality to assist (beginners) AspectJML programmers to see where the specified pointcuts intercept. Once pointcut language and quantification mechanism are understood, this tool is not required to reason about AspectJML in a modular way (as discussed in Section 4).

6. The HealthWatcher Case Study

Our evaluation of the XCS feature of AspectJML involves a medium-sized case study. The chosen system is a real health web-based complaint system, called Health Watcher (HW) [17, 46]. The main purpose of the HW system is to allow citizens to register complaints regarding health issues. This system was selected because it has a detailed requirements document available [17]. This requirements document describes 13 use cases and forms the basis for our JML specifications.

We analyzed the crosscutting contract structure of the HW system, comparing its specification in JML and AspectJML. Our results are available online at:

`http://www.cin.ufpe.br/%7ehemr/modularity14/.`

```
class Package {
    double width, height;
    //@ invariant this.width > 0 && this.height > 0;
    double weight;
    //@ invariant this.weight > 0;

    //@ requires width > 0 && height > 0;
    //@ requires width * height <= 400; // max dimension
    @Pointcut("execution(* *Size(double,double))")
    void sizes(double width, double height) {}
 Multiple markers at this line   h, double height){
 - formal unbound in
 pointcut                        ;
```

Figure 7. An example of a malformed pointcut declaration in AspectJML.

6.1 Understanding the Crosscutting Contract Structure

One of the most important steps in the evaluation is to recognize how the contract structure crosscuts the modules of the HW system. We now show some of the crosscutting contracts present in HW using the standard JML specifications.

Crosscutting preconditions

Crosscutting preconditions occur in the HW system's `IFacade` interface. This facade makes available all 13 use cases as methods. Consider the following code from this interface:

```
//@ requires code >= 0;
IteratorDsk searchSpecialitiesByHealthUnit(int code);

//@ requires code >= 0;
Complaint searchComplaint(int code);

//@ requires code >= 0;
DiseaseType searchDiseaseType(int code);

//@ requires code >= 0;
IteratorDsk searchHealthUnitsBySpeciality(int code);

//@ requires healthUnitCode >= 0;
HealthUnit searchHealthUnit(int healthUnitCode);
```

These methods comprise all the search-based operations that HW makes available. The preconditions of these methods are identical, as each requires that the input parameter, the code to be searched, is at least zero. However, in plain JML one cannot write a single precondition for all 5 search-based methods.

Crosscutting postconditions

Still considering the HW's facade interface `IFacade`, we focus now on crosscutting postconditions. First, we analyze the crosscutting contract structure for normal postconditions:

```
//@ ensures \result != null;
IteratorDsk searchSpecialitiesByHealthUnit(int code);

//@ ensures \result != null;
IteratorDsk searchHealthUnitsBySpeciality(int code);

//@ ensures \result != null;
IteratorDsk getSpecialityList()

//@ ensures \result != null;
IteratorDsk getDiseaseTypeList()

//@ ensures \result != null;
IteratorDsk getHealthUnitList()

//@ ensures \result != null;
IteratorDsk getPartialHealthUnitList()
```

As observed, all the methods in `IFacade` that return an object of type `IteratorDsk` should return a non-null object reference. In standard JML there are two more ways to express this constraint [9]. The first one uses the non-null semantics for object references. In this case we do not need to write out such normal postconditions to handle non-null. However, we can deactivate this option in JML if most object references in the system are possibly null. In this scenario, whenever we find a method that should return non-null, we still need to write these normal postconditions. So, by assuming that we are not using the non-null semantics of JML as default, these postconditions become redundant. The second option is to use the JML type modifier **non_null**; however, even this would lead to some (smaller) amount of repeated postconditions.

With respect to exceptional postconditions of `IFacade` interface, we found an interesting crosscutting structure scenario. Consider the following code:

```
//@ signals_only java.rmi.RemoteException;
void updateComplaint(Complaint q) throws
  java.rmi.RemoteException,...;

//@ signals_only java.rmi.RemoteException;
IteratorDsk getDiseaseTypeList() throws
  java.rmi.RemoteException,...;

//@ signals_only java.rmi.RemoteException;
IteratorDsk getHealthUnitList() throws
  java.rmi.RemoteException,...;

//@ signals_only java.rmi.RemoteException;
int insertComplaint(Complaint complaint) throws
  java.rmi.RemoteException,...;

... // all facade methods contain this constraint
```

As can be seen, these `IFacade` methods can throw the Java RMI exception `RemoteException` (see the methods throws clause). This exception is used as a part of the Java RMI API used by the HW system. Even though we list only four methods, all the methods contained in the `IFacade` interface contain this exception in their throws clause. Because of that, the **signals_only** clause is repeated for all methods in the `IFacade` interface. However, in JML one cannot write a single **signals_only** clause to constrain all such methods in this way.

Another example of exceptional postconditions occurs with the search-based methods discussed previously. All these search-based methods should have a **signals_only** clause that allows the `ObjectNotFoundException` to be thrown. As with the `RemoteException`, one cannot write this specification once and apply it to all search-based methods.

6.2 Modularizing Crosscutting Contracts in HW

To restructure/modularize the crosscutting contracts of the HW system, we use the XCS mechanisms of AspectJML. By doing this, we avoid repeated specifications, which is an improvement over standard DbC mechanisms. In the following, we show the details of how AspectJML achieves a better separation of the contract concern for this example.

Specifying crosscutting preconditions

We can properly modularize the crosscutting preconditions of HW with the following JML annotated pointcut in AspectJML:

```
//@ requires code >= 0;
@Pointcut("execution(* IFacade.search*(int))"+
  "&& args(code)")
void searchMeths(int code) {}
```

With this pointcut specification, we are able to locate the preconditions for all the search-based methods in a single place. To select the search-based methods, we use a property-based pointcut [21] that matches join points by using wildcards. Our pointcut matches any method starting with `search` and taking an **int** parameter. Before the executions of such intercepted methods, the precondition that constrains the code argument to be at least zero is enforced during runtime; if it does not hold, then one gets a precondition violation error.

Specifying crosscutting postconditions

Consider the modularization of the two kinds of crosscutting postconditions we discussed previously. For normal postconditions, we add the following code in AspectJML:

```
//@ ensures \result != null;
@Pointcut("execution(IteratorDsk IFacade.*(..))")
void nonNullReturnMeths() {}
```

With this pointcut specification, we are able to explicitly modularize the non-null constraint. The pointcut expression we use matches any method with any list of parameters returning `IteratorDsk`.

The AspectJML code responsible for modularizing the exceptional postconditions is similar:

```
//@ signals_only java.rmi.RemoteException;
@Pointcut("execution(* IFacade.*(..))")
void remoteExceptionalMeths() {}

//@ signals_only ObjectNotFoundException;
@Pointcut("execution(* IFacade.search*(..))")
void objectNotFoundExceptionalMeths() {}
```

These two specified pointcuts in AspectJML are responsible for modularizing the exceptional postconditions for methods that can throw `RemoteException` and methods that can throw `ObjectNotFoundException`, respectively. The first pointcut applies the specification for all methods in `IFacade`, whereas the second one intercepts just the search-based methods.

6.3 Reasoning About Change

The main benefit of AspectJML is to allow the modular specification of crosscutting contracts in an explicit and expressive way. The key mechanism is the quantification property [16, 52] inherited from AspectJ [21]. In addition to the documentation and modularization of crosscutting contracts achieved with AspectJML, another immediate benefit of using our approach is easier software maintenance. For example, if we add a new exception that can be thrown by all `IFacade` methods, instead of (re)writing a **signals_only** clause, we can add this exception to the **signals_only** list of the `remoteExceptionalMeths` pointcut. This pointcut can be reused whenever we want to apply constraints to methods already intercepted by the pointcut.

Another maintenance benefit occurs during system evolution. On one hand, we may add more methods in the `IFacade` interface to handle system's new use cases. On the other hand, we do not need to explicitly apply existing constraints to the newly added methods. The modularized contracts that apply to all methods also automatically apply to the newly added ones, with no cost. Finally, even if the crosscutting contracts are well documented by using JML specifications, the AJDT tool helps programmers to visualize the overall crosscutting contract structure. Just after a method is declared, we can see which crosscutting contracts apply to it through the cross-references feature of AJDT [23].

7. Discussion

This section discusses some issues with the AspectJML specification language, including limitations, compatibility, open issues, and related work.

7.1 Limitations of AspectJML

Even though AspectJML has the benefit of modularity when handling crosscutting contracts, there are some situations that AspectJML cannot currently deal with. In order to exemplify the main drawback, consider the following JML/Java code:

```
//@ requires x > 0;
public void m(int x){}

//@ requires x > 0;
//@ requires y > 0;
public void n(int x, int y){}

//@ requires y > 0;
public void o(double x, int y, double z){}

//@ requires z > 0;
public void p(double y, int z){}
```

In this code, we can observe that all formal parameters involving the Java primitive `int` types should be greater than zero (see the preconditions). In JML, we cannot write this precondition only once and apply it for all `int` arguments for the above methods. Unfortunately, this also cannot be done with AspectJML. The reason is that we cannot write a pointcut that matches all methods with `int` types in any position and associate a bound variable that can be used in the precondition. This is also a limitation of AspectJ's pointcut mechanism.

Another limitation of AspectJML is related to the crosscutting contract interfaces. Such interfaces are the ones we use to explicit make a crosscutting contract to be applied to several unrelated types. To enable the modular reasoning and checking of these contracts one just needs to implement such interfaces. The problem is that modular reasoning will be lost if a programmer makes a type implement one of these crosscutting contract interfaces by using AspectJ's `declare parents` feature. This feature would make the contracts modularized in a crosscutting contract interface to be implicit applied. Therefore, a programmer must take care of this risk if they decide to use AspectJ's feature combined with AspectJML.

7.2 AspectJML Compatibility

One of the goals of this work is to support a substantial user community. To make this concrete, we have chosen to design crosscutting contract specification in AspectJML as a compatible extension to JML using AspectJ's pointcut language. This takes advantage of AspectJ's familiarity among programmers. Our goal is to make programming and specifying with AspectJML feel like a natural extension of programming and specifying with Java and JML. The AspectJML/ajmlc compiler has the following properties:

- all legal JML annotated Java programs are legal AspectJML programs;
- all legal AspectJ programs are legal AspectJML programs;
- all legal @AspectJ programs are legal AspectJML programs;
- all legal Java programs are legal AspectJML programs; and
- all legal AspectJML programs run on standard Java virtual machines.

7.3 JML Versus AspectJ

We have discussed the main problems of dealing with contracts expressed in both JML and AspectJ. Indeed, this comparison was suggested by Kiczales and Mezini [23]. They asked researchers to explore what issues are better specified as contract/behavioral specifications and what issues are better addressed directly in pointcuts. In this context, AspectJML goes beyond their question in the sense that it combines both pointcuts and contracts. We showed that DbC is better used with a design by contract language, but for situations involving scattering of contracts it can be advantageous to provide a form of specified pointcuts to allow crosscutting contract specifications.

7.4 Open Issues

Our evaluation of AspectJML is limited to two systems, the delivery service system [35] and the Health Watcher [46]. Although we know of no scaling issues, larger-scale validation is still needed to analyze more carefully the benefits and drawbacks of AspectJML. Library specification and runtime checking studies are another interesting area for future work.

Another open issue, which we intend to address in future versions of AspectJML, is related to the pointcut parameters and methods with common argument types (see Section 7.1).

Two more important open issues that could be explored in AspectJML are related to specification and modular reasoning of AspectJ programs [40]. These are interesting because we can also program in AspectJ using AspectJML.

7.5 Related Work

As discussed throughout the paper, there are several works in the literature that argue in favor of implementing DbC with AOP [15, 21, 30, 41]. Kiczales opened this research avenue by showing a simple precondition constraint implementation in one of his first papers on AOP [21]. After that, other authors explored how to implement and separate the DbC concern with AOP [15, 21, 30, 40, 41]. All these works offer common templates and guidelines for DbC aspectization.

We go beyond these works by showing how to combine the best design features of a design by contract language like JML and the quantification benefits of AOP such as AspectJ. As a result we conceive the AspectJML specification language that is suitable for specifying crosscutting contracts. In AspectJML, one can specify crosscutting contracts in a modular way while preserving key DbC principles such as documentation and modular reasoning.

The work of Bagherzadeh *et al.* [2] contains "translucid" contracts that are grey-box specifications of the behavior of advice. Although which advice applies is unspecified, the specification allows modular verification of programs with advice, since all advice must satisfy the specifications given. The grey-box parts of translucid contracts are able to precisely specify control effects, for example specifying that a particular method must be called a certain number of times, and under certain conditions, which is not easy to specify with AspectJ or AspectJML. $Ptolemy_x$ [1] is an exception-aware extension to Ptolemy/translucid contracts [2]. As with AspectJML, Ptolemy$_x$ supports specification and modular reasoning about exceptional behaviors. The main difference is that AspectJML is used to specify and reason about Java code. On the other hand, Ptolemy$_x$ is used to specify and reason about event announcement and handling.

Pipa [53] is a design by contract language tailored for AspectJ. As with AspectJML, Pipa is an extension to JML. However, Pipa uses the same approach as JML to specify AspectJ programs, with just a few new constructs. AspectJML uses JML in addition to AspectJ's pointcut designators to specify crosscutting contracts.

As with our work with AspectJML, Lam, Kuncak, and Rinard [24] advocate that previous research in the field of aspect-oriented programming has focused on the use of aspect-oriented concepts in design and implementation of crosscutting concerns. Their experience indicates that aspect-oriented concepts can also be extremely useful for specification, analysis, and verification. In this sense, among other things, Lam, Kuncak, and Rinard designed constructs called *scopes* and *defaults* that can be used to improve the locality and clarity of specifications, and, at the same time, reducing the sizes of these specifications. These constructs cut across the preconditions and postconditions of procedures in a system. Like our work, their language provides a pointcut language to select where to apply constraints. The main difference is that their pointcut is not expressive as ours (since we reused the standard AspectJ pointcut language). For instance, in their language one cannot use wildcarding to select join points. Also, their pointcut language can apply to several modules, but this can break modular reasoning (which we preserve in AspectJML). Finally, their work is intended for specification and verification, whereas we are concerned with specification and runtime checking.

While AOP aims at the modularization of homogeneous *and* heterogeneous crosscutting concerns, feature-oriented programming (FOP) focuses on heterogeneous crosscutting concerns only, for which only lightweight language extensions are required. Contracts and their use for runtime assertions have also been studied in the context of FOP [50, 51]. We discussed specification clones in the base code, but they may also occur in crosscutting modules. Interestingly, some of these specification clones can actually be avoided by language constructs beyond quantification [51, 52]. A further challenge is to identify the crosscutting module that caused the violation of a contract. Behavioral feature interfaces have been proposed for localization by means of runtime assertions [50].

There are several other interface technologies that are related to ours [12, 20, 48–51]. However, none of them can modularize crosscutting contracts and keep DbC benefits such as documentation and modular reasoning at the same time. None of these checks contracts of base code.

8. Summary

AspectJML is a seamless aspect-oriented extension to JML. Specifying with AspectJML feels like a small extension of specifying with JML. AspectJML uses a mechanism called crosscutting contract specification (XCS). XCS enables one to explicit specify crosscutting contracts for Java code in a modular way. Also, runtime assertion checking is used to check the conformance of these crosscutting contracts during runtime.

Using AspectJML results in clean, well-modularized specifications of crosscutting contracts. In AspectJML, programmers do not need to use several syntactic constructs of AspectJ-like languages to enable crosscutting contract modularization. On the other hand, when written as AspectJML, the structure of a crosscutting contract is explicit and easy to understand, due to the benefits of DbC-style documentation.

Acknowledgements

We thank Eric Eide, Eric Bodden, Mario Südholt, Arndt Von Staa, David Lorenz and Mehmet Aksit for discussions (we had during the AOSD 2011, more specifically at the Miss 2011 workshop) about design by contract modularization in general.

Special thanks to Mira Mezini, Ralf Lämmel, Yuanfang Cai, and Shuvendu Lahiri for detailed discussions and for comments on earlier versions of this paper.

The work of Leavens was partially supported by US National Science Foundation grants CCF-10-17262 and CCF-1017334. Ricardo Lima is also supported by CNPq under grant No. 314539/2009-3. Also, the work of Rajan and Bagherzadeh was supported by US NSF grants CCF-11-17937 and CCF-08-46059.

References

[1] M. Bagherzadeh, H. Rajan, and A. Darvish. On exceptions, events and observer chains. In *Proceedings of the 12th annual international conference on Aspect-oriented software development*, AOSD '13, pages 185–196, New York, NY, USA, 2013. ACM.

[2] M. Bagherzadeh, H. Rajan, G. T. Leavens, and S. Mooney. Translucid contracts: Expressive specification and modular verification for aspect-oriented interfaces. In *Proceedings of the tenth international conference on Aspect-oriented software development*, AOSD '11, pages 141–152, New York, NY, USA, Mar. 2011. ACM.

[3] S. Balzer, P. T. Eugster, and B. Meyer. Can Aspects Implement Contracts. In *In: Proceedings of RISE 2005 (Rapid Implementation of Engineering Techniques*, pages 13–15, September 2005.

[4] M. Barnett, K. R. M. Leino, and W. Schulte. The Spec# programming system: an overview. In G. Barthe, L. Burdy, M. Huisman, J.-L. Lanet, and T. Muntean, editors, *Post Conference Proceedings of CASSIS: Construction and Analysis of Safe, Secure and Interoperable Smart devices, Marseille*, volume 3362 of *LNCS*. Springer-Verlag, 2005.

[5] J. Boner. Aspectwerks. http://aspectwerkz.codehaus.org/.

[6] L. C. Briand, W. J. Dzidek, and Y. Labiche. Instrumenting Contracts with Aspect-Oriented Programming to Increase Observability and Support Debugging. In *ICSM '05: Proceedings of the 21st IEEE International Conference on Software Maintenance (ICSM'05)*, pages 687–690, Washington, DC, USA, 2005. IEEE Computer Society.

[7] L. C. Briand, Y. Labiche, and H. Sun. Investigating the use of analysis contracts to improve the testability of object-oriented code. *Softw. Pract. Exper.*, 33:637–672, June 2003.

[8] L. Burdy, Y. Cheon, D. R. Cok, M. D. Ernst, J. R. Kiniry, G. T. Leavens, K. R. M. Leino, and E. Poll. An overview of JML tools and applications. *International Journal on Software Tools for Technology Transfer (STTT)*, 7(3):212–232, June 2005.

[9] P. Chalin and P. R. James. Non-null references by default in java: alleviating the nullity annotation burden. In *Proceedings of the 21st European conference on Object-Oriented Programming*, ECOOP'07, pages 227–247, Berlin, Heidelberg, 2007. Springer-Verlag.

[10] Y. Cheon and G. T. Leavens. A runtime assertion checker for the Java Modeling Language (JML). In H. R. Arabnia and Y. Mun, editors, *Proceedings of the International Conference on Software Engineering Research and Practice (SERP '02), Las Vegas, Nevada, USA, June 24-27, 2002*, pages 322–328. CSREA Press, June 2002.

[11] L. A. Clarke and D. S. Rosenblum. A historical perspective on runtime assertion checking in software development. *SIGSOFT Softw. Eng. Notes*, 31:25–37, May 2006.

[12] A. Costa Neto, R. Bonifácio, M. Ribeiro, C. E. Pontual, P. Borba, and F. Castor. A Design Rule Language for Aspect-oriented Programming. *J. Syst. Softw.*, 86(9):2333–2356, Sept. 2013.

[13] K. K. Dhara and G. T. Leavens. Forcing behavioral subtyping through specification inheritance. In *Proceedings of the 18th International Conference on Software Engineering, Berlin, Germany*, pages 258–267. IEEE Computer Society Press, Mar. 1996. A corrected version is ISU CS TR #95-20c, `http://tinyurl.com/s2krg`.

[14] M. Fähndrich, M. Barnett, and F. Logozzo. Embedded contract languages. In *Proceedings of the 2010 ACM Symposium on Applied Computing*, SAC '10, pages 2103–2110, New York, NY, USA, 2010. ACM.

[15] Y. A. Feldman et al. Jose: Aspects for Design by Contract80-89. *IEEE SEFM*, 0:80–89, 2006.

[16] R. E. Filman and D. P. Friedman. Aspect-Oriented Programming is Quantification and Obliviousness. Technical report, 2000.

[17] P. Greenwood, T. Bartolomei, E. Figueiredo, M. Dosea, A. Garcia, N. Cacho, C. Sant'Anna, S. Soares, P. Borba, U. Kulesza, and A. Rashid. On the Impact of Aspectual Decompositions on Design Stability: An Empirical Study. In *Proceedings of the 21st European conference on Object-Oriented Programming*, LNCS, pages 176–200. Springer-Verlag, 2007.

[18] S. Hanenberg and R. Unland. AspectJ idioms for aspect-oriented software construction. In *EuroPlop'03*, 2003.

[19] J. Hannemann and G. Kiczales. Design pattern implementation in Java and AspectJ. In *Proceedings of the 17th ACM SIGPLAN conference on Object-oriented programming, systems, languages, and applications*, OOPSLA '02, pages 161–173, New York, NY, USA, 2002. ACM.

[20] M. Inostroza, E. Tanter, and E. Bodden. Join point interfaces for modular reasoning in aspect-oriented programs. In *Proceedings of the*

19th ACM SIGSOFT symposium and the 13th European conference on Foundations of software engineering*, ESEC/FSE '11, pages 508–511, New York, NY, USA, 2011. ACM.

[21] G. Kiczales, E. Hilsdale, J. Hugunin, M. Kersten, J. Palm, and W. Griswold. Getting Started with AspectJ. *Commun. ACM*, 44:59–65, October 2001.

[22] G. Kiczales, J. Lamping, A. Mendhekar, C. Maeda, C. Lopes, J.-M. Loingtier, and J. Irwin. Aspect-oriented programming. In M. Aksit and S. Matsuoka, editors, *ECOOP'97 Object-Oriented Programming*, volume 1241 of *Lecture Notes in Computer Science*, pages 220–242. Springer Berlin / Heidelberg, 1997.

[23] G. Kiczales and M. Mezini. Aspect-oriented programming and modular reasoning. In *Proceedings of the 27th international conference on Software engineering*, ICSE '05, pages 49–58, New York, NY, USA, 2005. ACM.

[24] P. Lam, V. Kuncak, and M. Rinard. Crosscutting Techniques in Program Specification and Analysis. In *Proceedings of the 4th International Conference on Aspect-oriented Software Development*, AOSD '05, pages 169–180, New York, NY, USA, 2005. ACM.

[25] Y. Le Traon, B. Baudry, and J.-M. Jezequel. Design by contract to improve software vigilance. *IEEE Trans. Softw. Eng.*, 32(8):571–586, Aug. 2006.

[26] G. T. Leavens. JML's rich, inherited specifications for behavioral subtypes. In Z. Liu and H. Jifeng, editors, *Formal Methods and Software Engineering: 8th International Conference on Formal Engineering Methods (ICFEM)*, volume 4260 of *Lecture Notes in Computer Science*, pages 2–34, New York, NY, Nov. 2006. Springer-Verlag.

[27] G. T. Leavens, A. L. Baker, and C. Ruby. Preliminary design of JML: A behavioral interface specification language for Java. *ACM SIGSOFT Software Engineering Notes*, 2006.

[28] G. T. Leavens and D. A. Naumann. Behavioral subtyping, specification inheritance, and modular reasoning. Technical Report CS-TR-13-03a, Computer Science, University of Central Florida, Orlando, FL, 32816, July 2013.

[29] M. Lippert and C. V. Lopes. A study on exception detection and handling using aspect-oriented programming. In *Proceedings of the 22nd international conference on Software engineering*, ICSE '00, pages 418–427, New York, NY, USA, 2000. ACM.

[30] C. V. Lopes, M. Lippert, and E. A. Hilsdale. Design By Contract with Aspect-Oriented Programming. In *U.S. Patent No. 06,442,750*, issued August 27, 2002.

[31] M. Marin, L. Moonen, and A. van Deursen. A Classification of Crosscutting Concerns. In *ICSM '05: Proceedings of the 21st IEEE International Conference on Software Maintenance*, pages 673–676, Washington, DC, USA, 2005. IEEE Computer Society.

[32] B. Meyer. Applying "design by contract". *Computer*, 25(10):40–51, 1992.

[33] B. Meyer. *Eiffel: The Language*. Prentice-Hall, Inc., Upper Saddle River, NJ, USA, 1992.

[34] B. Meyer. *Object-Oriented Software Construction*. Prentice-Hall, PTR, 2nd edition, 2000.

[35] R. Mitchell, J. McKim, and B. Meyer. *Design by contract, by example*. Addison Wesley Longman Publishing Co., Inc., Redwood City, CA, USA, 2002.

[36] D. L. Parnas. On the criteria to be used in decomposing systems into modules. *Commun. ACM*, 15:1053–1058, December 1972.

[37] D. L. Parnas. Precise Documentation: The Key to Better Software. In S. Nanz, editor, *The Future of Software Engineering*, pages 125–148. Springer Berlin Heidelberg, 2011.

[38] H. Rebêlo, G. T. Leavens, and R. M. Lima. Client-aware Checking and Information Hiding in Interface Specifications with JML/Ajmlc. In *Proceedings of the 2013 Companion Publication for Conference on Systems, Programming, & Applications: Software for Humanity*, SPLASH '13, pages 11–12, New York, NY, USA, 2013. ACM.

[39] H. Rebelo, G. T. Leavens, R. M. F. Lima, P. Borba, and M. Ribeiro. Modular aspect-oriented design rule enforcement with XPIDRs. In *Proceedings of the 12th workshop on Foundations of aspect-oriented languages*, FOAL '13, pages 13–18, New York, NY, USA, 2013. ACM.

[40] H. Rebêlo, R. Lima, U. Kulesza, C. Sant'Anna, Y. Cai, R. Coelho, and M. Ribeiro. Quantifying the Effects of Aspectual Decompositions on Design By Contract Modularization: A Maintenance Study. *International Journal of Software Engineering and Knowledge Engineering*, 2013.

[41] H. Rebêlo, R. Lima, and G. T. Leavens. Modular Contracts with Procedures, Annotations, Pointcuts and Advice. In *SBLP '11: Proceedings of the 2011 Brazilian Symposium on Programming Languages*. Brazilian Computer Society, 2011.

[42] H. Rebêlo, R. Lima, G. T. Leavens, M. Cornélio, A. Mota, and C. Oliveira. Optimizing generated aspect-oriented assertion checking code for JML using program transformations: An empirical study. *Science of Computer Programming*, 78(8):1137 – 1156, 2013.

[43] H. Rebêlo, S. Soares, R. Lima, L. Ferreira, and M. Cornélio. Implementing Java modeling language contracts with AspectJ. In *Proceedings of the 2008 ACM symposium on Applied computing*, SAC '08. ACM, 2008.

[44] D. S. Rosenblum. A Practical Approach to Programming With Assertions. *IEEE Trans. Softw. Eng.*, 21(1):19–31, Jan. 1995.

[45] T. Skotiniotis and D. H. Lorenz. Cona: aspects for contracts and contracts for aspects. In *Companion to the 19th annual ACM SIGPLAN conference on Object-oriented programming systems, languages, and applications*, OOPSLA '04, pages 196–197, New York, NY, USA, 2004. ACM.

[46] S. Soares, E. Laureano, and P. Borba. Implementing distribution and persistence aspects with AspectJ. In *Proceedings of the 17th ACM SIGPLAN conference on Object-oriented programming, systems, languages, and applications*, OOPSLA '02, pages 174–190, New York, NY, USA, 2002. ACM.

[47] F. Steimann. The Paradoxical Success of Aspect-Oriented Programming. In *OOPSLA 2006: Proceedings of the 21st International Conference on Object-oriented Programming Systems, Languages, and Applications*, ACM SIGPLAN Notices, pages 481–497, New York, NY, Oct. 2006. ACM.

[48] F. Steimann, T. Pawlitzki, S. Apel, and C. Kästner. Types and modularity for implicit invocation with implicit announcement. *ACM Trans. Softw. Eng. Methodol.*, 20(1):1:1–1:43, July 2010.

[49] K. Sullivan, W. G. Griswold, H. Rajan, Y. Song, Y. Cai, M. Shonle, and N. Tewari. Modular Aspect-oriented Design with XPIs. *ACM Trans. Softw. Eng. Methodol.*, 20(2):5:1–5:42, Sept. 2010.

[50] T. Thüm, S. Apel, A. Zelend, R. Schröter, and B. Möller. Subclack: Feature-oriented Programming with Behavioral Feature Interfaces. In *Proceedings of the 5th Workshop on MechAnisms for SPEcialization, Generalization and inHerItance*, MASPEGHI '13, pages 1–8, New York, NY, USA, 2013. ACM.

[51] T. Thüm, I. Schaefer, M. Kuhlemann, S. Apel, and G. Saake. Applying design by contract to feature-oriented programming. In *Proceedings of the 15th international conference on Fundamental Approaches to Software Engineering*, FASE'12, pages 255–269, Berlin, Heidelberg, 2012. Springer-Verlag.

[52] M. T. Valente, C. Couto, J. Faria, and S. Soares. On the benefits of quantification in AspectJ systems. *Journal of the Brazilian Computer Society*, 16(2):133–146, 2010.

[53] J. Zhao and M. Rinard. Pipa: a behavioral interface specification language for AspectJ. In *Proceedings of the 6th international conference on Fundamental approaches to software engineering*, FASE'03, pages 150–165, Berlin, Heidelberg, 2003. Springer-Verlag.

A. Online Appendix

We invite researchers to replicate our case study. Source code of the JML and AspectJML versions of the running example and HW systems, and other resources are available at: `http://www.cin.ufpe.br/%7ehemr/modularity14/`.

Probabilistic Model Checking for Energy Analysis in Software Product Lines *

Clemens Dubslaff Sascha Klüppelholz Christel Baier
Technische Universität Dresden, Faculty of Computer Science, Germany
{dubslaff,klueppel,baier}@tcs.inf.tu-dresden.de

Abstract

In a *software product line (SPL)*, a collection of software products is defined by their commonalities in terms of features rather than explicitly specifying all products one-by-one. Several verification techniques were adapted to establish temporal properties of SPLs. Symbolic and family-based model checking have been proven to be successful for tackling the combinatorial blow-up arising when reasoning about several feature combinations. However, most formal verification approaches for SPLs presented in the literature focus on the *static* SPLs, where the features of a product are fixed and cannot be changed during runtime. This is in contrast to *dynamic* SPLs, allowing to adapt feature combinations of a product dynamically after deployment.

The main contribution of the paper is a compositional modeling framework for dynamic SPLs, which supports probabilistic and nondeterministic choices and allows for *quantitative analysis*. We specify the feature changes during runtime within an automata-based coordination component, enabling to reason over strategies how to trigger dynamic feature changes for optimizing various quantitative objectives, e.g., energy or monetary costs and reliability. For our framework there is a natural and conceptually simple translation into the input language of the prominent probabilistic model checker PRISM. This facilitates the application of PRISM's powerful symbolic engine to the operational behavior of dynamic SPLs and their family-based analysis against various quantitative queries. We demonstrate feasibility of our approach by a case study issuing an energy-aware bonding network device.

1. Introduction

In order to meet economic requirements and to provide customers individualized solutions, the development and marketing of modern hardware and software products often follows the concept of *product lines*. Within this concept, customers purchase a base system extendible and customizable with additional functionalities, called *features*. Although product lines are commonly established in both, hardware and software development, they have been first and foremost considered in the area of software engineering. A *software product line (SPL)* (see, e.g., [12]) specifies a collection of software systems built from features according to rules describing realizable feature combinations. Such rules for the composition of features are typically provided using *feature diagrams* [6, 29]. Feature combinations are often assumed to be static, i.e., some realizable feature combination is fixed when the product is purchased by a customer and is never changed afterwards. However, this do not faithfully reflect adaptations of modern software during its lifetime. For instance, when a software is updated or when a free trial version expires, features are activated or deactivated during runtime of the system. SPLs which model such adaptations are called *dynamic SPLs* [23], for which the design of specification formalisms is an active and emerging field in SPL engineering [16, 18, 25, 38].

The goal of this paper is provide a *compositional framework* for modeling *dynamic SPLs* which allows for a *quantitative analysis* in order to reason, e.g., about system's resource requirements.

Verification of SPLs. In order to meet requirements in safety-critical parts of SPLs or to guarantee overall quality, verification is highly desirable. This is especially the case for dynamic SPLs, where side-effects arising from dynamic feature changes are difficult to predict in development phases. Model checking [4, 9] is a fully automatic verification technique for establishing temporal properties of systems (e.g., safety or liveness properties). Indeed, it has been successively applied to integrate features in components and to detect feature interactions [36]. However, as observed by Classen et al. [10, 11], the typical task for reasoning about static SPLs is to solve the so-called *featured model-checking problem*:

> Compute the set of all feature combinations such that the considered temporal property φ holds for the corresponding software products.

This is in contrast to the classical model-checking problem that amounts to prove that φ holds for some fixed system, such as one software product obtained from a feature combination. The standard approach solving the featured model-checking problem is to verify the products in the SPL one-by-one (see, e.g., the product-line analysis taxonomy in [45]). However, already within static SPLs this approach certainly suffers from an exponential blow-up, since the number of different software products may rise exponentially in the number of features. To tackle this potential combinatorial blow-up, family-based [45] and symbolic approaches [32] are very successful. Within *family-based analysis*, all products in an SPL are checked at once rather than one-by-one. This requires a model which represents all behaviors of all the products of the SPL. In [10, 11], the concept of *featured transition systems (FTSs)* has been introduced to encode the operational behaviors of all products in an SPL. The transitions in an FTS are annotated by fea-

* This work has been partly supported by Deutsche Telekom Stiftung, the German Research Foundation DFG (SFB 912 HAEC, DFG-project QuaOS, DFG/NWO-project ROCKS) and the EU 7th Framework Programme under grant no. 295261 (MEALS).

MODULARITY '14, April 22–26, 2014, Lugano, Switzerland.

http://dx.doi.org/10.1145/2577080.2577095

ture combinations within which the transition can be taken. Based on symbolic techniques [32], the featured model-checking problem for SPLs represented by FTSs could be solved efficiently for both linear-time [10] and branching-time properties [11]. An extension of FTSs allowing for dynamic adaptions of feature combinations was presented by Cordy et al. [14], annotating further transition guards with possible feature combination switches.

Besides classical temporal properties, the quality of software products crucially depends on quantitative (non-functional) properties. While measurement-based approaches for reasoning about feature-oriented software have been studied intensively (see e.g. [34, 42, 43]), probabilistic model-checking techniques have been studied only recently. These use purely probabilistic operational models based on discrete-time Markov chains and probabilistic computation tree logic. The approach by Ghezzi and Sharifloo [22] relies on parametric sequence diagrams analyzed using the probabilistic model-checking tool PARAM. Recently, a family-based approach for Markov chains has been presented by [44].

Our Compositional Framework. For the compositional design of software products with parallel components, Markov chains are known to be less adequate than operational models supporting both, nondeterministic and probabilistic choices (see, e.g., [40]). A *Markov decision process (MDP)* is such a formalism, extending labelled transition systems by internal probabilistic choices taken after resolving nondeterminism between actions of the system. In this paper, we present a compositional framework for dynamic SPLs relying on MDPs with annotated costs, used, e.g., to reason about resource requirements, energy consumption or monetary costs. In particular, our contribution consists of

(1) feature modules: MDP-like models for the operational feature-dependent behavior of the components and their interactions,

(2) a parallel operator for feature modules that represents the parallel execution of independent actions by interleaving, supporting communication according to the handshaking principle and over shared variables, and

(3) a feature controller: an MDP-like model for the potential dynamic switches of feature combinations.

An SPL naturally induces a compositional structure over features, where features or collections thereof correspond to components. In our framework, these components are called feature modules (1), which can contain both, nondeterministic and probabilistic choices. The former might be useful in early design stages, whereas probabilistic choices can be used to model the likelihood of exceptional behaviors (e.g., if some failure appears) or to represent randomized activities (e.g., coin tossing actions to break symmetry). Both kinds of choices may depend on other features – for instance, whether another feature is activated during runtime or not.

Feature Modules are composed using a parallel operator (2), which combines the operational behaviors of all features represented by the feature modules into another feature module. This composition is defined upon compatible feature interfaces of the feature modules, which keep track of the features owned by the feature modules and those which the behavior of the feature modules depends on. Closest to our compositional approach with MDP-like models is the approach by [33] that works with nonprobabilistic finite-state machines and addresses conformance checking.

Feature activation and deactivation is described through feature controllers (3), which is a state-based model controlling valid changes in the feature combinations. As within feature modules, choices between feature combinations can be probabilistically (e.g., on the basis of statistical information on feature combinations and their adaptations over time) or nondeterministically (e.g., if feature changes rely on internal choices of the controller or are triggered from outside by an unknown or unpredictable environment) and combinations thereof. To the best of our knowledge, this concept is novel in the probabilistic setting and has also been only merely considered in the nonprobabilistic case [16].

The semantics of a feature module under a given feature controller is defined as a parallel composition of both formalisms, providing an elegant formalization of the feature module's behavior within the dynamic SPL represented by the feature controller. This parallel composition roughly arises by augmenting probabilistic automata [40] with feature interfaces. Note that our approach separates between computation and coordination [21, 35, 39], which allows for specifying features in the context of various different dynamic SPLs. Feature-oriented extensions of programming languages and specialized composition operators such as *superimposition* are an orthogonal approach [1–3, 30]. The effect of superimposition can be encoded into our framework, e.g., using techniques proposed by Plath and Ryan [36], but there is no direct support for composing feature modules using superimposition.

Quantitative Analysis. Fortunately, the semantics of feature modules under feature controllers rise a standard MDP, such that our approach permits the application of standard but sophisticated probabilistic model-checking techniques to reason about quantitative properties. This is in contrast to existing (nonprobabilistic) approaches, which require model-checking algorithms specialized for SPLs. Within our approach, temporal or quantitative queries such as "minimize the energy consumption until reaching a target state" or "maximize the utility value to reach a target state for a given initial energy budget" can be answered. Corresponding to the nonprobabilistic case, the solution of the featured model-checking problem would then provide answers of these queries for all initial feature combinations. In the setting of dynamic SPLs, we go a step further and define the *strategy synthesis problem* aiming to find an optimal strategy of resolving the nondeterminism between feature combination switches in the feature controller. This strategy includes the initial step of the dynamic SPL by selecting an initial feature combination, which suffices to solve the featured model-checking problem. However, our approach additionally provides the possibility to reason over worst-case scenarios concerning feature changes during runtime. Note that solving the strategy synthesis problem imposes a family-based analysis approach of the dynamic SPL, which is also novel in the nonprobabilistic setting.

As in the nonprobabilistic case, symbolic techniques can help to avoid the exponential blow-up when analyzing probabilistic SPLs. This is even more crucial for dynamic SPLs, since the number of feature changes during runtime also yield an exponential blow-up. Our compositional framework nicely fits with guarded-command languages such as the input language of the symbolic probabilistic model checker PRISM [28]. PRISM uses multi-terminal binary decision diagrams for the symbolic encoding of the probabilistic model and thus ensures a compact representation. We expressed a case study based on a real-case scenario from the hardware domain according to our framework to demonstrate applicability of PRISM. This case study details the energy-aware network device EBOND+, an extension of the recently presented EBOND device [24]. We explain how PRISM can be used to solve the aforementioned strategy synthesis problem w.r.t. to several quantitative queries formalizing requirements, e.g., on the energy consumption of the EBOND+ device. Our case study also illustrates that our approach is not restricted to SPLs, but can also be applied to product lines in general.

Outline. In Section 2 we briefly summarize basics on SPLs, feature models and relevant principles of MDPs and their quantitative analysis. The compositional framework for specifying feature combinations by means of feature modules and feature controllers as a formal operational model for dynamic features changes is presented in Section 3. We illustrate applicability of our approach within our energy-aware case study in Section 4. The paper ends with some concluding remarks in Section 5.

2. Preliminaries

Notations for Sets and Boolean Expressions. The powerset of a set X is denoted by 2^X. For convenience, we sometimes use symbolic notations based on Boolean expressions (propositional formulas) for the elements of 2^X, i.e., the subsets of X. Let $\mathbb{B}(X)$ denote the set of all Boolean expressions ρ built by elements $x \in X$ as atoms (Boolean variables) and the usual connectives of propositional logic (negation $\neg$, conjunction $\wedge$, etc.). The satisfaction relation $\models \subseteq 2^X \times \mathbb{B}(X)$ is defined in the obvious way. E.g., if $X = \{x_1, x_2, x_3\}$ and $\rho = x_1 \wedge \neg x_2$, then $Y \models \rho$ iff $Y = \{x_1\}$ or $Y = \{x_1, x_3\}$. To specify binary relations on 2^X symbolically, we use Boolean expressions $\rho \in \mathbb{B}(X \cup X')$, where X' is the set consisting of pairwise distinct, fresh copies of the elements of X. Then, the relation $R_\rho \subseteq 2^X \times 2^X$ is given by:

$$(Y, Z) \in R_\rho \quad \text{iff} \quad Y \cup \{z' : z \in Z\} \models \rho$$

E.g., the Boolean expression $\rho = (x_1 \vee x_3') \wedge \neg x_2$ represents the relation R_ρ consisting of all pairs $(Y, Z) \in 2^X \times 2^X$, where (1) $x_1 \in Y$ or $x_3 \in Z$ and (2) $x_2 \notin Y$. For $Y \subseteq X$, we use $Y = Y'$ as a shortform notation for the Boolean expression $\bigwedge_{y \in Y} y \leftrightarrow y'$.

Distributions. Let S be a countable nonempty set. A *distribution over* S is a function $\sigma : S \to [0,1]$ with $\sum_{s \in S} \sigma(s) = 1$. The set $\{s \in S : \sigma(s) > 0\}$ is called the *support of* σ and is denoted by $supp(\sigma)$. $Distr(S)$ denotes the set of distributions over S. Given $t \in S$, the distribution $Dirac[t] \in Distr(S)$ defined by

$$Dirac[t](t) = 1 \text{ and } Dirac[t](s) = 0 \text{ for all } s \in S \setminus \{t\}$$

is called the *Dirac distribution of t over S*. The *product* of two distributions $\sigma_1 \in Distr(S_1)$ and $\sigma_2 \in Distr(S_2)$ is defined as the distribution $\sigma_1 * \sigma_2 \in Distr(S_1 \times S_2)$, where $(\sigma_1 * \sigma_2)(s_1, s_2) = \sigma_1(s_1) \cdot \sigma_2(s_2)$ for all $s_1 \in S_1$ and $s_2 \in S_2$.

2.1 Feature Models

According to [12], a *software product line (SPL)* is a collection of software products, which have commonalities w.r.t. assets called *features*. When F denotes the set of all such features in an SPL, a *feature combination* is a subset C of F, which is said to be *valid* if there is a corresponding product in the SPL consisting exactly of the features in C. An SPL can hence be formalized in terms of a *feature signature* $(F, \mathcal{V})$, where $\mathcal{V}$ is the set of valid feature combinations. *Feature diagrams* [29] provide a compact representation of feature signatures via a tree-like hierarchical diagram (see, e.g., Figure 1). Nodes in feature diagrams correspond to features of F, where nodes with a circle on top denote optional features. If the node for feature f' is a son of the node for feature f, then feature f' requires f. Several types of branchings from a node for feature f towards its sons $f_1', \ldots, f_n'$ are possible. Standard branchings denote that all nonoptional sons are required by f (AND connective), connected branchings indicate that exactly one son is required by f (XOR connective) and solid ones require at least one son (OR connective). An additional arrow from a node for feature f towards a node for feature f' can be used to indicate that f' is required by f. Boolean expressions over F may be further used as constraints on possible feature combinations. For analyzing SPLs, various approaches annotating additional data to feature models were considered. E.g., [15] amends feature diagrams with statistical data, which yields probability distribution over valid feature combinations.

Static vs. Dynamic SPL. Usually, SPLs are static in the sense that a valid feature combination is fixed prior the execution of the system. SPLs allowing for activation and deactivation of features during runtime of a system are called *dynamic SPLs*. The common approach towards dynamic SPLs is to indicate disjoint sets of *dynamic features D* and *environment features E*, which respectively include features that can be activated or deactivated at runtime either by the system itself (features of D) or by the environment (features of E). Intuitively, an activation and deactivation of an environment feature may impose (de-)activations of dynamic features [14]. In [18] dynamic SPLs are formalized using a generalization of feature diagrams where dashed nodes represent elements of $D \cup E$. Costs for feature activations in dynamic SPLs have been considered in [46]. The following example details a dynamic SPL for a productivity system, provided by a feature diagram with annotated costs.

Example 2.1. Features of the dynamic SPL represented by the feature diagram shown in Figure 1 have underlined symbols used

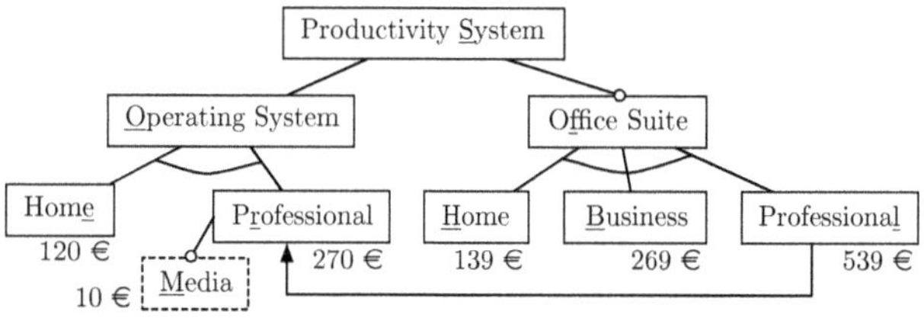

Figure 1. A feature diagram representing an SPL

as abbreviations, i.e., the set of features in the SPL would be $F = \{\mathrm{s, o, e, r, m, f, h, b, l}\}$. According to the semantics of feature diagrams, $\{\mathrm{s, o, e}\}$ (briefly written soe) is the smallest valid feature combination and, e.g., soefb describes a valid feature combination with a business feature in the office suite. The media center feature m is an optional environment feature, i.e., if the customer is unsatisfied with the media functionalities, she can downgrade to the plain professional version of the operating system and allowed to upgrade again if she changed her mind. Note that the professional office suite requires the professional operating system. Thus, the feature combination soefl is invalid but sorfl is valid.

2.2 Markov Decision Processes

The operational model used in this paper for modeling and analyzing the behavior of the instances represented by a dynamic SPL is given in terms of *Markov decision processes (MDPs)* [37]. We deal here with MDPs where transitions are labeled with decision identifiers and a cost value. MDPs with multiple cost functions of different types (e.g. for reasoning energy and memory requirements and utility values) can be defined accordingly. Formally, the notion of an MDP is a tuple

$$\mathcal{M} = (S, S^{init}, \mathsf{Moves}),$$

where S is a finite set of states, $S^{init} \subseteq S$ is the set of initial states and $\mathsf{Moves} \subseteq S \times \mathbb{N} \times Distr(S)$ specifies the possible moves of $\mathcal{M}$ and their costs. We require Moves to be finite and often write $s \xrightarrow{c} \sigma$ iff $(s, c, \sigma) \in \mathsf{Moves}$. Intuitively, the operational behavior of $\mathcal{M}$ is as follows. The computations of $\mathcal{M}$ start in some nondeterministically chosen initial state of S^{init}. If during $\mathcal{M}$'s computation the current state is s, one of the moves $s \xrightarrow{c} \sigma$ is selected nondeterministically first, before there is an internal probabilistic choice, selecting a successor state s' with probability $\sigma(s')$. Value c specifies the cost for taking the move $s \xrightarrow{c} \sigma$.

Steps of $\mathcal{M}$, written in the form $s \overset{c}{\hookrightarrow}_p s'$, arise from moves when resolving the probabilistic choice by plugging in some state s' with positive probability, i.e., $p = \sigma(s') > 0$. *Paths* in $\mathcal{M}$ are sequences of consecutive steps. In the following, we assume a finite path π having the form

$$\pi \; = \; s_0 \overset{c_1}{\hookrightarrow}_{p_1} s_1 \overset{c_2}{\hookrightarrow}_{p_2} s_2 \overset{c_3}{\hookrightarrow}_{p_3} \ldots \overset{c_n}{\hookrightarrow}_{p_n} s_n. \qquad (*)$$

We refer to the number n of steps as the length of π. If $0 \leq k \leq n$, we write $\pi[k]$ for the prefix of π consisting of the first k steps (then, $\pi[k]$ ends in state s_k). Given a finite path π, the probability $\Pr(\pi)$ is defined as the product of the probabilities in the steps of π and the accumulated costs $\text{cost}(\pi)$ are defined as the sum of the costs of π's steps. Formally,

$$\Pr(\pi) = p_1 \cdot p_2 \cdot \ldots \cdot p_n \text{ and } \text{cost}(\pi) = c_1 + c_2 + \ldots + c_n.$$

State $s \in S$ is called *terminal* if there is no move $s \xrightarrow{c} \sigma$. A path is *maximal*, if it is either infinite or ends in a terminal state. The set of finite paths starting in state s is denoted by $FPaths(s)$. Likewise, we write $Paths(s)$ for the set of all maximal paths starting in s.

Schedulers and Probability Measure. Reasoning about probabilities in MDPs requires the selection of an initial state and resolution of the nondeterministic choices between possible moves. The latter is formalized via *schedulers*, also called policies or adversaries, which take as input a finite path and decide which move to take next. For the purposes of this paper, it suffices to consider deterministic, possibly history-dependent schedulers, i.e., partial functions

$$\mathfrak{S} : FPaths \to \mathbb{N} \times Distr(S),$$

which are undefined for finite maximal paths and for which if $\mathfrak{S}(\pi) = (c, \sigma)$, then $s \xrightarrow{c} \sigma$ for all finite paths π that end in a nonterminal state s. A $\mathfrak{S}$*-path* is any path that arises when the nondeterministic choices in $\mathcal{M}$ are resolved by $\mathfrak{S}$. Thus, a finite path π as in $(*)$ is a $\mathfrak{S}$-path iff there are distributions $\sigma_1, \ldots, \sigma_k \in Distr(S)$ such that $\mathfrak{S}(\,\pi[k{-}1]\,) = (c_k, \sigma_k)$ and $p_k = \sigma_k(s_k)$ for all $1 \leq k \leq n$. Infinite $\mathfrak{S}$-paths are defined accordingly.

Given a scheduler $\mathfrak{S}$ and some initial state $s \in S^{init}$, the behavior of $\mathcal{M}$ under $\mathfrak{S}$ is purely probabilistic and can be formalized by a tree-like infinite-state Markov chain $\mathcal{M}_s^{\mathfrak{S}}$.[1] Using standard concepts, a probability measure $\mathbb{P}_s^{\mathfrak{S}}$ for measurable sets of maximal branches in the Markov chain $\mathcal{M}_s^{\mathfrak{S}}$ is defined and can be transferred to maximal $\mathfrak{S}$-paths in $\mathcal{M}$ starting in s. For further details we refer to standard text books such as [26, 31, 37].

Quantitative Properties and Queries. The concept of schedulers permits to talk about the probability of a measurable path property φ for fixed starting state s under a given scheduler $\mathfrak{S}$. Typical examples for such a property φ are reachability conditions of the following type, where T and V are sets of states:

- ordinary reachability: $\varphi = \Diamond T$ states that eventually some state in T will be visited
- constrained reachability: $\varphi = V \,\mathcal{U}\, T$ imposes the same constraint as $\Diamond T$ with the side-condition that all states visited before reaching T belong to V

For a worst-case analysis of a system modeled by an MDP $\mathcal{M}$, one ranges over all initial states and all schedulers (i.e., all possible resolutions of the nondeterminism) and considers the maximal or minimal probabilities for φ. If φ represents a desired path property, then $\mathbb{P}_s^{\min}(\varphi) = \inf_{\mathfrak{S}} \mathbb{P}_s^{\mathfrak{S}}(\varphi)$ is the probability for $\mathcal{M}$ satisfying φ that can be guaranteed even for the worst-case scenarios. Similarly, $\mathbb{P}_s^{\max}(\varphi) = \sup_{\mathfrak{S}} \mathbb{P}_s^{\mathfrak{S}}(\varphi)$ is the least upper bound that can be guaranteed for the likelihood of $\mathcal{M}$ to satisfy φ.

One can also reason about bounds for expected costs of paths in $\mathcal{M}$. We consider here accumulated costs to reach a set $T \subseteq S$ of target states from a state $s \in S$. Formally, if $\mathfrak{S}$ is a scheduler such that $\mathbb{P}_s^{\mathfrak{S}}(\Diamond T) = 1$, then the *expected accumulated costs* for reaching T from s under $\mathfrak{S}$ are defined by:

$$\mathbb{E}_s^{\mathfrak{S}}(\Diamond T) \;=\; \textstyle\sum_{\pi} \text{cost}(\pi) \cdot \Pr(\pi),$$

where π ranges over all finite $\mathfrak{S}$-paths with $s_n \in T$, $s_0 = s$ and $\{s_0, \ldots, s_{n-1}\} \cap T = \emptyset$. If $\mathbb{P}_s^{\mathfrak{S}}(\Diamond T) < 1$, i.e., with positive probability T will never be visited, then $\mathbb{E}_s^{\mathfrak{S}}(\Diamond T) = \infty$. Furthermore,

$$\mathbb{E}_s^{\min}(\Diamond T) = \inf_{\mathfrak{S}} \mathbb{E}_s^{\mathfrak{S}}(\Diamond T) \quad \text{and} \quad \mathbb{E}_s^{\max}(\Diamond T) = \sup_{\mathfrak{S}} \mathbb{E}_s^{\mathfrak{S}}(\Diamond T)$$

specify the greatest lower bound (least upper bound, respectively) for the expected accumulated costs reaching T from s in $\mathcal{M}$.

There are several powerful probabilistic model-checking tools that support the algorithmic quantitative analysis of MDPs against temporal specifications, such as formulas of linear temporal logic (LTL) or probabilistic computation-tree logic (PCTL) [5, 7]. In our case study, we will use the prominent probabilistic model checker PRISM [28] that offers a symbolic MDP-engine for PCTL, dealing with a compact internal representation of the MDP using multi-terminal binary decision diagrams. PCTL provides an elegant formalism to specify various temporal properties, reliability and resource conditions. For the purpose of the paper, the precise syntax and semantics of PCTL over MDPs is not relevant. We only give brief explanations for PCTL formula patterns and queries that will be used in our case study.

Let $q \in [0, 1]$ be a rational number that serves as a probability bound and let φ be a path property, e.g., one of the reachability conditions stated above. Then, the formula $\Phi = \exists \mathsf{P}_{>q}(\varphi)$ holds for a state s, denoted $s \models \Phi$, if $\mathbb{P}_s^{\mathfrak{S}}(\varphi) > q$ for some scheduler $\mathfrak{S}$. This is equivalent to $\mathbb{P}_s^{\max}(\varphi) > q$ for reachability as above (and all path conditions expressible in PCTL). Likewise, the P-operator can be used with nonstrict lower or upper probability bounds and universal rather than existential quantification over schedulers. We write $\mathcal{M} \models \Phi$ to indicate that all initial states of $\mathcal{M}$ satisfying Φ. $\mathsf{P}^{\max=?}[\varphi]$, respectively $\mathsf{P}^{\min=?}[\varphi]$ denote the PCTL-queries to compute for all states s the maximal, respectively minimal probability for φ. In our case study, we will also use queries of the form $\mathsf{E}^{\min=?}[\Diamond T]$, which amount computing the values $\mathbb{E}_s^{\min}(\Diamond T)$ for all states s defined above.

3. Compositional Framework

An SPL naturally induces a compositional structure, where features correspond to modules composed, e.g., along the hierarchy of features provided by feature diagrams. Thus, it is rather natural that our modeling framework for dynamic SPLs relies on a compositional approach. We formalize feature implementations by so-called *feature modules* that might interact with each other and can depend on the presence of other features and their current configurations. Dependencies between feature modules are represented in form of guarded transitions in the feature modules, which can impose constraints on the current feature combination and ask for synchronizing actions. The interplay of the feature modules can be also described by a single feature module, which arises from the feature implementations via parallel composition and hence only depends on the dynamic feature changes. Unlike other models for dynamic SPLs, there is no explicit representation of the dynamic feature combination changes inside the feature modules. Instead, we adopt the clear separation between computation and coordination as it is central for coordination languages [21, 35, 39]. In our approach, the dynamic activation and deactivation of features is represented in a separate module, called *feature controller*. This separation yields the usual advantages: feature modules can be replaced and reused for many scenarios that vary in constraints for switching feature combinations and that might even rely on different feature signatures.

We model both, feature modules and feature controllers, as MDP-like automata models with annotations for (possibly feature-dependent) interactions between modules and the controller. To

[1] Markov chains are MDPs that do not have any nondeterministic choices, i.e, where S^{init} is a singleton and $|\mathsf{Moves}(s)| \leq 1$ for all states $s \in S$.

reason about resource constraints, cost functions are attached to the transitions of both, the feature modules and the feature controller. Through parallel composition operators, the complete dynamic SPL has a standard MDP semantics, which facilitates the use of standard model-checking techniques for the functional and quantitative analysis. This is in contrast do other but similar but nonprobabilistic and noncompositional approaches, which require specialized feature-dependent analysis algorithms. We show that our approach towards dynamic SPLs is more expressive than existing approaches by providing embeddings into our framework. The compositional framework we present here aims also to provide a link between abstract models for feature implementations and the guarded command languages supported by state-of-the art probabilistic model checkers. As stated in the introduction, this approach is orthogonal to the compositional approaches for SPLs that have been proposed in the literature (see, e.g., [3, 27, 33, 36]) presenting an algebra for the nonprobabilistic feature-oriented composition of modules that covers several subtle implementation details.

3.1 Feature Modules

For our definitions, let us fix some feature signature $(F, \mathcal{V})$. To keep the mathematical model simple, we put the emphasis on the compositional treatment of features and therefore present first a data-abstract lightweight formalism for the feature modules. In this setting, feature modules can be seen as labeled transition systems, where the transitions have guards that formalize feature-dependent behaviors and are annotated with probabilities and costs to model stochastic phenomena and resource constraints.

We start with the definition of a feature interface that declares which features are "implemented" by the given feature module (called *own features*) and on which *external* features the behavior of the module depends on.

Definition 3.1 (Feature interface). *A feature interface is a pair* $\mathsf{F} = \langle \mathsf{OwnF}, \mathsf{ExtF} \rangle$ *consisting of two subsets* OwnF *and* ExtF *of* F *such that* $\mathsf{OwnF} \cap \mathsf{ExtF} = \varnothing$.

With abuse of notations, we often write F to also denote the set $\mathsf{OwnF} \cup \mathsf{ExtF}$ of features affected by the feature interface F. We now define feature modules as an MDP-like formalism according to a feature interface, where moves may depend on features of the feature interface and the change of own features can be triggered, e.g., from the environment.

Definition 3.2 (Feature module). *A* feature module *is a tuple* $\mathsf{Mod} = (\mathsf{Loc}, \mathsf{Loc}^{init}, \mathsf{F}, \mathsf{Act}, \mathsf{Trans})$, *where*

- Loc *is a set of locations,*
- $\mathsf{Loc}^{init} \subseteq \mathsf{Loc}$ *is the set of initial locations,*
- $\mathsf{F} = \langle \mathsf{OwnF}, \mathsf{ExtF} \rangle$ *is a feature interface,*
- Act *is a finite set of actions, and*
- $\mathsf{Trans} = \mathsf{TrAct} \cup \mathsf{TrSw}$ *is a finite transition relation.*

The operational behavior of Mod *specified through* Trans *is given by feature-guarded transitions that are either labeled by an action* (TrAct) *or by a switch event describing own features changes* (TrSw). *Formally:*

$$\mathsf{TrAct} \subseteq \mathsf{Loc} \times \mathbb{B}(\mathsf{F}) \times \mathsf{Act} \times \mathbb{N} \times Distr(\mathsf{Loc})$$

$$\mathsf{TrSw} \subseteq \mathsf{Loc} \times \mathbb{B}(\mathsf{F}) \times \mathbb{B}(\mathsf{OwnF} \cup \mathsf{OwnF}') \times \mathbb{N} \times Distr(\mathsf{Loc})$$

Recall that $\mathbb{B}(\cdot)$ *stands for the set of Boolean expressions over the augmented set of features.*

Let us go more into detail concerning the operational behavior of feature modules. Both types of transitions in Mod, action-labeled transitions and switch transitions, have the form $\theta = (\ell, \phi, *, c, \lambda)$, where

- ℓ is a location, called *source location* of θ,
- $\phi \in \mathbb{B}(\mathsf{F})$ is a Boolean expression, called *feature guard*,
- $c \in \mathbb{N}$ specifies the cost caused by executing θ,[2] and
- λ is a distribution over Loc specifying an internal choice that determines the probabilities for the successor locations.

For action-labeled transitions, the third component $*$ is an action $\alpha \in \mathsf{Act}$ representing some computation of Mod. Hence, wether an action-labeled is enabled or not depends on the current feature combination (fulfilling the feature guard or not) and on the interaction with other feature modules (see Section 3.2). For switch transitions, $*$ is a Boolean expression $\rho \in \mathbb{B}(\mathsf{OwnF} \cup \mathsf{OwnF}')$, enabling Mod to react or impose constraints on dynamic changes of features owned by Mod. In Section 3.3, we introduce feature controllers to describe the operational behavior of feature changes during runtime. A switch transition is then only enabled if the feature guard is fulfilled and the controller permits a change of own features of Mod as described by ρ. The precise meaning of switch transitions will become more clear from the operational behavior of Mod in the context of such controllers presented in Section 3.4.

Note that we defined feature modules in a generic way, such that feature modules need not to be aware of the feature signature and realizable feature switches, which makes them reusable for different dynamic SPLs.

3.2 Parallel Composition

We formalize the interactions of feature modules by introducing a parallel operator on feature modules. Thus, starting with separate feature modules for all features $f \in F$ one might generate feature modules that "implement" several features, and eventually obtain a feature model that describes the behavior of all "controllable" features of the SPL over the feature signature $(F, \mathcal{V})$. Additionally, there might be some features in the set of features F provided by an unknown environment, where no feature modules are given.

We now consider a parallel operator for two composable feature modules in the style of parallel composition of probabilistic automata [40, 41] using *synchronization* over shared actions (handshaking) and interleaving for all other actions. Let

$$\begin{aligned} \mathsf{Mod}_1 &= (\mathsf{Loc}_1, \mathsf{Loc}_1^{init}, \mathsf{F}_1, \mathsf{Act}_1, \mathsf{Trans}_1) \\ \mathsf{Mod}_2 &= (\mathsf{Loc}_2, \mathsf{Loc}_2^{init}, \mathsf{F}_2, \mathsf{Act}_2, \mathsf{Trans}_2), \end{aligned}$$

where $\mathsf{F}_i = \langle \mathsf{OwnF}_i, \mathsf{ExtF}_i \rangle$ and $\mathsf{Trans}_i = \mathsf{TrAct}_i \cup \mathsf{TrSw}_i$. Composability of Mod_1 and Mod_2 means that $\mathsf{OwnF}_1 \cap \mathsf{OwnF}_2 = \varnothing$. Own features of Mod_1 might be external for Mod_2 and vice versa, influencing each others behavior.

Definition 3.3 (Parallel composition). *Let* Mod_1, Mod_2 *be two composable feature modules as above. The* parallel composition *of* Mod_1 *and* Mod_2 *is defined as the feature module*

$$\mathsf{Mod}_1 \| \mathsf{Mod}_2 = (\mathsf{Loc}, \mathsf{Loc}^{init}, \mathsf{F}, \mathsf{Act}, \mathsf{Trans}),$$

where the feature interface $\mathsf{F} = \langle \mathsf{OwnF}, \mathsf{ExtF} \rangle$ *and the other components are defined as follows:*

$$\begin{aligned} \mathsf{Loc} &= \mathsf{Loc}_1 \times \mathsf{Loc}_2 \\ \mathsf{Loc}^{init} &= \mathsf{Loc}_1^{init} \times \mathsf{Loc}_2^{init} \\ \mathsf{OwnF} &= \mathsf{OwnF}_1 \cup \mathsf{OwnF}_2 \\ \mathsf{ExtF} &= (\mathsf{ExtF}_1 \cup \mathsf{ExtF}_2) \setminus \mathsf{OwnF} \\ \mathsf{Act} &= \mathsf{Act}_1 \cup \mathsf{Act}_2 \end{aligned}$$

The treansition relation $\mathsf{Trans} = \mathsf{TrAct} \cup \mathsf{TrSw}$ *is defined by the rules shown in Figure 2.*

[2] For simplicity, we deal here a single cost value for each guarded transition. Feature modules with multiple cost values will be considered in the case study and can be defined accordingly.

$$\frac{\alpha \in \mathsf{Act}_1 \setminus \mathsf{Act}_2,\ (\ell_1, \phi, \alpha, c, \lambda_1) \in \mathsf{TrAct}_1}{(\langle \ell_1, \ell_2 \rangle, \phi, \alpha, c, \lambda_1 * \mathit{Dirac}[\ell_2]) \in \mathsf{TrAct}} \qquad \frac{\alpha \in \mathsf{Act}_2 \setminus \mathsf{Act}_1,\ (\ell_2, \phi, \alpha, c, \lambda_2) \in \mathsf{TrAct}_2}{(\langle \ell_1, \ell_2 \rangle, \phi, \alpha, c, \mathit{Dirac}[\ell_1] * \lambda_2) \in \mathsf{TrAct}}$$

$$\frac{\alpha \in \mathsf{Act}_1 \cap \mathsf{Act}_2,\ (\ell_2, \phi_1, \alpha, c_1, \lambda_1) \in \mathsf{TrAct}_1,\ (\ell_2, \phi_2, \alpha, c_2, \lambda_2) \in \mathsf{TrAct}_2}{(\langle \ell_1, \ell_2 \rangle, \phi_1 \wedge \phi_2, \alpha, c_1 + c_2, \lambda_1 * \lambda_2) \in \mathsf{TrAct}}$$

$$\frac{(\ell_1, \phi, \rho, c, \lambda_1) \in \mathsf{TrSw}_1}{(\langle \ell_1, \ell_2 \rangle, \phi, \rho \wedge \mathsf{OwnF}_2 = \mathsf{OwnF}_2', c, \lambda_1 * \mathit{Dirac}[\ell_2]) \in \mathsf{TrSw}} \qquad \frac{(\ell_2, \phi, \rho, c, \lambda_2) \in \mathsf{TrSw}_2}{(\langle \ell_1, \ell_2 \rangle, \phi, \rho \wedge \mathsf{OwnF}_1 = \mathsf{OwnF}_1', c, \mathit{Dirac}[\ell_1] * \lambda_2) \in \mathsf{TrSw}}$$

$$\frac{(\ell_1, \phi_1, \rho_1, c_1, \lambda_1) \in \mathsf{TrSw}_1,\ (\ell_2, \phi_2, \rho_2, c_2, \lambda_2) \in \mathsf{TrSw}_2}{(\langle \ell_1, \ell_2 \rangle, \phi_1 \wedge \phi_2, \rho_1 \wedge \rho_2, c_1 + c_2, \lambda_1 * \lambda_2) \in \mathsf{TrSw}}$$

Figure 2. Rules for the parallel composition of feature modules

Obviously, $\mathsf{Mod}_1 \| \mathsf{Mod}_2$ is again a feature module. In contrast to the (nonprobabilistic) superimposition approach for composing modules representing feature implementations [30, 36], the parallel operator $\|$ is commutative and associative. More precisely, if Mod_i for $i \in \{1, 2, 3\}$ are pairwise composable feature modules, then:

$$\begin{aligned} \mathsf{Mod}_1 \| \mathsf{Mod}_2 &= \mathsf{Mod}_2 \| \mathsf{Mod}_1 \\ (\mathsf{Mod}_1 \| \mathsf{Mod}_2) \| \mathsf{Mod}_3 &= \mathsf{Mod}_1 \| (\mathsf{Mod}_2 \| \mathsf{Mod}_3) \end{aligned}$$

For the parallel composition of feature modules with multiple cost functions, one has to declare which cost functions are combined. This can be achieved by dealing with types (e.g., energy, money, memory requirements) of cost functions and accumulate costs of the same type.

3.3 Feature Controller

After we defined feature modules and described how their operational behavior is influenced via interacting with other feature modules, we now turn to feature controllers, which specify the rules for the possible changes of feature combinations during runtime of the system. We start with purely nondeterministic controllers switching feature combinations similar to [16] (Definition 3.4). Then, we extend such simple controllers by assigning probabilities to the feature switch events (Definition 3.5).

Definition 3.4. *A* simple feature controller *over the feature signature* $(F, \mathcal{V})$ *is a tuple*

$$\mathsf{Con} = (\mathcal{V}, \mathcal{V}^{init}, \mathsf{SwRel}),$$

where $\mathcal{V}^{init} \subseteq \mathcal{V}$ *is the set of* initial feature combinations *and* $\mathsf{SwRel} \subseteq \mathcal{V} \times \mathbb{N} \times \mathcal{V}$ *is a relation, called* (feature) switch relation, *that formalizes the possible dynamic changes of the feature combinations and their cost. We refer to elements in* SwRel *as* (feature) switch events *and require that* $(C, d_1, C'), (C, d_2, C') \in \mathsf{SwRel}$ *implies* $d_1 = d_2$.

If there are several switch events $(C, d_1, C_1), (C, d_2, C_2), \ldots$ that are enabled for the feature combination C, then the choice which switch event fires is chosen nondeterministically. This is adequate, e.g., to represent potential upgrades or downgrades of a software product or express environmental influences.

Although our focus is on reasoning about dynamic SPLs, we like to mention that our framework is also applicable for static SPLs, where one valid feature combination is selected initially and is never be changed at runtime. Static SPLs can easily be modeled using the simple feature controller $\mathsf{Con}_{\mathsf{static}} = (\mathcal{V}, \mathcal{V}, \varnothing)$, where the switch relation is empty.

The concept of simple feature controllers also covers the approach of [14, 18], where dynamic SPLs are represented by feature signatures $(F, \mathcal{V})$ extended with disjoint sets of dynamic features $D \subseteq F$ and environment features $E \subseteq F$. The features in $D \cup E$ can be activated or deactivated at any time, while the modes of all other features remain unchanged. This dynamic behavior of the feature combinations is formalized using the controller (we omit the cost values of switch events):

$$\mathsf{Con}_{D,E} = (\mathcal{V}, \mathcal{V}, \mathsf{SwRel}_{D,E}),$$

where $(C, C') \in \mathsf{SwRel}_{D,E}$ iff $\varnothing \neq C \ominus C' \subseteq D \cup E$ for all $C, C' \in \mathcal{V}$. Here, $C \ominus C'$ denotes the symmetric difference of C and C', i.e., $C \ominus C' = C \setminus C' \cup C' \setminus C$.

As already mentioned when detailing feature modules, switch events can require interactions between the feature controller and the feature modules. Thus, feature modules can trigger or prevent switch events by offering or refusing the required interactions with the feature controller. For example, suppose some software product is only distributed in a basic version. Potential upgrades after purchasing the software product will be triggered by the user, represented in our framework by some feature module.

There might be other switch events that are uncontrollable by the feature modules, e.g., the deactivation of features that are damaged due to environmental influences (electrical power outage, extreme hotness, etc.). Such switch events in the controller do not rely on interactions with the feature modules. Instead, statistical data might be available that permits to model the frequency of such uncontrollable switch events by probabilities. This leads to the more general concept of *probabilistic feature controllers*, where switch events are pairs (C, d, γ) consisting of a feature combination C, a cost value $d \in \mathbb{N}$ and a distribution γ over $\mathcal{V}$. Thus, probabilistic feature controllers can be seen MDPs with switch events as moves.

Definition 3.5 (Controller)**.** *A probabilistic feature controller over the signature* $(F, \mathcal{V})$, *briefly called* controller, *is a tuple* $\mathsf{Con} = (\mathcal{V}, \mathcal{V}^{init}, \mathsf{SwRel})$ *as in Definition 3.4, but*

$$\mathsf{SwRel} \subseteq \mathcal{V} \times \mathbb{N} \times \mathit{Distr}(\mathcal{V}).$$

Again, we require that the switch relation is finite and that (C, d_1, γ), $(C, d_2, \gamma) \in \mathsf{SwRel}$ *implies* $d_1 = d_2$.

Clearly, each simple feature controller Con can be seen as a (probabilistic feature) controller. For this, we just have to identify each switch event (C, d, C') with $(C, d, \mathit{Dirac}[C'])$. The following example shows a controller of our productivity system detailed already in Example 2.1.

Example 3.6. Let us consider the feature signature $(F, \mathcal{V})$, where $F = \{\mathrm{s, o, e, r, m, f, h, b, l}\}$ given by the feature diagram in Example 2.1 and the controller $\mathsf{Con}_{\mathrm{ps}}$ depicted in Figure 4 with the initial feature combinations soe, sor, sorm. States are valid feature combinations in $\mathcal{V}$ and arrows describe feature combination

$$\frac{(\ell,\phi,\alpha,c,\lambda)\in \mathsf{TrAct},\ \ C\models\phi}{(\langle \ell, C\rangle, c, \lambda * \mathit{Dirac}[C])\in \mathsf{Moves}} \qquad \frac{C \xrightarrow{d} \gamma,\ \ C\models\phi,\ \ \forall C'\in \mathit{supp}(\gamma). C\cap \mathsf{OwnF} = C'\cap \mathsf{OwnF}}{(\langle \ell, C\rangle, d, \mathit{Dirac}[\ell] * \gamma)\in \mathsf{Moves}}$$

$$\frac{(\ell,\phi,\rho,c,\lambda)\in \mathsf{TrSw},\ \ C\models\phi,\ \ C \xrightarrow{d} \gamma,\ \ \exists C'\in \mathit{supp}(\gamma).(C\cap \mathsf{OwnF} \neq C'\cap \mathsf{OwnF}),\ \ \forall C'\in \mathit{supp}(\gamma).(C,C')\in R_\rho}{(\langle \ell, C\rangle, c+d, \lambda * \gamma)\in \mathsf{Moves}}$$

Figure 3. Rules for the moves in the MDP Mod ⋈ Con

switches. These switches are amended with a probability, which is supposed to be estimated from statistical user data and costs for taking the switch (upgrade/downgrade). For instance, the step sor $\overset{\text{e},269}{\hookrightarrow}_{0.15}$ sorfb indicates that with probability 15%, a user is buying a business office feature (b) for 269 €, given she has a professional operating system (r). Although $\mathsf{Con}_{\mathrm{ps}}$ is purely probabilistic (i.e., $\mathsf{Con}_{\mathrm{ps}}$ can be seen as a Markov chain) in the sense that in all states precisely one move is enabled, it also formalizes the rules for upgrade or downgrade features. For better readability, self-loops with the remaining probability value are not depicted in this figure. Note that the media center feature (m) can be activated

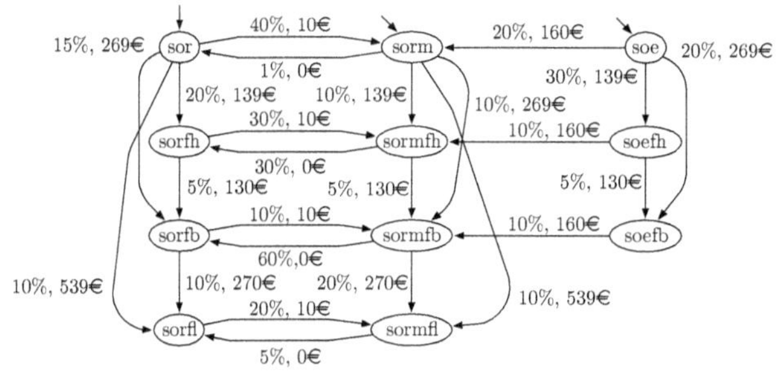

Figure 4. A probabilistic controller

and deactivated at any time if the professional operating system feature (r) is activated. Upgrades from the home edition (e) of the operating system are only possible to the professional edition including the media center feature (m). However, downgrading from the professional operating system (r) to the home edition (e) is prohibited. The home edition (h) of the office suite can only be upgraded to the professional one (l) if the operating system is professional (r).

3.4 MDP-semantics of Feature Modules

The semantics of a feature module Mod under some controller Con is given in terms of an MDP. If Mod stands for the parallel composition of all modules that implement one of the "internal" features of a given SPL and the controller Con specifies the dynamic adaptions of the feature combinations, then this MDP formalizes the operational behavior of the composite system. In what follows, we fix a feature module and a controller

$$\begin{aligned}\mathsf{Mod} &= (\mathsf{Loc}, \mathsf{Loc}^{init}, \mathsf{F}, \mathsf{Act}, \mathsf{Trans})\\ \mathsf{Con} &= (\mathcal{V}, \mathcal{V}^{init}, \mathsf{SwRel})\end{aligned}$$

as in Definition 3.2 and Definition 3.5 where $\mathsf{F}\subseteq F$. Intuitively, taking an action-labeled transition $(\ell,\phi,\alpha,c,\lambda)$ of Mod is a possible behavior of Mod in location ℓ, provided that the current state C of the controller Con (which is simply the current feature combination) meets the guard ϕ. Switch events of the controller can be performed independently from Mod if they do not affect the own features of Mod, whereas if they affect at least one feature in OwnF, the changes of the mode have to be executed synchronously.

Definition 3.7 (Semantics of feature modules). *Let* Mod *and* Con *be as before. The behavior of* Mod *under the controller* Con *is formalized by the MDP*

$$\mathsf{Mod} \bowtie \mathsf{Con} \;=\; (S, S^{init}, \mathsf{Moves}),$$

where $S = \mathsf{Loc}\times\mathcal{V}$, $S^{init} = \mathsf{Loc}^{init}\times\mathcal{V}^{init}$ *and where the move relation* Moves *is defined by the rules in Figure 3. In the last rule,* $\rho\in\mathbb{B}(\mathsf{OwnF}\cup\mathsf{OwnF}')$ *is viewed as a Boolean expression over* $F\cup F'$. *Thus,* ρ *specifies a binary relation* R_ρ *over* $2^F\times 2^F$.

Observe that due to the MDP semantics of feature modules under a controller, standard probabilistic model-checking techniques for the quantitative analysis can be directly applied. This includes properties about current feature combinations, since they are encoded into the states of the arising MDP.

3.5 Remarks on our Framework

Feature Modules with Variables. So far, we presented a lightweight data-abstract formalism for feature modules with abstract action and location names. This simplified the presentation of the mathematical model. From the theoretical point of view, feature modules in the sense of Definition 3.2 are powerful enough to encode systems where the modules operate on variables with finite domains. Even communication over shared variables can be mimicked by dealing with handshaking and local copies of shared variables. However, in case studies the explicit use of assignments for variables and guards for the transitions that impose constraints for local and shared variables is desirable; not only to avoid unreadable encodings, but also for performance reasons of the algorithmic analysis. Although message passing via channels would be more in the spirit of coordination paradigms, the concept of shared variables can help to generate more compact representations of the MDP for the composite system, which makes it useful for the application of model-checking tools. The formal definition of an extension of *feature modules by variables* is rather technical, but fairly standard. We present their syntax and MDP-semantics under a given controller in the accompanied technical report [19]. These extended feature modules directly yield a translation in PRISM's input language that we used in our case study described in the next section.

Other Variants. Besides amending feature modules by variables, the basic formalisms of our framework can be refined in various directions. We briefly mention here a few of them.

With the presented formalism the switch events appear as nondeterministic choices and require interactions between the controller and all modules that provide implementations for the affected features. Employing the standard semantics of MDPs, where one of the enabled moves is selected nondeterministically, this rules out the possibility to express that certain switch events might be unpreventable. Unpreventable switch events can be included into our framework, refining the concept of feature controllers by explicitly specifying which switch events must be taken whenever they are enabled in the controller. This could modeled by adding an extra transition relation for *urgent* switch events or prioritizing switches.

Instead of urgency or priorities, one might also keep the presented syntax of feature modules and controllers, but refine the

MDP-semantics by adding *fairness conditions* that rule out computations where enabled switch events are postponed ad infinitum.

Another option for refining the nondeterministic choices in the controller is the distinction between switch events that are indeed controllable by the controller and those that are triggered by the environment. This naturally leads to a game-based view of the MDP for the composite system (see also Section 5).

Controllers as Feature Modules. To emphasize the feature-oriented aspects of our framework, we used a different syntax for controllers and feature modules. Nevertheless, controllers can be viewed as special feature modules when we discard the concept of switch events and switch transitions and rephrase them as action-labeled transitions. To transform controllers syntactically to feature modules, we have to add the trivial guard and introduce names for all switch events. When turning the switch transitions of the feature modules into action-labeled transitions, matching names must be introduced to align the parallel operators $\|$ and $\bowtie$. Note that in the constructed feature modules, all features are external and the locations coincide with feature combinations. However, an extended version of controllers can also be considered, where in addition to feature combinations, arbitrary other internal locations of the controller can be specified.

4. Quantitative Feature Analysis

Within the compositional framework presented in the last section, let us assume that we are given feature modules $\mathsf{Mod}_1, \ldots \mathsf{Mod}_n$ which stand for abstract models of certain features $f \in F$ and a feature controller Con specifying the rules for feature combination changes. The feature set F might still contain other features where no implementations are given, which are external features controlled by the environment. Alternatively, one of the feature modules can formalize the interference of the feature implementations with a partially known environment, e.g., in form of stochastic assumptions on the workload or the frequency of user interactions. Applying the compositional construction by putting feature modules in parallel and joining them with the feature controller, we obtain an MDP of the form

$$\mathcal{M} = (\mathsf{Mod}_1 \| \ldots \| \mathsf{Mod}_n) \bowtie \mathsf{Con}.$$

This MDP $\mathcal{M}$ formalizes the operational behavior of a dynamic SPL and can now be used for quantitative analysis. Hence, the task of a quantitative analysis of dynamic SPLs is reduced to standard algorithmic problems for MDP and permits the use of generic probabilistic model-checking techniques. This is in contrast to other family-based model-checking approaches for SPLs, where feature-adapted algorithms were constructed [10, 11].

4.1 Quantitative Analysis and Strategy Synthesis Problem

A *quantitative worst-case analysis* in the MDP $\mathcal{M}$ that establishes least upper or greatest lower bounds for the probabilities of certain properties or for the expected accumulated costs by means of the queries $\mathsf{P}^{\max=?}[\varphi]$, $\mathsf{P}^{\min=?}[\varphi]$ or $\mathsf{E}^{\min=?}[\Diamond T]$ (see Section 2.2) can be carried out with standard probabilistic model-checking tools. These values provide guarantees on the probabilities under all potential resolutions of the nondeterministic choices in $\mathcal{M}$, possibly imposing some fairness constraints to ensure that continuously enabled dynamic adaptions of the feature combinations (switch events) cannot be superseded forever by action-labeled transitions of the feature modules.

Although the quantitative worst-case analysis can give important insights in the correctness and quality of an SPL, in our framework with separate specifications of the potential dynamic adaptions of feature combinations (the controller) and the implementations of the features (the feature modules), it appears naturally to go one step further by asking for *optimal strategies* for triggering switch events. Optimality can be understood with respect to queries like minimizing the probability for undesired behaviors or minimizing the expected energy consumption while meeting given deadlines, or maximizing the utility value when an initial energy budget is given.

Several variants of this problem can be considered. The basic variant that we address in our case study relies on the assumption that the nondeterminism in the MDP $\mathcal{M}$ for the composite system stands for decisions to be made by the controller, i.e., only the switch events appear nondeterministically, whereas the feature modules behave purely probabilistically (or deterministically) when putting them in parallel with the controller. More formally, we suppose that in each state s of $\mathcal{M}$, either there is a single enabled move representing some action-labeled transition of one or more feature modules or all enabled moves stand for switch events. In this case, an optimal strategy for the controller is just a scheduler for $\mathcal{M}$ that optimizes the quantitative measure of interest. Thus, the natural task that we address is the *strategy synthesis problem*, where $\mathcal{M}$ and some PCTL-query Φ as in Section 2 are given and the task is to construct a scheduler $\mathfrak{S}$ for $\mathcal{M}$ that optimizes the solution of the query Φ. Indeed, the standard probabilistic model-checking algorithms for PCTL are applicable to solve the strategy synthesis problem.

4.2 Case Study

In this section, we describe a case study to show the applicability of our framework to a real-case scenario. Our case study is based on EBOND, which is an energy-aware network device allowing for energy savings on the server-side [24]. The EBOND device supports bonding of (heterogenous) network interface cards (NICs) with different performance and energy characteristics into a single device. Individual NICs can be switched on at any time whenever more bandwidth is needed and switched off otherwise. In [24], simulation-based techniques were used to show that within EBOND, energy savings up to 75% can be achieved when demands for bandwidth varies, e.g., between day and night time.

***Original* EBOND.** The simulation in [24] was carried out for a fixed EBOND device with exactly two NICs. The first NIC requires much energy but supports up to 10 GBit bandwidth, whereas the second NIC is a slow 1 GBit NIC with low energy consumption. The NICs were only allowed to be used exclusively, i.e., the bonding of the two devices was not considered. Furthermore, three energy saving algorithms have been detailed:

(1) an *aggressive* algorithm, in which the 10GBit NIC is switched off whenever possible (i.e., the last observed bandwidth request is at most 1GBit),

(2) a *high saving* algorithm, which assumes a higher requested bandwidth, thus switching later to the slow NIC and earlier to the fast NIC, and

(3) a *balanced* algorithm, which behaves as the high saving algorithm, but introduces an additional cool-down phase delaying card switches even further.

The setting from [24] can be interpreted in terms of features, where we assume the energy saving algorithms to be enclosed in a coordination feature. The arising feature signature of this static SPL could be specified as a feature diagram shown in Figure 5. Note that the energy saving algorithm is chosen initially when the EBOND device is deployed.
The EBOND model operates in two phases, where a 5 minutes operating phase alternates with a reconfiguration phase, in which the active NIC is chosen by the energy saving algorithm. The analysis carried out in [24] issued the measurement of the energy con-

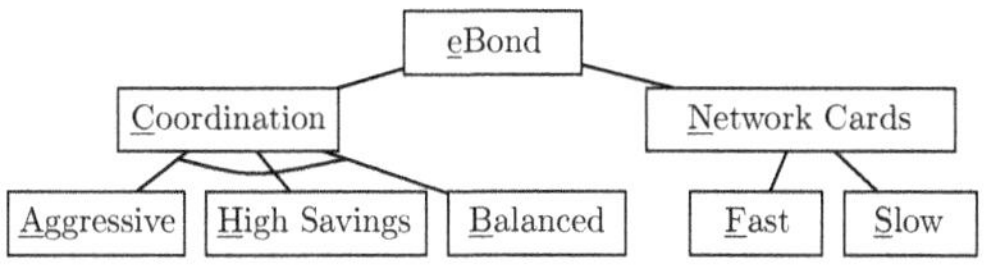

Figure 5. Feature diagram for an eBond product line

sumption for the different NICs in their sleeping mode and under load, as well as counting the number of service-level agreement (SLA) violations. An SLA violation was assumed to happen whenever the demanded bandwidth could not be delivered by the server, i.e., when the 1Gbit NIC has been activated by the energy saving algorithm but the requested bandwidth exceeds 1Gbit. The different energy saving algorithms have been simulated using bandwidth requirements from two real-case scenarios. In particular, the total energy consumption and number of SLA violations over 43 days have been detailed.

***Dynamic* EBOND+.** We extend the static SPL setting of EBOND towards a dynamic SPL, gaining more flexibility in bonding NICs. Our extended version, called EBOND+, allows for more than one NIC being active at the same time and involves dynamics by supporting to change the NIC combinations at runtime. We furthermore distinguish between a standard and a professional bundle which are for sale. In the standard bundle a costumer can plug up to two NICs, whereas the professional bundle supports up to three NICs. When buying an EBOND+ device, the costumer decides for either the standard or the professional bundle. We assume that this decision if fixed and that there is no upgrade option later on. Also the energy saving algorithm is fixed on purchase. For the NICs we support the same two types of cards as in the original EBOND. The customer selects on the number and type of NICs the EBOND+ device will be shipped with. The NICs can be bought or dropped also after the purchase. Interpreting each of the described functionality as features, the feature signature of EBOND+ can be specified by a feature diagram (see Figure 6). Note the additional constraint on the upper right of Figure 6, indicating that in the standard bundle only two NICs can be plugged into the system, i.e., if the standard bundle s is selected, it is not possible to purchase all three NICs.

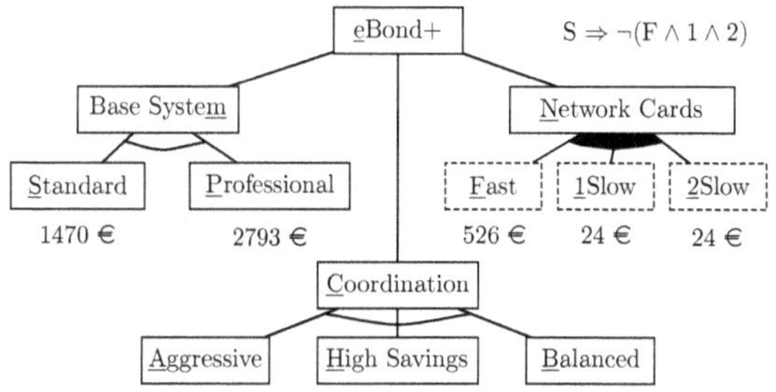

Figure 6. Feature diagram of the EBOND+ product line

We formalized the dynamic feature combination switches, i.e., plugging or unplugging NICs of the system, via a feature controller according to the framework developed in the previous section (see Section 3.3). The controller implements the constraints on plugging and unplugging NICs. We made the following assumptions on the dynamics of the feature switches: a NIC can only be bought (dropped) and plugged into (unplugged from) the device when there is a need, meaning that whenever the required bandwidth becomes either too high or too low w.r.t. the current configuration of the EBOND+ device. Furthermore, we assume that any change of the NICs requires a minimal amount of time. In contrast to the EBOND model, the EBOND+ model operates in three phases rather than two, as we introduce an additional feature controller step allowing dynamic feature switches. The initial phase is controlled by the costumer, who decides on the initial configuration of the EBOND+ device.

For the NICs, the energy saving algorithms and the system environment in terms of the requested bandwidth are formalized as feature modules in the spirit of our compositional framework. The standard or professional system features are only influencing the number of NIC features activated and are hence specified within the feature controller. For the operational behavior of the NICs we introduced a probabilistic choice with low probability modeling the possibility of failing network cards. In this case, the respective NIC feature is active but does not provide any functionality. The coordination features are implemented as for EBOND [24], where waking up and putting NICs into sleep follows a purely deterministic strategy (without any probabilistic or nondeterministic behavior). The environment feature, which models the requested bandwidth, is present in all valid feature combinations and behaves probabilistically. The exact distribution is derived from statistical user data.

***Reasoning over* EBOND+.** With the above model of the EBOND+ device, we obtain a standard MDP

$$\mathcal{M}_+ \;=\; (\underbrace{\mathsf{Fast}\|\mathsf{1Slow}\|\mathsf{2Slow}}_{\text{network cards}} \;\|\; \underbrace{\mathsf{A}\|\mathsf{H}\|\mathsf{B}}_{\text{coordination}} \;\|\; \underbrace{\mathsf{Env}}_{\text{environment}}) \bowtie \mathsf{Con}$$

having exactly one starting state, which yields the basis for any kind of quantitative analysis. We equip $\mathcal{M}_+$ with three different cost functions. Beyond the cost measures for the energy consumption of the active NICs and the number of SLA violations as considered in [24], we introduce here a third cost measure for money. Costs in terms of money include purchasing costs of the initial system, money spent for buying new NICs, paying the card switches as well as the cost of SLA violations. As SLA violations are rather expensive, it is clear that a customer tries to avoid SLA violations by purchasing a device whose reliability guarantees the desired throughput functionality. On the other hand, a customer also tries to save initial costs when buying the device. The strategy synthesis problem for $\mathcal{M}_+$ thus aims to find an optimal strategy (w.r.t. the introduced costs) for the customer resolving nondeterminism in the feature controller Con (plugging/unplugging NICs) to fulfill her needs assuming that the workload behaves as modeled by the environment feature Env.

In the analysis part of our EBOND+ case study, we consider four different strategy synthesis problems for $\mathcal{M}_+$ w.r.t. queries

$$\Phi_p = \mathsf{P}^{\max=?}[(\neg \mathit{Sla})\,\mathcal{U}\,T] \qquad \Phi_e = \mathsf{E}^{\min=?}_{\text{energy}}[\Diamond T]$$
$$\Phi_m = \mathsf{E}^{\min=?}_{\text{money}}[\Diamond T] \qquad \Phi_s = \mathsf{E}^{\min=?}_{\text{slavio}}[\Diamond T]$$

Here, the type of the expected minimal costs is annotated to the query (i.e., energy, money and slavio). Furthermore, *Sla* stands for the set of states in $\mathcal{M}_+$ where an SLA violation occurred and T for the set of states in $\mathcal{M}_+$ where some fixed time horizon is reached. Hence, the strategy synthesis problem for $\mathcal{M}_+$ corresponds to the optimization problem of maximizing the probability of not raising an SLA violation (i.e., reliability of the device), minimizing the expected energy consumption, money spent or percentage of SLA violations, respectively, all within the fixed time horizont.

4.3 Quantitative analysis of EBOND+ in PRISM

Using the compositional framework presented in Section 3, we modeled a parameterized version of EBOND+ within PRISM as MDP $\mathcal{M}_+$.All features were translated into individual PRISM modules, which results in $\mathcal{M}_+$ when parallel composed by PRISM. The types of NICs and their energy consumption profile are according to [24], i.e., the fast 10 GBit NIC corresponds to an Intel Ethernet Server Adapter X520-T featuring an E76983 CPU, whereas the remaining (at most two) NICs are supposed to be 1 GBit Intel EXPI9301CTBLK NICs with an E25869 CPU. The purchase costs for the system and the network cards (in €) are taken from a leading vendor's online store and an SLA violation is assumed to cost 200 € each. Whereas the coordination features were implemented according to the energy saving algorithms of EBOND, the environment feature modeling the bandwidth requirements differs. Instead of employing the statistical user data from one of the two setting addressed in [24], we assume a maximal bandwidth bound b [GBit/s]. Dependent on the current bandwidth requirements the bandwidth requirement rises and falls – the lower (higher) the current bandwidth is below (above) $b/2$, the higher is the probability that the environment requires more (less) bandwidth in the next phase.

Model Parameters. For the case study we fixed certain model parameters. First, we chose a time horizon of $T = 12$ hours and a delay of 20 minutes for reconfiguring the system. Other timing constraints are taken from the EBOND case study, involving a reconfiguration timer of 5 minutes and a cool-down timer of 30 minutes for the balanced coordination. For the high savings and balanced coordination feature, we assumed a predictor 10% hysteresis (also taken from EBOND). The probability that a NIC fails is set to 0.1%. Bandwidth values are evaluated with an accuracy of 100 MBit/s.

4.4 Empirical Evaluation.

In our experiments, we parameterized over the maximal bandwidth bound from values between 200 MBit/s and 7200 MBit/s, solving the strategy synthesis problem for $\mathcal{M}_+$ w.r.t. each query Φ_p, Φ_e, Φ_s and Φ_m as detailed above. The figures illustrate the influence the initial EBOND+ configuration when purchasing the system. The encoding is of the initial configurations is of the form "VW-X-Y", where V stands for the number of 10 GBit NICs, W stands for the number of 1 Gbit NICs, X ∈ {S,P} stands for either the standard or the professional bundle, and Y ∈ {A,H,B} stands for either the aggressive, high saving, or balanced energy saving algorithm.

Our results for all queries show that the chosen energy saving algorithm has a very similar influence on the results as determined in [24]. Although, our results indicate that there is no significant difference between the high savings and aggressive energy saving algorithm. The reason is that the aggressive energy saving algorithm relies mainly on switching cards as in EBOND, whereas in EBOND+ also bonding of two and more cards is supported.

Utility Analysis. We first look at Φ_p, i.e., the maximum probability of avoiding SLA violation within the given fixed time period, corresponding to a measure of reliability for an EBOND+ device. In Figure 7 it can be seen that when the maximal required

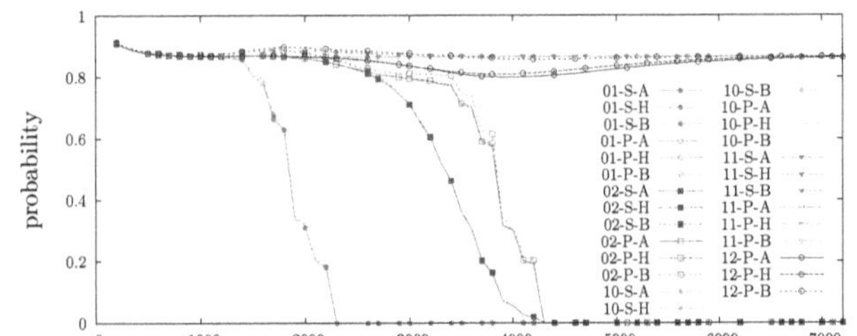

Figure 7. Evaluation of Φ_p for the different EBOND+ variants

bandwidth is low, the probability of avoiding an SLA violation within the considered time bound is nearly 90%, independent from the initial feature configuration. For initial feature combinations that have only one 1 GBit NIC activated, an SLA violation can hardly be avoided for maximal requested bandwidths greater than $b = 2$ GBit/s. This is due to the fact that the expected average bandwidth is $b/2 = 1$ GBit/s, which agrees with the maximal available bandwidth of the NIC. Within the 20 minutes required to change the initial feature combination and upgrade to more NICs, an SLA violation becomes very likely. The same phenomenon appears with only two 1 GBit NICs activated, but there the probability value drops below 50% at a maximal bandwidth of 4 GBit/s. Note that in this setting with the two 1 GBit NICs activated and being under load, only with the professional bundle the additional 10 GBit NIC can be bought and plugged, such that the impact of the slower NICs is superseded. With the fast NIC initially activated, the probability can be maximized always at around 88%, since the required bandwidth can always be complied up to the case the 10 GBit NIC fails. Note that whenever the balanced coordination feature is activated, the maximized probability avoiding an SLA violation is higher than within the other coordination features.

Energy Analysis. When turning to the minimization of the expected energy consumption, i.e., solving query Φ_e for $\mathcal{M}_+$, things are different as shown in Figure 8. Since the other cost measures

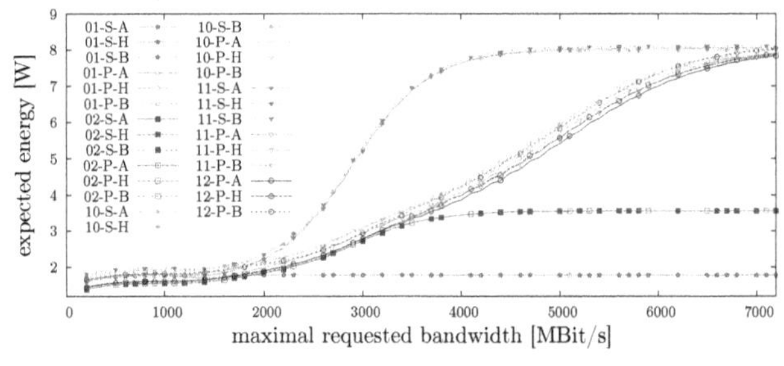

Figure 8. Evaluation of Φ_e for the different EBOND+ variants

are independent from the energy costs, the smallest configuration with only one slow card initially activated performs best with only 1.78 W energy consumption[3]. However, the standard bundles where the fast card is activated at the beginning have significant higher energy consumption for increasing maximal required bandwidth. This is due to the fact that the feature controller cannot unplug the fast NIC under load. For the same reason when activating a slow card in situations with maximal requested bandwidth above 2 GBit/s the fast card is very likely to be under load. Within a professional bundle, the feature controller is more flexible, allowing to plug the fast NIC on demand, such that the corresponding feature combinations have similar expected energy consumptions.

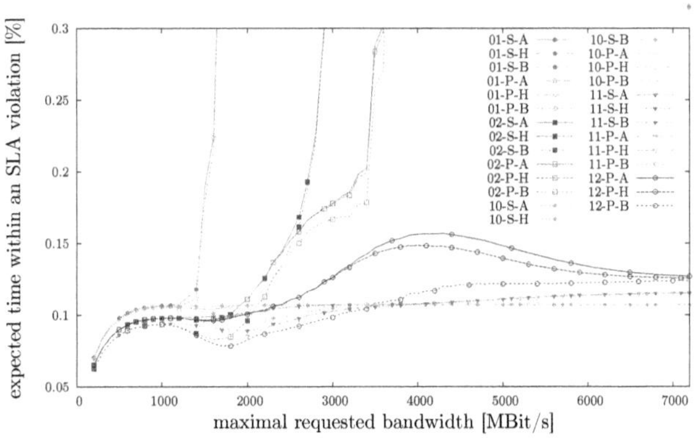

Figure 9. Evaluation of Φ_s for the different EBOND+ variants

[3] according to [24] the NIC requires 1.92 W on full load

SLA violation analysis. When minimizing the expected number of SLA violations, i.e., solving query Φ_s for $\mathcal{M}_+$, similar phenomena as within our utility analysis can be observed. In Figure 9 it can be seen that when choosing initial configurations with slow NICs, the expected percentage of time within an SLA violation rises significantly when the maximal required bandwidth exceeds the supported bandwidth of the activated NICs. When choosing an appropriate initial feature combination, the minimal expected time run with SLA violations is between 0.06% and 0.11%, which is in the range of the values from the EBOND case study [24]. Note that as in EBOND case study, the balanced energy saving algorithm minimizes SLA violations always best, followed by the high savings and aggressive energy saving algorithms.

Monetary Analysis. A novel aspect not considered in the case study by [24] is the expected run-time costs in terms of money. Figure 10 shows the results of evaluating query Φ_m for $\mathcal{M}_+$ minimizing the expected monetary costs for all initial feature combinations. As one expects, choosing a system with a fast 10 GBit NIC

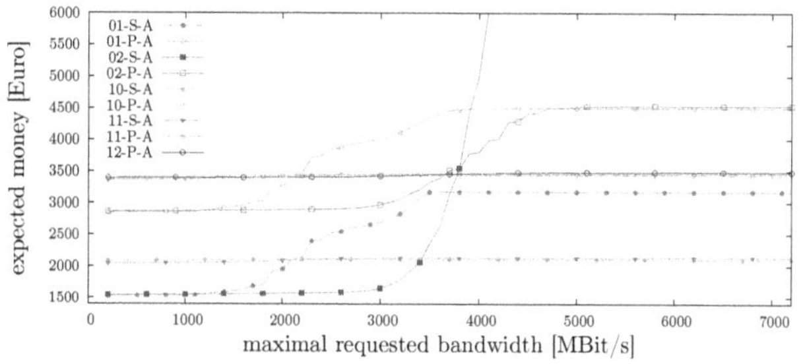

Figure 10. Evaluation of Φ_m for the different EBOND+ variants

does not yield to additional costs after the purchase, since SLA violations are unlikely (see utility analysis with evaluating Φ_p). However, when purchasing only slow cards, increasing the maximal required bandwidth leads to additional costs for SLA violation which may even supersede system configurations with higher initial costs. Thus, the customer may purchase a better performing but more expensive system if the maximal required bandwidth is high. However, if the maximal required bandwidth is below 2 GBit/s, it is always advisable to purchase the standard bundle with only one 1 GBit NIC, eventually plugging an additional 1 GBit NIC.

Statistical Evaluation. We analyzed the above queries on an Intel Xeon X5650 @ 2.67 GHz using PRISM 4.1 and employing the sparse engine with a precision of 10^{-5}. It is well-known that an explicit engine is usually faster than a symbolic one when many different probability values appear in the model. Due to the dynamic changes of bandwidth probabilities in the environment feature, this is also the case for our model. Hence, symbolic approaches are only used for the construction of the model and reachability analysis, which however have great impact on the instance of the strategy synthesis problem we considered in our case study. Due to the family-based symbolic representation, the complete model is small compared to the accumulated model size when constructing models for all initial feature combinations one-by-one. The model size also influences the time spent for the evaluation of the queries, as well as its maximal memory consumption. The logarithmically scaled Figure 11 shows a comparison of these characteristics, where solid curves stand for our family-based approach and the dashed ones for the one-by-one approach. In Table 1, these characteristics are exemplified with a fixed maximal bandwidth of 2.4 GBit/s. The entire computation for bandwidth constraints of 0.2 till 7.2 GBit/s in steps of 0.1 GBit/s took 123 hours of CPU time and consumed at most 6244 MBytes of memory using our approach, whereas the one-by-one approach took more than 782 hours with a maximal memory

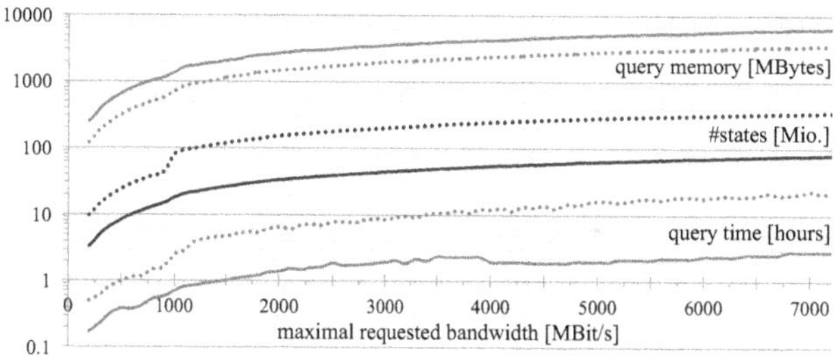

Figure 11. Statistical evaluation of the experiments

consumption of 3482 MBytes. All these statistics illustrate that the family-based approach for our framework outperforms the one-by-one approach and is around six times faster. Note that in our case study, we only considered 27 different feature combinations. Due to the exponential blow-up in the number of feature combinations, an even greater speed-up can be expected for bigger SPLs.

Table 1. Evaluation statistics (maximal bandwidth = 2.4 GBit/s)

	family-based ($\mathcal{M}_+$)	one-by-one
#states	37 Mio.	427 Mio.
query time	1.3 hours	6.9 hours
query memory	2970 MBytes	1680 MBytes

5. Conclusions

We presented a compositional modeling framework for dynamic SPLs that relies on dynamic adaptions of the feature combinations expressed by means of an MDP-like model. The feature implementations and the behavior of possibly unknown or only partially known implementations of external features are represented by separate automata with feature guards for the action-labeled transitions and special switch transitions for the dynamic activation or deactivation of own features. With the MDP-semantics of a dynamic SPLs, many feature-oriented problems are reducible to well-known algorithmic problems for MDPs and solvable with standard techniques. We illustrated this by means of an energy-aware network protocol. In this case study, we used probabilistic model checking for establishing several quantitative properties and addressed the strategy synthesis problem to generate an energy-efficient strategy for triggering feature combination changes.

There are many other interesting variants of the task to synthesize optimal strategies that are also solvable by known algorithms. One might distinguish between switch events that are indeed controllable and those that cannot be enforced or prevented, but are triggered by the environment. In this case, the MDP $\mathcal{M}$ can be seen as stochastic game-structure, where the controller and the environment are opponents and the task to generate an optimal strategy for the controller reduces to well-known game-based problems [8, 13, 17, 20]. Similarly, one might take into account that also the feature modules can behave nondeterministically. Depending on the meaning of the nondeterminism in the feature modules (e.g., implementation freedom or interactions with the environment), the nondeterministic choices in the feature modules can be classified into controllable and uncontrollable ones. Assuming that the controller and all feature modules build one coalition that aims to achieve some optimal value for a quantitative objective, no matter how the environment behaves, then again well-known algorithms for stochastic two-player games are applicable. This, and investigations on the scalability of our approach towards real-case dynamic SPLs with more features are left for further work.

Acknowledgements. We thank Marcus Daum and Steffen Märcker for their support concerning the case study.

References

[1] S. Apel and D. Hutchins. A calculus for uniform feature composition. *ACM Transactions on Programming Languages and Systems*, 32(5), 2010.

[2] S. Apel, F. Janda, S. Trujillo, and C. Kästner. Model superimposition in software product lines. In *ICMT'09*, volume 5563 of *LNCS*, pages 4–19, 2009.

[3] S. Apel, F. Janda, S. Trujillo, and C. Kästner. Model superimposition in software product lines. In *ICMT'09*, pages 4–19, Berlin, Heidelberg, 2009. Springer-Verlag.

[4] C. Baier and J.-P. Katoen. *Principles of model checking*. The MIT Press, 2008.

[5] C. Baier and M. Kwiatkoswka. Model checking for a probabilistic branching time logic with fairness. *Distributed Computing*, 11(3): 125–155, 1998.

[6] D. Benavides, S. Segura, and A. Ruiz-Cortés. Automated analysis of feature models 20 years later: A literature review. *Information Systems*, 35(6):615 – 636, 2010. ISSN 0306-4379.

[7] A. Bianco and L. de Alfaro. Model checking of probabilistic and nondeterministic systems. In *FSTTCS'95*, volume 1026 of *LNCS*, pages 499–513, 1995.

[8] K. Chatterjee, M. Jurdzinski, and T. Henzinger. Quantitative simple stochastic parity games. In *SODA'04*, pages 121–130. SIAM, 2004.

[9] E. M. Clarke, E. A. Emerson, and A. P. Sistla. Automatic verification of finite-state concurrent systems using temporal logic specifications. *ACM Trans. Program. Lang. Syst.*, 8:244–263, 1986.

[10] A. Classen, P. Heymans, P.-Y. Schobbens, A. Legay, and J.-F. Raskin. Model checking lots of systems: Efficient verification of temporal properties in software product lines. In *ICSE'2010*, pages 335–344. ACM, 2010.

[11] A. Classen, P. Heymans, P.-Y. Schobbens, and A. Legay. Symbolic model checking of software product lines. In *ICSE'2011*, pages 321–330. ACM, 2011.

[12] P. Clements and L. Northrop. *Software Product Lines : Practices and Patterns*. Addison-Wesley Professional, 2001.

[13] A. Condon. The complexity of stochastic games. *Information and Computation*, 96(2):203–224, 1992.

[14] M. Cordy, A. Classen, P. Heymans, A. Legay, and P.-Y. Schobbens. *Model Checking Adaptive Software with Featured Transition Systems*, volume 7740, pages 1–29. Springer Berlin Heidelberg, 2013.

[15] K. Czarnecki, S. She, and A. Wasowski. Sample spaces and feature models: There and back again. In *SPLC'08*, pages 22–31, 2008.

[16] F. Damiani and I. Schaefer. Dynamic delta-oriented programming. In *Proceedings of the 15th International Software Product Line Conference, Volume 2*, SPLC '11, pages 34:1–8, New York, 2011. ACM.

[17] L. de Alfaro and R. Majumdar. Quantitative solution of omega-regular games. In *STOC'01*, pages 675–683. ACM, 2001.

[18] T. Dinkelaker, R. Mitschke, K. Fetzer, and M. Mezini. A dynamic software product line approach using aspect models at runtime. In *Proceedings of the 1st Workshop on Composition and Variability*, März 2010.

[19] C. Dubslaff, S. Klüppelholz, and C. Baier. Probabilistic model checking for energy analysis in software product lines. Technical report, TU Dresden, 2013.

[20] J. Filar and K. Vrieze. *Competitive Markov Decision Processes*. Springer, 1997.

[21] D. Gelernter and N. Carriero. Coordination languages and their significance. *Communications of the ACM*, 35(2):96–107, 1992.

[22] C. Ghezzi and A. M. Sharifloo. Model-based verification of quantitative non-functional properties for software product lines. *Information & Software Technology*, 55(3):508–524, 2013.

[23] H. Gomaa and M. Hussein. Dynamic software reconfiguration in software product families. In *PFE*, pages 435–444, 2003.

[24] M. Hähnel, B. Döbel, M. Völp, and H. Härtig. ebond: Energy saving in heterogeneous r.a.i.n. In *Proceedings of the Fourth International Conference on Future Energy Systems*, e-Energy '13, pages 193–202, New York, NY, USA, 2013. ACM.

[25] S. Hallsteinsen, M. Hinchey, S. Park, and K. Schmid. Dynamic software product lines. *Computer*, 41(4):93–95, Apr. 2008. ISSN 0018-9162.

[26] B. Haverkort. *Performance of Computer Communication Systems: A Model-Based Approach*. Wiley, 1998.

[27] J. D. Hay and J. M. Atlee. Composing features and resolving interactions. In *SIGSOFT'00*, pages 110–119, New York, 2000. ACM. ISBN 1-58113-205-0.

[28] A. Hinton, M. Kwiatkowska, G. Norman, and D. Parker. PRISM: A tool for automatic verification of probabilistic systems. In H. Hermanns and J. Palsberg, editors, *TACAS'06*, volume 3920 of *LNCS*, pages 441–444. Springer, 2006.

[29] K. C. Kang, S. G. Cohen, J. A. Hess, W. E. Novak, and A. S. Peterson. Feature-oriented domain analysis (foda) feasibility study. Technical report, Carnegie-Mellon University Software Engineering Institute, November 1990.

[30] S. Katz. A superimposition control construct for distributed systems. *ACM Trans. Program. Lang. Syst.*, 15(2):337–356, Apr. 1993.

[31] V. Kulkarni. *Modeling and Analysis of Stochastic Systems*. Chapman & Hall, 1995.

[32] K. L. McMillan. *Symbolic Model Checking*. Kluwer Academic Publishers, 1993.

[33] J.-V. Millo, S. Ramesh, S. N. Krishna, and G. K. Narwane. Compositional verification of software product lines. In *IFM'13*, volume 7940 of *LNCS*, pages 109–123. Springer, 2013.

[34] M. Noorian, E. Bagheri, and W. Du. Non-functional properties in software product lines: A taxonomy for classification. In *SEKE'12*, pages 663–667. Knowledge Systems Institute Graduate School, 2012.

[35] G. A. Papadopoulos and F. Arbab. Coordination models and languages. *Advances in Computers*, 46:329–400, 1998.

[36] M. Plath and M. Ryan. Feature integration using a feature construct. *Science of Computer Programming*, 41(1):53 – 84, 2001.

[37] M. Puterman. *Markov Decision Processes: Discrete Stochastic Dynamic Programming*. John Wiley & Sons, Inc., New York, NY, 1994.

[38] M. Rosenmüller, N. Siegmund, S. Apel, and G. Saake. Flexible feature binding in software product lines. *Automated Software Engg.*, 18(2): 163–197, June 2011.

[39] J.-G. Schneider, M. Lumpe, and O. Nierstrasz. Agent coordination via scripting languages. In *Coordination of Internet Agents: Models, Technologies, and Applications*, pages 153–175, 2001.

[40] R. Segala. *Modeling and Verification of Randomized Distributed Real-Time Systems*. PhD thesis, MIT, 1995.

[41] R. Segala and N. A. Lynch. Probabilistic simulations for probabilistic processes. *Nordic Journal of Computing*, 2(2):250–273, 1995.

[42] N. Siegmund, M. Rosenmüller, M. Kuhlemann, C. Kästner, and G. Saake. Measuring non-functional properties in software product line for product derivation. In *APSEC'08*, pages 187–194. IEEE, 2008.

[43] N. Siegmund, M. Rosenmüller, C. Kästner, P. G. Giarrusso, S. Apel, and S. S. Kolesnikov. Scalable prediction of non-functional properties in software product lines: Footprint and memory consumption. *Information & Software Technology*, 55(3):491–507, 2013.

[44] M. Varshosaz and R. Khosravi. Discrete time Markov chain families: modeling and verification of probabilistic software product lines. In *SPLC'13*, pages 34–41. ACM, 2013.

[45] A. von Rhein, S. Apel, C. Kästner, T. Thüm, and I. Schaefer. The PLA model: On the combination of product-line analyses. In *Proceedings of VaMoS'13*, pages 14:1–8, New York, NY, USA, 2013. ACM.

[46] J. White, B. Dougherty, D. C. Schmidt, and D. Benavides. Automated reasoning for multi-step feature model configuration problems. In *SPLC'09*, pages 11–20, 2009.

Systematic Derivation of Static Analyses for Software Product Lines *

Jan Midtgaard
Dept. of Computer Science, Aarhus University
Aabogade 34, 8200 Aarhus N, Denmark
jmi@cs.au.dk

Claus Brabrand Andrzej Wąsowski
IT University of Copenhagen
Rued Langgaards Vej 7, 2300 Copenhagen S, Denmark
{brabrand,wasowski}@itu.dk

Abstract

A recent line of work *lifts* particular verification and analysis methods to Software Product Lines (SPL). In an effort to generalize such case-by-case approaches, we develop a systematic methodology for lifting program analyses to SPLs using abstract interpretation. Abstract interpretation is a classical framework for deriving static analyses in a compositional, step-by-step manner. We show how to take an analysis expressed as an abstract interpretation and lift each of the abstract interpretation steps to a family of programs. This includes schemes for lifting domain types, and combinators for lifting analyses and Galois connections. We prove that for analyses developed using our method, the soundness of lifting follows by construction. Finally, we discuss approximating variability in an analysis and we derive variational data-flow equations for an example analysis, a constant propagation analysis for a simple imperative language.

Categories and Subject Descriptors D.2.4 [*Software Engineering*]: Software/Program Verification; F.3.2 [*Theory of Computation*]: Semantics of Programming Languages —*Program Analysis*

General Terms Languages, Theory, Verification

Keywords Software Product Lines, Verification, Static Analysis, Abstract Interpretation

1. Introduction

The methodology of *Software Product Lines* (SPLs) [10] enables systematic development of *program families* by maximizing reuse in order to decrease development cost and time-to-market. The SPL method has grown in popularity over the last 20 years, especially in the domain of embedded systems, including safety critical systems with stringent quality requirements on produced code.

While program families can be implemented using domain specific languages and general purpose model transformation [19, 45], often it is possible to use simpler methods that are more easily amenable to testing and analysis. The most popular [31] implementation method relies on a simple form of two staged computation in preprocessor style: the programming language used (often C) is enriched with the ability to express simple compile time computations (often C preprocessor). At build-time, the source code is first configured, a variant describing a particular product is derived, and only then is this variant compiled or interpreted.

In this two-stage process the compiler handles only the second stage artifacts—the code of the actual product variant. Consequently, all its static analysis mechanisms (such as type checking, data and control-analyses) do not analyze the entire program source code, but only the variant specialized for a particular product. This is sufficient for analyses that aim for program optimization, but entirely unacceptable for analyses that aim at identifying program errors. Often, it is not feasible for the vendor shipping the code to analyze each of the variants separately, due to a combinatorial explosion of the number of products. For example, if variability is used to provide personalization of software for various users, it suffices to have 33 independent features to yield more configurations than people on the planet (2^{33}). As little as 320 optional features yield more configurations than the number of atoms in the universe. Now, the Linux kernel code base contains more than 10,000 configuration options [4]. The problem is particularly burning when runtime errors remain disguised because exhaustive analysis is not possible.

In the last decade, many existing program analysis and verification techniques have been *lifted* to work on program families leading to the emergence of so-called *family-based analyses* [47] (see the related work section for discussion of some of these). The main advantage of these analyses is that they do *not* work in two stages, but analyze the entire code base—all configuration variants at once—at a cost much lower than the accumulated cost of analyzing each of the product variants separately.

Unfortunately, along with the growth of the collection of available lifted analysis methods, a more fundamental worry became increasingly clear: does the variability challenge require redevelopment of the entire language and compiler engineering theory? In response, the industry initiated standardization efforts to codify common understanding of what variability in languages is (for example [29]). In research, a number of papers have started to appear that tackle the more fundamental question of "what is variability in a programming language?" [23, 24].

As part of this larger effort, we attack the problem by developing a systematic understanding of (1) how a single program analysis relates to the lifted analysis, (2) how programming language definitions (including semantics) are enriched with variability and (3) how a program analysis developed formally for a single program can be systematically lifted into a correct analysis for a set of programs.

We develop a systematic methodology for lifting single program analyses using abstract interpretation [13]. Abstract interpretation

* Supported by *The Danish Council for Independent Research* under the Sapere Aude scheme, projects SADL and VARIETE.

MODULARITY '14, April 22–26, 2014, Lugano, Switzerland.

http://dx.doi.org/10.1145/2577080.2577091

is a unifying theory of sound abstraction and approximation of structures; a well-established general framework, which can express many analyses (including data-flow analyses [13], control-flow analyses [37], model-checking [16, 17], and type checking [11]). Our method exploits knowledge about a single program analysis to obtain a family-based analyses. The family-based analyses derived using this method are not only sound, but also formally and intimately related to their single program origins. The method is applicable to any analysis expressible as an abstract interpretation. We contribute the following:

- A systematic method for compositional derivation of *sound* SPL analyses based on abstract interpretation.
- Understanding of the structure of the space of family-based analyses (how single program analyses induce family-based analyses, and which of their abstraction components can be reused at family level).
- Understanding of individual family-based analyses (in particular, precisely where analysis precision is lost).
- Transfer of the usual benefits of abstract interpretation to family-based analyses (for example, techniques for trading precision for speed and methods for proving analyses to be semantically sound).
- A step-by-step example-driven demonstration of how to derive a family-based analysis.

We have deliberately chosen a tutorial style of presentation for the introduction to systematic derivation of analyses (based on the calculational approach to abstract interpretation [12], on which our results are founded). For this reason, our results are postponed until Section 4, after SPLs and systematic derivation of analyses have been properly introduced (Sections 2 and 3). We hope that this presentation style maximizes the potential benefits of this paper for the research community developing product line analysis tools. We present a simple imperative language as the running example, formalize its semantics, derive a constant propagation analysis, and show how the whole derivation process and the resulting analysis can be lifted to the family level for analyzing SPLs.

2. From Programs to Software Product Lines

We begin with settling the programming language that we want to analyze. Then, we develop a formal understanding of its semantics (as we aim at provably sound analyses). Finally, we introduce static variability into the language, and into its formal semantics.

IMP Programs: Implementing Single Systems

We use a simple imperative language, IMP, as an example to demonstrate abstract interpretation. In this paper, IMP impersonates a regular general-purpose programming language, aimed at the development of single programs (as opposed to program families). IMP is a well established minimal language, used in teaching and research. We give a brief account of IMP, referring the interested reader to textbooks [41, 48] for more details. We stress that IMP is the running example in the paper. However the presented systematic methodology is not limited to IMP or its features.

Syntax. IMP is structured into two syntactic categories: expressions (integer constants, variables, and binary operations) and statements (no-ops, assignments, statement sequences, conditional statements, and while loops). Its abstract syntax is summarized using the following context free grammar:

$$e \quad ::= \quad n \mid \mathtt{x} \mid e_0 \oplus e_1$$

$$s \quad ::= \quad \mathtt{skip} \mid \mathtt{x} := e \mid s_0 \,;\, s_1 \mid \mathtt{if}\ e\ \mathtt{then}\ s_0\ \mathtt{else}\ s_1 \mid \mathtt{while}\ e\ \mathtt{do}\ s$$

$$\frac{}{\langle \mathtt{skip}, \sigma\rangle \to \sigma}\ \textsc{Skip} \qquad \frac{\mathcal{E}(e,\sigma) = v}{\langle \mathtt{x} := e, \sigma\rangle \to \sigma[\mathtt{x} \mapsto v]}\ \textsc{Assign}$$

$$\frac{\langle s_0, \sigma\rangle \to \langle s_0', \sigma'\rangle}{\langle s_0 \,;\, s_1, \sigma\rangle \to \langle s_0' \,;\, s_1, \sigma'\rangle}\ \textsc{Seq1}$$

$$\frac{\langle s_0, \sigma\rangle \to \sigma'}{\langle s_0 \,;\, s_1, \sigma\rangle \to \langle s_1, \sigma'\rangle}\ \textsc{Seq2}$$

$$\frac{\mathcal{E}(e,\sigma) = v \qquad v \neq 0}{\langle \mathtt{if}\ e\ \mathtt{then}\ s_0\ \mathtt{else}\ s_1, \sigma\rangle \to \langle s_0, \sigma\rangle}\ \textsc{If1}$$

$$\frac{\mathcal{E}(e,\sigma) = v \qquad v = 0}{\langle \mathtt{if}\ e\ \mathtt{then}\ s_0\ \mathtt{else}\ s_1, \sigma\rangle \to \langle s_1, \sigma\rangle}\ \textsc{If2}$$

$$\frac{\mathcal{E}(e,\sigma) = v \qquad v \neq 0}{\langle \mathtt{while}\ e\ \mathtt{do}\ s, \sigma\rangle \to \langle s \,;\, \mathtt{while}\ e\ \mathtt{do}\ s, \sigma\rangle}\ \textsc{While1}$$

$$\frac{\mathcal{E}(e,\sigma) = v \qquad v = 0}{\langle \mathtt{while}\ e\ \mathtt{do}\ s, \sigma\rangle \to \sigma}\ \textsc{While2}$$

Figure 1. Small-step structural operational semantics for IMP

In the above, n stands for an integer constant, $\mathtt{x}$ stands for a variable name, and $\oplus$ stands for a binary operator. The precise choice of available operators is immaterial for the remainder of the paper. We denote by *Stm* and *Exp* the set of all statements, s, and expressions, e, generated by the above grammar.

Semantics. A state of an IMP program is an abstraction of memory storage (a *store*) mapping variables to values (integer numbers). We write, *Store*, to denote the set of all possible stores. IMP expressions are computed in a given store, denoted by σ below. A function, $\mathcal{E}$, defined below by structural induction, maps an expression and a store to a value, thereby formalizing evaluation of expressions.

$$\begin{array}{ll} & \mathcal{E} : \mathit{Exp} \times \mathit{Store} \to \mathit{Val} \\ \mathit{Val} = \mathbb{Z} & \mathcal{E}(n,\sigma) = n \\ \mathit{Store} = \mathit{Var} \to \mathit{Val} & \mathcal{E}(\mathtt{x},\sigma) = \sigma(\mathtt{x}) \\ & \mathcal{E}(e_0 \oplus e_1,\sigma) = \mathcal{E}(e_0,\sigma) \oplus \mathcal{E}(e_1,\sigma) \end{array}$$

Figure 1 presents a small-step structural operational semantics for the language. Following the convention popularized by C, we model Boolean values as integers, with zero interpreted as false and everything else as true (see rules IF2 and WHILE2, respectively, IF1 and WHILE1). Note the two types of rules: the typical small-step rules (for instance, SEQ1 or SEQ2), which rewrite a complex statement into a simpler one, possibly updating the store; and the completion rules which execute a statement to completion producing a new store (for instance, SKIP or WHILE2).

Product Families: Lifting IMP to Staged Computation

Implementation of SPL Architectures [10] relies on the existence of a variability mechanism [19] that allows early, or *staged*, configuration of program functionality (i.e., ability to configure program behaviour at build time or compile time). This way, a single program can encode multiple variations of a software product, maximizing code reuse. An individual product is derived by specializing the multi-staged program at product derivation time, before it is built.

A simple form of two-staged computation involving a C-style preprocessor is the most common variability mechanism in practice [31]. We will now lift IMP from describing single programs to program families, admitting two-staged computation in this style.

$$
\begin{aligned}
P[\![\texttt{skip}]\!]_k &= \texttt{skip} \\
P[\![\texttt{x := } e]\!]_k &= \texttt{x := } e \\
P[\![s_0 \texttt{ ; } s_1]\!]_k &= P[\![s_0]\!]_k \texttt{ ; } P[\![s_1]\!]_k \\
P[\![\texttt{if } e \texttt{ then } s_0 \texttt{ else } s_1]\!]_k &= \texttt{if } e \texttt{ then } P[\![s_0]\!]_k \texttt{ else } P[\![s_1]\!]_k \\
P[\![\texttt{while } e \texttt{ do } s]\!]_k &= \texttt{while } e \texttt{ do } P[\![s]\!]_k \\
P[\![\texttt{\#if } \varphi\ s]\!]_k &= \begin{cases} P[\![s]\!]_k & k \models \varphi \\ \texttt{skip} & k \not\models \varphi \end{cases}
\end{aligned}
$$

Figure 2. Preprocessor from $\overline{\text{IMP}}$ to IMP for configuration, k.

The compile-time computation is controlled by a product configuration k—a set of product *features* that should be included in the build process. A finite set $\mathbb{F}$ of Boolean variables, f, describes available features, $f \in \mathbb{F}$. A configuration, k, is a subset of *selected* features: $k \subseteq \mathbb{F}$. We write $\mathbb{K}$ for the set of all valid configurations. We only consider valid configurations in the remainder of the paper.

The set of legal product configurations is typically described by a *feature model* [30] or a configuration model in another similar notation [4, 21]. The results of this paper are independent of the choice of configuration language syntax representing the set $\mathbb{K}$, as we are concerned with mathematical proofs more than with implementation details (so the set-theoretic view is simple and convenient). In practice, syntax of feature models can be easily related to sets of valid configurations [3]. An exhaustive account of feature modeling and domain modeling can be found in [19].

Syntax. The programming language $\overline{\text{IMP}}$ is our two-stage extension of IMP. Its abstract syntax includes the same expression and statement languages as IMP, but we add a new compile-time-conditional statement, with keyword `#if`. It takes a condition over features (φ) and a statement (s) that should be executed (included in the product) if the condition is satisfied by the product configuration.

$$
\begin{aligned}
s &::= \ \dots \mid \texttt{\#if } \varphi\ s \\
\varphi &::= \ f \in \mathbb{F} \mid \neg\varphi \mid \varphi_0 \wedge \varphi_1
\end{aligned}
$$

We also add a syntactic category of Boolean expressions (φ) to write compile-time propositional logic formulae over features. We write, $\overline{FeatExp}$, for the set of all Boolean expressions over features, and $\overline{Stm}$ for the set of all statements of $\overline{\text{IMP}}$. To stress the variability aspect, we will sometimes write $\bar{s}$ to denote a statement from $\overline{Stm}$ (despite the notational overhead). The set of expressions *Exp* remains the same as for IMP.

Observe that adding preprocessor directives to the abstract syntax of IMP was essentially a mechanical transformation of the grammar that will look similar for other, more complex languages.

Semantics: From $\overline{\text{IMP}}$ to IMP. $\overline{\text{IMP}}$'s semantics has two stages: first, given a configuration k compute an IMP program for a given product variant; second, execute the IMP program using regular IMP semantics. Below we present the first stage of $\overline{\text{IMP}}$'s semantics.

We capture the meaning of static conditional expressions over features using a *satisfiability relation*, $\models \subseteq \mathbb{K} \times FeatExp$, between configurations and Boolean expressions:

$$
\begin{aligned}
k \models f &\quad \text{iff} \quad f \in k \\
k \models \neg\varphi &\quad \text{iff} \quad k \not\models \varphi \\
k \models \varphi_0 \wedge \varphi_1 &\quad \text{iff} \quad k \models \varphi_0 \wedge k \models \varphi_1
\end{aligned}
$$

The semantics of the first stage of the computation—a simple preprocessor from $\overline{\text{IMP}}$ to IMP, is specified by the function $P : \overline{Stm} \to \mathbb{K} \to Stm$ in Figure 2. The semantic function P recursively pre-processes all sub-statements of its input. The last case checks whether a feature constraint is satisfied and, if so, it includes the guarded statement. Otherwise it reduces to `skip`, which has the effect of removing the guarded statement. Again, observe that the above rules are independent of the semantics of IMP, so specifying the semantics of the preprocessor is essentially a mechanical process.

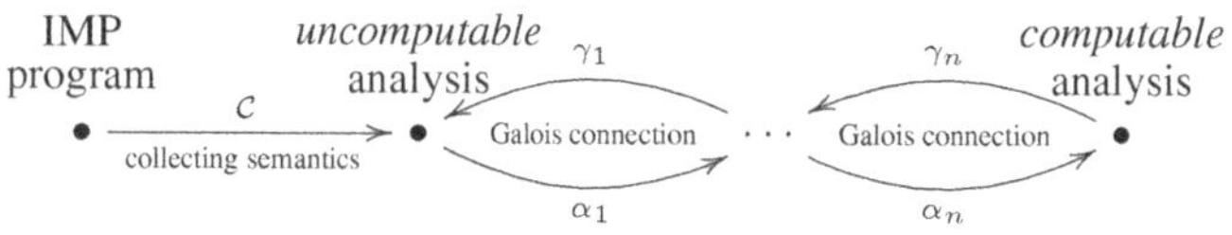

Figure 3. An overview of the abstract interpretation process.

3. Systematic Derivation of Analyses

In this section, we assume familiarity with *partial orders*, *complete lattices*, *monotone functions*, *fixed points*, and *the fixed-point theorem*. Appendix A of the accompanying technical report [39] summarizes these concepts.

We leave $\overline{\text{IMP}}$ aside for a few pages and work only with single programs and IMP in the following. We will systematically *derive* static analyses for IMP in a step-by-step compositional manner, using abstract interpretation. We include this section for pedagogical purposes. An analysis designer working with an existing language and analyses for which the abstract interpretation setup exists, would not need to do the work presented here. Instead, she would start right away with lifting the analyses to the family-based setting, following the steps outlined in Sect. 4.

We first introduce a so-called *collecting semantics* for IMP, which is the starting point in abstract interpretation. A collecting semantics takes a program as an argument and then defines how to "collect" information of interest in the given program. It can be seen as an analysis that does not introduce any imprecision (no approximation). Such an analysis is obviously *uncomputable*—it cannot be computed statically. Then, we introduce the notion of a so-called *Galois connection*—a pair of functions capturing information loss between two domains. Finally, we demonstrate how to combine collecting semantics and Galois connections to derive approximate, albeit computable analyses, which can statically determine dynamic properties of programs. An overview of this derivation process is shown in Fig. 3. We use a constant propagation analysis for IMP as the running example.

The process assumes that we have a semantics for our language (cf. Fig. 1), and define a compatible *collecting semantics*. A collecting semantics mimics the behavior of a structural-operational semantics, but with one important difference. Instead of working on *stores*, it works on *sets of stores*. In other words: our property of interest is the *possible* memories (modeled as a set of stores) that may arise at each program point. Furthermore, unknown program input can be modeled as *any* possible input (the set of stores in which a dedicated input variable can take on *any* run time value). Finally, the set of stores is naturally ordered under the subset ordering, $\subseteq$. In this way, the collecting semantics can already be thought of as a fully precise (but uncomputable) analysis. Then the actual computable analyses can be defined as approximations of this semantics.

The collecting semantics for IMP is given in Fig. 4. Going from the semantics to the collecting semantics is straightforward. The function $\mathcal{C}[\![s]\!]$ captures the effect of executing statement s on a set of input stores, by computing the set of possible output stores (memory contents after executing s). For instance, since the SKIP rule (cf. Fig. 1) does not modify the store, the corresponding case in the collecting semantics function becomes the identity function on sets of stores: $\lambda c.\, c$. The `if` case results in the *union* of the effect

$$
\begin{aligned}
\mathcal{C}[\![\texttt{skip}]\!] &= \lambda c.\, c \\
\mathcal{C}[\![\texttt{x := } e]\!] &= \lambda c.\, \{\sigma[\texttt{x} \mapsto v] \mid \sigma \in c \ \wedge\ v \in \mathcal{C}'[\![e]\!]\{\sigma\}\} \\
\mathcal{C}[\![s_0 \texttt{ ; } s_1]\!] &= \mathcal{C}[\![s_1]\!] \circ \mathcal{C}[\![s_0]\!] \\
\mathcal{C}[\![\texttt{if } e \texttt{ then } s_0 \texttt{ else } s_1]\!] &= \lambda c.\, \mathcal{C}[\![s_0]\!]\{\sigma \in c \mid 0 \notin \mathcal{C}'[\![e]\!]\{\sigma\}\} \\
&\quad \cup \mathcal{C}[\![s_1]\!]\{\sigma \in c \mid 0 \in \mathcal{C}'[\![e]\!]\{\sigma\}\} \\
\mathcal{C}[\![\texttt{while } e \texttt{ do } s]\!] &= \mathrm{lfp}\, \lambda\Phi.\, \lambda c.\, \{\sigma \in c \mid 0 \in \mathcal{C}'[\![e]\!]\{\sigma\}\} \\
&\quad \cup \Phi(\mathcal{C}[\![s]\!]\{\sigma \in c \mid 0 \notin \mathcal{C}'[\![e]\!]\{\sigma\}\})
\end{aligned}
$$

$$
\begin{aligned}
\mathcal{C}'[\![n]\!] &= \lambda c.\, \{n\} \\
\mathcal{C}'[\![\texttt{x}]\!] &= \lambda c.\, \{\sigma(\texttt{x}) \mid \sigma \in c\} \\
\mathcal{C}'[\![e_0 \oplus e_1]\!] &= \lambda c.\, \{v \mid v \in \{v_0\} \dot{\oplus} \{v_1\} \ \wedge\ \sigma \in c \ \wedge \\
&\qquad v_0 \in \mathcal{C}'[\![e_0]\!]\{\sigma\} \ \wedge\ v_1 \in \mathcal{C}'[\![e_1]\!]\{\sigma\}\}
\end{aligned}
$$

Figure 4. Collecting semantics for IMP where we have that $\mathcal{C}[\![s]\!] : 2^{Store} \to 2^{Store}$ and $\mathcal{C}'[\![e]\!] : 2^{Store} \to 2^{Val}$.

from the two corresponding rules (IF1 and IF2) with a contribution from s_0 (for the stores where the condition evaluates to a non-zero value) and one from s_1 (for the stores where the condition evaluates to zero). The only slightly more complex case is that of the `while` statement which is now given in a standard *fixed-point formulation* (see [39, Appendix A]). The case similarly combines the effects corresponding to the two rules (WHILE1 and WHILE2) although with an application of Φ to capture additional iterations of the loop. Observe, that the subordinate function $\mathcal{C}'[\![e]\!]$ does the same exercise for expressions. The symbol, $\dot{\oplus}$, denotes lifting of $\oplus$ to sets—an operator that produces a set of possible values of the expression for each combination of arguments from argument sets.

The collecting semantics captures precisely all executions of the structural operational semantics (SOS). Whenever a store is reachable by derivations of the SOS, then it is included in the corresponding denotation of the collecting semantics (and vice-versa). Formally:

Theorem 1 (Correctness of statement collecting semantics)**.**

$$\forall s \in \mathit{Stm}, c \in 2^{Store} : \ \mathcal{C}[\![s]\!]c = \{\sigma' \mid \sigma \in c \wedge \langle s, \sigma\rangle \to^* \sigma'\}$$

Importantly, given a statement, s, our collecting semantics $\mathcal{C}[\![s]\!] : 2^{Store} \to 2^{Store}$, and in particular the fixed point functional of the while rule:

$$\lambda\Phi.\, \lambda c.\, \{\sigma{\in}c \mid 0{\in}\mathcal{C}'[\![e]\!]\{\sigma\}\} \cup \Phi(\mathcal{C}[\![s]\!]\{\sigma{\in}c \mid 0{\notin}\mathcal{C}'[\![e]\!]\{\sigma\}\})$$

are now *monotone* functions over *complete lattices* (see [39, Appendix B] for proofs). By Tarski's Fixed-Point Theorem, they admit a unique least fixed point (cf. [39, Appendix A]). However, since these lattices have *infinite height*, it is not guaranteed that we can compute a fixed-point in finite time. Indeed, by reduction from the halting problem: if this analysis was *computable*, we would be able to decide whether an input program terminates by comparing the resulting store to lattice bottom. Since IMP is a Turing complete language, this cannot be the case; hence, the analysis must be *uncomputable*.

A *Galois connection* is a pair of functions, $\alpha : \mathbb{C} \to \mathbb{A}$ and $\gamma : \mathbb{A} \to \mathbb{C}$ (respectively known as the *abstraction* and *concretization* functions), connecting two partially ordered sets, $\langle \mathbb{C}, \leqslant\rangle$ and $\langle \mathbb{A}, \sqsubseteq\rangle$ (often called the *concrete* and *abstract* domain, respectively), such that:

$$\forall c \in \mathbb{C}, a \in \mathbb{A} : \quad \alpha(c) \sqsubseteq a \iff c \leqslant \gamma(a) \qquad (1)$$

which is often typeset as: $\langle \mathbb{C}, \leqslant\rangle \underset{\alpha}{\overset{\gamma}{\leftrightarrows}} \langle \mathbb{A}, \sqsubseteq\rangle$. Figure 5 illustrates a Galois connection graphically. For a concrete domain $\mathbb{C}$, we define

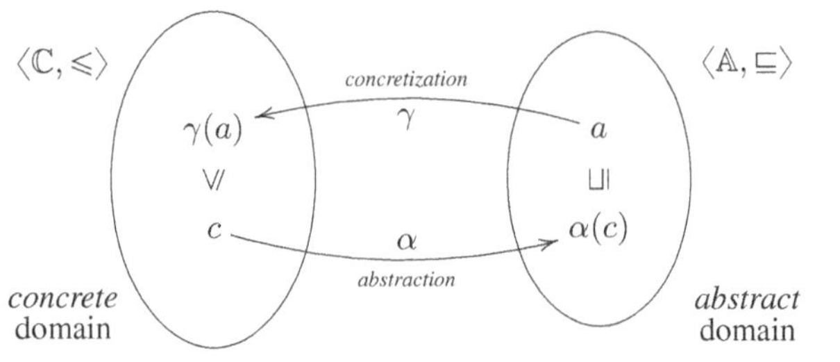

Figure 5. A *Galois connection* between a *concrete*, $\langle \mathbb{C}, \leqslant\rangle$, and an *abstract* domain, $\langle \mathbb{A}, \sqsubseteq\rangle$, connected via an *abstraction*, $\alpha : \mathbb{C} \to \mathbb{A}$, and a *concretization* function, $\gamma : \mathbb{A} \to \mathbb{C}$.

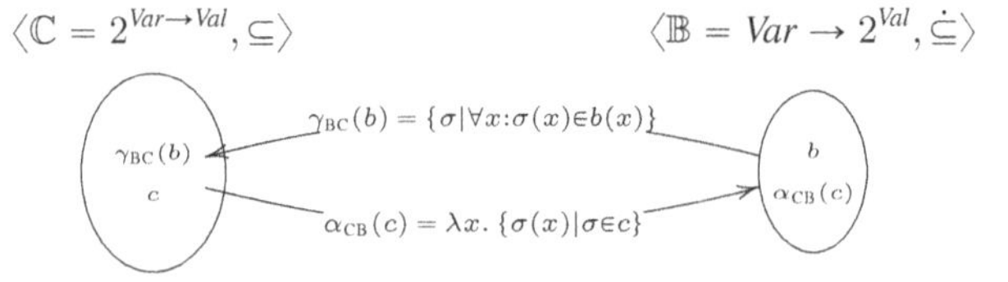

Figure 6. Galois connection between domains, $\mathbb{C}$ and $\mathbb{B}$: $\langle 2^{Var \to Val}, \subseteq\rangle \underset{\alpha_{\mathrm{CB}}}{\overset{\gamma_{\mathrm{BC}}}{\leftrightarrows}} \langle Var \to 2^{Val}, \dot{\subseteq}\rangle$.

abstraction and *concretization* functions to and from a more abstract domain $\mathbb{A}$, where information has been abstracted away. Later we will use the Galois connections to approximate an uncomputable analysis formulated over $\mathbb{C}$ with a computable analysis formulated over $\mathbb{A}$.

The seemingly innocent concept has a number of important properties [14]:

(i) α is *monotone*: i.e., $c \leqslant c' \Rightarrow \alpha(c) \sqsubseteq \alpha(c')$, for all $c, c' \in \mathbb{C}$;

(ii) γ is *monotone*; i.e., $a \sqsubseteq a' \Rightarrow \gamma(a) \leqslant \gamma(a')$, for all $a, a' \in \mathbb{A}$;

(iii) $\gamma \circ \alpha$ is *extensive*; i.e., $c \leqslant (\gamma \circ \alpha)(c)$, for all $c \in \mathbb{C}$;

(iv) $\alpha \circ \gamma$ is *reductive*; i.e., $(\alpha \circ \gamma)(a) \sqsubseteq a$, for all $a \in \mathbb{A}$;

(v) If $\mathbb{A}$ and $\mathbb{C}$ are *complete lattices*, then α is a *complete join morphism* (CJM), i.e.,

$$\alpha(\bigcup_{c \in \mathbb{C}} c) = \bigsqcup_{c \in \mathbb{C}} \alpha(c)$$

where $\cup$ and $\sqcup$ represent lattice joins in $\mathbb{C}$ and $\mathbb{A}$, respectively.

(vi) The composition of two Galois connections is itself a Galois connection (*closure under composition*):

$$\Big(\langle \mathbb{C}, \leqslant\rangle \underset{\alpha}{\overset{\gamma}{\leftrightarrows}} \langle \mathbb{B}, \subseteq\rangle \ \wedge\ \langle \mathbb{B}, \subseteq\rangle \underset{\alpha'}{\overset{\gamma'}{\leftrightarrows}} \langle \mathbb{A}, \sqsubseteq\rangle\Big) \Rightarrow \langle \mathbb{C}, \leqslant\rangle \underset{\alpha' \circ \alpha}{\overset{\gamma \circ \gamma'}{\leftrightarrows}} \langle \mathbb{A}, \sqsubseteq\rangle$$

Due to this last closure property, abstraction can be split into several steps by composing successive Galois connections that incrementally abstracts away information. Indeed, we will do exactly that in the derivation of a computable constant propagation analysis for the IMP language. Collectively, properties (i)–(iv) are equivalent to (1). Hence to test whether two functions form a Galois connection one can either check (1) or check properties (i)–(iv).

Let us now return to our IMP example and show how to use a Galois connection to abstract away information yielding a less precise analysis (although, in this case, still intractable).

Recall that the collecting semantics of a statement s works on sets of stores: it transforms sets of stores to sets of stores, cf. the

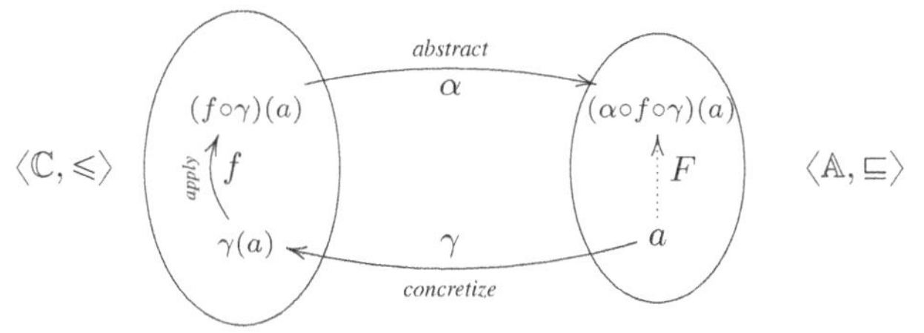

Figure 7. Abstract domain function, $F = \alpha \circ f \circ \gamma : \mathbb{A} \to \mathbb{A}$, *derived* from a concrete domain function, $f : \mathbb{C} \to \mathbb{C}$, via a round-trip in the Galois connection.

signature $2^{Store} \to 2^{Store}$ of $\mathcal{C}[\![s]\!]$ in Fig. 4. Figure 6 defines a Galois connection to abstract away information from sets of stores to multi-valued stores, so from $2^{Store} = 2^{Var \to Val}$ to $Var \to 2^{Val}$. Multi-valued stores are less precise than sets of stores, because they lose relational information about the values of different variables. Consider the (concrete) store set, $c = \{[x{\mapsto}1, y{\mapsto}2], [x{\mapsto}2, y{\mapsto}1]\}$, as an example. The abstraction function, α_{CB}, abstracts the store set c into $b = \alpha_{CB}(c) = [x{\mapsto}\{1,2\}, y{\mapsto}\{1,2\}]$. Like most *path-insensitive* program analyses, which merge and abstract away analysis information at control-flow confluence points (e.g., where `then` *joins* `else`), our abstract store b, will now have "forgotten" which values of variable x go with which values of y. Now if the next statement computes, say, multiplication $x * y$, the analysis will *conservatively over-approximate* the set of possible values to $\{1, 2, 4\}$, admitting *spurious values*, 1 and 4, in addition to the precise answer: $\{2\}$. The approximate response is bound to include the precise answer; in other words, we have a *sound* analysis: $\{2\} \subseteq \{1, 2, 4\}$.

Not only *values* can be abstracted from $\mathbb{C}$ to $\mathbb{A}$. In fact, also *functions* defined on the concrete domain, $f : \mathbb{C} \to \mathbb{C}$, can be abstracted to work on the abstract domain, $\alpha \circ f \circ \gamma = F : \mathbb{A} \to \mathbb{A}$. Figure 7 illustrates this process which transforms an argument, $a \in \mathbb{A}$, in three simple steps: (1) *concretize* a, $\gamma(a) \in \mathbb{C}$; (2) *apply* f, $(f \circ \gamma)(a) \in \mathbb{C}$; and (3) *abstract* the result, $(\alpha \circ f \circ \gamma)(a) \in \mathbb{A}$. Also, if f is monotone, then its composition with a monotone α and γ is monotone. In general, any monotone over-approximation of the composition is sufficient for a sound analysis.

In our case, we derive from, $\mathcal{C}[\![s]\!] : 2^{Var \to Val} \to 2^{Var \to Val}$, a function working on the abstracted domain, $\alpha_{CB} \circ \mathcal{C}[\![s]\!] \circ \gamma_{BC} : (Var \to 2^{Val}) \to (Var \to 2^{Val})$. This step is crucial—we use the Galois connection to derive a more abstract semantics (and thus a more approximating analysis) from the less abstract semantics (here the collecting semantics). Let us elaborate on this.

Cousot and Cousot [13] observed that even *fixed points* transfer from $\mathbb{C}$ to $\mathbb{A}$. If $\langle \mathbb{C}, \leqslant \rangle \underset{\alpha}{\overset{\gamma}{\leftrightarrows}} \langle \mathbb{A}, \sqsubseteq \rangle$ is a Galois connection whose domains, $\mathbb{C}$ and $\mathbb{A}$, are *complete lattices* and, f, is a *monotone* function on $f : \mathbb{C} \to \mathbb{C}$, then by the *fixed point transfer theorem* [13]:

$$\alpha(\mathrm{lfp}\, f) \sqsubseteq \mathrm{lfp}\, F \sqsubseteq \mathrm{lfp}\, F^{\#}$$

where $F = \alpha \circ f \circ \gamma$ and $F^{\#}$ is some monotone, conservative *over*-approximation of F; formally: $F \mathrel{\dot\sqsubseteq} F^{\#}$ (i.e., $\forall a \in \mathbb{A} : F(a) \sqsubseteq F^{\#}(a)$). Note that F represents the *best possible function* over the chosen abstract domain [14]. The above version of the fixed point transfer theorem still lets us approximate the desired fixed point. Under the stronger assumption that $\alpha \circ f = F \circ \alpha$ then a stronger version of the theorem guarantees that no approximation of the fixed point is taking place: $\alpha(\mathrm{lfp}\, f) = \mathrm{lfp}\, F$ [13].

The approach to abstract interpretation adopted in this paper, known as the *calculational approach* [12], advocates simple algebraic manipulation to obtain a *direct expression* for the function, F (if, indeed, it exists); or, a *sound approximation* thereof, $F^{\#}$. It is

$$
\begin{aligned}
\mathcal{B}[\![\texttt{skip}]\!] &= \lambda b.\, b \\
\mathcal{B}[\![\texttt{x := } e]\!] &= \lambda b.\, b[\texttt{x} \mapsto \mathcal{B}'[\![e]\!]b] \\
\mathcal{B}[\![s_0 \texttt{ ; } s_1]\!] &= \mathcal{B}[\![s_1]\!] \circ \mathcal{B}[\![s_0]\!] \\
\mathcal{B}[\![\texttt{if } e \texttt{ then } s_0 \texttt{ else } s_1]\!] &= \lambda b.\, \mathcal{B}[\![s_0]\!]b \mathrel{\dot\cup} \mathcal{B}[\![s_1]\!]b \\
\mathcal{B}[\![\texttt{while } e \texttt{ do } s]\!] &= \mathrm{lfp}\, \lambda\Phi.\, \lambda b.\, b \mathrel{\dot\cup} \Phi(\mathcal{B}[\![s]\!]b)
\end{aligned}
$$

$$
\begin{aligned}
\mathcal{B}'[\![n]\!] &= \lambda b.\, \{n\} \\
\mathcal{B}'[\![\texttt{x}]\!] &= \lambda b.\, b(\texttt{x}) \\
\mathcal{B}'[\![e_0 \oplus e_1]\!] &= \lambda b.\, \mathcal{B}'[\![e_0]\!]b \mathbin{\hat\oplus} \mathcal{B}'[\![e_1]\!]b
\end{aligned}
$$

Figure 9. Systematically derived *over-approximated* abstracted collecting semantics, $\mathcal{B}[\![s]\!] : (Var \to 2^{Val}) \to (Var \to 2^{Val})$ and $\mathcal{B}'[\![e]\!] : (Var \to 2^{Val}) \to 2^{Val}$.

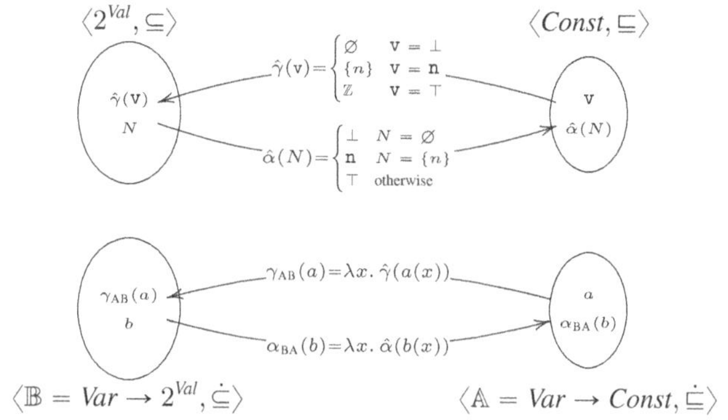

Figure 10. Galois connection: $\langle 2^{Val}, \subseteq \rangle \underset{\hat\alpha}{\overset{\hat\gamma}{\leftrightarrows}} \langle Const, \sqsubseteq \rangle$ (top diagram) along with its pointwise lifting (bottom diagram): $\langle Var \to 2^{Val}, \dot\subseteq \rangle \underset{\alpha_{BA}}{\overset{\gamma_{AB}}{\leftrightarrows}} \langle Var \to Const, \dot\sqsubseteq \rangle$.

thus a *systematic* (as in *"pen and paper"*) rather than *automatic* (as in *"computer generated"*) approach for *deriving* analyses.

Returning to our example, we now apply these ideas to our IMP analysis to obtain a *direct expression* for an over-approximation of $\alpha_{CB} \circ \mathcal{C}[\![s]\!] \circ \gamma_{BC}$ which we henceforth abbreviate, $\mathcal{B}[\![s]\!]$. Figure 8 illustrates how this may be done for the `if` case. Notice, how additional approximation is introduced (highlighted in boldface).

If we repeat this systematic derivation process for all the remaining cases, we can derive the over-approximated abstracted collecting semantics, $\mathcal{B}[\![s]\!]$, shown in Fig. 9 (where the case for `if` was the one we derived in Figure 8). Formally, $\mathcal{B}$ is related to $\mathcal{C}$ as follows:

Theorem 2 (Soundness of approximate statement semantics)**.**

$$\forall s \in Stm, b \in \mathbb{B} : (\alpha_{CB} \circ \mathcal{C}[\![s]\!] \circ \gamma_{BC})(b) \mathrel{\dot\subseteq} \mathcal{B}[\![s]\!]\, b$$

(See [39], for proof.) This is now starting to look like a conventional static analysis. However, it is still intractable. The program:

```
x := 1 ; while (1) x := x + 1
```

will give rise to an *infinite* multi-valued abstract store $b = [x \mapsto \{1, 2, 3, ...\}]$. Our next Galois connection will remedy this in abstracting our abstract domain, $Var \to 2^{Val}$, even further into a domain with *finite* height, thereby guaranteeing an analysis computable with a Kleene fixed point iteration.

Figure 10 presents a Galois connection between $\mathbb{B} = \mathrm{Var} \to 2^{Val}$ and $\mathbb{A} = \mathrm{Var} \to Const$, $\langle \mathbb{B}, \dot\subseteq \rangle \underset{\alpha_{BA}}{\overset{\gamma_{AB}}{\leftrightarrows}} \langle \mathbb{A}, \dot\sqsubseteq \rangle$, for abstracting the multi-valued store domain even further to a pointwise lifted constant propagation lattice (see Figure 11). If we now repeat the

$$
\begin{aligned}
&(\alpha_{\text{CB}} \circ \mathcal{C}[\![\texttt{if}\ e\ \texttt{then}\ s_0\ \texttt{else}\ s_1]\!] \circ \gamma_{\text{BC}})(b) && \text{(start of derivation)}\\
&= (\alpha_{\text{CB}} \circ (\lambda c.\, \mathcal{C}[\![s_0]\!]\{\sigma \in c \mid 0 \notin \mathcal{C}'[\![e]\!]\{\sigma\}\} \cup \mathcal{C}[\![s_1]\!]\{\sigma \in c \mid 0 \in \mathcal{C}'[\![e]\!]\{\sigma\}\}) \circ \gamma_{\text{BC}})(b) && \text{(by def. of } \mathcal{C}\text{, Fig. 4)}\\
&= \alpha_{\text{CB}}(\mathcal{C}[\![s_0]\!]\{\sigma \in \gamma_{\text{BC}}(b) \mid 0 \notin \mathcal{C}'[\![e]\!]\{\sigma\}\} \cup \mathcal{C}[\![s_1]\!]\{\sigma \in \gamma_{\text{BC}}(b) \mid 0 \in \mathcal{C}'[\![e]\!]\{\sigma\}\}) && (\beta\text{-reduction})\\
&= \alpha_{\text{CB}}(\mathcal{C}[\![s_0]\!]\{\sigma \in \gamma_{\text{BC}}(b) \mid 0 \notin \mathcal{C}'[\![e]\!]\{\sigma\}\}) \ \dot{\cup}\ \alpha_{\text{CB}}(\mathcal{C}[\![s_1]\!]\{\sigma \in \gamma_{\text{BC}}(b) \mid 0 \in \mathcal{C}'[\![e]\!]\{\sigma\}\}) && (\alpha_{\text{CB}} \text{ is a complete join morphism, p. 4 (v))}\\
&\dot{\subseteq}\ \alpha_{\text{CB}}(\mathcal{C}[\![s_0]\!](\gamma_{\text{BC}}(b))) \ \dot{\cup}\ \alpha_{\text{CB}}(\mathcal{C}[\![s_1]\!](\gamma_{\text{BC}}(b))) && \textbf{(over-approximation: } \mathcal{C} \textbf{ and } \alpha_{\text{CB}} \textbf{ monotone)}\\
&= (\alpha_{\text{CB}} \circ \mathcal{C}[\![s_0]\!] \circ \gamma_{\text{BC}})(b) \ \dot{\cup}\ (\alpha_{\text{CB}} \circ \mathcal{C}[\![s_1]\!] \circ \gamma_{\text{BC}})(b) && \text{(by def. of function composition)}\\
&\dot{\subseteq}\ \mathcal{B}[\![s_0]\!]\, b \ \dot{\cup}\ \mathcal{B}[\![s_1]\!]\, b && \text{(by inductive hypothesis: } \alpha_{\text{CB}} \circ \mathcal{C}[\![s_i]\!] \circ \gamma_{\text{BC}} \ \dot{\subseteq}\ \mathcal{B}[\![s_i]\!]\text{, twice)}\\
&= \mathcal{B}[\![\texttt{if}\ e\ \texttt{then}\ s_0\ \texttt{else}\ s_1]\!] b && \text{(by def. of } \mathcal{B}\text{)}
\end{aligned}
$$

Figure 8. Systematic derivation of *over-approximating* semantics, $\mathcal{B}[\![s]\!] : (\mathit{Var} \to 2^{\mathit{Val}}) \to (\mathit{Var} \to 2^{\mathit{Val}})$, for `if`, by abstracting collecting semantics, $\alpha_{\text{CB}} \circ \mathcal{C}[\![s]\!] \circ \gamma_{\text{BC}}$. Operators, $\dot{\cup}$ and $\dot{\subseteq}$, are extended to functions: $f \mathbin{\dot{\cup}} g = \lambda x.\, f(x) \cup g(x)$ and $f \mathrel{\dot{\subseteq}} g = \forall x.\, f(x) \subseteq g(x)$.

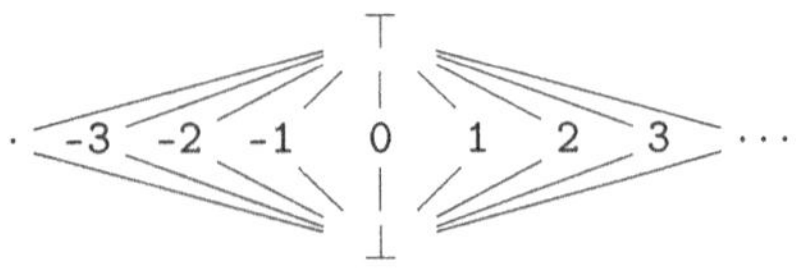

Figure 11. The constant propagation lattice: $\langle \mathit{Const}, \sqsubseteq \rangle$ with $\sqcup$ as its least upper bound operator (aka., *join*).

$$
\begin{aligned}
\mathcal{A}[\![\texttt{skip}]\!] &= \lambda a.\, a\\
\mathcal{A}[\![\texttt{x := } e]\!] &= \lambda a.\, a[\texttt{x} \mapsto \mathcal{A}'[\![e]\!]a]\\
\mathcal{A}[\![s_0\ \texttt{;}\ s_1]\!] &= \mathcal{A}[\![s_1]\!] \circ \mathcal{A}[\![s_0]\!]\\
\mathcal{A}[\![\texttt{if}\ e\ \texttt{then}\ s_0\ \texttt{else}\ s_1]\!] &= \mathcal{A}[\![s_0]\!] \mathbin{\dot{\sqcup}} \mathcal{A}[\![s_1]\!]\\
\mathcal{A}[\![\texttt{while}\ e\ \texttt{do}\ s]\!] &= \text{lfp}\, \lambda\Phi.\, \lambda a.\, a \mathbin{\dot{\sqcup}} \Phi(\mathcal{A}[\![s]\!]a)\\[1ex]
\mathcal{A}'[\![n]\!] &= \lambda a.\, \texttt{n}\\
\mathcal{A}'[\![\texttt{x}]\!] &= \lambda a.\, a(\texttt{x})\\
\mathcal{A}'[\![e_0 \oplus e_1]\!] &= \lambda a.\, \mathcal{A}'[\![e_0]\!]a \mathbin{\widehat{\oplus}} \mathcal{A}'[\![e_1]\!]a
\end{aligned}
$$

Figure 12. Constant propagation $\mathcal{A}[\![s]\!] : (\mathit{Var}{\to}\mathit{Const}) \to (\mathit{Var}{\to}\mathit{Const})$ and $\mathcal{A}'[\![e]\!] : (\mathit{Var}{\to}\mathit{Const}) \to \mathit{Const}$.

$$
\begin{aligned}
&(\alpha_{\text{BA}} \circ \mathcal{B}[\![\texttt{if}\ e\ \texttt{then}\ s_0\ \texttt{else}\ s_1]\!] \circ \gamma_{\text{AB}})(a) && \text{(start of derivation)}\\
&= (\alpha_{\text{BA}} \circ (\lambda b.\, \mathcal{B}[\![s_0]\!]b \ \dot{\cup}\ \mathcal{B}[\![s_1]\!]b) \circ \gamma_{\text{AB}})(a) && \text{(by def. of } \mathcal{B}\text{, Fig. 9)}\\
&= \alpha_{\text{BA}}(\mathcal{B}[\![s_0]\!](\gamma_{\text{AB}}(a)) \ \dot{\cup}\ \mathcal{B}[\![s_1]\!](\gamma_{\text{AB}}(a))) && (\beta\text{-reduction})\\
&= \alpha_{\text{BA}}(\mathcal{B}[\![s_0]\!](\gamma_{\text{AB}}(a))) \mathbin{\dot{\sqcup}} \alpha_{\text{BA}}(\mathcal{B}[\![s_1]\!](\gamma_{\text{AB}}(a))) && (\alpha_{\text{BA}} \text{ is a CJM, p. 4 (v))}\\
&\dot{\sqsubseteq}\ \mathcal{A}[\![s_0]\!]\, a \mathbin{\dot{\sqcup}} \mathcal{A}[\![s_1]\!]\, a && \text{(by inductive hypothesis, twice)}\\
&= \mathcal{A}[\![\texttt{if}\ e\ \texttt{then}\ s_0\ \texttt{else}\ s_1]\!]\, a && \text{(by def. of } \mathcal{A}\text{)}
\end{aligned}
$$

Figure 13. Systematic derivation of $\mathcal{A}[\![s]\!]$ from $\alpha_{\text{BA}} \circ \mathcal{B}[\![s]\!] \circ \gamma_{\text{AB}}$ for the `if` case.

$$
\begin{aligned}
[\![\texttt{skip}^{\ell}]\!]_{\mathsf{out}} &= [\![\texttt{skip}^{\ell}]\!]_{\mathsf{in}}\\[1ex]
[\![\texttt{x :=}^{\ell}\ e]\!]_{\mathsf{out}} &= [\![\texttt{x :=}^{\ell}\ e]\!]_{\mathsf{in}}[\texttt{x} \mapsto \mathcal{A}'[\![e]\!][\![\texttt{x :=}^{\ell}\ e]\!]_{\mathsf{in}}]\\[1ex]
[\![s_0^{\ell_0}\ \texttt{;}^{\ell}\ s_1^{\ell_1}]\!]_{\mathsf{out}} &= [\![s_1^{\ell_1}]\!]_{\mathsf{out}}\\
[\![s_1^{\ell_1}]\!]_{\mathsf{in}} &= [\![s_0^{\ell_0}]\!]_{\mathsf{out}}\\
[\![s_0^{\ell_0}]\!]_{\mathsf{in}} &= [\![s_0^{\ell_0}\ \texttt{;}^{\ell}\ s_1^{\ell_1}]\!]_{\mathsf{in}}\\[1ex]
[\![\texttt{if}^{\ell}\ e\ \texttt{then}\ s_0^{\ell_0}\ \texttt{else}\ s_1^{\ell_1}]\!]_{\mathsf{out}} &= [\![s_0^{\ell_0}]\!]_{\mathsf{out}} \mathbin{\dot{\sqcup}} [\![s_1^{\ell_1}]\!]_{\mathsf{out}}\\
[\![s_0^{\ell_0}]\!]_{\mathsf{in}} &= [\![\texttt{if}^{\ell}\ e\ \texttt{then}\ s_0^{\ell_0}\ \texttt{else}\ s_1^{\ell_1}]\!]_{\mathsf{in}}\\
[\![s_1^{\ell_1}]\!]_{\mathsf{in}} &= [\![\texttt{if}^{\ell}\ e\ \texttt{then}\ s_0^{\ell_0}\ \texttt{else}\ s_1^{\ell_1}]\!]_{\mathsf{in}}\\[1ex]
[\![\texttt{while}^{\ell}\ e\ \texttt{do}\ s^{\ell_0}]\!]_{\mathsf{out}} &= [\![s^{\ell_0}]\!]_{\mathsf{in}}\\
[\![s^{\ell_0}]\!]_{\mathsf{in}} &= [\![\texttt{while}^{\ell}\ e\ \texttt{do}\ s^{\ell_0}]\!]_{\mathsf{in}} \mathbin{\dot{\sqcup}} [\![s^{\ell_0}]\!]_{\mathsf{out}}
\end{aligned}
$$

Figure 14. Data-flow equations for constant propagation of Fig. 12

systematic derivation steps analogous to the steps of Figure 8 on the further abstracted analysis, $\alpha_{\text{BA}} \circ \mathcal{B}[\![s]\!] \circ \gamma_{\text{AB}}$, we can finally derive a *computable* constant propagation analysis as an over-approximation of $\alpha_{\text{BA}} \circ \mathcal{B}[\![s]\!] \circ \gamma_{\text{AB}}$, which we call $\mathcal{A}[\![s]\!]$—see Fig. 12. We show the derivation steps for the conditional statement in Fig. 13.

Since operators are functions, they too get abstracted by our Galois connection. Recall that our example uses $\dot{\oplus}$, the point-wise extension of the binary operator $\oplus$, defined as $V_0 \mathbin{\dot{\oplus}} V_1 = \{v_0 \oplus v_1 \mid v_0 \in V_0 \wedge v_1 \in V_1\}$. The abstract counterpart, $\widehat{\oplus}$, can be calculated by following the same recipe: $\hat{\alpha}(\hat{\gamma}(V) \mathbin{\dot{\oplus}} \hat{\gamma}(V')) \sqsubseteq V \mathbin{\widehat{\oplus}} V'$, i.e., by concretizing its arguments, performing the corresponding concrete operation, and finally abstracting the outcome. The resulting abstract operator, $\widehat{\oplus}$, can be computed effectively (in constant time) for all concrete binary operators:

$$
v_0 \mathbin{\widehat{\oplus}} v_1 = \begin{cases} \bot & \text{if } v_0 = \bot \vee v_1 = \bot\\ \texttt{n} & \text{if } v_0 = \texttt{n}_0 \wedge v_1 = \texttt{n}_1, \text{ where } \texttt{n} = \texttt{n}_0 \oplus \texttt{n}_1\\ \top & \text{otherwise} \end{cases}
$$

Finally, we write, $\dot{\sqcup}$, to denote the pointwise join in the $\mathit{Var} \to \mathit{Const}$ lattice: $a_0 \mathbin{\dot{\sqcup}} a_1 = \lambda\texttt{x}.\, a_0(\texttt{x}) \sqcup a_1(\texttt{x})$. This operator is then further lifted pointwise: $f \mathbin{\dot{\sqcup}} g = \lambda a.\, f(a) \mathbin{\dot{\sqcup}} g(a)$.

Since our domain now has a finite height, we have a tractable analysis. Indeed our example program from before gives rise to a *finite* abstract store, $a = [x \mapsto \top]$. Also, as a byproduct of the calculation, the analysis is provably sound:

Theorem 3 (Soundness of statement analysis)**.**

$$\forall s \in \mathit{Stm}, a \in \mathbb{A} : \ (\alpha_{\text{BA}} \circ \mathcal{B}[\![s]\!] \circ \gamma_{\text{AB}})(a) \mathrel{\dot{\sqsubseteq}} \mathcal{A}[\![s]\!]\, a$$

Notice again how this follows the recurring α-γ composition pattern. Also, Thm. 3 composes with the result of Thm. 2 yielding soundness of the analysis not only with respect to the approximate semantics $\mathcal{B}$, but also with respect to the original collecting semantics $\mathcal{C}$.

We may choose to implement the analysis in Figure 12 directly. Since the collecting semantics was compositional so is the resulting analysis, i.e., the analysis of straight-line code is straight-line (without fixed point computation), only loops require local fixed point computations. We may use Kleene's Fixed-Point Theorem to calculate these iteratively (cf. [39, Appendix A]).

To extract corresponding data-flow equations we assume the individual statements have been uniquely labelled with labels, ℓ,

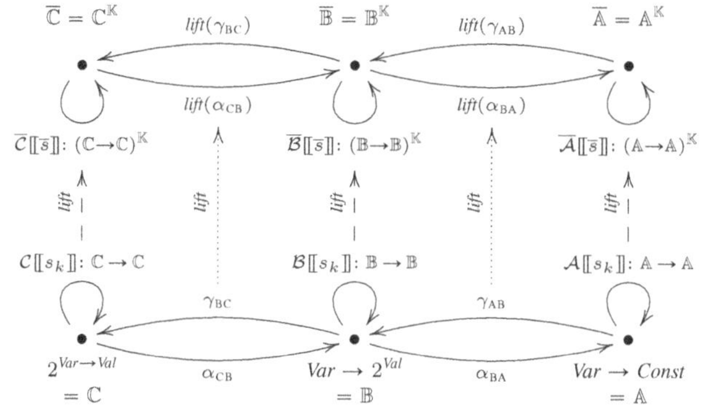

Figure 15. Abstract interpretation of programs (bottom line) along with *lifted* "variational abstract interpretation" of SPLs (top line).

to distinguish the individual flow to and from them and adapt $\mathcal{A}$ to work over these. The corresponding data-flow equations are shown in Fig. 14. Again the transformation from Fig. 12 to Fig. 14 is essentially mechanical. For each statement s^ℓ (program point) we generate two flow variables $[\![s^\ell]\!]_{\text{in}}$ and $[\![s^\ell]\!]_{\text{out}}$ for the input and output store, respectively. Then for each statement we simply write down that the input and output variable are related by an expression of the right-hand-side of the corresponding domain transformer in Fig. 12, where the input variable is substituted for the parameter, and the output variable for the value of the function (the same could be done for all expressions, but for brevity we refer directly to the semantics of expressions in Fig. 14). Observe that in the while equations the fixed point operator is stripped, and the value of the output variable is used for the recursive reference. The iteration used to compute the analysis result using these equations will handle the fixed point in the while rule at the meta-level. The iteration starts from the bottom value of the semantic domain assigned to all flow variables (if we disregard input), and stops when a fixed point is reached. Formally, a solution to the data-flow equations is sound with respect to the derived analysis:

Theorem 4 (Soundness of data-flow analysis)**.** *For all s^ℓ, such that $[\![s^\ell]\!]_{\text{in}}$, $[\![s^\ell]\!]_{\text{out}}$ satisfies the data-flow equations:*

$$\mathcal{A}[\![s^\ell]\!]([\![s^\ell]\!]_{\text{in}}) \dot{\sqsubseteq} [\![s^\ell]\!]_{\text{out}}$$

The resulting constant propagation analysis is the same as the data-flow analysis presented in, e.g., [6], but with one crucial difference; it has been *systematically derived* using the abstract interpretation framework, resulting in a *provably sound analysis*.

4. Systematic Derivation of Analyses for SPLs

We are now ready to discuss how the analysis obtained in Sect. 3 can be effectively lifted to work on Software Product Lines—the *variational abstract interpretation* for systematic derivation of analyses for SPLs. Figure 15 presents and relates the abstract interpretation of single programs and program families. The bottom part of the figure shows the derivation process for single programs presented in Sect. 3 (see also Fig. 3). The top part shows the same derivation process only lifted to work on SPLs. This top line of the workflow requires deriving the collecting semantics for the language with variability (in our example $\overline{\text{IMP}}$), and repeating the same abstraction steps as before at the level of program families. However, if we did this, we would almost completely ignore the artifacts accumulated during creation of the single program analysis! The core idea of the *variational abstract interpretation* is that the analyses at the single program level can be systematically lifted to

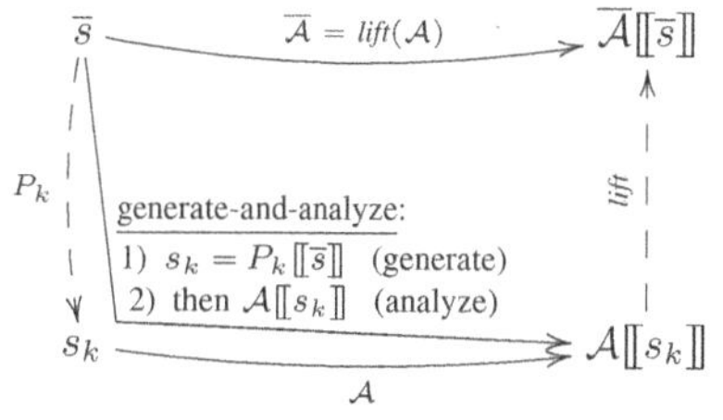

Figure 16. Generate-and-analyze vs. lifted analysis.

work on the family level without rerunning the entire derivation process: you arrive at the same, provably sound lifted analysis by commutation of the diagram.

The final constant propagation $\mathcal{A}$ can be lifted to family-based constant propagation $\overline{\mathcal{A}}$ by applying a lifting combinator (*lift*) to $\mathcal{A}$ and performing simplifying calculations. In the following, we discuss how this is done in detail and obtain a correctness result. We show how the domains of analyses, the analyses themselves (the transfer functions), and the Galois connections are lifted to the family level. Two kinds of upward arrows (dashed and dotted) lift us from the single program world to the program family world in Fig.15. There is a dashed upward arrow for lifting *analyses*, e.g. $\mathcal{A}[\![s]\!] : \mathbb{A} \to \mathbb{A}$ is lifted to $\overline{\mathcal{A}}[\![\overline{s}]\!] : (\mathbb{A} \to \mathbb{A})^{\mathbb{K}}$; and a dotted upward arrow for lifting *Galois connections*: $\mathbb{C} \underset{\alpha}{\overset{\gamma}{\leftrightarrows}} \mathbb{B}$ is *lifted* to $\overline{\mathbb{C}} \underset{lift(\alpha)}{\overset{lift(\gamma)}{\leftrightarrows}} \overline{\mathbb{B}}$. In the following we explain the meaning and interaction of these arrows.

4.1 Lifting Domains

We first lift the semantic domains. Recall that $\mathbb{K}$ denotes a finite set of valid configurations. A domain, $(\mathbb{C}, \sqsubseteq)$, is lifted to a *variability domain*, $(\overline{\mathbb{C}}, \dot{\sqsubseteq})$, by taking $\overline{\mathbb{C}}$ to be $\mathbb{C}^{\mathbb{K}}$ (i.e., a tuple of $|\mathbb{K}|$ copies of $\mathbb{C}$, one for each valid configuration), and lifting the ordering $\dot{\sqsubseteq}$ configuration-wise; i.e., $\overline{c} \dot{\sqsubseteq} \overline{c}' \equiv_{def}$ for all $k \in \mathbb{K} : \pi_k(\overline{c}) \sqsubseteq \pi_k(\overline{c}')$, where π_k selects the kth component of a tuple.

4.2 Lifting Analyses

The lifted domain representation, $\overline{\mathbb{A}} = \mathbb{A}^{\mathbb{K}}$, and Fig. 15 suggest that the lifted analysis, $\overline{\mathcal{A}}$, should be one complex function from $\mathbb{A}^{\mathbb{K}}$ to $\mathbb{A}^{\mathbb{K}}$. However, it turns out that using a tuple of $|\mathbb{K}|$ independent simple functions, $(\mathbb{A} \to \mathbb{A})^{\mathbb{K}}$, is a much better alternative. This models our intuition that lifting corresponds to running $|\mathbb{K}|$ analyses in parallel. Functions of type $(\mathbb{A} \to \mathbb{A})^{\mathbb{K}}$ are essentially a well behaved subset of functions from $\mathbb{A}^{\mathbb{K}}$ to $\mathbb{A}^{\mathbb{K}}$—namely those, for which the kth component of the function value only depends on the kth component of the argument. This warrants no problems with interference between configurations, which is critical for correctness of lifting.

To help readability, we introduce notational conventions that allow using tuples of functions, as if they were functions on tuples. We admit direct application of tuples of functions to tuples of arguments: if $\overline{f} : (\mathbb{A} \to \mathbb{A})^{\mathbb{K}}$ is a tuple of functions indexed by of $\mathbb{K}$, we write $\overline{f}(\overline{a})$ to mean the tuple of $|\mathbb{K}|$ values created by applying each function to the corresponding argument in the tuple of arguments: $\prod_{k \in K} \pi_k(\overline{f})(\pi_k(\overline{a}))$. Similarly, we overload the λ-abstraction notation, so creating a tuple of functions looks like creating a function on tuples: we write $\lambda\overline{a}.\ \prod_{k \in \mathbb{K}} f(\pi_k(\overline{a}))$ to mean $\prod_{k \in \mathbb{K}} \lambda a_k . f(a_k)$.

The straightforward way of analyzing a configuration, k, of an SPL, $\overline{s}$, using a conventional single-program analysis, $\mathcal{A}$, is to first *generate* product, $s_k = P_k[\![\overline{s}]\!]$, using the preprocessor; then, *analyze*

$$
\begin{aligned}
&\mathit{lift}(\mathcal{A})\llbracket \texttt{if}\ e\ \texttt{then}\ s_0\ \texttt{else}\ s_1 \rrbracket \\
&= \lambda\overline{a}.\ \prod_{k\in\mathbb{K}} \mathcal{A}\llbracket P\llbracket \texttt{if}\ e\ \texttt{then}\ s_0\ \texttt{else}\ s_1 \rrbracket_k \rrbracket(\pi_k(\overline{a})) && \text{(by def. of } \mathit{lift}\text{)} \\
&= \lambda\overline{a}.\ \prod_{k\in\mathbb{K}} \mathcal{A}\llbracket \texttt{if}\ e\ \texttt{then}\ P\llbracket s_0 \rrbracket_k\ \texttt{else}\ P\llbracket s_1 \rrbracket_k \rrbracket(\pi_k(\overline{a})) && \text{(by def. of } P\text{)} \\
&= \lambda\overline{a}.\ \prod_{k\in\mathbb{K}} (\mathcal{A}\llbracket P\llbracket s_0 \rrbracket_k \rrbracket \mathbin{\ddot{\sqcup}} \mathcal{A}\llbracket P\llbracket s_1 \rrbracket_k \rrbracket)(\pi_k(\overline{a})) && \text{(by def. of } \mathcal{A}\text{)} \\
&= \lambda\overline{a}.\ \prod_{k\in\mathbb{K}} \mathcal{A}\llbracket P\llbracket s_0 \rrbracket_k \rrbracket(\pi_k(\overline{a})) \mathbin{\dot{\sqcup}} \mathcal{A}\llbracket P\llbracket s_1 \rrbracket_k \rrbracket(\pi_k(\overline{a})) && \text{(by def. of } \ddot{\sqcup}\text{)} \\
&= \lambda\overline{a}.\ \prod_{k\in\mathbb{K}} \pi_k(\overline{\mathcal{A}}\llbracket s_0 \rrbracket\overline{a}) \mathbin{\dot{\sqcup}} \pi_k(\overline{\mathcal{A}}\llbracket s_1 \rrbracket\overline{a}) && \text{(by inductive hypothesis, twice)} \\
&= \lambda\overline{a}.\ \overline{\mathcal{A}}\llbracket s_0 \rrbracket\overline{a} \mathbin{\ddot{\sqcup}} \overline{\mathcal{A}}\llbracket s_1 \rrbracket\overline{a} && \text{(by def. of } \ddot{\sqcup}\text{)} \\
&= \overline{\mathcal{A}}\llbracket s_0 \rrbracket \mathbin{\ddot{\sqcup}} \overline{\mathcal{A}}\llbracket s_1 \rrbracket && (\eta\text{-reduce}) \\
&= \overline{\mathcal{A}}\llbracket \texttt{if}\ e\ \texttt{then}\ s_0\ \texttt{else}\ s_1 \rrbracket && \text{(by def. of } \overline{\mathcal{A}}\text{)}
\end{aligned}
$$

Figure 17. Deriving lifted constant propagation, $\overline{\mathcal{A}} = \mathit{lift}(\mathcal{A})$, for conditional statements: $\texttt{if}\ e\ \texttt{then}\ s_0\ \texttt{else}\ s_1$.

the generated product, s_k, using the conventional analysis: $\mathcal{A}\llbracket s_k \rrbracket$. This two stage process is depicted in Fig. 16 (cf. arrow labeled *generate-and-analyze*). However, it only analyzes *one* configuration of the SPL (the arrow ends up at the bottom part of Fig. 16).

To lift the analysis to the family level, we need to execute $\mathcal{A}$ for each of the valid configurations. Simply applying an analysis to *all* configurations, yields the formal specification of the lifting combinator for analyses. If $\mathcal{A}\llbracket s \rrbracket : \mathbb{A} \to \mathbb{A}$ is a single analysis function, then we require that its lifted version $\overline{\mathcal{A}}\llbracket \overline{s} \rrbracket : (\mathbb{A} \to \mathbb{A})^{\mathbb{K}}$ satisfies the following:

$$\overline{\mathcal{A}}\llbracket \overline{s} \rrbracket = \lambda\overline{a}.\ \prod_{k\in\mathbb{K}} \mathcal{A}\llbracket P\llbracket \overline{s} \rrbracket_k \rrbracket(\pi_k(\overline{a})) \tag{2}$$

The equation stipulates that running the aggregate analysis $\overline{\mathcal{A}}$ must be equivalent to running the original analysis $\mathcal{A}$ for each variant separately, after deriving it using the preprocessor P. An analysis $\overline{\mathcal{A}}$ satisfying (2) transforms a lifted store, $\overline{a} \in \overline{\mathbb{A}} = \mathbb{A}^{\mathbb{K}}$, into another lifted store, $\overline{a}' = \prod_{k\in\mathbb{K}} \mathcal{A}\llbracket P\llbracket \overline{s} \rrbracket_k \rrbracket \pi_k(\overline{a})$, of the same type. In other words, $\overline{\mathcal{A}}$ is a transformer between aggregated state of all configurations on entry to a given program point to a set of aggregated states of all configurations on the exit from that point.

This specification of lifting works for any single program analysis, not just for constant propagation. We formulate it as a general analysis-independent and language-independent combinator.

Definition 5. *The generic lifting of analysis, $\mathcal{X} : \mathbb{X} \to \mathbb{X}$, working on domain $\mathbb{X}$, is:*

$$\mathit{lift}(\mathcal{X})\llbracket \overline{s} \rrbracket \quad = \quad \lambda\overline{x}.\ \prod_{k\in\mathbb{K}} \mathcal{X}\llbracket P\llbracket \overline{s} \rrbracket_k \rrbracket(\pi_k(\overline{x}))$$

In Fig. 15 the dashed upward arrows represent applications of the above lifting combinator. They transform an analysis function (solid loop arrows at the bottom of the figure), to a *family-based* analysis (solid loop arrows at the top).

Unfortunately, Def. 5 cannot be used as a direct definition of analysis $\overline{\mathcal{A}}$ as it still depends on the single program analysis. Implementing $\overline{\mathcal{A}}$ naively, directly following (2), would merely apply the conventional analysis $|\mathbb{K}|$ times (one for each $k \in \mathbb{K}$). While this would give the correct results, it is not what we wanted! We seek an analysis that will analyse all configurations simultaneously. The question is how to obtain a definition of $\overline{\mathcal{A}}$ that is independent of $\mathcal{A}$, yet satisfies equation (2). To achieve this we simplify equation (2), similarly to how we simplified the composition of analysis functions with Galois connections. As such, our lifting is calculational in nature, following the natural steps in abstract interpretation. If

$$
\begin{aligned}
\overline{\mathcal{A}}\llbracket \texttt{skip} \rrbracket &= \lambda\overline{a}.\ \overline{a} \\
\overline{\mathcal{A}}\llbracket \texttt{x := } e \rrbracket &= \lambda\overline{a}.\ \prod_{k\in\mathbb{K}} (\pi_k(\overline{a}))[\texttt{x} \mapsto \pi_k(\overline{\mathcal{A}'}\llbracket e \rrbracket\overline{a})] \\
\overline{\mathcal{A}}\llbracket s_0\ \texttt{;}\ s_1 \rrbracket &= \overline{\mathcal{A}}\llbracket s_1 \rrbracket \circ \overline{\mathcal{A}}\llbracket s_0 \rrbracket \\
\overline{\mathcal{A}}\llbracket \texttt{if}\ e\ \texttt{then}\ s_0\ \texttt{else}\ s_1 \rrbracket &= \overline{\mathcal{A}}\llbracket s_0 \rrbracket \mathbin{\ddot{\sqcup}} \overline{\mathcal{A}}\llbracket s_1 \rrbracket \\
\overline{\mathcal{A}}\llbracket \texttt{while}\ e\ \texttt{do}\ s \rrbracket &= \mathrm{lfp}\,\lambda\overline{\Phi}.\ \lambda\overline{a}.\ \overline{a} \mathbin{\dot{\sqcup}} \overline{\Phi}(\overline{\mathcal{A}}\llbracket s \rrbracket\,\overline{a})
\end{aligned}
$$

$$\overline{\mathcal{A}}\llbracket \texttt{\#if}\ \varphi\ s \rrbracket = \lambda\overline{a}.\ \prod_{k\in\mathbb{K}} \begin{cases} \pi_k(\overline{\mathcal{A}}\llbracket s \rrbracket\overline{a}) & k \models \varphi \\ \pi_k(\overline{a}) & k \not\models \varphi \end{cases}$$

$$
\begin{aligned}
\overline{\mathcal{A}'}\llbracket n \rrbracket &= \lambda\overline{a}.\ \prod_{k\in\mathbb{K}} \texttt{n} \\
\overline{\mathcal{A}'}\llbracket \texttt{x} \rrbracket &= \lambda\overline{a}.\ \prod_{k\in\mathbb{K}} \pi_k(\overline{a})(\texttt{x}) \\
\overline{\mathcal{A}'}\llbracket e_0 \oplus e_1 \rrbracket &= \lambda\overline{a}.\ \prod_{k\in\mathbb{K}} \pi_k(\overline{\mathcal{A}'}\llbracket e_0 \rrbracket\overline{a}) \mathbin{\hat{\oplus}} \pi_k(\overline{\mathcal{A}'}\llbracket e_1 \rrbracket\overline{a})
\end{aligned}
$$

Figure 18. Lifted constant propagation analysis of $\overline{\text{IMP}}$ where, $\overline{\mathcal{A}}\llbracket \overline{s} \rrbracket : ((\mathit{Var} \to \mathit{Const}) \to (\mathit{Var} \to \mathit{Const}))^{\mathbb{K}}$ and $\overline{\mathcal{A}'}\llbracket \overline{e} \rrbracket : ((\mathit{Var} \to \mathit{Const}) \to \mathit{Const})^{\mathbb{K}}$.

$$
\begin{aligned}
\llbracket \texttt{skip}^{\ell} \rrbracket_{\overline{\mathsf{out}}} &= \llbracket \texttt{skip}^{\ell} \rrbracket_{\overline{\mathsf{in}}} \\
\underline{\forall k \in \mathbb{K}}\text{: } \pi_k(\llbracket \texttt{x :=}^{\ell}\ e^{\ell_0} \rrbracket_{\overline{\mathsf{out}}}) &= \pi_k(\llbracket \texttt{x :=}^{\ell}\ e^{\ell_0} \rrbracket_{\overline{\mathsf{in}}})[\texttt{x} \mapsto \pi_k(\overline{\mathcal{A}'}\llbracket e^{\ell_0} \rrbracket \llbracket \texttt{x :=}^{\ell}\ e^{\ell_0} \rrbracket_{\overline{\mathsf{in}}})] \\[4pt]
\llbracket s_0^{\ell_0}\ \texttt{;}^{\ell}\ s_1^{\ell_1} \rrbracket_{\overline{\mathsf{out}}} &= \llbracket s_1^{\ell_1} \rrbracket_{\overline{\mathsf{out}}} \\
\llbracket s_1^{\ell_1} \rrbracket_{\overline{\mathsf{in}}} &= \llbracket s_0^{\ell_0} \rrbracket_{\overline{\mathsf{out}}} \\
\llbracket s_0^{\ell_0} \rrbracket_{\overline{\mathsf{in}}} &= \llbracket s_0^{\ell_0}\ \texttt{;}^{\ell}\ s_1^{\ell_1} \rrbracket_{\overline{\mathsf{in}}} \\[4pt]
\llbracket \texttt{if}^{\ell}\ e\ \texttt{then}\ s_0^{\ell_0}\ \texttt{else}\ s_1^{\ell_1} \rrbracket_{\overline{\mathsf{out}}} &= \llbracket s_0^{\ell_0} \rrbracket_{\overline{\mathsf{out}}} \mathbin{\ddot{\sqcup}} \llbracket s_1^{\ell_1} \rrbracket_{\overline{\mathsf{out}}} \\
\llbracket s_0^{\ell_0} \rrbracket_{\overline{\mathsf{in}}} &= \llbracket \texttt{if}^{\ell}\ e\ \texttt{then}\ s_0^{\ell_0}\ \texttt{else}\ s_1^{\ell_1} \rrbracket_{\overline{\mathsf{in}}} \\
\llbracket s_1^{\ell_1} \rrbracket_{\overline{\mathsf{in}}} &= \llbracket \texttt{if}^{\ell}\ e\ \texttt{then}\ s_0^{\ell_0}\ \texttt{else}\ s_1^{\ell_1} \rrbracket_{\overline{\mathsf{in}}} \\[4pt]
\llbracket \texttt{while}^{\ell}\ e\ \texttt{do}\ s^{\ell_0} \rrbracket_{\overline{\mathsf{out}}} &= \llbracket s^{\ell_0} \rrbracket_{\overline{\mathsf{in}}} \\
\llbracket s^{\ell_0} \rrbracket_{\overline{\mathsf{in}}} &= \llbracket \texttt{while}^{\ell}\ e\ \texttt{do}\ s^{\ell_0} \rrbracket_{\overline{\mathsf{in}}} \mathbin{\ddot{\sqcup}} \llbracket s^{\ell_0} \rrbracket_{\overline{\mathsf{out}}} \\[4pt]
\underline{\forall k \in \mathbb{K}}\text{: } \pi_k(\llbracket \texttt{\#if}^{\ell}\ \varphi\ s^{\ell_0} \rrbracket_{\overline{\mathsf{out}}}) &= \pi_k(\llbracket s^{\ell_0} \rrbracket_{\overline{\mathsf{out}}}) \quad \text{if} \quad k \models \varphi \\
\underline{\forall k \in \mathbb{K}}\text{: } \pi_k(\llbracket \texttt{\#if}^{\ell}\ \varphi\ s^{\ell_0} \rrbracket_{\overline{\mathsf{out}}}) &= \pi_k(\llbracket \texttt{\#if}^{\ell}\ \varphi\ s^{\ell_0} \rrbracket_{\overline{\mathsf{in}}}) \quad \text{if} \quad k \not\models \varphi \\
\underline{\forall k \in \mathbb{K}}\text{: } \pi_k(\llbracket s^{\ell_0} \rrbracket_{\overline{\mathsf{in}}}) &= \pi_k(\llbracket \texttt{\#if}^{\ell}\ \varphi\ s^{\ell_0} \rrbracket_{\overline{\mathsf{in}}}) \quad \text{if} \quad k \models \varphi
\end{aligned}
$$

Figure 19. Flow equations for lifted constant propagation of Fig. 18.

we perform the composition and simplify the resulting expression systematically, we can eliminate the intermediate product generation step and obtain a direct expression as shown in Fig. 18 (corresponding to the top arrow in Fig. 16). It is essential to emphasize that this calculation, when completed for all cases, actually proves a theorem that the analyses specified in equation (2) and in Fig. 18 are the same:

Theorem 6. *The lifting of the constant propagation analysis is correct in the sense of requirement* (2), *so $\mathit{lift}(\mathcal{A}) = \overline{\mathcal{A}}$.*

The equality sign in this theorem captures that lifting has introduced no approximation: the family-based analyses obtained this way are as precise as running the original analysis for each configuration individually. In the appendix of the accompanying technical report [39] we prove this theorem for all three semantics. Here we briefly discuss it for constant propagation. Figure 17 illustrates how the calculation is done for conditional statements. In the fifth step we use the inductive hypothesis, which here means applying the definition of *lift* in the reverse direction to structurally smaller statements. Note that the pointwise join operator $\dot\sqcup$ defined in Section 3 is lifted to a join over tuples, $\ddot\sqcup$, defined as $\overline{a}_0 \ddot\sqcup \overline{a}_1 = \prod_{k\in\mathbb{K}} \pi_k(\overline{a}_0) \dot\sqcup \pi_k(\overline{a}_1)$. The operator is then further lifted pointwise to functions, $\ddot\sqcup$, as well.

The calculation looks similar for most other statements. The while-case is however non-trivial, due to the need of lifting the fixed point expressions. In particular, rather than to lift a fixed point computation to a tuple of fixed point computations, we wish to equate two fixed points. To do so, we define an abstraction, which projects a particular k configuration entry, along with the corresponding concretization function.

$$\alpha_k : \mathbb{A}^{\mathbb{K}} \to \mathbb{A} \qquad \gamma_k : \mathbb{A} \to \mathbb{A}^{\mathbb{K}}$$

$$\alpha_k(\overline{a}) = \pi_k(\overline{a}) \qquad \gamma_k(a) = \prod_{k'\in\mathbb{K}} \begin{cases} a & k = k' \\ \dagger & k \neq k' \end{cases}$$

Such projecting abstractions are well known to be Galois connections. We then lift this Galois connection to a Galois connection between monotone transfer functions [14]:

$$\alpha_\to : (\mathbb{A}^{\mathbb{K}} \xrightarrow{m} \mathbb{A}^{\mathbb{K}}) \to \mathbb{A} \xrightarrow{m} \mathbb{A} \qquad \gamma_\to : (\mathbb{A} \xrightarrow{m} \mathbb{A}) \to \mathbb{A}^{\mathbb{K}} \xrightarrow{m} \mathbb{A}^{\mathbb{K}}$$

$$\alpha_\to(\overline{\Phi}) = \alpha_k \circ \overline{\Phi} \circ \gamma_k \qquad \gamma_\to(\Phi) = \gamma_k \circ \Phi \circ \alpha_k$$

where we write $X \xrightarrow{m} Y$ for the domain of monotone function from X to Y. Then we show that

$$\alpha_\to \circ (\lambda\overline{\Phi}.\, \lambda\overline{a}.\, \overline{a} \ddot\sqcup \overline{\Phi}(\overline{\mathcal{A}}[\![s]\!]\overline{a})) = (\lambda\Phi.\, \lambda a.\, a \dot\sqcup \Phi(\mathcal{A}[\![P[\![s]\!]_k]\!]a)) \circ \alpha_\to$$

which we can use to transfer fixed points without needless approximation, using the stronger fixed point theorem (see Sec. 3).

$$\begin{aligned}
&\alpha_\to(\overline{\mathcal{A}}[\![P[\![\texttt{while}\ e\ \texttt{do}\ \overline{s}]\!]_k]\!]) \\
&= \alpha_\to(\overline{\mathcal{A}}[\![\texttt{while}\ e\ \texttt{do}\ P[\![\overline{s}]\!]_k]\!]) && \text{(by def. of } P\text{)} \\
&= \mathcal{A}[\![\texttt{while}\ e\ \texttt{do}\ P[\![\overline{s}]\!]_k]\!] && \text{(by above and stronger fixed point thm.)} \\
&= \mathcal{A}[\![P[\![\texttt{while}\ e\ \texttt{do}\ \overline{s}]\!]_k]\!] && \text{(by def. of } P\text{)}
\end{aligned}$$

We can now calculate the closed form for while loops in the same style as for conditional statements (using the above law in one of the rewrite steps). This proof method is independent of the transfer function (here $\mathcal{A}$). In the appendix of the accompanying technical report [39] we use it to lift fixed points for the other two semantics.

The resulting formulation in Fig. 18 no longer depends on $\mathcal{A}$, but specifies $\overline{\mathcal{A}}$ directly. Just like in Sect. 3, we can use this formulation to derive data flow equations. This is a fairly mechanical process that results in the equations of Fig. 19 (compare to figures 18, 14). As shown in previous work [5, 6], this simplified version can be implemented to run much faster than the naive approach. The obtained data-flow equations are now variability aware and provably sound:

Theorem 7. *(Soundness of lifted data-flow analysis) For all $\overline{s}^\ell$, such that $[\![\overline{s}^\ell]\!]_{\overline{\text{in}}}, [\![\overline{s}^\ell]\!]_{\overline{\text{out}}}$ satisfies the data-flow equations:*

$$\overline{\mathcal{A}}[\![\overline{s}^\ell]\!]([\![\overline{s}^\ell]\!]_{\overline{\text{in}}}) \ \ddot\sqsubseteq\ [\![\overline{s}^\ell]\!]_{\overline{\text{out}}}$$

An attentive reader may question if we obtained any aggregate analysis here. After all, the specification in Fig. 19 appears to be exponential in the size of the valid configurations. It is crucial to understand that this mathematical specification for computing aggregate analysis, is orthogonal to an implementation (including choices of data structures). In particular for SPL analysis in practice, many of the entries in the $\mathbb{K}$-indexed tuples and transfer functions will be identical (many program points are identical/act identically for most configurations). Thus they can be executed and represented efficiently, storing and running them once, instead of exponentially many times. This is also the reason why the analyses in [5, 6] are so efficient in practice.

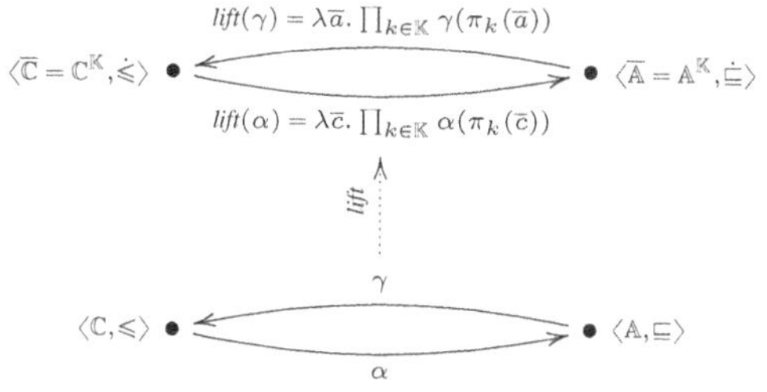

Figure 20. Pointwise lifting of a Galois connection.

4.3 Many Routes to Family-based Analysis

If we wanted to consider correctness of the lifted analysis $\overline{\mathcal{A}}$ using the classical abstract interpretation approach, we should devise a collecting semantics $\overline{\mathcal{C}}$ and a Galois connection relating them. If we wanted to follow the same incremental process as in Sect. 3, then we would need a chain of Galois connections:

$$\langle \overline{\mathbb{C}}, \dot\subseteq \rangle \underset{\overline{\alpha}_{\text{CB}}}{\overset{\overline{\gamma}_{\text{BC}}}{\leftrightarrows}} \langle \overline{\mathbb{B}}, \dot\subseteq \rangle \underset{\overline{\alpha}_{\text{BA}}}{\overset{\overline{\gamma}_{\text{AB}}}{\leftrightarrows}} \langle \overline{\mathbb{A}}, \ddot\sqsubseteq \rangle$$

Then, we would have to compute $\overline{\mathcal{A}}$ by composing these Galois connections with $\overline{\mathcal{C}}$ and prove that the resulting analysis is identical to the lifting of $\mathcal{A}$, so that the diagram in Fig. 15 commutes. A detailed development taking this route is available in the extended version [39]. But there is an easier route as we have just seen! Instead of devising the collecting semantics at family level, $\overline{\mathcal{C}}$, and then a sequence of Galois connections, we can obtain them all by lifting. The transfer functions, including the collecting semantics, can be lifted like in Sect. 4.3 (see [39]). We can lift the Galois connections using a third combinator:

$$\textit{lift}(\varphi) \;=\; \lambda\overline{d}.\, \prod_{k\in\mathbb{K}} \varphi(\pi_k(\overline{d})) \qquad (3)$$

Figure 20 illustrates the lifting of a Galois connection. By viewing *lift* (over a tuple) as a pointwise lifting (to configuration accepting functions) this is a well-known lifting of Galois connections [15]. This way, no invention of new analyses for the family level is needed. Instead, all analyses can be uniformly lifted and composed. This is by no means automatic, but it is systematic; it does not require any design effort, as the original analysis is a sufficient source of information for obtaining the family-based analysis.

The following theorem states that the result of lifting the final single-program analysis is equivalent to lifting and recalculating all intermediate steps. This result does not depend on any particular analysis. It states that if a static analysis $\mathcal{X}[\![s]\!]$ is obtained from a more concrete analysis $\mathcal{Y}[\![s]\!]$ by applying a Galois connection and simplifying (possibly with some approximation), then the lifting of this analysis can be soundly obtained by applying a lifted Galois connection to the lifting of $\mathcal{Y}$. Effectively, the diagram of Fig. 15 commutes. It is sound to develop the single program analysis and lift it as in Sect. 4.3, instead of lifting the collecting semantics and developing the entire analysis anew at the family level.

Theorem 8. *If for all programs s we have that $\alpha \circ \mathcal{Y}[\![s]\!] \circ \gamma \mathrel{\dot\sqsubseteq} \mathcal{X}[\![s]\!]$ then also for each program $\overline{s}$ with variability*

$$\textit{lift}(\alpha) \circ \textit{lift}(\mathcal{Y})[\![\overline{s}]\!] \circ \textit{lift}(\gamma) \ \ddot\sqsubseteq\ \textit{lift}(\mathcal{X})[\![\overline{s}]\!]$$

Moreover, if no approximation is introduced during the derivation of a single program analysis $\mathcal{X}$ (so that $\alpha \circ \mathcal{Y}[\![s]\!] = \mathcal{X}[\![s]\!] \circ \alpha$) then the lifting introduces no additional abstraction at the family level: $\textit{lift}(\alpha) \circ \textit{lift}(\mathcal{Y})[\![\overline{s}]\!] = \textit{lift}(X)[\![\overline{s}]\!] \circ \textit{lift}(\alpha)$. With this general theorem, the soundness for the example analysis now follows as a corollary from Thm. 2, 3, 6 and 8:

Corollary 9 (Soundness). *For all* $\overline{s} \in \overline{Stm}$:

$lift(\alpha_{BA} \circ \alpha_{CB}) \circ lift(\mathcal{C})[\![\overline{s}]\!] \circ lift(\gamma_{BC} \circ \gamma_{AB}) \ddot{\sqsubseteq} lift(\mathcal{A})[\![\overline{s}]\!] = \overline{\mathcal{A}}[\![\overline{s}]\!]$

4.4 Variability Relevant Abstractions

So far, we have argued that it is most practical to develop analyses for single programs, and then apply our lifting combinator to lift their definition to program families via a formal calculation. This process appears most straightforward, but it has one disadvantage: all the abstractions applied in the derivation of a single program analysis are unaware of variability. This way it is impossible to abstract over variability, which could sometimes be beneficial. For example, when the configuration space is too large, it may be difficult or impossible to represent lifted stores symbolically, so that they take little space in memory. Variability abstractions can only be applied at the family level: one needs an analysis formulated at the family level and then apply the variability aware abstraction to it, in the very same way as we applied usual abstractions on the single program level in Sect. 3.

Variability-aware abstractions can be plentiful. In this section we show one example: an abstraction that ignores a certain subset of features, presumably meant to have insignificant impact on the analysis results. Let $F \subset \mathbb{F}$ be a set of features that we deem relevant for the analysis. Then if $k \in \mathbb{K}$ is a valid configuration, $k \cap F$ is a simplification of this configuration to relevant features only. Let $\mathbb{K}_F$ be the set of valid configurations over relevant features (so $\mathbb{K}_F = \{k \cap F \mid k \in \mathbb{K}\}$). Let $\langle \mathbb{X}, \sqsubseteq \rangle$ stand for *any* complete lattice domain, which is lifted as usual, so $\overline{\mathbb{X}} = \mathbb{X}^{\mathbb{K}}$. We write $\overline{\mathbb{X}}_F$ for lifting $\mathbb{X}$ to the set of valid configurations over only the relevant features, so $\overline{\mathbb{X}}_F = \mathbb{X}^{\mathbb{K}_F}$. Both $\langle \overline{\mathbb{X}}, \dot{\sqsubseteq} \rangle$ and $\langle \overline{\mathbb{X}}_F, \dot{\sqsubseteq} \rangle$ are complete lattices. Clearly since the latter tracks the analysis values for a smaller set of configurations, it is a more abstract domain, thereby collapsing more information. Indeed, one can formulate abstraction and concretization functions between the two lifted domains:

$$\alpha_F(\overline{x}) = \prod_{k_F \in \mathbb{K}_F} \bigsqcup_{\{k \in \mathbb{K} \mid k_F = k \cap F\}} \pi_k(\overline{x}) \qquad (4)$$

$$\gamma_F(\overline{x}_F) = \prod_{k \in \mathbb{K}} \pi_{(k \cap F)}(\overline{x}_F) \qquad (5)$$

It is easy to show (see [39]) that $\langle \overline{\mathbb{X}}, \dot{\sqsubseteq} \rangle \underset{\alpha_F}{\overset{\gamma_F}{\leftrightarrows}} \langle \overline{\mathbb{X}}_F, \dot{\sqsubseteq} \rangle$ is a Galois connection. This Galois connection can be composed with any family-based analysis transfer function to produce a version of the analysis that is less precise regarding the set of valid configurations. In particular, it could be composed with our constant propagation analysis $\overline{\mathcal{A}}$. In the extreme case, if we ask for an analysis that is insensitive to all features (so $F = \emptyset$), we obtain an abstracted analysis, which conservatively detects which values are constant (same) in all configurations.

In general, the process of developing an analysis, which should abstract variability, starts at a single program level (Fig. 15). We recommend developing the analysis for single programs first, and then applying lifting at a convenient intermediate step. After lifting the intermediate analysis function, one can apply a variability abstraction (for example $\langle \overline{\mathbb{X}}, \dot{\sqsubseteq} \rangle \underset{\alpha_F}{\overset{\gamma_F}{\leftrightarrows}} \langle \overline{\mathbb{X}}_F, \dot{\sqsubseteq} \rangle$ presented above) and then continue applying the liftings of the remaining abstractions (Galois connections) to develop the final analysis. In simple words: it is possible to switch the level in Fig.15 at a convenient point, where abstracting over variability is beneficial for the design.

5. The Variational Abstract Interpretation Method

Let us summarize the methodology of developing analyses of program families. The main purpose of this section is to highlight the abstract steps and results of our method independently of the IMP language. The first three steps are the traditional steps of calculational abstract interpretation:

1. Develop formal operational semantics for your language.
2. Design collecting semantics for your language. Show equivalence of the operational and collecting semantics. Steps 1–2 are often given for existing established languages.
3. Specify a series of abstractions applied to the semantics in the form of Galois connections and compose them with the collecting semantics to obtain a single program analysis. The calculation of compositions includes developing an inductive proof that the resulting analysis is sound.

Once the single program analysis is establish we set off to develop the aggregate family-based analysis:

4. Extend the syntax of the language with a preprocessor, and give semantics to the preprocessor P mapping syntactic constructs with variability to syntactic constructs without variability. *Remark.* The preprocessor may apply to all syntactic categories of the language, and the language does not need to have any particular flavour. In the example we only applied the preprocessor to statements, and IMP was an imperative language—these choices were made purely for pedagogical reasons, and are not restrictions of variational abstract interpretation.
5. Apply the lifting combinator *lift* to the analysis calculated in step 3 above. *Remark.* In the paper we only applied *lift* to transfer functions, which were endofunctions. This is not a requirement. For example, when lifting expression semantics, we had to lift functions that given a store argument produce a simple value as a result (see [39]). So variational abstract interpretation can be applied not only to languages expressing computations (state transfers), but also to others, for example constraint languages.
6. Simplify the resulting function to obtain a lifted analysis that is formulated independently of the original single-program analysis (prove theorem akin to Thm. 6)
7. Soundness of the lifted analysis at the family level now follows from from combining the calculations in steps 3,6 with Thm. 8

For large configuration spaces it may be beneficial to include a variability abstraction in the process:

1. Decide at which point in the design of single program analysis the variability abstraction should be inserted. Compose the collecting semantics and all Galois connections until this point to obtain a partially specified analysis for single programs.
2. Apply the lifting combinator to the obtained analysis, and simplify the result to obtain the partially specified lifted analysis. As before, correctness follows from combining the previous calculations and Thm. 8.
3. Lift the remaining Galois connections to program families by applying our lifting combinator for Galois connections. By property of the lifting combinator, the lifted functions form composable Galois connections between lifted domains. Lifting is the only operation necessary, no properties of Galois connections need to be re-proven.
4. Formulate the Galois connection abstracting configurations. *Remark.* You may want to use the feature abstraction specified in equations (4) and (5), which is independent of $\overline{\text{IMP}}$ and the analysis domains used in our running example.
5. Compose the lifted Galois connections with the lifted partial analysis, in order to obtain the final formulation of the lifted analysis that includes variability abstraction. Soundness of the result follows from the soundness of the calculation argument and the soundness of the partially lifted analysis.

6. Related Work

We divide our discussion of related work into five categories; *abstract interpretation, lifting representations, lifting data-flow analyses, lifting other analyses*, and *multi-staged program analysis*.

Abstract interpretation: Abstract interpretation is a general theory that unifies *data-flow analysis* [13], *model checking* [16, 17], *type systems* [11], *verification* [18], and *testing* [28]. Our analyses have been developed using the classical Galois connection framework [13]. In particular, we follow the calculational and compositional approach advocated by Cousot [12]. With this approach, soundness follows from a systematic derivation. Indeed, this is the case for the data-flow analysis derived in Fig. 19. This approach has previously been used by the first author to derive, for instance, iterative graph algorithms [44] and modular control-flow analyses [38].

Lifting representations: Kästner et al. [33] show how languages with preprocessor syntax can be parsed and represented in syntax trees with variability, even if the preprocessor syntax is not properly nested in the main language syntax (as it was the case for IMP). Erwig and Walkingshaw [24] present the Choice Calculus, which can be seen as a more expressive and elegant version of a preprocessor with a fixed and well-defined semantics. It would be interesting to develop variational abstract interpretation further, to support richer preprocessors (like the Choice Calculus), and ill-formed preprocessor use. The former appears a rather straightforward extension, while the latter likely remains a challenge due to difficulty of defining semantics elegantly in a syntax-directed manner. One angle of attack would be to apply preprocessor normalization via rewrites as suggested by Garrido and Johnson [25, 26].

Lifting data-flow analysis: Previous work lifts data-flow analysis, resulting in *feature-sensitive* data-flow analysis [6], corresponding to our Figure 19. Lifted data-flow analyses are much faster than ones based on $|\mathbb{K}|$ runs of the naive generate-and-analyze strategy [6]. Indeed, inter-procedural application of the lifted analysis approach of SPL^{LIFT} [5] achieves several orders of magnitude speedups through the use of BDD-based sharing of configurations and encoding of lifted transfer functions and control-flow as graphs for which the fixed-point computation can be rephrased as graph reachability. This technique works for analyses phrased within the IFDS framework [43], a subset of data-flow analyses, which can then be transparently lifted without programmer intervention. Recently, larger SPLs based on C have been analyzed [36] via lifted type checking and liveness data-flow analysis.

Lifting other analyses: Recent work [47] has surveyed analysis strategies for SPLs and proposes a taxonomy of such which would classify our lifted analyses as *family-based analyses* (whereas the *generate-and-analyze* strategy yields a *product-based analysis*).

The approaches of *type checking*, *model checking*, and *verification* are complementary to abstract interpretation and share the commendable goal of detecting errors at compile-time as opposed to at runtime. There is work on lifting all of them in an attempt to find errors at SPL compile-time as opposed to at post product-instantiation time, when a product happens to be compiled, possibly long after it has been developed: *lifted type checking* [1, 32], *lifted well-formedness checking*[20], *lifted model checking* [8, 9, 27], and *lifted verification* [2, 35, 42]. With abstract interpretation, however, analysis soundness comes for free, by derivation—and as we have shown, even at the SPL level.

Safe composition [1, 22, 32, 34, 46] is about verification and safe generation of properties for SPL assets and aims to provide guarantees that only products where certain properties are obeyed can be generated. Errors detected include type and definition-usage errors (e.g., undeclared variables, undeclared fields, and unimplemented abstract methods). We complement this with an approach based on abstract interpretation with which analyses intercepting those kinds of errors can be derived.

Multi-staged program analysis: Our work is related to *multi-staged program analysis*, analyzing "programs that generate programs", e.g., [7, 40]. In the context of Software Product Lines, however, we are in a much simpler case where the first stage is significantly more restrictive than a Turing-complete programming language and can thus be dealt with without approximation. For SPLs, our approach is simpler and sufficient; and without loss of precision on the variability level.

7. Conclusion

We have shown how compositional and systematic derivation of static analyses based on abstract interpretation can be lifted to Software Product Lines. The result is variational abstract interpretation—a compositional and systematic approach for the derivation of variability-aware product line analyses, with the following distinctive components and properties:

- A scheme to lift domain types, and combinators for lifting analyses and Galois connections.
- A general soundness-by-construction result (Thm. 8), allowing to lift a formally developed analysis, without re-proving the entire abstract interpretation process. This crucially reuses all the effort invested in developing a single-program analysis, to obtain a provably sound family-based analysis.
- A possibility of incorporating abstractions that involve configuration space; including an example of one such abstraction.
- Precise control over precision of analyses (lifting does not lose any information *per se*).
- A scheme to obtain data-flow equations for family-based analyses from the abstract interpretation definition.

Variational abstract interpretation mixes language-independent and language-specific elements. The main language specific theorem (Thm. 6) needs to be proven for each new analysis. We have proven it for all the three semantics of our running example and extracted a general proof methodology presented in this paper. On the other hand, the main language-independent soundness theorem (Thm. 8) holds in general and needs not be re-proven.

Abstract interpretation is a unifying theory that allows the derivation of data-flow analyses, control-flow analyses, model checking, type systems, verification, and even testing. Hence, variational abstract interpretation tells us how to systematically obtain lifted versions of all such analyses. We believe that in this sense, variational abstract interpretation, contributes to the understanding of how variability affects analysis of programs in general.

Finally, since the lifting operator can be applied to a directly formulated analysis, we claim that the obtained insight into lifting extends beyond abstract interpretation. In particular, the *lift* combinator can be applied to analyses developed in an ad hoc process, without abstract interpretation, but represented as transfer functions (soundness of such lifting requires a separate argument though).

Acknowledgements. The authors thank Hans Erik Bugge Grathwohl and Aleksandar Dimovski for fruitful technical discussions.

References

[1] S. Apel, C. Kästner, A. Grösslinger, and C. Lengauer. Type safety for feature-oriented product lines. *Automated Software Engineering*, 17: 251–300, September 2010.

[2] S. Apel, H. Speidel, P. Wendler, A. von Rhein, and D. Beyer. Detection of feature interactions using feature-aware verification. In *ASE'11*, Lawrence, USA, November 2011. IEEE Computer Society.

[3] D. Batory. Feature models, grammars, and propositional formulas. In *9th International Software Product Lines Conference*, volume 3714 of *LNCS*, pages 7–20. Springer-Verlag, 2005.

[4] T. Berger, S. She, R. Lotufo, A. Wasowski, and K. Czarnecki. Variability modeling in the real: a perspective from the operating systems domain. In *ASE'10*, pages 73–82, 2010.

[5] E. Bodden, T. Tolêdo, M. Ribeiro, C. Brabrand, P. Borba, and M. Mezini. SPL^{LIFT} - statically analyzing software product lines in minutes instead of years. In *PLDI'13*, 2013.

[6] C. Brabrand, M. Ribeiro, T. Tolêdo, J. Winther, and P. Borba. Intraprocedural dataflow analysis for software product lines. *Transactions on Aspect-Oriented Software Development*, 10:73–108, 2013. Earlier version in AOSD 2012.

[7] W. Choi, B. Aktemur, K. Yi, and M. Tatsuta. Static analysis of multistaged programs via unstaging translation. *SIGPLAN Not.*, 46(1):81–92, Jan. 2011.

[8] A. Classen, P. Heymans, P.-Y. Schobbens, A. Legay, and J.-F. Raskin. Model checking lots of systems: efficient verification of temporal properties in software product lines. In *ICSE'10*, pages 335–344. ACM, 2010.

[9] A. Classen, P. Heymans, P.-Y. Schobbens, and A. Legay. Symbolic model checking of software product lines. In *ICSE'11*, pages 321–330, 2011.

[10] P. Clements and L. Northrop. *Software Product Lines: Practices and Patterns*. Addison-Wesley, 2001.

[11] P. Cousot. Types as abstract interpretations. In *POPL'97*, pages 316–331, 1997.

[12] P. Cousot. The calculational design of a generic abstract interpreter. In M. Broy and R. Steinbrüggen, editors, *Calculational System Design*. NATO ASI Series F. IOS Press, Amsterdam, 1999.

[13] P. Cousot and R. Cousot. Systematic design of program analysis frameworks. In *POPL'79*, pages 269–282, 1979.

[14] P. Cousot and R. Cousot. Abstract interpretation and application to logic programs. *Journal of Logic Programming*, 13(2–3):103–179, 1992.

[15] P. Cousot and R. Cousot. Higher-order abstract interpretation (and application to comportment analysis generalizing strictness, termination, projection and PER analysis of functional languages), invited paper. In *ICCL'94*, pages 95–112, Toulouse, France, May 1994.

[16] P. Cousot and R. Cousot. Refining model checking by abstract interpretation. *Autom. Softw. Eng.*, 6(1):69–95, 1999.

[17] P. Cousot and R. Cousot. Temporal abstract interpretation. In *POPL'00*, pages 12–25, 2000.

[18] P. Cousot, R. Cousot, J. Feret, L. Mauborgne, A. Miné, D. Monniaux, and X. Rival. The Astreé analyzer. In *ESOP'05*, pages 21–30, 2005.

[19] K. Czarnecki and U. Eisenecker. *Generative programming: methods, tools, and applications*. Addison-Wesley, 2000.

[20] K. Czarnecki and K. Pietroszek. Verifying feature-based model templates against well-formedness ocl constraints. In *GPCE'06*, pages 211–220, New York, NY, USA, 2006. ACM.

[21] K. Czarnecki, P. Grünbacher, R. Rabiser, K. Schmid, and A. Wasowski. Cool features and tough decisions: a comparison of variability modeling approaches. In *VaMoS'12*, pages 173–182, 2012.

[22] B. Delaware, W. R. Cook, and D. Batory. Fitting the pieces together: a machine-checked model of safe composition. In *ESEC/FSE'09*, pages 243–252, New York, NY, USA, 2009. ACM.

[23] B. Delaware, W. Cook, and D. Batory. Product lines of theorems. In *OOPSLA'11*, pages 595–608, New York, NY, USA, 2011. ACM.

[24] M. Erwig and E. Walkingshaw. The choice calculus: A representation for software variation. *ACM Trans. Softw. Eng. Methodol.*, 21(1):6:1–6:27, Dec. 2011.

[25] A. Garrido and R. E. Johnson. Refactoring C with conditional compilation. In *ASE'03*, pages 323–326. IEEE Computer Society, 2003. ISBN 0-7695-2035-9.

[26] A. Garrido and R. E. Johnson. Analyzing multiple configurations of a C program. In *ICSM'05*, pages 379–388. IEEE Computer Society, 2005. ISBN 0-7695-2368-4.

[27] A. Gruler, M. Leucker, and K. D. Scheidemann. Modeling and model checking software product lines. In *FMOODS'08*, pages 113–131, 2008.

[28] D. Guilbaud, E. Goubault, A. Pacalet, and B. S. F. Védrine. A simple abstract interpreter for threat detection and test case generation. In *WAPATV'01, with ICSE'01*, Toronto, 2001.

[29] IBM, Thales, F. FOKUS, and TCS. *Proposal for Common Variability Language (CVL) Revised Submission*, 2012.

[30] K. C. Kang, S. G. Cohen, J. A. Hess, W. E. Novak, and A. S. Peterson. Feature-Oriented Domain Analysis (FODA) feasibility study. Technical report, Carnegie-Mellon University Software Engineering Institute, November 1990.

[31] C. Kästner. *Virtual Separation of Concerns: Toward Preprocessors 2.0*. PhD thesis, University of Magdeburg, Germany, May 2010.

[32] C. Kästner and S. Apel. Type-checking software product lines - a formal approach. In *ASE'08*, pages 258–267, L'Aquila, Italy, 2008.

[33] C. Kästner, P. G. Giarrusso, T. Rendel, S. Erdweg, K. Ostermann, and T. Berger. Variability-aware parsing in the presence of lexical macros and conditional compilation. In *OOPSLA'11*, pages 805–824, Portland, OR, USA, 2011. ACM.

[34] C. Kästner, S. Apel, T. Thüm, and G. Saake. Type checking annotation-based product lines. *ACM Trans. Softw. Eng. Methodol.*, 21(3):14:1–14:39, July 2012.

[35] C. H. P. Kim, E. Bodden, D. Batory, and S. Khurshid. Reducing configurations to monitor in a software product line. In *1st International Conference on Runtime Verification (RV)*, volume 6418 of *LNCS*, Malta, November 2010. Springer.

[36] J. Liebig, A. von Rhein, C. Kästner, S. Apel, J. Dörre, and C. Lengauer. Scalable analysis of variable software. In *ESEC/FSE'13*, pages 81–91, New York, NY, 8 2013.

[37] J. Midtgaard and T. Jensen. A calculational approach to control-flow analysis by abstract interpretation. In *SAS'08*, volume 5079 of *LNCS*, pages 347–362, Valencia, Spain, July 2008. Springer-Verlag.

[38] J. Midtgaard, M. D. Adams, and M. Might. A structural soundness proof for Shivers's escape technique: A case for Galois connections. In *SAS'12*, volume 7460 of *LNCS*, pages 352–369, Deauville, France, Sept. 2011. Springer-Verlag.

[39] J. Midtgaard, C. Brabrand, and A. Wasowski. Systematic derivation of static analyses for software product lines. Technical Report TR-2014-170, IT University of Copenhagen, 2014.

[40] F. Nielson and H. R. Nielson. *Two-Level Functional Languages*. Cambridge Tracts in Theoretical Computer Science, vol. 34. Cambridge University Press, 1992.

[41] F. Nielson, H. R. Nielson, and C. Hankin. *Principles of Program Analysis*. Springer-Verlag, Secaucus, USA, 1999.

[42] H. Post and C. Sinz. Configuration lifting: Verification meets software configuration. In *ASE'08*, pages 347–350, L´Aquila, Italy, 2008. IEEE Computer Society.

[43] T. Reps, S. Horwitz, and M. Sagiv. Precise interprocedural dataflow analysis via graph reachability. In *POPL'95*, pages 49–61, New York, NY, USA, 1995. ACM.

[44] I. Sergey, J. Midtgaard, and D. Clarke. Calculating graph algorithms for dominance and shortest path. In *MPC'12*, volume 7342 of *LNCS*, pages 132–156, Madrid, Spain, June 2012. Springer.

[45] T. Stahl, M. Voelter, and K. Czarnecki. *Model-Driven Software Development: Technology, Engineering, Management*. John Wiley & Sons, 2006.

[46] S. Thaker, D. Batory, D. Kitchin, and W. Cook. Safe composition of product lines. In *GPCE'07*, pages 95–104, New York, NY, USA, 2007. ACM.

[47] T. Thüm, S. Apel, C. Kästner, M. Kuhlemann, I. Schaefer, and G. Saake. Analysis strategies for software product lines. Technical Report FIN-004-2012, School of Computer Science, University of Magdeburg, Germany, 2012.

[48] G. Winskel. *The Formal Semantics of Programming Languages*. Foundation of Computing Series. The MIT Press, 1993.

Aspectual Session Types

Nicolas Tabareau Mario Südholt
ASCOLA Team
Mines Nantes & Inria & LINA, Nantes, France
nicolas.tabareau@inria.fr
mario.sudholt@mines-nantes.fr

Éric Tanter *
PLEIAD Laboratory
Computer Science Department (DCC)
University of Chile
etanter@dcc.uchile.cl

Abstract

Multiparty session types allow the definition of distributed processes with strong communication safety properties. A global type is a choreographic specification of the interactions between peers, which is then projected locally in each peer. Well-typed processes behave accordingly to the global protocol specification. Multiparty session types are however monolithic entities that are not amenable to modular extensions. Also, session types impose conservative requirements to prevent any race condition, which prohibit the uniform application of extensions at different points in a protocol. In this paper, we describe a means to support modular extensions with *aspectual session types*, a static pointcut/advice mechanism at the session type level. To support the modular definition of crosscutting concerns, we augment the expressivity of session types to allow harmless race conditions. We formally prove that well-formed aspectual session types entail communication safety. As a result, aspectual session types make multiparty session types more flexible, modular, and extensible.

Categories and Subject Descriptors D.3.3 [*Programming Languages*]: Language Constructs and Features

Keywords session types, aspect-oriented programming

1. Introduction

Interaction protocols for the orchestrations of services, such as BPEL, are nowadays a common means to define Cloud-based applications. Most frequently, finite-state protocols are used to define interactions that are, however, not expressive enough to define many interaction patterns. More general approaches, such as communicating finite-state machines (CFSMs) are too expressive to support static correctness guarantees.

Session types [12] have been developed as an expressive means to define interaction protocols that provide correctness guarantees such as deadlock freedom, the absence of stuck messages, and the correctness of message reception by concurrent threads. In recent years, the expressivity of session types has been extended through the integration of multiple interaction parties, multiple roles, and the generalization of the underlying type system using a new subclass of CFSMs [7, 8, 13].

The main characteristic of multiparty session types consists in the provision of global types that define the overall interactions of a system and an automatic projection mechanism from a global type into local types. Local types define the interaction behavior of local processes, all of which, executed together, realize exactly the interaction behavior defined by the global type without any local process requiring any non-local interaction information.

The most recent version of session types developed by Deniélou and Yoshida [8] introduces more general parallel and choice flows that are expressed respectively using fork/joins and choice/merge nodes on the global type level and in a new class of graphs, the so-called multiparty session automata that constitute a subclass of communicating finite state machines (CFSMs). Global types with these generalized flows, the corresponding automata, local projections and processes have been shown to meet the three main correctness properties introduced above.

Despite these advances, session types suffer from a number of restrictions that hamper their adoption. First, session types do not support modular extensions. This is problematic because protocol-like service compositions are well-known to benefit from extension mechanism that allow functionalities to be added in a modular fashion. Otherwise the underlying protocols often have to be extensively rewritten, thus complexifying the protocol structure, a tedious and error-prone task. Aspect-oriented systems have been proposed for this purpose, notably to manipulate service orchestrations modularly, for example, using AO4BPEL [6] and in particular for the control of the QoS properties of orchestrations [2]. However, no aspect system exists that enables the modification of session types while maintaining their strong correctness guarantees.

Second, in order to guarantee strong properties such as deadlock freedom, session types generally have to impose restrictions on the interactions they support. One important restriction consists in the so-called *linearity* condition, which means that a participant should never be faced with two concurrent receptions where messages can have the same label. This is to forbid potential race conditions, which can lead to deadlocks. Thus, identical modifications that introduce the same new behavior in different threads cannot be expressed using session types because doing so directly breaks linearity.

We address these issues by introducing *aspectual session types* that enable the addition of new functionalities to multiparty generalized session types [8] in a modular way, supporting the introduction of uniform behavior in multiple places in session types. Intuitively, the latter is achieved by allowing race conditions between advice bodies, but by ensuring the preservation of the correctness conditions of session types by executing them in mutual exclusion.

* É. Tanter is partially funded by FONDECYT project 1110051.
This work is supported by the INRIA Associated Team REAL.

MODULARITY '14, April 22–26, 2014, Lugano, Switzerland.
Copyright © 2014 ACM 978-1-4503-2772-5/14/04. . . $15.00.
http://dx.doi.org/10.1145/2577080.2577085

Concretely, we provide the following contributions:

- We formally define *aspectual session types* that allow messages in session types to be matched and to introduce complex behavior in addition or in place of the matched messages.
- We explain a safe execution strategy for the weaving of advice at multiple places in session types and thus support a particular kind of race conditions, which we call *harmless race conditions*.
- We formally define the weaving of such aspects into global and local types by extending the formal framework of Deniélou and Yoshida [8].
- We provide a proof that the resulting types preserve all properties of session types despite the presence of harmless race conditions: absence of deadlocks, orphan messages (messages that will never be received) and the correct reception of messages in concurrent contexts (in the sense that messages of one thread can not be mistakenly received by another thread).

Section 2 briefly illustrates aspectual session types through examples. Section 3 provides the necessary background on generalized multiparty session types based on [8]. Section 4 introduces aspectual session types. Section 5 describes different properties of aspectual session types necessary for weaving to preserve the good properties of session types. Section 6 proves that harmless race conditions introduced by aspect weaving are indeed harmless: all properties are preserved. Section 7 describes an application of aspectual session types to data parallel programming. Section 8 discusses related work and Section 9 concludes.

2. Overview of Aspectual Session Types

We now provide an example-driven overview of the approach. Figure 1 presents the graphical representation of session types and aspects (their formal definitions are given in Appendix A). The exhaustive description of the formal syntax and semantics is developed in later sections.

A simple trade session. Figure 1a shows the graphical representation of a simple global type for a trade-like interaction, simplified and adapted from [8]. A seller S initially sends an item that contains its price to a broker B. The broker knows about an interested client C beforehand (no negotiation is taking place here) and then informs, in parallel, S whether the item is acceptably priced for C and the latter if he can purchase the item from the former.

Supporting modular extensions. Consider the introduction of a price negotiation between the broker and the client. This change would require the global interaction type to be rewritten[1]. In addition, the changes on the global types would cascade as changes to the corresponding local types, which in turn means that local processes have to be modified accordingly.

Aspectual session types enable modular extensions to existing session types. For instance, we can use the negotiation aspect shown in Figure 1b: this aspect matches the interaction `S`$\rightarrow$`B:Item` above the large delimited arrow and adds a negotiation loop after the interaction. The matched message is dynamically bound to the keyword proceed. Weaving of aspectual session types can be defined to ensure that modular extensions preserve the properties of well-formed session types.

The logging aspect shown in Figure 1c shows how multiple interactions, here B$\rightarrow$S or B$\rightarrow$C, may be matched through quantification, allowing the modular definition of a crosscutting concern.

[1] The original trade example in [8] includes the negotiation phase built in the interaction.

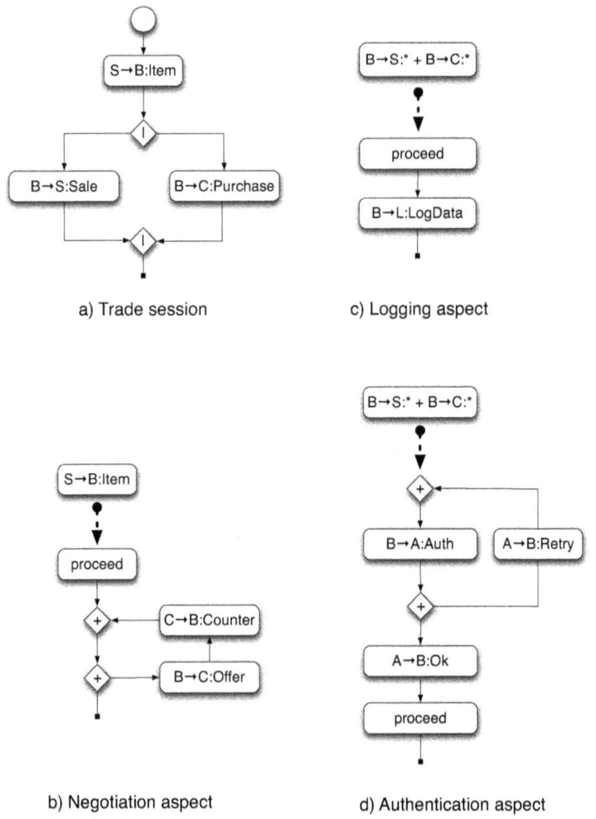

Figure 1: Graphical representation of the trade example, with three aspects

Allowing uniform behavior in parallel threads Once quantification is introduced, uniform behavior can be applied in parallel threads, as in the logging example. A more interesting example is an authentication aspect shown in Figure 1d: it introduces an interaction from the broker to an authentication server B$\rightarrow$A before each of the two messages B$\rightarrow$S and B$\rightarrow$C (represented by proceed). If applied to the base trading session (Figure 1a), it results in both branches after the fork to send two messages from B: respectively to A followed by one to S and to A followed by C.

Note that in these cases, the session types that result from weaving do not respect the traditional linearity condition of session types. Our approach however ensures that such weaving does produce correct session types. Aspectual session types therefore accommodate a strict superset of protocols compared to Daniélou's and Yoshida's session types [8].

3. Generalized Multiparty Session Types

This section briefly reviews the formal treatment of generalized multiparty session types based on the article of Deniélou and Yoshida [8]. We clearly identify the few points in which we depart from their definitions.

3.1 Global Types

The syntax of global session types is given in Figure 2. A global type **G** is a set of transitions $\overline{G}$ (the overbar denotes a possibly empty sequence), together with an *initial state* **x**. *State variables* **x** in $\overline{G}$ are the different states of the interaction. Transitions between states include coordination and communication among participants $\mathtt{p} \in \mathcal{P}$. The set of participants is fixed in a given interaction.

$\mathbf{G}$	$::=$	$\mathsf{def}\ \overline{G}\ \mathsf{in}\ \mathbf{x}$	Global Type
U	$::=$	$\langle \mathbf{G} \rangle \mid \mathit{bool} \mid \mathit{nat} \mid \ldots$	Sort
G	$::=$		Transition
	$\mid$	$\mathbf{x} = M; \mathbf{x}'$	Messages
	$\mid$	$\mathbf{x} \mid \mathbf{x}' = \mathbf{x}''$	Join
	$\mid$	$\mathbf{x} = \mathbf{x}' \mid \mathbf{x}''$	Fork
	$\mid$	$\mathbf{x} + \mathbf{x}' = \mathbf{x}'$	Merge
	$\mid$	$\mathbf{x} = \mathbf{x}' + \mathbf{x}''$	Choice
	$\mid$	$\mathbf{x} = \mathsf{end}$	End
M	$::=$	$\mathsf{p} \to \mathsf{p}' : l\langle U \rangle$	Labeled Message

Figure 2: Syntax of Global Session Types (adapted from [8])

$\mathbf{T}$	$::=$	$\mathsf{def}\ \overline{T}\ \mathsf{in}\ \mathbf{x}$	Local Type
T	$::=$		Local Transition
	$\mid$	$\mathbf{x} = M; \mathbf{x}'$	Message
	$\mid$	$\mathbf{x} = \mathbf{x}'$	Indirection
	$\mid$	$\mathbf{x} = \mathbf{x}' \oplus \mathbf{x}''$	Internal Choice
	$\mid$	$\mathbf{x} = \mathbf{x}' \& \mathbf{x}''$	External Choice
	$\mid$	$\mathbf{x} + \mathbf{x}' = \mathbf{x}'$	Merge
	$\mid$	$\mathbf{x} = \mathbf{x}' \mid \mathbf{x}''$	Fork
	$\mid$	$\mathbf{x} \mid \mathbf{x}' = \mathbf{x}''$	Join
	$\mid$	$\mathbf{x} = \mathsf{end}$	End
M	$::=$	$!\langle \mathsf{p}, l\langle U \rangle \rangle$	Send
	$\mid$	$?\langle \mathsf{p}, l\langle U \rangle \rangle$	Receive
	$\mid$	0	No Message

Figure 3: Syntax of Local Session Types (adapted from [8])

Compared to [8], we introduce a dedicated syntactic category M to describe messages, which we extend later. A message transition $\mathbf{x} = M; \mathbf{x}'$, with $M = \mathsf{p} \to \mathsf{p}' : l\langle U \rangle$, specifies that in state $\mathbf{x}$, the sender p can go to the continuation $\mathbf{x}'$ by sending a message labeled l (taken from a set $\mathbb{L}$) with payload argument type U. p' can go from $\mathbf{x}$ to $\mathbf{x}'$ by receiving the message, while other participants can freely go to state $\mathbf{x}'$. The choice transition $\mathbf{x} = \mathbf{x}' + \mathbf{x}''$ represents a choice made by exactly one participant to go to either $\mathbf{x}'$ or $\mathbf{x}''$. $\mathbf{x} = \mathbf{x}' \mid \mathbf{x}''$ represents forking the interactions in parallel threads. Forks are collected by joins, and choices are closed by merges. $\mathbf{x} = \mathsf{end}$ marks the end of the session.

3.2 Local Types

Figure 3 gives the syntax of local session types. Local types directly correspond to global types except for a couple of refinements. First, a message globally described as $\mathsf{p} \to \mathsf{p}' : l\langle U \rangle$ is reflected locally by a send action $!\langle \mathsf{p}', l\langle U \rangle \rangle$ on p, and by a receive action $?\langle \mathsf{p}, l\langle U \rangle \rangle$ on p'. Second, there are two variants of the global choice: the internal choice $\oplus$ is used on the participant that drives the choice, while the external choice $+$ is used on other participants, which are passive observers of the choice made by another participant.

Following our introduction of the category M for messages, we introduce 0 to denote the absence of action. We extend the congruence relation on local types $\equiv$ of [8] to account for the introduction of 0 for messages:

$$\mathbf{x} = 0; \mathbf{x}' \quad \equiv \quad \mathbf{x} = \mathbf{x}'$$

The projection from global types to local types $\upharpoonright$ is direct and given in Figure 4. As hinted previously, the local projection of a message is either a send, a receive or a null action. Fork, join, choice and merge transitions are projected as corresponding local operations. The only exception is the choice transition which is projected to either an internal or an external choice. The decision is based on whether or not the considered participant is the *active sender* at state $\mathbf{x}$. The computation of the active sender at state $\mathbf{x}$ where $\mathbf{x} = \mathbf{x}' + \mathbf{x}'' \in \overline{G}$ is expressed by an auxiliary function $\mathit{ASend}(\overline{G})(\mathbf{x})$, formally defined in [9, Figure 17], the companion appendix of [8]. This function asserts that there is a unique sender in each branch of a choice and identifies such sender. On the active sender, the choice is projected to an internal choice, while on other participants it is projected to an external choice.

$\mathsf{def}\ \overline{G}\ \mathsf{in}\ \mathbf{x} \upharpoonright \mathsf{p}$	$=$	$\mathsf{def}\ \overline{G} \upharpoonright_{\overline{G}} \mathsf{p}\ \mathsf{in}\ \mathbf{x}$
$\mathbf{x} = M; \mathbf{x}' \upharpoonright_{\overline{G}} \mathsf{p}$	$=$	$\mathbf{x} = M \upharpoonright \mathsf{p}; \mathbf{x}'$
$\mathsf{p} \to \mathsf{p}' : l\langle U \rangle \upharpoonright \mathsf{p}$	$=$	$!\langle \mathsf{p}', l\langle U \rangle \rangle$
$\mathsf{p} \to \mathsf{p}' : l\langle U \rangle \upharpoonright \mathsf{p}'$	$=$	$?\langle \mathsf{p}, l\langle U \rangle \rangle$
$\mathsf{p} \to \mathsf{p}' : l\langle U \rangle \upharpoonright \mathsf{p}''$	$=$	$0\ (\mathsf{p}'' \notin \{\mathsf{p}, \mathsf{p}'\})$
$\mathbf{x} \mid \mathbf{x}' = \mathbf{x}'' \upharpoonright_{\overline{G}} \mathsf{p}$	$=$	$\mathbf{x} \mid \mathbf{x}' = \mathbf{x}''$
$\mathbf{x} = \mathbf{x}' \mid \mathbf{x}'' \upharpoonright_{\overline{G}} \mathsf{p}$	$=$	$\mathbf{x} = \mathbf{x}' \mid \mathbf{x}''$
$\mathbf{x} = \mathbf{x}' + \mathbf{x}'' \upharpoonright_{\overline{G}} \mathsf{p}$	$=$	$\mathbf{x} = \mathbf{x}' \oplus \mathbf{x}''$ (if $\mathsf{p} = \mathit{ASend}(\overline{G})(\mathbf{x})$)
$\mathbf{x} = \mathbf{x}' + \mathbf{x}'' \upharpoonright_{\overline{G}} \mathsf{p}$	$=$	$\mathbf{x} = \mathbf{x}' \& \mathbf{x}''$ (otherwise)
$\mathbf{x} + \mathbf{x}' = \mathbf{x}'' \upharpoonright_{\overline{G}} \mathsf{p}$	$=$	$\mathbf{x} + \mathbf{x}' = \mathbf{x}''$
$\mathbf{x} = \mathsf{end} \upharpoonright_{\overline{G}} \mathsf{p}$	$=$	$\mathbf{x} = \mathsf{end}$

Figure 4: Projection Algorithm (adapted from [8])

3.3 Well-formedness

Deniélou and Yoshida provide an interpretation of local types as Communicating Finite State Machines (CFSM) that defines a formal semantics for global types. More precisely, they establish a correspondence between the local projections of a *well-formed global type* and a new class of CFSM named Multiparty Session Automata (MSA) that satisfy safety properties (free of deadlocks, orphan messages, and reception errors), as well as progress and liveness.

Deniélou and Yoshida then establish that all the good properties enjoyed by the MSAs generated from a well-formed global type $\mathbf{G}$ also hold in processes typed by the same $\mathbf{G}$. Well-formedness of global types is therefore the key from which all interesting properties are derived. Well-formedness of a global type is expressed in terms of three conditions: sanity, local choice and linearity.

Sanity. To prevent syntactic confusion about which continuations to follow at any given point, a global type $\mathsf{def}\ \overline{G}\ \mathsf{in}\ \mathbf{x}_0$ must satisfy a number of conditions: a) every state variable $\mathbf{x}$ except $\mathbf{x}_0$ appear exactly once on the left- and right-hand side of all transitions in $\overline{G}$; b) $\mathbf{x}_0$ appears exactly once, on the left-hand side; c) end appears at most once; d) transitions in $\overline{G}$ define a connected graph where threads are always collected by joins. Note that this last condition, called *thread correctness*, is less trivial to check. Deniélou and Yoshida present a polynomial verification algorithm based on Petri nets. Thread correctness expresses connectivity, the ability to reach end (liveness), and the fact that join transitions always correspond to concurrent threads.

Local choice. Introducing choices in an interaction must not induce confusion among participants. First, a choice must be local to a participant, meaning only one participant must proactively decide and act according to its decision. This is verified by the active sender computation ASend, discussed above. In addition, the choice must be propagated to the other participants, a condition called *choice awareness*. This is expressed with another function, Rcv, which ensures that each other participant is either oblivious to the choice (that is, it does not expect any message before the

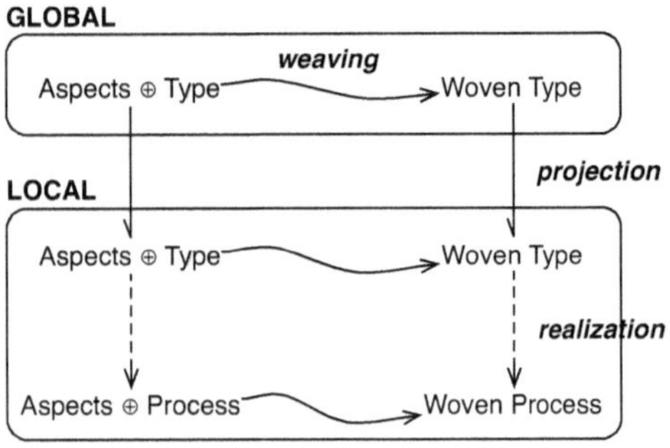

Figure 5: Aspectual Session Types: weaving, projection and realization

choice is merged), or expects messages with different labels in each branch. The definition of *Rcv* can be found in [8, page 7].

Linearity. To avoid race conditions in processes, participants should never be faced with two concurrent receptions where messages can have the same label. This linearity condition is enforced with another auxiliary function (not included here). Intuitively, linearity is to fork what choice awareness is to choice.

Well-formedness of a global type is defined as follows:

Definition 1 (Well-formedness). *A global type* **G** *is* well-formed *if it satisfies the* sanity, local choice *and* linearity *conditions.*

4. Aspectual Session Types

Programmers define global session types and global aspects. We define weaving at the global level. The global woven type is interesting for checking properties of the woven session (see next section), but it is not very practical for defining processes. Indeed, the local types obtained by projection of the global woven type contain all modifications made by aspects. This means that processes have to programmed as if aspect weaving was done by hand.

From a practical point of view, it is more interesting to first project the global session type and aspects to local types and aspects, realize them modularly, and then weave aspects.

Figure 5 depicts the different paths to deal with aspectual session types, starting from global aspects and session type, to obtain the local woven types and processes, either through weaving and projection, or vice versa, through projection and weaving. The realization of local types with processes is checked by a type system that is described in [8] and that we do not consider in this paper.

We define aspects and aspect weaving on global types in Section 4.1. The projection of the global woven type relies on the standard projection operation (Figure 4). In Section 4.2 we describe local aspects, the projection from global aspects to local ones, and local aspect weaving.

4.1 Aspects on Global Types

Syntax. Figure 6 presents the syntax of global aspectual session types $\mathbf{G}_a$. In addition to the base session type $\mathbf{G}$, the programmer can specify a number of aspects $\overline{A}$ of the form of pointcut/advice pairs $\langle pc, adv\rangle$. Messages are the only join points in this model. A pointcut specifies messages of interest, possibly using wildcards on the label (resp. payload type) to represent any label (resp. payload type). The disjunction of pointcuts is noted +, in line with the choice operator of session types. An advice is similar to a standard global type, except for the fact that it can use proceed as a message.

$\mathbf{G}_a$	::=	$\overline{A} \oplus \mathbf{G}$	Global Type with Aspects
A	::=	$\langle pc, adv\rangle$	Aspect
pc	::=	$\mathsf{p} \to \mathsf{p}' : l_*\langle U_*\rangle \mid pc + pc$	Pointcut
adv	::=	$\mathsf{def}\ \overline{G_a}\ \mathsf{in}\ \mathbf{x}$	Advice
G_a	::=	$\mathbf{x} = \mathsf{proceed}; \mathbf{x}' \mid G$	Advice Transition
l_*	::=	$l \mid *$	Labels with wildcard
U_*	::=	$U \mid *$	Sorts with wildcard

Figure 6: Syntax of Global Aspectual Session Types

$$\left.\begin{array}{r} match(\mathsf{p} \to \mathsf{p}' : l_*\langle U_*\rangle, \mathsf{p} \to \mathsf{p}' : l\langle U\rangle) \\ match(!\langle \mathsf{p}, l_*\langle U_*\rangle\rangle, !\langle \mathsf{p}, l\langle U\rangle\rangle) \\ match(?\langle \mathsf{p}, l_*\langle U_*\rangle\rangle, ?\langle \mathsf{p}, l\langle U\rangle\rangle) \end{array}\right\} \text{ if } l_* \in \{l, *\} \wedge U_* \in \{U, *\}$$

$$match(pc_1 + pc_2, M) \quad \text{if } match(pc_1, M) \vee match(pc_2, M)$$

Figure 7: Pointcut Matching

$$\text{(NG-Start)}\ \frac{\overline{A} \vdash \overline{G} \rightsquigarrow_N \overline{G'}}{\overline{A} \oplus \mathsf{def}\ \overline{G}\ \mathsf{in}\ \mathbf{x} \rightsquigarrow_N \mathsf{def}\ \overline{G'}\ \mathsf{in}\ \mathbf{x}}$$

$$\text{(NG-StepA)}\ \frac{A \vdash \overline{G} \rightsquigarrow_N \overline{G'} \qquad \overline{A} \vdash \overline{G'} \rightsquigarrow_N \overline{G''}}{A\overline{A} \vdash \overline{G} \rightsquigarrow_N \overline{G''}}$$

$$\text{(NG-StepG)}\ \frac{A \vdash G_1 \rightsquigarrow_N \overline{G_1'} \qquad A \vdash \overline{G_2} \rightsquigarrow_N \overline{G_2'}}{A \vdash G_1\overline{G_2} \rightsquigarrow_N \overline{G_1'}\,\overline{G_2'}}$$

$$\text{(NG-Skip)}\ \frac{G \neq \mathbf{x} = M; \mathbf{x}' \vee \neg match(pc, M)}{\langle pc, adv\rangle \vdash G \rightsquigarrow_N G}$$

$$\text{(NG-Weave)}\ \frac{\overline{G_A'} = localize(\overline{G_A}, \mathbf{x}) \qquad match(pc, M)}{\begin{array}{l}\langle pc, \mathsf{def}\ \overline{G_A}\ \mathsf{in}\ \mathbf{x}_A\rangle \vdash \mathbf{x} = M; \mathbf{x}' \rightsquigarrow_N \\ \quad \mathbf{x} = \mathbf{x}_A^{\mathbf{x}} \\ \quad \overline{G_A'}[\mathsf{proceed} \mapsto M][\mathsf{end} \mapsto \mathbf{x}']\end{array}}$$

Figure 8: Naive Global Weaving

Pointcut matching. Pointcut matching is straightforward, and defined in Figure 7. Only the first and last definitions apply to the case of global aspects. A pointcut matches a message if both participants are the same and if the pointcut label (resp. payload type) is either the wildcard $*$ or the same as the actual label (resp. payload type). Pointcut disjunction is interpreted as a disjunction of both branches.

Naive Weaving. Weaving of aspectual session types is defined in Figure 8. Aspects are woven one after the other in the order they appear in the list. So once an aspect is woven, it has no effect on the weaving of remaining aspects. This definition of weaving is called *naive*, noted $\rightsquigarrow_N$, because it is simple but can yield ill-formed types, as discussed below. The first three rules express the order of aspect weaving, which processes aspects one at a time and then treats one transition of G at a time. Rule (NG-Skip) applies whenever the transition is not a message or if the pointcut does not match the message. Rule (NG-Weave) specifies the rewriting of the transition $\mathbf{x} = M; \mathbf{x}'$ whenever the pointcut matches M. The rewriting replaces the original transition with the advice definitions, substituting $\mathbf{x}$ for $\mathbf{x}_A$, M for proceed, and $\mathbf{x}'$ for end in the advice body. Note that prior to substitution, all states in the advice body are renamed by annotating them with $\mathbf{x}$, as specified by the localize function:

$$localize(\overline{G}_A, \mathbf{x}) = \overline{G}_A[\mathbf{x}' \mapsto \mathbf{x}'^{\mathbf{x}}] \text{ for all } \mathbf{x}' \in \overline{G}_A$$

This ensures that the uniqueness of states is preserved when the advice is inserted several times within the same global session.

Illustration 1. Consider the naive weaving of the negotiation aspect on $\mathbf{G}_{\text{Trade}}$. The $\mathbf{x}_0$ in exponent comes from the localization process.

$$
\begin{array}{rcl}
A_{\text{nego}} \oplus \mathbf{G}_{\text{Trade}} \leadsto_N \mathsf{def} & & \\
\mathbf{x}_0 & = & \mathbf{x_A}^{\mathbf{x}_0} \\
\mathbf{x_A}^{\mathbf{x}_0} & = & \mathsf{S} \to \mathsf{B}\colon \mathit{Item}\langle \mathit{string}\rangle; \mathbf{x}_1^{\mathbf{x}_0} \\
\mathbf{x}_1^{\mathbf{x}_0} + \mathbf{x}_6^{\mathbf{x}_0} & = & \mathbf{x}_2^{\mathbf{x}_0} \\
\mathbf{x}_2^{\mathbf{x}_0} & = & \mathbf{x}_3^{\mathbf{x}_0} + \mathbf{x}_4^{\mathbf{x}_0} \\
\mathbf{x}_3^{\mathbf{x}_0} & = & \mathsf{B} \to \mathsf{C}\colon \mathit{Offer}\langle \mathit{nat}\rangle; \mathbf{x}_5^{\mathbf{x}_0} \\
\mathbf{x}_5^{\mathbf{x}_0} & = & \mathsf{C} \to \mathsf{B}\colon \mathit{Counter}\langle \mathit{nat}\rangle; \mathbf{x}_6^{\mathbf{x}_0} \\
\mathbf{x}_4^{\mathbf{x}_0} & = & \mathbf{x}_1 \\
\mathbf{x}_1 & = & \mathbf{x}_2 \mid \mathbf{x}_3 \\
\mathbf{x}_2 & = & \mathsf{B} \to \mathsf{S}\colon \mathit{Sale}\langle \mathit{boolean}\rangle; \mathbf{x}_4 \\
\mathbf{x}_3 & = & \mathsf{B} \to \mathsf{C}\colon \mathit{Purchase}\langle \mathit{boolean}\rangle; \mathbf{x}_5 \\
\mathbf{x}_4 \mid \mathbf{x}_5 & = & \mathbf{x}_6 \\
\mathbf{x}_6 & = & \mathsf{end} \quad \mathsf{in}\ \mathbf{x}_0
\end{array}
$$

Modulo congruence, this woven global type is the same as the trade session type with negotiation of [8], which is well formed. So it seems that naive aspect weaving provides a good way to enhance interactions while preserving well-formedness. However, the situation is not that simple, as shown by the following example.

Illustration 2. Consider the naive weaving of the authentication aspect on $\mathbf{G}_{\text{Trade}}$. The $\mathbf{x}_2$ and $\mathbf{x}_3$ in exponent come from two different applications of the localization process.

$$
\begin{array}{rcl}
A_{\text{auth}} \oplus \mathbf{G}_{\text{Trade}} \leadsto_N \mathsf{def} & & \\
\mathbf{x}_0 & = & \mathsf{S} \to \mathsf{B}\colon \mathit{Item}\langle \mathit{string}\rangle; \mathbf{x}_1 \\
\mathbf{x}_1 & = & \mathbf{x}_2 \mid \mathbf{x}_3 \\
\mathbf{x}_2 & = & \mathbf{x_A}^{\mathbf{x}_2} \\
\mathbf{x_A}^{\mathbf{x}_2} + \mathbf{x}_5^{\mathbf{x}_2} & = & \mathbf{x}_1^{\mathbf{x}_2} \\
\mathbf{x}_1^{\mathbf{x}_2} & = & \mathsf{B} \to \mathsf{A}\colon \mathit{Auth}\langle \mathit{string}\rangle; \mathbf{x}_2^{\mathbf{x}_2} \\
\mathbf{x}_2^{\mathbf{x}_2} & = & \mathbf{x}_3^{\mathbf{x}_2} + \mathbf{x}_4^{\mathbf{x}_2} \\
\mathbf{x}_3^{\mathbf{x}_2} & = & \mathsf{A} \to \mathsf{B}\colon \mathit{Retry}; \mathbf{x}_5^{\mathbf{x}_2} \\
\mathbf{x}_4^{\mathbf{x}_2} & = & \mathsf{A} \to \mathsf{B}\colon \mathit{Ok}; \mathbf{x}_6^{\mathbf{x}_2} \\
\mathbf{x}_6^{\mathbf{x}_2} & = & \mathsf{B} \to \mathsf{S}\colon \mathit{Sale}\langle \mathit{boolean}\rangle; \mathbf{x}_7^{\mathbf{x}_2} \\
\mathbf{x}_7^{\mathbf{x}_2} & = & \mathbf{x}_4 \\
\mathbf{x}_3 & = & \mathbf{x_A}^{\mathbf{x}_3} \\
\mathbf{x_A}^{\mathbf{x}_3} + \mathbf{x}_5^{\mathbf{x}_3} & = & \mathbf{x}_1^{\mathbf{x}_3} \\
\mathbf{x}_1^{\mathbf{x}_3} & = & \mathsf{B} \to \mathsf{A}\colon \mathit{Auth}\langle \mathit{string}\rangle; \mathbf{x}_2^{\mathbf{x}_3} \\
\mathbf{x}_2^{\mathbf{x}_3} & = & \mathbf{x}_3^{\mathbf{x}_3} + \mathbf{x}_4^{\mathbf{x}_3} \\
\mathbf{x}_3^{\mathbf{x}_3} & = & \mathsf{A} \to \mathsf{B}\colon \mathit{Retry}; \mathbf{x}_5^{\mathbf{x}_3} \\
\mathbf{x}_4^{\mathbf{x}_3} & = & \mathsf{A} \to \mathsf{B}\colon \mathit{Ok}; \mathbf{x}_6^{\mathbf{x}_3} \\
\mathbf{x}_6^{\mathbf{x}_3} & = & \mathsf{B} \to \mathsf{C}\colon \mathit{Purchase}\langle \mathit{boolean}\rangle; \mathbf{x}_7^{\mathbf{x}_3} \\
\mathbf{x}_7^{\mathbf{x}_3} & = & \mathbf{x}_5 \\
\mathbf{x}_4 \mid \mathbf{x}_5 & = & \mathbf{x}_6 \\
\mathbf{x}_6 & = & \mathsf{end} \quad \mathsf{in}\ \mathbf{x}_0
\end{array}
$$

In this case, naive weaving produces an ill-formed type, because it breaks linearity on $\mathsf{B} \to \mathsf{A}\colon \mathit{Auth}\langle \mathit{string}\rangle$ (explained in Section 3.3). We will come back to this in Section 5 when studying properties of aspectual session types. Note already that the size and complexity of the woven type can grow quickly.

$$
\begin{array}{rcll}
\mathbf{T}_a & ::= & \overline{A} \oplus \mathbf{T} & \text{Local Type with Aspects} \\
A & ::= & \langle pc, adv \rangle & \text{Aspect} \\
pc & ::= & !\langle \mathsf{p}, l_*\langle U_*\rangle\rangle \mid ?\langle \mathsf{p}, l_*\langle U_*\rangle\rangle & \text{Pointcut} \\
 & \mid & pc + pc \mid 0 & \\
adv & ::= & \mathsf{def}\ \overline{T_a}\ \mathsf{in}\ \mathbf{x} & \text{Advice} \\
T_a & ::= & \mathbf{x} = M_a; \mathbf{x}' \mid T & \text{Advice Transition} \\
M_a & ::= & \mathsf{proceed} \mid M & \text{Advice Message}
\end{array}
$$

Figure 9: Syntax of Local Aspectual Session Types

$$
\begin{array}{lcl}
\overline{A} \oplus \mathbf{G} \upharpoonright \mathsf{p} & = & \overline{A} \upharpoonright \mathsf{p} \oplus \mathbf{G} \upharpoonright \mathsf{p} \\
\langle pc, adv \rangle \upharpoonright \mathsf{p} & = & \langle pc \upharpoonright \mathsf{p}, adv \upharpoonright \mathsf{p} \rangle \\
pc + pc \upharpoonright \mathsf{p} & = & pc \upharpoonright \mathsf{p} + pc \upharpoonright \mathsf{p} \\
\mathsf{p} \to \mathsf{p}'\colon l_*\langle U_*\rangle \upharpoonright \mathsf{p} & = & !\langle \mathsf{p}', l_*\langle U_*\rangle\rangle \\
\mathsf{p} \to \mathsf{p}'\colon l_*\langle U_*\rangle \upharpoonright \mathsf{p}' & = & ?\langle \mathsf{p}, l_*\langle U_*\rangle\rangle \\
\mathsf{p} \to \mathsf{p}'\colon l_*\langle U_*\rangle \upharpoonright \mathsf{p}'' & = & 0\ (\mathsf{p}'' \notin \{\mathsf{p}, \mathsf{p}'\}) \\
\mathsf{proceed} \upharpoonright \mathsf{p} & = & \mathsf{proceed}
\end{array}
$$

Figure 10: Projection Algorithm for Aspects

4.2 Aspects on Local Types

Syntax. The syntax of local aspectual session types is given in Figure 9. Similarly to global aspectual session types, one can specify a set of aspects to weave on a local type. Local join points now denote message sending and reception. In addition to disjunction, we also include the null pointcut 0, which can appear via projection. As before, an advice body can include proceed.

We extend congruence naturally on local types to aspects, in particular to account for 0 in pointcuts:

$$
\begin{array}{rcll}
\langle pc, adv \rangle & \equiv & \langle pc', adv' \rangle & \text{if } pc \equiv pc' \wedge adv \equiv adv' \\
pc + 0 & \equiv & 0 + pc & \equiv \quad pc
\end{array}
$$

Projection. We extend the projection algorithm of Figure 4 to deal with the projection of aspects, shown in Figure 10. A message pointcut is projected as a message send pointcut on the sender, a message reception on the receiver, and 0 otherwise. The rest of the projection is straightforward. We call a projected aspect a *daemon aspect* when its projected pointcut is 0.

Local Weaving. Weaving of local aspectual session types is defined in Figure 11. Compared to global weaving, the novelty here is that it is possible for pointcuts to be projected to 0. Intuitively, this corresponds to advice actions that do not involve either of the participants in the intercepted message. The weaving of such daemon aspects is expressed by Rule (T-Daemon). Rule (T-NoDaemon) corresponds to the non-0 local pointcut case, which, together with rules (T-StepT), (T-Skip) and (T-Weave), is similar to the global weaving rules.

Weaving daemons is challenging because locally, there is no way to know precisely when these advice actions have to be performed. Therefore, they must possibly be realizable at any point, in parallel with the participant's original activity. This is why Rule (T-Daemon) rewrites the local type to introduce a fork that branches between the original activity (which starts at $\mathbf{x}$) and the advice activity[2]. In addition, the advice activity must possibly be executed several times. Therefore, in the advice body, end is substituted with

[2] Note that new participants introduced by aspects are initialized with local types $\mathsf{def}\ \mathbf{x} = \mathsf{end}\ \mathsf{in}\ \mathbf{x}$, so that the local weaving of projected advice is always defined.

$$
(\text{T-StepA})\ \frac{A \vdash \mathbf{T} \leadsto \mathbf{T}' \qquad \overline{A} \vdash \mathbf{T}' \leadsto \mathbf{T}''}{A\overline{A} \oplus \mathbf{T} \leadsto \mathbf{T}''}
$$

$$
(\text{T-Daemon})\ \frac{\mathbf{x}_0, \mathbf{x}_1, \mathbf{x}_E \text{ fresh in } \overline{T}, \overline{T}_A}{\begin{array}{ll} \langle 0, \mathsf{def}\ \overline{T}_A\ \mathsf{in}\ \mathbf{x}_A \rangle \vdash & \\ & \mathsf{def}\ \mathbf{x}_0 = \mathbf{x} \mid \mathbf{x}_1 \\ \mathsf{def}\ \overline{T}\ \mathsf{in}\ \mathbf{x} \leadsto & \quad \mathbf{x}_1 + \mathbf{x}_E = \mathbf{x}_A \\ & \quad \overline{T}_A[\mathsf{proceed} \mapsto 0][\mathsf{end} \mapsto \mathbf{x}_E] \\ & \quad \overline{T}\ \mathsf{in}\ \mathbf{x}_0 \end{array}}
$$

$$
(\text{T-NoDaemon})\ \frac{\langle pc, adv \rangle \vdash \overline{T} \leadsto \overline{T'} \qquad pc \neq 0}{\langle pc, adv \rangle \vdash \mathsf{def}\ \overline{T}\ \mathsf{in}\ \mathbf{x} \leadsto \mathsf{def}\ \overline{T'}\ \mathsf{in}\ \mathbf{x}}
$$

$$
(\text{T-StepT})\ \frac{A \vdash T_1 \leadsto \overline{T_1'} \qquad A \vdash \overline{T_2} \leadsto \overline{T_2'}}{A \vdash T_1\overline{T_2} \leadsto \overline{T_1'}\overline{T_2'}}
$$

$$
(\text{T-Skip})\ \frac{T \neq \mathbf{x} = M.\mathbf{x}' \vee \neg match(pc, M)}{\langle pc, adv \rangle \vdash T \leadsto T}
$$

$$
(\text{T-Weave})\ \frac{\overline{T}'_A = localize(\overline{T}_A, \mathbf{x}) \qquad match(pc, M)}{\begin{array}{l} \langle pc, \mathsf{def}\ \overline{T}_A\ \mathsf{in}\ \mathbf{x}_A \rangle \vdash \mathbf{x} = M.\mathbf{x}' \leadsto \\ \quad \mathbf{x} = \mathbf{x}_A^{\mathbf{x}} \\ \quad \overline{T}'_A[\mathsf{proceed} \mapsto M][\mathsf{end} \mapsto \mathbf{x}'] \end{array}}
$$

Figure 11: Local Weaving

a newly-introduced merge point that connects to the start of the advice $\mathbf{x}_A$. In effect, this weaving strategy serializes all advice executions in a given participant. Finally, because this rule applies in participants that are not involved in the intercepted message, proceed is replaced by the null message 0.

Illustration. We illustrate the local weaving on the negotiation aspect on the client side. It produces a daemon negotiation aspect for C that can be executed infinitely often in parallel with the *Purchase* interaction (′s are for states dealing with the daemon).

$$
\begin{array}{rcl}
\multicolumn{3}{l}{A_{\text{nego}} \upharpoonright \mathsf{C} \oplus \mathbf{G}_{\text{Trade}} \upharpoonright \mathsf{C} \leadsto \mathsf{def}} \\
\mathbf{x}'_0 & = & \mathbf{x}_0 \mid \mathbf{x}'_1 \\
\mathbf{x}'_1 + \mathbf{x}'_E & = & \mathbf{x}'_A \\
\mathbf{x}'_A + \mathbf{x}'_6 & = & \mathbf{x}'_2 \\
\mathbf{x}'_2 & = & \mathbf{x}'_3 + \mathbf{x}'_4 \\
\mathbf{x}'_3 & = & ?\langle B, Offer\langle nat \rangle \rangle; \mathbf{x}'_5 \\
\mathbf{x}'_5 & = & !\langle B, Counter\langle nat \rangle \rangle; \mathbf{x}'_6 \\
\mathbf{x}'_4 & = & \mathbf{x}'_E \\
\mathbf{x}_0 & = & \mathbf{x}_2 \mid \mathbf{x}_3 \\
\mathbf{x}_2 & = & \mathbf{x}_4 \\
\mathbf{x}_3 & = & ?\langle B, Purchase\langle boolean \rangle \rangle; \mathbf{x}_5 \\
\mathbf{x}_4 \mid \mathbf{x}_5 & = & \mathbf{x}_6 \\
\mathbf{x}_6 & = & \mathsf{end} \quad \mathsf{in}\ \mathbf{x}'_0
\end{array}
$$

Of course, in practice, the daemon will be executed only once for the global type $\mathbf{G}_{\text{Trade}}$, but this cannot be known locally.

Overall, the weaving of daemon advices introduces a mismatch between the global woven type and the local woven types. This means that weaving ($\leadsto$) and projection ($\upharpoonright$) do not commute: recalling Figure 5, the local types obtained by first weaving aspects in the global type and then projecting the woven type do not match the local types obtained by first projecting the aspects and global type and then locally weaving the aspects. In effect, the types obtained by local weaving describe a more parallel interaction than the interaction described by the global woven type.

This inevitable mismatch potentially breaks the connection between well-formedness of the global type and the desirable properties of local types. The most technical contribution of this work is to characterize sufficient conditions on aspectual session types for local aspect weaving to preserve the properties of the global woven type (Section 5), and to prove this proper relation between local and global weaving (Section 6).

5. Properties of Aspectual Session Types

Generalized multiparty session types come with a strong property: if a global type is well-formed, then the interaction of processes that realize the local projections of this type is free of deadlocks, free of orphan messages, and free of reception errors. Recall that well-formedness crucially relies on the local choice and linearity conditions (Section 3.3). To characterize sufficient conditions for aspect weaving to preserve the properties of the global woven type, we introduce two important conditions on aspects that deal with linearity and locality of choice:

- The *aspectual linearity* condition (Section 5.1) justifies that tagging makes sense.
- The *aspectual local choice* condition ensures that aspect weaving does not confuse participants by introducing opaque decisions (Section 5.2).

These two conditions are used to define well-formedness of aspectual session types in Section 5.4. We describe a correct version of global type weaving in Section 5.3, which refines naive weaving in order to address both conditions above. In Section 6, we formally prove that well-formedness of a global type with aspects effectively entails the same safety properties as that of global types.

5.1 Aspectual Linearity

Naive weaving produces a well-formed type in the negotiation example because the pointcut matches only one message. More generally, a sufficient condition to avoid race conditions for different advice executions is to rely directly on the linearity of global types. Namely, if the result of naive weaving is well-formed, two executions of the same advice can never run in parallel, and so there is no race condition between them. This restrictive but sufficient condition—a pointcut does not match two concurrent branches—is called *pointcut linearity*.

Definition 2 (Pointcut Linearity). *Let A be an aspect and $\mathbf{G}$ be a well-formed base type. A is* pointcut-linear *wrt $\mathbf{G}$ iff $A \oplus \mathbf{G} \leadsto_N \mathbf{G}'$ for some well-formed $\mathbf{G}'$.*

Of course, more interesting aspects can match different messages. For instance, the logging and authentication pointcuts match non-linearly as they match two different messages occurring in potentially-concurrent branches. In those cases, naive global weaving can lead to ill-formed global types that break linearity, as illustrated in Illustration 2 of Section 4.2.

Relaxing linearity with tagged weaving. The authentication and logging aspects introduce identical behaviors in different threads, but seem intuitively correct. This conflict reflects the fact that the linearity requirement is too strong in most cases, because advice is typically defined in a general manner, meant to react regardless of specific thread/choice contexts.

Technically, we can sidetrack the linearity issue with advice through *tagged weaving*: deploying a different version of an advice for each message that is matched. These different versions are obtained by using fresh labels tagged with the matched message. For instance, tagged weaving modifies the woven type of the authentication aspect on $\mathbf{G}_{\text{Trade}}$ (already presented in Illustration 2) by tagging each occurrence of *Auth*, *Ok* and *Retry* with the matched message:

$$
\begin{array}{lcl}
\multicolumn{3}{l}{A_{\text{auth}} \oplus \mathbf{G}_{\text{Trade}} \rightsquigarrow \mathsf{def}} \\
\ldots & & \text{(same definitions)} \\
\mathbf{x_1}^{\mathbf{x_2}} & = & \mathsf{B} \to \mathsf{A}\colon \mathit{Auth}^{\mathsf{B}\to\mathsf{S}:\ \mathit{Sale}\langle \mathit{boolean}\rangle}\langle \mathit{string}\rangle; \mathbf{x_2}^{\mathbf{x_2}} \\
\mathbf{x_3}^{\mathbf{x_2}} & = & \mathsf{A} \to \mathsf{B}\colon \mathit{Retry}^{\mathsf{B}\to\mathsf{S}:\ \mathit{Sale}\langle \mathit{boolean}\rangle}; \mathbf{x_5}^{\mathbf{x_2}} \\
\mathbf{x_4}^{\mathbf{x_2}} & = & \mathsf{A} \to \mathsf{B}\colon \mathit{Ok}^{\mathsf{B}\to\mathsf{S}:\ \mathit{Sale}\langle \mathit{boolean}\rangle}; \mathbf{x_6}^{\mathbf{x_2}} \\
\ldots & & \text{(same definitions)} \\
\mathbf{x_1}^{\mathbf{x_3}} & = & \mathsf{B} \to \mathsf{A}\colon \mathit{Auth}^{\mathsf{B}\to\mathsf{C}:\ \mathit{Purchase}\langle \mathit{boolean}\rangle}\langle \mathit{string}\rangle; \mathbf{x_2}^{\mathbf{x_3}} \\
\mathbf{x_3}^{\mathbf{x_3}} & = & \mathsf{A} \to \mathsf{B}\colon \mathit{Retry}^{\mathsf{B}\to\mathsf{C}:\ \mathit{Purchase}\langle \mathit{boolean}\rangle}; \mathbf{x_5}^{\mathbf{x_3}} \\
\mathbf{x_4}^{\mathbf{x_3}} & = & \mathsf{A} \to \mathsf{B}\colon \mathit{Ok}^{\mathsf{B}\to\mathsf{C}:\ \mathit{Purchase}\langle \mathit{boolean}\rangle}; \mathbf{x_6}^{\mathbf{x_3}} \\
\ldots & & \text{(same definitions)} \\
\mathbf{x}_6 & = & \mathsf{end} \quad \mathsf{in}\ \mathbf{x}_0
\end{array}
$$

By linearity of the initial global type, the same message cannot occur in two concurrent branches, so the same version of the advice cannot be executed twice in parallel. Therefore, well-formedness of the base type implies well-formedness of the tagged woven type. Note that tagging can only be done in the global type: in the local types, remote join points are not know, so it is impossible to relate messages properly.

Tagging is a technical device that sidetracks the strong linearity requirement but can obviously break the good properties of session types that are derived from well-formedness. For tagging to be compatible with linearity, the advice must satisfy an *advice linearity* condition. This condition ensures that even though tagging is not done locally, the locally-woven type *behaves as if* it were tagged. This property is proven in Section 6.4 by means of a simulation result.

Definition 3 (Advice Linearity). *Let $A = \langle pc, adv\rangle$ be an aspect and $\mathbf{G}$ be a well-formed base type, such that $\mathbf{G} = \mathsf{def}\ \overline{G}\ \mathsf{in}\ \mathbf{x}_0$. A is* advice-linear *wrt $\mathbf{G}$ iff $\mathbf{G}, A \vdash \mathit{UniqueMsg}$ and for all M such that match(pc, M), adv is single-threaded wrt M.*

Advice linearity relies on uniqueness of messages and single-threadedness. Both are formally defined in Appendix B. The first property ensures that two concurrent executions of a daemon can not interfere. An advice *adv* is said to be *single-threaded* wrt a message $M = \mathsf{p} \to \mathsf{p}'\colon l\langle U\rangle$ if, in the projections of $\mathit{adv}[\mathsf{proceed} \mapsto M]$ on p and p', there is only one thread communicating with daemon advices. That is $\mathit{adv}[\mathsf{proceed} \mapsto M] \upharpoonright \mathsf{p}, M \vdash \mathit{SgTh}(b_{\mathsf{p}})$ (resp. with p') with b_{p} or $b_{\mathsf{p}'}$ equal to false. The single-threaded condition ensures that the part of the advice that is not a daemon advice can not do a join on messages coming from different daemon advices, that are tagged with different labels.

Aspectual linearity follows from either pointcut linearity or advice linearity:

Definition 4 (Aspectual Linearity). *An aspect A satisfies the* aspectual linearity *condition wrt a base type $\mathbf{G}$ iff A is either pointcut-linear or advice-linear wrt to $\mathbf{G}$.*

5.2 Aspectual Local Choice

Aspect weaving introduces an extra implicit choice (is the original message happening, or is an aspect applied?), so it should not break the local choice condition. Informally, this means that participants that are not directly informed of the decision (the source and target of the intercepted message) should either not depend on the choice

$$
\text{(G-Start)}\ \frac{\overline{A} \vdash \overline{G} \rightsquigarrow \overline{G'}}{\overline{A} \oplus \mathsf{def}\ \overline{G}\ \mathsf{in}\ \mathbf{x} \rightsquigarrow \mathsf{def}\ \overline{G'}\ \mathsf{in}\ \mathbf{x}}
$$

$$
\text{(G-StepA)}\ \frac{A,\ \overline{G} \vdash \overline{G} \rightsquigarrow \overline{G'} \qquad \overline{A} \vdash \overline{G'} \rightsquigarrow \overline{G''}}{A\overline{A} \vdash \overline{G} \rightsquigarrow \overline{G''}}
$$

$$
\text{(G-StepG)}\ \frac{A,\ \overline{G} \vdash G_1 \rightsquigarrow \overline{G'_1} \qquad A,\ \overline{G} \vdash \overline{G_2} \rightsquigarrow \overline{G'_2}}{A,\ \overline{G} \vdash G_1\overline{G_2} \rightsquigarrow \overline{G'_1 G'_2}}
$$

$$
\text{(G-Skip)}\ \frac{G \neq \mathbf{x} = M; \mathbf{x}' \vee \neg \mathit{match}(pc, M)}{\langle pc, adv\rangle,\ \overline{G} \vdash G \rightsquigarrow G}
$$

$$
\text{(G-Weave)}\ \frac{\begin{array}{c} \mathit{match}(pc, M) \qquad M = \mathsf{p} \to \mathsf{p}'\colon l\langle U\rangle \\ \overline{G}'_A = \mathit{tag}(\mathit{localize}(\overline{G}_A, \mathbf{x}), M, \overline{G}) \\ \mathbf{x}_1, \mathbf{x}_2, \mathbf{x}_3, l' \text{ fresh in } \overline{G}, \overline{G}_A \end{array}}{\begin{array}{l} \langle pc, \mathsf{def}\ \overline{G}_A\ \mathsf{in}\ \mathbf{x}_A\rangle,\ \overline{G} \vdash \\ \mathbf{x} = M; \mathbf{x}' \rightsquigarrow \left[\begin{array}{l} \mathbf{x} = \mathbf{x}_1 + \mathbf{x}_A^{\mathbf{x}} \\ \mathbf{x}_1 = M\ [l \mapsto l']\ ; \mathbf{x}_2 \\ \overline{G}'_A\ [\mathsf{proceed} \mapsto M][\mathsf{end} \mapsto \mathbf{x}_3\ ] \\ \mathbf{x}_2 + \mathbf{x}_3 = \mathbf{x}' \end{array}\right. \end{array}}
$$

Figure 12: Global Weaving (tagging highlighted in blue with light gray boxes, local choice transformation highlighted in red with dark gray boxes)

taken or be explicitly informed of the choice.[3] To avoid introducing confusion by breaking locality of choice, aspect weaving should preserve the unique active senders and choice awareness conditions in the base type.

We could define aspectual local choice using modified definitions of *ASend* and *Rcv*. However, it is possible to check both properties by changing global weaving in a way that makes the implicit choice introduced by aspect weaving explicit, as discussed below. This implies that checking well-formedness on the global woven type ensures aspectual local choice.

5.3 Global Type Weaving Revisited

We now describe global type weaving (Figure 12) as a refinement and extension of naive global weaving, which includes both tagging and a transformation for aspectual local choice. The only rule that has to be changed wrt naive weaving is Rule (G-Weave).

The first change is the definition of $\overline{G}'_A$ (in blue), which deals with the tagging of labels. Advice tagging is defined in Figure 13. The second change in (G-Weave) is the "fake" choice introduced (in red) between the execution of the advice and the sending of a fresh version of M. Introducing this choice explicitly in the structure of the interaction ensures that well-formedness of the woven global type implies aspectual local choice.

We recursively extend the definition of aspectual linearity on global types with aspects. A global type with aspects $A\overline{A} \oplus \mathbf{G}$ satisfies the aspectual linearity condition if A satisfies the condition

[3] Note that our treatment of implicit choice would allow us to support pointcuts with dynamic conditions in a similar manner.

$$tag(\overline{G}_A, M, \overline{G}) = \overline{G}_A[l \mapsto l^M]\ \forall l \in F \quad \text{where } F = labels(\overline{G}_A) \setminus labels(\overline{G})$$

$$\begin{array}{rcl} labels(\overline{G}) & = & \bigcup_{G \in \overline{G}} labels(G) \\ labels(\mathbf{x} = \mathsf{p} \to \mathsf{p}' : l\langle U \rangle ; \mathbf{x}') & = & l \\ labels(G) & = & \emptyset \quad \text{if } G \neq \mathbf{x} = M; \mathbf{x}' \end{array}$$

Figure 13: Advice Tagging

wrt $\mathbf{G}$ and $\overline{A} \oplus \mathbf{G}'$ satisfies the aspectual linearity condition (where $A \oplus \mathbf{G} \rightsquigarrow \mathbf{G}'$).

Also, with the final definition of global type weaving, we can now formally define the aspectual local choice condition:

Definition 5 (Aspectual Local Choice). *An aspect A satisfies the* aspectual local choice *condition wrt a base type $\mathbf{G}$ iff $A \oplus \mathbf{G} \rightsquigarrow \mathbf{G}'$ and $\mathbf{G}'$ is well-formed*

This definition is naturally extended to an aspectual session type $\overline{A} \oplus \mathbf{G}$.

5.4 Well-formed Aspectual Session Types

To express well-formedness of aspectual session types, we introduce two sanity conditions, in addition to aspectual linearity and aspectual local choice. First, every advice must have an end so as to ensure that the constructions of (G-Weave), (T-Weave) and (T-Daemon) satisfy the sanity check for session types. Second, every message from/to a daemon advice must be fresh with respect to the base session type $\mathbf{G}$. Intuitively, a daemon adds an interaction that was not present and if it uses messages that are already in $\mathbf{G}$, it may break local choice or linearity.

Definition 6 (Well-formedness). *An aspectual session type $\overline{A} \oplus \mathbf{G}$ is* well-formed *when*

- *$\mathbf{G}$ is well-formed,*
- *every advice has an* end*,*
- *every message from/to a daemon advice is fresh wrt $\mathbf{G}$,*
- *$\overline{A} \oplus \mathbf{G}$ satisfies the aspectual linearity condition,*
- *$\overline{A} \oplus \mathbf{G}$ satisfies the aspectual local choice condition.*

6. Relating Local and Global Weaving

To compare local and global weaving, we need to define a formal semantics for local and global types. Following [8], we use the notion of Communicating Finite State Machines (CFSMs) to interpret local types and projections of global types.

In this section, we show that the interpretation of local woven types is simulated by the interpretation of the global woven type. This allows us to preserve all the properties satisfied by global types on a realization that is less sequential and that uses less labels.

Note that Sections 6.1 and 6.2 present background material directly based on [8]. Our contribution starts in Section 6.3.

6.1 Communicating Finite State Machines

Definition 7 (CFSM). *A communicating finite state machine is a finite state transition system $M = (\mathcal{Q}, C, q_0, \mathbb{L}, \delta)$ where $\mathcal{Q}$ is a finite set of states, $C = \{\mathsf{pq} \in \mathcal{P}^2 \mid \mathsf{p} \neq \mathsf{q}\}$, q_0 is the initial state, $\mathbb{L}$ is a finite set of labels, $\delta \subseteq \mathcal{Q} \times (C \times \{!, ?\} \times \mathbb{L}) \times \mathcal{Q}$ is a finite set of transitions.*

A transition of the form $\mathsf{pq}!l$ is called a *sending action* from participant p to participant q, and a transition of the form $\mathsf{pq}?l$ is called a *receiving action* from p by q. When the kind of action is not relevant, we use a, a' to range over sending or receiving actions.

A path in M is a finite sequence of states $q_0 \cdots q_n$ starting from the initial state q_0 such that $(q_i, a, q_{i+1}) \in \delta$.

Definition 8 (CS). *A (communicating) system $\mathcal{S} = (M_\mathsf{p})_{\mathsf{p} \in \mathcal{P}}$ is a tuple of CFSMs $M_\mathsf{p} = (\mathcal{Q}_\mathsf{p}, C, q_{0\mathsf{p}}, \mathbb{L}, \delta_\mathsf{p})$ that share the same channels.*

Given a CS $\mathcal{S}$, we note $\delta = \biguplus_{\mathsf{p} \in \mathcal{P}} \delta_\mathsf{p}$ the resulting transition on the system. A *configuration* of $\mathcal{S}$ is a couple $c = ((q_\mathsf{p})_{\mathsf{p} \in \mathcal{P}}, (\mathbf{w}_\mathsf{pq})_{\mathsf{p} \neq \mathsf{q} \in \mathcal{P}})$ where $q_p \in \mathcal{Q}_\mathsf{p}$ is a state and $\mathbf{w}_\mathsf{pq} \in \mathbb{L}^*$ is a queue of messages. The initial configuration of a system is $c_0 = ((q_{0\mathsf{p}})_{\mathsf{p} \in \mathcal{P}}, \overline{\varepsilon})$. There are two kinds of transitions t on a communicating system $\mathcal{S}$ from c to c', written $c \xrightarrow{t} c'$, that evolve in only one CFSM:

send. $t = (q_\mathsf{p}, \mathsf{pq}!l, q'_\mathsf{p}) \in \delta_\mathsf{p}$ with $q'_{\mathsf{p}'} = q_{\mathsf{p}'}$ for all $\mathsf{p}' \neq \mathsf{p}$ and $\mathbf{w}'_\mathsf{pq} = \mathbf{w}_\mathsf{pq}\, l$ and $\mathbf{w}'_{\mathsf{p}'\mathsf{q}'} = \mathbf{w}_{\mathsf{p}'\mathsf{q}'}$ for all $\mathsf{p}'\mathsf{q}' \neq \mathsf{pq}$.

receive. $t = (q_\mathsf{p}, \mathsf{pq}?l, q'_\mathsf{p}) \in \delta_\mathsf{p}$ with $q'_{\mathsf{p}'} = q_{\mathsf{p}'}$ for all $\mathsf{p}' \neq \mathsf{p}$ and $\mathbf{w}_\mathsf{pq} = l\, \mathbf{w}'_\mathsf{pq}$ and $\mathbf{w}'_{\mathsf{p}'\mathsf{q}'} = \mathbf{w}_{\mathsf{p}'\mathsf{q}'}$ for all $\mathsf{p}'\mathsf{q}' \neq \mathsf{pq}$.

The conditions on $\mathbf{w}_\mathsf{pq}$ express that a send performs an enqueue operation, and a receive performs a dequeue operation.

An *execution* of a CS is a sequence of transitions starting from the initial configuration:

$$c_0 \xrightarrow{t_0} c_1 \xrightarrow{t_1} \cdots \xrightarrow{t_{n-1}} c_n.$$

A configuration is *reachable* when there is an execution that leads to it. We note $RS(\mathcal{S})$ the set of reachable configurations of $\mathcal{S}$. A configuration $(\overline{q}, \overline{\varepsilon})$ is *final* when every state of $\overline{q}$ is final.

Property 1. *Let $\mathcal{S}$ be a communicating system and $c = (\overline{q}, \overline{\mathbf{w}})$ a configuration of $\mathcal{S}$. The following definitions follow [5]:*

- *c is a* deadlock configuration *if $\overline{\mathbf{w}} = \varepsilon$ and each state of $\overline{q}$ has only outgoing receiving transitions, i.e., all machine are blocked waiting for messages.*
- *c is an* orphan message configuration *if all states of $\overline{q}$ are final but the queue $\overline{\mathbf{w}}$ of messages is not empty.*
- *c is an* reception error configuration *if there exists a participant* p *which has only outgoing receiving transitions $(q_\mathsf{p}, \mathsf{qp}?l, q'_\mathsf{p}$ with $\mathbf{w}_\mathsf{qp} = l'\mathbf{w}'_\mathsf{qp}$ and $l \neq l'$.*

Property 2. *A communicating system $\mathcal{S}$ satisfies the* progress property *when for all $c \in RS(\mathcal{S})$, either c is final or $c \to c'$ for some configuration c'. It satisfies the* liveness property *when a final configuration can always be reached from any reachable configuration.*

6.2 Multiparty session automata

This section sums up the interpretation of generalized multiparty session types in terms of CFSMs called *multiparty session automata* (MSA), and the main properties satisfied by MSA.

In what follows, $\mathbf{X}$ denotes a collection of states of a local type connected by $\mid$ and $\mathbf{X}[-]$ a context with a hole. Given a list of local type $\overline{T}$, $\mathbf{X}$ comes with a notion of congruence $\equiv_{\overline{T}}$ defined in [8, page 11].

Given a local type $\mathbf{T} = \mathsf{def}\ \overline{T}\ \mathsf{in}\ \mathbf{x}_0$ obtained by projecting a global type $\mathbf{G}$ on a participant p, we define the CFSM $\mathcal{A}(\mathbf{T}) = (\mathcal{Q}, C, \mathbf{x}_0, labels(\mathbf{G}), \delta)$ as follows:

- $\mathcal{Q}$ is defined as the set of $\mathbf{X}$ build over states of $\mathbf{T}$, up to the congruence $\equiv_{\overline{T}}$,
- $C = \{\mathsf{pq} \mid \mathsf{p}, \mathsf{q} \in \mathbf{G}\}$,
- $(\mathbf{X}[\mathbf{x}], \mathsf{pp}'!l, \mathbf{X}[\mathbf{x}']) \in \delta$ iff $\mathbf{x} = !\langle \mathsf{p}', l\langle U \rangle \rangle ; \mathbf{x}' \in \overline{T}$,
- $(\mathbf{X}[\mathbf{x}], \mathsf{p}'\mathsf{p}?l, \mathbf{X}[\mathbf{x}']) \in \delta$ iff $\mathbf{x} = ?\langle \mathsf{p}', l\langle U \rangle \rangle ; \mathbf{x}' \in \overline{T}$.

A *multiparty session automaton* (MSA) is a communicating system of the form $(\mathcal{A}(\mathbf{G} \upharpoonright \mathsf{p}))_{\mathsf{p}\in\mathbf{G}}$ for a well-formed global type $\mathbf{G}$.

Below are the main properties satisfied by MSAs, proven in [8], which we want to extend to aspectual session types:

Theorem 1 (from [8]). *A multiparty session automaton is free from deadlock, orphan message, and reception error configurations. It satisfies the progress property, and when the global type that generated it contains* end, *it satisfies the liveness property.*

6.3 Aspectual multiparty session automata

Aspectual session types give rise to two kinds of communication systems, depending on whether we consider global or local weaving. The goal of this section and of Section 6.4 is to show that the system coming from global weaving, which inherits directly the properties of MSAs, can simulate the system coming from local weaving.

An *aspectual multiparty session automaton*, noted $\mathcal{A}(\overline{A}, \mathbf{G})$, is a MSA of a well-formed woven global type $\mathbf{G}'$, with $\overline{A} \oplus \mathbf{G} \rightsquigarrow \mathbf{G}'$ and $\overline{A} \oplus \mathbf{G}$ is well-formed.

A *locally woven multiparty session automaton* is a communicating system of the form $(\mathcal{A}(\mathbf{T}_\mathsf{p}))_{\mathsf{p}\in\mathbf{G}}$, where $(\overline{A} \oplus \mathbf{G} \upharpoonright \mathsf{p} \rightsquigarrow \mathbf{T}_\mathsf{p})_{\mathsf{p}\in\mathbf{G}}$ is a set of woven local types coming from a well-formed aspectual session type $\overline{A} \oplus \mathbf{G}$.

Advice atomic executions. We want to relate configurations in $(\mathcal{A}(\mathbf{T}_\mathsf{p}))_{\mathsf{p}\in\mathbf{G}}$ to configurations in $\mathcal{A}(\overline{A}, \mathbf{G})$. But configurations in $(\mathcal{A}(\mathbf{T}_\mathsf{p}))_{\mathsf{p}\in\mathbf{G}}$ are less sequential because daemon advices execute in parallel with the initial interaction. We first need to restrict the kind of configurations we have to deal with, by adding an atomicity condition that forces an interaction on an advice to be completed before another one starts.

Definition 9 (Advice atomic execution). *An execution e in $(\mathcal{A}(\mathbf{T}_\mathsf{p}))_{\mathsf{p}\in\mathbf{G}}$ is* advice atomic *when for any transition $c \xrightarrow{t} c'$ in e, with $t = (\mathbf{X}[\mathbf{x}], \mathsf{pq}!l, \mathbf{X}[\mathbf{x}'])$ between two states $\mathbf{x}$ and $\mathbf{x}'$ defined in $\mathbf{G}$, states present in c and c' are not localized states (of the form $\mathbf{x}_2^{\mathbf{x}_1}$, generated by Rule (T-Weave)), and states present in c that deal with daemon advice are all equal to their corresponding $\mathbf{x}_E$ (generated by Rule (T-Daemon)). By extension, we say that a configuration is* advice atomic *when it can be reached by an advice atomic execution.*

Of course, every configuration is not advice atomic, but using aspectual linearity, we can show that every configuration can be extended to a configuration that satisfies this atomicity.

Property 3. *Suppose $c \in RS((\mathcal{A}(\mathbf{T}_\mathsf{p}))_{\mathsf{p}\in\mathbf{G}})$. Then, c can be extended to $c \rightarrow^* c'$ such that c' can be reached by an advice atomic execution.*

Proof. We first show that two parallel executions of the same advice cannot interfere with each other.

Case of advice linearity. Using the unique message property, an execution of a daemon advice cannot be perturbed by message coming from other threads. Using the single-threaded condition, only one non-daemon advice (that is, the projection of an advice on one of the two participants of the matched message) can be waiting for a message coming from only one daemon at a time. It follows that two daemons of the same advice cannot interact in different threads at the same time.

Case of pointcut linearity. Using pointcut linearity, we know that two executions of the same advice cannot be done in parallel, because there is no race condition, even without tagging.

Using well-threadedness, we can reach the end state of every pending advice execution. Then, because every message of an advice is fresh (extra sanity condition), it can be commuted with the remaining interaction in the initial global type $\mathbf{G}$. □

6.4 Simulation of locally woven MSAs.

Intuitively, a communicating system $\mathcal{S}$ is simulated by a communicating system $\mathcal{S}'$ when every action performed in $\mathcal{S}$ can be replicated in some way in $\mathcal{S}'$. More formally, in our setting, a simulation $\mathcal{R}$ from $\mathcal{S}$ to $\mathcal{S}'$ is a relation between configurations of $\mathcal{S}$ and $\mathcal{S}'$ such that the initial configurations are related (i.e. $c_0 \mathcal{R} c_0'$) and when $c_1 \mathcal{R} c_1'$ and c_1 reduces in one step to c_2, there exists c_2' such that $c_2 \mathcal{R} c_2'$ and c_1' reduces (in 0, 1 or more steps) to c_2'. We illustrate this with the following diagrams:

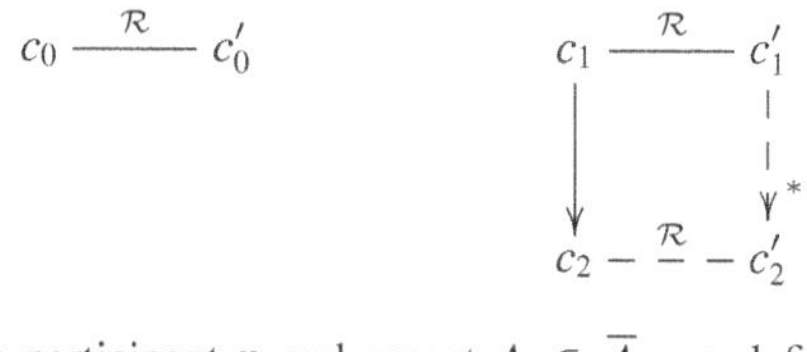

For any participant p and aspect $A \in \overline{A}$, we define a partial function σ_p^A from states of the CFSM of $\mathcal{A}(A, \mathbf{G})$ at p to states of the CFSM of $\mathcal{A}(\mathbf{T}_\mathsf{p})$ defined as the identity when $A \upharpoonright \mathsf{p}$ is not a daemon aspect, and—when it is a daemon aspect—defined as:

$$\begin{array}{rcll} \underline{\sigma}_\mathsf{p}^A([-]) & = & [-] & \\ \underline{\sigma}_\mathsf{p}^A(\mathbf{x}) & = & \mathbf{x} & \text{when } \mathbf{x} \in \mathbf{G} \\ \underline{\sigma}_\mathsf{p}^A(\mathbf{x}_1^{\mathbf{x}_2}) & = & \mathbf{x}_1 | \mathbf{x}_2 & \text{when } \mathbf{x}_1 \in A, \mathbf{x}_2 \in \mathbf{G} \\ \underline{\sigma}_\mathsf{p}^A(\mathbf{X}|\mathbf{X}') & = & \underline{\sigma}_\mathsf{p}^A(\mathbf{X}) | \underline{\sigma}_\mathsf{p}^A(\mathbf{X}') & \text{when at most one state of} \\ & & & \underline{\sigma}_\mathsf{p}^A(\mathbf{X}) \text{ or } \underline{\sigma}_\mathsf{p}^A(\mathbf{X}') \text{ is in } A \\ \underline{\sigma}_\mathsf{p}^A(\mathbf{X}) & & \multicolumn{2}{l}{\text{is otherwise undefined}} \end{array}$$

We then set $\sigma_\mathsf{p}^A(\mathbf{X}) = \underline{\sigma}_\mathsf{p}^A(\mathbf{X})|\mathbf{x}_E$ when $\underline{\sigma}_\mathsf{p}^A(\mathbf{X})$ contains no state in A, with $\mathbf{x}_A$ is the initial state of A. Otherwise, $\sigma_\mathsf{p}^A(\mathbf{X}) = \underline{\sigma}_\mathsf{p}^A(\mathbf{X})$. Note that σ_p^A is defined in two times using the auxiliary function $\underline{\sigma}_\mathsf{p}^A$ because a state of $\mathcal{A}(A, \mathbf{G})$ at p may contain no state of A, whereas every state of $\mathcal{A}(\mathbf{T}_\mathsf{p})$ contains exactly one state of A (even if just $\mathbf{x}_E$) because a daemon advice always executes in parallel with the rest of the local type.

This means that $\sigma_\mathsf{p}^A(\mathbf{X})$ is undefined when there is more than one execution of the daemon aspect in parallel because parallel executions of the daemon aspect are not possible in the locally woven type. It is also undefined when we are in a fresh (red) state of Rule (G-Weave), because such a state has been added to check the aspectual local choice condition, but it has no computational meaning and is not present in the locally woven type.

We extend the definition of σ_p to a list of aspects

$$\sigma_\mathsf{p}^\varepsilon = id \qquad \text{and} \qquad \sigma_\mathsf{p}^{A\overline{A}} = \sigma_\mathsf{p}^{\overline{A}} \circ \sigma_\mathsf{p}^A.$$

We now use σ_p to define the relation $\mathcal{R}_{Tag}$ between configurations of $(\mathcal{A}(\mathbf{T}_\mathsf{p}))_{\mathsf{p}\in\mathbf{G}}$ and configurations of $\mathcal{A}(\overline{A}, \mathbf{G})$ as

$$((\mathbf{X}_\mathsf{p})_{\mathsf{p}\in\mathcal{P}}, (\mathbf{w}_\mathsf{pq})_{\mathsf{p}\neq\mathsf{q}\in\mathcal{P}}) \mathcal{R}_{Tag} ((\mathbf{X}_\mathsf{p}')_{\mathsf{p}\in\mathcal{P}}, (\mathbf{w}_\mathsf{pq}')_{\mathsf{p}\neq\mathsf{q}\in\mathcal{P}})$$

exactly when

$$\forall \mathsf{p} \neq \mathsf{q} \in \mathcal{P},\ \mathbf{X}_\mathsf{p} = \sigma_\mathsf{p}^{\overline{A}}(\mathbf{X}_\mathsf{p}') \quad \text{and} \quad \mathbf{w}_\mathsf{pq} = untag(\mathbf{w}_\mathsf{pq}', \mathbf{G}).$$

where $untag(\mathbf{w}_\mathsf{pq}', \mathbf{G})$ is the function that removes in $\mathbf{w}_\mathsf{pq}'$ the tags introduced on labels not present in $\mathbf{G}$.

Theorem 2. *The relation $\mathcal{R}_{Tag}$ defines a simulation from advice atomic configurations of $(\mathcal{A}(\mathbf{T}_\mathsf{p}))_{\mathsf{p}\in\mathbf{G}}$ to configurations of $\mathcal{A}(\overline{A}, \mathbf{G})$.*

Proof. Initial configurations are in $\mathcal{R}_{Tag}$ because queues are empty and $\sigma_\mathsf{p}^{\overline{A}}$ is the identity on the initial state.

Suppose $c_1 \mathcal{R}_{Tag} c'_1$ and c_1 reduces in one step to c_2 with transition $t = (\mathbf{X}[\mathbf{x}_{1\mathrm{p}}], M, \mathbf{X}[\mathbf{x}_{2\mathrm{p}}]) \in \delta_{\mathrm{p}}$. By definition of $\mathcal{R}_{Tag}$, the configuration c'_n at p, say $\mathbf{X}'$, satisfies $\sigma^{\bar{A}}_{\mathrm{p}}(\mathbf{X}') = \mathbf{X}[\mathbf{x}_{1\mathrm{p}}]$. We proceed by case analysis on $\mathbf{X}[\mathbf{x}_{1\mathrm{p}}]$.

Case $\mathbf{x}_{1\mathrm{p}} = M; \mathbf{x}_{2\mathrm{p}} \in A \upharpoonright \mathrm{p}$, A is not a daemon at p.
M has been inserted in the interaction by Rule (T-Weave) for a certain matched message that is the projection of a global message, say M_G. Because the configuration is advice atomic, M_G is the only currently matched message in the interaction. By definition of σ_{p}, $\mathbf{X}'$ is of the form $\mathbf{X}'[\mathbf{x}_{1\mathrm{p}}]$. It is not difficult to check that

$$t' = (\mathbf{X}'[\mathbf{x}_{1\mathrm{p}}], tag(M, M_G, \overline{G}), \mathbf{X}'[\mathbf{x}_{2\mathrm{p}}]) \in \delta'_{\mathrm{p}}$$

and $c_2 \mathcal{R}_{Tag} c'_2$ with $c'_1 \xrightarrow{t'} c'_2$.

Case $\mathbf{x}_{1\mathrm{p}} = M; \mathbf{x}_{2\mathrm{p}} \in A \upharpoonright \mathrm{p}$, A is a daemon at p.
M has been inserted in the interaction by Rule (T-Daemon). By aspectual local choice, the daemon cannot be an active sender, so the interaction in the advice has already started on the sender of the matched message. Thus, $\mathbf{X}'$ is of the form $\mathbf{X}'[\mathbf{x}^{\mathbf{x}}_{1\mathrm{p}}]$. The state $\mathbf{x}^{\mathbf{x}}_{1\mathrm{p}}$ has been introduced by the localization process of Rule (G-Weave), for a matched pattern M_G (unique by advice atomicity). Again, it is easy to check that

$$t' = (\mathbf{X}'[\mathbf{x}^{\mathbf{x}}_{1\mathrm{p}}], tag(M, M_G, \overline{G}), \mathbf{X}'[\mathbf{x}^{\mathbf{x}}_{2\mathrm{p}}]) \in \delta'_{\mathrm{p}}$$

and $c_2 \mathcal{R}_{Tag} c'_2$ with $c'_1 \xrightarrow{t'} c'_2$.

Case $\mathbf{x}_{1\mathrm{p}} = M; \mathbf{x}_{2\mathrm{p}} \in G \upharpoonright \mathrm{p}$.
In this case, both interpretations do not coincide as local weaving may introduce daemons in parallel with the initial interaction. But c_1 is advice atomic, so there is no pending interaction in daemons advices, which means that $\mathbf{X}'$ is of the form $\mathbf{X}'[\mathbf{x}_{1\mathrm{p}}]$ and

$$t' = (\mathbf{X}'[\mathbf{x}_{1\mathrm{p}}], M, \mathbf{X}'[\mathbf{x}_{2\mathrm{p}}]) \in \delta'_{\mathrm{p}}$$

and $c_2 \mathcal{R}_{Tag} c'_2$ with $c'_1 \xrightarrow{t'} c'_2$.

□

6.5 Properties of locally woven MSAs

Aspectual multiparty session automata satisfy properties of Theorem 1 because they are just a particular kind of MSAs. But locally woven multiparty session automata are not proper MSAs because they may break the linearity property as they allow race conditions. In Section 6.3, we have shown that although more liberal, every configuration of a locally woven MSA can reach an advice atomic configuration that is a configuration in which all executions of advices have been done sequentially. Then, in Section 6.4, we have shown that advice atomic configurations of a locally woven MSA can be simulated by configurations of the corresponding aspectual MSA. As all properties of Theorem 1 are closed by reduction, we can directly deduce the main theorem of this paper.

Theorem 3 (Property of locally woven MSAs.). *A locally woven MSA is free from deadlock, orphan message, or reception error configurations. It satisfies the progress property, and when the global that generated it contains* end, *it satisfies the liveness property.*

7. Application: Data Parallel Programming Patterns and Mutualized Infrastructures

Data-parallel computations, notably the map-reduce paradigm, are mainly expressed in terms of the application of regular communication and computation patterns. Such computations are frequently performed using mutualized execution environments, such as private and public clouds.

Consider an interaction (Fig. 14a) where a client C may use different external services $\mathsf{S_e}$, $\mathsf{S'_e}$ depending on some internal choice.

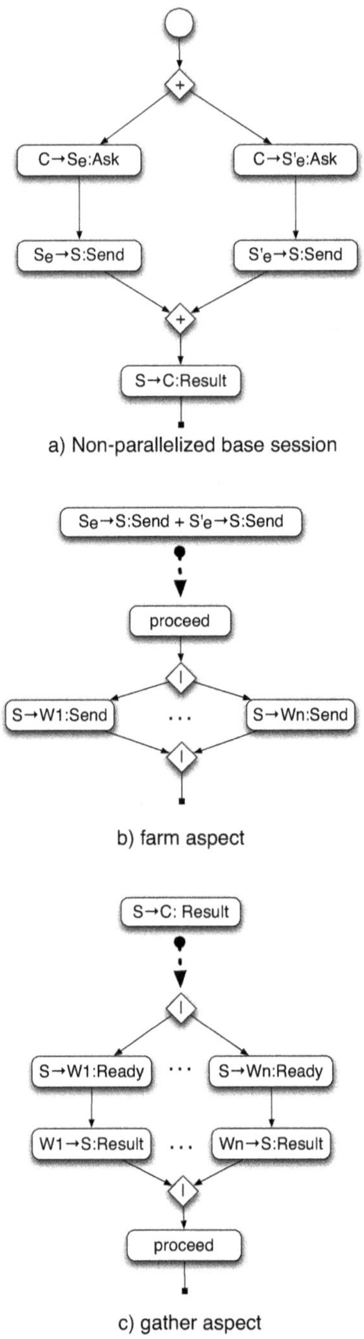

Figure 14: Managing data parallel computations

Then either of the two external service delegates the computation to the same, mutualized, service S. Finally, S sends the result to the client C. If the work can be performed by applying the same computation to small chunks of a large data set it is frequently performed in a data-parallel manner on many worker nodes. In this case, the first part of the computation (the initiation from the service S to workers Ws) can be performed using a "farm" pattern, while the second (involving the service S, the workers Ws and the client C) is termed a "gather" pattern.

Introducing such a data-parallel pattern directly in the session type greatly complicates its definition. With aspectual session types, the parallel interaction pattern is generated automatically using general-purpose aspects.

We can use the farm and gather aspect depicted in Figs 14b and c to introduce the farm/gather pattern without having to modify the base session. The farm aspect intercepts a send message to S from either the external service S_e or S'_e and transmits it to the worker nodes W1–Wn. The gather aspect intercepts the result message from S to C and informs all the worker nodes (by means of the interactions $S \rightarrow Wi$: *Ready*) and then gathers the partial results at C. Note that it is not possible to modify the gather aspect by omitting the interactions $S \rightarrow Wi$: *Ready* because the resulting gather aspect would not satisfy the aspectual local choice property. Indeed, daemons (here workers) can not initiate an advice interaction.

The naive weaving of these two aspects does not satisfy the traditional linearity condition on sessions (Section 3.3) because there are concurrent identical messages emissions on worker nodes on both branches (involving S_e or S'_e). This is because a worker node is not informed of the choice made by the client C. But with global weaving, those two branches are tagged with different names so linearity is preserved. We then need to check that concurrent invocations of a daemon worker remain separated. This is enforced by the message $S \rightarrow Wi$: *Ready* which forces the gather advice to be advice linear (Definition 3) by adding an explicit synchronization between S and Wi before the result is send.

8. Related Work

Our work is, to the best of our knowledge, the first approach investigating the benefits and limits of an integration of aspects with session types. Gay et al. [11] have presented a notion of modular session types: they aim at a seamless integration of object-oriented abstractions and the corresponding typing scheme with session types. In contrast to our work, their approach does not provide any support for the modular definition of crosscutting functionalities. Furthermore, they do not consider the extension of session types by harmless race conditions as we do.

There is also work that shares different specific features with our approach. In the following, we discuss work related to the expressivity of session types, previous application of aspects to (other) kinds of protocol, and studies on the relationship between session types and non-functional properties of interacting systems.

Expressivity of session types. Session types have been originally developed in order to precisely define typed interaction protocols between two partners [12]. Recently, their extension to multiparty protocols [8, 13] have significantly increased their expressivity. Furthermore, a kind of quantification in the form of roles has also been proposed [7]. However, none of these approaches provides the main benefits of aspectual session types: the definition of functionalities separated from a global session type in a modular way and the extension of the expressivity of session types by accepting certain interaction protocols that include race conditions.

Aspects over protocols. Several researchers have investigated the formal definition of aspects and their properties over different kinds of protocols, principally regular protocols (for instance [1, 10]). Since standard regular protocols do not obey the strong properties that session types enjoy, the integration of aspects is much simpler but may change the overall interaction structure in much less predictable ways.

There is also a significant body of work on programming extensions for protocol-like structures, notably in the context of web services and service compositions (for example [2, 6]). These approaches may modify (regular) service compositions in even more general ways and therefore do not, in general, preserve most correctness properties of the underlying protocols.

Session types and specific functionalities. Finally, some authors have explored the definition and properties over session types of functionalities that are not directly linked to the basic interaction structure. Capecchi et al. [3], for instance, have investigated security properties, notably information flow properties, over session types. Carbone et al. [4] consider the application of session types to the definition of exceptional behaviors. In contrast to our work, these approaches are specific to the functionalities they are interested in. Furthermore, they apply existing variants of session types and do not enhance their expressivity.

9. Conclusion

Session types provide clear benefits for the definition of protocol-like interactions in distributed systems, in particular, the static typability of multiparty interactions and a notion of projection that ensures the correct implementation of global interactions solely in terms of local processes.

We have proposed aspectual session types that augment the expressivity of generalized multiparty session types by allowing race conditions that are, as we show, harmless. Second, we support modular extensions of sessions, making it possible to bring the benefits of aspect orientation to the definition of distributed processes with strong communication safety properties.

As future work, we will study how to enhance quantification with wildcards on participants and dynamic conditions, and develop local aspect weaving at the level of processes.

References

[1] C. Allan, P. Avgustinov, et al. Adding trace matching with free variables to AspectJ. In Richard P. Gabriel, editor, *ACM Conference on Object-Oriented Programming, Systems and Languages (OOPSLA)*. ACM Press, 2005.

[2] F. Baligand, N. Rivierre, and T. Ledoux. A declarative approach for QoS-aware web service compositions. In *5th International Conference on Service-Oriented Computing, ICSOC 2007*, volume LNCS 4749. Springer, 2007.

[3] S. Capecchi, I. Castellani, M. Dezani-Ciancaglini, and T. Rezk. Session types for access and information flow control. In *CONCUR - Concurrency Theory, 21th International Conference*, LNCS 6269. Springer, 2010.

[4] M. Carbone, K. Honda, and N. Yoshida. Structured interactional exceptions in session types. In *CONCUR*, LNCS 5201. Springer, 2008.

[5] G. Cécé and A. Finkel. Verification of programs with half-duplex communication. *Information and Computation*, 202(2):166–190, 2005.

[6] A. Charfi and M. Mezini. Using aspects for security engineering of web service compositions. In *IEEE International Conference on Web Services, ICWS 2005*, 2005.

[7] P.-M. Deniélou and N. Yoshida. Dynamic multirole session types. In *Symposium on Principles of Programming Languages (POPL)*. ACM, 2011.

[8] P.M. Deniélou and N. Yoshida. Multiparty session types meet communicating automata. In *21st European Symposium on Programming (ESOP)*, LNCS 7211, page 194. Springer, 2012.

[9] P.M. Deniélou and N. Yoshida. Multiparty session types meet communicating automata. Technical report, Imperial College, London, 2012. http://www.doc.ic.ac.uk/ malo/msa/.

[10] R. Douence, P. Fradet, and M. Südholt. Composition, reuse and interaction analysis of stateful aspects. In *Proc. of 3rd Int. Conf. on Aspect-Oriented Software Development (AOSD)*. ACM, 2004.

[11] S. J. Gay, V. T. Vasconcelos, et al. Modular session types for distributed object-oriented programming. In *POPL'10*. ACM, 2010.

[12] K. Honda, Vasco T. Vasconcelos, and M. Kubo. Language primitives and type disciplines for structured communication-based programming. In *ESOP'98*, LNCS 1381, pages 22–38. Springer, 1998.

[13] K. Honda, N. Yoshida, and M. Carbone. Multiparty asynchronous session types. In *35th Symposium on Principles of Programming Languages (POPL)*. ACM, 2008.

$$
\begin{array}{l}
\mathbf{G}_{\text{Trade}} = \mathsf{def} \\
\quad \begin{array}{rcl}
\mathbf{x_0} & = & \mathsf{S} \rightarrow \mathsf{B}\colon \mathit{Item}\langle \mathit{string}\rangle; \mathbf{x_1} \\
\mathbf{x_1} & = & \mathbf{x_2} \mid \mathbf{x_3} \\
\mathbf{x_2} & = & \mathsf{B} \rightarrow \mathsf{S}\colon \mathit{Sale}\langle \mathit{boolean}\rangle; \mathbf{x_4} \\
\mathbf{x_3} & = & \mathsf{B} \rightarrow \mathsf{C}\colon \mathit{Purchase}\langle \mathit{boolean}\rangle; \mathbf{x_5} \\
\mathbf{x_4} \mid \mathbf{x_5} & = & \mathbf{x_6} \\
\mathbf{x_6} & = & \mathsf{end} \quad \mathsf{in}\ \mathbf{x_0}
\end{array}
\end{array}
$$

a) Global type for the trade session

$$
\begin{array}{l}
A_{\text{nego}} = \langle pc_{\text{nego}}, ad_{\text{nego}}\rangle \\
\mathit{where} \\
\quad pc_{\text{nego}} = \mathsf{S} \rightarrow \mathsf{B}\colon \mathit{Item}\langle \mathit{string}\rangle \\
\quad ad_{\text{nego}} = \mathsf{def} \\
\quad \begin{array}{rcl}
\mathbf{x_A} & = & \mathsf{proceed}; \mathbf{x_1} \\
\mathbf{x_1} + \mathbf{x_6} & = & \mathbf{x_2} \\
\mathbf{x_2} & = & \mathbf{x_3} + \mathbf{x_4} \\
\mathbf{x_3} & = & \mathsf{B} \rightarrow \mathsf{C}\colon \mathit{Offer}\langle \mathit{nat}\rangle; \mathbf{x_5} \\
\mathbf{x_5} & = & \mathsf{C} \rightarrow \mathsf{B}\colon \mathit{Counter}\langle \mathit{nat}\rangle; \mathbf{x_6} \\
\mathbf{x_4} & = & \mathsf{end} \quad \mathsf{in}\ \mathbf{x}_A
\end{array}
\end{array}
$$

b) Negotiation aspect

$$
\begin{array}{l}
A_{\text{log}} = \langle pc_{\text{log}}, ad_{\text{log}}\rangle \\
\mathit{where} \\
\quad pc_{\text{log}} = \mathsf{B} \rightarrow \mathsf{S}\colon * + \mathsf{B} \rightarrow \mathsf{C}\colon * \\
\quad ad_{\text{log}} = \mathsf{def} \\
\quad \begin{array}{rcl}
\mathbf{x_A} & = & \mathsf{proceed}; \mathbf{x_1} \\
\mathbf{x_1} & = & \mathsf{B} \rightarrow \mathsf{L}\colon \mathit{LogData}\langle \mathit{string}\rangle; \mathbf{x_2} \\
\mathbf{x_2} & = & \mathsf{end} \quad \mathsf{in}\ \mathbf{x}_A
\end{array}
\end{array}
$$

c) Logging aspect

$$
\begin{array}{l}
A_{\text{auth}} = \langle pc_{\text{auth}}, ad_{\text{auth}}\rangle \\
\mathit{where} \\
\quad pc_{\text{auth}} = \mathsf{B} \rightarrow \mathsf{S}\colon * + \mathsf{B} \rightarrow \mathsf{C}\colon * \\
\quad ad_{\text{auth}} = \mathsf{def} \\
\quad \begin{array}{rcl}
\mathbf{x_A} + \mathbf{x_5} & = & \mathbf{x_1} \\
\mathbf{x_1} & = & \mathsf{B} \rightarrow \mathsf{A}\colon \mathit{Auth}\langle \mathit{string}\rangle; \mathbf{x_2} \\
\mathbf{x_2} & = & \mathbf{x_3} + \mathbf{x_4} \\
\mathbf{x_3} & = & \mathsf{A} \rightarrow \mathsf{B}\colon \mathit{Retry}; \mathbf{x_5} \\
\mathbf{x_4} & = & \mathsf{A} \rightarrow \mathsf{B}\colon \mathit{Ok}; \mathbf{x_6} \\
\mathbf{x_6} & = & \mathsf{proceed}; \mathbf{x_7} \\
\mathbf{x_7} & = & \mathsf{end} \quad \mathsf{in}\ \mathbf{x}_A
\end{array}
\end{array}
$$

d) Authentication aspect

Figure 15: Formal definition of the trade example with aspects

A. Formal definition of the trade example

Figure 15 presents the formal definition of the trade example introduced in Section 2.

B. Formal definition of advice linearity

Figure 16 defines the uniqueness of messages. Figure 17 defines the computation of single threaded advice. Both definitions are expressed using auxiliary functions (respectively *Msg*, *STh*) that compute the result in their third argument and keep track of the protocol structure in the first two arguments. In Rule (STh-Join), the # operator denotes disjunction but is undefined when both arguments are true. This is to ensure that two branches that join can not both have an interaction with a daemon.

$$
(\text{Msg-Def})\ \frac{\begin{array}{c}\mathbf{G} = \mathsf{def}\,\overline{G}\ \mathsf{in}\ \mathbf{x} \qquad A = \langle pc, \mathsf{def}\,\overline{G_A}\ \mathsf{in}\ \mathbf{x}_A\rangle \\ \overline{G}, pc, \overline{G}_A \vdash \mathit{Msg}(\mathbf{x}_A, \varepsilon, \mathsf{M})\end{array}}{\mathbf{G}, A \vdash \mathit{UniqueMsg}}
$$

$$
(\text{Msg-Message})\ \frac{\begin{array}{c}\mathbf{x} = M; \mathbf{x}' \in \overline{G}_A \qquad M \neq \mathsf{proceed} \\ \overline{G}, pc, \overline{G}_A \vdash \mathit{Msg}(\mathbf{x}', \overline{\mathbf{x}}, \mathsf{M}')\end{array}}{\overline{G}, pc, \overline{G}_A \vdash \mathit{Msg}(\mathbf{x}, \overline{\mathbf{x}}, \{M\} \uplus \mathsf{M}')}
$$

$$
(\text{Msg-Proceed})\ \frac{\begin{array}{c}\mathbf{x} = \mathsf{proceed}; \mathbf{x}' \in \overline{G}_A \\ \overline{G}, pc, \overline{G}_A \vdash \mathit{Msg}(\mathbf{x}', \overline{\mathbf{x}}, \mathsf{M}') \\ \mathsf{M} = \{M \mid \mathbf{x} = M; \mathbf{x}' \in \overline{G} \wedge\ \mathit{match}(pc, M)\}\end{array}}{\overline{G}, pc, \overline{G}_A \vdash \mathit{Msg}(\mathbf{x}, \overline{\mathbf{x}}, \mathsf{M} \uplus \mathsf{M}')}
$$

$$
(\text{Msg-Choice})\ \frac{\begin{array}{c}\mathbf{x} = \mathbf{x}_1 + \mathbf{x}_2 \in \overline{G}_A \qquad \mathbf{x} \notin \overline{\mathbf{x}} \\ \overline{G}, pc, \overline{G}_A \vdash \mathit{Msg}(\mathbf{x}_1, \mathbf{x}\overline{\mathbf{x}}, \mathsf{M}_1) \\ \overline{G}, pc, \overline{G}_A \vdash \mathit{Msg}(\mathbf{x}_2, \mathbf{x}\overline{\mathbf{x}}, \mathsf{M}_2)\end{array}}{\overline{G}, pc, \overline{G}_A \vdash \mathit{Msg}(\mathbf{x}, \overline{\mathbf{x}}, \mathsf{M}_1 \cup \mathsf{M}_2)}
$$

$$
(\text{Msg-Fork})\ \frac{\begin{array}{c}\mathbf{x} = \mathbf{x}_1 \mid \mathbf{x}_2 \in \overline{G}_A \qquad \mathbf{x} \notin \overline{\mathbf{x}} \\ \overline{G}, pc, \overline{G}_A \vdash \mathit{Msg}(\mathbf{x}_1, \mathbf{x}\overline{\mathbf{x}}, \mathsf{M}_1) \\ \overline{G}, pc, \overline{G}_A \vdash \mathit{Msg}(\mathbf{x}_2, \mathbf{x}\overline{\mathbf{x}}, \mathsf{M}_2)\end{array}}{\overline{G}, pc, \overline{G}_A \vdash \mathit{Msg}(\mathbf{x}, \overline{\mathbf{x}}, \mathsf{M}_1 \uplus \mathsf{M}_2)}
$$

$$
(\text{Msg-Merge/Join})\ \frac{\begin{array}{c}\mathbf{x}_1 \mid \mathbf{x}_2 = \mathbf{x} \in \overline{G}_A \vee \mathbf{x}_1 + \mathbf{x}_2 = \mathbf{x} \in \overline{G}_A \\ \overline{G}, pc, \overline{G}_A \vdash \mathit{Msg}(\mathbf{x}, \overline{\mathbf{x}}, \mathsf{M})\end{array}}{\overline{G}, pc, \overline{G}_A \vdash \mathit{Msg}(\mathbf{x}_i, \overline{\mathbf{x}}, \mathsf{M}) \quad i \in \{1, 2\}}
$$

$$
(\text{Msg-Choice/Fork-Stop})\ \frac{\begin{array}{c}\mathbf{x} = \mathbf{x}_1 \mid \mathbf{x}_2 \in \overline{G}_A \vee \mathbf{x} = \mathbf{x}_1 + \mathbf{x}_2 \in \overline{G}_A \\ \mathbf{x} \in \overline{\mathbf{x}}\end{array}}{\overline{G}, pc, \overline{G}_A \vdash \mathit{Msg}(\mathbf{x}, \overline{\mathbf{x}}, \varepsilon)}
$$

$$
(\text{Msg-End})\ \frac{\mathbf{x} = \mathsf{end} \in \overline{G}_A}{\overline{G}, pc, \overline{G}_A \vdash \mathit{Msg}(\mathbf{x}, \overline{\mathbf{x}}, \varepsilon)}
$$

Figure 16: Unique messages

$$
(\text{STh-Def})\ \frac{\overline{T_A}, \mathbf{x}_A, M \vdash \mathit{STh}(\mathsf{end}, \varepsilon, b)}{\mathsf{def}\,\overline{G_A}\ \mathsf{in}\ \mathbf{x}_A, M \vdash \mathit{SgTh}(b)}
$$

$$
(\text{STh-Message})\ \frac{\mathbf{x} = ?\langle q, l\langle U\rangle\rangle; \mathbf{x}' \in \overline{T}_A \qquad \mathsf{q} \neq \mathsf{p}\ \text{or}\ \mathsf{p}'}{\overline{T_A}, \mathbf{x}_A, M \vdash \mathit{STh}(\mathbf{x}, \overline{\mathbf{x}}, \mathbb{T})}
$$

$$
(\text{STh-Message2})\ \frac{\begin{array}{c}\mathbf{x} = ?\langle q, l\langle U\rangle\rangle; \mathbf{x}' \in \overline{T}_A \qquad \mathsf{q} = \mathsf{p}\ \text{or}\ \mathsf{p}' \\ \overline{T}_A, \mathbf{x}_A, \mathsf{p} \rightarrow \mathsf{p}'\colon l\langle U\rangle \vdash \mathit{STh}(\mathbf{x}', \overline{\mathbf{x}}, b)\end{array}}{\overline{T_A}, \mathbf{x}_A, M \vdash \mathit{STh}(\mathbf{x}, \overline{\mathbf{x}}, b)}
$$

$$
(\text{STh-Merge})\ \frac{\begin{array}{c}\mathbf{x}_1 + \mathbf{x}_2 = \mathbf{x} \in \overline{T}_A \qquad \mathbf{x} \notin \overline{\mathbf{x}} \\ \overline{T_A}, \mathbf{x}_A, M \vdash \mathit{STh}(\mathbf{x}_1, \mathbf{x}\overline{\mathbf{x}}, b_1) \\ \overline{T_A}, \mathbf{x}_A, M \vdash \mathit{STh}(\mathbf{x}_2, \mathbf{x}\overline{\mathbf{x}}, b_2)\end{array}}{\overline{T_A}, \mathbf{x}_A, M \vdash \mathit{STh}(\mathbf{x}, \overline{\mathbf{x}}, b_1 \vee b_2)}
$$

$$
(\text{STh-Join})\ \frac{\begin{array}{c}\mathbf{x}_1 \mid \mathbf{x}_2 = \mathbf{x} \in \overline{T}_A \qquad \mathbf{x} \notin \overline{\mathbf{x}} \\ \overline{T_A}, \mathbf{x}_A, M \vdash \mathit{STh}(\mathbf{x}_1, \mathbf{x}\overline{\mathbf{x}}, b_1) \\ \overline{T_A}, \mathbf{x}_A, M \vdash \mathit{STh}(\mathbf{x}_2, \mathbf{x}\overline{\mathbf{x}}, b_2)\end{array}}{\overline{T_A}, \mathbf{x}_A, M \vdash \mathit{STh}(\mathbf{x}, \overline{\mathbf{x}}, b_1 \# b_2)}
$$

$$
(\text{STh-Fork/Choice})\ \frac{\begin{array}{c}\mathbf{x} = \mathbf{x}_1 \mid \mathbf{x}_2 \in \overline{T}_A \vee \mathbf{x} = \mathbf{x}_1 + \mathbf{x}_2 \in \overline{T}_A \\ \overline{T_A}, \mathbf{x}_A, M \vdash \mathit{STh}(\mathbf{x}, \overline{\mathbf{x}}, b)\end{array}}{\overline{T_A}, \mathbf{x}_A, M \vdash \mathit{STh}(\mathbf{x}_i, \overline{\mathbf{x}}, b) \quad i \in \{1, 2\}}
$$

$$
(\text{STh-Merge/Join-Stop})\ \frac{\mathbf{x}_1 \mid \mathbf{x}_2 = \mathbf{x} \in \overline{T}_A \vee \mathbf{x}_1 + \mathbf{x}_2 = \mathbf{x} \in \overline{T}_A \qquad \mathbf{x} \in \overline{\mathbf{x}}}{\overline{T_A}, \mathbf{x}_A, M \vdash \mathit{STh}(\mathbf{x}, \overline{\mathbf{x}}, \mathbb{F})}
$$

$$
(\text{STh-Init})\ \frac{}{\overline{T_A}, \mathbf{x}_A, M \vdash \mathit{STh}(\mathbf{x}_A, \overline{\mathbf{x}}, \mathbb{F})}
$$

$$
(\text{STh-End})\ \frac{\mathbf{x} = \mathsf{end} \in \overline{T}_A \qquad \overline{T_A}, \mathbf{x}_A, M \vdash \mathit{STh}(\mathbf{x}, \overline{\mathbf{x}}, b)}{\overline{T_A}, \mathbf{x}_A, M \vdash \mathit{STh}(\mathsf{end}, \overline{\mathbf{x}}, b)}
$$

Figure 17: Check for single-threadedness

JEScala: Modular Coordination with Declarative Events and Joins

Jurgen M. Van Ham[1,2] Guido Salvaneschi[1] Mira Mezini[1] Jacques Noyé[2]

[1] Software Technology Group, Technische Universität Darmstadt, Germany

[2] ASCOLA Team, Mines Nantes & Inria & LINA, Nantes, France

{vanham, salvaneschi, mezini}@informatik.tu-darmstadt.de, Jacques.Noye@mines-nantes.fr

Abstract

Advanced concurrency abstractions overcome the drawbacks of low-level techniques such as locks and monitors, freeing programmers that implement concurrent applications from the burden of concentrating on low-level details. However, with current approaches the coordination logic involved in complex coordination schemas is fragmented into several pieces including join patterns, data emissions triggered in different places of the application, and the application logic that implicitly creates dependencies among communication channels, hence indirectly among join patterns. We present JEScala, a language that captures coordination schemas in a more expressive and modular way by leveraging a seamless integration of an advanced event system with join abstractions. We validate our approach with case studies and provide a first performance assessment.

Categories and Subject Descriptors D.1.3 [*Software*]: Programming Techniques—Concurrent Programming; D.1.5 [*Software*]: Programming Techniques—Object-oriented Programming; D.3.3 [*Programming Languages*]: Language Constructs and Features

General Terms Languages

Keywords Scala; Event-driven Programming; Concurrency; Join Patterns

1. Introduction

Concurrency is required in a wide class of applications. However, writing correct concurrent software is hard. Conceptually, programmers are interested in the *coordination schemas* that an application must implement. For example, they want a *producer-consumer* model to correctly order data processing or *finite state machines* to regulate the progress of the program. Unfortunately, many synchronization primitives – like semaphores or monitors – are low-level and force programmers to focus on details – leading to error-prone code and reducing maintainability. For this reason, researchers have proposed language constructs that rise the level of abstraction and support high-level reasoning about concurrency. This includes Actors [18], Futures [1] and Join Patterns (Joins for short) [13].

MODULARITY '14, April 22–26, 2014, Lugano, Switzerland.

Copyright © 2014 ACM 978-1-4503-2772-5/14/04...$15.00.

http://dx.doi.org/10.1145/2577080.2577082

The Join Calculus [13] introduced join patterns and disjunctions thereof as key concepts for expressing the interaction among a set of processes that communicate by emitting data over communication channels. Since then these concepts have gained special attention because they combine abstraction and practicality – they are abstract enough to overcome the limitations of low-level constructs but still applicable in a wide variety of scenarios. As a result, several languages have been proposed to directly support joins (referred in the rest as *join languages*), including JoCaml [9], Join-Java [19], Polyphonic C# [2], the Join concurrency Library [33], Scala Joins [17] and JErlang [29].

In this paper, we argue that current join languages fall short with respect to capturing the whole logic of a coordination schema in a modular way due to the way they model channels and emissions. The latter are modeled either by method/function calls [2, 9, 19, 23, 26] or by explicitly triggered events [17]. In either case, the emission points need to be explicitly hardwired in the application code; in the case of method/function channels, the destination is hardwired too. As a result, the coordination logic gets fragmented into several pieces including the join patterns, different places in the application where data emission is triggered, and the application logic that implicitly creates dependencies among emissions, thus indirectly among joins. To infer the logic of a coordination schema, programmers have to *connect the dots* following the flow of the application and harvest how data emissions are related and interact. This hampers program understanding and makes programs harder to maintain and extend; since the coordination logic is not modularized, changes to the coordination schemas cannot benefit from local reasoning.

The design of the JEScala language proposed in this paper approaches this problem by exploring the synergy of Join Calculus concepts with the advanced event system of EScala [16]. The latter supports three kinds of events. In addition to explicitly triggered events, there are implicitly triggered events, referable points in the execution of the program similar to join points in aspect-oriented programming, as well as composite events that are declaratively defined by expressions correlating other events. The use of implicit events and composite events enables the modular definition of data emission sources together with the synchronization logic, capturing complex coordination schemas that would be otherwise scattered in the code base. In summary, the paper makes the following contributions:

- We motivate the need for abstractions to overcome deficiencies of current join languages regarding scattering of coordination logic.
- We present the design of JEScala, a language that exploits a seamless integration of an advanced event system with joins

processes

$P ::= 0$	empty process
$c(\tilde{d})$	emission of $\tilde{d}$ on c
$P_1 \& P_2$	parallel composition
$\texttt{def}\ D\ \texttt{in}\ P$	definition

definitions

$D ::= J \triangleright P$	reaction
$D_1 \| D_2$	disjunction

join patterns

$J ::= c(\tilde{d})$	reception of $\tilde{d}$ on c
$J_1 \& J_2$	synchronization

Figure 1. The basic constituents of the Join Calculus.

to capture coordination schemas in an expressive and modular way.

- We validate our approach with case studies that show the validity of our design and we provide a first performance assessment. The implementation of the language, the examples, and validation code are available in [20].

The paper is organized as follows. Section 2 motivates the work. Section 3 presents the design of JEScala and Section 4 key elements of its implementation. Section 5 validates the approach. Section 6 discusses related work. Section 7 summarizes the paper and outlines areas of future work.

2. Motivation

2.1 Basic Concepts of Join Languages

The Join Calculus The foundation for join languages is laid down by the Join Calculus [13, 21]. In its basic form [21] (see Figure 1), the calculus includes three kinds of constructs: *processes*, *definitions* and *join patterns*. Processes are the primary structuring entities. They communicate through asynchronous emissions of tuples of data across *channels*. In addition to emissions, processes are built from definitions and parallel compositions of other processes. An elementary definition, called *reaction*, associates a new process to a *join pattern*. A join pattern can be elementary or composite. An elementary pattern is simply a reception of a tuple, whereas a composite pattern synchronizes several receptions from different channels. A join pattern is *active* if there is data present on all referenced channels. In its general form, a definition is a *disjunction* of *reactions*, where a reaction associates a new process to a join pattern. A disjunction defines competing reactions. Here, the same channel may appear in different reactions. When several reactions are active, one of the reactions is chosen and the corresponding process spawned.

This basic calculus can be extended with, in particular, sequential composition of instructions and synchronous communications, using an implicit continuation channel to wait for a reply, getting back to the initial calculus of [13]. A fundamental property of the calculus, which makes it a practical foundation for concurrent and distributed programming languages, is that interprocess communication does not require global, distributed synchronization. Also, the join operator `&` turns out to be very expressive, combining atomically interprocess communication and synchronization.

Join Languages Channels can be implemented in various ways. In a functional setting, e.g., in JoCaml [9, 23] or Funnel [26], an elementary channel definition looks like a function definition and an emission like a function call. In an object-oriented setting, e.g., in Polyphonic C# [2] or Join Java [19], functions are replaced by methods. Reactions can then be seen as defining several functions or methods at once with a single shared body (a process in the calculus). In Scala Joins [17], method headers are replaced by *events*, objects of type `Event` that can then be used to build join patterns, associated to a body via a case clause. A case clause plays the same role as a multi-header method in Polyphonic C#. As in Polyphonic C#, an emission looks like a method invocation.

Disjunctions can take various forms. For instance, in JoCaml, Funnel and Scala Joins disjunctions are explicitly defined. In Polyphonic C#, disjunctions are implicit: If several reactions are defined in a class, they form a disjunction.

Concurrency In the following, we will focus on object-oriented languages and consider threads as the underlying support of concurrency, a choice shared by most object-oriented join languages. The concepts of the join calculus have also been combined with actors in JErlang [29], not an OO language, and Scala Joins (in Scala, threads and actors coexist).

In such join languages, writing concurrent programs does not require direct manipulation of threads any longer. Threads are implicitly created through asynchronous data emission or the use of parallel composition.

Depending on the language, all data emissions not returning any result are handled asynchronously, or the emissions have to be explicitly declared as asynchronous. This is in general done on the receiver's side. For instance, in Polyphonic C#, method headers can be qualified with the keyword `async`. In Scala Joins, this is a matter of defining an event as an instance of `AsyncEvent` (a subclass of `Event`) rather than `SyncEvent`. Whereas asynchronicity is useful for creating concurrency, synchronicity is useful when a result has to be returned. It is also useful for synchronization purposes: a thread can be blocked on data emission, waiting for a join pattern to be selected or, in other words, waiting for the complementary data receptions. As a result, join patterns can then be used both to synchronize threads and communicate between threads.

2.2 Limitation of Join Languages by Example

In this section, we discuss deficiencies in the design of applications that use existing join languages by means of a case study. In order to ease comparisons, we use a hypothetical language as a typical join language. We call it Polyphonic Scala as it relies on the syntax and semantics of Scala while implementing joins à la Polyphonic C#.

Case Study Our case study is a Web server that hosts two applications, an online booking application for flight tickets `OB` and a marketplace application `MP`[1] (Figure 2a). In both applications, client requests are managed by `handle` methods (Lines 3 and 10). Since the Web server shares the host with other services, we want to ensure that all services are responsive in the presence of a high number of requests. To do so, when the load is high, we limit the number of concurrently handled requests by controlling the execution frequency of `handle` methods[2]. This requires a coordination schema among the threads executing the components of Figure 2a.

Specifically, under high load, clients need to consume a token to be admitted into the server. When the load is high, client threads should block at the boundary of the `handle` method of each application, waiting for a token to be produced by the Token Generator (Line 16 in Figure 2a).

[1] In Scala, the keyword `object` introduces singleton classes.

[2] As in real Web servers, we assume that client connections not timely routed to applications are dropped after a timeout by the Web container.

```
1  object CL { // Coordination Logic
2    def OB_beforeHandle() { mayBlock() }
3    def MP_beforeHandle() { mayBlock() }
4    def mayBlock() {
5      if (systemLoadHigh())
6        RL.block()
7    }
8    def unblock() { RL.unblock() }
9  }
10
11 object RL { // Rate Limiter as 2-state Free-Busy FSM
12   def block():Unit & free():async {
13     // Stat.toBusy() // future extension
14     busy()
15   }
16   def unblock():async & busy():async {
17     // Stat.toFree() // future extension
18     free() // busy to free
19   }
20   def unblock():async & free():async {
21     // Stat.toFree() //future extension
22     free() // absorbed unblock
23   }
24   free() // initial state in constructor
25 }
```

(a)

```
1  object CL { // Coordination Logic
2    evt block = (OB.beforeSync(handle) || MP.beforeSync(handle)) &&
3                systemLoadHigh()
4    evt unblock = TG.beforeAsync(createToken)
5  }
6
7  object RL { // Rate Limiter as 2-state Free-Busy FSM
8    imperative async evt free[Unit], busy[Unit]
9    evt (toBusy, freed, absorbed) =
10     ( CL.block  & free
11     | CL.unblock & busy
12     | CL.unblock & free )
13   evt toFree = freed || absorbed
14   toBusy += ((arg:Any)=>busy())
15   toFree += ((arg:Any)=>free())
16   free() // initial state
17 }
```

(b)

Figure 4. Coordination logic with Polyphonic Scala (a) and JEScala (b).

```
1  // OnlineBooking App
2  object OB { //
3    def handle(...) = {
4      ...
5    }
6  }
7
8  // MarketPlace App
9  object MP {
10   def handle(...) = {
11     ...
12   }
13 }
14
15 // Token Generator
16 object TG extends Thread {
17   def createToken() = {
18     ...
19   }
20   override def run = {
21     while(true) {
22       sleep(1000)
23       createToken()
24     }
25   }
26 }
```

```
1  // OnlineBooking App
2  object OB {
3    def handle(...) = {
4      CL.OB_beforeHandle()
5      ...
6    }
7  }
8  // MarketPlace App
9  object MP {
10   def handle(...) = {
11     CL.MP_beforeHandle()
12     ...
13   }
14 }
15 // Token Generator
16 object TG extends Thread{
17   def createToken() = {
18     CL.unblock()
19     ...
20   }
21   ...
22 }
```

(a)   (b)

Figure 2. Web server: basic components (a) and instrumented components (b).

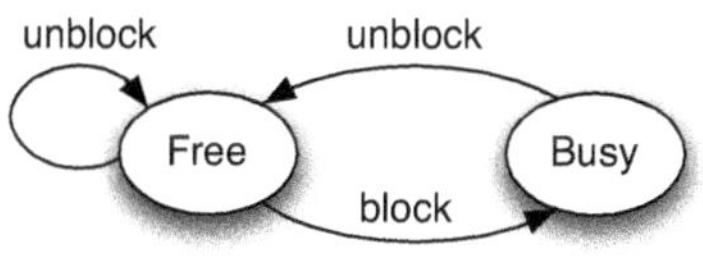

Figure 3. Rate limitation as a state machine

Instrumentation In order to be controlled by the coordination logic (implemented by the object CL in Figure 4a), the basic components of Figure 2a are instrumented as shown in Figure 2b.

The beforeHandle methods are called (Lines 4, 11) in the bodies of the handle methods to notify the coordination logic of the arrival of a new request to *one of* the applications. By calling a dedicated method of the coordination logic for each application, the coordination logic can be changed without requiring further changes to the web applications.

Similarly, the availability of new tokens is notified to the coordination logic by calling the unblock method each time a new token is about to be generated (Line 18).

Coordination Logic The top level of the coordination logic is implemented by the object CL (Lines 1–9 of Figure 4a), which turns the notifications from the basic components into calls to the object RL implementing rate limitation (Lines 11–25). Essentially, the calls from the web applications return immediately when the load is low, allowing the requests to be handled. They are turned into calls to the block method of the rate limiter otherwise. The calls to unblock are just forwarded to the rate limiter.

The role of the rate limiter is to delay returning from invocations to block until a token is available, that is, until an invocation to unblock occurs. We can represent the interaction between block and unblock calls as a state machine (Figure 3). When the rate limiter is in state Free (there is no application waiting for handling a request), calls to unblock are simply ignored, while calls to block switch the state to Busy (there is an application waiting). Then, a call to unblock brings back the rate limiter to state Free.

A common technique in join languages (see, for instance, [2, 17, 23]) represents states as pending data receptions. We apply it, with synchronous and asynchronous method calls, to the aforementioned state machine (see Figure 4a). A simple invariant underlies the technique: in the object implementing the state machine, there is always one single pending asynchronous method call. This pending call represents the current state. We refer to the corresponding methods (free and busy in our example) as *state methods*. The actions responsible for state transitions can be implemented by either synchronous or asynchronous method calls. We refer to these methods (`block` and `unblock`) as *action methods*. Each transition is implemented as a binary pattern between a state method and an action method (Lines 12, 16 and 20). The body executed when matching this pattern calls a state method. This maintains the invariant. The invariant is established when initializing the object by calling the state method for the initial state (`free`, Line 24). Note that a single pending call of a state method implies that the machine can handle only a single action at a time, the next action can only take place after the body has called a new state method.

Whereas the `unblock` method headers (Lines 16 and 20) are also declared as asynchronous in order not to block the token generator, calls to `block` are synchronous. The join pattern on Line 12 blocks the underlying thread until the state is free.

Discussion Even if the coordination schema is simple, its realization in Figure 4a has limitations.

First, the components to be coordinated are intrusively modified to add the notifications (Lines 4, 11, and 18 of Figure 2b) necessary to make observable the points in the execution that are relevant to the coordination schema. Further modifications may have to be considered, both in the application components and the coordination logic for further extensions. For instance, we will consider in Section 3.4 adding a component `Stat`, which will require the modifications commented out on Lines 13, 17 and 21.

Second, several indirections are needed: one to deal with requests to *any of* the applications (Lines 2 and 3 of Figure 4a) and another to take the load condition into account (Line 5). In the first case, the indirection implements a "union" semantics, which is not explicit in the code. Alternatively, the indirection can be suppressed by directly calling `mayBlock` within the applications. Yet, the cure is worse than the disease. In Figure 2b, the applications call distinct `beforeHandle` methods and the union of these calls is properly modularized within the coordination schema. Calling `mayBlock` directly from the applications would move part of the coordination logic (a call from *either* `OB` *or* `MP`) away from the coordination schema, and hardcode it into the coordinated components. As a result, it would be, for instance, impossible to implement a balancing strategy between `OB` and `MP` just by modifying the coordination code.

In summary, with only the abstractions from the join calculus, the logic of the coordination schema is hardly captured by the abstractions of the language. Instead, it must be harvested from the calls inserted within the coordinated components in order to capture the events of interest and the logic of corresponding (possibly multi-header) bodies in the coordination code. In addition, the application is not extensible and requires invasive changes to introduce new components.

3. A Rich Event System to the Rescue

3.1 On Events, Implicit Invocation and Joins

The requirements for both being able to capture and combine program execution points is, of course, highly reminiscent of the join points and pointcuts of Aspect-Oriented Programming (AOP). AOP would indeed make it possible to capture in a pointcut, in a non-intrusive way, the fact that a request is about to take place. It also makes it possible to combine such pointcuts in order to deal with several kinds of requests under a specific condition, namely the fact that the load is high. Unsurprisingly, assuming the availability of AOP facilities within Polyphonic Scala would improve the implementation of our case study.

Still, some discrepancy would remain between the composition of join points via pointcuts using logical operators and the composition of channel endpoints via the join operator. Our previous work on ECaesarJ [25] and EScala [16], which did not provide any support for concurrency, suggests a way to eliminate this discrepancy. The main idea behind this previous work is that the join points of AOP and the explicit triggering of events encountered in event-driven programming are of the same nature. A join point can be seen as an occurrence of an *implicit event* whereas an *explicit event* is explicitly triggered. Composite events can then be created by composing events through logical operators. The basic idea to solve our discrepancy issue is therefore twofold:

- Let us consider a data emission as triggering an explicit event.
- Let us consider the join operator as an additional composition operator.

Of course, this is not enough to get (implicit) concurrency: we also need a way to choose between synchronous and asynchronous event triggering, i.e. between sequentially proceeding with event handling or forking a new thread to deal with it.

All these ideas have been injected into EScala, leading to JEScala, described in detail in the next section. Using JEScala, our case study can be rewritten as shown in Figure 4b without the limitations previously discussed.

But, before presenting JEScala, let us first clarify what we mean by *event*. Indeed, this term can be confusing as, beyond the general idea that an event refers to a noteworthy state change, the semantics of event constructs varies a lot. In particular, the events of Scala Joins and the explicit events of (J)EScala share some common characteristics: they are instance members and triggered using method-call syntax. In both cases, events make it possible to split the traditional way methods are defined: the *event* itself corresponds to a method header and its *event handler* to a method body. In Scala Joins, these two parts have to be defined in the same class in order to be bound. This is quite different in (J)EScala where they can be defined in different classes and bound to each other in yet another class. There may also be different bindings, hence different handlers attached to the same event, resulting in some form of implicit invocation [15]. Hence, unlike languages that model channels with functions/methods, data is not sent to a single destination but to multiple destinations, i.e., triggering an event corresponds to an emission on multiple channels.

Implicit invocation is central to our event model. It exchanges the rigid connection between a sender and its single receiver for a flexible broadcast mechanism. Without modifying the sender, the group of receivers can be changed. Implicit invocation makes no assumption on the number of receivers. Therefore, it does not require to create dependencies that are not actually needed (e.g. a tracer can be detached). Receivers can be added and removed at runtime.

3.2 Basic Concepts of JEScala

JEScala combines asynchronous channels of join languages with implicit invocation of event systems. In addition to explicitly triggered events, JEScala supports EScala's implicit and composite events. However, unlike EScala's events, which are triggered only synchronously, in JEScala events are subject to both synchronous or asynchronous execution.

3.2.1 Asynchronous Events with Implicit Invocation

In the following, we present the event system of JEScala. For reference, the syntax of JEScala that is relevant for the discussion is given in Figure 5. JEScala inherits the event system of EScala, while extending it with asynchronous execution semantics. Yet, the extension is designed to ensure backward compatibility with EScala.

Imperative events In JEScala, the declaration of each explicitly triggered event begins with the keyword `imperative`, followed by an optional `sync` or `async` modifier. Hence, the programmer specifies whether an imperative event is handled synchronously or asynchronously at the declaration point of the event. Synchronicity is part of the interface of the entity declaring the event, documenting the fact that handlers may block or not the execution of the code that triggers the event. This does not, however, prevent a handler attached to a synchronous event to spawn a new computation via, for instance, the use of a Scala future or by triggering an asynchronous event.

For compatibility with EScala, if the synchronicity of events is not explicitly specified, they are assumed to be synchronous. As a result, each EScala program is a valid JEScala program with the same semantics.

Implicit events Implicit events make method executions observable a.k.a. join points in AOP parlance. EScala provides the implicit events `before(`*method-name*`)` and `after(`*method-name*`)` that are executed when a method enters – respectively, finishes – its execution[3]. We extended EScala's implicit events to account for synchronicity. In JEScala four implicit events are available: `beforeSync`, `beforeAsync`, `afterSync` and `afterAsync`. They all take a method name as argument. In the spirit of remaining compatible with EScala, the events `before(`*method-name*`)` and `after(`*method-name*`)` are still valid and mapped to the corresponding synchronous events.

Declarative events Like EScala, JEScala also supports declarative events defined in terms of event expressions. They are defined by composing other events through operators, like in e_1`||`e_2 (occurrence of one among e_1 or e_2), e_1`&&`p (e_1 occurs and the predicate p is satisfied[4]), e_1`.map(`f`)` (the event obtained by applying f to e_1). Declarative events have no synchronicity by themselves. Instead, they inherit the synchronicity of the event that triggers them. For example, the event e_1`&&`p is executed synchronously – respectively asynchronously – if e_1 is synchronous – respectively asynchronous. Note that there is no ambiguity, since the `||` composite event is triggered by one event only and inherits the synchronicity of that event.

This design choice requires more explanation. Providing a `sync/async` modifier for declarative events would make it possible to express event combinations like:

```
imperative async evt e1
sync evt e2 = e1 && (predicate)
```

whose semantics is unclear. The imperative event `e1` is asynchronous, so one expects that all the handlers bound (even indirectly) to the event are executed asynchronously. However `e2`, which depends on `e1`, is declared synchronous. This should imply that handlers attached to `e2` are executed immediately, which contradicts the modifier of `e1`. For this reason we decided to avoid explicit synchronicity for declarative events and let them inherit the synchronicity of the event that triggers them.

It still makes sense to force a declarative event to be asynchronous. To this aim, the prefix `!!` operator converts a possibly synchronous event expression into an asynchronous one.

Abstract events In EScala, it is possible to declare *abstract* events that are defined in concrete subclasses. In JEScala, the synchronicity of abstract events is not specified.

This design decision is motivated by the fact that an abstract event can be overridden by either a primitive or a composite event. Allowing synchronicity modifiers in abstract events would, for instance, allow one to define an abstract `sync` event and override

[3] Unlike most AOP languages, only methods declared in the interface of a class as such are observable outside the class.

[4] This filter operator is overloaded with the logical and operator. This is questionable and may change in future versions.

```
event-decl ::= prim-event | decl-event
prim-event ::= imperative [sync-modifier] evt event-name
decl-event ::= evt event-name = event-express
      | evt (event-name { , event-name}+ ) =
          (join-express { | join-express}+ )
event-express ::= [ obj-ref . ] event-name
      | event-prefix-operator event-express
      | event-express event-infix-operator event-express
      | event-express fun-operator fun
      | implicit-event
implicit-event ::= [ obj-ref . ] implicit-selector ( method-name )
implicit-selector ::= beforeSync | afterSync
      | beforeAsync | afterAsync
      | before | after
sync-modifier ::= sync | async

event-prefix-operator ::= !!
event-infix-operator ::= || | & | ...
fun-operator ::= map | && | ...
join-express ::= ( event-name { & event-name }+ )
```

Figure 5. The syntax of JEScala.

it in a subclass with a declarative event – running into the trouble previously described.

Actually, the synchronicity of an abstract event cannot be known until it has been defined. Defined as a primitive event, its synchronicity is known statically. Defined as a composite event, its synchronicity may not be known until runtime, depending on its definition and its evaluation.

3.2.2 Joins on Implicit and Declarative Events

As already mentioned, the key feature of JEScala is the combination of the rich event system described above with join concepts. This combination enables a succinct and well-localized definition of synchronization logic. For illustration, Figure 4b shows the implementation of the Web server example by using joins with implicit and declarative events.

The execution of `handle` in `OB` and `MP` is captured by the implicit events `OB.beforeSync(handle)` and `MP.beforeSync(handle)`, which are composed so that the declarative event `block` (Line 2) only fires when the load is high. The implicit event `TG.beforeAsync(createToken)` that captures the creation of a token is aliased to `unblock` (Line 4).

Finally, the state machine from Figure 3 is implemented as described in Section 2.2, except that state and action methods are replaced by *state* and *action events*: `free` and `busy` (declared Line 8), and `block` and `unblock` (defined in `CL` Lines 2 and 4). The implicit disjunction of Figure 4a is replaced by an explicit one (Line 9). Each alternative combines a state and an action event and triggers one of the events `toBusy`, `freed` or `absorbed` when it matches. These new events are necessary to attach a handler to each alternative and have the advantage that sharing can be made explicit, here by defining the event `toFree` that signals a transition to the `Free` state. Triggering the `free` event (Line 16) sets the initial state of the machine.

The implementation in Figure 4b has several design advantages compared to that in Figure 4a. The coordination logic is captured in one place (lines 2 – 17). There is no footprint of the coordination logic in the components to coordinate; all the execution points relevant to coordination are captured by implicit events. As a result, the coordination logic is properly modularized. and expressed declaratively, improving clarity and extensibility, e.g., the balancing strategy is clearly captured at Line 2 thanks to event expressions. Moreover, introducing an additional application in the coordination schema is e.g., as straightforward as adding a new im-

```
1  object CL {
2    evt blockOB = OB.beforeSync(handle)
3    evt blockMP = MP.beforeSync(handle)
4    evt unblock = TG.beforeAsync(createToken) map (()=>currentTime)
5  }
6  object RL {
7    imperative sync evt requestUnblockOB[Unit], requestUnblockMP[Unit]
8    imperative sync evt innerBlockOB[Unit], innerBlockMP[Unit]
9
10   CL.blockOB += ()=>{ requestUnblockOB(); innerBlockOB() }
11   CL.blockMP += ()=>{ requestUnblockMP(); innerBlockMP() }
12
13   evt _ = innerBlockOB & grantUnblockOB
14   evt _ = innerBlockMP & grantUnblockMP
15
16   evt (mayUnblockOB, mayUnblockMP) =
17       (requestUnblockOB & CL.unblock) |
18       (requestUnblockMP & CL.unblock)
19
20   evt grantUnblockOB = mayUnblockOB   && ((ts)=> !isExpired(ts))
21   evt expiredUnblockOB = mayUnblockOB && ((ts)=> isExpired(ts))
22   expiredUnblockOB += ()=>requestUnblockOB()
23
24   evt grantUnblockMP = mayUnblockMP   && ((ts)=> !isExpired(ts))
25   evt expiredUnblockMP = mayUnblockMP && ((ts)=> isExpired(ts))
26   expiredUnblockMP += ()=>requestUnblockMP()
27 }
```

Figure 6. Distributing load among Web applications in JEScala.

plicit event in Line 2. Given that events are values, the coordination schema can be a separate reusable component parameterized by events to coordinate. For the sake of simplicity, we have used singleton classes in our example. A more realistic implementation of the rate limiter would use a class with a primary constructor taking a `block` and an `unblock` event as parameters.

3.3 Advanced Use of Disjunctions

To introduce more abstractions of JEScala we extend the Web server example. So far, `OB` and `MP` clients have been served indistinctly. As a result, a high request rate in one application can significantly slow down the other. To address this issue, we shall introduce load distribution between `OB` and `MP`. Furthermore, we shall improve token generation to avoid that tokens accumulate when they are generated at a higher frequency than client arrivals – in the new version of the Web server, tokens simply expire after some time. The implementation of the extended Web server is shown in Figure 6. Instead of immediately discarding surplus `unblock` events by a state machine (Figure 3), this extension accumulates `unblock` events, which are consumed without effect after they expire. Since the example is not trivial, we start with a high-level description of the coordination schema. On arrival (exposed by events in Lines 2–3), each client is blocked until unblocking is granted (Lines 13–14). If two requests from different applications are performed, only one is chosen non-deterministically (Lines 16–18). The authorization to proceed is given only by not expired tokens. Token expiration is managed in Lines 20–26.

For a detailed description of the coordination schema of Figure 6, consider the flow of the events associated to `OB` (the event flow for `MP` is similar). When a client request for `OB` arrives, `blockOB` is synchronously triggered (Line 2). Its handler (Line 10) triggers `requestUnblockOB` and is blocked in the disjunction Line 17, waiting for an `unblock` event. The `unblock` events are generated by attaching a timestamp to events produced by the token generator (Line 4). When the disjunction pattern is selected, triggering a `mayUnblockOB` event, the handler proceeds but blocks at once on triggering the `innerBlockOB` event, involved in the disjunction Line 16. Concurrently, depending on whether the token is expired or not, either a `grantUnblockOB` event is triggered (Line 20) releasing the `blockOB` handler waiting at the disjunction Line 13 or a `requestUnblockOB` event is regenerated (Line 22) and the handler remains blocked at the disjunction Line 17. In the first case, the `blockOB` handler returns at once and the application can proceed.

The example in Figure 6 demonstrates several aspects of the design of JEScala.

Disjunctions consume and fire events Like in other join languages, disjunctions can be used to compose multiple conceptually-related join patterns; multiple join patterns in a disjunction can share an event (see e.g., Lines 13–14), consumed by the first matching pattern. If multiple patterns match, the one that fires is chosen non-deterministically. In JEScala, *disjunctions fire events*; it is possible to distinguish the join that fires by associating a specific event to each join in the disjunction (see e.g., Line 16). In other join languages when a join matches, a handler is executed. The model of JEScala is homogeneous: events generated by a disjunction can be freely composed with other events. For example, a union operator `||` can be used to merge the events from the same disjunction, if we do not need to distinguish among them. The same effect can be achieved in other join languages only by triggering the same emission from each handler registered to a join, which unnecessarily resorts to imperative code and bloats the coordination logic.

Multiple disjunctions inside the same class The example in Figure 6 shows another feature of JEScala. Many join languages group all join patterns defined in an object into a single *implicit* disjunction associated to the object. In JEScala, each disjunction *explicitly* defines a set of joins that are checked for a possible match. Therefore, JEScala allows one to define *multiple disjunctions inside the same class*. This fosters modularity. In case of complex coordination schemas, like in Figure 6, several disjunctions are required, with some of them (Lines 13-14) reduced to a single alternative.

In languages with implicit disjunctions, we would need both to create an artificial disjunction with two alternatives composing the two disjunctions with a single alternative (if we want to keep them in the same class) and split the coordination patterns into at least two separate classes in order to also implement the second disjunction (Line 16). In JEScala, disjunctions that logically belong to the same schema can be properly modularized inside the same class.

Supporting multiple disjunctions also affects the interaction between join abstractions and object-oriented inheritance. Consider the case in which the superclass defines a join pattern among events a, b, c, and d. If a developer adds a join on events a and b in a subclass, and the patterns of a class are implicitly correlated by a disjunction the join in the superclass may never trigger. The interaction between inheritance and join operators is subtle and can easily lead to deadlocks, e.g., in case c and d are synchronous events (the interested reader is referred to [2] for a detailed discussion). To tackle these issues, object-oriented join languages impose limitations on inheritance to prevent adding new joins in subclasses. In JoinJava, only final classes can define a join; in Polyphonic C# it is possible to override an inherited disjunction by replacing the associated handler, but it is not possible to add a join. Since in JEScala joins defined within a class are not implicitly correlated into a disjunction, classes can be freely extended regardless of the presence of disjunctions. Yet, advised by the lesson of existing join languages, we forbid breaking existing disjunctions by extending them with new joins. In our design, subclasses can only entirely override them.

3.4 Dynamic Registration of Handlers

While, in existing join languages, handlers are statically bound to join patterns, handlers in JEScala can be dynamically (un)registered. Figure 7 shows an extension of the Web server from Figure 4b that computes statistics about the queuing time of the

```
1  object Stat {  // Statistics
2    var sTime:timeStamp=null
3    def hdlToBusy:Unit={ // handler
4      sTime=currentTime  }
5    def hdlToFree:Unit=if (sTime!=null) {
6      log_busy(currentTime-sTime)
7      sTime=null  }
8
9    var isEnabled: Boolean = false
10   imperative sync evt enable[Unit]  // trigger to enable
11   imperative sync evt disable[Unit] // trigger to disable
12   evt doEnable = enable && ()=>!isEnabled // enable only once
13   evt doDisable = disable && ()=>isEnabled
14   // register an anonymous handler with doEnable event
15   doEnable  += ()=>{
16     isEnable=true
17     RL.toBusy += hdlToBusy _ // register with RL.toBusy event
18     RL.toFree += hdlToFree _  }
19   doDisable += ()=>{
20     RL.toBusy -= hdlToBusy _ // unregister
21     RL.toFree -= hdlToFree _
22     isEnabled = false  }
23 }
```

Figure 7. Dynamic handler registration in JEScala.

applications inside the server. Logging the time spent by the rate limiter (RL) in the busy state requires the observation of entering the states `Free` and `Busy` in the rate limiter. We prepared the code in Figure 4a by inserting explicit method calls into the `RL` component (Lines 13, 17 and 21). In JEScala, we just need to register additional handlers (Line 17) with the exposed events `toFree` and `toBusy` of RL without modifying the code of RL (Figure 4b). By using the declarative event `toFree` we can register each of our handlers with a single event with a descriptive name.

Triggering the `enable` event registers the handlers `toBusy` and `toFree`. Since we are not all the time interested in these statistics, triggering the `disable` event removes the handlers. The internal declarative events `doEnable` and `doDisable` prevent incorrect double registrations. The anonymous handler of `doEnable` registers the handlers from `Stat` with the exposed events from RL. Its counterpart for `doDisable` unregisters them. It also sets the `isEnabled` flag that is used by the filters defining `doEnable` and `doDisable`. An implementation in Polyphonic Scala, without declarative events, would need additional conditions in the methods `toBusy` and `toFree` to enable and disable statistics at runtime.

In other join languages, dynamic binding between join patterns and handlers can be obtained only by adding a layer of indirection with an intermediate handler that is responsible for notifying the right handler in case a certain condition is met. This approach has the drawback of moving the event logic from high-level operations among events to handlers. Further, it introduces a performance penalty, because the intermediate handler is *always* notified regardless of whether a reaction is needed. More importantly, this solution does not account for situations where the binding depends on the execution. JEScala solves these issues thanks to the uniform representation of join pattern outputs as events and dynamic event handler registration.

4. Implementation

The implementation of JEScala[5] required us to modify the EScala event system to support joins and asynchronous events. Before describing how these were implemented, we briefly summarize the mechanism behind the EScala event system [16].

[5] In its current version, this implementation is provided as a library, to be completed with compiler support, as was done for EScala, when a stable version of the new Scala compiler (2.11) is available.

EScala Event Propagation System in a Nutshell Internally, EScala events are organized in a graph. The graph is incrementally updated every time an event definition is executed by introducing a node for the newly defined event. Handlers are directly attached to each event node. Edges in the graph model dependencies between events. For example, the event `e3 = e1 || e2` creates a new node for `e3` that depends on the nodes previously created for `e1` and `e2`. Imperative events and implicit events (i.e. primitive events) are leaves in the graph since they are triggered directly. When a leaf event is triggered, the handlers to execute are collected. This process consists of a depth-first tree traversal of all nodes that are transitively reachable from the firing node, collecting the handlers associated to each visited node. Also, the process takes into account dynamic conditions introduced by event expressions. For example, a `filter` node can stop the evaluation along a branch if the condition is not satisfied. Finally, the collected handlers are executed in sequence. As an optimization, nodes are only *deployed* (i.e. take part to event triggering) if they have outgoing edges or handlers. Once deployed, they can be undeployed if the condition becomes false. This applies, for instance, to the `Stat` component of Figure 7.

Adding Asynchronous Event Handling In JEScala, collecting handlers applies to both synchronous and asynchronous primitive events. Differently from EScala, when the triggered event is asynchronous, a new thread is used to execute the collected set of handlers. As a result, the continuation of the code that triggers the event, and the handlers, can run concurrently. This also means that several collections may be active concurrently on the same graph, which requires us to make the process thread-safe. In particular, each new thread has access to its own buffer to collect handlers. Dynamic handler registration also requires that the handlers associated to an event are protected against concurrent accesses.

Handling disjunctions Disjunctions are implemented as sets of queues $q_1 ... q_n$, a queue q_i for each event e_i that appears in a pattern of the disjunction. When an event e_i is fired, it is stored with its arguments in the queue q_i and we check if a pattern can be completed with the new event. If none of the patterns can be completed, e_i remains in q_i. If a single pattern matches, the associated events are removed from the queue and the resulting event is fired. If multiple patterns match, one is chosen non deterministically and the associated events are removed.

Synchronous events that appear in a disjunction require a few additional steps. If the event is fired and none of the patterns applies, not only do we store the arguments, but we also block the thread and store it in the queue. Afterwards, when the pattern matches, one of the stored threads is chosen to execute the handlers of the resulting event (to be deterministic we select the thread of the first synchronous event in the pattern). To achieve a form of fairness, we randomly select among the patterns that can match when an event arrives.

The queues are new nodes in the event graph. By default, when a queue node is encountered during the collection step, queuing is not handled at once but postponed to handler execution by creating a new handler responsible for this queuing task. This is necessary so that synchronous events do not block the collection step.

Optimizations We applied a number of optimizations to increase the efficiency of asynchronous events. *Thread pool* (1) Asynchronous events need a thread to execute the handlers concurrently with the thread that triggers the event. Instead of creating a new thread every time, we recycle the thread from a thread pool. In case a number of handlers of asynchronous events are executed in parallel, no more threads are available, and some handlers may be delayed. Note, however, that this does not violate the semantics of asynchronous events, since the handler is still executed concurrently to the continuation of the caller. *Disj Only* (2) When an asynchronous event is fired and only propagated to disjunctions, enqueuing does not require a dedicated handler and can be part of the collection step. This optimization avoids the use of a separate thread for enqueuing. *Counters* (3) Event arguments are stored in the associated queue of a disjunction. However, if the event has no arguments, keeping a counter of the event occurrences is sufficient. Since synchronous events need to store the blocked threads anyway, a queue is still required, so the optimization is only applicable to asynchronous events. Note that in JEScala the synchronicity of an event cannot be determined statically. We apply the optimization when the event is trivially known to be asynchronous (it is a synchronous primitive event or the result of an event expression prefixed by the `!!` operator). Static analysis could be used to broaden the applicability of the optimization.

5. Evaluation

This section demonstrates the design advantages of JEScala in several small case studies and provides a preliminary performance evaluation. The code used for the evaluation is available online [20].

5.1 Qualitative Evaluation

We use several small case studies instead of a single larger one for two reasons. First, with several *synthetic* examples we can challenge JEScala with intentionally complex coordination schemas, while a *real* application would be probably less compelling from a coordination standpoint. Second, a larger example would dilute the coordination schema with the application logic. On the contrary, our studies distillate the essence of a coordination schema and sharpen the effects that we want to observe.

The case studies (Figure 8 Col. 1) include classic concurrency patterns (e.g., critical section, producer-consumer, actors), simulations that require coordination across several components (e.g., cellular automaton, binary adder, virus spreading over a complex network), and the Web server running example. Case studies also include client code that stresses the implemented features, e.g., threads accessing a critical section. The 2nd and 3rd columns in the figure report the number of threads and the number of components (classes and Scala objects) for each case study. We implemented each case study in JEScala and a subset JL (for Join Language) of JEScala excluding its specific features. JL programs are direct encodings of Polyphonic Scala programs (see Section 2) in JEScala.

For each implementation we measured the following metrics: lines of code ignoring comments and white spaces measured by CLOC[6], number of events, number of handlers and number of imperatively triggered events. To test the effect of different concurrency solutions, some case studies are implemented in both a single-threaded and a multithreaded version – marked with ST, respectively MT in the table. The need for coordination in a single-threaded context is not a contradiction, since a single thread must be "scheduled" to accomplish several tasks in a coordinated way. The variability between the ST and the MT versions does not affect our results significantly.

Based on the numbers reported in Figure 8, we make the following observations. Petri Nets and Parallel Graph Exploration use handlers to represent transitions, therefore we do not expect many differences between both implementations. JEScala captures coordination schemas in a more compact way; JEScala implementations have fewer lines of code (Columns LOC). The proportion of event declarations required by JEScala and by JL depends on the case study (Columns Events). JEScala implementations define fewer handlers (Columns Handlers). Furthermore, the number of statements in the code, where events are imperatively triggered are

[6] `httpc://cloc.sourceforge.net`

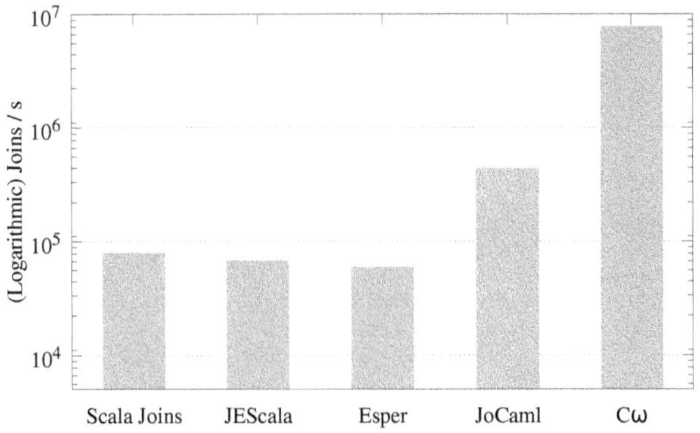

Figure 9. Performance of join languages.

considerably reduced in the JEScala versions (Columns Imp. Evts). The reduction of handlers and imperative events indicate that the coordination logic is moved from handlers and imperatively triggered events to declarative event expressions. As a consequence, developers do not risk forgetting firing events and coordination patterns are more composable, easier to extend, and express the intention of the programmer in a more declarative way.

5.2 Quantitative Evaluation

Our focus so far has been on the design of JEScala. To gain an idea about its performance, we implemented a number of benchmarks[7].

Comparison with other languages We initially compare JEScala with other languages that support joins. The benchmark consists of an automaton with n states. A transition fires when the join of the event associated to the current state and the event associated to the transition to another state fires. We measured the throughput (i.e., joined events per second) for Scala Joins, JEScala, the Esper complex event processing engine [11], JoCaml and $C\omega$ (Figure 9). Varying n from 1 to 5 (not shown) does not change the results significantly. Languages based on a dedicated compiler like JoCaml and $C\omega$ have the best performance. The results also show that performance degrades by increasing expressivity. This result is not surprising: for example $C\omega$ intentionally limits the constructs available to the programmer to achieve better performance [2]. At the opposite, Esper supports an extremely expressive language for event combination. JEScala exhibits a performance that minimally outperforms Scala Joins. However, JEScala is more expressive since it supports implicit invocation, event combination and real asynchronous events.

Effect of pattern complexity The complexity of the matching patterns has an impact on performance, which we measured with a dedicated benchmark. The size of the matching patterns in the benchmark increases; the cases $n = 3$ and $n = 4$ are shown in Figure 11a and Figure 11b. We measured the performance of each language for $n \in [2..6]$. The results for each language, normalized to the case $n = 2$, are in Figure 10. The benchmark shows performance degradation when the size of the pattern increases. $C\omega$ and JoCaml outperform JEScala, which however does better than Scala Joins.

Effect of optimizations To measure the effect of the optimizations for asynchronous events described in Section 4, we implemented a simple version of the rock-paper-scissors game. Two players running in different threads trigger an event that correspond to

[7] All measurements were performed on a MacBookPro6.2 with CPU I7 (2 cores, 2.66Ghz) with 8Gb ram, running OSX 10.6.8, Java 6 and Scala 2.10.

Case Study	Th.	Comp.	LOC JL	LOC JE	Events JL	Events JE	Handlers JL	Handlers JE	Imp. Evts JL	Imp. Evts JE
Critical Section (CS)	3	5	67	60	3	5	1	0	3	1
Alternating CS	3	4	49	42	7	8	5	1	8	3
Condition Variable	3	3	56	56	6	8	3	3	5	2
Monitor	6	7	86	80	9	10	3	1	7	2
Concurrent Barrier	2	3	46	37	4	4	1	0	3	0
Readers-Writer Lock	6	7	81	71	12	8	8	3	12	3
Threadsafe Counter	5	5	47	44	6	6	3	1	6	4
Hoare Cond. Crit. Region	4	7	90	71	7	9	4	1	7	2
Rendezvous	2	3	68	64	3	3	1	1	2	0
Concurrent Futures	2	3	58	48	7	7	3	3	5	2
Producer-Consumer (PC)	2	3	79	72	8	8	0	0	4	0
PC (Bounded Buffer)	4	4	72	68	7	7	2	2	5	3
Finite State Machine ST	1	2	76	66	14	11	11	5	12	6
Finite State Machine MT	4	4	74	64	14	11	11	5	12	6
Petri Net ST	1	2	46	44	9	12	13	14	9	8
Petri Net MT	3	2	56	54	11	14	12	11	9	8
Semaphore Petri Net	2	4	56	51	5	6	2	1	4	1
Tennis Players Petri Net	3	2	80	74	13	16	18	9	15	6
Agents (3 Ping-pong) ST	1	4	67	64	7	7	4	4	7	6
Agents (3 Ping-pong) MT	4	3	60	57	3	5	1	1	5	2
Agents (Token Ring) ST	1	4	54	54	7	6	4	4	5	4
Agents (Token Ring) MT	4	3	53	54	3	3	1	1	3	2
Elem. Cellular Automaton	1	3	87	84	8	11	4	1	9	2
Game Of Life	1	1	95	74	25	17	27	2	27	2
Shift Register	1	2	36	30	6	6	3	1	9	8
4 Bit Binary Adder	1	4	82	69	20	19	8	3	12	3
Logic Ports Circuit	3	4	70	64	10	7	7	1	7	1
Random Walks	7	8	185	179	16	16	12	3	17	4
Parall. Graph Explor.	21	20	184	181	9	10	5	6	10	7
Epidemic Model ST	1	11	184	172	18	16	16	4	18	6
Epidemic Model MT	11	11	190	178	18	16	16	4	18	6
Web Server	2	4	44	41	4	4	2	1	4	0
Web Server (Extended)	3	5	75	68	7	6	4	0	7	0
Web Server (Section 2.3)	4	5	111	97	18	18	8	4	16	8

Figure 8. Main metrics for the case studies.

rock, *paper* or *scissors*. A game component matches those events in a disjunction. Each pattern in the disjunction captures a possible combination. Depending on the matching pattern, the first or the second player wins. We measure the time required to run $5 \cdot 10^4$ games.

The results are in Figure 12a. Column *No Opt.* shows the non optimized version of JEScala. Subsequent columns show the effect of the *Counters* optimization, of the *Disj. Only* optimization, and of both optimizations in action. To give an intuition of what the values mean in absolute terms, the last two columns show the performance of Scala Joins in the same benchmark for events with and without parameters. The former is obtained by adding a dummy parameter to the event, which forces Scala Joins to switch off the *Counters* optimization, the latter shows the case in which the counters optimization is applied.

The dark bars in Figure 12a show the performance of JEScala when adding the *Thread Pool* optimization. Figure 12b focuses on this case. The *Thread Pool* optimization is by far the most important to improve the performance of JEScala, and it is sufficient to make JEScala faster than Scala Joins in the case of an event with a parameter (Figure 12a). However, other optimizations are also significant and further double the performance of JEScala.

6. Related work

Join languages Key design aspects of join languages are summarized in Figure 13. Most join languages are based on existing idioms (*Language* column). The *Channels* column shows how chan-

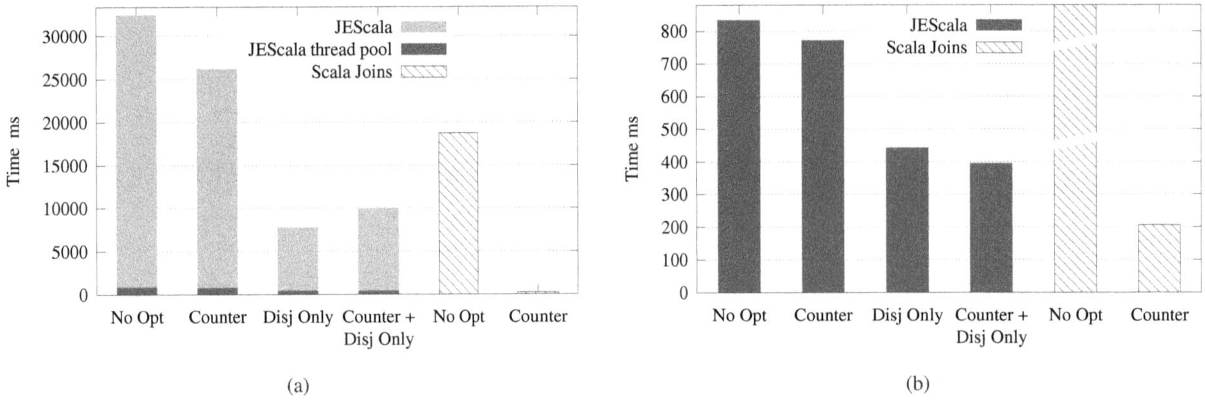

Figure 12. Optimization of asynchronous events in JEScala (a) zoom on the *Thread Pool* optimization (b).

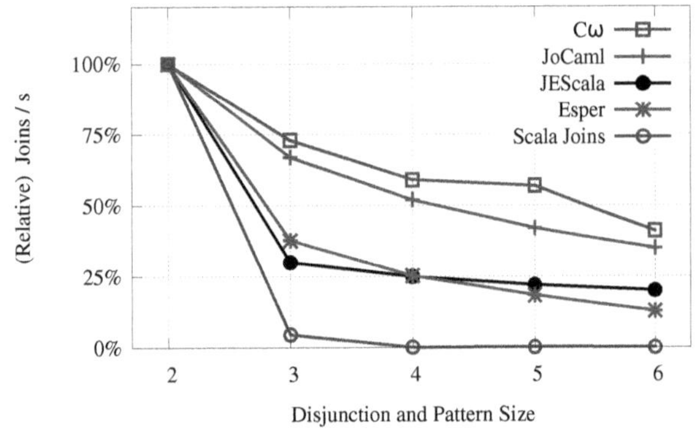

Figure 10. Effect of pattern complexity on performance.

```
var cnt:Long=0
//...evt decl
evt (toD,toC,toB,toA)=
    ( a & b )
  | ( c & a )
  | ( b & c )

toA += ()=>{ a(); cnt+=1 }
toB += ()=>{ b(); cnt+=1 }
toC += ()=>{ c(); cnt+=1 }
```

(a)

```
var cnt:Long=0
// ...evt decl
evt (toD,toC,toB,toA)=
    ( a & b & c)
  | ( d & a & b)
  | ( c & d & a)
  | ( b & c & d)
toA += ()=>{ a(); cnt+=1 }
...
toD += ()=>{ d(); cnt+=1 }
```

(b)

Figure 11. Benchmark: increasing complexity of matching patterns with n=3 (a) and n=4 (b).

nels are implemented. The *Sync* column indicates whether channels are synchronous or asynchronous. The *Disj* column shows how disjunctions are defined: through a specific explicit construct (*Explicit*) or, implicitly, via existing language abstractions. The *Matching* column shows how to select a reaction among active ones.

What sets JEScala truly apart from other join languages is its advanced event system that supports event composition and implicit events, in addition to imperatively triggered events. To the best of our knowledge, JEScala is the only language that explores the synergy between such an event system and join operators. The effect of using imperative events rather than method or function calls to implement channels was discussed in Section 2; the advantages of the synergy of implicit and declarative events with joins were discussed in Section 3.

The closest cousin of JEScala is the Scala library Scala Joins [17], since it also implements channels as events. Scala Joins demonstrate the use of extensible pattern matching to express joins and provides guards for join matching. Similarly to JEScala, disjunctions are explicit. Subclasses can redefine the disjunction in the superclass, but cannot modify it. However, unlike JEScala, the event model is simple: events must be declared together with the patterns they are involved in, including their synchronicity, and cannot be composed. When considering Scala Joins as a building block for implementing JEScala, the necessity of predefining the synchronicity of the events provided by the library turned out to be problematic for implementing JEScala declarative events, whose synchronicity may vary from one occurrence to the other.

Polyphonic C# [2] extends C# with advanced concurrency abstractions for asynchronous programming that are compiler-checked and optimized. Unlike JEScala it supports only one synchronous method per pattern and subclasses can change the body of a reaction but cannot extend disjunctions with new reactions. For our experiments we used the research language Cω [8], which offers the same extensions to C#. The Join Concurrency Library [33] provides a type-safe implementation of Polyphonic C# features by using C# 2.0 generics. The advantages are portability across the .NET platform and easier extensibility at the cost of fewer optimization opportunities. Further work [36] shows that impressive performance improvements can be achieved by fine-grained locking. Concurrent Basic [34] integrates the Join Concurrency Library into Visual Basic by including explicit channels and methods with multiple headers to define join patterns. Unlike JEScala, Concurrent Basic allows subclasses to add new reactions to existing disjunctions, as proposed in the Objective Join Calculus [14]. This however incurs the issues discussed in [2]. The latter is also true of JoinJava [19].

Funnel [26] is, as JoCaml, a language explicitly using the Join Calculus as its foundations (with the variation that only one synchronous channel is allowed in a join pattern). Unlike JoCaml, the language supports object-oriented programming with classes and inheritance on top of its functional basis.

In JErlang [29], channels are messages exchanged by actors. Erlang patterns are extended to express matching of multiple subsequent messages. Patterns are matched in their declaration order. JCThorn [27] extends the scripting language Thorn [3]. *Components* are actor-like containers for objects that share the same mailbox. JEScala implements a finer-grained event system and, unlike in JCThorn, concurrency abstractions and events are at the object granularity level. MogeMoge [24] is a prototype-based scripting language for game programming. Interactions are defined by asyn-

	Language	Channels	Sync	Disj.	Matching
JoCaml	Caml	Function	Async	Explicit	Non deterministic
Funnel	Funnel	Function/Method	Both	Explicit	Non deterministic
Polyphonic C#	C#	Method	Both	Object	Non deterministic
JoinJava	Java	Method	Both	Object	Both
Scala Joins	Scala	Imperative Event	Both	Explicit	Non deterministic
JErlang	Erlang	Message	Async	Actor	Deterministic
JCThorn	Thorn	Message	Async	Component	Deterministic
MogeMoge	MogeMoge	Join token	Async	Global	Deterministic
Join Conc. Lib.	.NET	Channel	Both	Explicit	Non deterministic
Concurrent Basic	Visual Basic	Channel	Both	Implicit	Non deterministic
JEScala	EScala	Advanced Events	Both	Explicit	Non deterministic

Figure 13. Languages implementing join abstractions.

chronous events called *join tokens* sharing a single global disjunction, the *token pool*.

Calculi JEScala has been designed in a pragmatic way. Proper theoretical foundations may bring a better understanding of its properties, in particular with respect to concurrency, with useful inspiration to be drawn from existing join-based calculi. We have already mentioned the objective join calculus [14], which deals with objects and inheritance. The aspect join calculus [35] may also be an interesting source of inspiration with respect to implicit invocation.

Other languages Pāñini [22] is a programming language that aims to coordinate concurrent components in a program by using explicit typed events, à la Ptolemy [32], except that these events are asynchronous, with a different meaning than the one we have used so far: events are fired synchronously with respect to their source but theirs handlers are executed asynchronously. However, no declarative ways of combining events are provided. Current versions of Pāñini aim at implicit concurrency [30, 31] with a programming style close to sequential programming. Using *capsules* to group objects into single threaded entities, which are combined into concurrent *systems*, results in coarse-grained concurrency compararable to actors [18]. Communication between capsules looks like method calls in a sequential program instead of asynchronous messages between actors.

Implicit invocation with traits [28] is another proposal based on explicit event types. There are no means of composition. The synchronicity of an event simply depends on whether it is associated to a block of code or not. In the first case, two synchronous, before and after, events are defined, otherwise a single asynchronous event is defined.

Join point interfaces [5] provide an interesting alternative to the event model of JEScala by using event types and still providing both explicit and implicit events, including declarative events. Also, this proposal is closer to Aspect-Oriented Programming than JEScala: its events (join points) can return a value and its handlers (advices) can be composed with `proceed`. However, it does not include any specific support for concurrency.

Other approaches Complex event processing (CEP) is about correlating time-changing streams of data. The available operators include joins with rich (and often subtle) semantic alternatives, typically applied to time windows. The interested reader is referred to [10] for an overview. Esper [11] is a CEP system implemented in Java. It is an enterprise-level product used in real applications with an expressive language and great emphasis on performance. As such, it is often used for comparison in CEP research, and was our choice as an indicator of the performance of CEP engines. Unlike join languages, most CEP solutions are not integrated into a programming language and applications interface with the CEP engine via SQL-like queries. A noticeable exception is EventJava [12].

Sequential and Parallel Object Monitors (SOM and POM) [6, 7] aim to to separate fine-grained synchronization concerns from the application logic. An *object monitor* is a programmable threadless scheduler that applies to reified calls to methods belonging to the object (or set of objects) the monitor is attached to. The framework is very expressive and makes it possible to implement, in Java, monitors able to deal with, among others, join patterns and disjunctions, with the possibility of providing different semantics, for instance in terms of determinacy. JEScala also deals with separation of concerns and concurrency but not at the same level and with a different purpose. Our concurrency abstractions are fixed and our interest is in seamlessly integrating them, at the language level, in order to improve modularity. Sometimes, but not always, both approaches almost completely overlap. For instance, in Java, it would make sense to write the rate limiter of Figure 4 as an object monitor (it would still require more programming). The mapping is less clear as soon as the rate limiter becomes more complex. On the one hand, the issue is not to systematically extract concurrency and, on the other hand, an issue is also to modularize the synchronization concern itself.

Finally, [4] introduces a rich programming model combining a form of implicit event types and aspects. Two salient features of the proposal are the possibility to define, within event declarations, side-effect-free code collecting data to be carried by the event as well as fine-grained means to control composition. Concurrency issues are not addressed.

7. Summary and Future Work

In this paper we have presented the design of JEScala, a language that combines the advanced event system of EScala with concurrency abstractions from the Join Calculus. We have shown that this solution captures coordination patterns in a way that is more compact and more declarative than existing join languages while preserving the OO style of modular reasoning (events are object members). Still, we have found that concurrency issues related to non-determinism and the mixing of synchronous and asynchronous events (a source of deadlocks) is challenging. We feel that JEScala provides an interesting practical language to study these issues.

Future work includes improving performance, providing compiler support as well as exploring the theroretical underpinning of JEScala. Finally, as already discussed in Section 6, CEP engines offer a richer semantics for event correlation than event-based languages – most noticeably, by including *time* in the form of various types of windows over the event streams. We plan to explore the semantic alternatives that joins offer in the context of event correlation over time windows. This field has been partially explored in CEP, but language integration of a flexible semantics for correlating events is still a research challenge.

Acknowledgments

This work has been partially supported by the German Federal Ministry of Education and Research (BMBF) under grant No. 16BY1206E ACCEPT and by the European Research Council, grant No. 321217.

References

[1] H. C. Baker, Jr. and C. Hewitt. The incremental garbage collection of processes. In *Symposium on Artificial intelligence and programming languages*, pages 55–59. ACM, 1977.

[2] N. Benton, L. Cardelli, and C. Fournet. Modern concurrency abstractions for C#. *ACM TOPLAS*, 26(5):769–804, Sept. 2004.

[3] B. Bloom, J. Field, N. Nystrom, J. Östlund, G. Richards, R. Strniša, J. Vitek, and T. Wrigstad. Thorn: robust, concurrent, extensible scripting on the JVM. In *OOPSLA '09*, pages 117–136. ACM, 2009.

[4] C. Bockisch, S. Malakuti, M. Akşit, and S. Katz. Making aspects natural: events and composition. In *AOSD '11*, pages 285–300. ACM, 2011.

[5] E. Bodden, E. Tanter, and M. Inostroza. Joint point interfaces for safe and flexible decoupling of aspects. *ACM TOSEM*, 2014. To appear.

[6] D. Caromel, L. Mateu, G. Pothier, and É. Tanter. Parallel object monitors. *Concurrency and Computation: Practice and Experience*, 20(12):1387–1417, July 2008.

[7] D. Caromel, L. Mateu, and É. Tanter. Sequential object monitors. In *ECOOP '04*, volume 3086 of *LNCS*, pages 316–340. Springer, 2004.

[8] Cω. Language Website. http://research.microsoft.com/en-us/um/cambridge/projects/comega/.

[9] S. Conchon and F. Le Fessant. JoCaml: mobile agents for Objective-Caml. In *ASAMA '99*, pages 22–29. IEEE Computer Society, 1999.

[10] G. Cugola and A. Margara. Processing flows of information: From data stream to complex event processing. *ACM Comput. Surv.*, 44(3):15:1–15:62, June 2012.

[11] EsperTech. Company Website. http://www.espertech.com.

[12] P. Eugster and K. R. Jayaram. EventJava: An extension of Java for event correlation. In *ECOOP '09*, volume 5653 of *LNCS*, pages 570–594. Springer, 2009.

[13] C. Fournet and G. Gonthier. The reflexive CHAM and the join-calculus. In *POPL '96*, pages 372–385. ACM, 1996.

[14] C. Fournet, C. Laneve, L. Maranget, and D. Rémy. Inheritance in the join calculus. In *Proceedings of the 20th Conference on Foundations of Software Technology and Theoretical Computer Science*, volume 1974 of *LNCS*, pages 397–408. Springer, 2000.

[15] D. Garlan and D. Notkin. Formalizing design spaces: Implicit invocation mechanisms. In *VDM '91*, volume 551 of *LNCS*, pages 31–44. Springer, 1991.

[16] V. Gasiūnas, L. Satabin, M. Mezini, A. Núñez, and J. Noyé. EScala: modular event-driven object interactions in Scala. In *AOSD '11*, pages 227–240. ACM, 2011.

[17] P. Haller and T. Van Cutsem. Implementing joins using extensible pattern matching. In *COORDINATION '08*, volume 5052 of *LNCS*, pages 135–152. Springer, 2008.

[18] C. Hewitt, P. Bishop, and R. Steiger. A universal modular ACTOR formalism for artificial intelligence. In *IJCAI '73*, pages 235–245. Morgan Kaufmann, 1973.

[19] G. S. Itzstein and M. Jasiunas. On implementing high level concurrency in Java. In *Advances in Computer Systems Architecture*, volume 2823 of *LNCS*, pages 151–165. Springer, 2003.

[20] The JEScala site. http://www.stg.tu-darmstadt.de/research, 2014.

[21] J.-J. Lévy. Some results in the join-calculus. In *TACS '97*, volume 1281 of *LNCS*, pages 233–249. Springer, 1997.

[22] Y. Long, S. L. Mooney, T. Sondag, and H. Rajan. Implicit invocation meets safe, implicit concurrency. In *GPCE '10*, pages 63–72. ACM, 2010.

[23] L. Mandel and L. Maranget. *The JoCaml language - Documentation and user's manual.* Inria, Aug. 2012. Release 4.00.

[24] T. Nishimori and Y. Kuno. Join token-based event handling: A comprehensive framework for game programming. In *SLE '11*, volume 6940 of *LNCS*, pages 119–138. Springer, 2011.

[25] A. Núñez, J. Noyé, V. Gasiūnas, and M. Mezini. *Aspect-Oriented, Model-Driven Software Product Lines - The AMPLE Way*, chapter Product Line Implementation with ECaesarJ. Cambridge University Press, 2011.

[26] M. Odersky. An introduction to functional nets. In *Applied Semantics*, volume 2395 of *LNCS*, pages 333–377. Springer, 2002.

[27] I. S. Paula. JCThorn: Extending Thorn with joins and chords. Master's thesis, Department of Computing, Imperial College London, 2010.

[28] T. Pawlitzki and F. Steimann. Implicit invocation of traits. In *SAC '10*, pages 2085–2089. ACM, 2010.

[29] H. Plociniczak and S. Eisenbach. JErlang: Erlang with joins. In *COORDINATION '10*, volume 6116 of *LNCS*, pages 61–75. Springer, 2010.

[30] H. Rajan, S. M. Kautz, E. Line, S. Kabala, G. Upadhyaya, Y. Long, R. Fernando, and L. Szakács. Capsule-oriented programming. Technical Report 13-01, Iowa State U., Computer Sc., 2013.

[31] H. Rajan, S. M. Kautz, and W. Rowcliffe. Concurrency by modularity: design patterns, a case in point. In *OOPSLA '10*, pages 790–805. ACM, 2010.

[32] H. Rajan and G. T. Leavens. Ptolemy: A language with quantified, typed events. In *ECOOP '08*, volume 5142 of *LNCS*, pages 155–179. Springer, 2008.

[33] C. Russo. The joins concurrency library. In *PADL '07*, volume 4354 of *LNCS*, pages 260–274. Springer, 2007.

[34] C. V. Russo. Join patterns for Visual Basic. In *OOPSLA '08*, pages 53–72. ACM, 2008.

[35] N. Tabareau. A theory of distributed aspects. In *AOSD '10*, pages 133–144. ACM, 2010.

[36] A. J. Turon and C. V. Russo. Scalable join patterns. In *OOPSLA '11*, pages 575–594. ACM, 2011.

Designing Information Hiding Modularity for Model Transformation Languages

Andreas Rentschler Dominik Werle Qais Noorshams Lucia Happe Ralf Reussner
Karlsruhe Institute of Technology (KIT)
76131 Karlsruhe, Germany
{rentschler, noorshams, happe, reussner}@kit.edu
dominik.werle@student.kit.edu

Abstract

Development and maintenance of model transformations make up a substantial share of the lifecycle costs of software products that rely on model-driven techniques. In particular large and heterogeneous models lead to poorly understandable transformation code due to missing language concepts to master complexity. At the present time, there exists no module concept for model transformation languages that allows programmers to control information hiding and strictly declare model and code dependencies at module interfaces. Yet only then can we break down transformation logic into smaller parts, so that each part owns a clear interface for separating concerns. In this paper, we propose a module concept suitable for model transformation engineering. We formalize our concept based on *cQVTom*, a compact subset of the transformation language QVT-Operational. To meet the special demands of transformations, module interfaces give control over both model and code accessibility. We also implemented the approach for validation. In a case study, we examined the effort required to carry out two typical maintenance tasks on a real-world transformation. We are able to attest a significant reduction of effort, thereby demonstrating the practical effects of a thorough interface concept on the maintainability of model transformations.

Categories and Subject Descriptors D.2.2 [*Software Engineering*]: Design Tools and Techniques—Modules and Interfaces; D.3.2 [*Programming Languages*]: Language Classifications—Specialized Application Languages

General Terms Design, Languages

Keywords Model-driven software engineering, model transformations, transformation languages, modularity, maintenance

1. Introduction

In software engineering circles, domain-specific languages (DSLs) have gained wide acceptance as a technique to improve the productivity and quality of software. This is particularly true for model-driven software engineering where models represent first-class artifacts. In this field, a multitude of specialized languages had been designed to transform models into other models and finally into code artifacts. These so-called transformation languages aim to ease development efforts by offering a succinct syntax to query from and map model elements between different modeling domains.

However, development and maintenance of model transformations themselves are expected to make up a substantial share of the lifecycle costs of software products that rely on model-driven techniques [20]. Much of the effort in understanding model transformations arises from complexity induced by a high degree of data and control dependencies. Complexity is connected to size, structural complexity and heterogeneity of models involved in a transformation. Visualization techniques can help to master this complexity [17, 20]. It is a fact that maintainability must already be promoted at the design-time of a software program [18]. As one solution to ease maintenance processes, modern programming languages feature concepts to decompose programs into modules or classes. In addition, the concept of interfaces helps to hide implementation details, thus making it easier for developers to understand a program, to locate concerns, and to adapt a program to new or changing requirements. These concepts reach back to the 1970s when Parnas proposed the information hiding principle as a key principle for software design [16]. Nowadays, they are well-accepted for their positive effect on maintainability [13].

At the present time, however, there exists no concept for model transformation languages that allows programmers to control information hiding and strictly declare model and code dependencies at module interfaces. Yet only then can we break down transformation logic into smaller parts, where each part owns a clear interface for separating concerns. To the same extent as for programs written in general-purpose languages, with a proper concept to encapsulate concerns, the effort required in understanding behavior and locating concerns in larger transformations can be significantly reduced.

Among the many DSLs that had been designed for model transformation programming, QVT, ETL, and ATL belong to the most popular and advanced ones. But all these and other proposed transformation languages lack a thorough module concept. QVT's concept of libraries, for example, does only allow to dissect a transformation into smaller parts. There are no explicit interfaces, and it is impossible to hide functionality. Thus, in order to understand a QVT transformation, it is necessary to read the full implementation.

What distinguishes transformation programs from general-purpose programs is that they operate on often large and structurally complex models. However, existing transformation languages merely provide weak encapsulation mechanisms: developers cannot specify what model elements a module is allowed to read, instantiate, or modify. By just looking at the interface of a module, one cannot tell its impact. But, as long as interfaces are not able to communicate on which of the models' elements a module operates, developers

MODULARITY '14, April 22–26, 2014, Lugano, Switzerland.
Copyright © 2014 ACM 978-1-4503-2772-5/14/04...$15.00.
http://dx.doi.org/10.1145/2577080.2577094

are struggling with understanding a module's impact on the overall transformation.

In this paper, we propose a module system that includes not only control dependencies as part of its interface contracts, but also data dependencies at the class-level of involved models. We formalize our approach by designing a minimal yet fully functional transformation language, Core QVT-Operational-Modular, short *cQVTom*, that is based on the conceptual core of QVT-Operational (QVTo) and that embraces an interface for rigorous specification of both control and data dependencies. The goal of our approach is to attest similar effects on model transformations as observed for modularized programs in general, namely improved understandability, maintainability and adaptability [18].

As a proof-of-concept and to validate the expected effects of our approach, we integrate our modular concept into the transformation language Xtend. We chose Xtend so we can reuse Java's interface and class concepts provided by Xtend's host language, Java, and adapt it to our needs. We carry out a case study on a real-world model-to-text transformation written in Xtend. For two typical maintenance scenarios, a refactoring and an evolution scenario, we can demonstrate how our approach helps to localize concerns already at the interface-level without examining the underlying implementation, thereby significantly reducing the effort as opposed to a previous, non-modularized version.

In summary, we make two different contributions: Firstly, we design a proper module concept for model transformation languages, which we formally define on a core subset of QVTo. Secondly, we validate our approach on a real-world model-to-text transformation written in Xtend. For this purpose, we implemented our concept for the Xtend language.

This paper is structured as follows. First, we motivate the difficulty of maintaining transformations in Section 2, and we present our idea in Section 3. In Section 4, we formalize the approach by providing syntax and a type system for a core subset of QVTo that is enriched with our module concept. Section 5 introduces our implementation into the Xtend language, and Section 6 studies effects of our approach on maintainability of a real-world transformation. In Section 7, related work is discussed. Finally, Section 8 presents conclusions and proposes directions for future work.

2. Maintenance of Model Transformations

In model-driven software engineering, models are considered to be first-class artifacts and are expected to evolve during their lifecycle. Whenever a model changes, all dependent artifacts of the model must be adapted for that change, including model instances and transformations that operate on the model (co-evolution). It is thus important that model transformations can be adapted with minimal effort. This effort can be minimized through a modular design, under the premise that the programming language supports adequate concepts for modularization.

By means of two realistic evolution scenarios, we identify issues that appear with existing module concepts of transformation languages. We chose an example transformation that is small enough to help clarify these issues while still presenting the core features of an imperative transformation language. Let us consider a unidirectional transformation between two similar models, one model describes simple activity diagrams, the other describes processes as chains of steps. Figure 1 uses a textual syntax that is part of the QVTo language [14] to define both models.

A transformation from activity to process models requires two mappings to be implemented. One mapping creates for each instance of `Activity` an instance of class `Process`, and another mapping is responsible for projecting any `Action` contained in an `Activity` to a `Step`, so that the `Step` is contained in the `Process` that had been created from the respective `Activity`. Since we

```
package ActivityModel {
  class Activity { composes actions : Action [*]; }
  class Action { references succ : Action [1]; }
  class StartAction extends Action { }
  class StopAction extends Action { }
}
package ProcessModel {
  class Process { composes steps : Step [*]; }
  class Step {
    references next : Step [1];
    composes isStart : Boolean [1];
    composes isStop : Boolean [1];
  }
}
```

Figure 1: Activity2Process example – Source and target models

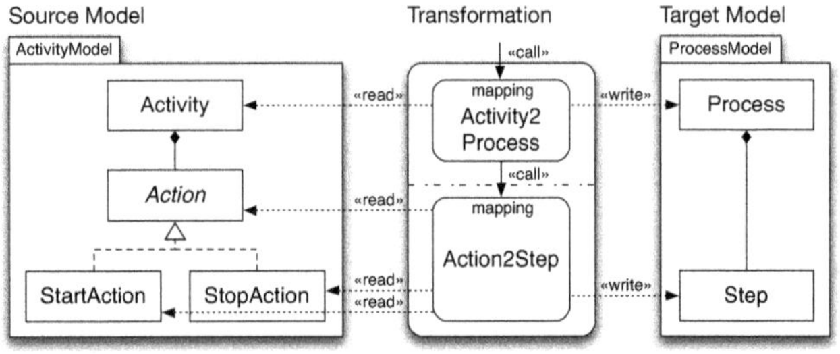

Figure 2: Activity2Process transformation

are anticipating that in the future both models might be extended with new entities, and that the exact behavior of these mappings might be subject to change, we find it reasonable to encapsulate each mapping in a separate module. Figure 2 depicts model and mapping dependencies that occur.

In QVTo, both mappings can be implemented as mapping operations and contained in two separate modules, a transformation and a library module. Because of QVTo's imperative nature, the transformation module must contain an entry point, the main function. The main function's signature declares input and output models as transformation parameters with a model type, also called the domains of a transformation. An implementation of the transformation module is given in Figure 3a. The latter mapping operation is factored out into an own module that is imported by the main module (Figure 3b).

Several weaknesses of this approach become evident when we consider two typical maintenance scenarios, refactoring and evolution. Failure to perform refactoring at periodic intervals usually results in accumulating technical debt. Evolution of transformations can be experienced even more frequently, emerging whenever any of the models change.

Refactoring modular structure. Suppose we want to rethink the way the transformation is currently structured. In our example, module `Activity2ProcessModule` is responsible for mapping an `Activity` to a `Process`, and module `Action2StepModule` for mapping instances of `Action` to instances of `Step`. Dependence information is only available by studying the actual implementation. Module clustering is generally determined by dependence metrics like coupling. In contrast to ordinary software, external dependencies are not only introduced by method calls, but also by references to model element. Without having an interface concept that incorporates both dimensions, control and data flow, it is hard to reason about modularity of model transformations. Furthermore, the subset of model elements a module does access is only by convention, it is neither programmatically declared nor automatically enforced.

Adapting to evolving models. Adding an attribute `name` to actions and steps requires the transformation to adapt accordingly

```
import Action2StepModule;
transformation Activity2ProcessModule(
  in a:ActivityModel, out p:ProcessModel)
  extends Action2StepModule;
main() {
   a.rootObjects()[Activity]->map Activity2Process();
}
mapping Activity::mapActivity2Process() : Process {
   result.steps := self.actions->map mapAction2Step();
}
```

(a) First module

```
transformation Action2StepModule(
  in a:ActivityModel, out p:ProcessModel);
mapping Action::mapAction2Step() : Step {
   -- result.name := self.name;
   result.next := self.succ.late resolveone(Step);
   result.isStart := self.oclIsTypeOf(StartAction);
   result.isStop := self.oclIsTypeOf(StopAction);
}
```

(b) Second module

Figure 3: Activity2Process example in QVTo

(Figure 3b, line 4). We cannot deduce from the transformation signature alone for what model parts each module is responsible. Because mapping implementations might internally access classes `Action` or `Step`, their signatures are neither informative enough. Developers need to check the full code to locate relevant spots before carrying out the requested change.

Other transformation languages, like ATL, ETL, Kermeta, and VIATRA2, provide even less sophisticated concepts than QVTo. In a classification from 2003 [6], Czarnecki observes that only some approaches support organization of rules into modules, he does not talk about information hiding aspects. Transformation languages that are hosted by an object-oriented language may exploit the available class mechanism, for example RubyTL for Ruby, SMTL for Scala, and Xtend for Java. But even Java's sophisticated class mechanism still does not offer a solution for model access control.

3. Modularity Tailored for Transformations

To solve mentioned issues, our idea is to introduce a proper interface concept that facilitates information hiding. Hiding the internal details of a piece of software from any other piece and encapsulating design decisions that are likely to change bring the following benefits (cf. MacCormack [13], Parnas [16]):

Encouraging deliberate designs. Implementations are type-checked against their interfaces to ensure contracts are met. This encourages developers to think about a modular design with encapsulated implementation decisions. It also prevents misuse by introducing unintended dependencies from external code.

Fostering team development. Initial development can be carried out more efficiently with a proper interface concept. As soon as a modular design has been created in terms of interfaces, multiple developers may work on implementing different parts of the project in parallel.

Making software easier to understand, use and reuse. Developers require less effort to understand software behavior when provided with a view that abstracts from implementation details. Interfaces offer an abstract and often sufficient description of a module's responsibilities and dependencies.

Simplifying modification and repair. If a decision is distributed over multiple modules, ripple-of-change effects occur when that decision is being modified. Localized design decisions help to limit ripple-of-change effect.

Facilitating variability through reconfiguration. Alternative implementations can be easily exchanged for design decisions that are encapsulated behind an interface. This is done by simply exchanging implementations of the same interface.

So that developers can exploit these benefits to the fullest, we expect a model transformation language to integrate a module concept that abides to the information hiding principle. Our understanding of the principle is described by these four rules:

R1: Segregation of interface and implementation. Implementation details (queries and helper methods, internal state) are hidden behind interfaces. Per required interface, a unique implementation exists.

R2: Conformance of interface and implementation. Implemented methods must conform to exported method signatures. This means that method name and the number of arguments have to be equal, and types must be substitutable according to Liskov (contravariance of argument types, covariance of return types). Any method used must be either defined locally in the implementation, or it must be defined in one of the imported interfaces.

R3: Method access control. Only methods that are either defined locally or by an imported interface are visible. Any other method is not visible and can therefore not be accessed.

R4: Model access control. Here, our domain-specific module concept is distinct from module concepts for general-purpose programming languages. In order to accommodate the central role of model references for transformation languages, interfaces must make the scope of model elements in a domain that can be referenced explicit. An implementation can access only model elements that are defined by exported interfaces. For greater flexibility, access restrictions on models should be definable not only at class-level but also at package-level. The latter is equivalent to explicitly stating any transitively nested classes.

Violation of interface contracts should be detected at design-time employing static type checking. A compile-time error should be issued if methods that are hidden are accessed, if model elements are referenced that are not declared as modifiable or readable, or if methods that are declared in an interface remain unimplemented or with incompatible signatures.

We propose a derivative of QVTo, we name it QVT-Operational-Modular (QVTom), that replaces the existing module concept with a more elaborate one. To give an idea of the notation, we rewrite the previous example in QVTom (cf. Figure 4). A `transformation module` must implement at least one interface and can depend on an arbitrary number of interfaces, stated by keywords `export` and `import`, respectively. A `transformation interface` must be exported by exactly one module implementation. An interface declares a transformation signature, which is a list of typed model parameters. Signatures of an implementation's exported interfaces must be identical, except for access restrictions. For each model parameter, directives `in/out/inout` indicate the direction, and access is restricted to the classes and packages listed in trailing square brackets `[]`. A package name is a shortcut for any directly or indirectly contained classes in the package. Any reference to a model element is put into the context of a model parameter, e.g. `Activity@a`. Modules must define at least the methods declared in an exported interface with compatible signature.

There has to be one dedicated interface `IMain` with exactly one mapping that forms the entry point of a transformation. This approach is borrowed from the Modula-3 language. In our example, module `Activity2Process` exports `IMain` (Figure 4a), so that mapping `mapActivity2Process` is the entry point.This mapping calls another mapping provided by interface `IAction2-Step`, and implemented by module `Action2Step` (Figure 4b).

```
transformation interface IMain(
    in a : ActivityModel[Activity],
    out p : ProcessModel[Process]) {
  mapping Activity@a::mapActivity2Process() : Process@p;
}
transformation module Activity2Process
    export IMain
    import IAction2Step {
  mapping Activity@a::mapActivity2Process() : Process@p {
      result.steps := self.actions->
        map IAction2Step::mapAction2Step();
  }
}
```

(a) First module

```
transformation interface IAction2Step(
    in a : ActivityModel[StartAction, StopAction],
    out p : ProcessModel[Step]) {
  mapping Action@a::mapAction2Step() : Step@p;
}
transformation module Action2Step
    export IAction2Step {
  mapping Action@a::mapAction2Step() : Step@p {
     result.name := self.name;
     result.next := self.succ.late resolveone(Step@p);
     result.isStart := self.oclIsTypeOf(StartAction@a);
     result.isStop := self.oclIsTypeOf(StopAction@a);
  }
}
```

(b) Second module

Figure 4: Activity2Process example in QVTom

Implementations of each interface are granted restricted read or read/write access to distinct subsets of the models, whereby access to a class automatically implicates access to the class's features. In the example, implementations of `IMain` can only access instances of `Activity`, and create or modify instances of `Process`. On the other hand, implementations of `IAction2Step` can only refer to instances of `StartAction` and `StopAction`, and create or modify objects of class `Step`. If the latter module implementation would define further queries or mappings, these would not be visible to the former module's implementation.

The purpose of a module system is namespace control and data abstraction. There are no extra semantics added besides definition and resolution of namespaces, access control on top of namespaces, and an aligned mechanism for entry point definition. Thus, QVTom programs can always be transformed into non-modular QVTom or QVTo programs by giving unique names to entities.

Revisiting both example scenarios from last section, we can easily see that the proposed module system brings certain benefits. Refactoring the modular structure requires less effort, as all of the information required for reasoning can be deducted from the interface definitions alone. When it comes to adapting the example to an evolving model, we can locate the affected module much quicker from reading the interface descriptions as well: only one of the two modules has access to subclasses of `Action`.

4. Core QVTom

In the style of Featherweight Java (FJ) [10] we formalize a minimal subset of QVTom that we call *Core QVTom* (*cQVTom*). Main purpose of cQVTom is to demonstrate the added modular system. While retaining core features of transformation languages, we skip several of QVTo's features that do not add to the general idea and should be integrable straightforwardly. In this section, based on the syntax, we present a calculus for type inference and prove its soundness. We guarantee that a well-typed program enforces information hiding postulated by the four rules from the previous section.

Core QVTom skips several metamodeling concepts (e.g., abstract classes, primitive types, multiplicities), many of QVTo's concepts (e.g., helpers, queries, constructors, variables and globals, superimposition, dispatching, guards and sections), and most concepts of the underlying *Object Constraint Language* (if, let, collection operations, stdlib functions). QVT's existing module concepts had been completely removed to be replaced by our concepts, e.g., import, access, extend, transform, main.

We realize modularity as a second-class module system. This means that the module system is segregated from the core language's system. Modular definitions are evaluated statically at compile-time, hence at runtime, expressions cannot reflect on modules nor can they manipulate them. If a program is well-typed it conforms to the information hiding rules. Later at runtime, the module structure can be ignored as it is no longer needed[1].

4.1 Syntax

The syntax is minimal, though expressive enough to demonstrate relevant features and interaction of the added features together with core features of QVTo. The abstract syntax is presented in Figure 5 using a variant of the Backus-Naur form. A transformation T comprises three parts, metamodel definitions, interface definitions, and module implementations, the latter defining mapping implementations with a minimal QVTo syntax.

Metavariables p, c, f, i, t, s, x range over unique names of packages, classes, fields, interfaces, domains, mappings, and both arguments and variables, respectively. Typing judgments on sequences are abbreviated, $\overline{P}$ is shorthand for whitespace-separated lists $P_1 \dots P_n$ with zero or a finite number of elements, analogous for $\overline{C}$, $\overline{F}$, $\overline{S}$, $\overline{O}$, $\overline{B}$. In order to hint the underlying concrete syntax, the overline operator with an overset comma denotes shorthand notation for comma-separated parameter lists, e.g., $\overset{,}{\overline{e}}$. The ? operator marks grammatical expressions as optional, the | operator separates alternative choices.

Metamodels are formulated with the same notation as described in the QVT specification, with one extension: Packages p not only define classes, they define subpackages as well. A class c can inherit from another class c', and define contained or referenced elements. A field f is typed with a class c and can have multiplicities 1 or $0..*$.

A module interface i specifies a list of model domains $\overline{t : p}$ the transformation unit is operating on, where a domain either acts as input or output (`in` or `out`). A domain owns a unique model domain identifier t that is part of any model element reference. In addition to root package p, the exact elements contained in the root package that are accessible by implementations must be declared in trailing square brackets. This can be a list of classes $\overline{c'}$ and packages $\overline{p'}$. Naming a package equals to naming all directly and indirectly contained classes in the package. Method signatures of mappings are identical to QVTo's syntax. Each metamodel element, the calling context c, parameters $\overline{c'}$ and the target element c'', is prefixed by the respective domain that marks the context, t, $\overline{t'}$, and t''.

A module m implements exactly one interface i. To do so, it can rely on one or more interfaces $\overline{j}$. This time, mapping signatures are supplemented by a list of statements. Assignment expressions can be used to setup fields of target model elements built from QVTo expressions. We have seven types of expressions in cQVTom: Querying a target object created from a source object, invoking a mapping s defined by an exported or imported interface j, checking the type of an expression, accessing a field f, instantiating a class c in domain t with constructor parameters $\overline{e}$, accessing the surrounding mapping's source context, and accessing an argument or variable x. This is a valid subset of QVTo's rich syntax. We now aim at showing how information hiding is enforced on this variety of concepts.

[1] Of course, one can defer static evaluation of information hiding to runtime.

Syntax:

$T ::= \overline{P}\ \overline{I}\ \overline{M}$	Transformation program
$P ::= \texttt{package}\ p\ \texttt{\{}\ \overline{P}\ \overline{C}\ \texttt{\}}$	Metamodel specification
$C ::= \texttt{class}\ c\ (\texttt{extends}\ c')^{?}\ \texttt{\{}\ \overline{F}\ \texttt{\}}$	Class declaration
$F ::= (\texttt{composes} \mid \texttt{references})\ f\ \texttt{:}\ c\ (\texttt{[1]} \mid \texttt{[*]})\texttt{;}$	Feature declaration
$I ::= \texttt{transformation interface}\ i\ \overline{((\texttt{in} \mid \texttt{out})\ t : p\ \texttt{[}\overline{p'}^{,}\ \overline{c}^{,}\texttt{]})}^{,}\ \texttt{\{}\ \overline{S}\ \texttt{\}}$	Module interface declaration
$S ::= \texttt{mapping}\ c\texttt{@}t\ \texttt{::}\ s\ \texttt{(}\overline{\texttt{in}\ c'\texttt{@}t'}^{,}\texttt{)}\ \texttt{:}\ c''\texttt{@}t''\texttt{;}$	Method signature declaration
$M ::= \texttt{transformation module}\ m\ \texttt{export}\ i\ (\texttt{import}\ \overline{j}^{,})^{?}\ \texttt{\{}\ \overline{O}\ \texttt{\}}$	Module implementation definition
$O ::= \texttt{mapping}\ c\texttt{@}t\ \texttt{::}\ s\ \texttt{(}\overline{\texttt{in}\ x : c'\texttt{@}t'}^{,}\texttt{)}\ \texttt{:}\ c''\texttt{@}t''\ \texttt{\{}\ \overline{B}\ \texttt{\}}$	Mapping implementation definition
$B ::= \texttt{result.}f\ \texttt{:=}\ E\texttt{;}$	Assignment
$E ::= E\texttt{.late resolveone}\texttt{(}c\texttt{@}t\texttt{)}$	Trace resolution call
$\mid E\texttt{->map}\ j\texttt{::}s\ \texttt{(}\overline{x}^{,}\texttt{)}$	Mapping invocation
$\mid E\texttt{.oclIsTypeOf(}c\texttt{@}t\texttt{)}$	Type checking
$\mid E\texttt{.}f$	Feature access
$\mid \texttt{new}\ c\texttt{@}t\texttt{(}\overline{E}^{,}\texttt{)}$	Class instantiation
$\mid \texttt{self}$	Context access
$\mid x$	Variable access

Metamodel primitives:

$$\texttt{package}\ \mathcal{G}\ \texttt{\{ class Object \{ \}; class Boolean \{ \}; class String \{ \}; \}}$$

Metamodel subtyping:

$$c <: c \qquad \frac{c <: c' \qquad c' <: c''}{c <: c''} \qquad \frac{\texttt{class}\ c\ \texttt{extends}\ c'\ \texttt{\{ ... \}}}{c <: c' \qquad c <: \texttt{Object}} \qquad \frac{\texttt{class}\ c\ \texttt{\{ ... \}}}{c <: \texttt{Object}}$$

Lookup of metamodel packages, classes and features:

$$\frac{\texttt{class}\ c\ (\texttt{extends}\ c')^{?}\ \texttt{\{...\}}}{\mathit{classes}_C(c) = c, \mathit{classes}_C\big((c')^{?}\big)}$$

$$\frac{\begin{array}{c}\texttt{package}\ p\ \texttt{\{}\ \overline{P}\ \overline{C}\ \texttt{\}} \\ \overline{P} = \overline{\texttt{package}\ p'\ \texttt{\{...\}}} \qquad \overline{C} = \overline{\texttt{class}\ c\ (\texttt{extends}\ c')^{?}\ \texttt{\{...\}}}\end{array}}{\mathit{packages}_P(p) = \overline{p'} \qquad \mathit{classes}_P(p) = \overline{c}, \big[_k\ \mathit{classes}_C\big((c'_k)^{?}\big)\ \big]}$$

$$\frac{\texttt{class}\ c\ (\texttt{extends}\ c')^{?}\ \texttt{\{}\ \overline{(\texttt{composes} \mid \texttt{references})\ f\ \texttt{:}\ c\ (\texttt{[1]} \mid \texttt{[*]})\texttt{;}}\ \texttt{\}}}{\mathit{features}_C(c) = \mathit{features}_C\big((c')^{?}\big), \overline{f : c}}$$

Lookup of declared and implemented mapping types:

$$\frac{\begin{array}{c}\texttt{transformation interface}\ i\ \ldots\ \texttt{\{}\ \overline{S}\ \texttt{\}} \\ S = \texttt{mapping}\ c\texttt{@}t\ \texttt{::}\ s\ \texttt{(}\overline{\texttt{in}\ c'\texttt{@}t'}\texttt{)}\ \texttt{:}\ c''\texttt{@}t''\end{array}}{\mathit{mappings}_I(i) = \bigcup_{S \in \overline{S}} \Big\{(i, s) \mapsto \big((c\texttt{@}t, \overline{c'\texttt{@}t'}) \mapsto c''\texttt{@}t''\big)\Big\}}$$

$$\frac{\begin{array}{c}\texttt{transformation module}\ m\ \ldots\ \texttt{\{}\ \overline{O}\ \texttt{\}} \\ O = \texttt{mapping}\ c\texttt{@}t\ \texttt{::}\ s\ \texttt{(}\overline{\texttt{in}\ x : c'\texttt{@}t'}\texttt{)}\ \texttt{:}\ c''\texttt{@}t''\ \texttt{\{...\}}\end{array}}{\mathit{mappings}_M(m) = \bigcup_{O \in \overline{O}} \Big\{(\texttt{this}, s) \mapsto \big((c\texttt{@}t, \overline{c'\texttt{@}t'}) \mapsto c''\texttt{@}t''\big)\Big\}}$$

Figure 5: cQVTom's syntax, subtyping rules, and auxiliary functions.

Module structure is well-formed:

$$\frac{\vdash \overline{I}\ \texttt{WF} \qquad \vdash \overline{M}\ \texttt{WF}}{\vdash T\ \texttt{WF}} \qquad (\text{WF-PROGRAM})$$

$$\frac{\begin{array}{c}\forall k : \overline{p'}_k \subset \mathit{packages_P}^{+}(p_k) \wedge \mathit{classes_C}^{*}(\overline{c}_k) \subset \mathit{classes_P}^{*}(\mathit{packages_P}^{+}(p_k)) \\ \Delta\big[_k\ (a_k,\ t_k) \mapsto \mathit{classes_C}^{*}(\overline{c}_k) \cup \mathit{classes_P}^{*}(\overline{p'}_k) \cup \mathit{classes_P}^{*}(\mathit{packages_P}^{+}(\overline{p'}_k)) \cup \mathit{classes_P}(\mathcal{G})\ \big] \vdash \overline{S}\ \texttt{WF}\end{array}}{\vdash \texttt{transformation interface}\ i\ \overline{(a = (\texttt{in} \mid \texttt{out})\ t : p\texttt{[}\overline{p'}\ \overline{c}\texttt{]})}\ \texttt{\{}\ \overline{S}\ \texttt{\}}\ \texttt{WF}} \qquad (\text{WF-INTERFACE})$$

$$\frac{\begin{array}{c}\texttt{transformation module}\ m\ \texttt{export}\ i\ \ldots\ \texttt{\{}\ldots\texttt{\}} \\ (\mathit{mappings_M}(m))(\texttt{this}, s) = (c_0 \texttt{@} t_0, \overline{c'_0 \texttt{@} t'_0}) \mapsto c''_0 \texttt{@} t''_0 \\ \Delta(\texttt{in}, t) \ni c \qquad \Delta(\texttt{in}, \overline{t'}) \ni \overline{c'} \qquad \Delta(\texttt{out}, t'') \ni c'' \\ c_0 \texttt{@} t_0 <: c \texttt{@} t \qquad \overline{c'} \texttt{@} \overline{t'} <: \overline{c'_0} \texttt{@} \overline{t'_0} \qquad c'' \texttt{@} t'' <: c''_0 \texttt{@} t''_0\end{array}}{\vdash \texttt{mapping}\ c\texttt{@}t\ \texttt{::}\ s\ \texttt{(}\overline{\texttt{in}\ c'\texttt{@}t'}\texttt{)}\ \texttt{:}\ c''\texttt{@}t''\ \texttt{WF}} \qquad (\text{WF-MAPPINGDECL})$$

$$\frac{\begin{array}{c}\texttt{transformation module}\ m'\ \texttt{export}\ i\ \ldots\ \texttt{\{}\ldots\texttt{\}} \Rightarrow m' = m \\ \texttt{transformation interface}\ i\ \overline{(a = (\texttt{in} \mid \texttt{out})\ t : p\texttt{[}\overline{p'}\ \overline{c}\texttt{]})}\ \texttt{\{}\ \overline{S}\ \texttt{\}} \\ \Delta\big[_k\ (a_k,\ t_k) \mapsto \mathit{classes_C}^{*}(\overline{c}_k) \cup \mathit{classes_P}^{*}(\overline{p'}_k) \cup \mathit{classes_P}^{*}(\mathit{packages}^{+}(\overline{p'}_k)) \cup \mathit{classes_P}^{*}(\mathcal{G})\ \big], \\ \Omega\big[\ (\cup_k \mathit{mappings_I}(\overline{j}_k)) \cup \mathit{mappings_M}(m)\ \big] \vdash \overline{O}\ \texttt{WF}\end{array}}{\vdash \texttt{transformation module}\ m\ \texttt{export}\ i\ (\texttt{import}\ \overline{j})^{?}\ \texttt{\{}\ \overline{O}\ \texttt{\}}\ \texttt{WF}} \qquad (\text{WF-MODULE})$$

$$\frac{\begin{array}{c}\Delta(\texttt{in}, t) \ni c \qquad \Delta(\texttt{in}, \overline{t'}) \ni \overline{c'} \qquad \Delta(\texttt{out}, t'') \ni c'' \\ \Gamma[\texttt{self} \mapsto c\texttt{@}t, \overline{x} \mapsto \overline{c'\texttt{@}t'}, \texttt{result} \mapsto c''\texttt{@}t''], \Delta, \Omega \vdash \overline{B}\ \texttt{WF}\end{array}}{\Delta, \Omega \vdash \texttt{mapping}\ c\texttt{@}t\ \texttt{::}\ s\ \texttt{(}\overline{\texttt{in}\ x : c'\texttt{@}t'}\texttt{)}\ \texttt{:}\ c''\texttt{@}t''\ \texttt{\{}\ \overline{B}\ \texttt{\}}\ \texttt{WF}} \qquad (\text{WF-MAPPINGIMPL})$$

$$\frac{\begin{array}{c}\Gamma(\texttt{result}) = c\texttt{@}t \qquad c_0 <: c' \qquad \Delta(\texttt{out}, t) \ni c \\ \mathit{features_C}(c) \ni f : c' \qquad \Gamma, \Delta, \Omega \vdash e_0 : c_0\texttt{@}t_0\end{array}}{\Gamma, \Delta, \Omega \vdash \texttt{result.}f\ \texttt{:=}\ e_0\texttt{;}\ \texttt{WF}} \qquad (\text{WF-ASSIGNMENT})$$

Expression typing and conformance checks:

$$\frac{\Gamma, \Delta, \Omega \vdash e_0 : c_0\texttt{@}t_0}{\Gamma, \Delta, \Omega \vdash e_0\texttt{.late resolveone}\ \texttt{(}c\texttt{@}t\texttt{)}\ \texttt{:}\ c\texttt{@}t} \qquad (\text{T-TRACERES})$$

$$\frac{\begin{array}{c}c_0 <: c \qquad \overline{c} <: \overline{c'} \\ \Omega(i, s) = (c\texttt{@}t, \overline{c'\texttt{@}t'}) \mapsto c''\texttt{@}t'' \\ \Gamma, \Delta, \Omega \vdash e_0 : c_0\texttt{@}t_0 \qquad \Gamma, \Delta, \Omega \vdash \overline{e} : \overline{c}\end{array}}{\Gamma, \Delta, \Omega \vdash e_0\texttt{->map}\ i\texttt{::}s\ \texttt{(}\overline{e}\texttt{)}\ \texttt{:}\ c''\texttt{@}t''} \qquad (\text{T-MAPPINGINV})$$

$$\frac{\Gamma, \Delta, \Omega \vdash e_0 : c_0\texttt{@}t_0 \qquad (\Delta(\texttt{in}, t) \cup \Delta(\texttt{out}, t)) \ni c}{\Gamma, \Delta, \Omega \vdash e_0\texttt{.oclIsTypeOf(}c\texttt{@}t\texttt{)} : \texttt{Boolean@}t_{\mathcal{G}}} \qquad (\text{T-TYPECHECK})$$

$$\frac{\begin{array}{c}\mathit{features_C}(c_0) = \overline{f} : \overline{c} \\ \Gamma, \Delta, \Omega \vdash e_0 : c_0\texttt{@}t_0 \qquad (\Delta(\texttt{in}, t_0) \cup \Delta(\texttt{out}, t_0)) \ni c_0\end{array}}{\Gamma, \Delta, \Omega \vdash e_0\texttt{.}f_i : c_i\texttt{@}t_0} \qquad (\text{T-FEATURE})$$

$$\frac{\Gamma, \Delta, \Omega \vdash \overline{e} : \overline{c'} \qquad \Delta(\texttt{out}, t) \ni c}{\Gamma, \Delta, \Omega \vdash \texttt{new}\ c\texttt{@}t(\overline{e}) : c\texttt{@}t} \qquad (\text{T-CLASSINST})$$

$$\frac{\Gamma(\texttt{self}) = c\texttt{@}t \qquad (\Delta(\texttt{in}, t) \cup \Delta(\texttt{out}, t)) \ni c}{\Gamma, \Delta \vdash \texttt{self} : c\texttt{@}t} \qquad (\text{T-CONTEXT})$$

$$\frac{\Gamma(x) = c\texttt{@}t \qquad (\Delta(\texttt{in}, t) \cup \Delta(\texttt{out}, t)) \ni c}{\Gamma, \Delta \vdash x : \Gamma(x)} \qquad (\text{T-VARIABLE})$$

Figure 6: cQVTom's typing rules.

For any metamodel defined, a package $\mathcal{G}$ introduces the primitive data types `Object`, `Boolean`, and `String`. Respective fields have been omitted for simplicity.

Like in FJ, a subtyping relationship between classes is established by an operator <: that is based on the `extends` keyword. Subtyping is reflexive, transitive, but also antisymmetric, i.e. no cycles are permitted. For convenience, any class except `Object` inherits from `Object` by default.

We introduce auxiliary methods for metamodel and mapping lookup. These methods are utilized by the typing rules hereinafter, they are defined in Figure 5 in the lower two sections. Function $classes_C$ maps a class to a list of inherited classes including itself. In case that $(\texttt{extends}\ c')^?$ is omitted, c' evaluates to `Object`, and $classes_C(\texttt{Object}) = \epsilon$. For a given package, functions $packages_P$ and $classes_P$ compute all packages and classes directly contained in the package, respectively. And finally, for a given class, function $features_C$ retrieves directly contained features. Note that here—and similarly in the rest of this paper—, for brevity, we abbreviate typing judgments on sequences, writing $\overline{f} : \overline{k}$ as shorthand for $f_1 : k_1, \ldots, f_n : k_n$ (cf. [10]). Function $mappings_I$ creates for a given interface identifier a function that relates pairs of interface and mapping identifiers to the mapping's signature type. Analogously, $mappings_M$ creates such a function for any mapping defined in a module implementation – here, we use `this` for identifying the interface whose implementation is currently being defined. For any of these functions being special kinds of binary relations, the $+$ operator denotes their transitive closure. The $*$ operator is short for a functional closure on sets, for instance, $classes_P{}^*(P) := \bigcup_{p \in P} classes_P(p)$.

4.2 Typing

We build a type system in the style of the classical Hindley-Milner type system. Several ideas and many notational elements are borrowed from FJ [10]. Primary judgment of our type system is that of type well-formedness with respect to the modular structure, $\vdash T$ WF. To attain this goal, we must judge about the typing of expressions to determine any explicit and implicit type references. We use a type system where typing relations take the form $\Gamma, \Delta, \Omega \vdash e : t$. This reads: "In a scoped type environment Γ, Ω, Δ of variables, methods, and model elements, the term e has type t".

We capture scoping information in a type environment that consists of three parts: a variable environment Γ, a method environment Ω, and a model element environment Δ. The variable environment is a function mapping identifiers in scope to types, $\Gamma ::= \emptyset \mid \Gamma, [_{k=0}^{n}\ v_k \mapsto c_k@t_k\ ]$. The method environment is more complex, it maps a pair of interface identifier and mapping identifier to a mapping's signature, $\Omega ::= \emptyset \mid \Omega, [_{k=0}^{n}\ (i, s_k) \mapsto \big((c_k@t_k, \overline{c'}_k@\overline{t'}_k) \mapsto c''_k@t''_k\big)]$. The model element environment is a function that captures accessible model elements, $\Delta ::= \emptyset \mid \Delta, [_{k=0}^{n}\ (a_k, t_k) \mapsto C_k]$, where a_k is the access type, `in` or `out`, t_k is the model domain identifier, the pair of both mapping to C_k, the list of class identifiers that are accessible as inquired.

Notation $\Gamma[x_0 \mapsto c_0@t_0, \ldots, x_n \mapsto c_n@t_n]$ is the type environment Γ updated at $x_k, k = 0..n$ to map x_k to $c_k@t_k$. For an overlined syntax expression $\overline{x : c@t}$ type variables are represented as sequences $(x_k)_{k=0}^{n}$, $(t_k)_{k=0}^{n}$, and $(c_k)_{k=0}^{n}$. Then, $\Gamma[\overline{x} : \overline{c@t}]$, $\Gamma[_k\ x_k \mapsto c_k@t_k]$, and $\Gamma[\{x_0 \mapsto c_0@t_0, \ldots, x_n \mapsto c_n@t_n\}]$ are short forms for the notation mentioned above.

Type inference rules are displayed in Figure 6. They are completely syntax directed, thus defining small-step semantics. As we already mentioned, our type system is designed to prove that a modular transformation program in cQVTom is well-formed regarding the information hiding principle. A transformation program T is only then well-formed if its interface definitions and module implementations are well-formed (WF-PROGRAM).

An interface signature defines a sequence of modeling domains on packages $\overline{p}$, and for each domain a list of packages $\overline{p'}$ and classes $\overline{c}$ on which access is opened up. These elements must be contained in the respective domain's root package p (WF-INTERFACE). An environment Δ is built that maps domain names to the list of accessible classes. Inside an interface definition, mapping signatures are declared. Any of these declared signatures must be implemented by a module m with compatible types, and any type used must be accessible (WF-MAPPINGDECL). Type conformance is checked according to the Liskov principle, and accessibility is checked based on the Δ environment.

There must be exactly one implementation per interface. A module inherits model visibilities from the interface it implements, so Δ is equally configured (WF-MODULE). The Ω environment is filled with methods provided by imported interfaces plus those defined locally. A mapping implementation must have any of its signature's type accessible. Two variables plus their respective types are added to its scope, `self` and `result` (WF-MAPPINGIMPL). In the body of a mapping, the target object's features can be initialized. It must be a valid feature of the object's type, both sides of the assignment must have matching types, and the result's type must be write accessible. (WF-ASSIGNMENT).

Expression typing is obvious, insofar that we infer for each syntactical element related types, and check that the element is visible and excels a valid accessibility mode. Trace resolution and mapping invocation (T-TRACERES, T-MAPPINGINV) do not require access rights as they delegate type access to external modules. Even so must we ensure that parameter types are compatible. Global type classes are accessed via a global domain identifier $t_{\mathcal{G}} : \mathcal{G}$, rule T-TYPECHECK gives an example of use. Access to a feature demands read access only to the parent type (T-FEATURE). If an object is created, we check if its type is write accessible (T-CLASSINST). Context and variables are checked if they are in scope and their type is read accessible (T-CONTEXT, T-VARIABLE).

4.3 Properties

Soundness of the semantics with respect to a type system generally means that "well-typed programs cannot go wrong". Since we only focus on soundness of modular concepts added by us, soundness means that well-typed programs at runtime do not hurt any of our four principles. In the following, we formalize our four rules, and provide a proof sketch for each of them.

R1: Segregation of interface and implementation. Modules that implement the same interface can be exchanged while maintaining type conformance.

THEOREM 4.1. *For any pair of transformations T and T', where*

$$T = \overline{P}\,\overline{I}\,M_0 \ldots M_i \ldots M_n$$

$$T' = \overline{P}\,\overline{I}\,M_0 \ldots M'_i \ldots M_n\,,$$

with module implementations M_i, M'_i of the same name $m = m'$, both exporting the same interface $i = i'$, and both being well-formed, i.e., $\vdash M$ WF and $\vdash M'$ WF, we can say that $\vdash T$ WF $\Leftrightarrow \vdash T'$ WF.

PROOF. In the scope of an implementation definition, methods and model types only can (and must be) dereferenced by an interface name, i.e. $j :: s$ and $c@t$, at the syntactical level. No assumptions concerning the actual implementation are made. Required and provided method signatures must be compatible in terms of Liskov's substitution principle, as encoded by rules WF-MAPPINGDECL for module implementations and T-MAPPINGINV for method invocations. Therefore, any module implementation remains independent of any other module implementations. □

R2: Conformance of interface and implementation. A program is only then well-formed if there exists exactly one implementation per interface. If an interface misses an implementation potential method calls cannot be resolved. If an interface is implemented multiple times it is not clearly expressed which implementation to choose resulting in nondeterministic behavior.

THEOREM 4.2. *For any interface $i \in I$, there exists exactly one implementation $m \in M$ for i. For this implementation we can find exactly one bijective mapping between implementation and interface methods $f_{m,i} : O|_m \rightarrow S|_i$, so that each method $o \in O|_m$ maps to a method $s \in S|_i$ with equal name and an equal number of arguments, $o = s$ and $|\overline{c'_o}| = |\overline{c'_s}|$, and signature types are pairwise compatible according to Liskov (contravariant argument types, covariant return types).*

PROOF. Suppose for an implementation $m \in M$ of interface $i \in I$ exists another implementation $m' \in M$ of that same interface. Then, implementations m, m' must be the same, as guaranteed by rule WF-MODULE: $m = m'$. In addition, WF-MAPPINGDECL guarantees that for any method implementation (which there must be exactly one, as we have just shown), type conformance constraints according to Liskov are met. □

R3: Method access control. In an implementation, only model types or mappings are referenced that are imported by the prefixed interface, and the interface is imported by the implemented interface.

THEOREM 4.3. *For any implementation of a module m,*

$$\texttt{transformationmodule}\ m\ \texttt{export}\ i\ (\texttt{import}\ \overline{j})^?,$$

if a method implementation $o \in O|_m$ references a method $j' :: o$ that is not locally defined, $j' \neq \texttt{this}$, then $j' \in \overline{j}$, and the signature of o is compatible (regarding to Liskov's substitution principle) to the signature of o specified in the interface j'.

PROOF. Only mapping invocation expressions may refer to methods. There are two cases, either a called mapping o is defined locally (dereferenced using $\texttt{this}::o$), or the mapping is dereferenced by an interface with notation $i::o$. By inquiring the Ω environment, rule T-MAPPINGINV ascertains that only methods in scope (i.e., local or imported ones) are referenced. The same rule tests for type conformance, as well. □

R4: Model access control. In an implementation, only model types are referenced for read or write access in a specific domain if the respective access mode is declared for this model type and domain type in the interface implemented by the implementation.

THEOREM 4.4. *For any expression's inferred type, $\vdash e : c@t$, model type c must be defined as read-accessible in the respective domain t by the surrounding module's interface, except if access is delegated to another module. It must be write-accessible if features are created or modified. Additionally, for any parameter being part of a mapping or OCL operation's signature, its type $c@t$ must be defined as accessible with the correct mode (read- or write-accessible for context and input parameters, write-accessible for output and return parameter types) in the respective domain t by the surrounding module's interface.*

PROOF. For any expression that is defined in the syntax, a type is inferred by an expression typing rule. There, we can find a precondition in the form of $c \in \Delta(\texttt{in}, t) \cup \Delta(\texttt{out}, t)$ for read access checks, and $c \in \Delta(\texttt{out}, t)$ for write access checks, depending on the underlying dynamic semantics; Exceptions are T-TRACERES and T-MAPPINGINV which delegate to external modules. The same is true for method parameters (rules WF-MAPPINGDECL, WF-MAPPINGIMPL) and assignments (rule WF-ASSIGNMENT). □

Type Soundness. A program is considered as being well-typed if and only if it does not hurt the information hiding principle.

COROLLARY 4.5. *Let T be a transformation program in valid cQVTom syntax. If $\vdash T$ $\texttt{WF}$, transformation T does not hurt the principle of information hiding as described by rules R1 to R4.*

PROOF. From the proofs of theorems 4.1 to 4.4 immediately follows soundness of our module concept. □

Decidability. Because type inference rules are syntax directed, there is only one conclusion for each syntactic form. Evaluation will only get stuck if one of two kinds of premises remains unfulfilled, type conformance or accessibility. If and only if our type system terminates on a program with $\vdash T$ $\texttt{WF}$, it is well-formed. Hence the type system is decidable, and an efficient implementation exists.

5. Implementation in Xtend

For validation purposes, we prototypically implemented a transformation language *Xtend2m*[2] that includes our module concept. Xtend2m augments the *Xtend* language[3] for model-to-model (M2M) and model-to-text (M2T) transformations on EMF-based Ecore models. EMF maps Ecore metamodels to Java types. Xtend is a statically typed language that compiles to ordinary Java code. It features template expressions for M2T and cached methods for M2M, and because it is built with the Xtext framework, it comes with full-featured Eclipse editors and can be easily extended and customized. Extensibility was the primary reason we decided to use the Xtend language for a prototypical implementation of our concepts.

We exploit the fact that Xtend programs are 100% compatible with Java's type system: We utilize Java interfaces as module interfaces and Java classes as module implementations. Mapping operations are Java methods inside a class. As a consequence, Java's type checker automatically ensures that a module conforms to its interface, and enforces that only mappings marked as public are accessed from outside.

However, there are four weaknesses. First, cached methods only take care that, for a certain parameter set, the previously created element is returned instead of a new one. Second, model access restrictions can not be declared for an interface, and implementations are not statically checked for violations against restrictions. Third, module implementations must be kept independent from each other. This issue is already tackled by standard dependency injection APIs, but it is not checked if the imported interface is actually a transformation interface. And fourth, Xtend does not prescribe how a transformation's entry point must look like.

To mark classes and interfaces as transformation concepts, and to include access declarations and mapping methods with QVTo-like tracing, we designed six dedicated Java annotations. Based on these annotations, we were able to make use of an Xtend feature called *Active Annotations*. This mechanism gives language developers the chance to intercept static code analysis and transpilation to Java for two purposes. On the one hand, we can perform static type checking, and in cases of any semantic issues we can create appropriate compiler warnings and errors. These issues are then displayed at the corresponding location in the Eclipse editor. On the other hand, we can manipulate transpilation, for example, we are able to inject code into methods with a certain annotation.

Figure 7 again shows the Activity2Process transformation from the introduction, but this time it is implemented in Xtend2m rather than QVTom. All the annotations used there are going to be explained in the following paragraphs.

[2] Sources are available at `qvt.github.io/xtend2m`.

[3] Xtend is hosted at `xtend-lang.org`

```
@TransformationInterface
@ModelIn(#["activitymodel.Activity",
          "activitymodel.Action"])
@ModelOut(#["processmodel.Process"])
interface IActivity2Process extends MainMethod {
  def Process mapActivity2Process(Activity self)
}
@TransformationModule
class Activity2Process implements IActivity2Process {
  @Import extension IAction2Step

  @Creates(typeof(Process))
  override Process mapActivity2Process(Activity self) {
    result.steps = self.actions.map[mapAction2Step]
  }

  override main(List<List<EObject>> input) {
    val activity = input.head.
      filter(typeof(Activity)).head
    activity2Process(activity)
    doLateResolution
  }
}
```

(a) First module

```
@TransformationInterface
@ModelIn(#["activitymodel.StartAction",
          "activityModel.StopAction"])
@ModelOut(#["processModel.Step"])
interface IAction2StepModule {
  def Step mapAction2Step(Action self)
}
@TransformationModule
class Action2Step implements IAction2Step {
  @Creates(typeof(Step))
  override Step mapAction2Step(Action self) {
     result.name = self.name
     self.succ.lateResolveOne [ result.next = it ]
     result.isStart = self instanceof StartAction
     result.isStop = self instanceof StopAction
  }
}
```

(b) Second module

Figure 7: Activity2Process example in Xtend2m

Interfaces must be indicated with `@TransformationInterface`, and classes with `@TransformationModule`. Control dependencies can be declared via `@Import`, and are mapped by the transpiler to an ordinary `@Inject`. At the same time, transformation modules are automatically injected with a factory for model creation, a module configuration class and a tracing API. Type checking makes sure that an interface implemented or imported by a transformation module is in any case annotated as a transformation interface. A dedicated interface `IMain` constitutes the entry point. A transformation is only valid if this interface is implemented by exactly one module.

We replaced cached methods with our own concept. Methods annotated with `@Creates(typeof(T))` automatically create an instance of T that is registered at our tracing API. Later on, trace resolution can be conducted in the style of QVTo, for example by calling `lateResolveOne`. In contrast to QVTo, late resolution must be triggered by an explicit call to `doLateResolution`. Any referenced model types from inside a method are checked if they are declared as accessible by the interface the surrounding module implements.

Access control can be declared for module interfaces via two annotations, `@ModelIn` and `@ModelOut`. These are parameterized by a list of model element classes. All classes in a package can be declared using a wildcard operator, `myPackage.*`.

At this time, the dependency injection framework has not been informed about available implementations. Xtend programs are typically orchestrated from a workflow script written for the *Model Workflow Engine* (MWE2). We built a customized workflow component that initiates the wiring and then executes the transformation. So that this can happen, module implementations must be registered. Concerning the introductory *Activity2Process* example, a workflow script must register implementations for two interfaces, `IMain` and `IAction2Step` (Figure 8).

```
module Activity2ProcessTransformation
Workflow {
  // load metamodels ActivityModel.ecore, Process.ecore
  // load ActivityModel instance into slot "inputModel"
  :
  component = xtend2m.mwe.ModuleLoader {
    input  = "inputModel"
    output = {
      package = "processmodel"
      slot    = "outputModel" }
    transformationModule = "Activity2Process"
    transformationModule = "Action2Step"
  }
  // persist ProcessModel from slot "outputModel"
  :
}
```

Figure 8: Activity2Process example – MWE2 workflow definition

As we have shown, transformations written in Xtend2m share all modular concepts of QVTom and key QVTo concepts. Because Xtend already comes with template expressions built-in, not only M2M, but also M2T transformations can be written. One difference concerning our module concept is that no metamodel represents the target, hence access restrictions cannot be declared.

6. Validating our Approach

To validate our approach, we chose a transformation that is practically used in a larger research project on software architecture simulation, the Palladio approach[4]. For this transformation, we are able to show that maintenance effort is significantly smaller if a transformation is structured based on our module concept.

The *Palladio* approach [1] enables the prediction of extra-functional properties at the design-time of component-based software. By analyzing simulation results, performance, scalability and reliability problems can be detected at an early stage in the development process. Component-based software architectures and typical usage scenarios are first modeled in the *Palladio Component Model* (PCM). Instances of this model are then translated to simulation code that is based on the *SimuCom* simulation framework. Other targets exist as well, for instance mappings to Plain Old Java Objects (POJO), to Enterprise Java Beans (EJB3), and to a performance prototype (ProtoCom).

Technically, the program for translating architectural models to simulation code had been implemented as an M2T transformation written in Xpand and Xtend1, both being predecessors of Xtend2[5]. M2T transformations are special cases of M2M transformations, where the target model are textual artifacts. Xpand and Xtend2 are both template-based languages, meaning that transformation logic is embedded into static text with the help of meta-tags.

We examined two maintenance scenarios that appeared recently during development. The first scenario deals with the process of refactoring the modular structure of the transformation. The second scenario is about adapting the transformation for a new requirement. We will demonstrate that the effort involved in identifying bad smells and locating concerns can be dramatically reduced with a proper modular structure and descriptive module interfaces.

[4] For details on Palladio, see `palladio-simulator.com`.

[5] As we discuss the dated dialect *Xtend1*, we refer to Xtend as *Xtend2*.

Table 1: SimuCom transformation – Data dependencies per module

Xtend Module	reliability.*	resourceenv.*	system.*	seff.*	usagemodel.*	repository.*	LOC
M_1: Allocation							7
M_2: Build			✗			✗	157
M_3: Calculators				✗	✗		32
⋮							
M_{10}: Dummies			✗			✗	89
M_{11}: JavaCore				✗		✗	244
M_{12}: JavaNamesExt	✗		✗		✗	✗	278
M_{13}: PCMExt			✗	✗	✗	✗	480
M_{14}: ProvidedPorts						✗	260
M_{15}: Repository						✗	120
M_{16}: Resources				✗		✗	27
M_{17}: SEFFBody	✗			✗		✗	220
⋮							
M_{23}: SimAllocations		✗	✗			✗	111
M_{24}: SimCalculators				✗	✗	✗	86
M_{25}: SimCalls				✗		✗	286
⋮							
M_{32}: SimResources		✗					252
M_{33}: SimSEFFBody	✗			✗		✗	252
M_{34}: SimSensors							35
M_{35}: SimUsage			✗		✗	✗	253
⋮							
M_{39}: SimUsageFactory			✗		✗	✗	91
LOC (Σ)							4987
Modules (Σ)	4	2	11	13	9	30	
LOC (%)	18%	7%	35%	42%	28%	87%	
Modules (%)	10%	5%	28%	33%	23%	77%	

6.1 Scenario 1: Refactoring the modular structure

One of the more recent development tasks in the Palladio project was to migrate the meanwhile deprecated Xpand templates to the Xtend2 language. Transformation templates were already modularized using the template method pattern, with the result that variants share common parts, and concretize by implementing abstract methods. Yet, former modularization did not use Java interfaces to declare which public methods implementations must provide, and in Java, it is not possible to restrict access to model elements.

Next, we utilized the Xtend2m add-on to declare proper interfaces. Results of a precursive analysis of data dependencies are depicted in Table 1 in the form of a dependence matrix. The table lists for select modules which of the six PCM packages it references. The PCM is packetized by six modeling aspects, a structural view (repository.*), a behavioral view (seff.*), an assembly view (system.*), a usage view (usagemodel.*), a resource view (resourceenvironment.*), and a view on reliability annotations (reliability.*). For instance, PCM's reliability concepts are handled—and thus referenced—by four modules: M_{12}, M_{17}, M_{28}, and M_{33} (M_{28} has been omitted in this view). These four modules share 18% of the overall 4987 lines of code (LOC).

While modules $M_1,\ldots,M_{22}$ act as generic templates for various targets including SimuCom, modules $M_{23},\ldots,M_{39}$ refine these to produce SimuCom target code. For example, M_{23} extends M_1 in order to implement several abstract methods.

According to the table, most packages reference model elements from only few packages. This indicates a low coupling regarding data dependencies. Particularly JavaNamesExt and PCMExt (M_{12} and M_{13}) exhibit a high degree of coupling. Both modules depend on four PCM packages and are called by most other modules. Inspecting their code quickly reveals that the two modules had been used to collect helper methods. This design decision issues from Xpand's inability to mix template expressions with utility functions. Both modules used to be implemented in Xtend1. However, with the advent of Xtend2, template expressions and functions are mixable. Because almost all methods are only required by single modules, they can be moved to the respective module without breaking the code.

In this example, we identified a bad smell just from studying dependencies declared in module interfaces. Thus we were able to reduce the coupling and increase cohesion between modules, making the overall transformation better understandable and maintainable. Without descriptive interfaces, we would have to reverse-engineer data dependencies manually, with the risk of missing some dependencies. On the other hand, our type interference system statically analyzes implementations against declared interfaces and identifies violations automatically.

6.2 Scenario 2: Locating concerns

In the Palladio model, software components can realize component interfaces. Interfaces in turn can extend other interfaces. When a component realizes such a chain of interfaces, it must provide operations for any interface along that inheritance chain. Until recently[6], our transformations were not aware of inheritance chains. A first step to correct the transformations is to locate places in the code where interfaces are handled. In the PCM, three manifestations of interfaces exist, all being descendants of class `Interface`, namely `OperationInterface`, `InfrastructureInterface`, and `EventGroup`. All four model elements are part of the structural view, and therefore belong to the repository.* namespace. Without having data dependencies declared, we must investigate the full code to track down relevant places. Since the SimuCom transformation employs our module concept, we can narrow down possible locations of concern by just studying module descriptions.

By looking at a transformation's module interfaces, we can tell if a module is actually authorized to access these interface concepts. With dependencies declared at the package-level, we would have to check modules with access to the repository namespace, being 30 out of 39 modules (see Table 1). Since we already have the transformation's model dependencies declared at the class-level, we can narrow down the number of modules we need to consider even further. Table 2 displays for relevant modules if they access any `Interface`-related class residing in the repository namespace. There are only 14 modules whose implementation must be examined further, reducing the amount of code to 39%. In the end, we had to edit four among these to get our task done.

Without a modular structure based on a descriptive module concept, developers need to fall back to a text-based search. However, a word-based search for "interface" leads to many false positives, because semantics are ignored. With our proposed blackbox module concept, maintenance of model transformations takes significantly less effort than with existing module concepts that do not account for data and control dependencies at the interface-level.

7. Related Work

Early formal treatment of modular concepts as they appear in general-purpose programming languages had been carried out by Burstall and Lampson [3]. More recently, modularity has been discovered as beneficial for domain-specific languages as well, for example Kang and Ryu introduced modularity to the JavaScript language [11].

The initial European workshop on composition of model transformations in 2006 marked major interest in the topic for the first time. Since then, compositionality of model transformations has been under steady research, albeit most compositional approaches

[6] `sdqbuild.ipd.kit.edu/jira/browse/PALLADIO-165`

Table 2: SimuCom transformation – Change impact analysis

Xtend Module	<: repository.Interface	Had to modify?
M_1: Allocation		
M_2: Build	✗	
⋮		
M_6: ComposedStructure	✗	
M_7: ContextPattern	✗	
M_8: DataTypes		
M_9: DelegatorClass	✗	✗
M_{10}: Dummies	✗	
M_{11}: JavaCore	✗	✗
M_{12}: JavaNamesExt		
M_{13}: PCMExt		
M_{14}: ProvidedPorts	✗	✗
M_{15}: Repository	✗	✗
⋮		
M_{19}: Sensors	✗	
M_{20}: System		
M_{21}: Usage	✗	
M_{22}: UserActions		
⋮		
M_{27}: SimContextPattern		
M_{28}: SimDummies	✗	
M_{29}: SimJavaCore	✗	
M_{30}: SimProvidedPorts	✗	
M_{31}: SimRepository	✗	
M_{32}: SimResources		
⋮		
Modules (Σ)	14	4
LOC (%)	39%	14%
Modules (%)	36%	10%

Table 3: Comparison of concepts for internal composition

Concept	QVTom	Xtend2	Kermeta	QVTr	QVTo	ATL	ETL	VIATRA2
Modules	✓	✓ class	✓ class	✓ library	✓ library	✓ module	✓ *files*	✓ namespace
Import mechanisms	✓	✓ extends	✓ inherits	✓ import	✓ access, extend	✓ uses	✓ import	✓ import
Rule inheritance	–	–	–	(✓) *unimpl.*	✓ inherits	✓ extends	✓ extends	–
Rule merging	–	–	–	–	✓ merges	–	–	–
Superimposition	–	✓ override	✓ *implicit*	(✓) *implicit*	✓ extends	✓ *implicit*	✓ *implicit*	✓ *model+ data*
Qualified namespace	✓	✓ package	✓ package	(✓) *models*	(✓) *models*	(✓) *models*	(✓) *models*	(✓) *models?*
Explicit interfaces	✓	✓ interface	✓ abstract class	–	–	–	–	–
Traces	✓	(✓) *only local*	–	–	–	–	–	–
Methods	✓	✓ def	✓ *implicit*	–	–	–	–	–
Model elements	✓	(✓) import	–	–	–	–	–	–
Information hiding	✓	✓ private	–	–	–	–	–	–

focus on reusability. In Belaunde's article on QVTo's compositional abilities [2], the author distinguishes between coarse-grained and fine-grained techniques, also known as internal and external composition. The former work on transformations and whole models, whereas the latter work at the level of mappings and model elements.

7.1 Reuse

Olsen et al. investigate possible ways to improve reusability of transformations [15], compositional techniques being among them. A more up-to-date survey and far more detailed classification of reuse techniques is given by Wimmer et al. [23, 24]. They observe that module mechanisms should support definition of access rights and restricted inheritance options. None of the presented fine-grained compositional mechanisms seems to possess blackbox characteristics. We believe the main reason is that techniques which aim at better reuse rely on invasive whitebox mechanisms, whereas we concentrate on improving maintainability. In fact, we deliberately decide in favor of maintainability: Because our approach introduces static dependencies to model elements, we even hinder reuse over metamodels, yet we can improve evolvability, understandability and type-safety.

7.2 Internal composition

Original work on modularity had been carried out in the 1990s in the field of Graph Rewriting Systems, surveyed by Heckel et al. [7]. Hiding of rewrite rules seems to be possible in all of the discussed approaches, but hiding of typed graph structures remains unsupported. More recently, Klar et al. [12] transferred MOF's package management to manage rules in MOFLON, a Triple Graph Grammar dialect. They have reuse in mind, and although rules can be hidden from imports there is no explicit interface concept.

Stratego/XT supports "meta-model extensibility through generator extensibility" [9], also known as horizontal modularity. Our approach still requires the respective modules to be modified when the models change, yet our descriptive interface helps to locate the affected modules with less effort.

Cuadrado and Molina added a rule organization mechanism called *phasing* [4] to RubyTL, a DSL embedded into Ruby. Phasing is a whitebox technique to promote modularity and internal transformation composition. Common code can be factored out, as one phase may refine rules of another phase. A phase has a scope (a pivot point, i. e. an element in the source metamodel from which a rule evolves), a precondition, by-value parameters, and a scheduling script for ordering sub-phases and binding parameters. However, their concept does not include interface descriptions to make data and rule dependencies between phases explicit.

Table 3 compares typical modularity features between languages we perceived to be most interesting and our proposed derivate, QVTom. A checkmark indicates full support, partial support if bracketed, and either the respective keyword or possible limitations are stated below. All of the observed languages support modularity to some extent.

Most concentrate on whitebox techniques for reuse matters, for example inheritance, merging, and superimposition of rules. Superimposition had been first introduced by Wagelaar to ATL and QVT [22], a technique to overlay sets of rule definitions on top of each other. QVTo is said to have an OO heritage [2] and thus only supports inheritance and superimposition.

When it comes to interface concepts, only few languages provide concepts to make traces, methods, or model elements explicit. Only internal DSLs are able to hide implementation details by exploiting concepts of high-level languages, for instance Xtend and RubyTL. Rules in Kermeta are defined as class methods in UML, so inheritance, interfaces and other UML concepts can be exploited. To our knowledge, QVTom and the Xtend2m prototype are the only approaches that introduce blackbox modularity.

7.3 External composition

The key characteristic of any external composition mechanism is that only whole transformations operating on complete models can be chained, whereas we aim at supporting finer-grained compositionality. Both *QVT and ATL* already bring along integrated blackbox composition mechanisms for orchestrating complete transformations. There is no interface concept for language constructs.

Several approaches are concerned with compositionality at the transformation level, also known as blackbox composition, mostly aiming at reusability of transformations. The most notable ones are UniTI [21] integrated into Eclipse AM3 as a GMM4CT plug-in, Wires* and TraCo. All of them follow the data-driven programming paradigm, component instances are executed as soon as models are present at all of the available input ports. None of them offers a language concept for binding model concepts, which has only recently been proposed by Cuadrado et al. [5]. While UniTI supports a shared tracing model, it is not possible to explicitly share single traces based on concepts.

TraCo is a transformation composition framework that showcases safe composition through contractual interfaces [8]. TraCo's interfaces only provide for full models, it has neither built-in support for model access policies, nor does it include mapping operations. A TraCo component is purely data-driven, it cannot refer to external mappings or externally generated traces. A notable field of application is to ensure that only valid transformation variants can be built from available components. With our approach, type-safe configuration of variants could be performed similarly at design-time. Because our binding is resolved before runtime, there is no runtime validation intended.

8. Conclusions and Outlook

In this paper, we have introduced a novel module concept that is specially tailored for model transformations. The concept makes data and control dependencies between modules explicit, it provides interface descriptions that can hide implementation details from module users. Implementations are statically checked if they actually meet contractual obligations defined by provided interfaces. We formalized the underlying type system, and, as a proof-of-concept, integrated this approach into the Xtend language. In a case study on a real-world M2T transformation, we have shown that our module system is able to effectively reduce the effort of locating concerns involved in typical evolution scenarios.

In the near future, we plan to carry out additional case studies on M2M transformations. We are currently working on an integration of our concept into the QVTo language. Modularizing existing transformations could be assisted by an automatic clustering algorithm, provided that we can find metrics to assess cohesion and coupling of mappings. Finally, several features of common module systems remain yet unsupported. For example, only implementations can define import dependencies, modules cannot form a hierarchy. Additionally, data dependencies could be augmented with syntactic sugar, e.g. a postponed plus operator could automatically include subclasses of a named class, following a similar feature in Kermeta. Also, behavioral contracts in the spirit of Meyer's Design by Contract could complement our concept, as already proposed by Vallecillo et al. [19] for monolithic transformations.

Acknowledgments

This research has been funded by the German Research Foundation (DFG) under grant No. RE 1674/5-1.

References

[1] S. Becker, H. Koziolek, and R. Reussner. The Palladio Component Model for model-driven performance prediction. *Journal of Systems and Software*, 82(1):3–22, Jan. 2009.

[2] M. Belaunde. Transformation composition in QVT. In *Proc. 1st Europ. Workshop on Composition of Model Transformations (CMT'06)*, TR-CTI, pages 39–46. Centre for Telematics and Information Technology, Univ. of Twente, June 2006. URL `doc.utwente.nl/66171/`.

[3] R. M. Burstall and B. W. Lampson. A kernel language for abstract data types and modules. In *Proc. Int'l Symp. on Semantics of Data Types*, volume 173 of *LNCS*, pages 1–50. Springer, 1984.

[4] J. S. Cuadrado and J. G. Molina. Modularization of model transformations through a phasing mechanism. *Software and System Modeling*, 8 (3):325–345, 2009.

[5] J. S. Cuadrado, E. Guerra, and J. de Lara. Generic model transformations: *Write once, reuse everywhere.* In *Proc. 4th Int'l Conf. Theory and Practice of Model Transformations (ICMT'11)*, volume 6707 of *LNCS*, pages 62–77. Springer, 2011.

[6] K. Czarnecki and S. Helsen. Feature-based survey of model transformation approaches. *IBM Systems Journal*, 45(3):621–646, 2006.

[7] R. Heckel, G. Engels, H. Ehrig, and G. Taentzer. Classification and comparison of module concepts for graph transformation systems. In *Handbook of Graph Grammars and Computing by Graph Transformations, Volume 2: Applications, Languages, and Tools*, chapter 1. World Scientific, Oct. 1999. ISBN 9810240201.

[8] F. Heidenreich, J. Kopcsek, and U. Aßmann. Safe composition of transformations. *Journal of Object Technology*, 10:7: 1–20, 2011.

[9] Z. Hemel, L. C. L. Kats, D. M. Groenewegen, and E. Visser. Code generation by model transformation: A case study in transformation modularity. *Software and System Modeling*, 9(3):375–402, 2010.

[10] A. Igarashi, B. C. Pierce, and P. Wadler. Featherweight Java: A minimal core calculus for Java and GJ. *ACM Trans. Program. Lang. Syst.*, 23 (3):396–450, 2001.

[11] S. Kang and S. Ryu. Formal specification of a JavaScript module system. *SIGPLAN Not.*, 47(10):621–638, Oct. 2012. ISSN 0362-1340.

[12] F. Klar, A. Königs, and A. Schürr. Model transformation in the large. In *Proc. 6th Joint Meeting of the Eur. Software Engineering Conf. and the ACM SIGSOFT Int'l Symp. on Foundations of Software Engineering (ESEC/SIGSOFT FSE'07)*, pages 285–294. ACM, 2007.

[13] A. MacCormack, J. Rusnak, and C. Baldwin. The impact of component modularity on design evolution: Evidence from the software industry. *Harvard Business School Technology & Operations Mgt. Unit Research Paper*, No. 08-038, 2007.

[14] Object Management Group. MOF 2.0 Query/View/Transformation, version 1.1. URL `www.omg.org/spec/QVT/1.1/`, Jan. 2011.

[15] G. K. Olsen, J. Aagedal, and J. Oldevik. Aspects of reusable model transformations. In *Proc. 1st Europ. Workshop on Composition of Model Transformations (CMT'06)*, TR-CTI, pages 21–26. Centre for Telematics and Information Technology, Univ. of Twente, June 2006. URL `doc.utwente.nl/66171/`.

[16] D. L. Parnas. On the criteria to be used in decomposing systems into modules. *Commun. ACM*, 15(12):1053–1058, 1972.

[17] A. Rentschler, Q. Noorshams, L. Happe, and R. Reussner. Interactive visual analytics for efficient maintenance of model transformations. In *Proc. 6th Int'l Conf. on Theory and Practice of Model Transformations (ICMT'13)*, volume 7909 of *LNCS*, pages 141–157. Springer, 2013.

[18] K. J. Sullivan, W. G. Griswold, Y. Cai, and B. Hallen. The structure and value of modularity in software design. *SIGSOFT Softw. Eng. Notes*, 26(5):99–108, Sept. 2001. ISSN 0163-5948.

[19] A. Vallecillo, M. Gogolla, L. Burgueño, M. Wimmer, and L. Hamann. Formal specification and testing of model transformations. In *12th Int'l School on Formal Methods for the Design of Computer, Communication, and Software Systems (SFM'12)*, volume 7320 of *LNCS*, pages 399–437. Springer, 2012.

[20] M. van Amstel and M. G. J. van den Brand. Model transformation analysis: Staying ahead of the maintenance nightmare. In *Proc. 4th Int'l Conf. on Theory and Practice of Model Transformations (ICMT'11)*, volume 6707 of *LNCS*, pages 108–122. Springer, 2011.

[21] B. Vanhooff, D. Ayed, S. V. Baelen, W. Joosen, and Y. Berbers. UniTI: A unified transformation infrastructure. In *Proc. 10th Int'l Conf. on Model Driven Engineering Languages and Systems (MODELS'07)*, volume 4735 of *LNCS*, pages 31–45. Springer, 2007.

[22] D. Wagelaar. Composition techniques for rule-based model transformation languages. In *Proc. 1st Int'l Conf. on Theory and Practice of Model Transformation (ICMT'08)*, volume 5063 of *LNCS*, pages 152–167. Springer, 2008.

[23] M. Wimmer, G. Kappel, A. Kusel, W. Retschitzegger, J. Schönböck, and W. Schwinger. Fact or fiction - reuse in rule-based model-to-model transformation languages. In *Proc. 5th Int'l Conf. Theory and Practice of Model Transformations (ICMT'12)*, volume 7307 of *LNCS*, pages 280–295. Springer, 2012.

[24] M. Wimmer, G. Kappel, A. Kusel, W. Retschitzegger, J. Schönböck, W. Schwinger, D. S. Kolovos, R. F. Paige, M. Lauder, A. Schürr, and D. Wagelaar. Surveying rule inheritance in model-to-model transformation languages. *Journal of Obj. Techn.*, 11(2):3: 1–46, 2012.

JavaScript Module System: Exploring the Design Space

Junhee Cho   Sukyoung Ryu
KAIST
{ssaljalu, sryu.cs}@kaist.ac.kr

Abstract

While JavaScript is one of the most widely used programming languages not only for web applications but also for large projects, it does not provide a language-level module system. JavaScript developers have used *the module pattern* to avoid name conflicts by themselves, but the prevalent uses of multiple libraries and even multiple versions of a single library in one application complicate maintenance of namespace. The next release of the JavaScript language specification will support a module system, but the module proposal in prose does not clearly describe its semantics. Several tools attempt to support the new features in the next release of JavaScript by translating them into the current JavaScript, but their module semantics do not faithfully implement the proposal.

In this paper, we identify some of the design issues in the JavaScript module system. We describe ambiguous or undefined semantics of the module system with concrete examples, show how the existing tools support them in a crude way, and discuss reasonable choices for the design issues. We specify the formal semantics of the module system, which provides unambiguous description of the design choices, and we provide its implementation as a source-to-source transformation from JavaScript with modules to the plain JavaScript that the current JavaScript engines can evaluate.

Categories and Subject Descriptors D.3.3 [*Programming Languages*]: Language Constructs and Features

Keywords JavaScript, module system, source-to-source transformation

1. Introduction

JavaScript [4] was originally developed as a simple scripting language but now it is one of the most widely used programming languages. The main advantage of using JavaScript in web documents is to support dynamic interaction with users. JavaScript enables dynamic partial updates of web documents by communicating with servers through HTTP and updating web documents via browser APIs for Document Object Model (DOM) [25]. Thanks to the capability, 98 out of the 100 most visited websites according to Alexa [11] use JavaScript [8], and its use outside client-side web programming keeps growing. Large stand-alone projects such as node.js [12] for building scalable network applications use JavaScript and web applications on various platforms including Samsung Smart TV SDK [21] and Tizen SDK [5].

MODULARITY '14, April 22–26, 2014, Lugano, Switzerland.

http://dx.doi.org/10.1145/2577080.2577088

```
<!DOCTYPE html><html>
<head>
  <script src="http://code.jquery.com/jquery-1.9.1.js">
  </script>
</head>
<body>
<div id="log"><h3>Before $.noConflict(true)</h3></div>
<script src="http://code.jquery.com/jquery-1.6.2.js">
</script>
<script>
var $log = $( "#log" );
$log.append( "2nd loaded jQuery version ($): " +
             $.fn.jquery + "<br>" );
/* Restore globally scoped jQuery variables to
   the first version loaded (the newer version) */
jq162 = jQuery.noConflict(true);
$log.append( "<h3>After $.noConflict(true)</h3>" );
$log.append( "1st loaded jQuery version ($): " +
             $.fn.jquery + "<br>" );
$log.append( "2nd loaded jQuery version (jq162): " +
             jq162.fn.jquery + "<br>" );
</script></body></html>
```

Figure 1. Multiple versions of jQuery in one HTML document, an excerpt from the jQuery API document [14]

However, JavaScript does not provide any language-level module system. Simple scripts may not need to maintain namespace but a module system is necessary for programming in the large. Because JavaScript does not have the standard libraries, JavaScript developers use more than a dozen libraries: jQuery [13] focuses on improving the interaction between JavaScript and HTML, MooTools [24] emphasizes animation supports, Prototype [23] focuses on adding new features to JavaScript, and other libraries have their own strength. Due to the lack of the single standard libraries, JavaScript developers often use multiple sets of third-party libraries with duplicated functionalities in one project to selectively use functionalities from them. Similarly, some JavaScript projects use even multiple versions of a single library to use both new API functions introduced in a newer version and old API functions deprecated in the newer version. While multiple versions of a single library obviously share symbols with the same names, different libraries often use the same symbol names too, which lead to name conflicts when a single project uses them. For example, because both jQuery and Prototype use the symbol $, if an HTML document includes both libraries by `<script>` tags, the library included later overrides the symbol $ from the other library with its own $. Figure 1 shows an example from the jQuery API document [14], which uses multiple versions of a single library and resolves name conflicts explicitly; it loads two versions of jQuery, `jquery-1.9.1.js` and `jquery-1.6.2.js`, and then re-

```
var module = function () {
  var privateVar = "accessible only from within module";
  function privateMethod() {
    alert("accessible only from within module");
  }
  return {
    publicProp: "accessible as module.publicProp",
    publicMethod: function() {
      alert(privateVar);
      privateMethod();
      alert("accessible as module.publicMethod");
    };
  };
}();
```

Figure 2. JavaScript module pattern

stores jQuery's globally scoped variables to the first loaded jQuery, `jquery-1.9.1.js`, by `jQuery.noConflict(true)`.

To alleviate the problem, the JavaScript community has used the "module pattern" [19]. The module pattern is to use functions to simulate modules by assigning an anonymous function to a namespace object and adding "private" members to the function. For example, Figure 2 shows a simple use of the module pattern where the anonymous function returns an object with public members which may use private members defined in the function. The module pattern provides some forms of namespace manipulation but such a programming pattern is verbose and error prone, and programmers are responsible for checking that they follow the pattern correctly.

Given the growing popularity of JavaScript as a general purpose language for programming in the large and the need for a standard, language-level support for namespace manipulation, the next release of JavaScript (JavaScript.next) plans to include a module system. The ECMAScript Harmony proposals [2] are a collection of proposals for the next ECMA-262 language specification, and most of the proposals have already been incorporated into the ECMAScript 6 specification draft [3]. While the Harmony proposals include a module proposal [10], the proposal description is very brief and informal. Even in the ECMAScript 6 specification draft, the sections related to modules are empty. The Harmony module proposal describes only the high-level ideas and the design principles of the module system succinctly; it does not specify the complete semantics of modules especially the various interactions with the existing JavaScript language features.

Despite of the current status of the module proposal, the long-awaited module system gets eagerly adopted in various ways. Kang and Ryu [16] present a formalization of the core Harmony module proposal that does not include dynamic module loading. They introduce a formal specification and implementation of the module system by desugaring JavaScript extended with modules to λ_{JS} [9], a core-calculus of JavaScript. The Traceur [6] compiler translates a JavaScript.next program to a JavaScript program, which enables developers to use the new JavaScript.next features in advance. It provides various new features including a module system and asks for user inputs to reflect the feedback in the ECMAScript standards process. Among many variant languages of JavaScript, TypeScript [18] is a typed superset of JavaScript that compiles to plain JavaScript. It supports classes, modules, and interfaces to improve static checking and verification of TypeScript programs.

Unfortunately, the immature status of the Harmony proposal causes discrepancies between the various module extensions of JavaScript. While Kang and Ryu's module system clearly describes the module semantics via desugaring to λ_{JS}, because the semantics of λ_{JS} is very different from that of JavaScript, it is difficult for JavaScript developers to understand the semantics in terms of λ_{JS}. On the contrary, Traceur and TypeScript do not describe their module systems clearly; Traceur partially implements the module proposal and TypeScript provides some variant of the proposal.

In this paper, we investigate the design issues of the JavaScript module system with concrete code examples. While one of the goals of the module system is orthogonality from existing features, the informal proposal reveals some ambiguous semantics of the module system and interactions with existing features. First, naïve source-to-source transformations by Traceur and TypeScript provide inconsistent semantics of import and export statements. For example, when a Traceur module imports an exported variable from another module, the importing module assigns the current value of the variable to the imported variable without any connection to the exported variable, which does not satisfy the module proposal. Second, the proposal specifies the semantics when there are conflicts between import declarations, but it does not specify any semantics when there are conflicts between function, variable, module, and import declarations. Third, while every JavaScript object has its prototype[1], a module instance object that is a first-class object that reflects the exported bindings of an evaluated module does not have any prototype. The unique difference of module instance objects from ordinary JavaScript objects leads to peculiar semantics of module instance objects. Finally, the module proposal does not specify the interactions between module declarations and dynamic code generation functions such as `eval`. We believe that an exploration of the design space will help the ECMAScript committee to design the module system more clearly and reasonably, and the third-party developers to support the module system correctly.

To rigorously discuss and describe the JavaScript module system, we present a formal specification of the module system via source-to-source transformation rules. Because the ECMAScript language specification describes the semantics informally in prose, we developed a formal specification and implementation of a Scalable Analysis Framework for ECMAScript (SAFE) [17] and made it publicly available [15]. We provide a formal specification and an implementation of the module system by extending SAFE with the rewriting rules from JavaScript with modules to the plain JavaScript. By supporting JavaScript.next features today via source-to-source translation precisely, JavaScript application developers can try future features in advance and contribute their feedback to the design of JavaScript.next, and JavaScript engine developers can apply the same technique to their existing engines without modifying the current implementation largely. Our implementation of the module system is also available to the public via the SAFE repository.

The contributions of this paper are as follows:

- We describe design issues of the JavaScript module system with concrete examples, and we discuss reasonable design choices.
- We present a formal specification of the module system, which enables to discuss various design choices formally.
- We provide an implementation of the module system so that JavaScript developers can try future JavaScript features today and JavaScript engine developers can support the features today.

The remainder of this paper is organized thus. In Section 2, we introduce design issues in the JavaScript module system with the comparison of how Traceur and TypeScript support the module system, and we discuss the design issues and reasonable choices. Section 3 describes a formalization of the module system and it addresses some of alternative semantics depending on the design choices. It also proves two safety properties of the module system: validity of module environments and isolation of namespaces. In Section 4, we describe our implementation of the module system

[1] Each JavaScript object has an internal link to its *prototype* as a way of inheritance and a list of prototype links is a *prototype chain*.

```
(function Foo() {
    var foo = "foo", bar = 42;
    (function Bar() {
        bar;            // undefined;
        var bar = "bar";
        bar;            // "bar";
    })();
})();
```

Figure 3. Static variable declaration in a function scope

```
(function Foo() {
    var foo = "foo", bar = 42;
    (function Bar() {
        var bar;        // variable declaration
        bar;            // not yet initialized
        bar = "bar";    // variable initialization
        bar;            // after initialization
    })();
})();
```

Figure 4. Same semantics with Figure 3

```
(function Foo() {
    var foo = "foo", bar = 42;
    (function Bar() {
        bar;            // 42;
        eval("var bar = 'bar';");
        bar;            // "bar";
    })();
})();
```

Figure 5. Dynamic variable declaration in a function scope

and discuss limitations of our approach. Section 5 discusses related work and we conclude in Section 6.

2. Design Issues in the JavaScript Module System

The brief informal description of the Harmony module proposal leads to discrepancies between implementations of the module system. Both Traceur and TypeScript provide inconsistent semantics for import and export declarations, for example. To make the module proposal more elaborate and precise, and to prevent the current module implementations from diverging from the proposal semantics, we discuss four important design issues:

- Unclear semantics of import and export declarations
- Incomplete semantics of name conflict resolution
- Inconsistent semantics of prototypes of module instance objects
- Unclear semantics of the module system in the argument of the `eval` function

We describe each design issue, compare the semantics supported by Traceur and TypeScript, discuss possible semantics that are compliant to the Harmony proposal, and propose a reasonable semantics among the alternatives.

2.1 Import and Export Declarations

Design Issue The Harmony proposal does not describe the semantics of the import and export declarations completely. The proposal specifies their semantics as follows:

```
module Foo {
    export var foo = "foo", bar = 42;
    module Bar {
        export bar;
        bar;                    // 42;
        eval("var bar = 'bar';");
        bar;                    // 42? "bar"?
    }
    export Bar;
}
Foo.Bar.bar;                    // 42? "bar"?
```

Figure 6. Dynamic variable declaration in a module scope

> "Export declarations declare that a top-level declaration in a module is visible externally to the module."
>
> "Import declarations bind another module's exports as local variables."

Because the Harmony proposal does not specify the interactions between the import and export declarations and other existing JavaScript features, there are several cases where the semantics is not clear.

First, the proposal does not provide a clear semantics of the interactions between the evaluation of import and export declarations and that of variable and function declarations. Before describing the interactions, let us review the JavaScript semantics for the evaluation of variable and function declarations. When a JavaScript engine evaluates a program code or a function body code, it first binds all the variable and function declarations in the code and then evaluates the code. For a variable declaration with an initialization expression, the variable declaration is conceptually divided into a variable declaration without any initialization expression and an assignment expression to bind the initialization expression to the variable. Thus, variable and function declarations are bound before actually evaluating any other statements; in a single scope, variables or functions may be used before their definitions textually. For example, Figure 3 shows that two occurrences of `bar` in the body of the function `Bar` evaluate to different values. The first reference to `bar` evaluates to `undefined` because it is already declared but not yet initialized, and the second reference to `bar` evaluates to `"bar"` because it is initialized with the value. In effect, the code in Figure 4 has the same semantics with the one in Figure 3. On the other hand, a variable declaration in a code string passed to the `eval` function as its argument is not evaluated as a variable declaration in the enclosing code; the variable declaration is bound after evaluating the `eval` function call, which behaves differently from static variable declarations. Consider the example in Figure 5. The first reference to `bar` evaluates to 42 instead of `undefined` because the variable `bar` is not yet declared in the body of the function `Bar` because the `eval` function call is not yet evaluated.

Second, similarly for the first case, the proposal does not specify the semantics of the interactions between the import and export declarations and other declarations in a module scope. Because a module scope is analogous to a function scope as the module pattern illustrates, a similar issue arises: what happens when the evaluation of the `eval` function declares a variable that is already declared in the module scope? It is not clear whether a variable declared by the `eval` call shadows the already declared variable with the same name. It is not clear either whether such a dynamic variable declaration should affect the values of the exported variables. For example, consider the example in Figure 6. The second reference to `bar` in the module `Bar` and the property access to `Foo.Bar.bar` outside the module may evaluate to `42` if the dy-

```
module Foo {
    var foo = "foo";
    module Bar {
        export var foo = "bar", bar = "bar";
        eval("delete foo; delete bar;");
    }
    export { foo, Bar };
}
Foo.Bar.foo;            // "bar"? undefined? error?
Foo.Bar.bar;            // "bar"? undefined? error?
```

Figure 7. Export declarations and the `eval` function

```
module Foo {
  export var foo = 42;
  export function inc() { foo++; }
}
import foo from Foo;
Foo.inc();
foo;                    // 43
```

Figure 8. Changing the value of an exported name

```
var Foo = (function() {
  "use strict";
  var foo = 42;
  function inc() { foo++; }
  return Object.preventExtensions(Object.create(
    null,
    { foo: { get: function() { return foo; },
             enumerable: true },
      inc: { get: function() { return inc; },
             enumerable: true }
    }));
}).call(this);
var foo = Foo.foo;
Foo.inc();
foo;                    // 42
```

Figure 9. Translation of Figure 8 by Traceur

namic variable declaration does not have any effects; both of them may evaluate to "bar" if the dynamic variable declaration affects even the exported name. Or, the second reference to `bar` may evaluate to "bar" and `Foo.Bar.bar` may evaluate to 42, if the dynamic variable declaration is in effect only in a module scope.

Finally, the proposal does not describe what happens when the evaluation of the `eval` function deletes variables that are exported to out of the module scope, as Figure 7 illustrates. Depending on the semantics, `Foo.Bar.foo` may evaluate to "bar" if the `eval` function call does not delete the variable `foo`, it may evaluate to `undefined` if the call deletes the variable, or it may throw an error if the semantics disallows such a delete operation.

Semantics in Traceur and TypeScript Based on the Harmony proposal, both Traceur and TypeScript translate an import declaration to an assignment expression, assigning the current value bound to the exported name to the imported name, which does not reflect any future changes of the value of the exported name. Figure 8 presents a simple module declaration of `Foo` exporting a variable `foo` and a function `inc`. The top-level imports `foo` from the module `Foo`, increments the value of `foo` by calling the exported function `inc`, and gets the value of the imported `foo`. According to the

```
var Foo;
(function (Foo) {
    Foo.foo = 42;
    function inc() { Foo.foo++; }
    Foo.inc = inc;
})(Foo || (Foo = {}));
var foo = Foo.foo;
Foo.inc();
foo;                    // 42
```

Figure 10. Translation of Figure 8 by TypeScript

semantics in the Harmony proposal, the value of `foo` should be 43. However, both Traceur and TypeScript do not preserve the semantics. Figure 9 presents the translated version of the original code in Figure 8 by Traceur. Traceur uses the module pattern by creating an anonymous function, which uses the strict mode and returns a new object with two properties: `foo` and `inc`. It creates a new object by extending `Object` with `preventExtensions` to faithfully simulate read-only module instance objects. Similarly, Figure 10 presents the translated version of the original code by TypeScript. Unlike Traceur, TypeScript simply uses the traditional module pattern without any particular method for prohibiting future updates to the module object. Also, TypeScript uses a different concrete syntax for import declarations. More importantly, both of them produce "wrong" results 42, because the translation is merely desugaring an import declaration to an assignment expression without maintaining a reference to the original exported name.

Interestingly, Traceur and TypeScript behave differently for the aforementioned examples. For the code example in Figure 6, Traceur evaluates both of them to 42, but TypeScript evaluates them to `undefined` because their simple translation does not handle nested variable declarations correctly. Similarly for the code in Figure 7, Traceur throws a syntax error for trying to delete `foo` in strict mode, but TypeScript evaluates it to "bar".

Semantics Compliant to Harmony Our formal semantics correctly preserves the semantics of the Harmony proposal. We provide a high-level explanation here and describe it formally in Section 3. We translate an export declaration to a pair of an exported name and its enclosing environment record, either a declarative environment record for a module scope or an object environment record for a module instance object, and we translate any references to the exported name to references to the name in the environment record. One might think that our translation is unnecessarily complicated and it is enough to translate an export declaration to simply a getter property in a module instance object rather than an assignment as in Traceur and TypeScript. Indeed, with such a translation, the value of the exported name would be always in synch with the value of the original variable. However, maintaining only a module instance object may lose connections to variables declared by `eval` function calls; it will refer to the new variable declared by `eval` calls rather than the variable declared in an enclosing scope. On the contrary, our translation mechanism always gets the correct value even in the presence of `eval` function calls.

An analogous problem arises with import declarations and we translate import declarations similarly to the export declarations. Instead of translating an import declaration to a property access in a module instance object, we translate an import declaration to a pair of an imported name and the module instance object that includes the imported entity, and we translate the references to the imported name to references to the property name in the module instance object, which always produces correct values.

```
foo();                              // "foo";
bar;                                // undefined;
function foo() { return "bar"; }
function foo() { return "foo"; }
var foo, bar = "foo", bar = "bar";
function bar() { return 42; }
bar;                                // "bar";
```

Figure 11. Name conflicts between functions and variables

```
function foo() { return "bar"; }
function foo() { return "foo"; }
function bar() { return 42; }
var foo, bar, bar;
foo();                              // "foo";
bar;                                // undefined;
bar = "foo";
bar = "bar";
bar;                                // "bar";
```

Figure 12. Same semantics for Figure 11

2.2 Name Conflict Resolution

Design Issue While one of the main goals of the module system is to avoid name conflicts, the Harmony proposal does not specify a name resolution mechanism precisely. A program may have various kinds of name conflicts between declarations in a program or a module: function declarations, variable declarations, module declarations, export declarations, and import declarations. The Harmony proposal describes a name conflict resolution mechanism between export declarations and between import declarations, but it does not describe any name conflict resolution mechanism between other kinds of declarations. To make things more complicated, the binding and evaluation order of declarations in a JavaScript program is different from their textual order.

Before describing name conflict resolution mechanisms, let us review the JavaScript semantics for evaluation of variable and function declarations again in more detail. As we discussed in Section 2.1, regardless of the textual order of function and variable declarations in a single scope, all the function declarations are evaluated first, all the variable declarations are bound and initialized to `undefined` next, and the remaining statements including the assignments from the variable declarations with initialization expressions, if any, are evaluated in their textual order. When there are name conflicts between function declarations, the function declaration that comes later in textual order overrides the other function declaration. Name conflicts between variable declarations have no effects in terms of name binding, but if both declarations have initialization expressions they are evaluated in order during the evaluation of the remaining statements. Similarly, when a function declaration and a variable declaration with an initialization expression declare the same name f, the function declaration is evaluated first and binds the name f and the initialization expression of the variable declaration overrides the function declaration.

For example, Figure 11 shows a JavaScript code with name conflicts between various declarations. According to the JavaScript semantics, the code example has the same semantics with the code example in Figure 12. The second function declaration overrides the first function declaration with the same name; variables are declared right after evaluating function declarations and initialized to `undefined`. Note that variable declarations do not override function declarations.

```
module Foo {
    export function toString() { return 42; }
}
module Bar {}
"" + {};                       // "[object Object]";
"" + Foo;                      // "42";
"" + Bar;                      // TypeError
```

Figure 13. Modules with and without `toString`

Semantics in Traceur and TypeScript Again, Traceur and TypeScript behave differently for name conflict resolution. Because Traceur uses the module pattern, it does not distinguish between module declarations and variable declarations with initialization expressions; a module declaration is translated to a variable declaration with an anonymous function expression as its initialization expression, and resolution of any name conflicts with it behaves just like for variable declarations following the JavaScript semantics. On the contrary, while TypeScript also uses the module pattern, it does not allow name conflicts with entities of different types; it syntactically rejects any name conflicts with different declarations.

Semantics Compliant to Harmony While the proposal does not provide a clear semantics for resolving name conflicts between various declarations including module declarations, we found that several options are incomparably reasonable in the sense that they are consistent with the JavaScript name resolution semantics. We may want to evaluate module declarations earlier than other declarations just like function declarations. We may also want to evaluate import and export declarations before other declarations; we may want to evaluate module, import and export declarations in any order, or we may want to evaluate module declarations before import and export declarations.

In our formalization of the module system, we chose to let one kind of declarations override other kinds of declarations: module declarations override the other kinds of declarations, import declarations override function and variable declarations, and function declarations override variable declarations. We made this design choice because we consider that module and import declarations are more important than local declarations, and a module declaration is more important than an import declaration which is simply an alias of a name in a module instance object. We do not argue that this design choice is the best option; rather, we provide our formalism as a starting point for any other researchers and developers to extend and modify according to their preferred design decisions.

2.3 Prototypes of Module Instance Objects

Design Issue While every JavaScript object has the `Object` prototype object as the top of its prototype chain, the Harmony proposal makes an exception for module instance objects:

> "A module instance object is a prototype-less object that provides read-only access to the exports of the module."

However, the unique characteristic of module instance objects may cause confusion when they are used with ordinary JavaScript objects, which does not satisfy one of the design goals of the Harmony module proposal: orthogonality from existing features.

Because `Object` provides default implementations for the `toString` and `valueOf` properties, every ordinary JavaScript object uses them unless some object in its prototype chain or the object itself provides its own implementations. For example, as Figure 13 shows, when we concatenate a string with an object, the object is implicitly converted to a string by calling the function bound to the `toString` property and concatenated to the given string. JavaScript developers use such implicit type conversions heavily without worrying about the existence of the `toString` property, but module instance objects now break such programming. As in Figure 13, concatenation of a string to a module may result in a string or the `TypeError` exception depending on the existence of the `toString` property in the module instance object.

Semantics in Traceur and TypeScript Indeed, this feature is one of the sources to make differences between the module semantics of Traceur and TypeScript. While Traceur throws the `TypeError` exception for concatenating an empty string to the `Bar` module, TypeScript produces the `"[object Object]"` string.

Semantics Compliant to Harmony Our formalization of the module system is compliant to the Harmony proposal. However, we note that the proposed semantics in the proposal could be confusing to JavaScript developers as we described so far, and it might be a reasonable alternative to make module instance objects have the `Object` prototype object as their prototype object.

2.4 `eval` Function

Design Issue Though we used the `eval` function in our code examples so far, the Harmony proposal does not specify the interactions between the module system and the `eval` function clearly. While the proposal states that:

> "Reflective evaluation, via `eval` or the module loading API starts a new compilation and linking phase for the dynamically evaluated code."

it does not specify the semantics of module declarations, export declarations, and import declarations when they are evaluated by the `eval` function, which is not straightforward.

For example, whether the evaluation of an export declaration by the `eval` function affects the enclosing scope is debatable because it may require changes in the read-only module instance object that is already *sealed*. Since the `[[Extensible]]` internal property of a sealed object has the `false` value, we cannot add new properties to a sealed object. Also, since every property of a sealed object has the `false` value for its `[[Configurable]]` internal property, we cannot delete or modify the property. Therefore, prohibiting the evaluation of export and import declarations by the `eval` function from affecting the enclosing scope may be a reasonable option.

Semantics in Traceur and TypeScript Similarly for the case in Section 2.2, Traceur and TypeScript behave differently. Because module bodies are translated to strict code in Traceur, new declarations evaluated by the `eval` function do not affect the enclosing scope, and the `eval` function rejects any inputs of the extended syntax with the module system. On the contrary, TypeScript does not allow inputs of the extended syntax with the module system either but it does not signal any error.

Semantics Compliant to Harmony In our formalization, we chose to evaluate module, import, and export declarations by the `eval` function only when the function is called either in the global scope or in a module scope. Because module declarations can appear only at the top level of a program or a module body, we believe this design choice is consistent with the module proposal. If the `eval` function is called from a scope that is not the global scope or a module scope, evaluation of the function ignores any module, import, and export declarations in the input string.

3. Formalization of the JavaScript Module System

In this section, we describe the formalization of the JavaScript module system. Due to space limitations, we discuss only the central parts related to the design issues discussed in Section 2, and we refer the interested readers to our companion report [1].

Our formalization of the JavaScript module system translates JavaScript programs extended with the module system to plain JavaScript programs, which is based on our previous work [16] that translates JavaScript programs with modules to λ_{JS} programs. The contributions of the formalization in this paper over the previous work are as follows:

- It provides a semantics that is much closer to the JavaScript semantics. While λ_{JS} was proposed as "the essence of JavaScript," its semantics is very different from the JavaScript semantics. It is a simple extension of the lambda calculus, and the "desugaring" process is not really a syntactic simplification but rather a compilation. As the authors of λ_{JS} specified in their paper, type checking of translated λ_{JS} programs does not directly correspond to type checking of the original JavaScript programs. Although a small calculus may be useful for reasoning and proving some properties of JavaScript, the big gap between the source JavaScript language and the target λ_{JS} language makes it hard to understand and connect the relationships between original JavaScript programs and their translated λ_{JS} versions for JavaScript developers. Because the source-to-source translation in this paper describes the module semantics in terms of JavaScript, the language that the developers are already familiar with, it is more easily understandable.
- It enables more efficient and practical implementations. Because the generated λ_{JS} programs are huge and they manipulate large immutable objects, execution of λ_{JS} programs is impractically slow and it consumes a lot of memory. Instead, the source-to-source translation can take advantage of existing efficient JavaScript engines. For example, developers may write JavaScript programs with modules, translate them into plain JavaScript using the module rewriter described in Section 4, and run the translated programs on any JavaScript engine.
- It supports the `eval` function with one restriction. While λ_{JS} does not support the `eval` function at all, the source-to-source translation can utilize the ability of executing JavaScript code after translation. One restriction is that temporary helper function names should not conflict with the names introduced by the the `eval` function calls during module translation, which one can easily satisfy by using long strings of complicated characters for the helper function names.
- It is more flexible and adaptable in that it can address the design choices discussed in Section 2. Because the translation captures JavaScript-specific features in translated versions, it shows the design issues explicitly as we describe in Section 3.2.
- Because the formalization is built on top of the previous work [16], we can reuse much of the machinery developed there. For example, we reuse the module environment construction and the proofs of the validity checks.

3.1 JavaScript Module System

Our formalization describes the Harmony module proposal. Module declarations and import declarations can appear only at the top level of a program or a module body, and export declarations can appear only at the top level of a module body. The formalization builds on top of SAFE [17], which provides both a formal specification and implementation of JavaScript. We describe the module system using the Intermediate Representation (IR) syntax of SAFE; SAFE formally specifies compilation steps from JavaScript Abstract Syntax Tree (AST) to IR, and dynamic semantics of IR. We extend the syntax of JavaScript with module support as presented in Figure 14.

Before describing the translation from JavaScript with modules to plain JavaScript, let us review the semantics of the JavaScript

Program	::=	*SourceElement**
SourceElement	::=	*Statement*
	|	*VariableDeclaration*
	|	*FunctionDeclaration*
	|	*ImportDeclaration*
	|	*ModuleDeclaration*
ModuleDeclaration	::=	`module` *Identifier* { *ModuleBody* }
ModuleBody	::=	*ModuleElement**
ModuleElement	::=	*SourceElement*
	|	*ExportDeclaration*
ExportDeclaration	::=	`export` *ExportSpecifierSet* (, *ExportSpecifierSet*)* ;
	|	`export` *VariableDeclaration*
	|	`export` *FunctionDeclaration*
	|	`export get` *Identifier* () { *FunctionBody* }
	|	`export set` *Identifier* (*Identifier*) { *FunctionBody* }
ExportSpecifierSet	::=	{ *ExportSpecifier* (, *ExportSpecifier*)* } (`from` *Path*)?
	|	*Identifier* (`from` *Path*)?
	|	* (`from` *Path*)?
ExportSpecifier	::=	*Identifier* (: *Path*)?
Path	::=	*Identifier*(. *Identifier*)*
ImportDeclaration	::=	`import` *ImportClause* (, *ImportClause*)* ;
ImportClause	::=	*Path* `as` *Identifier*
	|	*ImportSpecifierSet* `from` *Path*
ImportSpecifierSet	::=	{ *ImportSpecifier* (, *ImportSpecifier*)* }
	|	*Identifier*
ImportSpecifier	::=	*Identifier* (: *Identifier*)?

Figure 14. Syntax of the module system

module system. When a JavaScript engine evaluates a program with modules, it first statically constructs a *module environment* which holds all the names in the global object and modules, and all the import and export relations. Then, it evaluates module, import, function, and variable declarations, and statements in order. When it evaluates module declarations, it first instantiates every module by constructing a *module scope* and a *module instance object*. Each module declaration introduces a new scope called a module scope, and its module body is evaluated in the module scope. An evaluated module called a module instance object contains lexically encapsulated members and exported bindings. An evaluation of a module results in a JavaScript object that reflects the exported bindings of a module instance object. After instantiating the modules, a JavaScript engine initializes all the module bindings and makes all the module instance objects read-only. Initializing a module binding is to evaluate the statements in the module body in its module scope. For mutually recursive import statements, function, variable, and nested module declarations are evaluated in the module scope, and the getters for the exported names are set in the module instance object. Finally, it seals all the module instance objects to make them read-only and substitutes each imported name with its canonical name of which the imported name is an alias.

$$(\Sigma, \phi), p \rightarrow_m \mathit{MDecl}[\![p]\!](\Sigma, \phi)$$

$$\mathit{MDecl}[\![s_1 \cdots s_n]\!](\Sigma, \phi) = \mathit{MDecl}[\![s_1]\!](\Sigma, \phi) \cdots \mathit{MDecl}[\![s_n]\!](\Sigma, \phi)$$

$$\begin{array}{l}
\mathit{MDecl}[\![\texttt{module } M \ \{s_1 \cdots s_n\}]\!](\Sigma, \phi) = \\
\quad \texttt{var } M = \texttt{new (function(f, p) \{} \\
\qquad\qquad \texttt{f.prototype} = \texttt{p;} \\
\qquad\qquad \texttt{return f;} \\
\qquad \texttt{\}} \ (f, p))\ ()\texttt{;} \\
\quad \texttt{Object.seal(}M\texttt{);}
\end{array}$$

$$\begin{array}{l}
\text{where } f = \texttt{function() \{} \\
\quad \mathit{QName}[\![\mathit{FDecl}[\![s_1 \cdots s_n]\!](\Sigma, \phi')]\!](\mathit{QNEnv}(\Sigma, \phi')) \\
\quad \mathit{QName}[\![\mathit{VDecl}[\![s_1 \cdots s_n]\!](\Sigma, \phi')]\!](\mathit{QNEnv}(\Sigma, \phi')) \\
\quad \mathit{QName}[\![\mathit{MDecl}[\![s_1 \cdots s_n]\!](\Sigma, \phi')]\!](\mathit{QNEnv}(\Sigma, \phi')) \\
\quad \mathit{QName}[\![\mathit{Exports}[\![s_1 \cdots s_n]\!](\Sigma, \phi')]\!](\mathit{QNEnv}(\Sigma, \phi')) \\
\quad \texttt{this.update}M = \texttt{function(arguments) \{} \\
\qquad \mathit{QName}[\![\mathit{Others}[\![s_1 \cdots s_n]\!](\Sigma, \phi')]\!] \\
\qquad\qquad (\mathit{QNEnv}(\Sigma, \phi')) \\
\quad \texttt{\};} \\
\texttt{\}}
\end{array}$$

$$\text{and } p = \begin{cases} \texttt{Object.prototype} & \text{if } \phi = \epsilon \\ \phi & \text{otherwise} \end{cases}$$

$$\text{and } \phi' = \begin{cases} M & \text{if } \phi = \epsilon \\ \phi.M & \text{otherwise} \end{cases}$$

$$\mathit{MDecl}[\![d]\!](\Sigma, \phi) = \texttt{;} \qquad \text{if } d \notin \mathit{ModuleDeclaration}$$

Figure 15. Module translation

Translation of a program p consists of several phases as follows:

$$\frac{(\Sigma, \phi), p \rightarrow_f p_f \qquad (\Sigma, \phi), p \rightarrow_v p_v \qquad (\Sigma, \phi), p \rightarrow_m p_m \qquad (\Sigma, \phi), p \rightarrow_u p_u \qquad (\Sigma, \phi), p \rightarrow_s p_s}{(\Sigma, \phi), p \rightarrow p_f \ p_v \ p_m \ p_u \ p_s}$$

Before translating the program, we build a module environment Σ, which maps all the names in p to their unique qualified names, as described in the previous work [16]. For given Σ and a path from the top-level ϕ, which is the empty path ϵ for p, we first translate declarations: function declarations by the $\rightarrow_f$ rule, variable declarations by the $\rightarrow_v$ rule, and module declarations by the $\rightarrow_m$ rule. Then, we initialize module instance objects by the $\rightarrow_u$ rule, and rename all the imported names in top-level variable declarations, function declarations, and statements with their corresponding exported names by the $\rightarrow_s$ rule.

Translation of a module declaration uses the module pattern. As Figure 15 describes, for given Σ and ϕ, translation of a module declaration "`module` M $\{s_1 \cdots s_n\}$" uses a function scope to represent a module scope. Because any function value is an object in JavaScript, we translate a module declaration to a variable declaration initialized with the `new` statement using a function as a constructor. Specifically, in Figure 15, the declaration of a module M is translated to the declaration of a variable M which constructs a function object.[2] The function sets up its prototype object, which we discuss in Section 3.2. Then, it returns a module instance object f with exported names as its properties; in the body

[2] While the function translates its `arguments` variable as a pair of a getter and a setter to avoid name conflicts, we omit the translation for presentation brevity.

$$(\Sigma, \phi), p \rightarrow_f \mathit{FDecl}[\![p]\!](\Sigma, \phi)$$

$$\mathit{FDecl}[\![s_1 \cdots s_n]\!](\Sigma, \phi) = \mathit{FDecl}[\![s_1]\!](\Sigma, \phi) \cdots \mathit{FDecl}[\![s_n]\!](\Sigma, \phi)$$

$$\mathit{FDecl}[\![(\texttt{export})\ \texttt{function}\ f(x_1, \cdots, x_n)\ \{s_1 \cdots s_k\}]\!](\Sigma, \phi) = \texttt{function}\ f(x_1, \cdots, x_n)\ \{s_1 \cdots s_k\}$$

$$\mathit{FDecl}[\![d]\!](\Sigma, \phi) = ; \quad \text{if } d \notin \mathit{FunctionDeclaration}$$

Figure 16. Function translation

$$(\Sigma, \phi), p \rightarrow_v \mathit{VDecl}[\![p]\!](\Sigma, \phi)$$

$$\mathit{VDecl}[\![s_1 \cdots s_n]\!](\Sigma, \phi) = \texttt{var}\ x_1, \cdots, x_k \quad \text{where } x_i \in \mathit{VName}[\![s_1 \cdots s_n]\!](\Sigma, \phi) \wedge 1 \leq i \leq k$$

Figure 17. Variable translation

$$\mathit{Others}[\![s_1 \cdots s_n]\!](\Sigma, \phi) = \mathit{Others}[\![s_1]\!](\Sigma, \phi) \cdots \mathit{Others}[\![s_n]\!](\Sigma, \phi)$$

$$\mathit{Others}[\![(\texttt{export})\ \texttt{var}\ x_1 (= e_1), \cdots, x_n (= e_n)]\!](\Sigma, \phi) = x_{i_1} = e_{i_1}; \cdots x_{i_k} = e_{i_k}; \quad \text{where } \exists\, e_{i_j} \wedge i_1 \leq i_j \leq i_k$$

$$\mathit{Others}[\![s]\!](\Sigma, \phi) = s \quad \text{if } s \in \mathit{Statement}$$

$$\mathit{Others}[\![d]\!](\Sigma, \phi) = ; \quad \text{if } d \notin (\mathit{VariableDeclaration} \cup \mathit{Statement})$$

Figure 18. Other declaration translation

$$\frac{(\Sigma, \phi), s_i \rightarrow_u s'_i \qquad 1 \leq i \leq n}{(\Sigma, \phi), s_1 \cdots s_n \rightarrow_u s'_1 \cdots s'_n}$$

$$\frac{(\Sigma, \phi.M), s_i \rightarrow_u s'_i \qquad 1 \leq i \leq n}{(\Sigma, \phi), \texttt{module}\ M\ \{s_1 \cdots s_n\} \rightarrow_u \phi.M.\texttt{update}M();\ \texttt{delete}\ \phi.M.\texttt{update}M;\ \texttt{Object.freeze}(\phi.M);\ s'_1 \cdots s'_n}$$

$$\frac{d \notin \mathit{ModuleDeclaration}}{(\Sigma, \phi), d \rightarrow_u ;}$$

Figure 19. Module initialization

$$\frac{\{i_1, \cdots, i_k\} = \{i \mid s_i \notin \mathit{ModuleDeclaration} \wedge s_i \notin \mathit{ImportDeclaration} \wedge 1 \leq i \leq n\}}{(\Sigma, \phi), s_1 \cdots s_n \rightarrow_s \mathit{QName}[\![s_{i_1} \cdots s_{i_k}]\!](\mathit{QNEnv}(\Sigma, \phi))}$$

Figure 20. Module renaming

$$\mathit{Exports}[\![s_1 \cdots s_n]\!](\Sigma, \phi) = \mathit{Exports}[\![s_1]\!](\Sigma, \phi) \cdots \mathit{Exports}[\![s_n]\!](\Sigma, \phi)$$

$$\mathit{Exports}[\![\texttt{export}\ \{x\}]\!](\Sigma, \phi) = \mathit{Exports}[\![\texttt{export}\ \{x\texttt{:}\ x\}]\!](\Sigma, \phi)$$

$$\mathit{Exports}[\![\texttt{export}\ \{x\texttt{:}\ \phi'\}]\!](\Sigma, \phi) = \mathit{Export}(\texttt{get}, x, ()\{\texttt{return}\ \mathit{lookup}[\![\phi']\!](\Sigma, \phi);\})$$

$$\mathit{Exports}[\![\texttt{export get}\ f()\{s_1 \cdots s_n\}]\!](\Sigma, \phi) = \mathit{Export}(\texttt{get}, f, ()\{\mathit{Exports}[\![s_1]\!](\Sigma, \phi) \cdots \mathit{Exports}[\![s_n]\!](\Sigma, \phi)\})$$

$$\mathit{Exports}[\![\texttt{export set}\ f(x)\{s_1 \cdots s_n\}]\!](\Sigma, \phi) = \mathit{Export}(\texttt{set}, f, (x)\{\mathit{Exports}[\![s_1]\!](\Sigma, \phi) \cdots \mathit{Exports}[\![s_n]\!](\Sigma, \phi)\})$$

Export(*accessor*, *f*, *ftn*) =

```
var $desc =
    Object.getOwnPropertyDescriptor(this, "f");
delete this.f;
if (typeof $desc == "undefined")
  $desc = {configurable : true};
$desc.accessor = function ftn;
Object.defineOwnProperty(this, "f", $desc);
```

Figure 21. Export translation (partial)

of the function object f, the declarations and statements are reordered as we discuss in Section 3.2. Function declarations come first, if any, variable declarations, sub-module declarations, export declarations, and statements, if any, follow in order. As Figure 16 describes, *FDecl* collects function declarations including exported ones without the `export` keyword, and *VDecl* shown in Figure 17 collects variable names in M by using the helper function *VName* and declares them. Note that any initialization expressions in variable declarations are deferred to statements. All the names in each function, variable, and module declarations in M are replaced with their unique qualified names by using the helper functions *QName* and *QNEnv*. We omit the definitions of the helper functions in this paper due to space limitations, and refer the interested readers to our companion report [1]. As we discuss in Section 3.2, *Exports* makes getters for exported names. Because of nested modules and mutually-dependent modules, the translation resolves names that appear in declarations and statements in different scopes at different phases. It creates a temporary function update$M$ to replace the names in the remaining declarations and statements with their unique qualified names after constructing module instance objects; the $\rightarrow_u$ rule calls this function to initialize module instance objects. We assume that the translator chooses update$M$ as a non-conflicting name with any names in the program. Figure 18 presents *Others* which collects the initialization expressions in variable declarations and the statements in M. We make the module instance object read-only by calling `Object.seal`, which finishes translation of a module declaration.

Now that all module instance objects finished declaration of their functions, variables, and sub-modules, the $\rightarrow_u$ rule presented in Figure 19 initializes each module instance object recursively; it calls the temporary function update$M$ to perform renaming in the module scope, deletes the temporary function object update$M$, and freezes the module instance object. Finally, the $\rightarrow_s$ rule presented in Figure 20 renames all the imported names in top-level variable declarations, function declarations, and statements with their corresponding exported names.

3.2 Formal Specification of the Design Issues

Let us revisit the design issues in the JavaScript module system discussed in Section 2, and explain the issues and our design decisions in the context of the formal specification.

Import and Export Declarations To correctly preserve the semantics of the import and export declarations in the Harmony proposal, we translate an export declaration to a pair of an exported name and its enclosing environment record, and we translate any

{`[[Class]]` : "Module", `[[Extensible]]` : true, `[[Prototype]]` : *#ObjectPrototype*, `[[Scope]]` : {}, `@property` : {}}	{`[[Class]]` : "Module", `[[Extensible]]` : true, `[[Prototype]]` : *#Null*, `[[Scope]]` : {}, `@property` : {}}

Figure 22. Module instance objects with/without prototype object

references to the exported name to references to the name in the environment record. In the formalization, we represent a pair of an exported name and its enclosing environment record as an accessor property in a module instance object. As Figure 21 describes, an exported name x_i in a module instance object ϕ is translated to a getter named x_i of the object, where $lookup[\![\phi']\!](\Sigma, \phi)$ returns the unique qualified name denoted by ϕ'. We show translation of some export declarations in Figure 21 for presentation brevity; translation of other export declarations is very similar. Then, any reference to x_i becomes a getter call on the module instance object ϕ, which preserves the semantics even when the `eval` function call creates a new value with the same name x_i. Similarly, references to imported names become getter calls on module instance objects, which preserves the semantics even in the presence of `eval` function calls.

Name Conflict Resolution As we discussed in Section 2.2, the proposal does not provide a clear semantics for resolving name conflicts between various declarations. While several options are incomparably reasonable, we chose a specific precedence so that module declarations override the other kinds of declarations and function declarations override variable declarations. Figure 15 describes this precedence in the body of f. We made this design choice because we consider that module declarations are more important than function or variable declarations. One can make different design decisions by changing the order of declarations in the body of f.

According to the Harmony proposal, the translation should instantiate and initialize modules in their textual order. At the same time, because the proposal allows nested modules and mutually-dependent modules, we may not have all the information to resolve names by a single scan of a program. Thus, name resolution for the JavaScript module system requires several steps: we first build a module environment Σ to collect all the names, create module instance objects possibly uninitialized, and finish initialization and freeze all the module instance objects.

Prototypes of Module Instance Objects As we discussed in Section 2.3, the proposed semantics of the prototypes of module instance objects in the proposal could be confusing or rather unintuitive to JavaScript developers. As a reasonable alternative semantics, in the formalization in Figure 15, the function object representing a module scope takes p as its second argument, which denotes its prototype object. If a module is declared at the top-level of a program, its module instance object sets its prototype object with `Object.prototype`. Otherwise, a module instance object sets its prototype object with its enclosing module instance object. For a compliant semantics to the Harmony proposal, one may not set the prototype object of a module instance object.

More concretely, Figure 22 shows module instance objects with the empty scope and the empty property as placeholders. The value of the `[[Class]]` internal property is `"Module"` and the value of the `[[Extensible]]` internal property is `true` until the objects are sealed. The left module instance object represents the semantics where its prototype object is `Object.prototype` just like other JavaScript objects and the right module instance object represents the semantics where it does not have its prototype object as the Harmony proposal specifies. In Figure 22, *#ObjectPrototype* denotes the location of the `Object` prototype object and *#Null* denotes that the object does not have its prototype object.

$$\frac{\begin{array}{c}\Gamma = (H, A, tb, \Sigma, \phi) \qquad (v_1, v_3) = isEval(\Gamma, y, z_1, z_2) \\ inModScope(H, A) \qquad \Sigma' = Env[\![v_3]\!](\Sigma, \phi) \\ (H, A, tb, \Sigma', \phi), x = \texttt{eval}(v_1, v_3) \rightarrow_e (H', A'), ct\end{array}}{\Gamma, x = y(z_1, z_2) \rightarrow_e (H', A'), ct}$$

$$\frac{\begin{array}{c}\Gamma = (H, A, tb, \Sigma, \phi) \qquad (v_1, v_3) = isEval(\Gamma, y, z_1, z_2) \\ \neg\, inModScope(H, A) \qquad v_4 = RemoveModule(v_3) \\ \Gamma, x = \texttt{eval}(v_1, v_4) \rightarrow_e (H', A'), ct\end{array}}{\Gamma, x = y(z_1, z_2) \rightarrow_e (H', A'), ct}$$

$$\frac{\begin{array}{c}\Gamma = (H, A, tb, \Sigma, \phi) \qquad \Gamma, y \rightarrow_e \#GlobalEval \\ \Gamma, z_1 \rightarrow_e v_1 \qquad v_1 \in Loc \qquad \Gamma, z_2 \rightarrow_e v_2\end{array}}{isEval(\Gamma, y, z_1, z_2) = (v_1, ToString(H, v_2))}$$

$$\frac{}{inModScope(H, \#Global)}$$

$$\frac{\begin{array}{c}l \in dom(H) \qquad H(l) \in Object \\ H(l).[[\texttt{Class}]] = \text{“Module”} \qquad H(l).[[\texttt{Scope}]] = A\end{array}}{inModScope(H, A)}$$

Figure 23. Evaluation of the `eval` function

`eval` Function Because module declarations can appear only at the top level of a program or a module body, our formalization chose to evaluate module, import, and export declarations by the `eval` function only when the function is called either in the global scope or in a module scope. Figure 23 describes the semantics of the `eval` function call.

The first rule describes the case when the `eval` function is called in the global scope or in a module scope. Under the evaluation context Γ, which consists of a heap H, an execution environment A, the value of `this` *tb*, a module environment Σ, and a path from the top level ϕ, it first checks whether the function being called is the global `eval` function by *isEval*. The third rule defines *isEval*, which makes sure that the global `eval` function denoted by *#GlobalEval* is being called, and returns a pair of valid arguments to the function. The fourth and the fifth rules define *inModScope*, which checks whether the function is being called in the global scope or in a module scope. When the `eval` call is *inModScope*, it updates the module environment by *Env* to treat the string argument of the `eval` function just like a JavaScript code and evaluates it. After evaluating the function call, it produces (H', A'), a heap and an execution environment that may be updated during the evaluation, and the function call result *ct*.

The second rule describes the case when the `eval` function is called locally. Then, it removes any module-related declarations from the input string by *RemoveModule* and evaluates it. We omit the definitions of the helper functions for presentation brevity.

As an alternative semantics, one may want to allow evaluation of the `eval` function to declare modules, imports, and exports. We can support such a semantics in the formalization by replacing the first and the second rules with the following:

$$\frac{\begin{array}{c}\Gamma = (H, A, tb, \Sigma, \phi) \qquad (v_1, v_3) = \mathit{isEval}(\Gamma, y, z_1, z_2) \\ \Sigma' = \mathit{Env}[\![v_3]\!](\Sigma, \phi) \\ (H, A, tb, \Sigma', \phi), x = \texttt{eval}(v_1, v_3) \rightarrow_e (H', A'), ct\end{array}}{\Gamma, x = y(z_1, z_2) \rightarrow_e (H', A'), ct}$$

In other words, the alternative semantics evaluates the string argument of the `eval` function without checking whether it is being called in the global scope or in a module scope by *inModScope*.

3.3 Validity Properties of the JavaScript Module System

Because our formalization is built on top of the previous work [16], we can reuse the machinery used to prove the properties of valid programs. For a valid JavaScript program p that may declare and use modules, its translated program in JavaScript does not include any free variables.

Property 1 (Validity of Translation Rules). *For a valid program p, evaluating its translated version does not cause any error due to free variables.*

Proof Sketch. Let $FV(s)$ denote the set of the free variables in a statement s. For each evaluation rule:

$$\forall H, A, tb, \Sigma, \phi, s.$$
$$(H, A, tb, \Sigma, \phi), s \rightarrow_e (H', A'), ct \text{ for some } H', A', ct$$

we show that the evaluation does not add new free variables. Assume that the property is false, that is, the translated version p' causes an error due to a free variable. By the properties of free variables and because evaluations do not add new free variables, $FV(p')$ includes the free variable causing the error during evaluation of p'. Because p is a valid program, we can show that $FV(p) = \emptyset$, which makes the assumption false. Thus, the translated version of a valid program does not cause an error due to a free variable. □

In a valid program p, the module scopes are correctly *isolated* from outside.

Property 2 (Isolation of Module Scopes). *When a module M declares a variable x but does not export it, the module-scope variable x does not affect outside its enclosing module M.*

Proof Sketch. Let $p(v)$ be `module` M {`var` x = v;} p. By establishing the exact module environments for p and $p(v)$, we can show that the module environment of $p(v)$ is a simple extension of the module environment of p. We can also show that two environments $\mathit{Env}[\![p]\!]$ and $\mathit{Env}[\![p(v)]\!] \backslash \mathit{Env}[\![p]\!]$ are disjoint. Therefore, we can show that any translation of $p(v)$ shares a similar structure that is independent of the choice of v. By showing that the translation of p by the $\rightarrow_s$ rule under the module environment Σ derived from the translation of $p(v)$ does not contain any occurrence of $M.x$, we can finish the proof. □

4. Implementation of the JavaScript Module System

We implemented the JavaScript module system on top of SAFE [17] as a source-to-source translator and made it publicly available [15]. Figure 24 illustrates a high-level architecture of the important parts of SAFE. The architecture accepts a JavaScript program, translates it through AST, IR, and Control Flow Graph (CFG), each of which is utilized by various analyses and tools. For example, AST suites best for clone detection and pretty printing the original JavaScript program; IR works best for evaluation and test data generation; and CFG works best for type-based analysis and bug detection among others. For presentation brevity, we omit other features of SAFE such as Web IDL [26] supports. Figure 25 presents the extended architecture of SAFE with support for the module system. The dotted boxes denote extended parts to support the module system, and the *ModuleRewriter* phase translates an AST that may include module syntax into another AST that does not include any module syntax. Due to space limitations, we omit the details of *ModuleRewriter*, but discuss its properties and limitations. JavaScript engine developers can evaluate their implementations and ours to articulate and discuss ambiguous semantics from the Harmony proposal. Because our implementation is open sourced, the developers can apply our technique to their engines. Or, they can even use our *ModuleRewriter* as a preprocessor to support the module system as a sort of macros.

As we discussed in Section 3.1, the translation mechanism is based on the module pattern. Because translation of a module consists of instantiation and initialization, the control should reenter the function scope at initialization, which is not available with JavaScript objects. Therefore, our implementation creates a temporary object in the global scope which has temporary functions created from the module scope at instantiation time, and it calls the temporary functions to initialize the modules at initialization time. We implement import statements by replacing the references to imported names with the corresponding property accesses to the module instance objects. Figure 26 presents a translated code of the example in Figure 8 in plain JavaScript by *ModuleRewriter*.

The limitations of *ModuleRewriter* are due to the quirky dynamic semantics of JavaScript: the `eval` function and the `with` statement. First, *ModuleRewriter* does not handle the references to imported names in a string passed to the `eval` function as an argument. Because *ModuleRewriter* statically collects the references to imported names and replaces them to corresponding property accesses to module instance objects at compile time, it should be able to collect the references to imported names from a string at compile time. Secondly, the `with` statement takes an object, called a *with object*, and introduces the properties of the with object to the environment at run time, which basically supports dynamic scoping. The properties of the with object shadow any bindings with the same name in the enclosing context. Therefore, a reference to an identifier may evaluate to an entity defined in the enclosing context or to a property in the with object. Because it is not possible to determine whether an identifier refers to an imported name at compile time, it is not possible to replace identifiers in the `with` statement. Thanks to Park *et al.* [20], we can desugar most of the `with` statements at compile time; for example, we can desugar the following `with` statement:

```
with (o) { x = 42; }
```

to the following code without using the `with` statement:

```
("x" in o ? o.x : x) = 42;
```

preserving the semantics. Indeed, the SAFE architecture includes the `with` rewriter implementation by default. Therefore, *ModuleRewriter* can handle the `with` statements unless they call dynamic code generation functions such as the `eval` function.

5. Related Work

The ECMAScript Harmony proposal [2] describes the new features adopted in the next release of ECMAScript such as modules, classes, generators, and block scoped bindings. Most of the proposal have already been incorporated into the ECMAScript 6 language specification draft, but the module proposal [10] is not yet included. The module proposal provides a brief, high-level description of the JavaScript module system but the informal specification in prose does not explain the module semantics precisely.

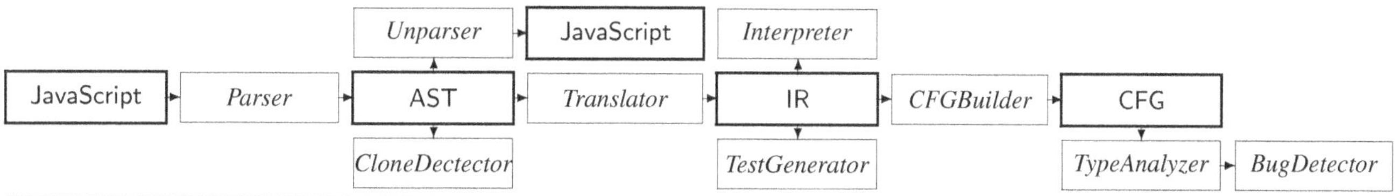

Figure 24. SAFE architecture

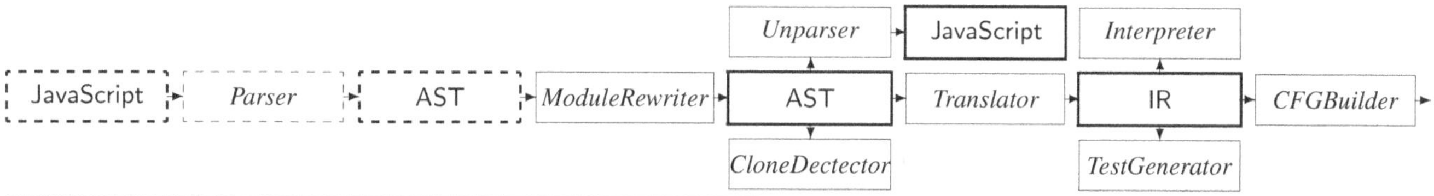

Figure 25. SAFE architecture with module support

Kang and Ryu [16] designed a formal specification and implementation of a JavaScript module system based on the Harmony proposal. They formalized and implemented their module system using λ_{JS} [9], which is a core calculus of ECMAScript 3. While they provide a small set of conventional formal semantics rules of λ_{JS} and translation rules from JavaScript to λ_{JS}, the implementation is impractically slow. They described the formal semantics of the module system as a set of translation rules from JavaScript with modules to λ_{JS}, and they implemented the module system by extending the translation rules. While the formalization and implementation are solid and rigorous, the practicality of their approach is not clear. Because the semantics of λ_{JS} is very much different from the original JavaScript, the big gap between JavaScript and λ_{JS} makes it hard for JavaScript developers to understand and connect the relationships between original JavaScript programs and their translated λ_{JS} versions. Because the generated λ_{JS} programs are huge, executing λ_{JS} programs has been absurdly slow. On the contrary, our formalization is similarly rigorous but much easier to understand because it is a source-to-source translation, and our implementation is much more efficient and practical.

Traceur [6] is a compiler developed by Google that compiles JavaScript.next code into one in ECMAScript 5. While their implementation is written in JavaScript of size more than 20,000 lines, they do not provide any formal specification or a detailed description of the system. As we have seen in this paper, the module implementation in Traceur does not satisfy the semantics in the Harmony module proposal in many cases.

TypeScript is a superset of JavaScript that supports a type system for static checking and verification. It also provides some features of JavaScript.next including the module system, and it compiles a TypeScript program into a plain JavaScript program. Unlike Traceur, supporting JavaScript.next closely today is not one of the main goals of TypeScript. It focuses more on type inference and type annotation for better static checking and analysis. Thus, its module support is more premature than Traceur, often leads to different semantics from the Harmony module proposal. It supports somewhat different module syntax and it does not support mutually recursive imports, for example.

While both Traceur and TypeScript support very premature module systems with different semantics from the Harmony proposal without any detailed description of them, our module system is formally specified and implemented preserving the semantics of the Harmony proposal. Our implementation is built on top of SAFE, a scalable analysis framework for JavaScript, which provides various facilities for JavaScript program manipulation. Because the implementation of the SAFE architecture uses tools to automatically generate AST nodes by ASTGen [22] and parsers by Rats! [7], it is easily adaptable to any syntax changes and extensions. The various components of SAFE such as the unparser to pretty print plain JavaScript syntax, the interpreter to evaluate JavaScript programs, and the `with` rewriter to desugar the `with` statements away have greatly improved the quality and productivity of our implementation.

6. Conclusion

JavaScript is now one of the most widely used programming languages from small scripts embedded in web documents to large stand-alone projects such as web applications and compilers. The lack of any language-level module system in JavaScript has caused many problems and an ad-hoc programming pattern, which finally introduces a language-level module system to JavaScript in the next release of the ECMAScript language specification. Even though the ECMAScript Harmony proposal for the next release includes a JavaScript module system, its current status is not yet ready to be incorporated into the language specification draft. Its brief, informal description of the module system does not specify the module semantics precisely, which often leads to ambiguous or unclear interactions with existing language features. Thus, even Traceur from Google and TypeScript from Microsoft do not support the module system semantics correctly yet.

In this paper, we investigate and describe design issues with the JavaScript module system with concrete code examples. We explain each issue using the results from Traceur and TypeScript and discuss reasonable design decisions for the issues. We present a formal specification of the module system as a source-to-source transformation from JavaScript with modules to plain JavaScript. We also provide an open-source implementation of the module system so that JavaScript developers can use the future module system in advance and JavaScript engine developers can take advantage of our implementation techniques. We believe that our discussion on the design issues of the module system and its formal specification and implementation will help the designers of the Harmony proposal and the developers of the proposal to understand the module system more clearly. Because our module system is not particularly tied to JavaScript, we expect that it will be applicable to other scripting languages such as Python and Ruby.

```
var __initarg = {},
    __initfun = {},
    __extmod = {},
    __intmod = {},
    __Object = Object,
    Foo, foo;
Foo = __extmod.Foo = new (function(arguments) {
  function inc() { foo ++; }
  var inc, foo;
  __intmod.Foo = {
      get inc() { return inc; },
      get foo() { return foo; }
  };
  (function (__this) {
    var __desc =
      __Object.getOwnPropertyDescriptor(__this, "foo");
    delete __this.foo;
    if(typeof __desc == "undefined")
      __desc = { configurable : true };
    __desc.get = (function foo() {
      return __intmod.Foo.foo;
    });
    __Object.defineProperty(__this, "foo", __desc);
  })(this);
  (function (__this) {
    var __desc =
      __Object.getOwnPropertyDescriptor(__this, "inc");
    delete __this.inc;
    if(typeof __desc == "undefined")
      __desc = { configurable : true };
    __desc.get = (function inc() {
      return __intmod.Foo.inc;
    });
    __Object.defineProperty(__this, "inc", __desc);
  })(this);
  __initfun.Foo = (function(arguments) {
      foo = 42;
  });
  __initarg.Foo = {
      get arguments() { return arguments; },
      set arguments(x) { arguments = x; }
  };
})({
  get arguments() { return arguments; },
  set arguments(x) { arguments = x; }
   });
__Object.seal(Foo);
__initfun.Foo.call(this, __initarg.Foo);
Foo.inc();
__intmod.Foo.foo;
```

Figure 26. Translation of Figure 8 by *ModuleRewriter*

Acknowledgments

This work is supported in part by Korea Ministry of Education, Science and Technology(MEST) / National Research Foundation of Korea(NRF) (Grants NRF-2011-0016139 and NRF-2008-0062609), Samsung Electronics, S-Core, and Google.

References

[1] Junhee Cho and Sukyoung Ryu. JavaScript module system: Exploring the design space (extended with proofs). `http://plrg.kaist.ac.kr/research/publications`.

[2] ECMA. Harmony proposals. `http://wiki.ecmascript.org/doku.php?id=harmony:proposals`.

[3] ECMA. Harmony proposals – draft specification for ES.next (Ecma-262 Edition 6). `http://wiki.ecmascript.org/doku.php?id=harmony:specification_drafts`.

[4] ECMA. *ECMA-262: ECMAScript language specification*. 5th edition, December 2009.

[5] Linux Foundation. Tizen: an open source, standards-based software platform for multiple device categories. `https://www.tizen.org`.

[6] Google. Traceur-compiler: Google's vehicle for JavaScript language design experimentation. `https://code.google.com/p/traceur-compiler/`.

[7] Robert Grimm. Rats! – an easily extensible parser generator. `http://cs.nyu.edu/~rgrimm/xtc/rats.html`.

[8] Salvatore Guarnieri, Marco Pistoia, Omer Tripp, Julian Dolby, Stephen Teilhet, and Ryan Berg. Saving the world wide web from vulnerable JavaScript. In *Proceedings of the 20th Internaional Symposium on Software Testing and Analysis*, 2011.

[9] Arjun Guha, Claudiu Saftoiu, and Shriram Krishnamurthi. The essence of JavaScript. In *Proceedings of the 24th European Conference on Object-Oriented Programming*, 2010.

[10] Dave Herman and Sam Tobin-Hochstadt. Harmony proposals – modules. `http://wiki.ecmascript.org/doku.php?id=harmony:modules`.

[11] Alexa Internet. Alexa. `http://www.alexa.com`.

[12] Joynet. Node.js. `http://nodejs.org/`.

[13] jQuery Foundation. jQuery. `http://jquery.com/`.

[14] jQuery Foundation. `jQuery.noConflict()`. `http://api.jquery.com/jQuery.noConflict/`.

[15] PLRG @ KAIST. SAFE: Scalable Analysis Framework for ECMAScript. `http://safe.kaist.ac.kr`.

[16] Seonghoon Kang and Sukyoung Ryu. Formal specification of a JavaScript module system. In *Proceedings of the 2012 ACM SIGPLAN Conference on Object-Oriented Programming, Systems, Languages, and Applications*, 2012.

[17] Hongki Lee, Sooncheol Won, Joonho Jin, Junhee Cho, and Sukyoung Ryu. SAFE: Formal specification and implementation of a scalable analysis framework for ECMAScript. In *Proceedings of the 19th International Workshop on Foundations of Object-Oriented Languages*, 2012.

[18] Microsoft. TypeScript. `http://www.typescriptlang.org`.

[19] Eric Miraglia. A JavaScript module pattern. `http://www.yuiblog.com/blog/2007/06/12/module-pattern/`.

[20] Changhee Park, Hongki Lee, and Sukyoung Ryu. All about the `with` statement in JavaScript: Removing `with` statements in JavaScript applications. In *Proceedings of the Dynamic Language Symposium 2013*, 2013.

[21] Samsung Electronics. Samsung Smart TV. `http://developer.samsung.com/smarttv`.

[22] Brian R. Stoler, Eric Allen, and Dan Smith. ASTGen. `http://sourceforge.net/projects/astgen`.

[23] Prototype Core Team. Prototype. `http://prototypejs.org/`.

[24] The MooTools Dev Team. MooTools: a compact JavaScript framework. `http://mootools.net`.

[25] W3C. Document Object Model (DOM). `http://www.w3.org/DOM/`.

[26] W3C. Web IDL. `http://www.w3.org/TR/WebIDL`.

Modular Specification and Dynamic Enforcement of Syntactic Language Constraints when Generating Code

Sebastian Erdweg
TU Darmstadt, Germany

Vlad Vergu
TU Delft, Netherlands

Mira Mezini
TU Darmstadt, Germany

Eelco Visser
TU Delft, Netherlands

Abstract

A key problem in metaprogramming and specifically in generative programming is to guarantee that generated code is well-formed with respect to the context-free and context-sensitive constraints of the target language. We propose *typesmart constructors* as a dynamic approach to enforcing the well-formedness of generated code. A typesmart constructor is a function that is used in place of a regular constructor to create values, but it may reject the creation of values if the given data violates some language-specific constraint. While typesmart constructors can be implemented individually, we demonstrate how to derive them automatically from a grammar, so that the grammar remains the sole specification of a language's syntax and is not duplicated. We have integrated support for typesmart constructors into the run-time system of Stratego to enforce usage of typesmart constructors implicitly whenever a regular constructor is called. We evaluate the applicability, performance, and usefulness of typesmart constructors for syntactic constraints in a compiler for MiniJava developed with Spoofax and in various language extensions of Java and Haskell implemented with SugarJ and SugarHaskell.

Categories and Subject Descriptors D.2.4 [*Software/Program Verification*]: Programming by contract; I.2.2 [*Automatic Programming*]: Program transformation; D.3.4 [*Processors*]: Run-time environments

General Terms Languages, Design

Keywords typesmart constructors; dynamic analysis; program transformation; generative programming; well-formedness checks; abstract syntax tree; Spoofax; SugarJ

1. Introduction and motivating example

Metaprograms process other programs as data, for example, to realize program optimizations, to compile a program to another language, or to inject monitoring code. A traditional problem of metaprogramming is to guarantee that generated code is well-formed according to the syntax and type system of the target language. Such a guarantee is important because it provides valuable feedback to developers of metaprograms and rules out a whole

MODULARITY '14, April 22–26, 2014, Lugano, Switzerland.
Copyright is held by the owner/author(s). Publication rights licensed to ACM.
ACM 978-1-4503-2772-5/14/04...$15.00.
http://dx.doi.org/10.1145/2577080.2577089

```
compile1 :
  Lambda(x, atype, rtype, body)
  ->
  |[ new lambda.Function<~atype, ~rtype>{
       public ~rtype apply(~atype ~x) { ~cbody; }
     }
  ]|
  where cbody := <compile> body
```

```
compile2 :
  Lambda(x, atype, rtype, body)
  ->
  NewInstance(
    None(),
    ClassOrInterfaceType(
      TypeName(
        PackageOrTypeName(Id("lambda")),
        Id("Function")),
      Some(TypeArgs([atype, rtype]))),
    [],
    Some(ClassBody(
      [MethodDec(
        MethodDecHead(
          [Public()], None(), rtype, Id("apply"),
          [Param([], atype, Id(x))], None()),
        cbody)])))
  where cbody := <compile> body
```

Figure 1. Compilation of a lambda expression to Java by transformation of the syntax tree, with and without using concrete syntax.

class of errors that would lead to subsequent metaprogramming tools to fail or even to unsound behavior of the generated program at its run time.

For example, consider the program transformations compile1 and compile2 displayed in Figure 1. Both transformations are implemented in the strategic term-rewriting language Stratego [27] and compile a lambda expression to one and the same anonymous Java class. The lambda expression binds variable x of type atype and has body body with result type rtype. From such a lambda expression, each transformation generates an anonymous class instance of interface lambda.Function and defines a public method apply that takes a parameter corresponding to the lambda-bound variable. The body of the generated method is defined by a recursive call of the transformation on the body of the lambda expression.

The second transformation compile2 uses untyped abstract syntax (similar to s-expressions) to describe the generated code. As the abstract syntax of the target language Java is rather complicated, it is very easy to accidentally generate ill-formed code in compile2. For example, a missing Id tag around a name such as "lambda" or a forgotten None or Some, which are used to represent optional nodes. Such little mistakes are hard to trace and can entail severe problems that may break the rest of the processing pipeline, such as a static analysis or a pretty printer that expect syntactically well-formed code as input. The first transformation compile1 avoids some of these mistakes by using concrete Java syntax in the generation template, which is parsed with an enriched Java grammar before the transformation is applied [26]. For example, the parser will automatically produce a well-formed abstract syntax tree for the qualified name lambda.Function that contains all necessary Id tags.

However, despite using concrete syntax and a parser, even compile1 is not safe at all and can generate ill-formed code: When splicing external data into a generation template (designated by ~ in the template of compile1), the injected data must match the expected syntactic form. For example, both transformations assume that the types of lambda expressions have a Java encoding, because atype and rtype are injected unchanged into the generated Java code. Whether this is true or not cannot be answered by looking at Figure 1 alone. Instead, a (potentially global) data-flow analysis is necessary to statically determine the type encoding of the lambda expressions that are passed to compile as input. Similarly, compile assumes that the recursive compile call on the lambda-expression body results in a valid Java method body. Again, a data-flow analysis is required to ensure this statically. These examples only consider the syntactic structure of generated code; guaranteeing that generated code is well-typed would be even harder. In particular, due to Stratego's sophisticated language features (for example, rule overloading, generic traversals, or dynamically scoped rewrite rules), an efficient static analysis would be hard to design and most likely very specific to the Stratego language and not reusable for other metaprogramming systems. Stratego is not the only metaprogramming system that fails to guarantee the well-formedness of generated code. In particular, metaprograms written in similarly flexible programming languages such as Python, Ruby, or JavaScript exhibit the same problem.

We propose *dynamic checking* of language-specific invariants on generated code at construction time using *typesmart constructors*. A typesmart constructor is a conventional function that acts like a regular constructor and creates data values. However, in contrast to a regular constructor, a typesmart constructor may reject the creation of a value if this would violate a language-specific invariant. For example, a typesmart version of the constructor Param used in the generated method header in Figure 1 would reject the construction of parameters where the parameter name is not wrapped in an Id syntax-tree node or where the parameter type atype is not a well-formed syntax tree representing a Java type. To communicate metadata about a program (such as a syntactic sort or type), typesmart constructors read and write annotations on the abstract syntax tree. For example, the typesmart version of constructor Param would query the annotation of atype to identify its syntactic sort.

In this paper, we particularly focus on the syntactic well-formedness of generated programs and how to *modularly specify and enforce* syntactic well-formedness with typesmart constructors. Typically, a language's syntax is specified centrally by a grammar. It is bad practice to duplicate such specification because this impedes consistency and maintainability. Instead, we want to retain the grammar as a modular specification of a language's syntax: Typesmart constructors should neither duplicate information of the grammar, nor should the grammar be coupled to typesmart constructors. To this end, we devised a transformation that extracts the conditions for syntactic well-formedness from a grammar and generates corresponding typesmart constructors automatically. For enforcing the generation syntactically well-formed programs , the application of typesmart constructors in place of regular constructors should be transparent to developers of program transformations and should not require any change to existing transformations. To achieve this, we designed runtime-system support for typesmart constructors that does not rely on the user's discipline and that can be activated and deactivated modularly. In summary, we make the following contributions:

- We propose typesmart constructors for dynamically checking language-specific well-formedness criteria on generated code. Typesmart constructors are applicable in any metaprogramming system
- We designed and implemented a transformation that automatically derives typesmart constructors from a language's syntax definition to dynamically check the syntactic structure of generated code.
- We incorporated support for typesmart constructors in the runtime system of Stratego to transparently enforce the usage of typesmart constructors in place of regular constructors. This establishes the global invariant that all generated code is well-formed at all times, and transformations do not have to be adapted.
- We evaluate the applicability, performance, and usefulness of typesmart constructors for syntactic constraints by investigating their application in a compiler for MiniJava written in Stratego and in various language extensions of Java and Haskell implemented in SugarJ and SugarHaskell. Using typesmart constructors, we found 27 bugs in existing, tested program transformations.

In this paper, we explore the standard trade-off between static and dynamic analyses: On the one hand, dynamic analyses are easier to define and understand than static data-flow analyses (in particular, if sophisticated metalanguage features should be supported). On the other hand, static analyses deliver feedback at an earlier stage and do not entail any runtime overhead. We see this work as an initial step to support sophisticated language-specific invariants in metaprogramming systems with sophisticated metalanguage features. We envision future work on hybrid analyses that reduce the runtime overhead and deliver feedback earlier when possible, and on dynamic analyses that enforce semantic properties of a language at program-generation time.

2. Typesmart constructors

Consider a constructor C with signature

```
C :: A -> B.
```

A typesmart constructor for C is any function f with signature

```
f :: A -> (fail or B*)
```

that satisfies

```
f(a) = fail  or  f(a) = C(a).
```

Here, B* denotes the type B augmented with annotations of auxiliary data such as the syntactic sort or the type of a term. We assume term equality (=) ignores annotations. Accordingly, a typesmart constructor for C behaves exactly like C except that it may fail or annotate auxiliary data to the constructed value.

Typesmart constructors can be used to enforce invariants about constructed data. For example, here are two typesmart list constructors that enforce that all list elements are even integers:

```
nil() = Nil()
cons(x, xs) =
  if x % 2 == 0
    then Cons(x, xs)
    else fail
```

Similar functionality is supported by contracts on structures in Racket [21]. Indeed, typesmart constructors can be seen as a form of flat contracts [11] for constructors. However, in contrast to contracts, typesmart constructors are allowed to modify the resulting value by adding annotations. For example, we can use annotations to efficiently ensure that the tail of the constructed list consists of even integers as well:

```
nil() = Nil()
cons(x, xs) =
  if x % 2 == 0 && get-anno(xs, "list-of-even") == True
    then put-anno(Cons(x, xs), "list-of-even", True)
    else fail
```

Functions get-anno and put-anno read and write a named annotation of a term, respectively. Without annotations, the typesmart constructor cons would have to recheck the tail of the list each time another element is added, which would change the asymptotic complexity of cons from constant to linear.

An important property of tree-like terms is that they are always built bottom-up. Accordingly, the arguments of a constructor have themselves been previously constructed by other constructors, which may have been typesmart or regular ones. We use annotations in typesmart constructors for three purposes:

- To ensure that the arguments of a typesmart constructor have themselves been constructed by a typesmart constructor.
- To ensure that all required invariants have been enforced on arguments of a typesmart constructor.
- And more generally, to provide a channel of communication from children to parents during the construction of terms.

We can leverage these properties of typesmart constructors to enforce invariants about terms. For the special and important case where we generate programs, we can use typesmart constructors to enforce language-specific constraints. In this paper, we focus on the enforcement of syntactic language constraints.

3. Typesmart constructors for syntactic language constraints

Let us consider a simple language with variables, expressions, and statements (names in curly braces denote the desired constructor names):

```
Var ::= String    {Var}
Exp ::= Var       {VarExp}
      | Integer   {Num}
      | Exp + Exp {Add}
Stm ::= Var = Exp {Assign}
      | Stm; Stm  {Seq}
```

We can define the typesmart constructors for this language as shown in Figure 2. Each constructor checks that its arguments have the appropriate sort. For example, the constructor for assignments requires that the first argument is a variable and the second argument is an expression. An assignment itself is of sort statement. Essentially, the typesmart constructors of Figure 2 ensure that all generated programs adhere to the above grammar.

In statically typed programming languages, the syntactic structure of our simple language can be easily encoded using, for example, algebraic data types. This would statically guarantee that all generated programs adhere to the grammar. We are interested in achieving similar guarantees in dynamically typed languages with sophisticated language features such as generic traversals. Enforcing syntactic constraints with typesmart constructors poses the following challenges:

```
var(v) =
  if is-string(v)
    then put-anno(Var(v), "sort", "Var")
    else fail
varexp(v) =
  if get-anno(v, "sort") == "Var"
    then put-anno(VarExp(v), "sort", "Exp")
    else fail
num(n) =
  if is-integer(n)
    then put-anno(Num(n), "sort", "Exp")
    else fail
add(e1, e2) =
  if get-anno(e1, "sort") == "Exp" &&
     get-anno(e2, "sort") == "Exp"
    then put-anno(Add(e1, e2), "sort", "Exp")
    else fail
assign(v, e) =
  if get-anno(v, "sort") == "Var" &&
     get-anno(e, "sort") == "Exp"
    then put-anno(Assign(v, e), "sort", "Stm")
    else fail
seq(s1, s2) =
  if get-anno(s1, "sort") == "Stm" &&
     get-anno(s2, "sort") == "Stm"
    then put-anno(Seq(s1, s2), "sort", "Stm")
    else fail
```

Figure 2. Typesmart syntax constructors for a simple language with variables, expressions, and statements.

- Not all terms correspond to user-defined sorts. For example, no user-defined sort exists for lists [a,b,c], tuples (a,b,c), or optional elements None() and Some(t). Moreover, the constructors for lists, tuples, and optional terms are inherently polymorphic. For example, for any nonterminal S, the constructor Some generates a term of sort S? given a term of sort S.
- Many languages allow the injection of terms without delimiting constructors. For example, it is often the case that any valid term of sort Variable can be used as a valid term of sort Expression. Typesmart constructors need to consider such injections when checking the sorts of the constructor arguments.
- If a constructor occurs multiple times in a grammar (for example, due to language composition), the constructor may be able to produce terms of alternative sorts for the same arguments. Technically, such a term would be valid with respect to all alternative sorts and no preference can be safely made at this point.

We resolve these issues by (i) built-in support for primitive polymorphic term constructors for lists, tuples, and optionals, (ii) explicit support for a subsort relation that corresponds to term injections, and (iii) alternative result sorts for constructor calls that satisfy multiple productions simultaneously (similar to union types). We provide these features as a library that implementors of typesmart constructors for syntactic constraints can use. In the following, we present the exact definition of this library.

3.1 A library for checking syntax sorts

We define an auxiliary library that provides a high-level function has-sort(t, s) -> Bool to check whether term t has sort s. Function has-sort supports primitive polymorphic terms, alternative sorts, and checks a term with respect to subsorting. To this end, has-sort is configurable with a user-defined subsort relation.

We define function has-sort formally via inference rules. Figure 3 shows the abstract representation of terms t and sorts s that we use in the definition of has-sort. A term is either constructed

$c ::= \mathit{string}$	constructors	
$t ::= c(t, \ldots, t)$	constructed	$s ::= \mathit{string}$
$\mid \mathit{string}$	string literals	$\mid \mathsf{String}$
$\mid [t, \ldots, t]$	lists	$\mid \mathsf{List}(s)$
$\mid (t, \ldots, t)$	tuples	$\mid \mathsf{Tuple}(s, \ldots, s)$
$\mid \mathsf{None} \mid \mathsf{Some}(t)$	optionals	$\mid \mathsf{Option}(s)$
	alternatives	$\mid \mathsf{Alt}(s, s)$

Figure 3. Abstract syntax for terms t and sorts s.

$$\textsc{String}\ \frac{\mathit{is\text{-}string}(t)}{t : \mathsf{String}} \qquad \textsc{List}\ \frac{t_1 : s \quad \cdots \quad t_n : s}{[t_1, \ldots, t_n] : \mathsf{List}(s)}$$

$$\textsc{Tuple}\ \frac{t_1 : s_1 \quad \cdots \quad t_n : s_n}{(t_1, \ldots, t_n) : \mathsf{Tuple}(s_1, \ldots, s_n)}$$

$$\textsc{Opt1}\ \frac{}{\mathsf{None} : \mathsf{Option}(s)} \qquad \textsc{Opt2}\ \frac{t : s}{\mathsf{Some}(t) : \mathsf{Option}(s)}$$

$$\textsc{Alt1}\ \frac{t : s_1}{t : \mathsf{Alt}(s_1, s_2)} \qquad \textsc{Alt2}\ \frac{t : s_2}{t : \mathsf{Alt}(s_1, s_2)}$$

$$\textsc{Anno}\ \frac{\mathit{get\text{-}anno}(\texttt{"sort"}, t) \equiv s}{t : s}$$

$$\textsc{Sub}\ \frac{t : s_1 \quad s_1 <: s_2}{t : s_2} \qquad \textsc{Trans}\ \frac{s_1 <: s_2 \quad s_2 <: s_3}{s_1 <: s_3}$$

Figure 4. Definition of function has-sort, written as $t : s$.

through a constructor application, or it is a list, a tuple, or an optional term None or Some(t). A sort is either a user-defined sort or represents a list, a tuple, an option, or an alternative of two other sorts. We define function has-sort in Figure 4, where we write a call has-sort(t, s) in relational style $t : s$.

The definition of has-sort is mostly straight-forward. A literal string has sort String, a list with elements of sort s has sort List(s), an Option sort describes terms None and Some, a tuple has sort Tuple with matching component sorts. For alternatives Alt(s_1, s_2), it suffices if the term has either sort s_1 or sort s_2. If a term already has a sort annotation (that is, it was constructed by a typesmart constructor), we compare the annotated sort to the required one s in rule Anno. To support terms annotated with alternative sorts, we use a special equivalence relation $\equiv$ that has special treatment for alternative sorts:

$$\textsc{Eq1}\ \frac{s_1 \equiv s}{\mathsf{Alt}(s_1, s_2) \equiv s} \qquad \textsc{Eq2}\ \frac{s_2 \equiv s}{\mathsf{Alt}(s_1, s_2) \equiv s}$$

That is, if the constructed term adheres to multiple sorts, it suffices if one of them matches the required sort s. Otherwise, the equivalence relation checks for syntactic equality.

Finally, function has-sort as defined in Figure 4 employs a subsumption rule Sub: If a term t has sort s_1 and sort s_1 is a subsort of sort s_2, then t also has sort s_2. Here, the subsort relation corresponds to valid term injections. For example, if our language allows the occurrence of variables in expressions Exp ::= Var, then Var would be subsort of Exp (Var <: Exp). The subsort relation is transitive as declared by rule Trans. Apart from that, the subsort relation is unspecified and can be configured according to the syntactic constraints of a language, as we show in the following example.

3.2 Example language and example term construction

Using the function has-sort and the subsort relation, we can implement typesmart constructors that comply with the challenges from the beginning of this section. Let us consider the following small example language that highlights issues we observed in grammars of real-world languages.

```
Var    ::= String                    {Var}
Exp    ::= Var
         | "[" Exp* "]"              {Exps}
Param  ::= String                    {Var}
Proc   ::= "proc" Param? "=" Exp     {Proc}
```

Programs of this language are described with primitive terms for lists (Exp*) and optionals (Param?), perform term injection of variables into expressions, and variables and parameters share the constructor name Var and can be used interchangeably. Using the library from the previous subsection, we can define typesmart constructors for this language as follows:

```
var(v) =
  if is-string(v)
    then put-anno(Var(v), "sort", Alt("Var","Param"))
    else fail
exps(xs) =
  if has-sort(xs, List("Exp"))
    then put-anno(Exps(xs), "sort", "Exp")
    else fail
proc(p, e) =
  if has-sort(p, Option("Param")) && has-sort(e, "Exp")
    then put-anno(Proc(p,e), "sort", "Proc")
    else fail
Var <: Exp = True
```

These typesmart constructors require all features our has-sort library provides: primitive terms, term injection, and alternative sorts. Let us illustrate these features by constructing the term:

Proc(Some(Var("x")), Exps([Var("y")]))

1. The term Var("x") gets assigned sort Alt("Var","Param") since "x" is a string.
2. The term Some(Var("x")) has sort Option(Alt("Var","Param")).
3. The term Var("y") gets assigned sort Alt("Var","Param") since "y" is a string.
4. The term [Var("y")] has sort List(Alt("Var","Param")).
5. The term Exps([Var("y")]) gets assigned sort "Exp" since the argument to Exps is a list of expressions as checked by has-sort(xs, List("Exp")): According to the definition of has-sort in Figure 4, this holds if all elements of xs have sort Exp. However, the only element of xs is Var("y"), which has a sort that does not match: Alt("Var","Param") $\not\equiv$ "Exp". Therefore, we cannot use rule Anno just yet. Instead, we first have to apply rule Sub using Var <: Exp to get Var("y") : "Var", which we can discharge using Anno and Alt("Var","Param") $\equiv$ "Var".
6. The full term Proc(Some(Var("x")), Exps([Var("y")])) has sort "Proc": We first check the optional parameter, which succeeds due to rules Opt2, Anno, and Alt("Var","Param") $\equiv$ "Param". Then we check the body Exps(...), which succeeds immediately using Anno since it has a sort annotation Exp as required.

From this example term construction, we observe that at the time we constructed the Var terms, we did not yet know whether we need the terms as variables or as parameters. Since the Var terms adhere to the structure of both sorts (the abstract syntax overlaps), we marked the terms with an alternative sort that allows their usage in either contexts. Indeed, this was required in our example, because Var("x") was used as a parameter whereas Var("y") was used as a variable. Furthermore, we observe that due to alternative sorts and subsorts, there is quite a number of different cases to consider when checking the sort of an argument. For example, for the body of a procedure, valid argument sorts are Exp, Var, Alt("Var","Param"), but not Param and not Proc. Our library function has-sort greatly reduces the effort of writing typesmart constructors by taking care of all alternatives for saturating a sort requirement.

Nevertheless, the implementation of manual typesmart constructors is tedious, does not reflect the enforced language constraints declaratively, and duplicates knowledge about the syntax of the target language. In the subsequent section, we show that the grammar of the target language in fact can serve as a declarative and modular specification for typesmart constructors that enforce the corresponding syntactic constraints.

4. Deriving typesmart syntax constructors

A grammar should be the ultimate reification of all syntactic constraints a language possesses. Typesmart constructors enforce the syntactic constraints of a language dynamically while programs of the language are generated. In the previous section, we required the manual implementation of typesmart constructors. This limited modularity of the language definition since knowledge about the syntactic constraints is duplicated in the grammar and typesmart constructors. Moreover, the procedural implementation of typesmart constructors is neither declarative nor simple (as we shall see below).

We have developed a transformation that automatically derives typesmart constructors from a language's grammar. Our transformation assumes a grammar defined with SDF [25]. From such a grammar, it generates typesmart constructors as follows.

Regular productions with constructor (`N ::= rhs {C}`). From the right-hand side rhs, we extract the expected argument sorts (as of Figure 3) of the constructor C. First, all lexical tokens are removed; they are not part of the abstract syntax tree that we are constructing. For the rest of rhs, a nonterminal name is its own sort, an optional expression e? has sort Option of the sort of e, a list e* has sort List of the sort of e, and so on.

We generate exactly one typesmart constructor for each constructor for a given arity (number of arguments sorts). The typesmart constructor uses function has-sort (Section 3.1) to test each actual argument for conformance to the expected argument sort. If multiple productions define the same constructor C with the same arity, the single typesmart constructor we generate will test the actual arguments against each list of expected argument sorts. If the actual arguments conform to no production, the typesmart constructor fails and rejects the building of an ill-formed term. If the actual arguments conform to exactly one production, the typesmart constructor returns a term of the result sort of this production. If the actual arguments conform to multiple productions, the typesmart constructor returns a term of an alternative sort Alt(s_1, s_2) with one alternative per successful production.

For example, for the productions

```
A ::= "(" A A ")" {C}
B ::= "{" B B "}" {C}
```

we generate a single typesmart constructor

```
c(x,y) =
  if has-sort(x, "A") && has-sort(y, "A")
   then if has-sort(x, "B") && has-sort(y, "B")
          then put-anno(C(x,y), Alt("A", "B"))
          else  put-anno(C(x,y), "A")
   else if has-sort(x, "B") && has-sort(y, "B")
          then put-anno(C(x,y),"B")
          else fail
```

If the constructor arguments fit both productions, the resulting tree has an alternative sort. Otherwise, if the arguments only fit one production, the resulting tree has the sort this production. If the arguments match neither production, the typesmart constructor fails.

As the number of constructor arguments and the number of productions with equally-named constructors grows, the implementation of the corresponding typesmart constructor becomes tedious and error-prone. For example, the largest typesmart constructor generated for Java has 7 arguments and comprises more than 30 lines of code. Since our transformation generates these constructors from a grammar automatically, language developers do not have to bother with the implementation details of typesmart constructors.

Injection productions (`N ::= A`). We use injection productions to define the subsort relation, over which function has-sort is parameterized. For each injection production N ::= A, we add the fact (A <: N) to the definition of the subsort relation (<:). In addition, we augmented function has-sort to check for cyclic injections when using rule SUB. Otherwise, an infinite loop A <: B <: A <: ... would make our dynamic analysis loop.

Lexical productions (`N ::= [a-z]+`). SDF supports lexical productions, which do not yield nodes in the abstract syntax tree. Instead, a lexical production always yields a string literal representing the parsed fragment of the input string. To support lexical productions in typesmart constructors, we install the nonterminal of a lexical production as a subsort of the sort String (N <: String).

Renamed nonterminals. SDF supports the renaming of nonterminals when importing a module. This provides a means for avoiding name clashes between nonterminals defined in independent modules. For example, one module may define a production Exp ::= Exp "+" Exp {Plus}. Another module may want to use a renamed version JavaExp of nonterminal Exp like this: Body ::= JavaExp {Body}. However, this is problematic for the typesmart constructor of Body, which expects a single argument of the renamed sort JavaExp. However, the concrete argument will have sort Exp. Essentially, the original and the renamed nonterminal are equivalent: We can use either original or renamed sort where the other one is expected. We encode this equivalence using the subsort relation: For each renaming of N to N', we install N as a subsort for N' and vice versa (N <: N' and N' <: N). The check for cyclic injections applies here as well to prevent infinite looping.

Implementation. We implemented the derivation of typesmart constructors as a Stratego transformation that accepts an SDF grammar as input and outputs Stratego code that implements the generated typesmart constructors. For evaluation, we applied our transformation to a composed grammar consisting of productions for SDF and Stratego, which results in 5595 source lines of Stratego code implementing a total of 361 typesmart constructors and installing a total of 262 subsort relationships. Furthermore, we applied our transformation to a grammar for Java, which results in 3989 source lines of Stratego code implementing a total of 206 typesmart constructors and installing a total of 307 subsort relationships. Given that the grammar provides a full specification of the syntactic constraints of a language, all of this generated code provides useful but redundant information. We would not have wanted to implement typesmart constructors for these languages by hand, and our generator provides required tool support for automatically deriving typesmart constructors from a grammar. Especially, this permits the modular evolution of the grammar, since typesmart constructors can simply be regenerated.

5. Run-time support for typesmart syntax constructors in Stratego

The idea of typesmart constructors is applicable in any language that provides an explicit notion of construction. However, manually applying typesmart constructors is cross-cutting the whole transformation: Every occurrence of a regular constructor must be replaced by a typesmart constructor. Moreover, the well-formedness of generated code relies on the users' discipline to actually call typesmart constructors in place of regular constructors. Especially, when using third-party libraries, such discipline cannot be expected.

To remedy this situation, we integrated support for typesmart constructors into the runtime system of Stratego. Specifically, we modified the way Stratego terms are constructed such that a call to a regular constructor is *always* redirected to the corresponding typesmart constructor. Since this redirection is modularly defined, automatic, and transparent to users, we obtain the following advantages: (i) transformations do not have to be changed in any way, (ii) transformations can rely on the global guarantee that all abstract syntax trees represent syntactically well-formed programs during the whole execution, and (iii) dynamic checks can be modularly activated and deactivated. In this section, we describe the augmented architecture of the Stratego runtime system.

Stratego [27] is a declarative language for the transformation of syntax trees. Conceptually, the runtime system of Stratego can be separated into two components: (i) the abstract syntax trees, generally referred to as *terms*, and (ii) the rewriting rules that transform terms. Stratego terms are immutable data objects that may have attachments. Attachments are used to store metadata about a term as required in different execution contexts, such as parent attachments pointing to the parent of a node or origin information establishing a link back from the result of a transformation to its input.

The Stratego runtime system produces terms via *term factories*. A term factory provides methods for the construction of different term types (integer, string, list, tuple, constructor application) and produces the required term. Following the decorator pattern, a basic term factory may be wrapped by other term factories to realize alternative semantics, such as installing attachments for parent references or for origin tracking.

When executing a Stratego transformation, a single term factory is associated to the execution context of the Stratego runtime system. All term construction required by the transformation is delegated to this term factory. To enforce the application of typesmart constructors in place of regular constructors, we implemented a special term factory for typesmart term construction and changed the Stratego runtime system to use this term factory by default. In summary, the runtime support for typesmart constructors comprises the following components:

Typesmart term factory. A designated term factory for typesmart term construction that delegates term construction to typesmart constructors if available.

Term-sort attachment. Term metadata that indicates the sort of the term. This attachment is read and installed by typesmart constructors.

Typesmart primitives. Primitive functions for setting and retrieving term-sort attachments (`put-anno` and `get-anno` in our previous examples), and a primitive function for intentionally building an unsafe term. The latter primitive may only be used within typesmart constructors to build the resulting term after the arguments have been checked.

Has-sort library. The library described in Section 3.1, which is used within typesmart constructors.

Typesmart constructors. Language-specific typesmart constructors of the form described in Section 2. These may be automatically generated from an SDF syntax definition by our generator described in Section 4.

Caching typesmart term factory. A term factory which caches sorts of successfully constructed terms for later reuse without repeating validation.

When a user transformation requests the construction of a term $C(t_1, \ldots, t_n)$, this request is served by the augmented Stratego runtime system as follows.

1. The execution context dispatches the construction request to its term factory. Let us assume this term factory is a simple typesmart term factory without caching.
2. The typesmart term factory checks whether a typesmart constructor for constructor C with arity n exists. We represent typesmart constructors as regular Stratego transformations named `smart-` followed by the name of the constructor. Accordingly, we check for the existence of a Stratego transformation `smart-`C with arity n in the execution context.
   (a) If no transformation `smart-`C with arity n exists, then no typesmart factory has been defined for C. The typesmart term factory then calls a standard term factory that creates an unchecked term and returns it to the user's transformation. For example, this happens for lists, tuples, and optionals.
   (b) If a transformation `smart-`C with arity n exists, the typesmart term factory dispatches the construction of $C(t_1, \ldots, t_n)$ to this transformation as described in Section 3 with details as follows.
3. In the second case (b), the typesmart constructor checks the constructor arguments using a Stratego implementation of function `has-sort`. The subsort relation that `has-sort` uses is provided through additional transformation definitions in the execution context. Function `has-sort` uses a primitive function to retrieve the sort attachment of a term. If all arguments conform to the expected sorts, the typesmart constructor uses a primitive function to build an unchecked term through a standard term factory (this is needed to avoid cycles). Subsequently, the typesmart constructor applies a primitive function to install the result sort as a term-sort attachment. This term is returned.
4. A successful invocation of a typesmart constructor indicates a morphologically correct term and results in the term with installed term-sort attachment. A failed invocation of a typesmart constructor indicates a violation of the term signature and causes the execution of the transformation to be aborted.

In essence, the typesmart term factory only dispatches calls to typesmart constructors which are responsible for the actual verification and construction of terms.

Furthermore, we provide a term factory that caches the result sort of typesmart constructors to alleviate the runtime overhead of typesmart constructors. Our cache assumes that the result sort of a typesmart term construction only depends on the constructor name, the constructor's arity, and the sorts of the constructor arguments. This assumption holds for all typesmart constructors generated by our tool from an SDF grammar (Section 4). When the construction of a term is requested, the caching term factory checks whether a construction with the same constructor name, arity, and argument sorts occurred before. If not (cache miss), then the construction is delegated to the non-caching typesmart term factory. We cache the sort of the resulting term in an internal map. If a construction with the same constructor name, arity, and argument sorts occurred before (cache hit), we retrieve the result sort from the internal map, build an unchecked term, and install the cached result sort.

Thus, a cache hit avoids calling out to the Stratego transformation implementing the typesmart constructor, which furthermore avoids running function has-sort on all arguments.

Through the integration of typesmart constructors at the Stratego level, any technology building on top of Stratego enjoys dynamic enforcement of syntactic language constraints, too. Notably, Spoofax [16] and SugarJ [8] use Stratego as a metalanguage for the implementation of language analyses and semantics. We evaluate typesmart constructors and our implementation in Stratego through application in Spoofax and SugarJ.

6. Case studies

We evaluate the applicability and usefulness of the typesmart constructors by using them inside Spoofax [16] and SugarJ [7, 8]. Spoofax is a language workbench for agile development of external textual languages with IDE support. SugarJ is an extensible language that encapsulates language extensions as regular base-language modules that can be activated via import statements. Both Spoofax and SugarJ use Stratego as underlying term transformation language with which a language developer/extender can define static analyses, program semantics, and semantic editor services.

We extended Spoofax such that it generates typesmart constructors from SDF definitions as explained in Section 4. This generation step is applied during compilation of a Spoofax language project. The typesmart constructors are compiled and loaded together with the user-supplied syntax, analysis rules, semantics, and editor services. We employ the instrumented Stratego runtime system described in Section 5 to transparently enforce syntactic validity during analysis, desugaring, and while executing semantic editor services.

We extended the SugarJ system to generate and use typesmart constructors for the base language. A SugarJ language extension extends the base language by defining additional syntax (as an SDF grammar), additional static analysis for the extended syntax (in Stratego), a desugaring from the extended syntax to the base language (in Stratego), and editor services for the extended syntax. We modified SugarJ to generate additional typesmart constructors for every user-defined extension. When an extension is activated via an import statement, we merge the typesmart constructors of the base language with the typesmart constructors of the extension. Again, we use the augmented runtime system of Stratego to transparently enforce syntactic validity.

To evaluate the applicability and usefulness of typesmart constructors, we applied them in Spoofax and SugarJ. In Spoofax, we applied typesmart constructors in a project that implements a compiler for a subset of Java. In SugarJ, we applied typesmart constructors for validating language extensions of Java and Haskell (transformations are implemented in Stratego). In addition, we evaluated the performance implications of typesmart constructors by measuring and comparing the execution time of a lambda-calculus compiler running with regular constructors only, with typesmart constructors, and with cached typesmart constructors.

6.1 MiniJava compiler

We evaluated the Spoofax integration of typesmart constructors by application to the Spoofax-based MiniJava implementation. The MiniJava compiler is a Stratego program that transforms MiniJava programs into their equivalent counterpart written in the Jasmin assembler language [1] for the Java Virtual Machine. The transformation translates a MiniJava syntax tree into Jasmin syntax tree, which is subsequently pretty-printed. As described above, we generated a library of Jasmin and MiniJava typesmart constructors from syntax definitions of Jasmin and MiniJava, respectively.

[1] http://jasmin.sourceforge.net

The MiniJava compiler was implemented, maintained, and thoroughly tested by a Stratego and Spoofax expert. Accordingly, we expected that the MiniJava compiler produces syntax trees that conform to the syntactic constraints of Jasmin. We tested the MiniJava compiler by applying it to 233 programs written in MiniJava. To our surprise, this gradually uncovered more than 20 bugs in the Jasmin generator, which we repaired. The uncovered defects caused morphologically incorrect Jasmin ASTs to be generated by the compiler. We describe the errors we found below.

The majority of violations involved missing constructors that wrap references to classes, fields, and labels. For example, we changed the compiler as follows:

```
Reference("java/io/PrintStream")
   ⇝ Reference(CRef("java/io/PrintStream"))

GOTO(end)
   ⇝ GOTO(LabelRef(end))
```

When working with abstract syntax trees, this is a typical problem: The abstract syntax requires more intermediate nodes than seems necessary for a programmer. Therefore, it is easy to forget some of these nodes, such as LabelRef. Note that using concrete syntax in the generation template [26] would only have resolved the former violation but not the latter violation, because the sort of end is unknown at compile time.

Another significant part of the morphological errors were caused by mismatching types, such as integers used instead of strings, and ill-placed or missing constructors:

```
ALOAD(n)
   ⇝ ALOAD(VarNum(<int-to-string> n))

JBCVarDecl(
  VarNum(n), x, <to-jbc> t,
  LabelRef(START()), LabelRef(END()))
⇝
JBCVarDecl(
  <int-to-string> n, x, JBCFieldDesc(<to-jbc> t),
  LabelRef(START()), LabelRef(END()))
```

In the MiniJava compiler, the generated Jasmin code is forwarded to a rather permissive pretty-printer that only locally applies formatting rules that do not capture nor rely on the hierarchical structure of the tree. We suspect that the errors we found remained hidden until now because the pretty-printer accepts these ill-formed syntax trees and emits syntactically correct concrete Jasmin syntax. For example, the trees LabelRef(end) and end are pretty-printed to the same string. Furthermore, we believe that the relatively low severity of the defects we found is due to compiler having been heavily tested prior to this evaluation. We believe that the high number of uncovered bugs to be indicative of the prevalence of bugs in other code generators that use abstract syntax.

In different application scenarios, the bugs we found could have been severe. Especially, forwarding ill-formed code to another program transformation, for example a byte-code verifier or optimizer, may lead these tools to fail. Such bugs are very hard to track down, because a developer needs to manually retrace the data flow of the generated program to discover where the ill-formed term was originally constructed. Typesmart constructors reject ill-formed programs right away when they are constructed. This provides precise and early feedback to developers.

6.2 Language extensions of Haskell and Java

We applied typesmart constructors to language extensions developed with SugarHaskell [10] and SugarJ [8], which both are developed as instances of our framework for syntactic language extensibility [9]. This led to the discovery of a number of bugs in previously developed and tested language extensions. We describe the errors we found below.

In a SugarHaskell language extension that introduces special syntax for "idiomatic brackets", we found a bug related to constructor and variable symbols in Haskell. At many places, the Haskell grammar distinguishes constructor symbols (starting with an upper-case character) from variable symbols (starting with a lower-case character). We failed to retain this distinction in our desugaring. We had to rewrite the production of the language extension and the desugaring to retain this distinction:

```
"(|" Exp Qop Exp "|)" -> Exp {"IdiomBrack"}
  ⤳ "(|" Exp Qvarsym Exp "|)" -> Exp {"VarIdiomBrack"}

<apply-effect> (BinCon(op), [e1, e2])
  ⤳ <apply-effect> (BinOp(op), [e1, e2])
```

The first change restricts the production for idiomatic brackets to only permit variable symbols, and the second change designates this symbol as a user-defined operator instead of a constructor in the generator. Would we break this distinction between constructors and variables (as the original code did), this may have far-reaching consequences. For example, subsequent optimizations may assume that constructor calls can be executed cheaply, whereas regular function calls should be inlined or are subject to further optimization if they are recursive. An optimization that transforms the program accordingly would probably fail. Our typesmart constructors notified us of the error immediately when the program was generated, instead of silently failing such that the error could have only been noticed when a generated and optimized program fails to perform as fast as expected.

Another two errors occurred in auxiliary functions that construct Haskell terms using fold functions. In the first case, we tried to construct a qualified module identifier from a list of strings using foldr1 from the standard Stratego library. This failed because foldr1 passes a singleton list containing the last list element to the argument functions. However, our function expected the last list element directly, and thus failed to unpack the singleton list. This led to the construction of the ill-formed term QModId("Control", ["Applicative"]). The revised version correctly generates QModId("Control", "Applicative").

```
foldr1(id, \(x,y) -> QModId(x,y)\)
  ⤳ foldr1(\[x] -> x\, \(x,y) -> QModId(x,y)\)
```

In the second case, we tried to construct a pair-wise sequence of toplevel declarations from a list of declarations. This failed because we used foldr instead of foldr1 to prevent the empty list ending up as a declaration.

```
foldr(id,\(x,y) -> TopdeclSeq(x,y)\)
  ⤳ foldr1(\[x] -> x\,\(x,y) -> TopdeclSeq(x,y)\)
```

Finally, similar as in the MiniJava compiler, we found a few instances of missing constructor applications that were supposed to wrap expression literals, variable symbols in expressions, etc.

We also applied typesmart constructors to three Java extensions implemented with SugarJ: tuple notation, lambda expressions, and literal XML. We did not discover any additional syntactic errors in code generated from these extensions for our test programs. Since we only used a handful of test inputs for our language extensions, it might well be that the test coverage was too low. Alternatively, the generators indeed are safe and produce well-formed programs.

6.3 Performance benchmarks

We evaluated the performance penalty introduced by typesmart constructors. We benchmarked the performance of a compiler from lambda expressions to Java similar to the one in Figure 1. We compared the execution time of the generator for three lambda expressions of increasing size in four scenarios: (*nocheck*) no typesmart constructors, (*check*) non-cached typesmart constructors, (*cache*) cached typesmart constructors reset prior to execution, (*persist*) cached typesmart constructors with cache preservation across transformations. We repeated each execution three times and averaged the results, thus 36 total executions were performed. Table 1 summarizes the timings and cache statistics observed.

	S			M			L		
	T	H	M	T	H	M	T	H	M
nocheck	0.023	-	-	0.026	-	-	0.033	-	-
check	1.493	-	-	2.153	-	-	8.170	-	-
cache	1.207	30	32	1.167	63	32	1.193	405	35
persist	0.015	62	0	0.02	95	0	0.04	440	0

Table 1. Benchmarks results where S, M and L are a small, a medium, and a large input lambda expression; T, H and M are execution times in seconds, cache hits, and cache misses.

We observed that typesmart constructors without any form of caching (case *check*) introduce a large time penalty that is non-linearly related to the the size of the input program. The execution overhead is proportional to the number of terms constructed. The execution overhead also depends on the target language and more specifically on its syntax specification in SDF: The more alternative productions there are per sort, the higher the average number of checks a typesmart constructor has to perform. In our benchmark, we generate programs of the Java language, which has a rather large grammar of 1164 source lines of code.

Results from caching scenarios (*cache*) and (*persist*) show that term-sort caching as described in Section 5 is not only beneficial but necessary for performance. This necessity is clear from the approximately 50% cache hit to miss rate for even the smallest test case and up to 92% for the largest test case. The high cache hit ratios suggest two conclusions. Firstly, the overhead introduced by the typesmart constructors is significant for small transformations producing very heterogenous ASTs. For these short running transformations that cover many different constructors, the caching is unlikely to yield significant improvements. Secondly, larger transformations benefit from caching after the initial period required to fill up the cache. Furthermore, results from scenario (*persist*) confirm that the typesmart term factory does not induce any overhead by itself.

In future work, we want to investigate the application of *hybrid analysis* to reduce the runtime overhead of typesmart constructors. In many cases, typesmart constructors can be checked statically based on partial information. In particular, we can statically check syntax trees that occur literally in a transformation. Even in build patterns that integrate dynamically computed trees into a static skeleton, we can check the skeleton except for the immediate vicinity of the dynamic data. We expect that hybrid analysis can significantly reduce the runtime overhead of typesmart constructors while providing the same guarantees and supporting the same flexibility for transformation languages.

7. Discussion

In this section, we reflect on typesmart constructors and discuss support for potential problematic scenarios, additional application areas, and future extensions of the concepts presented in this paper.

7.1 Mixing typesmart and non-typesmart constructors

Typesmart rely on the assumption that (i) terms are built bottom-up and that (ii) subterms are built via typesmart constructors as well. While the first assumption is ubiquitous for the construction of tree-shaped data, the second assumption may fail to hold in some scenarios. For example, a legacy transformation libraries may employ internal, intermediate representations that are not accompanied by typesmart constructors. Multiple issues can arise when using such a legacy library together with a library that employs typesmart constructors.

First, if a non-typesmart term is used as a typesmart constructor argument, the argument is going to be rejected because it lacks a sort annotation. Most likely, this behavior is intended and correctly notifies the programmer that an unexpected term ended up as argument to the typesmart constructor. In some rare cases, however, it is possible that the unchecked argument in fact is well-formed and adheres to the expected sort. For example, this happens in Spoofax when a term is deserialized from an external ressource (e.g., loaded from a file). To ensure that the term indeed adheres to the sort requirement of the typesmart constructor, we can simply rebuild (that is, clone) it in the current execution using a typesmart term factory. If the term is well-formed, this must succeed and the term can afterwards be used like any other checked term.

Second, the legacy library might try to construct terms with typesmart constructors that the second library introduced. Since the legacy library was not aware of the additional constraints, it may attempt to temporarily create ill-formed terms. For example, some existing Stratego pretty-print libraries operate by incrementally stringifying a term bottom-up: `Plus(Plus(1, 2), 3)` transforms to `Plus("1+2", 3)`, which is illegal since the first argument of `Plus` is not of expression sort. For libraries that produce ill-formed intermediate terms but can be trusted to eventually provide well-formed result terms, we added a primitive second-order Stratego transformation `finally-typesmart(s)`. This transformation takes another transformation `s` as argument and executes it in an execution context with a standard term factory that does not perform any typesmart syntax checking. This allows us, for example, to call legacy pretty-print libraries that eventually yield a simple string. After transformation `s` yields a resulting tree, **finally**-typesmart checks the well-formedness of the generated tree by rebuilding (cloning) it as described in the previous paragraph.

Third, another problem occurs if the legacy library internally uses a constructor that is independently introduced as a typesmart constructor in the new library. To ensure composability of independently declared constructors, we introduced alternative sorts in Section 3: All equally-named constructors are represented by a single typesmart constructor that, given the actual argument terms, returns a term with all valid result sorts as alternatives. This pattern fails when two equally-named constructors exist but only one of them is typesmart. As described in Section 5, the typesmart term factory will execute the one typesmart constructor independent of which constructor was intended to be used. Thus, the typesmart constructor shadows the non-typesmart one. If these constructors do not incidentally expect the same argument sorts, the transformations of the legacy library are bound to fail. We have no clear solution for this scenario so far. One possibility might be to limit scope of typesmart constructors such that the legacy library is not included. We plan to further investigate the integration typesmart and non-typesmart transformations in our future work.

7.2 Typesmart constructors in OO languages

In this paper, we mainly explored the application of typesmart constructors in the transformation language Stratego. However, the ideas behind typesmart constructors can be applied in any language with a notion of construction. In particular, typesmart constructors can be used in object-oriented (OO) languages.

In dynamically typed OO languages such as Ruby, Python, or JavaScript, arguments of constructors are not checked at object-creation time at all, but only when a member of an argument is required. When encoding the abstract syntax of a programming language as a class hierarchy in a dynamically typed OO language, we can use typesmart constructors to check the argument types at object-creation time. We can even allow the class hierarchy to deviate from the abstract syntax by again relying on annotations to store an object's sort (implemented as a member of the object). Moreover, the instrumentation of the Stratego runtime system (Section 5) can be mirrored for other languages to transparently apply typesmart constructors when available and to cache the checking of syntax sorts. This way, existing generators can remain unchanged and we can ensure the invariant that all objects that represent programs are well-formed with respect to the syntactic constraints of the language. This enables safer metaprogramming in dynamically typed OO languages. Furthermore, typesmart constructors can also be useful in statically typed OO languages if the class hierarchy is less precise than the syntactic constraints we want to enforce.

```
data Annotated a = Annotated { val :: a, freevars :: [String] }
put-freevars a vars = Annotated a vars

data Exp = Var String | Lam String AExp | App AExp AExp
type AExp = Annotated Exp

var :: String -> Annotated Exp
var s = put-freevars (Var s) [s]

lam :: String -> Annotated Exp -> Annotated Exp
lam s e = put-freevars (Lam s e) (delete s (freevars e))

app :: Annotated Exp -> Annotated Exp -> Annotated Exp
app e1 e2 = put-freevars (App e1 e2)
                         (freevars e1 'union' freevars e2)

finalize :: Annotated Exp -> Either Exp String
finalize e = case freevars e of
             [] -> Left (val e)
             xs -> Right ("Error: free variables " ++ show xs)
```

Figure 5. Typesmart constructors in Haskell that guarantee closed terms (no free variables).

7.3 Mixing concrete and abstract syntax

As illustrated in Section 1, the use of concrete syntax in generation templates can preclude some well-formedness issues that arise when using abstract syntax. However, concrete syntax alone cannot guarantee the generation of syntactically well-formed code because spliced program fragments must be checked to match the expected sort.

In Stratego, a generation template that uses concrete syntax is preprocessed into a generation template that uses the corresponding abstract syntax [26]. Since the preprocessed template uses regular constructors, the modified Stratego runtime system would impose typesmart constructors also for those subterms where concrete syntax guarantees well-formedness. However, it is fairly straightforward to modify the preprocessor for concrete-syntax templates such that only spliced program fragments are checked, whereas all other subterms are built without run-time checking. Indeed, this resembles a hybrid analysis that can significantly improve run-time performance for transformations that employ lots of concrete syntax in generation templates.

7.4 Typesmart constructors for semantic constraints

Eventually, we want to use typesmart constructors not only to enforce syntactic constraints of a language, but also to enforce semantic constraints. We want to guarantee that only programs can be generated that adhere to semantic properties of a language such as name resolution or type checking. Syntactic constraints are relatively easy to enforce because they are *context-free*. This means that we can check whether a term is well-formed only by inspecting the term; we need no knowledge about how the term is used in different contexts. Semantic properties tend to be *context-sensitive* in nature. For example, for type checking we cannot give a final answer when only seeing a variable term. It depends on whether this variable is bound and used with the same type consistently.

Typically, semantic properties are enforced by traversing a term top-down. This way, it is possible to keep track of the context while going down. For example, a type checker keeps track of the bound variables and their types. When reaching a variable term, it suffices to look up the variable type in the accumulated context. However, we want to check programs while they are generated, and programs are generated bottom-up.

While the investigation of typesmart constructors for semantic constraints is not the focus of our present work, we discuss some early ideas here. First, since we cannot change the order in which terms are generated, we must adapt the checking of the semantic properties. Second, to make the order of checking semantic properties independent of the order in which knowledge about the program becomes available, we want to use a constraint system as explored before by Miao and Siek [19]. A constraint system has the advantage that additional constraints can be generated at any time. Nevertheless, whenever a new constraint is added to the constraint system, we can test whether the current problem is still satisfiable. This way, we hope to find ill-formed programs as soon as a constraint violation manifests, while allowing required knowledge for saturating constraints to emerge later on during the program generation.

For example, consider the Haskell program in Figure 5 that implements three typesmart constructors to ensure that generated lambda-calculus programs are closed terms, that is, they do not contain free variables. This is a simple, but context-sensitive property. Essentially, the construction of a term always yields the constructed term and a *residual constraint system* that has to be satisfied by the surrounding context. In our example, the residual constraints is simply a list of free variables, that have to be bound before the term conforms to the semantic property of being closed. Every occurrence of a variable adds a constraint. Every occurrence of a lambda saturates a constraint. As soon as a term has an empty list of free variables, it is well-formed. Otherwise, we never know whether additional context becomes available later on or whether the term is indeed ill-formed. To this end, we defined a function `finalize` that enforces the saturation of all constraints and reports an error otherwise. In our future work, we want to investigate whether typesmart constructors can be effectively used for enforcing semantic properties when generating programs.

8. Related Work

Using smart constructors to enforce data invariants has a long tradition and is a popular idiom in functional programming. The use smart constructors goes at least back to Stephen Adams, who used smart constructors to ensure tree balancing in the definition of an efficient set representation [1]. Our work on typesmart constructors goes considerably beyond traditional smart constructors: First, we allow typesmart constructors to annotate the constructed trees, which enables checking of data invariants without recursing into subtrees. Second, we integrate support for typesmart constructors into the run-time system to globally and transparently enforce invariants.

Smart constructors can also be used to implement local optimizations such as constant folding. For example, Elliott, Finne, and De Moore use optimizing smart constructors to compile the embedded language Pan [6]. In contrast, typesmart constructors must either fail or behave exactly as the corresponding regular constructor. Thus, typesmart constructors cannot be used to implemented optimizations directly. However, optimizing constructors call regular constructors after optimization has finished. By replacing these regular constructors with typesmart constructors (either manually or transparently by our run-time system), it is possible to combine the benefits of optimizing constructors and typesmart constructors.

Most related approaches for guaranteeing the syntactic or semantic well-formedness of generated programs significantly restrict the expressiveness of the metaprogramming language. For example, MetaML [22] supports type-safe run-time staging, MacroML [12] supports type-safe compile-time staging, and SoundExt [18] supports type-safe compile-time staging based on user-defined type rules. However, the expressiveness of the employed transformation languages is limited: MetaML and MacroML support no inspection of input terms; SoundExt supports inspection but requires small-step rewrite rules and cannot handle generic traversals. Language embeddings in form of generalized algebraic data types do not support flexible traversal and generation patterns as well as language composition.

To address metalanguages with sophisticated metalanguage features such as generic traversals or generating programs of composed languages, we explore the application dynamic analyses. In particular, typesmart constructors can be used for dynamic analysis in any metaprogramming system that has or can be retrofitted with a notion of term construction. Furthermore, typesmart constructors are independent of high-level language features such as generic traversals, because eventually all program generation is handled by term constructors.

Static checking of syntactic language constraints. The need for dynamic checking of term well-formedness is caused by the introduction of generic traversal strategies that do not fit in traditional static type systems. Traditional algebraic specification/rewrite languages such as OBJ [14], ASF [23], and later Maude [5] are statically typed. However, these languages have limited expressiveness that can be handled by type systems with first-order types extended with variations on subtyping such as injections and order-sorted algebra. For example, in ASF+SDF function signatures are defined with grammar productions, such as `"compile" "(" DslExp ")" -> JavaExp`. Rewrite rules (equations) are typechecked by parsing, avoiding the need for dynamic type checking. However, the first-order nature of these type systems does not admit the definition of generic, reusable transformation functions, leading to boilerplate code for e.g. traversals. Extensions such as ELAN's [3] congruence operators and ASF's traversal functions [24] fit within the first-order type system, but thereby limit the traversals that can be expressed.

Rascal [17] is the successor of ASF+SDF. Instead of defining transformation functions as extension of the object grammar, it provides a separate statically typed general-purpose language with domain-specific features to express metaprogramming. Rascal supports generic traversals via a built-in visitor pattern that allows the modification of the visited tree. Rascal's type system requires that the modified tree component has the same type as the original one. While this ensures that all generated trees are syntactically well-formed, it limits the flexibility of the transformation because it is not possible to transform a tree from one type to another.

The generalized (traversal) strategies of the Stratego [27] language provide an expressive and flexible transformation language, but is not covered by static type systems. This paper provides an approach to catch syntactic type errors in Stratego programs using a programmable dynamic type system.

Template engines. Template engines such as StringTemplate and Xpand generate code by directly composing strings. While these engines may guarantee type-safe input access, no checks are done on the output. Repleo [2] is a template engine that *does* provide syntactic guarantees about the output generated by templates. Partly this is based on the concrete object syntax approach also applied in ASF+SDF. This approach is extended by reparsing the result of strings that are substituted into the holes of a template. In contrast, the approach in this paper is based on tree rewritings, where the syntactic category of intermediate trees does not change and, thus, does not have to be rechecked. Repleo provides an interesting mix of static and dynamic analysis. Static analysis for parsing the template modulo splices, and dynamic analysis for checking the spliced strings. Our typesmart constructors can benefit from such a hybrid analysis as well, which could be achieved by partially evaluating the application of type smart constructors in statically known term fragments.

Stratego's concrete object syntax [26] provides partial static checking of syntactic templates in rewrite rules by parsing term fragments written in the concrete syntax of the object language. However, this technique fails to check the composition of term fragments. The dynamic approach in this paper checks all constructed terms and is complementary to concrete-syntax templates.

TemplateHaskell [20] is a template engine for Haskell. It provides syntactic safety via algebraic data types. Templates ensure scoping and type-safety statically up to spliced values, which are defined in a quotation monad that only ensures referential transparency statically and defers type checking until after the outermost splice has been computed.

Dynamic analysis. Miao and Siek explore dynamic type checking in the context of metaprogramming [19]. After every evaluation step of the metaprogramming language, they check the type of the generated code artifact by collecting and resolving constraints incrementally. Miao and Siek apply their technique in an idealized metaprogramming language [13] that resembles C++ metaprogramming and does not support materialization, introspection, or transformation of programs as data (e.g., abstract syntax trees cannot be manipulated directly). For this reason, the question of syntactic well-formedness does not even arise. In contrast, we explore dynamic checking of language-specific constraints in metaprogramming systems that permit arbitrary manipulation of code.

The `format-check` tool of Stratego/XT [4] checks terms against a signature by means of a full term traversal. This can be applied after a transformation or between stages of a transformation pipeline to ensure that a term conforms to the expected syntax. This approach can be used to catch errors in transformations. However, it can be hard to trace back a signature violation to an actual error in a transformation rule. Kalleberg and Visser [15] describe weaving of format checkers into Stratego programs as a case study of an experimental aspect-oriented extension of Stratego. A joinpoint on term construction can be used to inject the application of smart constructors as an alternative mechanism to our term factory replacement. In addition to the delivery mechanism, typesmart constructors apply to all intermediate terms and use annotations to avoid duplicate effort in analyzing the same subterms multiple times. Moreover, we mark a term with an alternative result sort if there is an overlap of signatures. This enables us to check and annotate terms despite the lack of context information.

Dynamic contracts as, for example, used in Racket [11, 21] also provide a programmable interface for run-time checking of structures. One important difference to our work is that contracts may not annotate the checked term. In contrast, we use annotations as a communication channel from subterms to parents. Moreover, contracts in Racket need to be manually programmed. We focus on dynamic analysis of metaprograms that generate other programs and provide a generator of typesmart constructors from a language's syntax definition.

9. Conclusion

We propose a novel approach for safe metaprogramming using dynamic analyses and typesmart constructors. A dynamic analysis is relatively easy to define since it can inspect run-time values. We explore the application of dynamic analyses for program generation, where the analysis is executed at program-construction time and can reject a partially generated program as soon as a violation manifests. In particular, we propose typesmart constructors as a mechanism to realize dynamic analyses for program generation. We demonstrate how to implement typesmart constructors for validating the syntactic well-formedness of generated programs and provide a tool to derive such typesmart constructors automatically from the syntactic definition of the target language. The caching of typesmart syntax checks ensures moderate run-time overhead and enables scalability to large generated programs. In our evaluation, we successfully applied typesmart constructors in Spoofax and SugarJ and found errors in preexisting program transformations.

Acknowledgments

We thank the anonymous reviewers for their helpful feedback.

References

[1] S. Adams. Functional pearls: Efficient sets–a balancing act. *Functional Programming*, 3(4):553–562, 1993.

[2] J. Arnoldus, J. Bijpost, and M. van den Brand. Repleo: A syntax-safe template engine. In *Proceedings of Conference on Generative Programming and Component Engineering (GPCE)*, pages 25–32. ACM, 2007.

[3] P. Borovanský, C. Kirchner, H. Kirchner, P.-E. Moreau, and C. Ringeissen. An overview of elan. *Electronic Notes in Theoretical Computer Science*, 15, 1998.

[4] M. Bravenboer, K. T. Kalleberg, R. Vermaas, and E. Visser. *Stratego/XT Reference Manual*, 2003–2008.

[5] M. Clavel, S. Eker, P. Lincoln, and J. Meseguer. Principles of maude. *Electronic Notes in Theoretical Computer Science*, 4:65–89, 1996.

[6] C. Elliott, S. Finne, and O. De Moor. Compiling embedded languages. *Functional Programming*, 13(3):455–481, 2003.

[7] S. Erdweg. *Extensible Languages for Flexible and Principled Domain Abstraction*. PhD thesis, Philipps-Universiät Marburg, 2013.

[8] S. Erdweg, T. Rendel, C. Kästner, and K. Ostermann. SugarJ: Library-based syntactic language extensibility. In *Proceedings of Conference on Object-Oriented Programming, Systems, Languages, and Applications (OOPSLA)*, pages 391–406. ACM, 2011.

[9] S. Erdweg and F. Rieger. A framework for extensible languages. In *Proceedings of Conference on Generative Programming and Component Engineering (GPCE)*, pages 3–12. ACM, 2013.

[10] S. Erdweg, F. Rieger, T. Rendel, and K. Ostermann. Layout-sensitive language extensibility with SugarHaskell. In *Proceedings of Haskell Symposium*, pages 149–160. ACM, 2012.

[11] R. B. Findler and M. Felleisen. Contracts for higher-order functions. In *Proceedings of International Conference on Functional Programming (ICFP)*, pages 48–59. ACM, 2002.

[12] S. Ganz, A. Sabry, and W. Taha. Macros as multi-stage computations: Type-safe, generative, binding macros in MacroML. In *Proceedings of International Conference on Functional Programming (ICFP)*. ACM, 2001.

[13] R. Garcia and A. Lumsdaine. Toward foundations for type-reflective metaprogramming. In *Proceedings of Conference on Generative Programming and Component Engineering (GPCE)*, pages 25–34. ACM, 2009.

[14] J. Goguen, C. Kirchner, H. Kirchner, A. Mégrelis, J. Meseguer, and T. Winkler. An introduction to OBJ 3. In *Conditional Term Rewriting Systems*, pages 258–263. Springer, 1988.

[15] K. T. Kalleberg and E. Visser. Combining aspect-oriented and strategic programming. *Electronic Notes in Theoretical Computer Science*, 147(1):5–30, 2006.

[16] L. C. L. Kats and E. Visser. The Spoofax language workbench: Rules for declarative specification of languages and IDEs. In *Proceedings of Conference on Object-Oriented Programming, Systems, Languages, and Applications (OOPSLA)*, pages 444–463. ACM, 2010.

[17] P. Klint, T. van der Storm, and J. Vinju. Rascal: A domain-specific language for source code analysis and manipulation. In *Proceedings of Conference on Source Code Analysis and Manipulation (SCAM)*, pages 168–177, 2009.

[18] F. Lorenzen and S. Erdweg. Modular and automated type-soundness verification for language extensions. In *Proceedings of International Conference on Functional Programming (ICFP)*, pages 331–342. ACM, 2013.

[19] W. Miao and J. G. Siek. Incremental type-checking for type-reflective metaprograms. In *Proceedings of Conference on Generative Programming and Component Engineering (GPCE)*, pages 167–176. ACM, 2010.

[20] T. Sheard and S. Peyton Jones. Template meta-programming for Haskell. In *Proceedings of Haskell Workshop*, pages 1–16. ACM, 2002.

[21] T. S. Strickland, S. Tobin-Hochstadt, R. B. Findler, and M. Flatt. Chaperones and impersonators: run-time support for reasonable interposition. In *Proceedings of Conference on Object-Oriented Programming, Systems, Languages, and Applications (OOPSLA)*, pages 943–962. ACM, 2012.

[22] W. Taha and T. Sheard. MetaML and multi-stage programming with explicit annotations. *Theoretical Computer Science*, 248(1-2):211–242, 2000.

[23] M. van den Brand, A. van Deursen, J. Heering, H. De Jong, et al. The ASF+SDF Meta-Environment: A component-based language development environment. In *Proceedings of Conference on Compiler Construction (CC)*, volume 2027 of *LNCS*, pages 365–370. Springer, 2001.

[24] M. G. J. van den Brand, P. Klint, and J. J. Vinju. Term rewriting with traversal functions. *Transactions on Software Engineering Methodology (TOSEM)*, 12(2):152–190, 2003.

[25] E. Visser. *Syntax Definition for Language Prototyping*. PhD thesis, University of Amsterdam, 1997.

[26] E. Visser. Meta-programming with concrete object syntax. In *Proceedings of Conference on Generative Programming and Component Engineering (GPCE)*, volume 2487 of *LNCS*, pages 299–315. Springer, 2002.

[27] E. Visser, Z.-E.-A. Benaissa, and A. P. Tolmach. Building program optimizers with rewriting strategies. In *Proceedings of International Conference on Functional Programming (ICFP)*, pages 13–26. ACM, 1998.

Author Index

Aotani, Tomoyuki 85
Bacon, Jean 37
Bagherzadeh, Mehdi 157
Baier, Christel 169
Brabrand, Claus 181
Chavez, Christina von F. G. 121
Chiba, Shigeru 13
Cho, Junhee 229
Churchill, Martin 145
Cornélio, Márcio 157
da Silva, Bruno C. 121
Dubslaff, Clemens 169
Ducasse, Stéphane 1
Eichberg, Michael 61
Erdweg, Sebastian 241
Figueiredo, Eduardo 109
Figueroa, Ismael 133
Garcia, Alessandro 61
Gurgel, Alessandro 61
Hanenberg, Stefan 99
Happe, Lucia 217
Hintz, Gerold 25
Ichikawa, Kazuhiro 13
Kamina, Tetsuo 85
Klüppelholz, Sascha 169
Leavens, Gary T. 157
Lima, Ricardo 157
Macia, Isela 61
Maia, Marcelo de A. 49
Masuhara, Hidehiko 85
Mezini, Mira 25, 61, 205, 241
Midtgaard, Jan 181
Mitschke, Ralf 61
Mosses, Peter D. 145
Nierstrasz, Oscar 1
Noorshams, Qais 217
Noyé, Jacques 205
Pasquier, Thomas F. J.-M. 37
Rajan, Hridesh 157
Rebêlo, Henrique 157
Rentschler, Andreas 217
Reussner, Ralf 217
Ryu, Sukyoung 229
Salvaneschi, Guido 25, 205
Sant'Anna, Claudio N. 121
Scholtes, Ingo 73
Schrijvers, Tom 133
Schweitzer, Frank 73
Shand, Brian 37
Silva, Luciana Lourdes 49
Souza, Carlos 109
Spiza, Samuel 99
Südholt, Mario 193
Tabareau, Nicolas 133, 193
Tamai, Tetsuo 85
Tanter, Éric 133, 193
Teruel, Camille 1
Tessone, Claudio Juan 73
Thüm, Thomas 157
Torrini, Paolo 145
Valente, Marco Tulio 49
Van Ham, Jurgen M. 205
Vergu, Vlad 241
Visser, Eelco 241
von Staa, Arndt 61
Wąsowski, Andrzej 181
Werle, Dominik 217
Wernli, Erwann 1
Zanetti, Marcelo Serrano 73
Zimmerman, Daniel M. 157

www.ingramcontent.com/pod-product-compliance
Lightning Source LLC
Chambersburg PA
CBHW061359210326
41598CB00035B/6037
* 9 7 8 1 4 5 0 3 3 0 7 7 0 *